INTERNATIONAL BUSINESS

Competing in the Global Marketplace

IRWIN TITLES IN INTERNATIONAL BUSINESS AND ECONOMICS

Appleyard and Field,
International Economics,
1992

Ball and McCulloch,
International Business:
Introduction and Essentials,
Fifth Edition, 1993

Bartlett and Ghoshal,
Transnational Management:
Text Cases and Readings
in Cross-Border Management,
1992

Beamish, Killing,
Lecraw, and Crookell,
International Management:
Text and Cases,
Second Edition, 1994

Bornstein,
Comparative Economic Systems:
Models and Cases,
Sixth Edition, 1989

Cateora,
International Marketing,
Eighth Edition, 1993

Grosse and Kujawa,
International Business:
Theory and Managerial Applications,
Second Edition, 1992

Lindert,
International Economics,
Ninth Edition, 1991

Mueller, Gernon, and Meek,
Accounting:
An International Perspective,
Second Edition, 1991

Robock and Simmonds,
International Business and
the Multinational Enterprise,
Fourth Edition, 1989

INTERNATIONAL BUSINESS
Competing in the Global Marketplace

Charles W. L. Hill
University of Washington

Burr Ridge, Illinois
Boston, Massachusetts
Sydney, Australia

Senior sponsoring editor: Craig Beytien
Developmental editors: Karen E. Perry/Lara Vergoth
Marketing manager: Kurt Messersmith
Project editor: Stephanie M. Britt
Production manager: Diane Palmer
Designer: Laurie Entringer
Art coordinator: Mark Malloy
Compositor: Better Graphics, Inc.
Typeface: 10/12 Goudy
Printer: Von Hoffmann Press

Library of Congress Cataloging-in-Publication Data

Hill, Charles W. L.

International business : competing in the global marketplace / Charles W.L. Hill.

p. cm.

ISBN 0-256-11292-4 0-256-15682-4 (international ed.)
0-256-17509-8 (Postscript)

1. International business enterprises—Management.
2. Competition, International. I. Title.

HD62.4.H55 1994
658'.049—dc20 93-7559

Printed in the United States of America
2 3 4 5 6 7 8 9 0 VH 0 9 8 7 6 5 4

For June Hill and Mike Hill,
my parents

About the Author

Charles W. L. Hill is professor of management and organization at the University of Washington's graduate school of business. He received a Ph.D. in economics from the University of Manchester Institute of Science and Technology (UMIST) in Great Britain and has taught there and at Texas A&M University, Michigan State University, and the University of Washington. His research interests center on strategic management and international business. The author of more than 30 research papers in academic journals, including the *Academy of Management Journal*, the *Academy of Management Review*, *Organization Science*, and the *Strategic Management Journal*, Professor Hill has served on the editorial boards of six journals, including those of the *Academy of Management Journal*, *Organization Science*, and the *Strategic Management Journal*. Currently he is a consulting editor for the *Academy of Management Review*.

Preface

International Business: Competing in the Global Marketplace is intended for the first international business course at either the undergraduate or the M.B.A. level. My goal in writing this book has been to set a new standard for international business textbooks: I have attempted to write a book that (1) is comprehensive and up-to-date, (2) goes beyond an uncritical presentation and shallow explanation of the body of knowledge, (3) maintains a tight, integrated flow between chapters, (4) focuses managerial implications, and (5) makes important theories accessible and interesting to students.

COMPREHENSIVE AND UP-TO-DATE

To be comprehensive, an international business textbook must:

- Explain how and why the world's countries differ.
- Present a thorough review of the economics and politics of international trade and investment.
- Explain the functions and form of the global monetary system.
- Examine the strategies and structures of international businesses.
- Assess the special roles of an international business's various functions.

This textbook does all of these things. Too many other textbooks pay scant attention to the strategies and structures of international businesses and to the implications of international business for firms' various functions. This omission is a serious deficiency, because the students in these international business courses will soon be international managers, and they will be expected to understand the implications of international business for their organization's strategy, structure, and functions. This book pays close attention to these issues.

Comprehensiveness and relevance also require coverage of the major theories. Although many international business textbooks do a reasonable job of reviewing long-established theories (e.g., the theory of comparative advantage and Vernon's product life-cycle theory) they tend to ignore such important newer work as:

- The new trade theory and strategic trade policy.
- Michael Porter's theory of the competitive advantage of nations.
- Robert Reich's recent work on national competitive advantage.
- The market-imperfections approach to foreign direct investment that has grown out of Ronald Coase and Oliver Williamson's work on transaction-cost economics.
- Bartlett and Ghoshal's research on the transnational corporation.
- The writings of C. K. Prahalad and Gary Hamel on core competencies, global competition, and global strategic alliances.

The failure of many books to discuss such work is a serious deficiency considering how influential these theories have become. A major proponent of strategic trade policy, Laura Tyson, is chairperson of President Clinton's Council of Economic Advisors. Robert Reich is Secretary of Labor in the Clinton administration. Porter's book has influenced the debate on trade and competitiveness. Ronald Coase won the 1992 Nobel Prize in economics, giving the market-imperfections approach new respectability. The work of Bartlett, Ghoshal, Hamel, and Prahalad is having an important impact on business practice.

I have incorporated all relevant state-of-the-art work at the appropriate points in this book. For example, in Chapter 4, "International Trade Theory," in addition to such standard theories as the theory of comparative advantage and the Heckscher–Ohlin theory, there is a detailed discussion of the new trade theory and Porter's theory of national competitive advantage. In Chapter 5, "The Political Economy of International Trade," the pros and cons of strategic trade policy are discussed. In Chapter 6, "Foreign Direct Investment," the market-imperfections approach is reviewed. Chapters 12 and 13, which deal with the strategy and structure of international businesses, draw on Bartlett and Ghoshal's work, and Prahalad and Hamel's research on strategic alliances is examined in Chapter 14.

Finally, in light of the fast-changing nature of the international business environment, every effort is being made to ensure that this book is as up-to-date as possible as it goes to press. Thus, for example, the student will find a detailed outline of the NAFTA, a discussion of the prospects for the EC after the partial breakdown of the European exchange rate mechanism late in 1992, a review of the concurrent problems with the Maastricht Treaty, and an examination of the political and economic turmoil occurring in the newly independent states of the former Soviet Union.

BEYOND UNCRITICAL PRESENTATION AND SHALLOW EXPLANATION

Many issues in international business are complex and thus necessitate considerations of pros and cons. To demonstrate this to students, I have adopted a critical approach that presents the arguments for and against economic theories, government policies, business strategies, organizational structures, and so on.

Related to this, I have attempted to explain the complexities of the many theories and phenomena unique to international business so that the student might fully comprehend the statements of a theory or the reasons a phenomenon is the way it is. These theories and phenomena are typically explained in more depth in this book than they are in competing textbooks, the rationale being that a shallow explanation is little better than no explanation at all. In international business, a little knowledge is indeed a dangerous thing.

INTEGRATED PROGRESSION OF TOPICS

Many textbooks lack a tight, integrated flow of topics from chapter to chapter. In this book students are told in Chapter 1 how the book's topics are related to each other. Integration has been achieved by organizing the material so that each chapter builds on the material of the previous ones in a logical fashion.

Part One Chapter 1 provides an overview of the key issues to be addressed and explains the plan of the book.

Part Two Chapters 2 and 3 focus on national differences in political economy and culture. Most international business textbooks place this material at a later point, but I believe it is absolutely vital to discuss national differences first. After all, many of the central issues in international trade and investment, the global monetary system, international business strategy and structure, and international business operations arise out of national differences in political economy and culture. To fully understand these issues, students must first of all appreciate the differences in countries and cultures.

Part Three Chapters 4 through 8 investigate the political economy of international trade and investment. The purpose of this part is to describe and explain trade and investment environment in which international business occurs.

Part Four Chapters 9 through 11 describe and explain the global monetary system, laying out in detail the monetary framework in which international business transactions are conducted.

Part Five In Chapters 12 through 14 attention shifts from the environment to the firm. Here the book examines the strategies and structures that firms adopt in order to compete effectively in the international business environment.

Part Six In Chapters 15 through 20 the focus narrows further to investigate business operations. These chapters explain how firms can perform their key functions—manufacturing, marketing, R&D, human resource management, accounting, and finance—in order to compete and succeed in the international business environment.

Throughout the book, the relationship of new material to topics discussed in earlier chapters is pointed out to the students to reinforce their understanding of how the material comprises an integrated whole.

FOCUS ON MANAGERIAL IMPLICATIONS

Many international business textbooks fail to discuss the implications of the various topics for the actual practice of international business. This does not serve the needs of business school students who will soon be practicing managers. Accordingly, the usefulness of this book's material in the practice of international business is discussed explicitly. In particular, at the end of each chapter in Parts Two, Three, and Four—where the focus is on the environment of international business, as opposed to particular firms—there is a section entitled *Implications for Business.* In this section, the managerial implications of the material discussed in the chapter are clearly explained. For example, Chapter 4, "International Trade Theory," ends with a detailed discussion of the various trade theories' implications for international business management.

In addition, each chapter begins with a case that illustrates the relevance of the chapter material to the practice of international business. Chapter 11, "The Global Capital Market," for example, opens with a case that describes how a Belgium biotechnology company used the global capital market to raise funds that could not have been raised in Belgium's illiquid capital market.

ACCESSIBLE AND INTERESTING

The international business arena is fascinating and exciting, and I have tried to communicate my enthusiasm for it to the student. Learning is easier and better if the subject matter is communicated in an interesting, informative, and accessible manner. One technique I have used to achieve this is weaving interesting anecdotes into the narrative of the text—stories that illustrate theory. Just how well this objective has been achieved will be revealed by time and student feedback. I am confident, however, that this book is far more accessible to students than its competitors. For those of you who view such a bold claim with skepticism, I urge you to read the sections in Chapter 1 on the globalization of the world economy, the changing nature of international business, and how international business is different.

SUPPORT MATERIAL

Instructor's Manual and Test Bank

The Instructor's Manual, prepared by Duane Helleloid of the University of Washington, contains chapter overviews, teaching suggestions, lecture notes, video notes, and a test bank of multiple-choice, short-answer, and essay questions.

Computest

A computerized version of the test bank is available and allows the instructor to generate random tests and to add his or her own questions.

Teletest

Customized exam preparation is furnished by the publisher.

Transparency Package

A set of full-color transparencies contains key figures and maps from the book as well as additional lecture enhancers.

Videos

Four videotape segments bring the fast-changing world of international business into the classroom for students. Highlighting major sections of the book, these videos focus on such topics as international trade, global manufacturing, and Coca-Cola's entry into Japan.

Global Business Insights

Recent articles from the *Los Angeles Times* provide students with additional, real-life illustrations of the concepts covered in the book. Chosen for their currency and level of interest, they will stimulate and enhance classroom discussions.

The Software Toolworks World Atlas

An atlas, almanac, and world fact book, the *World Atlas* is a powerful computer-based reference tool that combines state-of-the-art maps of every country in the world with a database of international information.

ACKNOWLEDGMENTS

Numerous people deserve to be thanked for their assistance in preparing this book. First, thank you to all of the people at Irwin who have worked with me on the project:

Craig Beytien, Sponsoring Editor
Karen Perry and Lara Vergoth, Developmental Editors
Stephanie Britt, Project Editor
Laurie Entringer, Designer
Mark Malloy, Assistant Art Manager
Diane Palmer, Production Manager

Second, my thanks go to the reviewers, who provided good feedback that helped to shape the book. They are

Suhail Abboushi, Duquesne University
Thomas Becker, Florida Atlantic University
Dharma de Silva, Wichita State University
Gary Dicer, University of Tennessee
Ben Kedia, Memphis State University
Kamlesh Mehta, St. Mary's University
William Renforth, Florida International University
John Stanbury, Indiana University at Kokomo

Third, thank you to my M.B.A. research assistant, Maria Gonzalez, for her assistance in preparing the manuscript. And last, but by no means least, I thank my wife, Alexandra, and my daughters, Charlotte and Elizabeth, for their support and, indeed, for giving me the strength to write this book.

Charles W. L. Hill

Brief Table of Contents

Table of Contents

INTERNATIONAL BUSINESS
Competing in the Global Marketplace

INTRODUCTION

We live in a world where the only constant is change. This presents a problem for international business books, where we always make an attempt to be as current as possible on multilateral and regional trade agreements, international political and economic developments, the evolution of the international monetary system, and the development of new business strategies and structures for competing in the global marketplace. Because the international economic and political scene evolves so quickly, any international business book is out of date the moment it is published. Since the final draft of this book was completed in mid-1993, there have been a number of developments with important implications for enterprises trying to compete in the global economy. In this postscript we review these developments and discuss their implications. The developments include:

- Completion of the Uruguay Round of GATT negotiations and an agreement to create a new international institution, the World Trade Organization (WTO), to implement the GATT.
- The emergence of serious trade tensions between the United States and Japan over the limited foreign access to Japan's market.
- The ratification of the North American Free Trade Agreement (NAFTA) by the U.S. Congress, which effectively removed the final impediment to the formation of the world's largest free-trade area.
- The ratification of the Maastricht treaty by the 12 members of the European Community (EC). The Maastricht treaty lays out a framework and timetable for a much closer economic and political union between EC member-countries. Symbolically, the EC also changed its name to the European Union (EU) at this time.
- A March 1994 agreement among existing EU members to enlarge the EU to include four new members: Norway, Sweden, Finland, and Austria (subject to approval by the voters of those countries).
- The virtual collapse of the European Monetary System (EMS) following a wave of speculative pressure in the international currency markets.
- Growing economic and political turmoil in many countries formerly part of the Soviet Union and most seriously in Russia, where the risk of political anarchy and economic collapse seems very real.

In this postscript, as of mid-1994, we review these developments and flesh out their implications for material discussed in earlier chapters of this book. We will deal with the issues in the order that they were listed.

GATT: THE DEAL IS DONE

The history and functions of the GATT were discussed in detail in Chapter 5. Established in 1947, the GATT is a multilateral agreement whose objective is liberalizing world trade by eliminating tariffs, subsidies, import quotas, and the like. The process of tariff reduction has been spread over eight rounds. The last round, the Uruguay Round, was launched in 1986, completed on December 15, 1993, and formally signed by member-states at a meeting in Marrakesh, Morocco, on April 15, 1994. The Uruguay agreement now has to be ratified by the governments of the 117 member-countries before being formally put into effect on July 1, 1995.

By all accounts, reaching a final agreement on the Uruguay Round was an extremely difficult process. For some time, it looked as though an agreement might be impossible, which raised fears of trade wars and economic depression. The main impediment to reaching agreement was a long-standing dispute between the United States and the European Community on agricultural subsidies. An agreement had to be reached before December 16, when the "fast-track negotiating authority" granted to the U.S. president, Bill Clinton, by the U.S. Congress would have expired. Had this authority expired, any agreement would have required approval from the U.S. Congress as a whole, rather than only the president—a much more difficult proposition that could effectively have stalled the talks. An eleventh-hour compromise on agricultural subsidies, which reduced the level of subsidies significantly but not as much as the United States had initially wanted, saved the day.

Main Components of the GATT Deal

Some of the most important components of the December 15 agreement are detailed in Table P.1.[1] In brief, if ratified by all member-nations, the Uruguay Round will have the following effects: tariffs on industrial goods will be reduced by more than one-third from their present level; agricultural subsidies will be substantially reduced; for the first time, GATT fair trade and market access rules will be extended to cover a wide range of services; GATT rules will also be extended to enhance protection for patents, copyrights, and trademarks (intellectual property); barriers on trade in textiles will be significantly reduced over 10 years; GATT rules will in general be much clearer and stronger; a World Trade Organization (WTO) will be created to implement the GATT agreement.

Services and Intellectual Property

In the long run, the extension of GATT rules to services and intellectual property may be particularly significant. Up to now, GATT rules have only applied to industrial goods (manufactured goods and commodities). In 1992, world trade in services amounted to $900 billion out of a total of $3,580 billion. Extending GATT rules to this important trading arena could significantly increase both the total share of world trade accounted for by services and the overall volume of world trade. Moreover, the extension of GATT rules to cover intellectual property will make it much easier for high-technology companies to do business in developing nations where intellectual property rules have historically been poorly enforced. In particular, high-technology companies will now have a mechanism to force countries to prohibit the piracy of intellectual property (e.g., the illegal copying of books, computer software, and music recordings, or infringing on patents).

[1] Table P.1 is based on "The GATT Deal," a special report in the *Financial Times*, December 16, 1993, pp. 4–7.

Table P.1:
Main Features of the December 15, 1993, GATT Agreement

Up to Now	The 1993 Agreement	Main Impact
Industrial Tariffs		
Backbone of previous GATT rounds. Tariffs on industrial goods average 5% in industrialized countries—down from 40% in the late 1940s.	Rich countries will cut tariffs on industrial goods by more than one-third. Tariffs will be scrapped altogether on over 40% of manufactured goods.	Easier access to world markets for exports of industrial goods. Lower prices for consumers.
Agriculture		
High farm subsidies and protected markets in United States and EU lead to overproduction and dumping.	Subsidies and other barriers to trade in agricultural products will be cut over six years. Subsidies will be cut by 20%. All import barriers will be converted to tariffs and cut by 36%.	Better market opportunities for efficient food producers. Lower prices for consumers. Restraint of farm subsidies war.
Services		
GATT rules do not extend to services. Many countries protect service industries from international competition.	GATT rules on fair trade principles extended to cover many services. Failure to reach agreement on financial services and telecommunications. Special talks will continue.	Increase in trade in services. Further liberalization of trade in services now seems likely.
Intellectual Property		
Standards of protection for patents, copyrights, and trademarks vary widely. Ineffective enforcement of national laws a growing source of trade friction.	Extensive agreements on patents, copyrights, and trademarks. International standards of protection and agreements for effective enforcement established.	Increased protection and reduction of intellectual property piracy will benefit producers of intellectual property (e.g. computer software firms, performing artists). Will increase transfer of technology.
Textiles		
Rich countries have restricted imports of textiles and clothing through bilateral quotas under Multi-Fiber Arrangement (MFA).	MFA quotas progressively dismantled over 10 years and tariffs reduced. Normal GATT rules will apply at end of 10 years.	Increased trade in textiles should benefit developing countries. Reduced prices for consumers worldwide.
GATT Rules		
GATT remains the same as when drafted in 1947 even though many more countries have entered the world trading community and trade patterns have shifted.	Many GATT rules revised and updated. They include codes on customs valuation and import licensing, customs unions and free trade areas, and rules dealing with waivers from GATT regulations.	Greater transparency, security, and predictability in trading policies.
World Trade Organizations (WTO)		
GATT originally envisioned as part of an International Trade Organization. ITO never ratified and GATT applied provisionally.	GATT becomes a permanent world trade body covering goods, services, and intellectual property with a common disputes procedure. WTO to implement results of Uruguay Round.	More effective advocacy and policing of the international trading system.

The World Trade Organization (WTO)

The clarification and strengthening of GATT rules and the creation of the World Trade Organization (WTO) hold out the promise of more effective policing and enforcement of GATT rules. By promoting trade, the WTO should have a beneficial effect on overall economic growth and development. The WTO will act as an umbrella organization that will encompass the GATT along with two new sister bodies: one on services and the other on intellectual property. The WTO will take over responsibility for arbitrating trade disputes and monitoring the trade policies of member-countries. While the WTO will operate as GATT now does in dispute settlement—on the basis of consensus—member-countries will no longer be able to block adoption of arbitration reports. Arbitration panel reports on trade disputes between member-countries will be automatically adopted by the WTO unless there is a consensus to reject them. Countries found by the arbitration panel to violate GATT rules may appeal to a permanent appellate body of the WTO, but its verdict will be binding. If offenders fail to comply with the recommendations of the arbitration panel, trading partners will have the right to compensation or, as a last resort, to impose commensurate trade sanctions. Every stage of the procedure will be subject to strict time limits. Thus, the WTO will have something that the GATT never had—teeth.[2]

Implications of the GATT Deal

Some of the general implications of the GATT deal are noted in Table P.1. On balance, the world is significantly better off with a GATT deal than without one. Without the deal there was a very real possibility that the world might have slipped into increasingly dangerous trade wars, which might have triggered a substantial recession. With a GATT deal concluded, the current world trading system looks secure, and there is a good possibility that the world economy will now grow faster than it would have otherwise. Estimates on the overall impact of the GATT agreement, however, are not that dramatic. Three studies undertaken in mid-1993 (before the agreement was finalized)—one by the Organization for Economic Cooperation and Development (OECD), one by the World Bank, and one by the GATT Secretariat—have estimated that the deal will add between \$213 billion and \$274 billion in 1992 U.S. dollars to aggregate world income by 2002—or about 0.75 percent to 1 percent of gross global income by that time.[3] However, others argue that these figures underestimate the potential gain because they do not factor in the gains from the liberalization of trade in services, stronger trade rules, and greater business confidence. Including such factors, it is claimed that due to the GATT agreement global economic output could be as much as 8 percent higher than it would otherwise have been by 2002.[4] Whatever figure is closer to the truth, recall what a successful GATT agreement helps avoid—the risk of a trade war that might reduce global economic growth and raise consumer prices.

As for individual firms, some clear winners emerge—and also some that have not done so well in the GATT deal. Two big winners in the United States are Caterpillar, Inc., and John Deere & Co., both manufacturers of heavy construction equipment. The GATT deal eliminates import tariffs on the construction equipment and engines these

---

[2] Frances Williams, "WTO—New Name Heralds New Powers," *Financial Times*, December 16, 1993, p. 5. Frances Williams, "GATT's Successor to Be Given Real Clout," *Financial Times*, April 4, 1994, p. 6.

[3] The studies are: (i) OECD and the World Bank, *Trade Liberalization: The Global Economic Implications*, Paris and Washington, 1993; (ii) OECD, *Assessing the Effects of the Uruguay Round*, Paris, 1993; (iii) GATT Secretariat, *Background Paper: The Uruguay Round*, GATT, 1993.

[4] Martin Wolf, "Doing Good Despite Themselves," *Financial Times*, December 16, 1993, p. 15.

companies produce. Caterpillar estimates that the deal will add $125 million to its $10 billion annual sales and result in 800 more jobs at Caterpillar with a further 1,600 jobs at Caterpillar's suppliers. Other big winners include many small exporters around the world, who, in addition to falling tariffs, will find that GATT contains simplified import licensing rules and steps for harmonizing customs procedures. These rules promise to simplify exporting procedures—procedures that raise exporting costs and are thought to deter many small firms from getting into the export business.

On the other hand, not everyone is pleased with the deal. While pharmaceutical companies are pleased that drug tariffs will be phased out over the next few years, they expressed disappointment that it will take 10 years to phase in patent protection for their products (weak patent protection in many countries has led to local competitors violating patents and copying the successful drugs of multinational pharmaceutical firms). Among the disappointed were financial services companies—particularly big banks. They had hoped for elimination of many of the barriers that prevent them from selling their financial services across borders, but a failure to reach agreement resulted in financial services being specifically excluded from the extension of GATT rules to services. The Hollywood film and television industry was also disappointed. Hollywood had hoped to use the GATT to break down European quotas that limit the number of U.S. movies broadcast on European TV, but opposition from the French government led to this issue being dropped in a last-minute compromise.[5]

For the Future

Although the Uruguay Round has now been agreed to in principle by all member-states, it still has to be formally ratified by the governments of each member-state. The plan is to complete ratification before the end of 1994 so the new set of regulations can take effect on July 1, 1995. However, in the United States, the world's largest trading nation, congressional passage of the Uruguay Round implementing legislation will not be easy. The Clinton administration faces opposition from a number of influential special interests in Congress who fear that they will lose under the new agreement. This includes the agricultural lobby, which will see significant reductions in subsidies, and many business and labor groups who see the pact as diluting U.S. trade laws. For example, labor groups and some businesses argue that in virtually every area, current U.S. law provides the domestic industry with greater remedies against injurious unfair trade than will exist under the new Uruguay Round regime.[6] Despite such opposition, most observers believe that the Uruguay Round legislation will ultimately pass the U.S. Congress, although it may be a bumpy ride.

Once in effect, the 1994 GATT deal still leaves a lot to be done on the international trade front. Substantial trade barriers still remain in areas such as financial services and broadcast entertainment—although these seem likely to be reduced eventually. More significantly, perhaps, there is still a whole range of issues that GATT, and now the WTO, have yet to discuss—but increasingly will need to. Three of the most important areas for future development are environmentalism, workers' rights, and foreign direct investment.[7]

---

[5] Brent Bowers, "For Small Firms, Big Gains Are Seen in the Fine Print," *The Wall Street Journal*, December 16, 1993, p. A12. Staff reporters, "U.S. Business Like Trade Pact as a Whole: But Not Some Parts," *The Wall Street Journal*, December 16, 1993, pp. A3, A13.

[6] Nancy Dunne, "U.S. Farm Interests Fire Warning Shot," *Financial Times*, April 15, 1994, p. 8.

[7] Frances Williams, "Trade Round Like This May Never Be Seen Again," *Financial Times*, December 16, 1993, p. 7.

High on the list of the WTO's future concerns will be the interaction of environmental and trade policies and how to best promote sustainable development and ecological well-being without resorting to protectionism. In particular, the WTO will have to find ways to cope with the increasingly strident claims by environmentalists that expanded international trade encourages companies to locate factories in areas where they are freer to pollute.

Paralleling environmental concerns are concerns that free trade encourages firms to shift production to countries with low labor costs where workers' rights are routinely violated. The United States has repeatedly and unsuccessfully pressed for discussion of common international standards on workers' rights—an idea strongly opposed by poorer nations who fear that it is another excuse for protectionism by the rich.

GATT regulations have never been extended to embrace foreign direct investment. Given the globalization of production that we are now witnessing in the world economy, barriers to foreign direct investment seem antiquated and yet are still widespread (see Chapter 7 for details). Currently many countries place limits on investment by foreign companies in their economies (e.g., local content requirements, local ownership rules, and even outright prohibition). Extending GATT to embrace foreign direct investment might require countries to grant establishment rights to foreign companies.

TWO TRADE DISPUTES

The ink on the December 15th GATT agreement had hardly dried when the burst of euphoria that followed the agreement was dampened by the development of two potentially serious trade disputes, one between the United States and Japan and the other between Britain and Malaysia. Both disputes demonstrate how far the world trading system has to go before reality matches the ideals that GATT has been striving toward for over half a century.

Japan and the United States: Numerical Targets and Cellular Phones

The United States and Japan boast one of the largest bilateral trading relationships in the world. It is also a trading relationship that many see as lopsided, with Japan exporting nearly $60 billion more goods to the United States than it imports from the United States. The trade dispute had its roots in a series of talks between Japan and the United States begun in mid-1993. The subject of these talks was Japan's trade imbalance with the United States and steps that might be taken to open up the Japanese market to more foreign goods and services. In particular, the Clinton administration felt that various nontariff (administrative) trade barriers worked to exclude foreign companies from competing effectively in Japan's automobile, construction, telecommunications, insurance, and medical equipment industries (for details of nontariff trade barriers see Chapter 5).

For months, the U.S. government has been pushing the Japanese government to agree to set numerical targets for foreign imports. The model was a 1991 agreement between Japan and the United States to increase foreign access to Japan's semiconductor market. That agreement contained an *expectation* that due to improved market access, by the end of 1992, foreign companies would be able to gain 20 percent of the Japanese market for semiconductors. The United States chose to view the 20 percent figure as a *target*—as opposed to an expectation—and when the 20 percent figure was reached they jumped to the conclusion that numerical targets work, much to the horror of the

Japanese, who had never seen the 20 percent figure as a target.[8] The Japanese resisted the whole idea of numerical targets for what they saw as a very rational reason: Japan has a free-market economy, and in a free-market economy the government cannot, and should not, tell consumers and companies how much of a foreign product to buy. To complicate matters, the government of Morihiro Hosokawa, then in power, was a fragile coalition and Hosokawa was under strong domestic pressure to stand up to the United States on the issue of numerical targets. The net result was that the Japanese refused to budge and on February 11, 1994, the market access talks collapsed.

The American response was swift—on February 15th the U.S. government announced its intent to introduce formal trade sanctions against Japan for protecting its cellular telephone market. The United States stated that within 30 days it would produce a list of Japanese companies that would be punished with trade sanctions unless Japan opened its cellular telephone market. The cellular telephone market was chosen because it was relatively easy to make a case that administrative trade barriers had made it difficult for the U.S. cellular phone company, Motorola, Inc., to gain market share in Japan. Japan had originally agreed to open up a big part of the cellular telephone market to Motorola in 1989. At that time, the Japanese cellular phone service company, IDO, was building a mobile phone system using a rival technology developed by Nippon Telegraph and Telephone (NTT) to serve the highly populated Tokyo–Nagoya corridor. Under pressure from the Japanese government, IDO agreed to build a separate system using Motorola's technology. However, IDO could not easily afford to build two systems, so it concentrated on the NTT technology. Consequently, as of January 1994 it had 400 base stations for the NTT-compatible system compared with 110 for the Motorola system. This meant that the NTT phones could be used in 94 percent of the area, compared with 61 percent for the Motorola phones. Given this disparity, it is unsurprising that more than 310,000 customers have chosen NTT-compatible phones and only 10,000 use the Motorola phones. According to the U.S. government, the resulting lack of sales violated the comparable market access that Japan promised in 1989.[9]

According to many observers, the real agenda of the U.S. government was to create uncertainty and anxiety in Japan about Washington's next move. The uncertainty would drive up the value of the Japanese yen, thereby making Japan's exports more expensive and further hurting Japan's troubled exporting companies—companies already mired in their deepest recession since World War II. The net effect, it was hoped, would force the Japanese to return to the bargaining table and make concessions on the key issue of numerical targets.[10]

The U.S. government increased the pressure on Japan in early March when it revived a trade law known as "Super 301" that had lapsed in 1990. Super 301 is a provision in U.S. trade law that allows individuals or the government to retaliate against "unjustifiable, unreasonable, or discriminatory traders abroad." While few believe that the U.S. will actually apply Super 301, they see the revival of this law as another step in the game of piling pressure on the Japanese in an attempt to bring them back to the bargaining table with concessions.

---

[8] Michiyo Nakamoto, "Japan 'Trapped' by Chip Import Deal," *Financial Times*, March 23, 1994, p. 4.

[9] Andrew Pollack, "The Trade Frustrations of Motorola," *The New York Times*, February 16, 1994, p. C4.

[10] Thomas Friedman, "United States Hoping to Use Fears of Trade War to Pressure Japan," *The New York Times*, February 16, 1994, pp. C1, C4.

While there is still no sign that the Japanese are willing to give ground on numerical targets, there are signs that the Japanese are willing to make some important concessions to avoid getting drawn into a costly trade war; to this extent, the U.S. tactics might be viewed as eliciting the desired response. On March 13, 1994, Japan announced that it had brokered a deal between Motorola and IDO that would increase Motorola's access to the Japanese market. The deal calls for IDO to bring forward its investment in 159 more base stations for the Motorola phone system and to complete that investment by autumn of 1995. IDO also agreed to reallocate some of its radio frequency used by NTT to Motorola. The Japanese government further agreed to monitor IDO's progress in achieving these goals and to provide IDO with low interest rate loans to help it make the accelerated investments.[11]

On March 30, 1994, the Japanese government followed up by unveiling a package of market-opening measures intended to increase imports, reduce its current account surplus, boost the domestic economy, and open up markets to foreign competition through deregulation. The main thrust of the package was streamlining or eliminating many of the bureaucratic procedures used in the past to block foreign competition in certain sectors. However, the package did not include the numerical targets that the United States had been requesting, and U.S. officials expressed only lukewarm approval of the package.[12]

As of early May 1994, this dispute is still ongoing. A final resolution seems some way off, although most analysts doubt that the Unites States and Japan will enter into a tit-for-tat trade war. To complicate matters further, in early April, Japan's prime minister, Morihiro Hosokawa, a champion of deregulation in Japan, was forced to resign following allegations that he was involved in a long-standing corruption scandal that has already forced three prime ministers out of office since 1991. The political uncertainty following Hosokawa's resignation seems likely to push any resolution of the still-simmering trade dispute between the United States and Japan even further off into the future.

Britain and Malaysia

In mid-February of 1994, a British paper, *The Sunday Times*, ran an article alleging that a £1 billion ($750m) sale of defense equipment by British companies to Malaysia was secured only after bribes had been paid to Malaysian government officials, and after the British Overseas Development Administration (ODA) had agreed to approve a £234 million grant to the Malaysian government for a hydroelectric dam of dubious (according to *The Sunday Times*) economic value. The clear implication was that U.K. officials, in their enthusiasm to see British companies win a large defense contract, had yielded to pressures from "corrupt" Malaysian officials for bribes—both personal and in the form of the £234 million development grant.[13]

What happened next took everyone by surprise—the Malaysian government promptly announced a ban on the import of all British goods and services into Malaysia and demanded an apology from the British government. Officially the ban only applied to government orders for British goods and services, with the private sector left free to buy as it chose. However, British companies with experience in the region are nervous that the private sector will follow the government's lead in shunning British products. At stake is as much as £4 billion in British exports and construction activities in Malaysia, and a presence in one of the world's fastest-growing developing economies (Malaysia's econom-

---

11 Michiyo Nakamoto, "Cell Phone Pact Lifts U.S. Threat against Tokyo," *Financial Times*, March 14, 1994, p. 1.

12 Emiko Terazono, "Japan Trade Package Yields to U.S. Demands on Imports," *Financial Times*, April 30, 1994, pp. 1, 4.

13 Keiran Cooke, "Honeypot of as Much as $4 Billion down the Drain," *Financial Times*, February 26, 1994, p. 4.

ic growth has averaged 8 percent per annum since 1989). In announcing the ban, Malaysia's prime minister, Dr. Mahathir Mohamad, noted that the British media portrays Malaysians as corrupt because "they are not British and not white" and that "we believe the foreign media must learn the fact that developing countries, including a country led by a brown moslem, have the ability to manage their own affairs successfully."[14]

The British government responded by stating that it could not tell the British press what to publish or not to publish, to which Dr. Mahathir replied that there would be "no contracts for British press freedom to tell lies." At the same time, the British government came under attack from members of its Parliament who suspect that the government did act unethically and approve the ODA hydroelectric grant to help British companies win orders in Malaysia. As of May 1994, no quick resolution is in sight. What the dispute demonstrates, however, is that for all of the moves toward global economic integration, trade between nations is still very much subject to the whims of the governments involved.

REGIONAL ECONOMIC INTEGRATION: NAFTA, THE EU, AND APEC

Over the last 12 months the pace of regional economic integration has accelerated worldwide (see Chapter 8 for background). One significant development was in North America, where the North American Free Trade Agreement (NAFTA) was ratified by the U.S. Congress after bitter debate. In Europe, significant developments included the ratification of the Maastricht treaty by the member-nations of the European Community, which subsequently changed its name to the European Union (EU), and a decision to enlarge the EU to 16 nations. In the Asian Pacific region, the Asia Pacific Economic Cooperation group (APEC) emerged as a forum within which intraregional trade issues could be discussed.

NAFTA

The background to NAFTA was discussed in Chapter 8 (see pages 235–38). When Chapter 8 was written NAFTA had been agreed to in principle but not yet ratified by the governments of the three countries involved: Canada, Mexico, and the United States. The United States and Canada entered into a free trade agreement in 1989, and NAFTA involved an extension of that agreement to include Mexico. Both Canada and Mexico had committed themselves to NAFTA by the fall of 1993, leaving only the U.S. government to signal its intention to go forward with the agreement. The Clinton administration had already committed itself to NAFTA, and passage by the U.S. Senate looked likely, but the agreement faced stiff opposition in the U.S. House of Representatives. The vote on NAFTA in the House of Representatives was scheduled for November 17, 1993. Only hours before the vote the outcome was still in doubt, and then a last-minute round of lobbying by President Clinton, which included numerous side deals to sway the support of wavering representatives, led to a final surge of votes for NAFTA and the bill passed the House by a comfortable margin.

The NAFTA agreement became law on January 1, 1994. The contents of the NAFTA agreement include:

- NAFTA abolishes, within 10 years, tariffs on 99 percent of the goods traded between Mexico, Canada, and the United States.

[14] Keiran Cooke, "Arrogance of the West Riles a Maverick," *Financial Times*, February 26, 1994, p. 4. Robert Peston, "Malaysia PM Says Die Is Cast over U.K. Ban," *Financial Times*, March 17, 1994, p. 1.

- NAFTA removes most barriers on the cross-border flow of services, allowing financial institutions, for example, unrestricted access to the Mexican marketplace by 2000.
- NAFTA contains provisions to protect intellectual property rights (copyrights, trademarks, and patents).
- NAFTA removes most restrictions on foreign direct investment between the three member-countries, although special treatment (protection) will be given to Mexican energy and railway industries, American airline and radio communications industries, and Canadian culture.
- NAFTA allows each country to apply its own environmental standards, provided such standards have a scientific basis. Lowering standards to lure investment is described as inappropriate.
- NAFTA establishes two commissions with the power to impose fines and remove trade privileges when environmental standards or legislation involving health and safety, minimum wages, or child labor are ignored.

Opinions remained divided on the consequences of the NAFTA agreement. Those who opposed NAFTA claimed that ratification would be followed by an exodus of jobs from the United States and Canada into Mexico as employers sought to profit from Mexico's lower wages and looser environmental and labor laws. According to one extreme opponent, Ross Perot, up to 5.9 million U.S. jobs would be lost to Mexico after NAFTA. Most economists dismiss these numbers as absurd and alarmist. They point out that Mexico would have to run a bilateral trade surplus with the United States of close to $300 billion for job loss on such a scale to occur—about the size of Mexico's present gross domestic product (GDP). In other words, the scenario is completely implausible.

More sober estimates of the impact of NAFTA range from a net creation of 170,000 jobs in the United States (due to increased Mexican demand for U.S. goods and services) and an increase of $15 billion per year to the United States and Mexican GDP, to a net loss of 490,000 U.S. jobs. To put these numbers in perspective, employment in the U.S. economy is predicted to grow by 18 million over the next 10 years. As most economists repeatedly stress, in the grand scheme of things NAFTA will have a small impact on both Canada and the United States. It could hardly be any other way, since the Mexican economy is at present only 5 percent the size of the U.S. economy. Indeed, the country that is really taking the economic leap of faith by signing NAFTA is neither Canada nor the United States but Mexico. Falling trade barriers will now expose Mexican firms to highly efficient U.S. and Canadian competitors that, when compared to the average Mexican firm, have far greater capital resources, access to highly educated and skilled work forces, and greater technological sophistication. The short-run outcome is bound to be painful economic restructuring and unemployment in Mexico. But if economic theory is any guide, in the long run, there should be dynamic gains in the efficiency of Mexican firms as they adjust to the rigors of a more competitive marketplace. To the extent that this happens, an acceleration of Mexico's long-term rate of economic growth will follow, and Mexico might yet become a major market for Canadian and U.S. firms.[15]

For the future, the big issue now confronting NAFTA is enlargement. Following approval of NAFTA by the U.S. Congress, a number of other Latin American countries

[15] *The Economist*, "NAFTA: The Showdown," November 13, 1993, pp. 23–36. Susan Garland, "Sweet Victory," *Business Week*, November 29, 1993, pp. 30–31.

indicated their desire to eventually join NAFTA. Currently the governments of both Canada and the United States are adopting a wait-and-see attitude. Getting NAFTA approved was such a bruising political experience that neither the Canadian nor the U.S. government has a desire to repeat the process anytime soon. Nevertheless, the U.S. government has signaled its willingness to begin earnest negotiations with Chile in 1995 regarding that country's possible entry into NAFTA.

The European Union

The December 1991 Maastricht treaty was meant to usher in a new era of ever-closer economic and political cooperation for the 12 member-states of the European Community—including plans for monetary union and closer political union (see Chapter 8, pages 232–34). Before becoming law, however, the treaty had to be ratified by each member-state, and there the treaty ran into problems. Danish voters initially rejected the treaty by a narrow margin, the British House of Commons refused to pass the treaty unless some modifications were made, French voters approved the treaty by the narrowest of margins, while in Germany the treaty was challenged on the grounds that it violated the German constitution. Just as damaging to the vision of monetary and political union laid out in the Maastricht treaty was the partial collapse of the European Monetary System in late 1992, which highlighted the difficulties of achieving monetary union (see Chapter 10, pages 304–307 and the case *Chaos in the Currency Markets*, pages 337–41) and the failure of the 12 EC countries to agree on a common foreign policy position toward the political turmoil in the former Yugoslavia (Bosnia-Herzegovina)—a sign of the impediments in the way of any attempt to achieve political union.

To answer Danish and British objections to some of the items contained in the Maastricht agreement, the treaty was subsequently renegotiated to allow for greater flexibility in the timetable for economic and political union. Although the goal of monetary union was set for 1999, both Britain and Denmark were allowed to temporarily opt out of any such union if they did not feel ready to participate. With this commitment in hand, the British House of Commons voted to approve the Maastricht treaty, while Danish voters signaled their acceptance of the revised pact in a national referendum. The last impediment to ratification of the Maastricht treaty was removed on October 12, 1993, when Germany's Constitutional Court ruled that the treaty did not violate the German constitution.

With all 12 EC countries having finally agreed to the terms of the treaty, it went into force on January 1, 1994. In a symbolic gesture to emphasize the importance of the Maastricht treaty, the European Community also changed its name at this point to the European Union (EU). Skepticism remains as to whether the timetable for closer economic and political union laid out in the treaty will be met. According to the treaty, to achieve monetary union by 1999, member-countries must achieve low inflation rates and a stable exchange rate and limit public debt to 60 percent of a country's gross domestic product. No country at present meets all criteria and precious few seem likely to within the Maastricht timetable—in which case monetary union will not occur in 1999 (for a discussion of the implications of European monetary union, see page 232 and pages 304–307).

The other big issue that the EU must now grapple with is enlargement. After a bitter dispute between the existing 12 members, in March 1994 they agreed to enlarge the EU to include Austria, Finland, Sweden, and Norway. Most of the opposition to enlargement came from Britain, which worried that enlargement, and a subsequent reduction in its voting power in the EU's top decision-making body, the Council of Ministers, would limit its ability to block EU developments that it did not like. Britain backed down in the face of strong opposition from other EU members and agreed to enlargement. Voters in the four countries approved for entry must now give their verdicts on joining the EU. If they approve the terms of admission to the EU negotiated by their respective governments, on January 1, 1995, the Europe of 12 will become the Europe of 16. Next the EU must consider likely membership applications from Hungary, Poland, the Czech Republic, and Slovakia.[16]

Asia Pacific Economic Cooperation

Asia Pacific Economic Cooperation (APEC) was founded in 1990 at the suggestion of Australia. APEC has 16 member-states including such economic powerhouses as the United States, Japan, and China. Collectively, the 16 member-states account for half of the world's gross national product (GNP), 40 percent of world trade, and most of the growth in the world economy. The stated aim of APEC is to increase multilateral cooperation in view of the economic rise of the Pacific nations and the growing interdependence within the region. United States support for APEC was also based on the belief that it might be a viable strategy for heading off any moves to create Asian groupings from which the United States would be excluded.

Interest in APEC was heightened considerably in November 1993 when the heads of APEC member-states met for the first time for a two-day conference in Seattle. The run up to the meeting produced a debate over the likely future role of APEC. One view was that APEC should commit itself to the ultimate formation of a free-trade area. Such a move would transform the Pacific Rim from a geographical expression into the world's largest free-trade area. Another view was that APEC would only produce hot air and lots of photo opportunities for its leaders. The APEC meeting ultimately produced little more than some vague commitments from member-states to work closely together for greater economic integration and a general lowering of trade barriers. However, significantly, member-states did not rule out the possibility of closer economic cooperation in the future, and analysts speculated that any failure of GATT negotiations might lead to a move to turn APEC into a free-trade area. For now this scenario looks unlikely—particularly since the Uruguay Round of GATT was finally completed in December 1993. Even so, APEC is worth tracking, for there is a remote possibility that it might ultimately develop into an international trade institution similar in form to NAFTA.[17]

THE COLLAPSE OF THE EUROPEAN MONETARY SYSTEM

The European Monetary System (EMS) of the European Community was created in March 1979. The objectives of this fixed exchange rate system included creating a zone of monetary stability in Europe, controlling inflation through the imposition of monetary discipline, and paving the way for the establishment of a single European Union currency by 1999 as specified in the Maastricht treaty. The EMS permitted the currencies of member-countries to fluctuate within a 2.25 percent band vis-à-vis a central rate that was linked to Germany's deutschmark. (For details see pages 304–307. Also see pages 301–304 for a discussion of the arguments for and against fixed exchange rates.)

The system appeared to work reasonably well until mid-1992—then it began to unravel. The central cause seems to have been high German interest rates. In 1991 and

---

[16] *The Economist*, "From the Arctic to the Mediterranean," March 5, 1994, pp. 52, 57. Lionel Barber, "More Does Not Mean Merrier," *Financial Times*, March 14, 1994, p. 13.

[17] *The Economist*, "Aimless in Seattle," November 13, 1993, pp. 35–36.

1992, the German central bank, the Bundesbank, sharply raised interest rates to hold German inflation in check. The high interest rates increased demand for the German deutschmark (D-mark), primarily because financial institutions could earn a higher interest rate by holding their money in German D-marks than in other European currencies. In order to stay within the 2.25 percent band and maintain the value of their currencies against the D-mark, other EMS members were forced to raise their interest rates. The result was a credit squeeze that depressed business and consumer demand in Europe and contributed to a severe economic recession. However, this did not stop the rise of the D-mark on foreign exchange markets, and by September 1992, both Britain and Italy were having difficulty keeping their currencies within the 2.25 percent band. Sensing that both currencies would have to be devalued, speculators started to buy D-marks and sell British pounds and lire. This increased the downward pressure on the pound and lira, and despite heavy buying of pounds and lire by the central banks of Britain and Italy, the slide in the value of their currencies against the D-mark continued. Defeated, both Britain and Italy withdrew from the EMS in mid-1992 (see the case *Chaos in the Currency Markets*, pages 337–41).

With Britain and Italy out of the system, speculative pressure eased and the system appeared to return to something approaching equilibrium. However, the fault lines that appeared in the EMS in September 1992 widened again during 1993. By July 1993, German interest rates were still high, as was demand for German D-marks, and the French franc was now under speculative pressure. The Bank of France responded by raising key interest rates, hoping to stem the flow of funds from francs to D-marks, but funds continued to flow to D-marks. Betting that France would have to devalue the franc against the D-mark, speculators began to sell francs and buy D-marks in large quantities. To defend the value of the franc and keep it within the 2.25 percent band permitted by the EMS, the Bank of France was forced to enter the foreign exchange markets, buying francs and selling D-marks. At one point on Friday, July 30, 1993, the Bank of France was reportedly selling $100 million a minute in borrowed foreign exchange trying to stop the franc from falling below its floor of FFr3.4305 to the D-mark permitted by the EMS. By the end of that day, the amount of foreign exchange deployed by the Bank of France to hold the franc's EMS parity is thought to have exceeded FFr300 billion (more than $50 billion). Heavy borrowing from Germany's Bundesbank and other central banks wiped out France's foreign currency reserves and left the Bank of France with a FFr180 billion deficit.[18]

The following day, July 31, the European Community's monetary committee, linking the Finance Ministry and central bank officials from the 12 member-countries, assembled to discuss the crisis. Faced with the impending collapse of the system, the committee bowed to the inevitable and decided that all currencies except the D-mark and the Dutch guilder were to abandon their existing 2.25 percent fluctuation band and move to 15 percent.

Widening the permitted fluctuation bands to 15 percent meant that the EMS now existed in name only. This action also amounted to an admission that the EMS had failed to create a zone of monetary stability in Europe. To critics of fixed exchange rate systems, the collapse of the EMS seemed to confirm their argument that fixed exchange rate systems are unmanageable and can be blown apart by speculative pressures. Moreover, the collapse of the EMS cast a pall over the plans laid out in the Maastricht treaty to achieve monetary union by 1999. The EMS was envisaged as the vehicle that would

---

[18] David Marsh, "Faultlines Show in Franco-German Unity," *Financial Times*, December 23, p. 4.

move the EU toward monetary union, but with the EMS in tatters, it is no longer clear how this can be achieved.[19]

THE BUMPY ROAD TO ECONOMIC REFORM: GROWING CHAOS IN RUSSIA

In mid-1993, it was still possible to talk with some optimism about the business opportunities bought about by the new world order that followed the dramatic collapse of Eastern Europe's Communist regimes and finally the Soviet Union itself. It is no longer possible to be so optimistic. Although some of the former Communist states of Eastern Europe have managed their transformation to a market economy with a degree of success—particularly Poland, the Czech Republic, and Hungary—many others have been far less successful. Russia, by far the largest of the former Communist states, where events have taken a marked turn for the worse, is an example of the lack of success in transforming to a market economy.

Russia's problems are both political and economic. Taken together they present a disturbing picture that demonstrates just how risky investment can be in these areas of the world. On the political front, the reform-minded government of the current Russian president, Boris Yeltsin, has tried for two years to push reform programs through the Russian Parliament, with only limited success. Opposition came from an intransigent block of Russian nationalists and former communists who seemed determined to block any reform efforts. Frustrated by continual opposition, on September 21, 1993, Yeltsin dissolved Parliament, only to face an occupation of the Parliament building by a large number of dissenting politicians and their supporters. After failing to persuade the occupiers to vacate the building and after the leaders of the occupation called for the overthrow of Yeltsin's government, Yeltsin ordered in troops and, in the bloody melee that followed, the occupation was forcibly ended. Yeltsin's victory proved short-lived, for subsequent election for a new Parliament held on December 12, 1993, produced a strong showing for three antireform parties—the inappropriately named Liberal Democratic Party (actually a neo-fascist nationalist party), the Communist Party of Russia, and the Agrarian Party. The pro-Yeltsin parties, Russia's Choice and Yabloko, received less than 30 percent of the vote.

With the influence of the reform forces in Russia visibly weakened after the December elections, reform slowed still further and economic chaos increased. In February 1994, Russian economic production fell 24 percent compared with the same period a year earlier. The production of oil, Russia's most precious commodity because it is by far the most tradable, continued to fall rapidly—down more than 14 percent in the first two months of 1994 compared with the same period in 1993. Since early 1992, Russia's oil production has been cut in half. The Russian budget is a mess; the 1994 budget calls for expenditure of Rbs183,000 and income of Rbs120,000, resulting in a deficit that amounts to 9 percent of Russia's gross national product. The real deficit might be two or even three times this amount, because a rising tide of bankruptcies and growing unemployment is predicted to cause a slump in government tax revenues—a fact conveniently ignored in the budget document. Given the inability of Russia to raise funds on the international capital market, the only way of financing such a huge budget deficit will be by printing money. The result will probably be an increase in inflation, which in February 1994 was already running at a rate of 10 percent *per month*. If inflation in Russia

---

[19] *The Economist*, "Europe's Monetary Future," October 23, pp. 25–27.

accelerates again, and it is currently down from 25 percent per month in February 1993, the free fall in the value of the Russian ruble on the foreign exchange markets will continue. Since April 1991, the ruble has lost 90 percent of its value against major currencies such as the U.S. dollar (for the link between the money supply, inflation rates, and foreign exchange rates see pages 268–74).

Given the state of the Russian economy, it is not surprising that no western companies have made very large commitments to Russia in recent years. While changes in the economic policies of China, India, and Vietnam have produced an excited buzz about investment possibilities, there is very little foreign investment activity in Russia. The one bright spot is that some progress has been made toward the privatization of Russia's state-owned enterprises. By February 1994, nearly 80 percent of Russia's small enterprises had been auctioned off to private owners, and 14,000 medium and large-sized concerns have also gone through the privatization process. However, the financial condition of many of the privatized enterprises is generally no better—and sometimes worse—than that of their state counterparts, so any vitality that these enterprises might inject into Russia's failing economy may be some years off. In sum, the Russian experience of its shift to a more market-based economic system is very discouraging—and it makes much of the optimism about business opportunities in Russia that followed the 1991 collapse of the Soviet Union seem misplaced.[20]

CONCLUSION

While this postscript is current as of May 1994, there is little doubt that the ongoing evolution of the world's political and economic systems will continue to produce surprises that will outdate some of the topical material contained in this book. Among the events on the horizon to keep in view are

- The continuing economic and political turmoil in Russia and other states of the former Soviet Union. Developments here could shatter post-Cold War assumptions about the decline in political and military tensions among the world's major states.
- The upcoming battle in the U.S. Congress to ratify the Uruguay Round of the GATT. Look for a repeat of the NAFTA debate.
- The ongoing trade dispute between the United States and Japan over market access.
- Increasing volatility in the world's financial and currency markets as the continuing emergence of a truly global capital market facilitates the flow of vast quantities of capital across national borders in pursuit of higher long-term returns or speculative gains. The havoc that speculative money wreaked on the European Monetary System could be a foreshadow of things to come.

---

[20] John Lloyd, "A Push and They All Fall Down," *Financial Times*, April 22, 1994, p. 17. *The Economist*, "Russia's Bankruptcy Bears," March 19, 1994, pp. 79–80.

PART ONE

Introduction and Overview

Overview and Plan of the Book

KODAK VERSUS FUJI

INTRODUCTION

THE GLOBALIZATION OF THE WORLD ECONOMY

Declining Trade and Investment Barriers
The Role of Technological Change
Implications for Management

THE CHANGING NATURE OF INTERNATIONAL BUSINESS

The Changing World Output and World Trade Picture
The Changing Foreign Direct Investment Picture
The Changing Nature of the Multinational Enterprise
The Changing World Order

HOW INTERNATIONAL BUSINESS IS DIFFERENT

ORGANIZATION OF THIS BOOK

The Environmental Context
The Firm
Business Operations

SUMMARY OF CHAPTER

DISCUSSION QUESTIONS

CHAPTER 1

KODAK VERSUS FUJI

Kodak first started selling photographic equipment in Japan in 1889, and by the 1930s, it had a dominant position in the Japanese market. Then came World War II and the subsequent occupation of Japan. In the aftermath of the war, U.S. occupation forces persuaded most U.S. companies, including Kodak, to leave Japan to give the war-torn local industry a chance to recover. Kodak reluctantly handed over the marketing of its products to Japanese distributors. Effectively priced out of the market by tariff barriers, over the next 35 years Fuji gained a 70 percent share of the market while Kodak saw its share slip to a miserable 5 percent. Then, in the early 1980s, Fuji launched an aggressive export drive, attacking Kodak in the North American and European markets where for decades

Kodak had enjoyed a lucrative dominance in color film. Fuji's onslaught squeezed Kodak's margins, took market share, and forced the company to slash costs. • With their backs to the wall, Kodak's top executives admitted to themselves that their company faced a global challenge from Fuji that would only grow. They also realized that repeated rounds of trade negotiations had dismantled most of the postwar trade barriers that had protected the Japanese film market from foreign competition. Deciding that a good offense is the best defense, in 1984 Kodak set out to invade its rival's home market. Over the next six years, Kodak spent an estimated $500 million in Japan. At a time when Fuji was committed to heavy spending on promotion abroad, Kodak outspent Fuji in Japan by a ratio of more than 3 to 1. It erected mammoth $1 million neon signs as landmarks in many of Japan's big cities. It sponsored sumo wrestling, judo, and tennis tournaments, and even the Japanese team at the 1988 Seoul Olympics, a neat reversal of Fuji's 1984 coup when it won the race to become the official sponsor of the Los Angeles Olympics. • Kodak realized that to make any headway in Japan, it had to control its own distribution and marketing channels. Rather than go it alone, Kodak established a joint venture with its distributor, Nagase Sangyo, an Osaka-based trading company specializing in chemicals. Kodak also realized that it would not succeed in Japan unless it thought and acted just like a Japanese company. Today, apart from a small unit that liaises with Kodak's headquarters in Rochester, New York, all of Kodak's employees in Japan are Japanese, complete with a Japanese boss and Japanese management. There are only 30 foreigners among Kodak's 4,500 employees in Japan. So thoroughly Japanese has Kodak become that it even has its own *keiretsu* (family of suppliers with cross-holdings in each other). • All of this activity has bought success. Between 1984 and 1990, Kodak's sales in Japan soared sixfold to an estimated $1.3 billion. Kodak's share of sales to amateur photographers has grown by a steady 1 percent each year for the past six years. Kodak now has a 15 percent share of that market and may well overtake second-place Konica within the next few years. Kodak's success has been even more impressive in Tokyo, where it now has 35 percent of the amateur market. In addition, Kodak now has 85 percent of the market for medical X-ray film and photographic supplies to the graphic arts and publishing industries. Perhaps the most important effect of Kodak's Japanese thrust, however, is that Fuji's margins in Japan have been squeezed. Kodak has put Fuji on the defensive, forcing it to divert resources from overseas to defend itself at home. By 1990, some of Fuji's best executives had been pulled back to Tokyo. *"The Revenge of Big Yellow,"* The Economist, *November 10, 1990, pp. 77–78.*

INTRODUCTION

An **international business** is any firm that engages in international trade or investment. *International trade* occurs when a firm exports goods or services to consumers in another country. *International investment* occurs when a firm invests resources in business activities outside its home country. The two firms discussed in the opening case, Kodak and Fuji, are both international businesses. Both export, and both have invested in activities outside their home countries.

This book is about the issues confronting managers in an international business, whether that business is small or large. It is about the problems managers face when they try to export to another country or invest in another country. It is about policy issues related to a firm's strategy, organizational structure, manufacturing, materials management, marketing, R&D, human relations, finance, and accounting that arise in an international business. A central presumption of the book is that to understand these issues and problems, one must first understand the economic, political, and cultural environment within which international business takes place. One must understand how countries differ and what these differences imply for an international business. One must understand the political and economic context within which international trade and investment occur. And, one must understand the nature of the world monetary system, including, most important, the mechanisms governing currency exchange rates between countries. Accordingly, the first half of this book deals with the environmental context of international business, while the second half focuses explicitly on the issues and problems confronting managers in an international business.

One point that must be made immediately is that the international business environment is changing rapidly. We outline the reasons for this in the next section when we consider the globalization of the world economy. In subsequent chapters of the first half of the book, we elaborate on the nature and implications of the forces for change in the world economy. For now, note that changes in the international business environment are forcing many firms to think of the world as one vast market. For example, as suggested by the story of Fuji and Kodak in the opening case, competition in many industries is now a global game in which the same competitors confront each other in various nations. At the same time, despite all the talk in the popular press about the globalization of world markets, the "global village," the "global factory," and "global products" (e.g., Coca-Cola, Levi's jeans, and Sony Walkmans), national differences still exist and have a profound effect on the way business is conducted in different nations. Thus, the opening case tells us that to compete successfully in Japan, Kodak realized it had to think and act just like a Japanese company. The tension between the need to view the world as a single market and the need to be responsive to differences between countries is fundamental in international business. As a theme, it will reoccur often throughout this book, particularly in the second half of the book when we look at issues pertaining to managing an international business.

The remainder of this chapter is divided into four sections. The first section discusses the forces for change in the world economy. The second section discusses the changing nature of international business. The third section outlines how international business differs from business in a purely domestic context. The fourth section provides an outline of the chapters that make up this book and explains how the topics in each chapter relate to an integrated whole.

THE GLOBALIZATION OF THE WORLD ECONOMY

A popular feeling is that something fundamental is happening in the world economy. The term *global shift* has been coined by one author to capture the essence of the change.[1] We seem to be witnessing the globalization of markets and production. With regard to the **globalization of markets,** it has been argued that we are moving away from an economic system in which national markets are distinct entities, isolated from each other by trade barriers and barriers of distance, time, and culture, and toward a system in which national markets are merging into one huge global marketplace. According to this view, the tastes and preferences of consumers in different nations are beginning to converge on

[1] P. Dicken, *Global Shift* (New York: Guilford Press, 1992).

some global norm. Thus, in many industries it is no longer meaningful to talk about the "German market," "the American market," or the "Japanese market"; there is only the "global market." The global acceptance of Coca-Cola, Levi's jeans, Sony Walkmans, and McDonald's hamburgers exemplifies this trend.[2] It is important not to push this view too far, however. As we shall see in later chapters, very significant differences in consumer tastes and preferences between national markets still remain in many industries. These differences frequently require that marketing strategies and product features be customized to local conditions. Notwithstanding this, however, there is no doubt that there are more global markets today than at any previous period in history.

As for the **globalization of production,** it has been observed that increasingly, individual firms are dispersing parts of their production process to various locations around the globe to take advantage of national differences in the cost and quality of production factors (e.g., labor, energy, land, capital). As a consequence, it is no longer always meaningful to talk about "American products," "German products," or "Japanese products." Consider General Motor's (GM) Pontiac Le Mans, which is commonly perceived as an "American product." Based upon its comparison of production factor costs and quality in various countries, GM has dispersed many of the Le Mans production activities to other countries. As a result, of the $20,000 paid to GM for a Le Mans,

- About $6,000 goes to South Korea, where the Le Mans is assembled.
- $3,500 goes to Japan for advanced components (engines, transaxles, and electronics).
- $1,500 goes to Germany, where the Le Mans was designed.
- $800 goes to Taiwan, Singapore, and Japan for small components.
- $500 goes to Great Britain for advertising and marketing services.
- About $100 goes to Ireland for data processing services.
- The remaining $7,600 goes to GM and to the lawyers, bankers, and insurance agents that GM uses in the United States.

So is the Le Mans an "American product"? Obviously not; but neither is it a "Korean product," a "Japanese product," nor a "German product." Like an increasing number of the products that we buy today, it is, in fact, a *global product.* (Box 1.1 presents further illustrations of this phenomenon.)[3]

It is also important to stress that the globalization of production is not limited to large firms like General Motors. An increasingly large number of medium-sized and small firms are also engaged in global production. For example, Swan Optical, a U.S. manufacturer of eyeglasses, generated revenues of $20 million in 1990. Hardly a giant, yet Swan is a global company with manufacturing and design operations in Hong Kong, mainland China, Japan, France, and Italy.[4]

Two factors seem to underlie the trend toward globalization of markets and production. The first is the decline in barriers to the free flow of goods, services, and capital that has occurred since the end of World War II. The second factor is the dramatic developments in communication, information, and transportation technologies in the same period.

---

[2] T. Levitt, "The Globalization of Markets," *Harvard Business Review,* May–June 1983, pp. 92–102.

[3] R. B. Reich, *The Work of Nations* (New York: Alfred A. Knopf, 1991).

[4] C. S. Trager, "Enter the Mini-Multinational," *Northeast International Business,* March 1989, pp. 13–14.

How "American" Are Cars Sold in America?

BOX 1.1

In 1992 the *Detroit Free Press* constructed an Index of American Content for 29 cars sold in the United States. The index reflects four weighted factors: whether the car is sold by a U.S.-based company, where it was designed and engineered, where it was assembled, and how many of its parts were made in the United States. The index score would be zero for a car with no U.S. content and 100 for a car with all U.S. content. The index, shown in the table, contained some surprises. For example, some "Japanese" cars, such as the Mazda Navajo, the Nissan Quest, and the Honda Accord Wagon, had greater "American" content than cars widely perceived as "American built," such as GM's Pontiac Le Mans, Chrysler's Dodge Stealth, and Ford's Mercury Capri. Ford's Mercury Capri came in with the lowest ranking for a U.S.-nameplate car (18). The Capri is, in fact, designed in Italy; its engine and drive train are made in Japan, and the car itself is assembled in Australia. The Capri's only U.S. part may be its Ford nameplate.

Car	Index Score	Car	Index Score
Ford Taurus	100	Honda Accord Wagon	65
Pontiac Bonneville	100	Geo Prizm	64
GM Saturn	100	Honda Civic	46
Ford Escort	95	Nissan Sentra	46
Chevrolet Cavalier	93	Mazda 626	46
Plymouth Acclaim	93	Honda Accord	46
Cadillac Allante	83	Pontiac Le Mans	35
Ford Probe	78	Dodge Stealth	28
Mazda Navajo	75	Mercury Capri	18
Mercury Villager	73	Nissan Maxima	17
Nissan Quest	72	Acura Legend	8
Ford Crown Victoria	70	Mazda 323	8
Plymouth Laser	[illegible]	Mazda MX-3	8
Mercury Tracer	65	Nissan 300ZX	8

Source: "Cars: American Style," The Seattle Times, *March 27, 1992, pp. D7, D8.*

Declining Trade and Investment Barriers

During the 1920s and 30s many of the nation-states of the world erected formidable barriers to international trade and investment. Many of these barriers took the form of high tariffs on imports of manufactured goods. The typical aim of such tariffs was to protect domestic industries from "foreign competition." One of their consequences, however, was "beggar thy neighbor" retaliatory trade policies with countries progressively raising trade barriers against each other. Ultimately, this depressed world demand and contributed to the Great Depression of the 1930s.

Having learned from this experience, after World War II, the advanced industrial nations of the West—under U.S. leadership—committed themselves to the goal of removing barriers to the free flow of goods, services, and capital between nations. The goal of removing barriers to the free flow of goods was enshrined in the treaty known as the General Agreement on Tariffs and Trade (GATT). Under the umbrella of GATT, there has been a significant lowering of barriers to free flow of goods in the half-century since World War II. More recently, attempts have been made to expand the GATT umbrella to include services. At the same time, many countries have been progressively

Figure 1.1
The Growth of World Trade and World Output

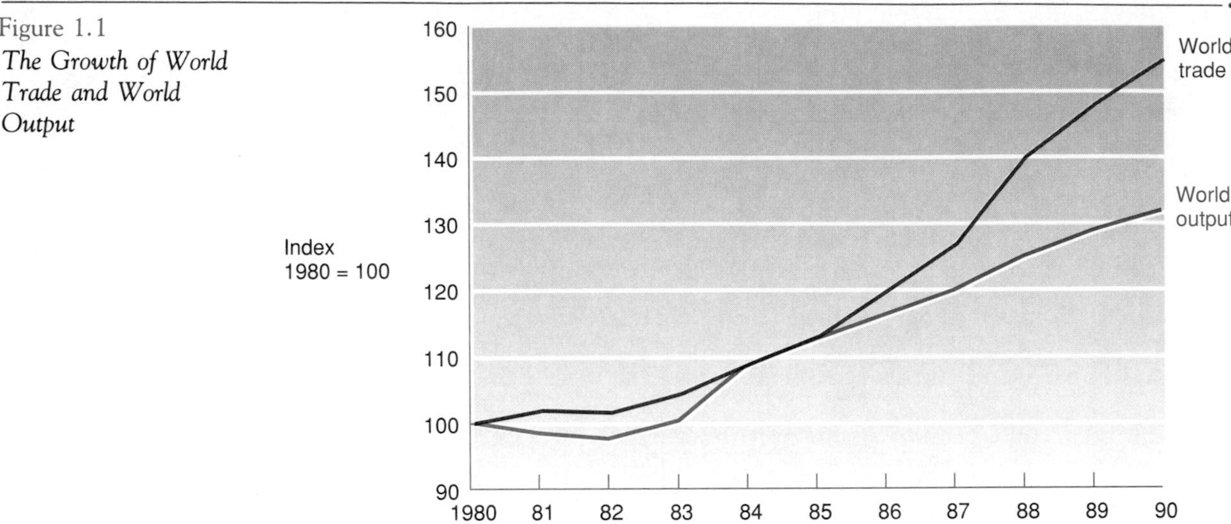

Source: World Bank, World Development Report, 1992, *Tables 1.4, 1.7*

removing restrictions on capital inflows and outflows. During 1991 alone, for example, 34 countries, rich and poor, made 82 changes to their laws governing foreign direct investment. All but two of those changes made the laws less restrictive, thereby encouraging both outward investment by domestic firms and inward investment by foreign firms.[5]

These trends facilitate both the globalization of markets and the globalization of production. Increasingly, the lowering of trade barriers enables firms to view the world, rather than a single country, as their market. The lowering of trade barriers also enables firms to base individual production activities at the optimal location for that activity, serving the world market from that location. Thus a firm might design a product in one country, produce component parts in two other countries, assemble the product in yet another country, and then export the finished product around the world.

There is plenty of hard evidence that the lowering of trade barriers has facilitated the globalization of production. For example, over the last decade the volume of world trade grew faster than the volume of world output. Between 1980 and 1990, total world output grew by 32 percent, while world trade grew by more than 55 percent. (See Figure 1.1.)[6] What these figures imply is that more and more firms are doing what GM does with the Pontiac Le Mans and dispersing manufacturing, marketing, and design activities around the globe to the optimal location for each activity.

Consistent with this trend, the evidence suggests that **foreign direct investment (FDI)** is playing an increasing role in the global economy as firms ranging in size from General Motors to Swan Optical increase their cross-border investments. Between 1984 and 1989, the flow of new FDI worldwide rose at an annual rate of 29 percent, three times the growth rate of international trade. The major investors have been U.S. companies investing in Europe and (increasingly) Japan and Japanese and European companies

---

5 "Another World," The Economist, *World Economy Survey,* September 19, 1992, pp. 15–18.

6 The Economist, *The Economist Book of Vital World Statistics* (New York: Random House, 1990).

investing in the United States.[7] For example, Japanese auto companies have been investing rapidly in U.S.-based auto assembly operations.

Another consequence of the lowering of trade barriers and the resulting globalization of production is that imports are penetrating more deeply into the world's largest economies. In 1970 imports were equivalent to 4.1 percent of the U.S. gross national product (GNP). In 1980 to 9.1 percent; and in 1989 to more than 18 percent. In Japan, which is scarcely noted for its imports, imports rose from 10 percent of GNP in 1970 to 12 percent in 1980, and to around 13 percent in 1989. More important perhaps, in 1989 for the first time ever manufactured goods, rather than raw materials, accounted for more than half of Japan's imports.[8] The growth of imports is a natural by-product of the growth of world trade and the trend toward manufacturing component parts, or even entire products, overseas before shipping them back home for final sale.

Finally, the globalization of markets and production, and the resulting growth of world trade, foreign direct investment, and imports all imply that firms around the globe are finding their home markets under attack from foreign competitors. This is true in Japan, where Kodak has taken market share in the film industry away from Fuji in recent years, in the United States where Japanese automobile firms have taken market share away from GM, Ford, and Chrysler, and in Western Europe where the once-dominant Dutch company, Philips, has seen its market share in the consumer electronics industry taken by Japan's JVC, Matsushita, and Sony. The bottom line is that the growing integration of the world economy into a single, huge marketplace is increasing the intensity of competition in a wide range of manufacturing and service industries.

Having said all of this, it would be a mistake to take declining trade barriers for granted. As we shall see in the following chapters, protectionist pressures are once more on the rise in the United States and elsewhere. Although a return to the "beggar thy neighbor" trade policies of the 1920s and 30s is unlikely, it is not clear whether the political majority in the industrialized world favors further reductions in trade barriers. If trade barriers decline no further, at least for the time being, a temporary limit may have been reached in the globalization of both markets and production.

The Role of Technological Change

Whereas the lowering of trade barriers made globalization of markets and production a theoretical possibility, technological change made it a tangible reality. Since the end of World War II, there have been major advances in communications, information processing, and transportation technology. Perhaps the single most important innovation is the development of the microprocessor, which enabled the explosive growth of high-power, low-cost computing, vastly increasing the amount of information that can be processed by individuals and firms. Moreover, the microprocessor underlies many recent advances in communications technology. Over the last 30 years global communications have been revolutionized by developments in satellite and optical fiber technology. Satellites and optical fibers can carry hundreds of thousands of signals simultaneously. Both of these technologies rely upon the microprocessor to encode, transmit, and decode the vast amount of information that flows along these electronic highways.

In addition to these developments, several major innovations in transportation technology have occurred since World War II. In economic terms, the most important are probably development of commercial jet aircraft and superfreighters and the introduction of containerization, which greatly simplifies transshipment from one mode of

---

[7] "Foreign Investment and the Triad," *The Economist*, August 24, 1991, p. 57.

[8] "Managing Your Oyster," *The Economist*, October 28, 1989, p. 78.

Figure 1.2 *The Shrinking Globe*

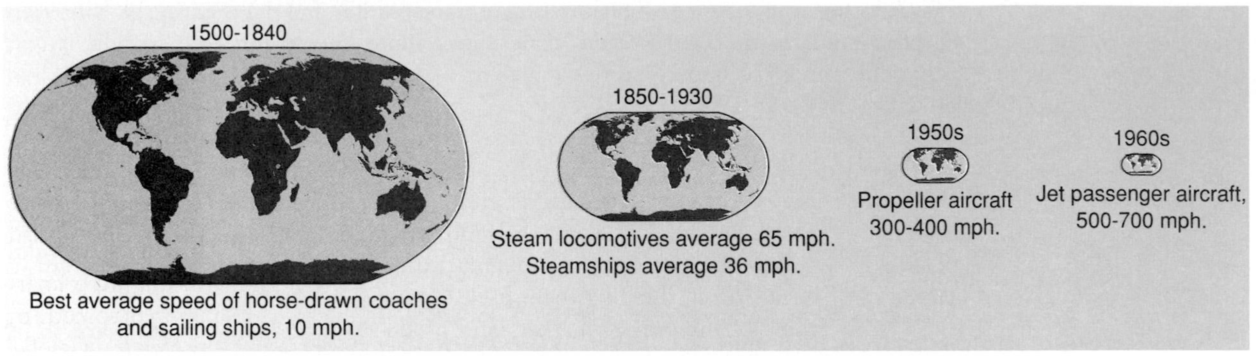

Source: P. Dicken, Global Shift *(New York: Guilford Press, 1992), p. 104*

transport to another. Most significant, the advent of commercial jet travel, by reducing the time needed to get from one location to another, has effectively shrunk the globe (see Figure 1.2). As a consequence of jet travel, New York is now "closer" to Tokyo than it was to Philadelphia in the Colonial days.

Implications for the Globalization of Production

As a result of the technological innovations discussed above, the real costs of information processing and communication have fallen dramatically in the last two decades. This has made it possible for a firm to manage a globally dispersed production system. Indeed, a worldwide communications network has become essential for many international businesses. For example, Texas Instruments (TI), the U.S. electronics firm, has approximately 50 plants in some 19 countries. A satellite-based communications system allows TI to coordinate, on a global scale, its production planning, cost accounting, financial planning, marketing, customer service, and personnel management. The system consists of more than 300 remote job-entry terminals, 8,000 inquiry terminals, and 140 mainframe computers. The system enables managers of TI's worldwide operations to send vast amounts of information to each other instantaneously and to effect tight coordination between the firm's different plants and activities.[9]

A similar example is that of another U.S. electronics firm, Hewlett-Packard, which uses satellite communications and information processing technologies to link its worldwide operations. Hewlett-Packard has new-product development teams composed of individuals based in different countries (e.g., Japan, the United States, Great Britain, and Germany). When developing new products, these individuals use teleconferencing technologies to "meet" on a weekly basis. They also communicate with each other daily via telephone, electronic mail, and fax. Communication technologies have enabled Hewlett-Packard to increase the integration of its globally dispersed operations and to reduce the time needed for developing new products.[10]

In addition to communications and information processing technology, the development of commercial jet aircraft has helped knit together the worldwide operations of many international businesses. Using jet travel, an American manager need spend a day

[9] Dicken, *Global Shift.*

[10] Interviews with Hewlett-Packard personnel by the author.

at most traveling to her firm's European or Asian operations. This enables her to oversee a globally dispersed production system.

Implications for the Globalization of Markets

The same technological innovations have also facilitated the globalization of markets. Low-cost jet travel has resulted in the mass movement of people between countries. This has reduced the cultural distance between countries and is bringing about some convergence of consumer tastes and preferences. At the same time, global communications networks and global media are creating a worldwide culture. U.S. television networks such as CNN, MTV, and HBO are now received in many countries around the world, and Hollywood films are shown the world over. In any society the media are primary conveyers of culture; as global media develop, we must expect the evolution of something akin to a global culture. A logical result of this evolution is the emergence of global markets for consumer products. Indeed, the first signs that this is occurring are already apparent. It is now as easy to find a McDonald's restaurant in Tokyo as it is in New York, to buy a Sony Walkman in Rio as it is in Berlin, and to buy Levi's jeans in Paris as it is in San Francisco.

On the other hand, we must be careful not to overemphasize this trend. While modern communications and transport technologies are ushering in the "global village," very significant differences remain between countries in culture, consumer preferences, and the ways in which business is conducted. As we shall see in subsequent chapters, a firm that ignores these differences does so at its peril.

Implications for Management

The trend toward globalization of production and markets has several important implications for the manager of an international business. The manager of today's firm operates in an environment that offers more opportunities but one that is more complex and competitive than the one her predecessor faced a generation ago. Opportunities are greater because the movement toward free trade has opened up many formerly protected national markets. The potentials for export, for making direct investments overseas, and for dispersing productive activities to the optimal locations around the globe are now all greater than ever before. The environment is more complex because today's manager often must meet the challenges of doing business in countries with radically different cultures and of coordinating globally dispersed operations. The environment is more competitive because, in addition to domestic competitors, the modern manager must also deal with cost-efficient foreign competitors. It is these management issues that we will address throughout this book.

THE CHANGING NATURE OF INTERNATIONAL BUSINESS

Hand in hand with the trends toward globalization of markets and of production, there has been a fairly dramatic change in the nature of international business over the last 30 years or so. As late as the 1960s four stylized facts described much of international business. The first fact was U.S. dominance in the world economy and world trade picture. The second fact was U.S. dominance in the world foreign direct investment picture. Related to this, the third fact was the dominance of large, multinational U.S. firms on the international business scene. The fourth fact was that roughly half of the globe—the centrally planned economies of the Communist world—was off-limits to Western international businesses. All four of these stylized facts are changing. We look at each in turn.

Figure 1.3 *The Changing Pattern of World Output*

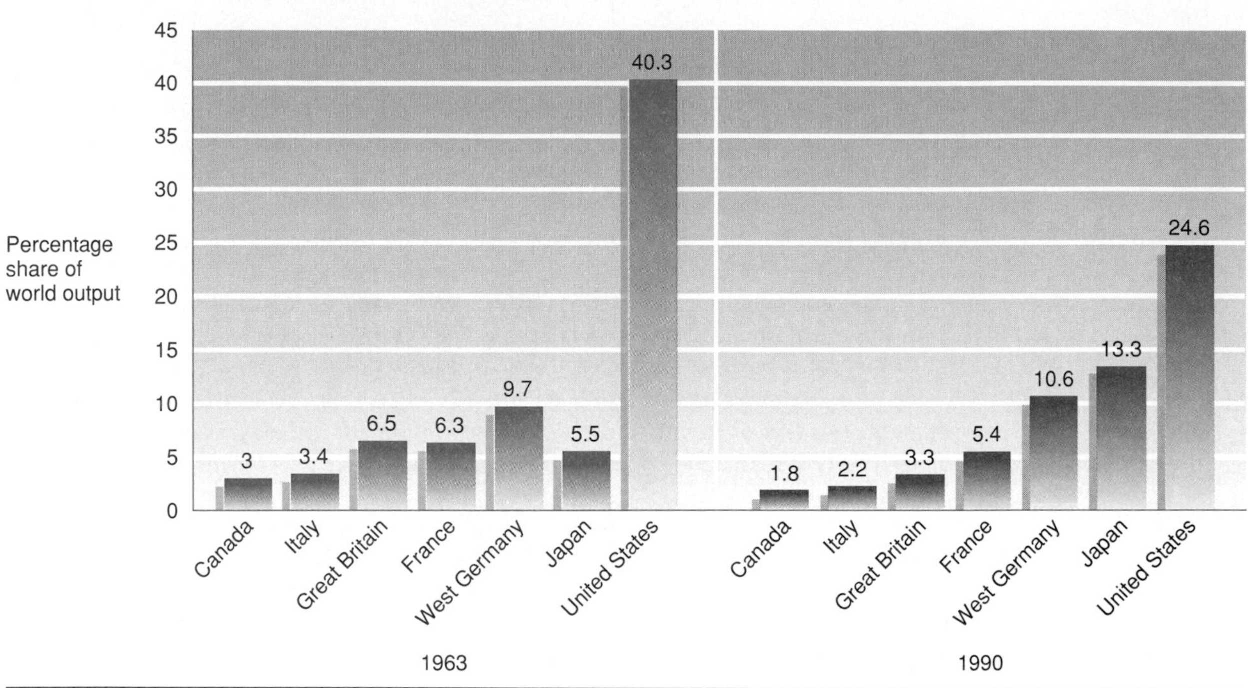

Source: World Bank, World Development Report, *various issues.*

The Changing World Output and World Trade Picture

In the early 1960s the United States was still by far the world's dominant industrial power. In 1963, for example, the United States accounted for 40.3 percent of world manufacturing output. However, by 1990 the United States accounted for only 24 percent (see Figure 1.3). This decline in the U.S. position was not an absolute decline, since the U.S. economy grew at a relatively robust average annual rate of 2.8 percent in the 1965–90 time period. Rather, it was a relative decline, reflecting the faster economic growth of several other economies, most notably that of Japan. As can be seen from Figure 1.3, in the 1963–90 time period, Japan's share of world manufacturing output increased from 5.5 percent to 13.3 percent. Other countries that markedly increased their share of world output include South Korea and Taiwan.

Reflecting the relative decline in U.S. dominance, by the end of the 1980s its position as the world's leading exporter was threatened. During the 1960s the United States routinely accounted for 20 percent of world exports of manufactured goods. Figure 1.4 reports manufacturing exports as a percentage of the world total in 1991. As can be seen, the U.S. share of world exports of manufactured goods had slipped to 12 percent by 1991. The United States was followed by Germany, which accounted for 11.4 percent of world exports, and Japan with 8.9 percent.[11]

Over the last thirty years U.S. dominance in export markets has waned as Japan, Germany, and a number of newly industrialized countries such as South Korea and Taiwan have taken a larger share of world exports. Given the rapid economic growth rates now being experienced by countries such as China, Thailand, and Indonesia,

[11] "U.S. Takes Lead Back in Exports," *The New York Times,* March 18, 1992, p. C1.

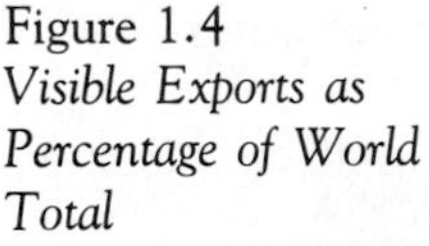
Figure 1.4
Visible Exports as Percentage of World Total

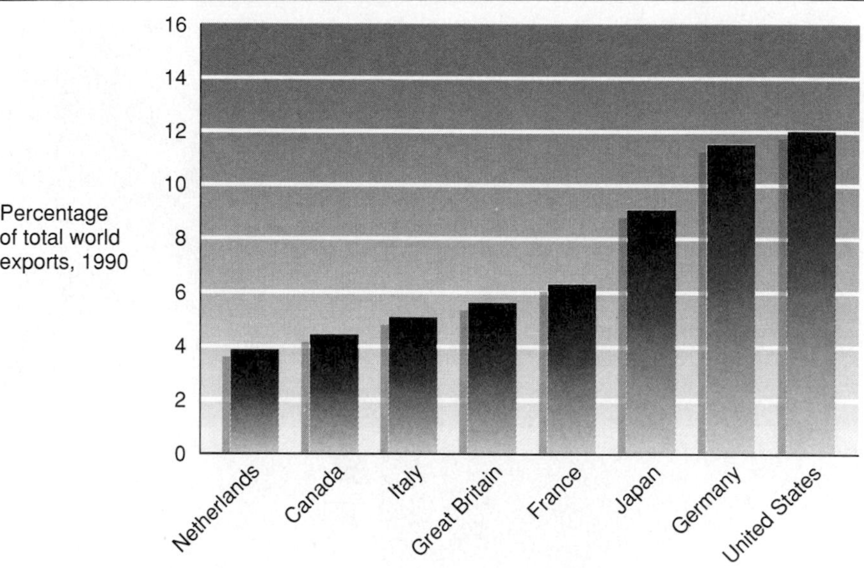

Source: World Bank, World Development Report, 1992.

further relative declines in the U.S. share of world output and world exports seem likely. By itself, however, this is not necessarily a bad thing. The relative decline of the United States reflects the growing industrialization of the world economy, as opposed to any absolute decline in the health of the U.S. economy.

In sum, what now seems to be happening is that the world is shifting from a global economy in which the United States was the dominant "hub" to a global economy with three equally important regional hubs of economic activity (see Figure 1.5). One of these hubs is North America, which currently includes the United States and Canada but may also include Mexico if the North American Free Trade Agreement (NAFTA) is expanded to incorporate that country (as now seems likely). The second hub is the 12-nation European Community (EC), which includes among its members the major industrial nations of Great Britain, France, Germany, and Italy. The third hub is centered on East and Southeast Asia. Japan is currently the dominant economic power in this hub, with South Korea, Taiwan, Singapore, and Hong Kong playing supporting roles. However, the rapid economic development of mainland China during the 1980s suggests that China may well develop into a major economic power early in the next century. During the decade of the 1980s, for example, the Chinese economy grew at an annual average rate of 11.4 percent, compared to a Japanese growth rate of 4.1 percent and a U.S. growth rate of 3.0 percent.[12]

The Changing Foreign Direct Investment Picture

Reflecting the dominance of the United States in the global economy, U.S. firms accounted for 66.3 percent of worldwide foreign direct investment in the 1960s. British firms were second, accounting for 10.5 percent while Japanese firms were a distant eighth, with only 2 percent. The dominance of U.S. firms was so great that in Europe books were written about the economic threat posed to Europe by U.S. corporations.[13]

[12] The Economist, *Book of Vital World Statistics* (New York: Random House, 1990).

[13] One of the classics being J. J. Servan-Schreiber, *The American Challenge* (New York: Atheneum, 1968).

Figure 1.5
The Triad of Economic Power (1990 data; $ millions)

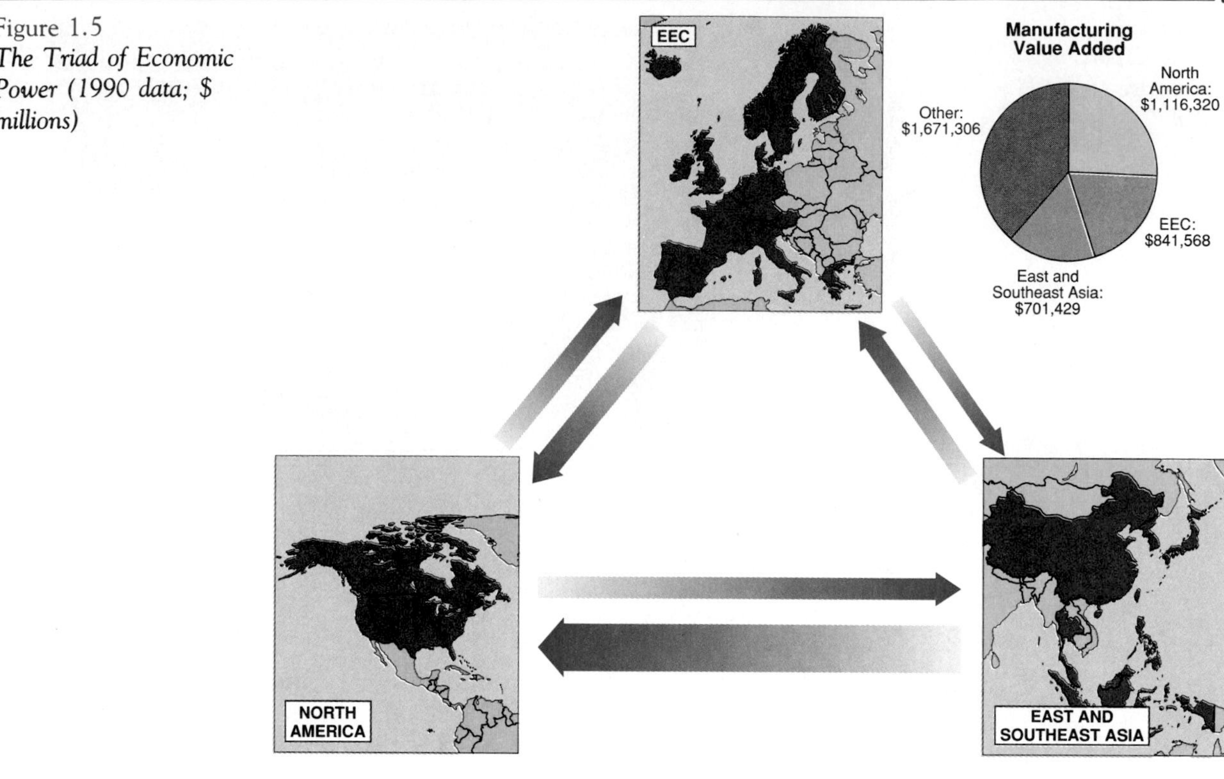

Source: P. Dicken, Global Shift *(New York: Guilford Press, 1992), p. 45.*

Several European governments, most notably that of France, talked of limiting inward investment by U.S. firms in their economies.

However, as the barriers to the free flow of goods, services, and capital fell, and as other countries increased their shares of world output, non-U.S. firms increasingly began to invest across national borders. The motivation for much of this foreign direct investment by non-U.S. firms was the desire to disperse production activities to optimal locations. Thus, for example, during the 1970s and 80s Japanese firms began to shift labor-intensive manufacturing operations from Japan to other Southeast Asian countries where labor costs were lower. In addition, given that the world was developing into a tripolar global economy with hubs in Europe, North America, and Southeast Asia (see Figure 1.5), many Japanese and European firms decided it was important to have a presence in each hub as a hedge against the emergence of trade barriers between hubs. Thus Japanese firms have invested in North America and Europe, and many European firms have invested in Southeast Asia and North America.

The consequences of these developments are mapped out in Figures 1.6a and 1.6b. Figure 1.6a shows how the source of foreign direct investment changed between the mid-1970s and the early 1990s. Figure 1.6b shows which countries this investment was targeted at. A number of interesting trends can be seen in Figures 1.6a and 1.6b. First, note that by 1990–91 the share of worldwide foreign direct investment accounted for by U.S. firms had fallen to 16 percent, down from 47 percent in the 1975–79 period. Second, notice the rise in foreign direct investment by Japanese firms. In the 1975–79 period Japanese firms accounted for 6 percent of total foreign direct investment outflows;

Figure 1.6a *Foreign Direct Investment Outward Flow from the Larger Industrial Countries*

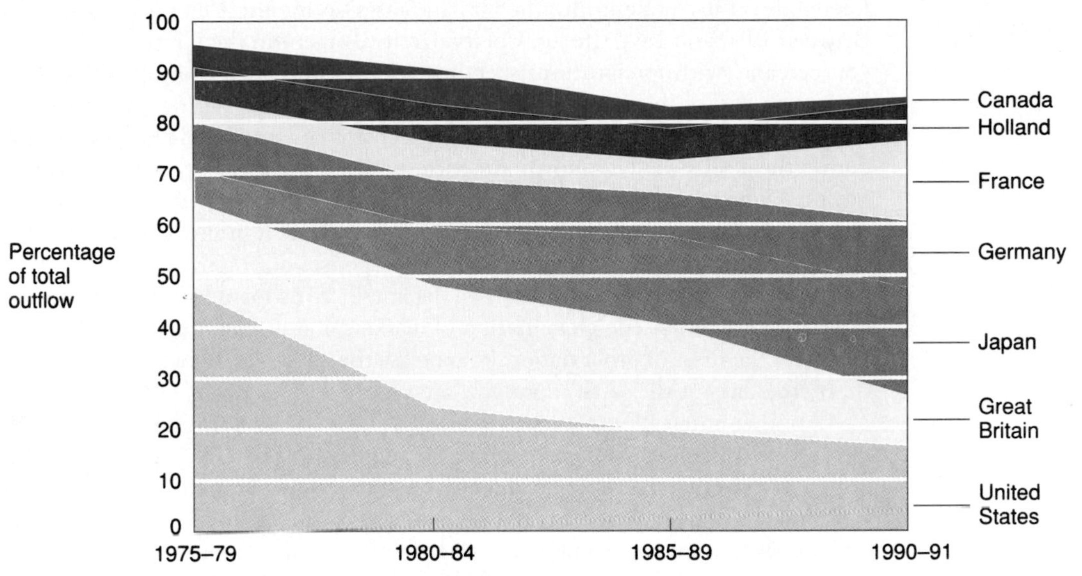

Source of data: The Economist, *September 19, 1992, p. 17.*

Figure 1.6b *Foreign Direct Investment Inflows into the Larger Industrialized Countries*

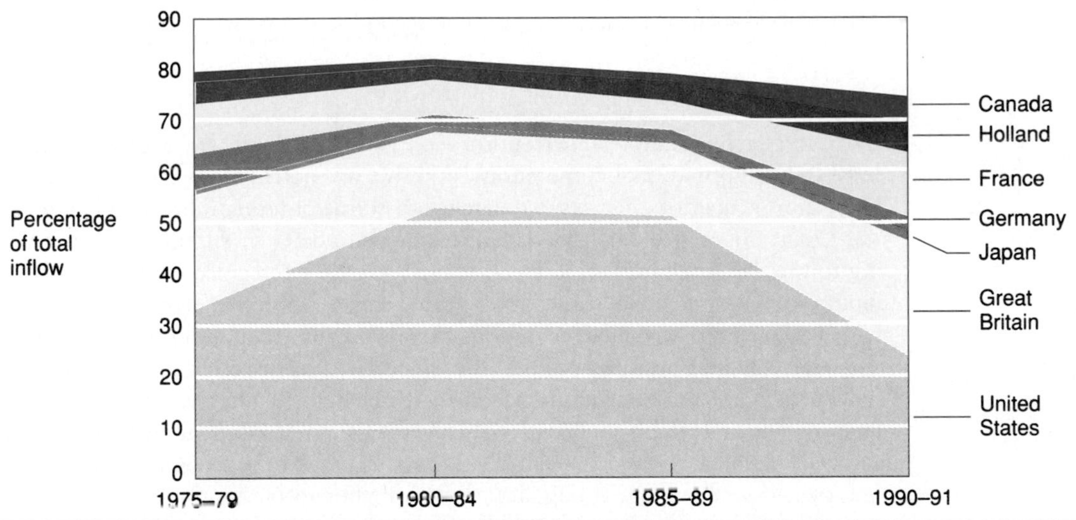

Source of data: The Economist, *September 19, 1992, p. 17.*

by 1990–91, their share was 21 percent. During much of the 1980s, British firms were also major foreign investors, accounting for about 20 percent of all direct foreign investment. By 1990–91, however, the British share had slipped to 10 percent.

Figure 1.6b shows that from 1975 onward, over half of total foreign direct investment was directed at two countries, the United States and Great Britain. The attraction of the United States was its status as the world's largest and richest free-market economy; that of Great Britain, its low-cost location for serving the European market. The surge in foreign direct investment into the United States during the 1980s is particularly striking. Between 1980 and 1990 the stock of foreign investment in the United States increased by 480 percent, with foreign firms spending $400 billion on acquiring and/or establishing businesses.[14] The biggest investors in the United States during this period were the British, Dutch, and Japanese. In total, 43 percent of Japanese direct foreign investment during the 1980s went to North America, with 96 percent of that going to the United States.[15] The high level of direct foreign investment by Japanese firms was the cause of much concern in the U.S. Congress, even though British firms were the largest investors in the United States during the 1980s.[16] In response, during the early 1990s there seems to have been a marked slowdown in Japanese investment in the United States. In general, however, as the globalization of markets and production continues, it is logical to expect the firms of other nations to increase their level of foreign direct investment. In short, the days of the U.S. monopoly are over.

Another interesting feature revealed in Figure 1.6b is the relative lack of foreign direct investment into Germany and Japan between 1975 and 91. In the 1990–91 period, only 2.5 percent of all foreign direct investment was directed at Germany, and only 1.5 percent at Japan. The low level of foreign direct investment into Japan is particularly striking given the surge of outward investment by Japanese firms in recent years. We shall look again at this disparity in Chapter 6 when we discuss the theory of foreign direct investment. For now, note that very few formal barriers to inward foreign direct investment have existed in Japan since the early 1980s, so it would be wrong to attribute this disparity to formal investment barriers.

The Changing Nature of the Multinational Enterprise

Two trends are worthy of note here. The first is the rise of non-U.S. multinationals, particularly Japanese multinationals. The second is the growth of mini-multinationals.

Non-U.S. Multinationals

In the 1960s the widespread perception was that international business was dominated by large U.S. multinational corporations, and this was actually not far off the mark. With U.S. firms accounting for approximately two thirds of foreign direct investment during the 1960s, one would *expect* most multinationals to be U.S. enterprises. Indeed, according to the data presented in Table 1.1, in 1973, 48.5 percent of the world's 260 largest multinationals were U.S. firms. The second-largest source country was Great Britain, with 18.8 percent of the largest multinationals. Japan accounted for only 3.5 percent of the world's largest multinationals at the time. The large number of U.S. multinationals reflected U.S. economic dominance in the three decades after World War II, while the large number of British multinationals reflected that country's industrial dominance in the early decades of the 20th century.

By 1991, however, things had shifted significantly. In that year U.S. firms accounted for 32.8 percent of the world's 500 largest multinationals, followed by Japan with 22.2 percent. Great Britain, accounting for 8.6 percent, was a distant third. Although the two sets of figures in Table 1.1 are not strictly comparable (the 1973 figures are based

---

[14] "Foreign Investors Drawn to Low Prices for Assets Due to Weak Dollar," *Industry Week*, October 7, 1991, p. 35.

[15] "Direct Foreign Investment," *Business Tokyo*, May, 1991, p. 13.

[16] For an example of the reaction to this trend see M. Tolchin and S. Tolchin, *Buying into America* (New York: Times Books, 1988).

Table 1.1
The National Composition of the Largest Multinationals

	Of the Top 260 in 1973	Of the Top 500 in 1991
United States	126 (48.5%)	164 (32.8%)
Japan	9 (3.5%)	111 (22.2%)
Great Britain	49 (18.8%)	43 (8.6%)
France	19 (7.3%)	30 (6%)
Germany	21 (8.1%)	30 (6%)
Sweden	8 (3.1%)	17 (3.4%)
Canada	4 (1.5%)	18 (3.6%)

Source: 1973 data from Hood and Young, The Economics of the Multinational Enterprise *(New York: Longman, 1979), Table 1.3; 1991 figures from "The Global 500,"* Fortune, *July 29, 1991, pp. 238–46.*

on the largest 260 firms, whereas the 1991 figures are based on the largest 500 firms), they illustrate the trend very well. In particular, the globalization of the world economy, together with Japan's rise to the top rank of economic powers, has resulted in a relative decline in the dominance of U.S. (and, to a lesser extent, British) firms in the global marketplace.

The relative decline in the dominance once enjoyed by U.S. multinationals is even more striking when one looks at individual industries. Take semiconductors as an example. In 1975, the two dominant multinationals in this industry were both U.S. firms: Motorola and Texas Instruments. Now the list of key global players also includes NEC, Fujitsu, Hitachi, and Toshiba, all of them Japanese firms. A similar trend is seen in consumer electronics. In 1975 the key global players were General Electric and RCA, both U.S. multinationals. The list now also includes two Japanese firms, Matsushita and Sony, and the Dutch firm Philips.[17] Although this development may make Americans uncomfortable, it should be noted that the decline in the U.S. position was probably inevitable with the emergence of industrialized countries such as Japan. What it does mean, however, is that U.S. businesses now face a far more competitive environment than the one they faced in the 1950–80 period.

The Rise of Mini-Multinationals

Another trend in international business has been the growth of medium-sized and small multinationals (*mini-multinationals*). When people think of international businesses they tend to think of firms like Exxon, General Motors, Ford, Fuji, Kodak, Matsushita, Procter & Gamble, Sony, and Unilever—large, complex multinational corporations with operations that span the globe. Although it is certainly true that most international trade and investment is still conducted by large firms, it is also true that many medium-sized and small businesses are increasingly involved in international trade and investment. As an example, consider Lubricating Systems, Inc., of Kent, Washington. In 1991, Lubricating Systems, which manufactures lubricating fluids for machine tools, employed 25 people and generated sales of $6.5 million. Hardly a large, complex multinational, yet more than $2 million of the company's sales were generated by exports to a score of countries from Japan to Israel and the United Arab Emirates. Moreover, Lubricating Systems is now setting up a joint venture with a German company to serve the European market.[18] As another example consider Lixi, Inc., a small U.S. manufac-

[17] C. K. Prahalad and Y. L. Doz, *The Multinational Mission* (New York: The Free Press, 1987).

[18] R. A. Mosbacher, "Opening Up Export Doors for Smaller Firms," *Seattle Times*, July 24, 1991, p. A7.

turer of industrial X-ray equipment. In 1991, 70 percent of Lixi's $4.5 million in revenues came from exports to Japan.[19] Or take G. W. Barth, a manufacturer of cocoa-bean roasting machinery based in Ludwigsburg, Germany. Employing just 65 people in 1990, it captured 70 percent of the global market for cocoa-bean roasting machines.[20] The point is, international business is conducted not just by large firms but also by medium-sized and small enterprises.

It is difficult to say just how important the growth of mini-multinationals actually is, primarily because hard statistical data on this phenomenon is sparse. However, the data we do have suggests that the mini-multinationals are an important, often-overlooked part of the international business scene. For example, according to a United Nations report, 23 percent of all Japanese firms with foreign operations employed fewer than 300 people in 1984, and 78 percent of British firms with investments abroad employed fewer than 500 people.[21]

The Changing World Order

Between 1989 and 1991 a series of remarkable democratic revolutions swept the communist world. For reasons that are explored in more detail in Chapter 2, in country after country throughout Eastern Europe and eventually in the Soviet Union itself, communist governments collapsed like the shells of rotten eggs. The Soviet Union is now history, having been replaced by 15 independent republics. Czechoslovakia has divided itself into two states, while Yugoslavia has dissolved into a bloody civil war among its five successor states.

Many of the former communist nations of Europe and Asia seem to share a commitment to democratic politics and free market economics. If this continues, the opportunities for international businesses may be enormous. For the best part of half a century these countries were essentially closed to Western international businesses. Now they present a host of export and investment opportunities. Just how this will play itself out over the next 10 to 20 years is difficult to say. The economies of most of the former communist states are in very poor condition, and their continued commitment to democracy and free market economics cannot be taken for granted. Indeed, disturbing signs of growing unrest and totalitarian tendencies are seen in many Eastern European states. Thus, the risks involved in doing business in such countries are very high, but then again, so may be the returns.

In addition to these changes, more quiet revolutions have been occurring in China and Latin America. Their implications for international businesses may be just as profound as the collapse of communism in Eastern Europe. China suppressed its own prodemocracy movement in the bloody Tiananmen Square massacre of 1989. Despite this, China seems to be moving progressively toward ever-greater free market reforms. The southern Chinese province of Guangong, where these reforms have been pushed the furthest, now has the fastest growing economy in the world. (In 1991 Guangong's economy grew 13.5 percent.)[22] If what is now occurring in southern China continues, and particularly if it spreads throughout the country, China may move from Third World to industrial superpower status even more rapidly than Japan did. The potential consequences for Western international business are enormous. On the one hand, with 1.1 billion people, China represents a huge and largely untapped market. Reflecting

---

19 "Small Companies Learn How to Sell to the Japanese," *Seattle Times,* March 19, 1992.

20 W. J. Holstein, "Why Johann Can Export but Johnny Can't," *Business Week,* November 4, 1991, pp. 64–65.

21 "Come Back Multinationals," *The Economist,* November 26, 1988, p. 73.

22 P. Engardio and L. Curry, "The Fifth Tiger Is on China's Coast," *Business Week,* April 6, 1992, pp. 42–43.

this, between 1983 and 1991 annual foreign direct investment in China increased from less than $2 billion to $11.8 billion.[23] On the other hand, China's new firms are already proving to be very capable competitors, and there is a real possibility that they will take global market share away from Western and Japanese enterprises. Thus the changes in China are creating both opportunities and threats for established international businesses.

As for Latin America, here too both democracy and free market reforms seem to have taken hold. For decades most Latin American countries were ruled by dictators, many of whom seemed to view Western international businesses as instruments of imperialist domination. Accordingly, they restricted direct investment by foreign firms. In addition, the poorly managed economies of Latin America were characterized by low growth, high debt, and hyperinflation—all of which discouraged investment by international businesses. Now all of this seems to be changing. Throughout most of Latin America, debt and inflation are down, governments are selling off state-owned enterprises to private investors, foreign investment is welcomed, and the region's economies are growing rapidly. These changes have increased the attractiveness of Latin America, both as a market for exports and as a site for foreign direct investment. For example, in 1991 U.S. firms sold $58 billion worth of goods to Latin America, an 18 percent increase from 1990 and approximately two thirds of the amount that they sold to the European Community. In addition, investment by U.S. firms in Latin America increased from $29 billion in 1987 to $49 billion in 1991.[24] Thus, the changes in Latin America have created enormous opportunities for international businesses that did not exist a decade ago. At the same time, given the long history of economic mismanagement in Latin America, there is no guarantee that these favorable trends will continue. As in the case of Eastern Europe, substantial opportunities are accompanied by substantial risks.

HOW INTERNATIONAL BUSINESS IS DIFFERENT

How do we justify a whole book on international business? The task of managing an international business differs from that of a purely domestic business in many ways. At the most fundamental level, the differences arise from the simple fact that *countries* are different. Countries differ in their cultures, political systems, economic systems, legal systems, and levels of economic development. Despite all the talk about the emerging global village, and despite the trends toward globalization of markets and production, many of these differences are very profound and enduring. (Box 1.2 provides an example of how countries differ.)

Differences between countries require that an international business vary its practices country by country. Marketing a product in Brazil may require a different approach than marketing the product in Germany; managing U.S. workers might require different skills than managing Japanese workers; maintaining close relations with a particular level of government may be very important in Mexico and irrelevant in Great Britain; the business strategy pursued in Canada might not work in South Korea; and so on. Managers in an international business must not only be sensitive to these differences, they must also adopt the appropriate policies and strategies for coping with them. Much of this book is devoted to explaining the sources of these differences and the methods for coping with them successfully.

---

23 N. D. Kristof, "Foreign Investors Pouring into China," *The New York Times,* June 12, 1992, p. C1.

24 S. Baker et al., "Latin America: The Big Move to Free Markets," *Business Week,* June 15, 1992, pp. 50–62.

Differences in National Wealth

BOX 1.2

As has been pointed out, countries differ along a whole range of dimensions. Here we examine differences in wealth and living standards, one of the most fundamental differences among nations. Differences in national wealth are strongly correlated with all sorts of other national differences, such as those in literacy rate, education level, health care provision, and life expectancy.

Which is the world's richest nation? The answer depends upon how you define *rich*. The conventional way of defining wealth is in terms of gross domestic product (GDP) per person. This definition, however, does not take into account differences in the cost of living between countries. In recent years the United Nations has begun to calculate estimates of GDP per head adjusted for the cost of living. These estimates are known as purchasing power parity (PPP) indicators. The PPP indicators are scaled so that the United States equals 100. For example, the PPP indicators tell us is that in 1988 the Japanese, with a GDP per head of $23,325, were numerically better off than Americans, whose GDP per head was $19,815. When the high cost of living in Japan is taken into account by the PPP, however, the Japanese are shown as significantly worse off. In 1988 the Japanese PPP was 71.5, compared to 100 for the United States.

The table provides the GDP per head in 1970 and 1988 and the 1988 PPP indicators for selected countries. What do these figures tell us about the relative change in the position of the United States and Japan over the last 20 years? What are the implications of these figures for managers of an international luxury-goods firm who must decide which markets to export to?

	GDP per Head		
Country	**1970 ($)**	**1988 ($)**	**1988 PPP**
Brazil	450	2,451	24.5
Ethiopia	60	114	1.6
France	2,831	17,004	69.5
Germany, West	3,049	19,743	73.8
Great Britain	2,209	14,477	66.1
India	100	335	4.7
Indonesia	90	473	9.4
Ireland	1,315	9,181	40.9
Japan	1,930	23,325	71.5
Mexico	710	2,102	26.3
Philippines	230	662	10.7
Portugal	700	4,017	33.8
Switzerland	3,350	27,748	87.0
United States	4,922	19,815	100.0

Source: The Economist, Book of Vital World Statistics (*New York: Random House, 1990*).

A further way in which international business differs from domestic business is the greater complexity of managing an international business. In addition to the problems that arise from the differences between countries, a manager in an international business is confronted with a whole range of other issues that the manager in a domestic business never confronts. An international business must decide where in the world to site its production activities in order to minimize costs and to maximize value added. Then it must decide how best to coordinate and control its globally dispersed production activities (which, as we shall see later in the book, is not a trivial problem). An international business also must decide which foreign markets to enter and which ones to avoid. Moreover, it must choose the appropriate mode for entering a particular foreign country. Is it best to export its product to the foreign country? Should the firm allow a local firm to produce its product under license in that country? Should the firm enter into a joint venture with a local firm to produce its product in that country? Or should the firm set up a wholly owned subsidiary to serve the market in that country? As we shall see, the choice of entry mode is critical, because it has major implications for the long-term health of the firm.

Another way international business is different is that the conduct of business involves transactions across national borders. Because it is involved in international trade and investment, an international business must deal with government restrictions on international trade and investment. It must find ways to work within the limits imposed by specific governmental interventions in the international trade and investment system. As this book explains, despite the fact that many governments are nominally committed to free trade, their interventions to regulate cross-border trade and investment are actually substantial. International businesses must develop strategies and policies for dealing with this.

In addition, cross-border transactions also require that money be converted from the firm's home currency into a foreign currency and vice versa. Since currency exchange rates are not stable over time but vary in response to changing economic conditions, an international business must develop policies for dealing with exchange rate movements. A firm that adopts a wrong policy can lose large amounts of money, whereas a firm that adopts the right policy can actually increase the profitability of its international transactions.

In sum, international business is different from domestic business for at least four reasons: (1) countries are different, (2) the range of problems confronted by a manager in an international business is wider, and the problems themselves more complex than those confronted by a manager in a domestic business, (3) an international business must find ways to work within the limits imposed by government intervention in the international trade and investment system, and (4) international transactions involve converting money into different currencies. In this book we examine all of these issues in depth.

ORGANIZATION OF THIS BOOK

The remainder of this book is divided into 19 chapters within five parts. Chapters 2 to 11 deal with the environmental context within which international transactions are conducted. Chapters 12 to 14 take a firm-level view of the strategy and structure of international business. Chapters 15 to 20, on business operations, examine how individual business functions are performed within an international business. Thus the book starts out looking at the environment; then it looks at the firm, and finally it looks at individual operations within a firm (see Figure 1.7). Put another way, the book begins by discussing the international business environment before examining specific strategies, structures, and operational policies that firms must adopt in order to survive and prosper in that environment.

The Environmental Context

As illustrated in Figure 1.8, discussion of the environmental context of international business is further subdivided into three parts in this book. Part Two deals with country factors, Part Three deals with the global trade and investment environment, and Part Four looks at the global monetary system.

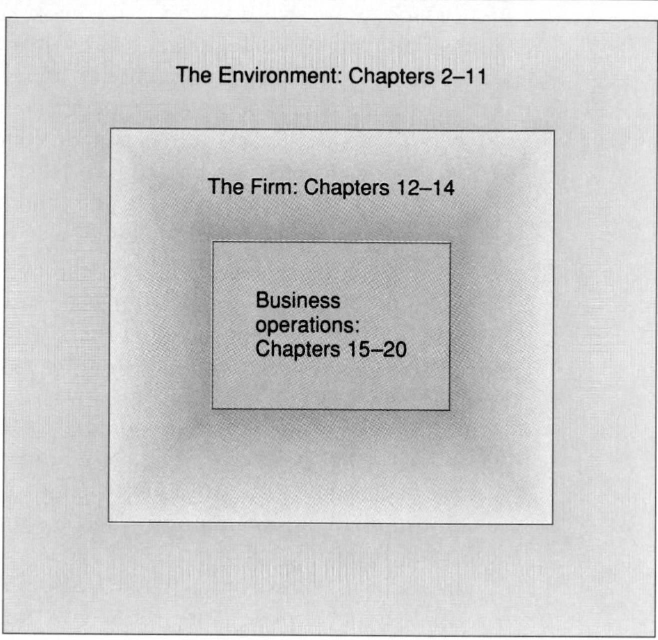

Figure 1.7
The Structure of the Book

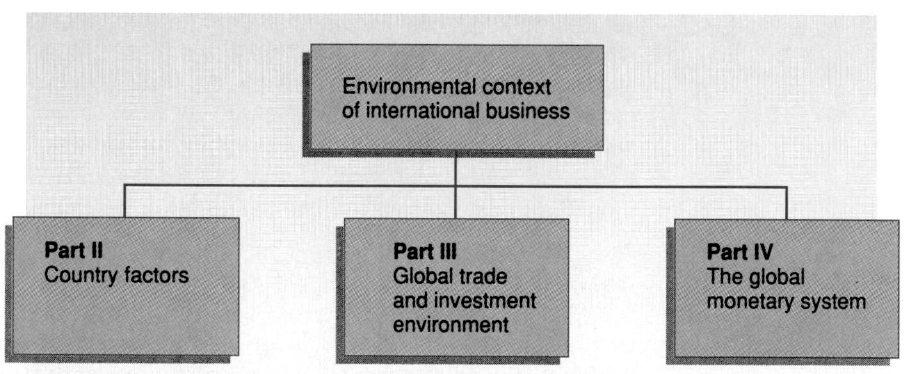

Figure 1.8
The Environmental Context of International Business

Country Factors

As noted in the previous section, international business is different because countries are different. Taking this as our cue, we start by discussing country factors. Chapter 2 looks at the foundations of national differences in political and economic systems. We discuss the different political, economic, and legal systems found in the world and outline the implications of these differences for an international business. Chapter 3 looks at the foundations of national differences in culture. We identify the various factors of a society that make up its culture (e.g., social structure, religion, language, education), identify how these differ from country to country, and explain the implications of these differences for the practice of international business.

The Global Trade and Investment Environment

We begin this part in Chapter 4 by reviewing the economic theories of international trade. These theories form the basis of the intellectual case for free trade. As such, they are the driving force behind the General Agreement on Trade and Tariffs (GATT), which establishes the "rules of the game" for international trade. In Chapter 5 we move from theory to practice by taking a close look at the political economy of international trade. Although the theory of international trade advocates *unrestricted* free trade, in practice, all countries use policies to restrict certain imports and to protect their producers in certain sectors. In Chapter 5 we review the various instruments of governmental trade policy that international businesses are likely to encounter. We also look at the international trade framework of the 1990s (including the current state of GATT), and we discuss the case for and against government regulation of international trade through trade policy.

In Chapter 6 we switch our attention to the economic theories of foreign direct investment (FDI). These theories outline the conditions under which it makes sense for a firm to establish operations in a foreign country, as opposed to exporting goods and services from its home country or licensing a foreign firm to produce its output. As such, the theories help to identify with some precision the conditions under which it is and is not profitable for a firm to engage in FDI. Chapter 7 takes a look at the political economy of foreign direct investment. Governments around the world have adopted a variety of postures toward FDI, ranging from—at one extreme—a free market view of laissez-faire toward it to—at the other extreme—a radical view that prohibits FDI under all circumstances. In this chapter we look at the political ideology that determines a government's attitudes toward FDI. We review the costs and benefits of FDI both to the host country (the country receiving FDI) and to the home country (the source country for FDI). We also look at the various policy instruments that governments adopt for regulating FDI.

Chapter 8 is the last chapter that deals explicitly with the global trade and investment environment. The focus of Chapter 8 is on regional economic integration—the emergence of regional trade blocks. The ultimate purpose of regional economic integration is to remove all barriers to the free flow of goods, services, and factors of production between countries within a region, thereby enabling member countries to realize the gains from trade that are discussed in detail in Chapter 4. The most comprehensive regional grouping in the world is the European Community (EC); however, even the EC falls a long way short of the theoretical ideal. Other regional groupings include the emerging North American Free Trade Association (NAFTA) and regional groupings in Latin America and Asia. In Chapter 8 the case for regional economic integration is discussed. We take a close look at economic integration in the EC and review regional economic integration elsewhere.

The Global Monetary System

The last component of the environmental context of international business that we examine is the global monetary system. Different countries have different currencies. To engage in international trade and investment a firm must change its money from one currency into another. This process is complicated by the fact that exchange rates are not stable; they vary over time. Chapter 9 explains how money can be converted from one currency to another by using the foreign exchange market. The chapter also outlines the economic theories that explain how exchange rates are determined.

Chapter 10 builds upon Chapter 9 by taking a close look at the international monetary system, of which the foreign exchange market is just one part. The international monetary system plays a key role in the workings of the foreign exchange market. Currently, the world has a floating exchange rate regime, as opposed to a fixed exchange rate regime (which existed from 1945 until 1973). In Chapter 10 the pros and cons of these regimes are debated. We also look at the role of the International Monetary Fund and the World Bank in the international monetary system.

Chapter 11 looks at another component of the global monetary system, the global capital market. A striking development of the last 20 years has been the rapid growth of the global capital market. It is now possible for firms to raise funds not just from domestic investors, but also from foreign investors in foreign capital markets. In Chapter 11 we review the reasons for the growth of the global capital market and discuss the attractions of the market to international businesses. We also look at various components of the market, including most importantly, the Eurocurrency market, the international bond market, and the international equity market.

The Firm

Chapters 12 to 14 deal with the strategy and structure of international business. Chapter 12 focuses on the strategy of international business. The chapter opens with a general discussion of the role of strategy—the purpose of which is to help a firm maximize its value added. Then we look at the different ways in which firms can profit from international expansion. Next, the pros and cons of various strategies pursued by international businesses are reviewed. The chapter also discusses how international businesses must respond to pressures for local responsiveness and for cost efficiency, and how these pressures can place conflicting demands upon the firm.

Chapter 13 builds upon Chapter 12 by looking at the structure of international business. A central theme is that a firm's structure must be matched to its strategy if the firm is to survive. We consider the basic dimensions of structure and control that firms must work with, focusing attention on the implications of the various dimensions of structure and control for an international business. We then pull all of this material together in a synthesis that reviews the structures and controls that international businesses must operate with if they are to survive.

Chapter 14 focuses upon the alternative **entry modes** for firms entering a foreign market—exporting, licensing, franchising, a joint venture with a local firm, and setting up a wholly owned subsidiary. We compare and contrast these entry modes, highlight the advantages and disadvantages of each, and identify factors that help determine the appropriate mode in a given situation. Chapter 14 also looks at the topic of global strategic alliances—alliances with actual or potential competitors. We discuss the pros and cons of strategic alliances and provide some steps firms can take to help make these alliances work.

Business Operations

The remaining six chapters of the book focus on business operations. Throughout these chapters, a deliberate attempt is made to relate the material to the material in the earlier chapters on the environment, the strategies, and the structure of international business.

Chapter 15 looks at exporting, importing, and countertrade. This is a "nuts-and-bolts chapter." It explains how to identify export opportunities, how to finance exports and imports, and the types of public and private assistance that is available to help exporters. The chapter also deals with the issue of **countertrade**—the exchange of goods for goods; essentially a bartering arrangement. Countertrade is used when a firm trades with a country whose currency is not freely convertible into other currencies. We discuss the growth of countertrade, the types of countertrade, and the pros and cons of using countertrade.

Chapter 16 looks at manufacturing and materials management in an international business. The chapter opens with a discussion of the factors that determine the optimal global location for manufacturing facilities. For example, we try to identify the factors that might influence a U.S. firm's decision to manufacture component parts in Hong Kong, rather than Germany. The chapter then moves on to discuss the issue of **make or buy decisions**—that is, whether the firm will produce its own component parts or contract them out to independent suppliers. Make or buy decisions of international businesses are complicated by the volatile nature of the international political economy, exchange-rate movements, temporal changes in relative factor costs, and the like. In this chapter we look at the arguments for making components internally, the arguments for contracting out component manufacturing to independent suppliers, and the inevitable trade-offs involved in these decisions. The chapter closes with a detailed discussion of how to coordinate a globally dispersed manufacturing and supply system. This final section is principally about the central role of materials management in an international business.

Chapter 17 looks at marketing and R&D in an international business. We begin by reviewing the debate on the globlization of markets. Then we look in turn at the four elements of the **marketing mix**—product attributes, distribution strategy, communication strategy, and pricing strategy. The marketing mix is the set of choices that determine a firm's offer to its target market(s). Firms often vary their marketing mix from country to country in light of differences in national culture, economic development, product standards, distribution channels, and so on. The chapter discusses how this is done. The chapter closes with a discussion of new product development in an international business and of the implications of this for the organization of the R&D firm's function.

Chapter 18 looks at the human resource management (HRM) function. Staffing, management development, performance evaluation, and compensation activities are complicated in an international business by the profound differences between countries in labor markets, culture, legal systems, economic systems, and the like. We discuss the strategic role of HRM in an international business and then turn our attention to four major tasks of the function: staffing policy, management training and development, performance appraisal, and compensation policy. The chapter closes with a look at international labor relations and at the desirable relationship between a firm's labor relations and its strategy.

Chapter 19 focuses on accounting within the multinational firm. We look at how and why accounting standards differ from country to country and at the efforts now underway to harmonize accounting practices across countries. We discuss the rationale behind the practice of producing consolidated accounts for a multinational firm and we look at the problems associated with currency translation. The chapter closes with a detailed look at several issues relating to the use of accounting-based control systems within an international business.

The final chapter, Chapter 20, is concerned with financial management in an international business. We explain how decisions about investments, financing, and money management in an international business are complicated by the fact that countries differ in their currencies, tax regimes, levels of political and economic risk, and so on. We discuss how financial managers can consider all of these factors when deciding where to invest the firm's scarce financial resources, how the firm's foreign investments can be financed, how the flow of funds within the firm can be managed, and how best to protect the firm from various political and economic risks it is exposed to (including foreign exchange risk) in the process.

SUMMARY OF CHAPTER

The purpose of this chapter has been to set the scene for the rest of the book. We have looked at the globalization of the world economy, discussed the changing nature of international business, explained the differences between international business and domestic business, outlined the material to be discussed in the book, and shown how this material fits together in an integrated whole. These major points were made in the chapter:

1. Over the last two decades we have witnessed the globalization of markets and production.
2. The globalization of markets implies that national markets are merging into one huge marketplace. However, it is important not to push this view too far.
3. The globalization of production implies that firms are basing individual productive activities at the optimal world locations for the particular activities. As a consequence, it is increasingly irrelevant to talk about "American" products, "Japanese" products, or "German" products, since these are being replaced by "global" products.
4. Two factors seem to underlie the trend toward globalization: declining trade barriers and changes in communication, information, and transportation technologies.
5. Since the end of World War II there has been a significant lowering of barriers to the free flow of goods, services, and capital. More than anything else, this has facilitated the trend toward the globalization of production and has enabled firms to view the world as a single market.
6. As a consequence of the globalization of production and markets, in the last decade, world trade has grown faster than world output, foreign direct investment has surged, imports have penetrated more deeply into the world's industrial nations, and competitive pressures have increased in industry after industry.
7. The development of the microprocessor and related developments in communications and information processing technology have helped firms to link their worldwide operations into sophisticated information networks. Jet air travel, by shrinking travel time, has also helped to link the worldwide operations of international businesses. These changes have enabled firms to achieve tight coordination of their worldwide operations and to view the world as a single market.
8. Over the last three decades a number of dramatic changes have occurred in the nature of international business. In the 1960s, the U.S. economy was dominant in the world, U.S. firms accounted for most of the foreign direct investment in the world economy, U.S. firms dominated the list of large multinationals, and roughly half the world—the centrally planned economies of the communist world—was closed to Western businesses.
9. By the end of the 1980s, the U.S. share of world output had been cut in half, with major shares of world output being accounted for by Western European and Southeast Asian economies. The U.S. share of worldwide foreign direct investment had also fallen, by about two thirds. Moreover U.S. multinationals were now facing competition from a large number of Japanese and European multinationals. In addition, the emergence of mini-multinationals was noted.
10. The most dramatic environmental trend has been the collapse of communist power in Eastern Europe, which has created enormous long-run opportunities for international businesses. In addition, the move toward free market economies in China and Latin America is creating opportunities (and threats) for Western international businesses.
11. International business is different from domestic business for at least four reasons: (*i*) because countries are different, (*ii*) because the range of problems confronted by a manager in an international business is wider and the problems themselves more complex than those confronted by a manager in a domestic business, (*iii*) because an international business must find ways to work within the limits imposed by governments' intervention in the international trade and investment system, and (*iv*) because international transactions involve converting money into different currencies.
12. This book begins by discussing the environmental context of international business and then moves on to discuss the strategies, structures, and operational policies that firms must adopt in order to survive and prosper in that environment.

DISCUSSION QUESTIONS

1. Describe the shifts in the world economy over the last 30 years. What are the implications of these shifts for international businesses based in North America?
2. "The study of international business is fine if you are going to work in a large multinational enterprise, but it has no relevance for individuals who are going to work in small firms." Critically evaluate this statement.
3. How have changes in technology contributed to the globalization of markets and of production? Would the globalization of production and markets have been possible without these technological changes?
4. "Ultimately, the study of international business is no different from the study of domestic business. Thus, there is no point in having a separate course on international business." Critically evaluate this statement.

PART TWO

Country Factors

National Differences in Political Economy

TURMOIL IN THE FORMER SOVIET UNION

INTRODUCTION

POLITICAL ENVIRONMENT

Collectivism and Individualism
Democracy and Totalitarianism
The Complexions of Government
Why Does It All Matter?

ECONOMIC ENVIRONMENT

Economic Systems
Economic Development

LEGAL ENVIRONMENT

Patents, Copyrights, and Trademarks
Product Safety and Product Liability
Contract Law

THE NEW WORLD ORDER

Eastern Europe
Asia
Latin America
Africa
Implications

IMPLICATIONS FOR BUSINESS

Attractiveness
Ethical Issues

SUMMARY OF CHAPTER

DISCUSSION QUESTIONS

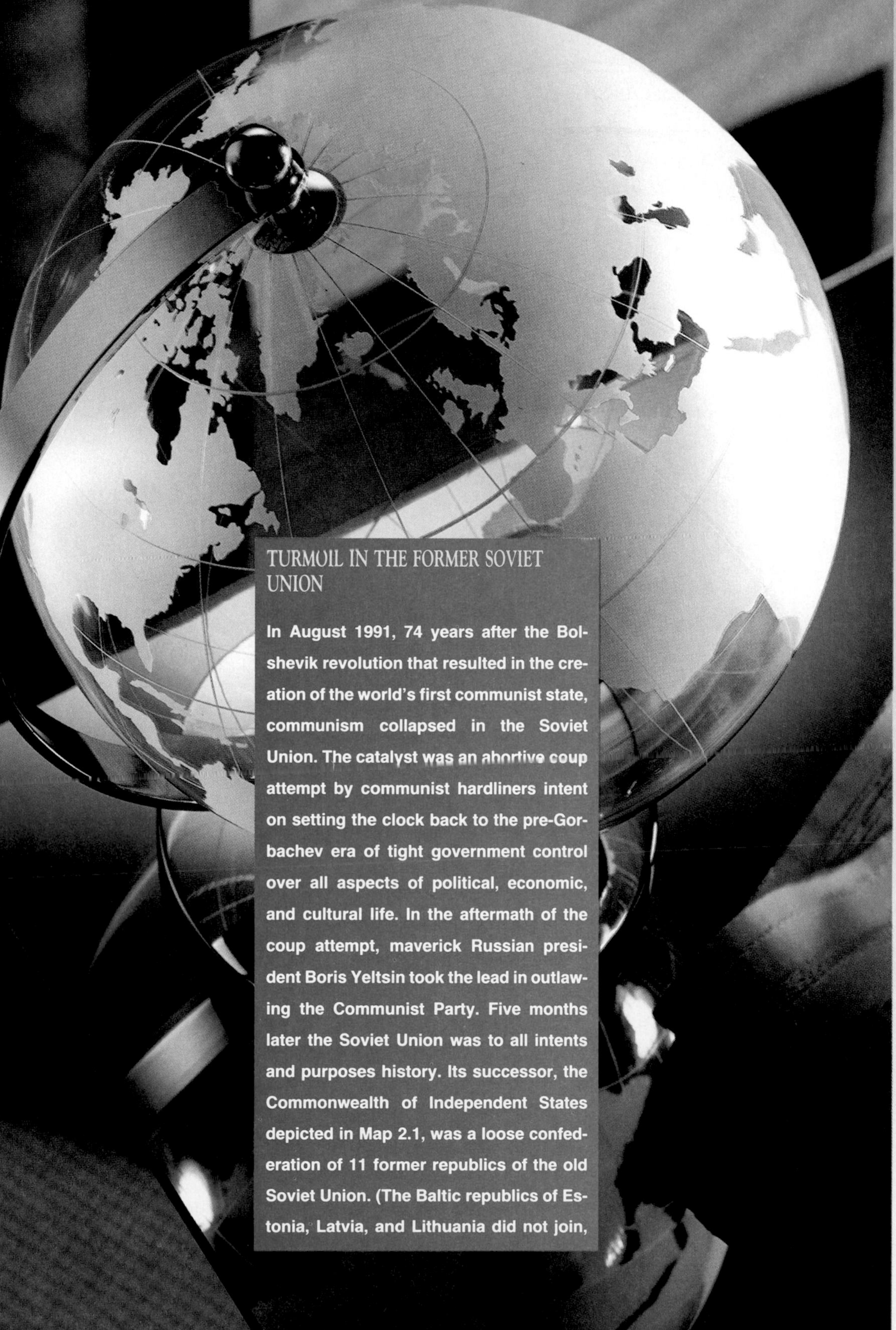

CHAPTER 2

TURMOIL IN THE FORMER SOVIET UNION

In August 1991, 74 years after the Bolshevik revolution that resulted in the creation of the world's first communist state, communism collapsed in the Soviet Union. The catalyst was an abortive coup attempt by communist hardliners intent on setting the clock back to the pre-Gorbachev era of tight government control over all aspects of political, economic, and cultural life. In the aftermath of the coup attempt, maverick Russian president Boris Yeltsin took the lead in outlawing the Communist Party. Five months later the Soviet Union was to all intents and purposes history. Its successor, the Commonwealth of Independent States depicted in Map 2.1, was a loose confederation of 11 former republics of the old Soviet Union. (The Baltic republics of Estonia, Latvia, and Lithuania did not join,

Map 2.1 *Commonwealth of Independent States (CIS)*

and neither did the southern republic of Georgia.) • Collectively the 11 republics pledged themselves to adopt democratic political institutions and free market economic systems. While moves toward greater democracy had been under way since 1985, until 1992 the republics had made only the most elementary steps toward freeing their economies from centralized control by state bureaucrats. By 1992 the republics were rushing headlong toward adopting free market economic institutions. Russia led the way in early 1992 by removing centralized controls over prices and legalizing private ownership. Privatization of state-owned enterprises was planned for 1992 and 1993. However, with no practical knowledge of how a market economy actually works, of how to set prices, or of what profit is, the early results have been nothing short of chaos. The removal of price controls and the tendency of the Russian government to print money at a furious pace caused inflation to soar to an annual rate of more than 1,000 percent in early 1992. Hyperinflation transformed the Russian ruble into a worthless currency with no real value on international exchange markets. This makes it difficult for Russia to buy goods from the rest of the world (since nobody wants to take the worthless ruble as payment). • In addition, the republics' lack of a legal system for regulating business transactions and competition in a market economy has resulted in a version of capitalism that has more in common with the American gold rush of the mid-19th century than with the modern day capitalism of the industrialized West. Too many of the former Soviet Union's new entrepreneurs are reportedly con artists who operate in the murky world of bribery, blackmail, and double-cross. Unless the governments of the republics enact legislation to protect consumers from con artists, popular sentiment may turn against the democratic free market reforms currently underway. • To make matters worse, the political future of the Commonwealth of Independent States is far from secure. In spite of the 11 member-republics' pledge to cooperate closely and to maintain some Commonwealthwide institutions (such as unified armed forces), centrifugal forces may tear the Commonwealth apart. One reason this may occur is the immense disparity in size, culture, and wealth of the 11 member-states. Russia, with a population of 150 million, is three times as populous as the next-largest republic, the Ukraine. It has twice the income per head of the poorest republic, Tajikistan. Whereas Russia, Belorussia, and Azerbaijan are ethnically fairly homogeneous—three quarters of their populations are of the dominant ethnic nationality—in Kazakhstan and Kirgizia the dominant ethnic nationality represents little more than half of the populations. Moreover, whereas Russia, Belorussia, and the Ukraine have historic, cultural, and religious ties to Europe, the central Asian republics of Kazakhstan, Turkmenistan, Tajikistan, and Kirgizia are predominantly Muslim. Their historic and cultural ties are to Muslim states such as Iran and Iraq. • For Western companies seeking to do business in this area of the world, the economic and political turmoil is very troubling. One of the main problems is that the rules of the game are ill defined and seem to change constantly. Consider the case of Chevron. In 1989 Chevron reached an agreement with the government of the Soviet Union to invest millions of dollars in a joint venture with a Soviet state enterprise to extract oil from the huge Tenghiz field in Kazakhstan. The deal was blessed personally by Soviet president Mikhail Gorbachev and backed by "rock solid" financial guarantees from the Soviet government. Now, however, both the Soviet government and Gorbachev are gone, and the financial guarantees are worthless. Following the abortive coup, Kazakhstan nationalized the oil field and demanded that Chevron renegotiate the deal directly with the Kazakhstan government. The Kazakhs complained that the deal made by the Soviet government did not give them a big enough cut of Chevron's export earnings. To back up their demands, the Kazakhs hired a British law firm to assess the fairness of the project and threatened to throw the Tenghiz oil field open to international tender if Chevron did not meet their demands. Thus, as a result of changes in the political map, Chevron could be forced to write off an investment that has already consumed tens of millions of dollars. At the very best, Chevron will end up with a less profitable venture than it would have had. •

A further problem facing Western businesses is how to conduct business in a country where the currency is worthless. The solution that most companies are adopting is barter. Although this is by no means the best solution (given a choice, most companies would prefer a hard currency such as the dollar), it is better than being paid in rubles. Take Polaroid, for example. The company imports camera parts into Russia, assembles them, and sells them on the Russian market. In return, Polaroid purchases printed circuit boards (which it also uses for camera production) and plastic videocassette cases and exports them to the West for hard currency. The only problem with this agreement is that Polaroid cannot meet the Russian demand for cameras, since, given the barter arrangement, the number of cameras it can sell is limited by the number of videocassette cases and circuit boards it can sell in the West. • As for the future, Western companies doing business in the republics of the former Soviet Union have good reason to be concerned. Many commentators feel that if the reforms currently underway in the new Commonwealth do not bear fruit quickly, a popular backlash might result in the likes of Boris Yeltsin being replaced by leaders less committed to democracy and free markets. If that happens, those Western companies that have invested heavily in the republics could be big losers. In particular, many could see their assets nationalized. On the other hand, if the reforms take hold, several of the republics—including the large Russian and Ukrainian republics—could develop into modern industrialized states and those Western companies that invested early could reap significant rewards. Western companies, therefore, find themselves confronting a very difficult dilemma.

Sources: "Remaking the Soviet Union," The Economist, *July 31, 1991, pp. 21–23; R. Brady and P. Galuszka, "Let's Make a Deal—But a Smaller One,"* Business Week, *January 20, 1992, pp. 44–45; R. Brady and P. Galuszka, "The Soviet Lurch toward Capitalism,"* Business Week, *October 21, 1991, pp. 50–51; D. Robinson, "Polaroid Develops Profitable Venture in USSR despite Perils with Ruble,"* Journal of Commerce, *September 30, 1991, pp. 1, 3.*

INTRODUCTION

As noted in Chapter 1, international business is much more complicated than domestic business because countries differ in many ways. Different countries have different political environments, economic environments, and legal environments. Cultural practices can vary dramatically from country to country, as can the education and skill level of the population, and different countries are at different stages of economic development. All of these differences have major implications for the practice of international business. They have profound impacts upon the benefits, costs, and risks of doing business in different countries, upon the way operations in different countries should be managed, and upon the strategy that international firms should pursue in different countries. The international manager with no awareness of or appreciation for these differences is like a fool walking in front of a buffalo stampede; he is likely to get trampled very quickly. Accordingly, one of the principal functions of this chapter and the next is to develop an awareness of and appreciation for the significance of such differences.

In this chapter we focus our attention upon the differing political, economic, and legal environments of countries. We also explore how these differences influence the benefits, costs, and risks associated with doing business in different countries, and how they impact upon management practice and strategy. In Chapter 3 we will look at how differences in such factors as culture, religion, and education influence the practice of international business.

The opening case illustrates that the costs and risks of doing business in a country are influenced by its political, economic, and legal environment. In the case of the newly independent republics of the former Soviet Union, it is clear that the lack of a well-developed market system, the absence of a legal framework for regulating business transactions in a market economy, and the general political and economic turmoil have increased both the costs and the risks of doing business in that part of the world. Firms like Chevron and Polaroid would not face problems of the magnitude described if the various republics of the former Soviet Union had well-established market systems, stable economic and political systems, and well-established bodies of law for regulating business transactions and protecting consumers. The opening case also illustrates that management practice and strategy are influenced by country circumstances. Polaroid's decision to embrace a barter agreement was clearly a strategic response to the rampant inflation in the Russian republic.

With these issues in mind, this chapter is structured as follows. First, we will look at the different political systems that international managers might encounter around the world. Second, we will consider the different economic systems that international managers might encounter and review the profound differences that exist in the economic well-being of different nation states. Third, we will look at the different legal environments that face an international business. Fourth, we will consider the implications for international business of the "new world order" that began to emerge after the Eastern European revolutions of 1989. Finally, we will discuss the implications of all of these factors for the practice of international business.

POLITICAL ENVIRONMENT

Because a country's economic and legal systems are in a large part determined by its political system, we must understand the nature of different political systems before we examine different economic and legal systems. Political systems can be assessed according to two *related* dimensions. The first dimension is the degree to which they emphasize collectivism, as opposed to individualism. The second dimension is the degree to which they are either democratic or totalitarian. These dimensions are interrelated; systems that emphasize collectivism tend to be totalitarian, whereas systems that place a high value on individualism tend to be democratic. However, there is much variation; some democratic societies emphasize a mix of collectivism and individualism, and some totalitarian societies are not collectivist.

Collectivism and Individualism[1]

Political systems that emphasize collectivism stress the primacy of collective goals over individual goals; that is, that the needs of society as a whole are more important than individual freedoms. In such circumstances, an individual's right to do something may be restricted on the grounds that it runs counter to "the good of society." Advocacy of collectivism can be traced back to the ancient Greek philosopher Plato (428–347 B.C.), who argued in *The Republic* that individual rights should be sacrificed for the good of the majority and that property should be owned in common. In modern times the collectivist mantle has been picked up by socialists.

Socialism

Socialists trace their intellectual roots back to Karl Marx (1818–1883). Marx's basic argument is that in a capitalist society in which individual freedoms are not restricted, the few benefit at the expense of the many. While successful capitalists will accumulate considerable wealth, Marx postulated, the wages earned by most workers in a capitalist society will be forced down to subsistence levels. Marx argued that capitalists expropriate for their own use the value created by workers while paying workers only subsistence wages in return. Put another way, according to Marx, the pay workers receive does not reflect the full value of their labor. In order to correct this perceived wrong, Marx advocated state ownership of the basic means of production, distribution, and exchange. His logic was that if the state owned the means of production, the state could ensure that workers were fully compensated for their labor. Thus, the idea is to manage state-owned enterprises to benefit society as a whole, rather than individual capitalists.

[1] For a discussion of the philosophical roots of collectivism and individualism see H. W. Spiegel, *The Growth of Economic Thought* (Durham, N.C.: Duke University Press, 1991). An easily accessible discussion of the weaknesses of collectivism and the strengths of individualism can be found in M. Friedman and R. Friedman, *Free to Choose* (London: Penguin Books, 1980).

In the early 20th century, the socialist ideology split into two broad camps. On the one hand there were **Communists**, who believed that socialism could only be achieved through violent revolution and totalitarian dictatorship. On the other hand, there were the **Social Democrats**, who committed themselves to achieving socialism by democratic means and turned their back upon violent revolution and dictatorship. Both versions of socialism have waxed and waned during the 20th century.

The communist version of socialism reached its high point in the late 1970s, when the majority of the world's population lived in communist states. The countries under communist rule at that time included the U.S.S.R. and its Eastern European client nations (e.g., Poland, Czechoslovakia, Hungary), China, the Southeast Asian nations of Cambodia, Laos, and Vietnam, various African nations (e.g., Angola, Mozambique), and the Latin American nations of Cuba and Nicaragua. By 1992, however, communism was in retreat worldwide. Most significantly, the U.S.S.R. had collapsed and had been replaced a collection of 15 democratically inclined independent republics, while communism had been swept out of Eastern Europe by the largely bloodless revolutions of 1989. Many feel it is now only a matter of time before communism collapses in China, the last remaining major communist power.

Social democracy also seems to have passed its high-water mark, although its ideology may prove to be more enduring than communism. Social democracy has had perhaps its greatest influence in such democratic Western nations as Australia, Great Britain, France, Germany, Norway, Spain, and Sweden, where social democratic parties have occasionally held political power. Other countries where social democracy has had an important influence include India and Brazil. Consistent with their Marxist roots, many social democratic governments have nationalized private companies in certain industries, transforming them into state-owned enterprises to be run for the "public good, rather than private profit." In Great Britain, for example, by the end of the 1970s, state-owned companies had monopolies in the telecommunications, electricity, gas, coal, railway, and shipbuilding industries as well as substantial interests in the oil, airline, auto, and steel industries.

History has shown, however, that far from being in the public interest, state ownership of the means of production often runs counter to the public interest. In many countries the performance of state-owned companies has been poor. Protected from significant competition by their monopoly position and guaranteed government financial support, many state-owned companies have become inefficient. In the end, individuals have paid for the luxury of state ownership through higher prices and higher taxes. Social democratic parties in a number of Western democracies were voted out of office in the late 1970s and early 1980s. They were succeeded by political parties—such as Great Britain's Conservative Party and Germany's Christian Democratic Party—that were more committed to free market economics. These administrations have spent most of the last decade selling off state-owned enterprises to private investors (a process referred to as *privatization*). Thus in Great Britain the Conservative government of Margaret Thatcher sold off the state's interests in telecommunications, electricity, gas, shipbuilding, oil, airlines, autos, and steel to private investors. Moreover, even those social democratic parties that remain in power now seem to be committed to greater private ownership (as is the case in Australia and Sweden).

Individualism

Like collectivism, individualism can be traced back to an ancient Greek philosopher, in this case Plato's disciple Aristotle (384–322 B.C.). In contrast to Plato, Aristotle argued that individual diversity and private ownership are desirable. In a passage that might have been taken from a speech by Margaret Thatcher or Ronald Reagan, he argued that private property is more highly productive than communal property and will thus make for progress. According to Aristotle, communal property receives little care, whereas property that is owned by an individual will receive the greatest care and therefore be most productive.

After sinking into oblivion for the best part of two millennia, individualism was reborn as an influential political philosophy in the Protestant trading nations of England and the Netherlands during the 16th century. The philosophy was refined in the work of several British philosophers, including David Hume (1711–1776), Adam Smith (1723–1790), and John Stuart Mill (1806–1873). The philosophy of individualism had a profound influence upon those in the American colonies who sought independence from Britain. Indeed, individualism underlies the ideas expressed in the Declaration of Independence. In more recent years the philosophy has been championed by several Nobel Prize-winning economists, including Milton Friedman, Friedrich Hayek, and James Buchanan.

Individualism has two central tenets. The first is an emphasis upon the importance of guaranteeing individual freedom and self-expression. As John Stuart Mill put it,

> the sole end for which mankind are warranted, individually or collectively, in interfering with the liberty of action of any of their number is self-protection. . . . The only purpose for which power can be rightfully exercised over any member of a civilized community, against his will, is to prevent harm to others. His own good, either physical or moral, is not a sufficient warrant. . . . The only part of the conduct of any one, for which he is amenable to society, is that which concerns others. In the part which merely concerns himself, his independence is, of right, absolute. Over himself, over his own body and mind, the individual is sovereign.[2]

The second tenet of individualism is that the welfare of society is best served by allowing people to pursue their own economic self-interest, as opposed to having some collective body such as government dictate what is in society's best interest. Or as Adam Smith put it in a famous passage from *The Wealth of Nations,* an individual who intends his own gain is

> led by an invisible hand to promote an end which was no part of his intention. Nor is it always worse for the society that it was no part of it. By pursuing his own interest he frequently promotes that of the society more effectually than when he really intends to promote it. I have never known much good done by those who effect to trade for the public good.[3]

The central message of individualism, therefore, is that individual economic and political freedoms are the ground rules upon which a society should be based. This puts individualism into direct conflict with collectivism, which asserts the primacy of the collective over the individual. In no small way, this ideological conflict has influenced the recent history of the world. The Cold War, for example, was essentially a war between collectivism, championed by the U.S.S.R., and individualism, championed by the United States.

In practical terms, individualism translates into an advocacy for democratic political systems and free market economics. Viewed this way, we can see that the waning of

---

[2] J. S. Mill, *On Liberty* (London: Longman's, 1865), p. 6.

[3] A. Smith, *The Wealth of Nations,* vol. 1, p. 325.

collectivism in the late 1980s and early 1990s accompanied the ascendancy of individualism. A wave of democratic ideals and free market economics is currently sweeping away socialism and communism worldwide. The changes of the last few years go beyond the dramatic revolutions in Eastern Europe and the former Soviet Union to include a move toward greater individualism in Latin America and in some of the social democratic states of the West (e.g., Great Britain and Sweden). This is not to claim that individualism has finally won a long battle with collectivism—it has not—but as a guiding political philosophy, there is no doubt that individualism is on the ascendancy. This is good news for international business, since in direct contrast to collectivism, the probusiness and pro-free trade values of individualism create a favorable environment for international business.

Democracy and Totalitarianism

Democracy and totalitarianism are at opposite ends of the political dimension. The democratic-totalitarian dimension is not independent of the collectivism-individualism dimension. Democracy and individualism go hand in hand, as do the communist version of collectivism and totalitarianism. However, gray areas also exist; collective values may predominate in a democratic state, and a totalitarian state may be hostile to collectivism and encourage some degree of individualism—particularly in the economic sphere. (E.g., Chile in the 1980s was ruled by a military dictatorship that encouraged economic freedom but not political freedom.)

Democracy

The pure form of democracy, as originally practiced by several city-states in ancient Greece, is based upon a belief that citizens should be directly involved in decision-making processes. In complex advanced societies with populations in the tens or hundreds of millions, this is simply impractical. Accordingly, most modern democratic states practice what is commonly referred to as **representative democracy**. In a representative democracy citizens periodically elect individuals to represent them. These elected representatives then form a government, whose function is to make decisions on behalf of the electorate. A representative democracy rests upon the assumption that if elected representatives fail to perform this job adequately, they can and will be removed from office at the next election.

In order to guarantee that elected representatives can be held accountable for their actions by the electorate, an ideal representative democracy includes a number of safeguards in its constitutional law. These include (1) an individual's right to freedom of expression, opinion, and organization; (2) free news media; (3) regular elections in which all eligible citizens are allowed to vote; (4) universal adult suffrage; (5) limited terms for elected representatives; (6) a fair court system that is independent of the political system; (7) a nonpolitical state bureaucracy; (8) a nonpolitical police force and armed service; and (9) relatively free access to state information.[4]

Totalitarianism

In a totalitarian dictatorship a single political party, individual, or group of individuals monopolizes political power in the state, neither recognizing nor permitting opposition.

---

[4] R. Wesson, *Modern Government—Democracy and Authoritarism*, 2nd ed. (Englewood Cliffs, N.J.: Prentice Hall, 1983).

All of the constitutional guarantees upon which representative democracies are built—such as an individual's right to freedom of expression and organization, free news media, and regular elections—are denied to the citizens. In most totalitarian states political repression is widespread, and those who question the right of the rulers to rule find themselves imprisoned, or worse.

In the world today there are four major forms of totalitarianism. Until recently the most widespread was **communist totalitarianism.** As discussed earlier, communism is a version of collectivism that advocates that socialism can only be achieved through totalitarian dictatorship. Communism, however, is in decline worldwide, and many of the old communist dictatorships have collapsed since 1989. The major exceptions to this trend (so far) are China, Vietnam, Laos, North Korea, and Cuba, although in all of these states clear signs exist that the Communist party's monopoly on political power is under attack.

A second form of totalitarianism might be labeled **theocratic totalitarianism.** Theocratic totalitarianism is found in states where political power is monopolized by a party, group, or individual that governs according to religious principles. The most common form of theocratic totalitarianism is the one based upon Islam, exemplified by states such as Iran and Saudi Arabia. In these states not only is freedom of political expression restricted, so is freedom of religious expression, while the laws of the state are based upon Islamic principle.

A third form of totalitarianism might be referred to as **tribal totalitarianism.** Tribal totalitarianism is found principally in African countries such as Zimbabwe, Tanzania, Uganda, and Kenya. The borders of most African states reflect the administrative boundaries drawn by the former European colonial powers, rather than tribal or ethnic realities. Consequently, the typical African country contains a number of ethnic groups. Tribal totalitarianism occurs when a political party that represents the interests of a particular tribe (not necessarily the majority tribe) monopolizes power. Such one party states are scattered throughout Africa.

A fourth form of totalitarianism might be described as **right-wing totalitarianism.** A common feature of most right-wing dictatorships is an overt hostility to communism. Right-wing dictatorships generally permit individual economic freedom but restrict individual political freedom on the grounds that it would lead to a rise of communism. Many right-wing totalitarian governments are backed by the military, and indeed, the government may be made up of military officers. Until the early 1980s, right-wing dictatorships (many of them military dictatorships) were common throughout Latin America. They were also found in several Asian countries, particularly in South Korea, Taiwan, Singapore, Indonesia, and the Philippines. Since the early 1980s, however, this form of government has been in retreat. The majority of Latin American countries are now genuine multiparty democracies, while significant political freedoms have been granted to the political opposition in countries such as South Korea, Taiwan, and the Philippines.

The Complexions of Government

One way of assessing the complexion of a government is to examine its attitude toward economic and political freedom. For example, consider Figure 2.1; here economic freedom is plotted on the horizontal axis, and political freedom on the vertical axis. Communist totalitarian states like Cuba, in which collectivism predominates over individualism, score low on both dimensions and thus are found in the bottom left corner of the figure. Representative democracies in which governments adhere to individualism and oppose collectivism, such as the United States, Germany, and (since the early 1980s) Great Britain, appear in the top right corner of the figure.

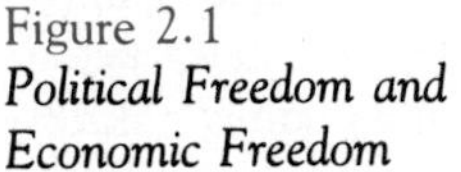

Figure 2.1
Political Freedom and Economic Freedom

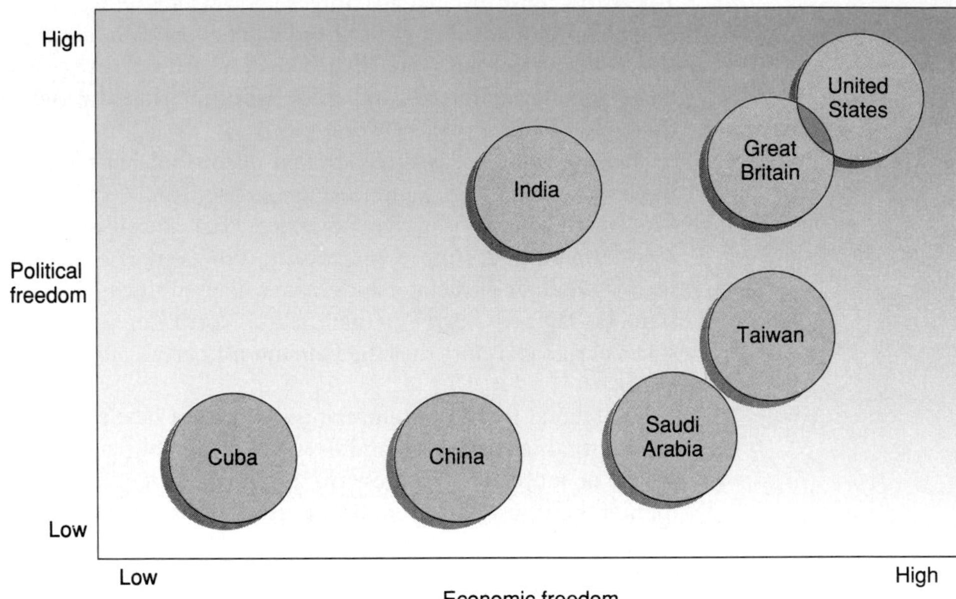

However, there are many other countries whose position is not so clear-cut. Take China, for example. China is still a communist totalitarian state, so it scores low on the political freedom dimension; but it is a totalitarian state that is nevertheless now granting significant economic freedoms to individuals. (Recent developments in China are discussed later in this chapter.) Thus, on the economic freedom dimension China scores relatively high (compared to Cuba, for example). Another interesting case is India. India is a representative democracy in which collective ideals have been influencing political policy ever since the country gained independence from the British in 1947. As a result, state-owned companies account for the majority of production in the telecommunications, electricity, gas, oil, airline, steel, and shipbuilding industries. Thus, although India scores high on a political freedom dimension, it does not do so well on the economic freedom dimension. Taiwan is in just the opposite situation. Taiwan has vigorously encouraged economic freedoms, but its quasi-democratic government limits the ability of the political opposition to gain power. Thus Taiwan scores high on the economic freedom dimension and relatively low on the political freedom dimension. Then there is the case of Saudi Arabia. Saudia Arabia is a procapitalist state that permits considerable economic freedoms, but it is also a theocratic totalitarian state with limited political freedom.

Map 2.2 illustrates the political freedom dimension as of 1991. The map charts political freedom on a scale from 1 for the highest degree of political freedom to 7 for the lowest. Among the criteria for a high rating are recent free and fair elections, a parliament with effective power, a significant opposition, and recent shifts in power through elections. Factors contributing to a lower rating include military or foreign control, the denial of self-determination to major population groups, and a lack of decentralized political power. Countries that have become independent since 1945 are indicated by their date of independence.

Map 2.2 *Political Freedom in 1991*

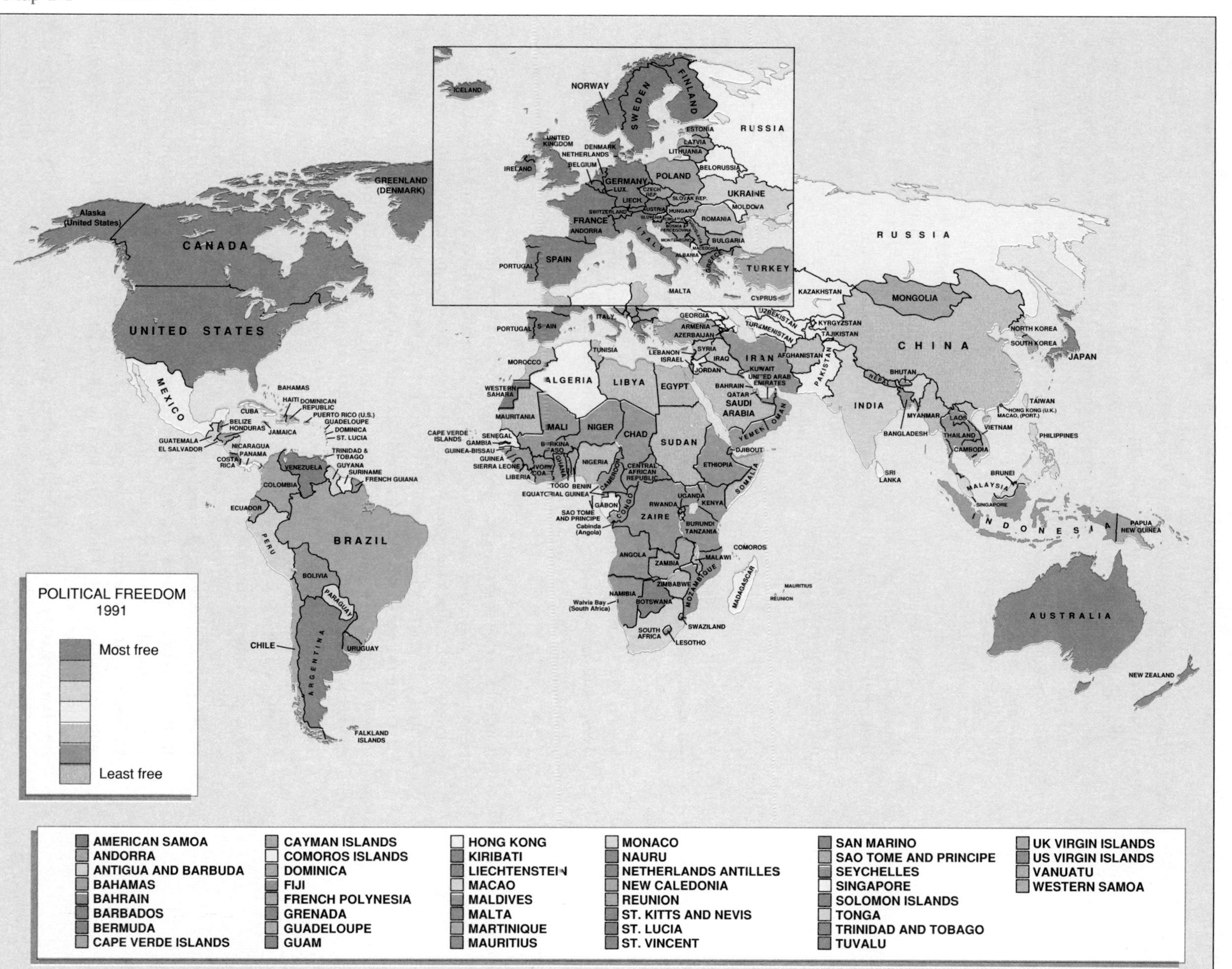

Source: Map data from Freedom Review *23, no. 1 (January–February 1992), pp. 17–19.*

Why Does It All Matter?

At this point you may be wondering what all of this has to do with international business. We discuss this issue in depth in the Implications for Business section at the end of the chapter, but it seems appropriate to consider a couple of points now. First, a political environment that encourages economic freedom is clearly more attractive to an international business than one that restricts economic freedoms. When economic freedoms are restricted, so may be the ability of an international business to operate efficiently. For example, it is much easier to do business in Germany than it is in Cuba, China, or India—precisely because the state accounts for so much economic activity in those nations.

Second, the issue of whether to do business in countries that do not grant their citizens political freedoms and that routinely violate their human rights, raises difficult and complex **ethical issues** for international business. Should a U.S. firm do business in China, given that the Chinese government continues to imprison and execute its political opponents? Is a U.S. firm supporting a totalitarian dictatorship by investing in that country, or can the investment be justified on grounds that it might help change the dictatorship from within, thereby bringing about greater political freedoms? We will return to this issue later.

ECONOMIC ENVIRONMENT

We consider two features of a country's economic environment in this section. The first is the nature of a country's economic system—whether it is a free market system, a command economy, or a combination of the two. The second feature is the level of economic development of a country. It should be noted at the outset that these two aspects of a country's economic environment are not independent. As we shall see, there are reasons for supposing that the level of economic development is influenced by the country's type of economic system.

Economic Systems

It should be clear from the previous section that a profound linkage exists between political ideology and economic systems. In countries where individual goals are given primacy over collective goals, we are likely to find free market economic systems. In contrast, in countries where collective goals are given preeminence, the state may well have taken control over the commanding heights of the economy, and markets are likely to be restricted rather than free. More specifically, we can identify three broad types of economic system: a market economy, a command economy, and a mixed economy.

Market Economy

In a pure market economy, the goods and services the country produces and their quantity are not planned by anyone. Rather, these things are determined by the interaction of supply and demand and are signaled to producers through the price system. If demand for a product exceeds supply, prices will rise, signaling producers to produce more. If supply exceeds demand, prices will fall, signaling producers to produce less. Consumers are sovereign in this system. The purchasing patterns of consumers, as signaled to producers through the mechanism of the price system, determine what and how much is produced.

For a market to work in this manner there must be no restrictions on supply. A restriction on supply occurs when a market is monopolized by a single firm. In such circumstances, rather than increasing output in response to increased demand, a monopolist might restrict output and let prices rise. This allows the monopolist to take a greater profit on each unit it sells. Although this is good for the monopolist, it is bad for the consumer, who must pay higher prices. Moreover, it is probably bad for the welfare of society. Since, by definition, a monopolist has no competitors, it has no incentive to search for ways of lowering its costs of production. Rather, it can simply pass on cost increases to consumers in the form of higher prices. The net result is that the monopolist is likely to become increasingly inefficient, producing high-priced low-quality goods, and that society is likely to suffer as a consequence.

Given the dangers inherent in monopoly, the role of government in a market economy is to encourage vigorous competition between producers. Governments do this by outlawing monopolies and restrictive business practices designed to monopolize a market (e.g., U.S. antitrust laws serve this function). The institution of private ownership also serves to encourage vigorous competition and economic efficiency. Private ownership ensures that entrepreneurs have a right to the profits generated by their own efforts. This gives entrepreneurs an incentive to search for better ways of serving consumer needs—whether that be through introducing new products, by developing more efficient production processes, by better marketing and after-sales service, or simply through managing their businesses more efficiently than their competitors manage theirs. In turn, the constant improvement in product and process that results from the existence of such an incentive has been argued to have a major positive impact upon economic growth and development.[5]

Command Economy

In a pure command economy, the goods and services that a country produces, the quantity in which they are produced, and the prices at which they are sold are all planned by the government. Consistent with the collectivist ideology, the objective of a command economy is for government to allocate resources for "the good of society." In addition, all businesses are state-owned in a pure command economy, the rationale being that the government can then direct them to make investments that are in the best interests of the nation as a whole.

Command economies are typical in communist countries, where collectivist goals are given priority over individual goals. However, a good deal of government planning, mixed with some state ownership, has also been undertaken in several democratic nations by socialist-inclined governments. France and India, in particular, have experimented with extensive government planning and state ownership, although government planning has recently fallen into disfavor in both countries.

Although the objective of a command economy is to mobilize economic resources for the public good, in practice, just the opposite seems to occur. State-owned enterprises in a command economy have little incentive to control costs and to be efficient, since they cannot fail as businesses. Moreover, the abolition of private ownership removes the incentive for individuals to look for better ways of serving consumer needs; hence there is a general absence of dynamism and innovation in command economies. Instead of growing and becoming more prosperous, they tend to be characterized by economic stagnation. (Some evidence to support this is presented later.)

---

[5] For a detailed but accessible elaboration of this argument, see Friedman and Friedman, *Free to Choose*.

Mixed Economy

Between market economies and command economies can be found mixed economies. In a mixed economy, certain sectors of the economy are left to private ownership and free market mechanisms, while other sectors are characterized by significant state ownership and government planning. Mixed economies have been relatively common among the social democratic states of Western Europe, but they are becoming less so. Great Britain, France, Italy, and Sweden can all be classified as mixed economies. In these countries the government intervenes in those sectors where it feels that private ownership is not in the best interests of society. For example, Great Britain and Sweden both have extensive state-owned health systems that provide free universal health care to all citizens (actually it's not really free, since it is financed through taxes.) In both countries it is felt that government has a moral obligation to provide for the health of its citizens. One consequence is that private ownership of health care operations is very restricted in both countries.

In mixed economies, governments also tend to take into state ownership troubled firms whose continued operation is felt to be vital to national interests. For example, the French automobile company, Renault, is state-owned. The government took over the company when it ran into serious financial problems. Reasoning that the social costs of the unemployment that might result if Renault collapsed were unacceptable, the French government nationalized the company in order to save it from bankruptcy. Of course, Renault's competitors weren't exactly thrilled by this move, since they now must compete with a company whose costs are subsidized by the French government.

Economic Development

Different countries have dramatically different levels of economic development. One of the most common measures of economic development is a country's gross domestic product (GDP) per head of population. GDP is often regarded as a yardstick for the economic activity of a country; it measures the total value of the goods and services produced annually. Map 2.3 summarizes the GDP per head of the world's nations in 1991. As can be seen, countries like the United States, Canada, and Germany are among the richest on this measure, while the large countries of China and India are among the poorest.

GDP-per-head figures, such as those upon which Map 2.3 is based, can be misleading, however, since they do not take into account differences in the cost of living. For example, although the 1991 GDP per head of Switzerland, at $30,304, exceeded the 1991 GDP per head of the United States, which was $22,049, the higher cost of living in Switzerland meant that U.S. citizens could actually afford more goods and services than Swiss citizens. As noted in Box 1.2 of Chapter 1, to account for differences in the cost of living, the United Nations (UN) has calculated a purchasing power parity index (PPP), which adjusts GDP per head for the cost of living. This index allows for a direct comparison of living standards in different countries. The index is scaled so that an indicator of 100 is assigned to the country with the highest PPP (which happens to be the United States). The PPP index for selected countries is summarized in Figure 2.2. As can be seen, there are striking differences in standard of living among countries. For example, Figure 2.2 suggests that the average Indian citizen can afford to consume only 4.7 percent of the goods and services consumed by the average U.S. citizen. Given this, despite its large population, India is unlikely to be a lucrative market for the consumer products produced by many U.S. international businesses.

A problem with the data presented in both Map 2.3 and Figure 2.2 is that they give a very static picture of development. They tell us, for example, that China is much poorer

Map 2.3 *1991 GDP per Capita (in U.S. $)*

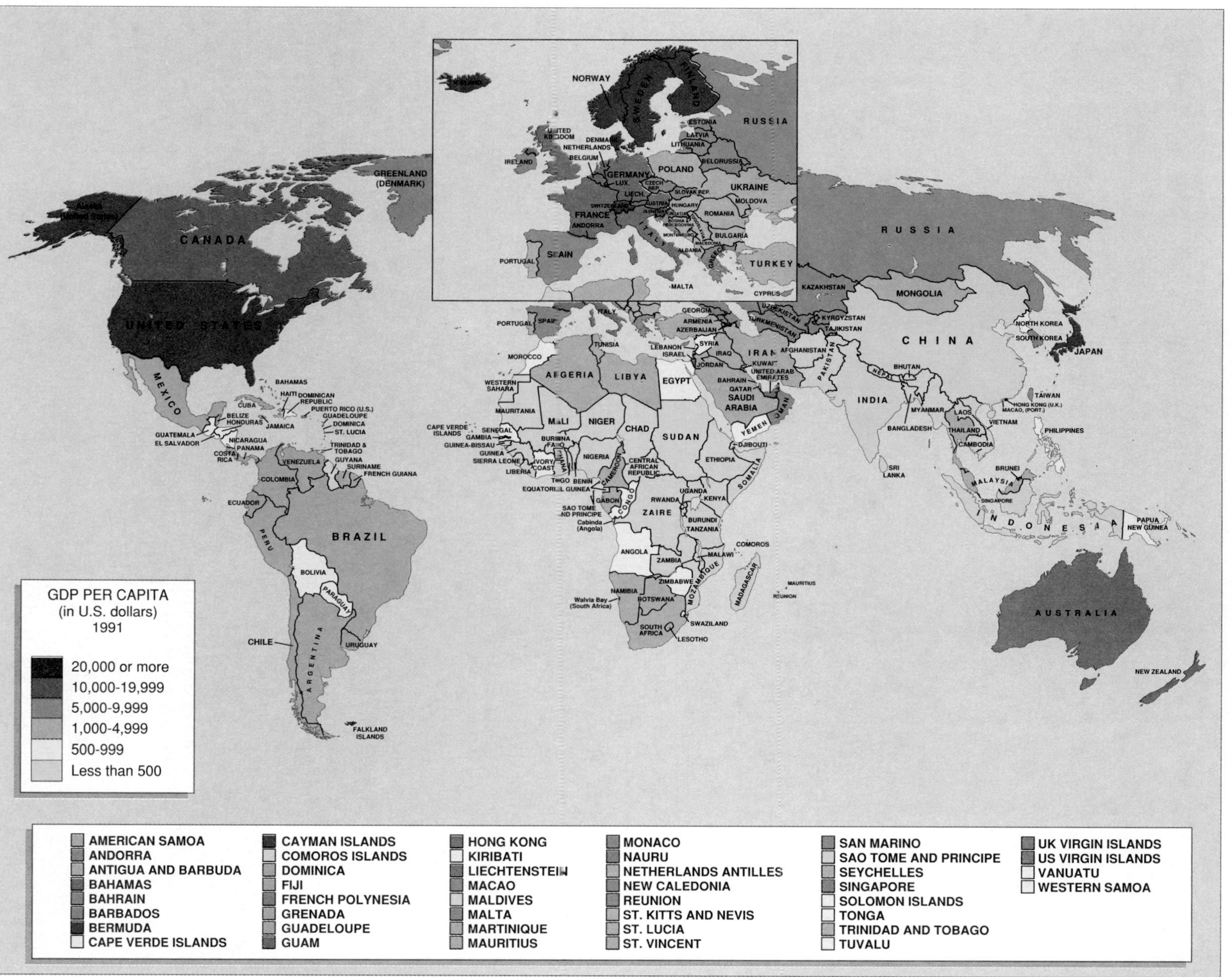

Source: *Map data from World Bank,* World Development Report, 1992.

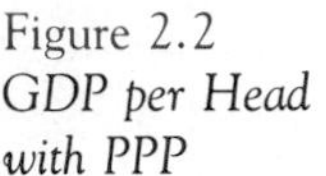

Figure 2.2
GDP per Head with PPP

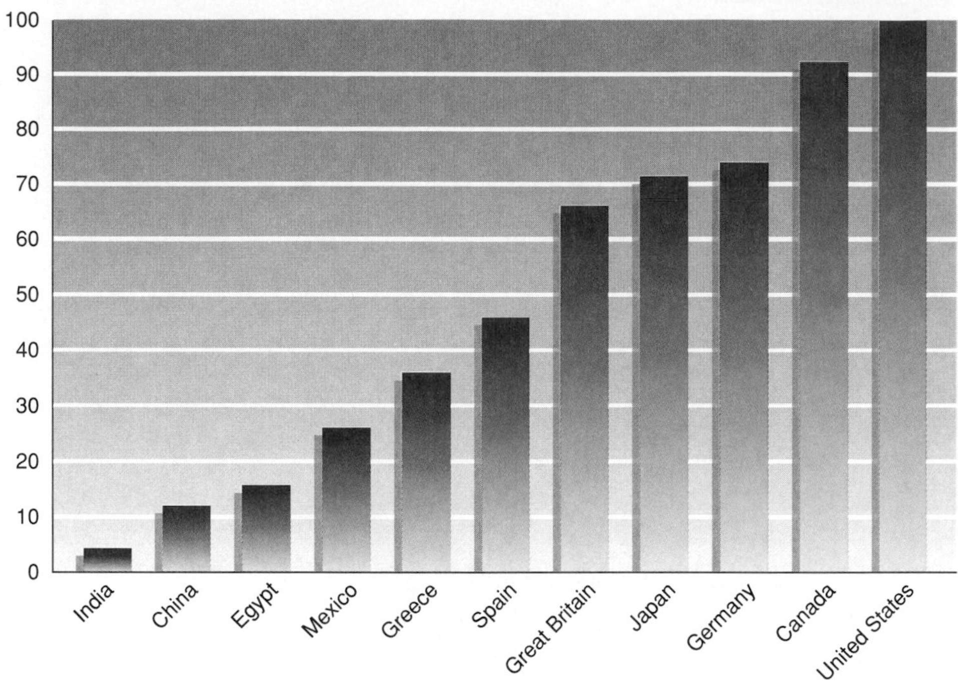

Source: The Economist, Book of Vital World Statistics *(London: Economist Books, 1990), p. 41.*

than the United States, but they do not tell us if China is closing the gap. To assess this, we must look at the economic growth rates achieved by different countries. Figure 2.3 summarizes the growth in GDP achieved by a number of countries between 1980 and 1990. As the figure shows, the economies of some currently very poor countries like China and India are growing more rapidly than those of many of the advanced nations of the West. Consequently, they may in time become advanced nations themselves—and huge markets for the products of international businesses. Given their potential, some international businesses may decide to start getting a foothold in these markets now. Even though their current contribution to an international firm's revenues might be small, their future contributions could be large.

A number of other indicators can also be used to evaluate both a country's level of economic development and its likely future growth rate. These include literacy rates, the number of people per doctor, infant mortality rates, life expectancy, calorie (food) consumption per head, car ownership per 1,000 people, and education spending as a percentage of GDP. In an innovative attempt to assess the impact of factors such as these upon the quality of life in a country, in 1990 the United Nations published its first **human development index.** This index is based upon three measures: life expectancy, literacy rates, and whether average incomes—based on PPP estimates—are sufficient to meet the basic needs of life in a country (adequate food, shelter, and health care). The human development index is scaled from 0 to 100. Countries scoring less than 50 are classified as having low human development (the quality of life is poor), those scoring from 50 to 80 are classified as having medium human development, while those countries that score above 80 are classified as having high human development. The scores of selected countries are summarized in Table 2.1. Also given in Table 2.1 are figures for population and for population doubling time (the number of years in which the popula-

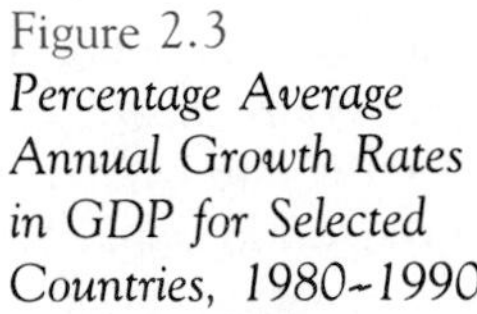
Figure 2.3
Percentage Average Annual Growth Rates in GDP for Selected Countries, 1980–1990

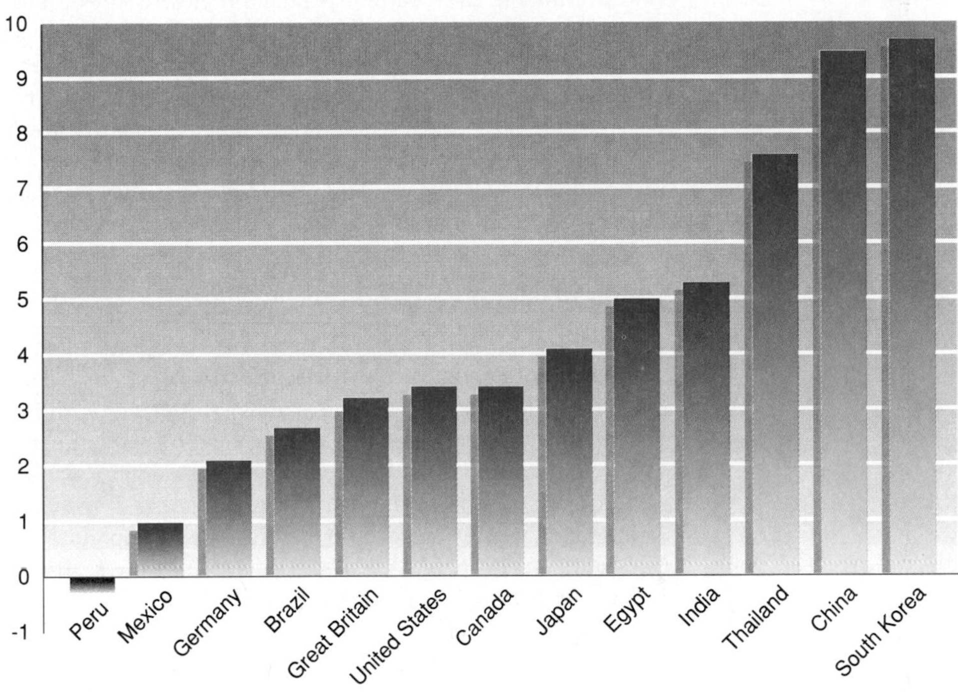

Source: World Bank, World Development Report, 1992, *Table 2.*

Table 2.1
Human Development Index and Population Statistics for Selected Countries

Country	Human Development Index	Population (millions)	Population Doubling Time (years)
Japan	99.6	124.0	174
Canada	98.3	26.8	63
Great Britain	97.0	57.5	231
Germany	96.7	79.5	174
United States	96.1	252.5	87
Hungary	91.5	10.5	1,000
Mexico	87.6	90.0	32
Malaysia	80.0	17.9	29
Brazil	78.4	155.0	39
Thailand	78.3	56.8	50
China	71.6	1,151.0	44
Indonesia	59.1	193.6	39
India	43.9	866.0	37
Pakistan	42.3	117.5	28
Nigeria	32.3	88.5	23
Bangladesh	31.8	116.6	30
Zaire	29.4	37.8	21
Mozambique	23.9	15.1	15
Afghanistan	21.2	16.5	14
Chad	15.7	5.1	33

Sources: The Economist, Book of Vital World Statistics, 1990 *(Economist Books), p. 228; and World Bank.* World Development Report, 1992.

tion will double given current population growth rates). The disturbing fact revealed by the table is that some of the world's poorest countries, as measured by the human development index, are not only heavily populated, but they also have rapidly expanding populations. Given this, the quality of life in such countries may deteriorate over the next few decades. If this occurs, the implications for the rest of the world could be profound and could include widespread famine and war. In such circumstances, the underdevelopment of the Third World may hold back the continuing economic growth of the world's advanced industrialized nations.

What Determines Economic Growth Rate?

The question arises as to what determines a country's economic growth rate. This is valuable information for an international business to have. Other things being equal, economies that are likely to grow rapidly offer more profit potential for international businesses than economies that are unlikely to grow. The question, however, is not easy to answer. In truth, a large number of factors—political system, economic system, legal system, education level, infrastructure, natural resources, and others—all contribute to economic growth. **Capacity for growth** is also important. The United States, with its high standard of living, has less capacity for growth than countries such as China or India, which cannot even provide for the basic needs of their populations at this time.

Despite the complexity of this issue, one variable seems to stand out. In general, countries with market economies appear to achieve greater sustained economic growth rates than countries with command economies. The vibrant economic growth of Western Europe after 1945 and the stagnation of the command economies of Eastern Europe at the same time provide an interesting contrast in the relative merits of market and command economies. Another example is seen in comparing the performance of North Korea's command economy with that of South Korea's market economy. In 1960, South Korea's GNP per person was about $675 in today's money, probably not that much more than in communist North Korea. Since then the South's real GNP has grown by 8.4 percent a year, giving each citizen a share of GNP equal to $4,550 by 1989. In contrast, the GNP per head in North Korea was less than $1,000 in 1989.[6] China's spurt of economic growth during the 1980s, for example (see Figure 2.3), can also be attributed to a pragmatic decision by the communist government to move away from a command economy and toward a market economy. (This is discussed in more detail later in the chapter.)

LEGAL ENVIRONMENT

The legal environment of a country is of immense importance to international business. A country's laws regulate business practice, define the manner in which business transactions are to be executed, and set down the rights and obligations of those involved in business transactions. Needless to say, the legal environments of different countries differ in significant ways. Differences in the structure of law can have an important impact upon the attractiveness of a country as an investment site and/or market.

Like the economic environment of a country, the legal environment is in part influenced by the political environment. Specifically, it is the government of a country that defines the legal framework within which firms do business, and the laws that

6 "Taiwan and Korea: Two Paths to Prosperity," *The Economist*, July 14, 1990, pp. 19–20.

regulate business in a country usually reflect the dominant political ideology. For example, collectivist-inclined totalitarian states tend to enact laws that severely restrict private enterprise, whereas laws enacted by governments in democratic states where individualism is the dominant political philosophy tend to favor private enterprise and the consumer.

The variation in the structure of law between countries is a massive topic that warrants a textbook in its own right. Here we will simply focus upon three issues that illustrate the variations and their effects on the practice of international business. These issues are (1) laws governing patents, copyrights, and trademarks; (2) laws covering product safety and product liability; and (3) contract law.

Patents, Copyrights, and Trademarks

A patent grants the inventor of a product or process exclusive rights to the manufacture, use, or sale of the invention. Copyrights are the exclusive legal rights of authors, composers, playwrights, artists, and publishers to publish and dispose of their work as they see fit. Trademarks are designs and names, often officially registered, by which merchants or manufacturers designate and differentiate their products (e.g., Christian Dior clothes, McDonald's restaurants). More generally, the purpose of patents, copyrights, and trademarks is to protect **intellectual property** (ideas).

The intent of intellectual property laws is to reward the originator of a new invention, book, musical record, clothes design, restaurant chain, and the like, for his or her idea and effort. As such, they are a very important stimulus to innovation and creative work. They provide an incentive for people to search for novel ways of doing things and they reward creativity. For an example, consider innovation in the pharmaceutical industry. A patent grants the developer of a new drug a 17-year monopoly in production of that drug. This gives pharmaceutical firms an incentive to undertake the expensive, difficult, time-consuming basic research required to develop and test new drugs. (Estimates are that $100 million in R&D and 12 years are needed to get a new drug on the market.) Without the guarantees provided by patents, it is unlikely that companies would commit themselves to extensive basic research.[7]

Intellectual property rights differ greatly from country to country. Most seriously for international businesses, some countries take a very relaxed view of intellectual property laws and are generally unwilling to enforce them, or even to recognize the legitimacy of foreign patents, copyrights, and trademarks. This encourages piracy of intellectual property. China and Thailand have recently been among the worst offenders in Asia. In China, for example, bookstores commonly maintain a section that is closed to foreigners. Ostensibly reserved for sensitive political literature, this section more often displays illegally copied textbooks. Pirated computer software is also widely available in China. Similarly, the streets of Bangkok, the capital of Thailand, are lined with stands selling pirated copies of Rolex watches, Levi's jeans, videotapes, and computer software. More generally, estimates suggest that Asian violations of intellectual property rights are costing U.S. computer software companies $6 billion annually and U.S. pharmaceutical companies at least $500 million annually.[8]

International businesses have a number of alternatives in dealing with such violations. First, firms can push for international agreements to ensure that intellectual

---

[7] Indeed, Douglass North has argued that correct specification of intellectual property rights is one factor that lowers the costs of doing business and, thereby, stimulates economic growth and development. See D. North, *Institutions, Institutional Change, and Economic Performance* (Cambridge, U.K.: Cambridge University Press, 1991).

[8] M. Magnier, "U.S. Gains in Effort to Protect Intellectual Property in Asia," *Journal of Commerce,* February 3, 1992, pp. 1A, 3A; and "Economy of the Mind," *The Economist,* December 23, 1989, pp. 99–101.

Does the United States Have Too Many Lawyers?

In early 1992 Vice President Dan Quayle addressed the annual convention of the American Bar Association. He caused an uproar by drawing a link between the number of lawyers in the United States and poor competitiveness. "Does America," he asked, "really need 70 percent of the world's lawyers? Is it healthy for our economy to have 18 million new lawsuits coursing through the system annually?" He went on to characterize America's legal system as a "self-inflicted competitive disadvantage costing $300 billion a year."

Is Dan Quayle right? A close look at the figures suggests that the answer is both yes and no. The United States does have a lot of lawyers, although the correct figure is 30 percent of the world's total, not 70 percent, as Quayle asserted. As shown in the table, the United States has more lawyers per 100,000 people than any other industrialized country. (It has nearly twice as many per 100,000 people as Germany and three times as many as Japan.) Also shown in the table are tort costs as a percentage of Gross National product (GNP). Tort costs are the liability costs arising from suits involving product liability and medical malpractice. Rising tort costs were the main target of Quayle's criticism. As can be seen, U.S. tort costs amount to about 2.4 percent of GNP, many times the percentage in other industrialized countries. So the costs of law suits would seem to put the United States at a competitive disadvantage.

On the other hand, Quayle's estimate that these costs amount to $300 billion per year is an overstatement. More sober estimates are that total tort costs amount to around $100 billion per year. Since some of these costs would arise in less litigious societies as well, Quayle's $300 billion figure is almost certainly a gross exaggeration. Nonetheless, it is clear that legal costs are significantly higher in the United States than in other advanced industrialized societies and that this translates into something of a competitive disadvantage. For example, medical malpractice insurance costs the average U.S. doctor about $16,000 per year, compared to about $1,600 per year for the average doctor in Western Europe.

property rights are strictly enforced, and this is occurring. Second, firms may decide to stay out of countries where intellectual property laws are lax, rather than risk having their ideas stolen by local entrepreneurs. (Such reasoning partly underlay decisions by Coca-Cola and IBM to pull out of India in the early 1970s.) Third, firms can devote resources to ensuring that pirated copies of their products produced by businessmen in countries where intellectual property laws are lax do not turn up in their home market or in third countries. Microsoft, for example, recently discovered that pirated Microsoft software produced illegally in Thailand was being sold worldwide (including in the U.S.) as the real thing.

Product Safety and Product Liability

Product safety laws set certain safety standards to which a product must adhere. Product liability involves holding a firm and its officers responsible when their product causes injury, death, or damage. Product liability can be much greater if a product does not conform to required safety standards. There are both civil and criminal product liability laws. Civil laws call for payment and money damages. Criminal liability laws result in fines or imprisonment. Both civil and criminal liability laws are probably more extensive in the United States than in any other country, although many other Western nations

BOX 2.1

Country	Lawyers per 100,000 Population	Tort costs as Percent of GNP
United States	312	2.4
Belgium	213	0.5
Germany	190.1	0.45
Canada	168.5	0.55
Australia	145.7	0.3
Great Britain	134	0.45
Japan	106	0.35
Spain	84.6	0.35
Italy	81.2	0.45
Denmark	58.7	0.35
Switzerland	51.4	0.7
France	49.1	0.55

Source: "A Survey of the Legal Profession," The Economist, *July 18, 1992, pp. 4, 13.*

The interesting question, of course, is why are legal costs so much higher in the United States? Experts argue that the high costs have little to do with differences in liability law across countries, which are minimal. Rather, they point out that in the United States juries decide tort cases and, more significantly, set damages. In most other countries judges do these things. Juries tend to be less objective and more prone to emotional arguments than judges in awarding damages in liability cases, particularly when those cases involve "pain and suffering." The result: jury awards in the United States have risen sharply in real terms since the mid-1970s. Whereas Quayle might be correct in arguing that high tort costs in the United States place the country at a competitive disadvantage, although he almost certainly exaggerates the size of the effect, he is perhaps wrong to blame the problem on "too many lawyers." Rather, the problem may be due to a legal system that allows juries, not judges, to fix damage awards in tort cases.

Sources: "A Survey of the Legal Profession," The Economist, *July 18, 1992, pp. 1–18; and P. Huber and R. Litan,* The Liability Maze. *(Washington, D.C.: The Brookings Institution, 1992.)*

also have comprehensive liability laws. Liability laws are typically least comprehensive in less developed nations.

A boom in product liability suits and awards in the United States has resulted in dramatic increases in the cost of liability insurance. In turn, many business executives argue that the high costs of liability insurance in the United States are making U.S. businesses less competitive in the global marketplace. This view was supported by the Bush administration. Vice President Dan Quayle argued that the United States has too many lawyers and that product liability awards are too large. According to Quayle, the result is that product liability insurance rates are typically much lower overseas, thereby giving foreign firms a competitive advantage. For further details see Box 2.1.

The competitiveness issue apart, country differences in product safety and liability laws raises an important ethical issue for U.S. firms doing business abroad. Specifically, when U.S. product safety laws are tougher than those of a foreign country (as is typically the case), and/or when liability laws are more lax, should a U.S. firm doing business in that country adhere to the more relaxed local standards, or should it adhere to the standards of its home country? Although the ethical thing to do is undoubtedly to adhere to home-country standards, U.S. companies have been known to take advantage of lax safety and liability laws to do business in a manner that would not be allowed back home.

Contract Law

A contract is a document that specifies the conditions under which an exchange is to take place and the rights and obligations of the parties to the exchange. Many business transactions are regulated by some form of contract. Contract law is the body of law that governs contract enforcement. The parties to an agreement normally resort to contract law when one party feels the other has violated either the letter or the spirit of an agreement.

Contract law can differ significantly across countries, and as such it effects the kind of contracts an international business should use to safeguard its position. The main differences are due to differences in legal tradition. There are two main legal traditions in the world today, the **common law system** and the **civil law system.** The common law system evolved in England over hundreds of years and is the basis of laws in most of Britain's former colonies, including the United States. Common law is based on tradition, precedent, and custom. When law courts interpret common law, they do so with regard to these characteristics. Civil law, on the other hand, is based on a very detailed set of laws that are organized into "codes." Among other things, these codes define the laws that govern business transactions. When law courts interpret civil law, they do so with regard to these codes. More than 80 countries, including Germany, France, Japan, and Russia, operate within a civil law system. Since common law tends to be relatively ill specified, contracts drafted under a common law framework tend to be very detailed with all contingencies spelled out. In civil law systems, however, contracts tend to be much shorter and less specific, since many of the issues typically covered in a common law contract are already covered in a civil code.

THE NEW WORLD ORDER

During the late 1980s and early 1990s a wave of democratic revolutions swept the world. In country after country totalitarian governments collapsed and were replaced by democratically elected government typically more committed to free market capitalism than their predecessors. The change was most dramatic in Eastern Europe, where the collapse of communism brought an end to the Cold War and led to the breakup of the Soviet Union, but similar changes were occurring throughout the world during this period. Across much of Asia, Latin America, and Africa there was a marked shift toward greater democracy and free market capitalism. In this section we discuss these changes and explore their implications for the future of international business.

Eastern Europe

After World War II, Soviet-backed communists took power in eight Eastern European states—Poland, Czechoslovakia, East Germany, Hungary, Rumania, Bulgaria, Albania, and Yugoslavia. This set the scene for 40 years of ideological conflict between the Communist bloc, dominated by the Soviet Union, and the democratic West. The conflict did not begin to thaw until 1985 when Mikhail Gorbachev became general secretary of the Soviet Communist Party and began his program of *perestroika.* By that time the gulf between the vibrant, wealthy economies of the West and the stagnant economies of the communist East had become so immense that even the most hard-line communist ideologue could not have failed to notice. With the tacit support of Gorbachev, several of the communist regimes of Eastern Europe began to loosen their repressive economic and political systems in an attempt to revive their stalled economies. What they discovered, however, was that once the "genie" of freedom had been let out of the bottle it could not easily be put back in. During 1989 communist government after communist government fell like dominoes.

The change was smoothest and most gradual in Bulgaria, Hungary, and Poland, where the forces of democracy had been gaining ground since the early 1980s. In all three countries the communists (sometimes under new names) were simply voted out of office. Faced with huge street demonstrations that would have been unthinkable a year before, the communist governments of Czechoslovakia and East Germany collapsed like eggshells. In Rumania the communist dictator, Nicolae Ceauşescu, resorted to military force to try to put down street demonstrations. The result was a short and bloody civil war that ended with Ceauşescu's overthrow and execution.

By the end of 1989 only Yugoslavia and backward Albania remained under communist rule. In 1991 the Yugoslavian federation disintegrated into a civil war between its constituent republics. Albania held its first elections since 1945, and although the Communist party held onto power by a thin margin, its days seemed numbered. The biggest change in 1991, however, occurred in the Soviet Union itself. By 1991 the U.S.S.R. had already moved significantly down the road toward political—but not economic—freedom. Faced with the breakup of the U.S.S.R. into quasi-independent, democratically inclined states, the old communist hard-liners attempted to remove Mikhail Gorbachev from power. The coup d'etat attempt, badly planned from the start, collapsed when it became apparent that much of the military was not going to support the coup plotters. The end result was that the Communist party was outlawed and the reform movement gained strength. On January 1, 1992, the U.S.S.R. passed into history, to be replaced by 15 independent republics, 11 of which elected to remain associated as a Commonwealth of Independent States (see opening case).

Asia

No less significant changes were taking place in Asia during the 1980s and early 90s. Shifts toward greater political democracy occurred in the Philippines, Thailand, Taiwan, and South Korea. In Vietnam, long a U.S. pariah, the ruling Communist party removed many price controls and began to shift toward a market economy. In North Korea, still one of the most repressive of communist regimes, signs of a thaw in relations with their longtime capitalist enemy, South Korea, could be seen. The most momentous changes in Asia, however, were probably those that occurred in China.

In 1979 the communist government of China started to shift the Chinese economy from a pure command economy to a mixed economy. The government began by permitting private ownership of farmland and allowing free markets for farm products. The growth rate of farmers' output quadrupled, from 2 percent a year in 1958–78 to 8 percent a year in 1979–84. In 1984 the agricultural reforms were extended to the cities. Private ownership was allowed in a number of industries, the number of products allocated through central planning was reduced from 250 to 20, and free markets were allowed to function in a wide range of industries. Perhaps the most important reform at this time, however, was the creation of a number of special economic zones. In these zones, free markets were allowed to operate without any restrictions, private ownership was allowed, and foreign companies were permitted to invest. Three of the original four economic zones were set up in the southern province of Guangdong (which adjoins Hong Kong). Since then, Guangdong has had the fastest-growing economy in the world, with economic growth rates of over 20 percent per year in the late 1980s.[9] The clear message contained in this story is that the shift toward free market economics, by creating incentives for entrepreneurial activity, is sending China hurtling down a road that has already been taken by many of its Asian neighbors, including Japan, Taiwan, and South Korea.

Like much of Eastern Europe in 1989, China also was swept by a wave of protests in favor of greater political democracy. Unlike Eastern Europe, however, in China the democracy movement was violently suppressed by the brutal 1988 massacre in Tiananmen Square. This was initially accompanied by a scaling back of China's promarket reforms. Fortunately, the scaling back seems to have been a temporary phenomenon, for China now seems to be back on the road to economic reform, and many longtime observers believe that political reform will follow within a decade.[10]

Latin America

In Latin America, too, a shift toward greater democracy and a greater commitment to free market economics occurred during the late 1980s and early 90s. At the beginning of the 1980s, almost all Latin American countries were dictatorships, most of them of the military variety (although communists held sway in Nicaragua and Cuba). By the early 1990s, however, almost all of the countries had democratic governments. (In 1992 Peru's democratically elected president suspended many democratic institutions, however, and communists still ruled in Cuba.)

Under these dictatorships, Latin American countries had been erecting high barriers to imports and foreign direct investment for decades. The feeling was that allowing free trade and investment would result in domination by Western—particularly U.S.—multinational firms. Thus, in the interest of preserving their "national sovereignty," many Latin countries severely restricted trade and investment. At the same time, socialist-inclined governments in several countries took major corporations into state ownership. These policies manifestly failed to deliver economic growth and, in fact, seem to have had the opposite effect.

The tide began to turn in Chile in the 1970s when that country, under the government of a rather unsavory military dictatorship, shifted sharply in the direction of a free market economy. The largest shift, however, occurred in 1989 when Mexico, then run by the civilian government of President Salinas, moved toward a more free market economy. Under Salinas the Mexican government privatized many state-owned enterprises, repealed many laws that had limited foreign direct investment, cut import tariffs to world levels, and committed Mexico to joining the North American Free Trade Agreement (NAFTA) with the United States and Canada (discussed in Chapter 8). A host of other countries are now following Mexico's lead, including, most notably, the two Latin American giants of Argentina and Brazil.

Africa

In Africa, as elsewhere in the world, there are signs of a shift toward more democratic modes of government and free market economics. Most African countries gained their

---

[9] A. Tanzer, "The Mountains Are High, the Emperor Is Far Away," *Forbes,* August 5, 1991, pp. 70–75; and "China's Economy: They Couldn't Keep It Down," *The Economist,* June 1, 1991, pp. 15–18.

[10] "China Swings Back to Reform," *The Economist,* February 1, 1992, pp. 35–36.

independence from colonial powers, particularly Great Britain, France, and Portugal, in the 1950s and 1960s. Originally there were high hopes that the newly independent nations of Africa would become Western-style democracies, but this did not happen. Instead most of them rapidly became one-party states ruled by authoritarian leaders. Moreover, most of these leaders adhered to socialist theories and applied them to the running of their countries. One result was 30 years of economic mismanagement and consequent stagnation while much of the rest of the world experienced tangible growth.

Now there are signs that socialism and totalitarianism are in retreat in Africa, just as elsewhere. This is illustrated in Map 2.4, which indicates those countries where contested elections have been held in the last five years and those countries where contested elections seem likely to take place reasonably soon. Map 2.4 also identifies those countries that have agreements in place with the International Monetary Fund (IMF). The role of the IMF is discussed in Chapter 11. For now, it is important to note that the IMF is an international institution that lends money to indebted nations. One of its lending conditions is that the borrowing country agree to implement free market reforms. Thus, the number of African countries with IMF agreements in place is one index of the size of the shift away from socialism and toward free market economics in Africa.

Implications

What are the implications of these geopolitical changes for international business? For one thing, it would seem that the ideological conflict between collectivism and individualism that characterized the 20th century is winding down. The democratic free market ideology of the West has won the Cold War and has never been more widespread than it is in the early 1990s. Although command economies and totalitarian dictatorships still exist around the world, for the time being at least, the tide is running in favor of democracy and free markets.

The implications for business are enormous. For the best part of 50 years, half the world was closed to Western businesses. Now all of that is changing. Although many of the national markets of Eastern Europe, Latin America, Africa, and Asia may still be undeveloped and impoverished, they are potentially enormous. With a population of 1.1 billion, the Chinese market alone is potentially bigger than that of the United States, the European Community, and Japan combined! In Latin America there are another 400 million potential consumers. Obviously it is unlikely that China, Russia, Poland, or any of the other states now moving toward a free market system will attain the living standards of the West anytime soon. Nevertheless, the upside potential is so large that companies need to consider making inroads now.

Just as the upside potential is large, however, so are the risks. Take the countries of Eastern Europe and the newly independent states of the former Soviet Union as an example. They all profess a desire to move toward a free market economic system, but do they know what that means? After decades of central planning and tight control over prices, markets are poorly understood, *profit* is still too often a dirty word, and the laws required to regulate business transactions, which we take for granted in the West, are largely absent. (Box 2.2 offers an example.) And what about political freedoms? Faced with economic chaos, there is no guarantee that democracy will thrive. Totalitarian dictatorships could return, although it is unlikely they would be of the communist variety. Put another way, while the long-term potential for economic gain from investment in the world's new market economies is large, the risks associated with any such investment are also substantial. It would be foolish to ignore them.

Map 2.4 *Democracy in Africa*

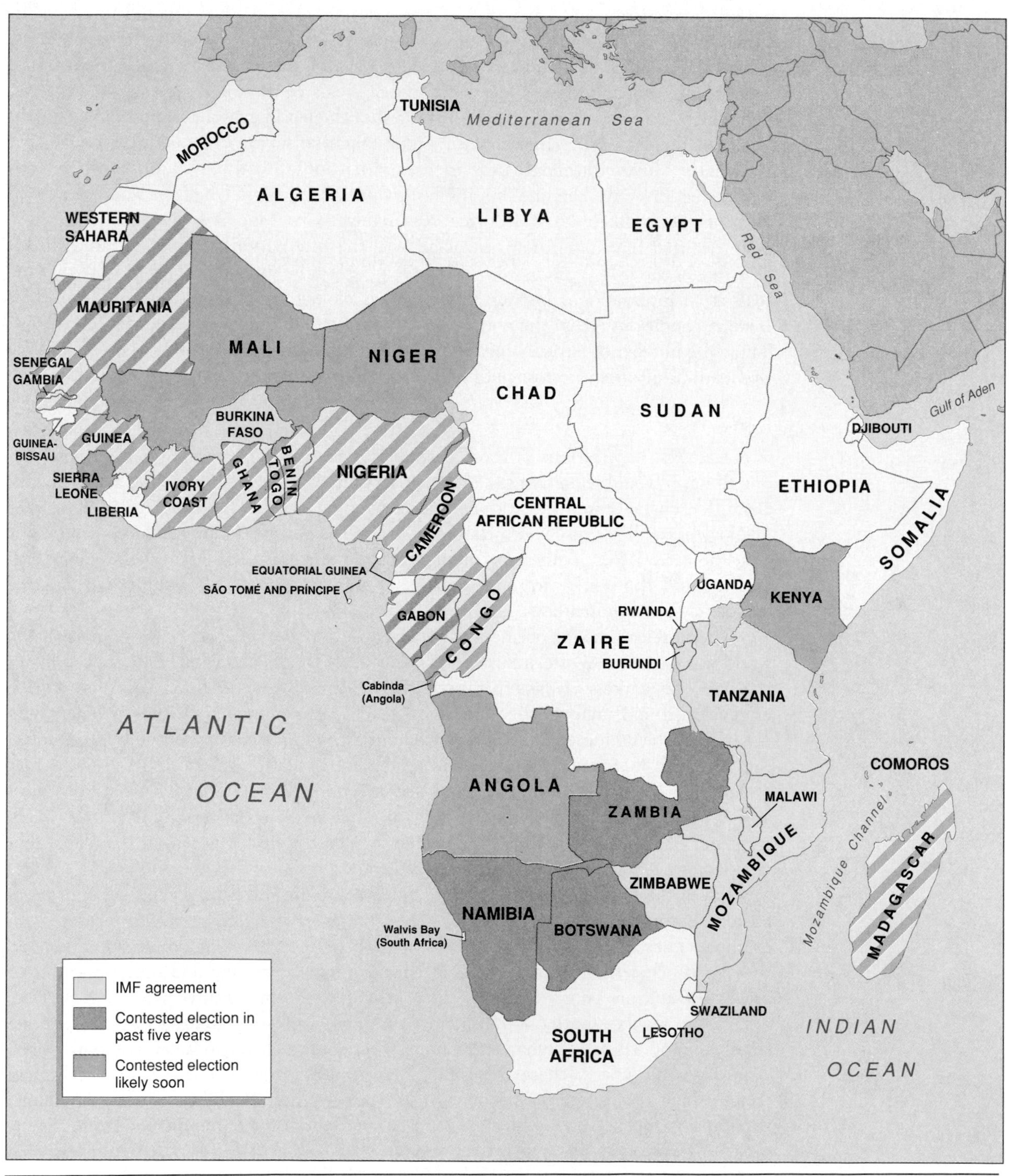

Source: Map data from "Democracy in Africa," The Economist, *February 22, 1992, pp. 17–18.*

BOX 2.2

Chiquita in Czechoslovakia

Chiquita Brands International, Inc., is one of the world's largest and most successful marketers of bananas. The company has been doing business in Czechoslovakia for about ten years, operating until recently through a foreign trade organization. Although it was never satisfied with the sales prowess of the bureaucrats that ran the organization, under the communist system of central planning and state monopolies Chiquita had little choice. The 1989 collapse of communism in Czechoslovakia gave Chiquita the chance to strike out on its own, and in December 1990 it set up a wholly owned, direct sales operation in Prague. However, the dawn of capitalism in Czechoslovakia did not bring smooth sailing. In postcommunist Czechoslovakia, chaos rules.

The old retail and warehouse system of distribution under the communist system is breaking up, but an efficient system has yet to emerge to replace it. Chiquita is trying to determine whether it should deal directly with retailers or continue to deal with the central warehouses even though they will eventually break up. Another option is for Chiquita to enter into a joint venture with one or more of the private warehouses that are now springing up, but the company is nervous about diversifying into warehousing, a business it knows little about.

Then there is the issue of pricing. Chiquita has discovered that after decades of communism, the Czechoslovakian public does not understand why something of better quality should cost more. Originally Chiquita had hoped to sell its premium-grade bananas in Czechoslovakia, but it was forced to switch to its lower grade after finding that consumers simply were not prepared to pay more for better quality.

Price fluctuations are also a new concept for retailers used to central planning. Retailers are given a price on Thursdays and asked to place their orders. The retailers tend to take several days to think about the price, however, not realizing that in a capitalist system the prices of commodities such as bananas can fluctuate day to day.

Chiquita management believes that it could be four years before the Czechoslovakian market begins to appreciate better fruit, and another four years before the country begins to function like a true capitalist society. On a more mundane level, setting up an office in Prague has proved difficult. The construction and renovation job was poorly done and behind schedule. Then the company tried to open a bank account. It got as far as being issued an account number, and then was told for several weeks that the account wasn't usable! Despite these setbacks, Chiquita is betting that in the long run Czechoslovakia will become a profitable market for its high-quality bananas.

Source: Mark Magnier, "Chiquita Bets Czechoslovakia Can Produce Banana Bonanza," Journal of Commerce, *August 29, 1991, pp. 1, 3.*

IMPLICATIONS FOR BUSINESS

The implications of a country's political-economic-legal environment for international business fall into two broad categories. First, the political, economic, and legal environment of a country clearly influences its *attractiveness* as a market and/or investment site. More precisely, the benefits, costs, and risks associated with doing business in a country are in part a function of the country's political, economic, and legal environment. Second, the political, economic, and legal environment of a country can raise important *ethical issues* that have implications for the practice of international business. We shall consider each of these categories in turn.

Attractiveness

In general, the overall attractiveness of a country as a market and/or investment site depends upon balancing the likely long-term benefits of doing business in that country against the likely costs and risks. Let us consider the determinants of benefits, costs, and risks.

Benefits

In the most general sense, the potential long-run monetary benefits of doing business in a country are a function of the size of the market, the present wealth (purchasing power) of consumers in the market, and the likely future wealth of the consumers. Although some markets are very large as measured by the number of consumers (e.g., China and India), low living standards may imply limited purchasing power and, therefore, a relatively small market in economic terms. While international businesses need to be aware of this distinction, they also need to keep in mind the likely future prospects of a country. In 1960, for example, South Korea was viewed as just another impoverished Third World nation. By 1988 it was the world's 18th-largest economy in terms of GDP. If present trends continue through the year 2000, it will be one of the ten largest economies in the world and the fourth-largest trading nation after Japan, the United States, and Germany. International firms that recognized South Korea's potential in 1960 and began to do business there then may have reaped greater benefits than firms that wrote off South Korea as just another Third World nation.

By identifying a potential economic star and investing in it early, an international firm may be able to build up brand loyalty and gain valuable experience in that country's business practices. These things will pay substantial dividends if that country is subsequently able to achieve sustained high economic growth rates. In contrast, late entrants may find that they lack the necessary brand loyalty and experience with business practices to achieve a significant presence in the market. Put differently, in the language of business strategy, early entrants into potential future economic stars may be able to reap substantial **first-mover advantages,** whereas late entrants may fall victim to **late-mover disadvantages.**[11]

Earlier in the chapter it was argued that one reasonably good predictor of a country's economic prospects is its economic system. Put simply, other things being equal, on average, free market–oriented countries achieve greater economic growth rates than do command economies. It follows that this and market size (in population terms) are probably reasonably good indicators of the potential long-run benefits of doing business in a country.

Costs

The costs of doing business in a country are determined by a number of political, economic, and legal factors. With regard to political factors, the costs can be increased by a need to pay off the politically powerful in order to be allowed by the government to conduct business there. As a general rule, the need to pay what are essentially bribes is greater in closed, totalitarian states than in open, democratic societies, where politicians are held accountable by their electorates. Of course, whether a company should actually

---

[11] For a discussion of first-mover advantages see M. Liberman and D. Montgomery, "First Mover Advantages," *Strategic Management Journal* 9, Summer special issue (1988), pp. 41–58.

pay such bribes is an important ethical issue. This and other ethical considerations are discussed in the next subsection.

With regard to economic factors, one of the most important variables is the sophistication of a country's economy. It may well be more costly to do business in relatively primitive or undeveloped economies because of the lack of infrastructure and supporting businesses. At the extreme, an international firm may have to provide its own infrastructure and supporting business if it wishes to do business in a country. For example, when McDonald's decided to open its first restaurant in Moscow, it found—much to its initial dismay—that in order to serve food and drink indistinguishable from that served in McDonald's restaurants elsewhere, it had to vertically integrate backward to supply its own needs. The quality of Russian-grown potatoes and meat was simply too poor. Thus, to protect the quality of its product, McDonald's established its own dairy farms, cattle ranches, vegetable plots, and food-processing plants within Russia. This made the costs of doing business there higher than it is in more sophisticated economies where high-quality inputs could be purchased on the open market.

As for legal factors, it can be more costly to do business in a country where local laws and regulations set strict standards for product safety, safety in the workplace, environmental pollution, and the like (since adhering to such regulations is costly). It can also be more costly to do business in a country like the United States, where the absence of a cap on damage awards has brought spiraling liability insurance rates. Moreover, it can be more costly to do business in a country that lacks well-established laws for regulating business practice (as is the case in many formerly communist nations). In the absence of a well-developed body of business contract law, international firms may have no satisfactory way to resolve contract disputes and so may routinely face large losses from contract violations. Similarly, if local laws fail to adequately protect intellectual property, "theft" of the business's intellectual property—with all that this means in terms of lost income—can result.

Risks

The risks of doing business in a country also are determined by a number of political, economic, and legal factors. On the political front, there is the issue of **political risk.** Political risk has been defined as the likelihood that political forces will cause drastic changes in a country's business environment that adversely affects the profit and other goals of a particular business enterprise.[12] So defined, political risk tends to be greater in countries experiencing social unrest and disorder, or in countries where the underlying nature of society makes the likelihood of social unrest high. Social unrest typically finds expression in strikes, demonstrations, terrorism, and in some cases violent conflict. Such unrest is more likely in countries that contain more than one ethnic nationality (e.g., Yugoslavia), in countries where competing ideologies are battling for political control (e.g., the United Kingdom in the early 1970s and Iran in the late 1970s), and in countries where economic mismanagement has created high inflation and falling living standards (e.g., the U.S.S.R. in the early 1990s).

Social unrest can result in abrupt changes in government and government policy or, in some cases, in protracted civil strife. By its very nature, such strife tends to have

[12] S. H. Robock, "Political Risk: Identification and Assessment," *Columbia Journal of World Business,* July/August 1971, pp. 6–20.

negative economic implications that may well affect the profit goals of business enterprises. For example, in the aftermath of the 1979 Islamic revolution in Iran, the Iranian assets of numerous U.S. companies were seized by the new Iranian government without compensation. Similarly, today the violent disintegration of the Yugoslavian federation has precipitated a collapse in the Yugoslavian economy and, consequently, a collapse in the profitability of investments in that country. A current example of how social unrest and civil strife can affect the investment policies of international business is given in Box 2.3.

On the economic front, **economic risks** arise from economic mismanagement by a country's government. Economic risks can be defined as the likelihood that economic mismanagement will cause drastic changes in a country's business environment that adversely affects the profit and other goals of a particular business enterprise. Of course, economic risks are not independent of political risk. Economic mismanagement may give rise to significant social unrest and hence political risk (as in the case of Zaire; see Box 2.3). Nevertheless, economic risks are worth emphasizing as a separate category, since there is not always a one-to-one relationship between economic mismanagement and social unrest. The most visible indicator of economic mismanagement tends to be a country's inflation rate.

On the legal front, risks exist when a country's legal system fails to provide adequate safeguards for contract violations or protection of intellectual property rights. When legal safeguards are weak, firms are more likely to break contracts and/or steal intellectual property to serve their own interests. Thus, legal risks might be defined as the likelihood that a trading partner will opportunistically break a contract or expropriate intellectual property rights. When legal risks in a country are high, an international business might hesitate to enter into a long-term contract or a joint venture agreement with a firm in that country. For example, when the Indian government passed a law requiring all foreign investors to enter into joint ventures with Indian companies, U.S. companies such as IBM and Coca-Cola closed down their investments in India. They did this because they believed the Indian legal system did not adequately protect their intellectual property rights. Thus, a very real danger existed that the Indian partners of IBM and Coca-Cola would expropriate their intellectual property—the core of their competitive advantage.

Overall Attractiveness

Evaluating the overall attractiveness of a country as a potential market and/or investment site for an international business requires balancing the benefits, costs, and risks of doing business there. These factors are summarized in Figure 2.4. As a general point, it should be noted that the costs and risks associated with doing business in a foreign country are typically lower in economically advanced, politically stable, democratic nations, whereas they are greater in less developed, politically unstable nations. The calculus is complicated, however, by the fact that the potential *long-run* benefits bear little relationship to a nation's current stage of economic development or political stability. Rather, they are dependent upon likely future economic growth rates. In turn, among other things, economic growth appears to be a function of a free market system and a country's capacity for growth, which may be greater in less-developed nations. This leads to the conclusion that, other things being equal, the benefit–cost–risk tradeoff is likely to be most favorable in politically stable, developing nations with free market systems. It is likely to be least favorable in politically unstable, developing nations with mixed or command economies.

BOX 2.3

Social Unrest in Zaire

Spreading social unrest in Zaire has been accelerating a trend toward declining foreign investment in the central African nation. In recent years Zaire has been plagued by rampant inflation, widespread government corruption, and widespread unrest. In 1991 the annual inflation rate exceeded 1000 percent. In the same year the government announced increases in personal and company tax rates in an attempt to compensate for its inefficient operations. In response, widespread rioting and looting broke out. Zairean troops, who had not been paid by the government for months, were joined by civilian bands as they ransacked commercial districts and private homes throughout the country. As the unrest spread, Western governments moved to evacuate thousands of foreign residents from Zaire.

One clear response to the political instability has been a dramatic decline in foreign investment. In 1985 U.S. companies invested $145 million in Zaire. In 1990 this had fallen to $60 million, and it fell steeply in 1991 to under $10 million. Moreover, total global investment in Zaire has been negative in recent eras, as foreign investors take their money out of the country (see the figure).

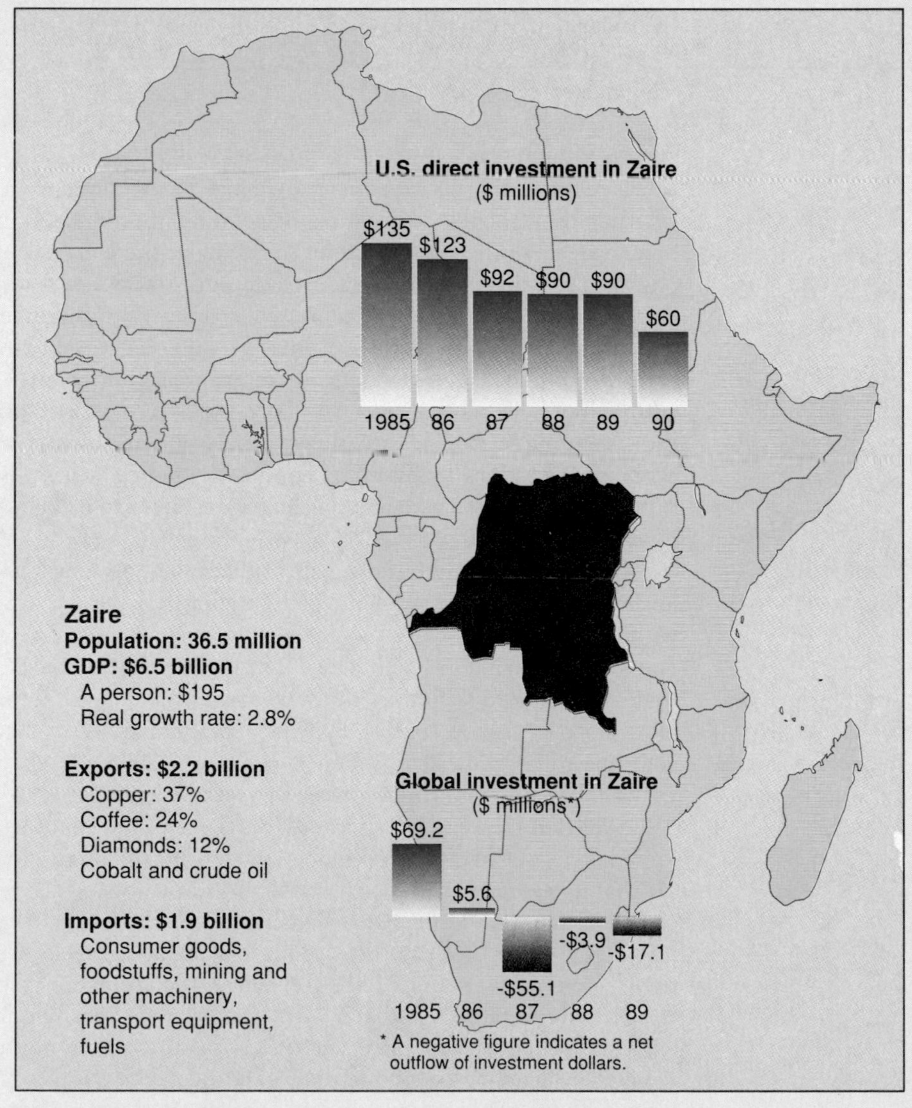

Source: P. L. Green, "Strife in Zaire Speeds Decline in Investment," Journal of Commerce, *September 30, 1991, pp. 1A, 3A.*

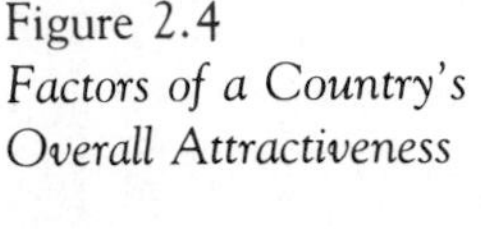
Figure 2.4
Factors of a Country's Overall Attractiveness

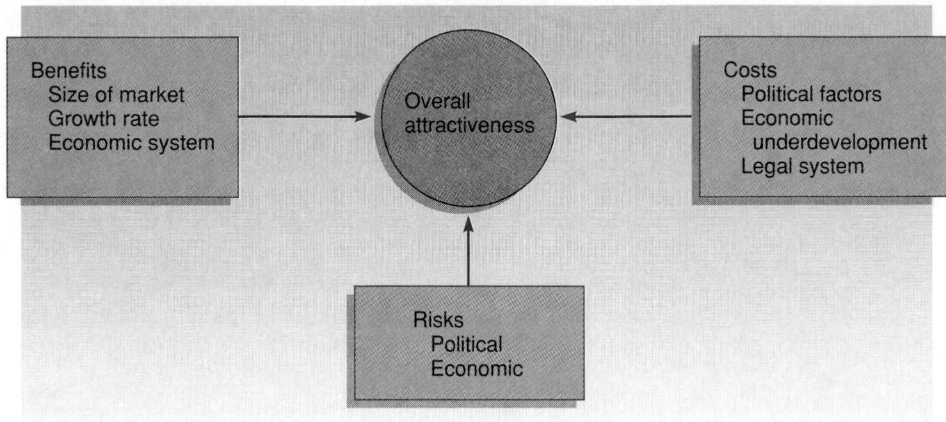

Ethical Issues

Country differences give rise to some particularly interesting and contentious ethical issues. One of the major ethical dilemmas facing firms from Western democracies is whether they should do business in totalitarian countries that routinely violate the human rights of their citizens. Not surprisingly, there are two sides to this issue. On the one hand is the argument that investing in totalitarian countries provides comfort to dictators and can help prop up repressive regimes. Without investment by Western firms, it is claimed, many repressive regimes would collapse and be replaced by more democratically inclined governments. In recent years, firms that have invested in Chile, China, Iraq, and South Africa have been targets of such criticisms. Interestingly enough, the current move to dismantle the apartheid systems in South Africa is being credited to economic sanctions by Western nations, including a lack of investment by Western firms. This, say those who argue against investment in totalitarian countries, proves that investment boycotts work.

On the other hand is the argument that investment by a Western firm, by raising the level of economic development of a totalitarian country, can help to change it from within. Proponents of this argument note that economic well-being and political freedoms often go hand in hand. Thus, for example, when arguing against attempts to apply trade sanctions to China in the wake of the violent 1989 government crackdown on prodemocracy demonstrators, the Bush administration claimed that U.S. firms should continue to be allowed to invest in mainland China, since greater political freedoms would follow the resulting economic growth.

Since both positions appear to have merit, it would be extremely difficult to formulate a general ethical opinion of what firms should do. Indeed, it is probably fair to say that unless mandated by government (as in the case of investment in South Africa), each firm must make its own judgments about the ethical implications of investing in totalitarian states on a case-by-case basis. The more repressive the regime, however, and the less amenable it seems to be to change, the stronger is the case for not investing.

Another interesting ethical issue is whether an international firm should adhere to the same standards of product safety, work safety, and environmental protection that are required in its home country. This is of particular concern to firms headquartered in the United States, where product safety, worker safety, and environmental protection laws are among the world's toughest. Should U.S. firms investing in less-developed countries adhere to tough U.S. standards, even though local laws do not require them to do so?

Again there is no easy answer. While on the face of it the argument for adhering to U.S. standards might seem strong, on closer examination, the issue becomes more complicated. What if adhering to U.S. standards would make the foreign investment unprofitable, thereby denying the foreign country much needed jobs? What then is the ethical thing to do—to adhere to U.S. standards and not invest, thereby denying people jobs; or to adhere to local standards and invest, thereby providing jobs and income? As with many ethical dilemmas, there is no easy answer. Each case needs to be assessed on its own merits.

A final ethical issue is that of bribes. Should an international business pay bribes to government officials in order to gain market access to a foreign country? To most Westerners, bribery seems corrupt and morally repugnant, so one's answer might initially be no. In many parts of the world, however, payoffs to government officials are a part of life. Moreover, a decision not to invest if bribes are required ignores the fact that such investment can bring substantial benefits to the local populace in terms of income and jobs. Given this, from a purely ethical standpoint, perhaps the practice of giving bribes, a lesser evil, is the price of doing a greater good (assuming that the investment creates jobs where none existed before). Again, given the complexity of the issue, generalization is difficult. One thing seems certain, however; it is clearly unethical to go around offering bribes. Responding to a request for a bribe is, perhaps, a different issue.

SUMMARY OF CHAPTER

The objective of this chapter has been to review the variation in political, economic, and legal systems among countries and to examine some of the implications of these differences for the practice of international business. In particular, we have noted that the potential benefits, costs, and risks of doing business in a country are a function of its political, economic, and legal environment. More specifically, we have made the following points in this chapter:

1. Political systems can be assessed according to two related dimensions: the degree to which they emphasize collectivism as opposed to individualism, and the degree to which they are democratic or totalitarian.
2. Collectivism is an ideology that views the needs of the society as being more important than the needs of the individual. This philosophy underlies both communism and social democracy. Collectivism translates into an advocacy for state intervention in economic activity and, in the case of communism, a totalitarian dictatorship.
3. Individualism is an ideology based on an emphasis of the primacy of individual freedoms in the political, economic, and cultural realm. Individualism translates into an advocacy for democratic ideals and free market economics.
4. Democracy and totalitarianism are at opposite ends of a political spectrum. In a representative democracy, citizens periodically elect individuals to represent them, and political freedoms are guaranteed by a constitution. In a totalitarian state, political power is monopolized by a party, group, or individual, and basic political freedoms are denied to citizens.
5. One way of assessing the complexion of a government is to examine its attitude toward economic and political freedoms. Whereas some countries guarantee both political and economic freedoms, and others deny individuals both types of freedom, in many countries the picture is more ambiguous. In some states political freedoms are denied, but economic freedoms are encouraged. In other countries political freedoms are encouraged, but economic freedoms are denied.
6. There are three broad types of economic system: a market economy, a command economy, and a mixed economy. In a market economy prices are free of any controls, and private ownership is predominant. In a command economy prices are set by central planners, productive assets are owned by the state, and private ownership is forbidden. A mixed economy has elements of both a market economy and command economy.
7. A country's level of economic development depends upon the standard of living its citizens can achieve. A country's future economic potential depends upon its economic growth rate and its capacity for growth. Other things being equal, a country's economic growth rate appears to be a positive function of the degree to which a free market system is allowed to exist. Countries with free market systems tend to grow faster than countries with command economies.
8. Differences in the structure of law between countries

can have important implications for the practice of international business.

9. The degree to which intellectual property rights are protected varies dramatically from country to country, as do product safety and product liability legislation and the nature of contract law.
10. In the late 1980s and early 90s a new world order emerged. Communism collapsed in Eastern Europe and the Soviet Union and was retreating elsewhere. Democratic free market ideals gained wider influence than at any time in world history. Due to the ideological conflict between individualism and collectivism, for almost 50 years nearly half the world had been closed to western business. With the current decline of collectivism, this is changing, creating new opportunities and risks for international business.
11. Evaluating the attractiveness of a country as a market and/or investment site involves balancing the likely long-run benefits of doing business in that country against the likely costs and risks.
12. The benefits of doing business in a country are a function of the size of the market (population), its present wealth (purchasing power), and its growth prospects. By investing early in countries that are currently poor but nevertheless growing rapidly, firms can gain first-mover advantages that will pay back substantial dividends in the future.
13. The costs of doing business in a country tend to be greater in those countries where political payoffs are required to gain market access, where supporting infrastructure is lacking or underdeveloped, and where adhering to local laws and regulations is costly.
14. The risks of doing business tend to be greater in countries (*i*) that are politically unstable, (*ii*) that are subject to economic mismanagement, and (*iii*) where the legal system does not provide safeguards for contract violations or theft of intellectual property rights.
15. Country differences give rise to several ethical dilemmas, including (*i*) should a firm do business in a repressive totalitarian state; (*ii*) should a firm conform to its home country's product, workplace, and environmental standards when they are not required by the host country's laws; and (*iii*) should a firm pay bribes to government officials in order to gain market access?

DISCUSSION QUESTIONS

1. Free market economies stimulate greater economic growth, whereas command economies stifle growth! Discuss.
2. During the late 1980s and early 90s China has been routinely cited by various international organizations (e.g., Amnesty International and Freedom Watch) for major human rights violations, including torture, beatings, imprisonment, and execution of political dissidents. Despite this, in 1991 China was the recipient of record levels of foreign direct investment, principally from firms based in democratic societies such as the United States, Japan, and Germany. Evaluate this trend from an ethical perspective. If you were the CEO of a firm that had the option of making a potentially very profitable investment in China, what would you do?
3. You are the CEO of a company that is going to invest $100 million in either Russia or Brazil. Both alternatives promise the same long-run return, so your decision of which investment to make must be driven by considerations of risk. Assess the risks of doing business in each of these nations. Which investment would you favor, and why?

National Differences in Culture

CHAPTER 3

INNOCENTS ABROAD—HARRY AND SALLY IN SAUDI ARABIA

In 1980 Harry Jones and Sally Smith founded Diagnostica, Inc., to manufacture electronic health care equipment. Since then the growth of the company has far exceeded their expectations. By 1990 the Kentucky company had annual revenues of $35 million and a nationwide sales force. Recently they got an opportunity to break into the lucrative international market when a Saudi government agency invited them to compete for a contract to supply the Saudi health care system with diagnostic equipment. At over $30 million, the estimated value of the contract, this deal could help propel Diagnostica into the big league of electronic diagnostic equipment producers. Diagnostica submitted samples of its products along with proposed prices to the government agency. Harry and Sally were delighted a few weeks later when they learned that Diagnostica had been selected as one of the two finalists for the contract. In order to win the contract, they would now have to go to Riyadh, the desert capital of Saudi Arabia, to negotiate the contract terms. • Neither Harry nor Sally had been outside the United States before, so both were excited at the prospect of seeing the land of Lawrence of Arabia. Unfortunately for them, their knowledge of Saudi Arabia was limited to David Lean's epic film. Their plans were to fly out Monday morning, arrive in Riyadh Tuesday evening after a 20-hour flight, spend Wednesday through Friday negotiating, and return on Saturday. • Their trouble started in London, where they were to change planes. The flight from Washington, D.C., to London arrived on time, but departure of the connecting flight was delayed. Consequently, they didn't arrive in Riyadh until 4:00 A.M. Wednesday. It took them two and a half hours to get through customs and immigration procedures, which left them with just an hour to make the first meeting, scheduled for 7:30 A.M. Jet-lagged Harry and Sally decided to go straight to the government offices, as they would wait until that evening to check into their hotel. They quickly changed into their business suits in the airport restrooms (Sally putting on a new knee-length dress she had bought for the trip) and then they went outside into the 110° heat. • Harry hailed a cab outside the airport, and they jumped in. "Take us to the Ministry of Health, please," said Harry. The driver looked puzzled and raised his hands to show that he did not understand. "The Ministry of Health," repeated Harry with slow deliberation. The driver smiled, nodded, and drove off. Forty-five minutes later, they pulled up in front of an impressive, official-looking building. "Some place," said Sally, who was now perspiring heavily. (The taxi had no air-conditioning.) Harry paid the driver, and they entered the foyer of the Ministry of Defense. They didn't discover their mistake until they asked at the desk for Muhumad Oman, their Saudi contact. "We have no one of that name here," said the male receptionist, casting a disapproving eye at Sally. • Ten minutes later they were in another taxi, speeding across town to the Ministry of Health. They arrived by 8:00 A.M., thirty minutes late. "Great start," grunted Harry. "Harry Jones and Sally Smith to see Muhumad Oman," announced Harry to the male receptionist. The receptionist looked confused, but he picked up a telephone and spoke with someone in Arabic for about ten minutes. "The Sheikh will see you now, Mr. Jones," he said when he put down the phone. "The lady can wait in the reception room off to your left." "But I am scheduled to meet with Muhumad Oman as well!" gasped a puzzled Sally. "Sorry, Madam," replied the polite but firm receptionist. "Women are not allowed to participate in business meetings." Harry rolled his eyes as Sally sulked off to get a cab to the hotel. • Ten minutes later Harry finally met Muhumad Oman. Sheikh Oman, as every one called him, spoke impeccable English and was dressed in an elegant European manner. Thank God, thought Harry. "I'm sorry I'm so late. Our plane was delayed in London," Harry said. "It's of no concern," replied Muhumad Oman. "Would you like to join me in a cup of coffee before we begin our discussions?" "I'd rather not," replied Harry. "All that caffeine's not good for you." Sheikh Oman frowned and raised an eyebrow. "All right then," he said. "Let us begin." • The next four hours with Muhumad Oman and his four assistants were difficult for Harry. He was tired and hungry, and what's more, Muhumad Oman never once gave him a direct answer to his questions. Harry, who prided himself on his forthright, direct manner, was stumped. The negotiations seemed to be going nowhere. Then at 1:00 in the afternoon Muhumad Oman called the meeting to a halt. "I think we need to discuss your offer among ourselves," said

Oman. "Let us plan to meet again at 8:00 A.M. tomorrow." • What offer? thought Harry as he hailed a cab. I never got that far. • On the way to the hotel Harry asked the driver to stop at a roadside food stand. He was damn hungry, having not eaten since dinner on the plane the previous evening. He bought something that looked vaguely like a cross between a burrito and a hot dog and wolfed it down. Not bad food, he thought, although it's a little spicy. • Harry found Sally in her room. She was not happy. She had tried to go swimming in the hotel pool, but had learned that "women's hour" is between 4:00 and 5:00 P.M. "I think I'll just stay in my room and watch CNN," said Sally. An exhausted Harry commiserated and went to his room to get an hour's sleep. He quickly fell asleep and did not wake until 11:00 that evening. I must have been really tired, thought Harry. He stood up, suddenly felt horribly sick, and proceeded to deposit his lunch all over the floor. Four hours later Harry was still feeling somewhat sick, and now he had another problem; he couldn't get back to sleep. Damn, he thought, it's three in the morning, and I have to be at the Ministry of Health by eight. I'm going to be in no shape to negotiate. He was right; he wasn't. • The negotiations on the second day were every bit as difficult as they were the first, plus Harry had to make frequent trips to the bathroom. "Look, Muhumad," said an exasperated Harry after three hours of fruitless negotiations, "I think we need to set a deadline for finishing the negotiations on prices. Let's say by 3:00 this afternoon. And then we can move on to discuss the service agreements." Oman and his colleges exchanged glances. Then Oman turned to Harry and said, "Mr. Jones, we do not think it is appropriate to fix a deadline. Please remember that *we* are the *customers* here." Harry realized that he had just made a blunder, although he didn't know what kind of one. "Okay," he said, unsuccessfully stifling a yawn, "have it your way." They did. By 5:00 P.M. they had finally agreed on a price—one that was not favorable to Diagnostica. Harry was so tired that he just gave up fighting and agreed. • "Well," said Harry, "now that we have reached an agreement on price, perhaps we can tackle the service agreements tomorrow?" All of the Saudis looked shocked. "Mr. Jones, tomorrow is the *Sabbath*," said Sheikh Oman. "It is a day for Allah, not for business. We will meet again on *Saturday*." "Oh," said Harry, "but we are scheduled to fly back to the States on Saturday." "Then you had better change your arrangements, hadn't you, Mr. Jones?" replied an obviously irritated Muhamad Oman. Harry did, but it didn't help Diagnostica win the contract. • After two more days of negotiations, during which Sally grew increasingly irritated at the "sexist attitudes of these people" and Harry never did manage to find his equilibrium, an assistant of Sheikh Oman politely informed Harry that the terms he had offered them were not good enough and that the contract would be awarded to a company from England. Defeated and dejected, Harry and Sally finally left for home on Monday, but it took them two weeks to get there. Their plane was hijacked over Jordan by terrorists demanding the release of some colleagues being held in an Italian prison for a previous hijacking attempt. But that's another story. *This account is only partly fiction. Some of the blunders made by Harry and Sally occurred to people known to the author on their first business trip abroad.*

INTRODUCTION

In Chapter 2 we saw how national differences in political, economic, and legal systems influence the benefits, costs, and risks associated with doing business in different countries. We also explored how such differences impact upon management practice and strategy. In this chapter we will explore how cultural differences impact upon the practice of international business. In particular, we will explore two main issues.

First, we will explore the relationship between culture and the costs of doing business in a country. Put simply, the culture of some countries supports the capitalist mode of production and lowers the costs of doing business there. Cultural factors can help firms based in such countries to achieve a competitive advantage in the world economy. We shall see how this is probably the case for Japan; cultural factors seem to have lowered the costs of doing business there, which has helped many Japanese businesses achieve a competitive advantage in the world economy. We will also look at how cultural factors can raise the costs of doing business in a country, making it more difficult for that country's firms to achieve a competitive advantage in the world economy. For example, the emphasis on class conflict in Great Britain makes it more difficult for firms there to achieve cooperation between management and labor. Class conflict has been reflected in a large number of labor disputes in Great Britain. In many countries, such as Switzerland, Norway, Germany, and Japan, class conflict is virtually unknown.

The second issue we shall explore in this chapter is *cross-cultural literacy,* one requirement for successfully doing business in a variety of cultures. That is, to understand how the culture of a country can affect the practice of business. In these days of global communications, rapid transportation, and global markets, when the era of the global village seems just around the corner, it is all too easy to overlook the cultural differences of countries. Yet in practice, cultural differences remain deep and profound. The importance of cross-cultural literacy cannot be overemphasized. Without it, businesspeople can make blunders that will jeopardize lucrative opportunities.

The opening case illustrates how a lack of cross-cultural literacy can doom a business deal. Harry and Sally made several fundamental mistakes. The first was for Sally to accompany Harry on a business trip. Saudi Arabia is an Islamic state in which women are still denied equal rights with men. Sally's very presence was bound to confuse and irritate their Muslim hosts. A second mistake was Sally's dress; knee-length apparel is frowned upon in Saudi Arabia, where Islamic convention demands that women remain covered from head to foot when outside. A third mistake was the failure to plan for the debilitating effects of jet lag. The 11-hour time difference between the eastern United States and Saudi Arabia effectively turns night into day. Even the most experienced international traveler needs a day or so to adjust to the new time zone. A fourth mistake was Harry's refusal to take coffee from Sheikh Oman, since an offer of coffee is a gesture of friendship in Saudi Arabia. Harry's tactless rejection of this offer was a personal affront to Sheikh Oman. A fifth mistake was for Harry to eat street food. Sampling local foods is one of the fascinations of travel, but a business traveler on a tight schedule cannot afford the risk. The potential costs of a bad meal are too great, as Harry found out. A sixth mistake was Harry's attempt to set a deadline for the negotiations, because Arabs generally dislike deadlines. An Arab faced with a deadline tends to feel threatened and backed into a corner; he is unlikely to react well. A seventh mistake was Harry and Sally's failure to account for Friday's being the Islamic Sabbath in their plans. With this many blunders, it is not surprising that Harry and Sally failed to clinch the deal of their dreams.[1]

We open this chapter with a general discussion of what culture actually is. What we shall discover is that a country's culture is defined by its value systems and norms. In turn,

---

[1] Some of these culturally bound conventions are discussed in D. A. Ricks, *Big Business Blunders: Mistakes in Multinational Marketing* (Homewood, Ill.: Dow-Jones Irwin, 1983).

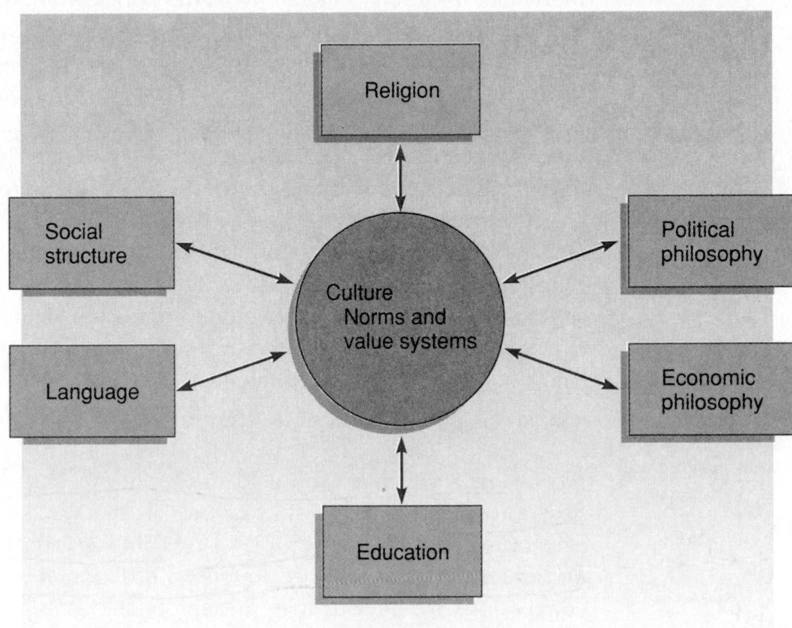

Figure 3.1
The Determinants of Culture

the value systems and norms of a country are influenced by such factors as social structure, religion, language, education, political philosophy, and economic philosophy. Countries differ from each other because of these factors (see Figure 3.1). We discussed national differences in political and economic philosophy in detail in Chapter 2, so we will not review them here. Bear in mind, however, that the factors discussed in Chapter 2 also influence the culture of a country. In this chapter we focus our attention on cultural differences among countries and their implications for business practice.

WHAT IS CULTURE?

Culture has been defined as that complex whole which includes knowledge, belief, art, morals, law, custom, and other capabilities acquired by people as members of society.[2] Culture shapes individual human behavior by identifying appropriate and inappropriate forms of human interaction. Individuals learn culture in the course of everyday living by interacting with those around them; they become *socialized*. This learning starts at an early age and generally stays with people for the rest of their lives. In turn, they transmit culture to others, particularly to their offspring, through direct instruction and through the behaviors they consciously and unconsciously encourage and discourage.

Values

The fundamental building blocks of a culture are its values and norms. **Values** are abstract ideas about what society believes to be good, right, and desirable; they form the cultural bedrock of a society. They provide the context within which a society's norms are established and justified. They include a society's attitudes toward such concepts as

[2] E. B. Tylor, *Primitive Culture* (London: Murray, 1871).

individual freedom, democracy, truth, justice, honesty, loyalty, social obligations, collective responsibility, the role of women, love, sex, marriage, and so on. They are invested with considerable emotional significance; people argue, fight, and even die over values such as "freedom." Not surprisingly, values are reflected in the political and economic system of a society. As we saw in Chapter 2, democratic free market capitalism reflects a philosophical value system that emphasizes individual freedom. Values are not necessarily static, but change in a country's value system can be slow and painful for the society. In the 1960s, for example, American values toward the role of women, love, sex, and marriage underwent significant changes. Much of the social turmoil of that time reflected these changes. Similarly, today the value system of many formerly communist states such as Russia are undergoing significant changes as those countries move away from a value system that emphasizes collectivism toward one that emphasizes individualism. Social turmoil is inevitable in this process.

Norms

Norms are social rules and guidelines that prescribe appropriate behavior in particular situations. Norms shape the actions of people toward one another. Norms can be categorized as either *folkways* or *mores*. **Folkways** are the routine conventions of everyday life. Generally, folkways are actions of little moral significance. Rather, they are social conventions for such things as appropriate dress, social etiquette, "table manners," neighborly behavior, and the like (for some examples see Box 3.1). Folkways define the way people are expected to behave, but violations of them are not normally a serious matter. People who violate folkways may be thought of as eccentric or ill-mannered, but seldom as evil or bad. In many countries foreigners may be initially excused for violating folkways, but repeated violations may not be excused.

Unlike folkways, **mores** are norms that are seen as central to the functioning of a society and to its social life. They have much greater significance than folkways. Accordingly, the violation of mores can be expected to bring serious retribution. Mores include such things as prohibitions against theft, adultery, incest, and cannibalism. In many societies mores have been enacted into law; for example, all advanced societies have laws against theft, incest, and cannibalism. However, there are also many differences among societies in mores. In America, for example, drinking alcohol is widely accepted, whereas in Saudi Arabia it violates important social mores and is punishable by imprisonment (as many Western citizens working in Saudi Arabia have learned to their distress).

The Formation of Values and Norms

The values and norms of a society do not appear out of nowhere fully formed. They are evolutionary products of a number of factors at work in a society. These factors include the prevailing political and economic philosophies, the social structure of a society, the dominant religion, the language, and education. We discussed political and economic philosophy at length in Chapter 2. All that needs to be stated here is that such philosophy clearly influences the value systems of a society. For example, the values in the former Soviet Union toward freedom, justice, and individual achievement were clearly different from those in the United States, precisely because each country operated according to a different political and economic philosophy (i.e., collectivism versus individualism).

Now let us go on to examine the influence of cultural factors in more depth. Throughout the chapter, bear in mind that the "chain of causation" goes two ways. That is, although such factors as social structure and religion clearly influence the values and

BOX 3.1

Some Examples of Folkways: Attitudes towards Time, Gift Giving, and the Exchange of Business Cards

Time

Norms regarding punctuality differ significantly from country to country. In the United States people tend to be very time-conscious. Conscientious Americans arrive a few minutes early for business appointments, because being late is considered poor etiquette. When invited to dinner at someone's home, it is considered polite to arrive on time, or just a few minutes late. In many other countries attitudes toward time are very different. It is not necessarily a breach of etiquette to arrive a little late for a business appointment; indeed, it might be considered impolite to arrive early. As for dinner invitations, arriving on time may be very bad manners. In Great Britain, for example, when someone says, "come for dinner at seven," what they mean is, "Come between 7:30 and 8:00." The guest who arrives at 7:00 is likely to find an unprepared and embarrassed host. Similarly, when an Argentinian says, "Come for dinner anytime after eight," what they mean is, "do not come at 8:00; that would be far too early!"

Gift Giving

The norms of gift giving also vary significantly from country to country. In Great Britain for example, when invited to someone's home for dinner it is not necessary to bring a gift, but it is polite to offer to bring a bottle of wine and to ask the host in advance what kind of wine they would like. In contrast, in Japan it is considered rude *not* to bring a gift when invited to someone's home, and it is equally rude to offer in advance to bring something for the dinner table, such as wine.

Exchanging Business Cards

When businesspeople in the United States meet, they often exchange business cards, typically at the conclusion of a meeting and without giving the exchange much thought. In Japan, in contrast, the exchange of business cards is regarded as a part of the introduction. Moreover, the order of exchange is important. The lower-status person must offer his or her card first. Only then will the higher-status individual take out his or her card and offer it. It is considered respectful for the lower-status individual to examine the business card of the higher-status person with considerable interest while holding it reverently with both hands.

norms of a society, it is also true that the values and norms of a society can influence the social structure and religion.

SOCIAL STRUCTURE

A society's "social structure" is its basic social organization. Although there are many aspects of social structure, two dimensions have particular importance when explaining differences between cultures. The first dimension is the degree to which the basic unit of social organization is the individual, as opposed to the group. Whereas Western societies tend to emphasize the primacy of the individual, many Asian societies—particularly the Japanese—emphasize the primacy of the group. The second dimension is the degree to which a society is stratified into classes or castes. Some societies are characterized by a fairly high degree of social stratification and relatively low mobility between classes (e.g., those of India and, to a lesser extent, Great Britain), while other societies are characterized by a low degree of social stratification and high mobility between stratas (e.g., Japan and the United States). We will consider each of these dimensions in turn.

Individuals and Groups

A group is an association of two or more individuals who have a shared sense of identity and who interact with each other in structured ways based on a common set of expectations about each other's behavior.[3] Human social life is group life. Individuals are involved in families, work groups, social or recreational groups, and so on. Societies differ, however, regarding the degree to which the group is viewed as the primary means of social organization. In some societies individual attributes and achievements are regarded as more important than group membership; in other societies just the reverse is true. For some research relating to this, see Box 3.2.

The Individual

In Chapter 2 we discussed individualism as a political philosophy. It is important to realize, however, that individualism is not just an abstract political philosophy. It is far more than that. In many Western societies the individual, as opposed to the group, is the basic building block of social organization. This is reflected not just in the political and economic organization of society but also in the way in which people perceive themselves and relate to each other in social and business settings. In the value systems of Western societies, for example, great emphasis is placed upon individual achievement. The social standing of an individual is not so much a function of their employer as it is of their individual performance in their particular work setting.

The emphasis placed upon individual performance in many Western societies has both beneficial and harmful aspects. In the United States, for example, the emphasis on individual performance finds expression in an admiration for "rugged individualism" and entrepreneurship. One beneficial consequence of this is the high level of entrepreneurial activity in the United States and other Western societies. New products and new ways of doing business have repeatedly been created in the United States by entrepreneurial individuals (e.g., personal computers, photocopiers, computer software, biotechnology, supermarkets, and discount retail stores). Indeed, there is little doubt that the dynamism of the U.S. economy owes much to the philosophy of individualism.

On the other hand, the philosophy of individualism also finds expression in a high degree of managerial mobility between companies, and this is not always a good thing. Although moving from company to company may benefit individual managers who are trying to build impressive résumés, it is not necessarily beneficial to U.S. companies. Such lack of employee loyalty and commitment to an individual company and the tendency to seek and accept advancement opportunities is seen by some to produce managers who have good general skills but who lack the in-depth knowledge, experience, and network of interpersonal contacts that come from years of working within the same company. Company-specific experience, knowledge, and personal contacts are probably all good things, since they may increase a manager's ability to perform his or her job effectively. A manager may draw upon past experience, knowledge, and a network of contacts, to find solutions to current problems. It follows that U.S. companies may suffer if their managers lack these things.

Moreover, the emphasis upon individualism may make it difficult to build teams within an organization for performing collective tasks. If individuals are always competing with each other to demonstrate superior individual performance, they may be unable to simultaneously cooperate. On this point, it is interesting to note that a recent study of U.S. competitiveness by MIT concluded that one factor that is hurting US firms in the global economy is a failure to achieve cooperation both within a company (e.g., between

---

[3] N. Goodman, *An Introduction to Sociology* (New York: Harper Collins, 1991).

functions, between management and labor) and between companies (e.g., between a firm and its suppliers). Given the emphasis on individualism in the U.S. value system, perhaps this failure is not surprising.[4] Put another way, the emphasis upon individualism in the United States, while helping to create a dynamic, entrepreneurial economy, may also raise the costs of doing business due to its adverse impact upon managerial continuity and cooperation.

Having said this, it should be noted that there is a positive aspect of high managerial mobility. Moving from firm to firm exposes U.S. executives to different ways of doing things. The ability to compare and contrast different firms' business practices allows executives to identify effective practices and techniques that can be profitably applied to other firms.

The Group

In sharp contrast to the Western emphasis on the individual, in many Asian societies the group is the primary unit of social organization. This is particularly true in Japan, where an individual's social status is determined as much by the standing of the group to which he or she belongs as by his or her individual performance. In traditional Japanese society the group was the family or village to which an individual belonged. Today the group is more likely to be the work team or business organization to which an individual belongs. In a now classic study of Japanese society, Nakane has noted how this expresses itself in everyday life:

> When a Japanese faces the outside (confronts another person) and affixes some position to himself socially he is inclined to give precedence to institution over kind of occupation. Rather than saying, "I am a typesetter" or "I am a filing clerk," he is likely to say, "I am from B Publishing Group" or "I belong to S company."[5]

Nakane goes on to observe that the primacy of the group to which an individual belongs often evolves into a deeply emotional attachment in which identification with the group becomes all-important in one's life. Put another way, one of the central values of Japanese culture is the importance attached to group membership. This clearly has beneficial implications for business firms (it lowers the costs of doing business). Strong identification with the group is argued to create pressures for mutual self-help and collective action. If the worth of an individual is closely linked to the achievements of the group (e.g., the firm), as Nakane maintains is the case in Japan, this creates a strong incentive for individual members of the group to work together for the common good. In other words, the failures of cooperation that the MIT study found in many U.S. firms may not be a problem in Japanese firms. Indeed, there is evidence that the competitive advantage of many Japanese enterprises in the global economy is based partly upon their ability to achieve close cooperation of individuals within companies and between companies. This ability to cooperate is apparent in the widespread utilization of self-managing work teams within Japanese organizations, the close cooperation between functions within Japanese companies (such as between manufacturing, marketing, and R&D) and the cooperation between a company and its suppliers in such areas as design, quality control, and inventory reduction.[6] In all of these cases, cooperation is driven by the desire to improve the performance of the group (i.e., the business firm) to which individuals belong.

---

[4] M. L. Dertouzos, R. K. Lester, and R. M. Solow, *Made in America* (Cambridge, Mass.: MIT Press, 1989).

[5] C. Nakane, *Japanese Society* (Berkeley: University of California Press, 1970).

[6] For details see M. Aoki, *Information, Incentives, and Bargaining in the Japanese Economy* (Cambridge, U.K.: Cambridge University Press, 1988); and Dertouzos et al., *Made in America.*

Hofstede's Dimensions of National Culture

One of the most famous studies of the relationship between national culture and values in the workplace was undertaken by Geert Hofstede. As part of his job as a psychologist for a large multinational company, over the 1967–73 period Hofstede collected data on employee attitudes and values from more than 100,000 employees representing 40 nationalities. This data enabled him to compare the dimensions of national cultures.

Two of the dimensions he used to describe national culture were **individualism versus collectivism** and **large or small power distance.** The "individualism versus collectivism" dimension focused upon the relationship between the individual and his or her fellows. Each country was assigned a score between 0 and 100. At the high end of the scale were societies in which the ties between individuals were very loose and individual achievement and freedom were highly valued. At the low end of the scale were societies in which the ties between individuals were very tight. In such societies people are born into collectives, such as extended families, and everyone is expected to protect the interests of his or her collective.

A Power Distance × Individualism–Collectivism Plot for 50 Countries & 3 Regions

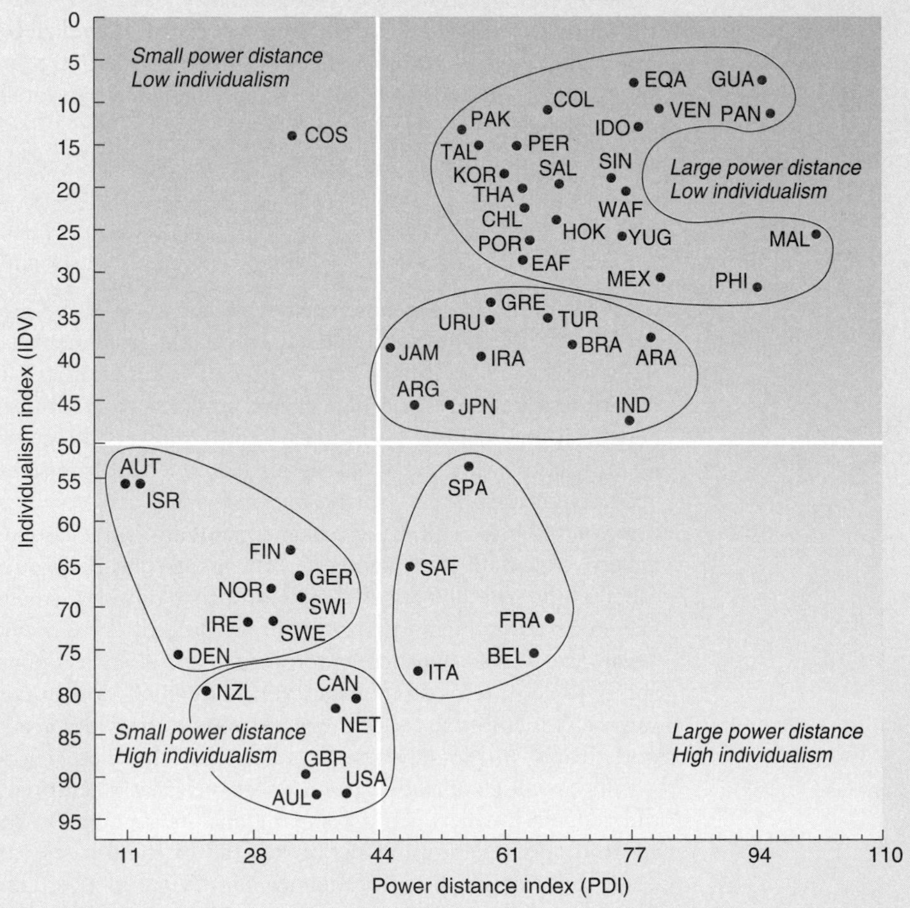

The "power distance" index focuses upon how a society deals with the inequality among people in physical and intellectual capabilities. Again each country was assigned a score between 0 and 100. At the high end of the scale were societies in which these inequalities are allowed to grow over time into inequalities of power and wealth. At the low end of the scale were societies that attempt to remove such inequalities.

The figure reproduces Hofstede's results for these two dimensions. What we find is that advanced Western nations such as the United States, Canada, and Great Britain score high on the individualism scale and relatively low on the power distance scale. At the other extreme are a group of Latin American and Asian countries that emphasize individualism over collectivism and that score high on the power distance scale.

Key

- ARA Arab countries (Egypt, Lebanon, Libya, Kuwait, Iraq, Saudi Arabia, United Arab Emirates)
- ARG Argentina
- AUL Australia
- AUT Austria
- BEL Belgium
- BRA Brazil
- CAN Canada
- CHL Chile
- COL Colombia
- COS Costa Rica
- DEN Denmark
- EAF East Africa (Kenya, Ethiopia, Zambia)
- EQA Equador
- FIN Finland
- FRA France
- GBR Great Britain
- GER Germany
- GRE Greece
- GUA Guatemala
- HOK Hong Kong
- IDO Indonesia
- IND India
- IRA Iran
- IRE Ireland
- ISR Israel
- ITA Italy
- JAM Jamaica
- JPN Japan
- KOR South Korea
- MAL Malaysia
- MEX Mexico
- NET Netherlands
- NOR Norway
- NZL New Zealand
- PAK Pakistan
- PAN Panama
- PER Peru
- PHI Philippines
- POR Portugal
- SAF South Africa
- SAL Salvador
- SIN Singapore
- SPA Spain
- SWE Sweden
- SWI Switzerland
- TAI Taiwan
- THA Thailand
- TUR Turkey
- URU Uruguay
- USA United States
- VEN Venezuela
- WAF West Africa (Nigeria, Ghana, Sierra Leone)
- YUG Yugoslavia

Source: G. Hofstede, *"The Cultural Relativity of Organizational Practices and Theories,"* Journal of International Business Studies, *Fall 1983, pp. 75–89.*

The high value placed on group identification in many Asian cultures could be expected to discourage managers and workers from moving from company to company. Indeed, this is the case in Japan, where lifetime employment with one company is the norm in certain sectors of the economy. (It has been estimated that between 20 and 40 percent of all Japanese employees have formal or informal lifetime employment guarantees.) One result of the lifetime employment system is that over the years managers and workers build up knowledge, experience, and a network of interpersonal business contacts. All of these things can help managers to perform their jobs more effectively and to achieve cooperation with others in the organization.

However, the primacy of the group is not beneficial in all respects. Just as U.S. society is characterized by a great deal of dynamism and entrepreneurship, reflecting the value placed on individualism, so Japanese society is characterized by a corresponding lack of dynamism and entrepreneurship. Although it is not clear how this will play itself out in the long run, it is quite possible that due to the cultural emphasis upon individualism, the United States will continue to create more new industries than will Japan. Put another way, for *cultural* reasons the United States may continue to be more successful than Japan at pioneering radically new products and new ways of doing business. At the same time and for some of the same cultural reasons, the costs of doing business may continue to be lower in Japan than in the United States.

Social Stratification

All societies are stratified on a hierarchical basis into social classes; that is, into social strata. These strata are typically based on such characteristics as family background, occupation, and income. Individuals are born into a particular stratum; they become a member of the social class to which their parents belong. Individuals born into strata toward the top of the social hierarchy tend to have better life chances than individuals born into strata toward the bottom. They are likely to have a better education, better health, a higher standard of living, and better work opportunities. Although all societies are stratified to some degree, societies differ in two related ways that are of interest to us here. First, they differ in the degree of *social mobility* between social strata, and second, they differ in the *significance* attached to social strata in business contexts.

Social Mobility

The term **social mobility** refers to the ability of individuals to move out of the social class into which they are born. This varies significantly from society to society. The most rigid system of stratification is a **caste system.** A caste system is a *closed* system of stratification in which social position is determined by the family into which a person is born and from which movement is usually not possible during an individual's lifetime (i.e., social mobility is very limited). Often a caste position carries with it a specific occupation. Members of one caste might be shoemakers, members of another caste might be butchers, and so on. These occupations are embedded in the caste and passed down to succeeding generations. Although the number of societies with caste systems has diminished rapidly during the 20th century, one major example still remains: India. India has four main castes and several thousand subcastes. Even though the caste system was officially abolished in 1949, two years after India became independent, it is still a powerful force in Indian society. This is especially true in rural areas, where occupation and marital opportunities are still largely related to caste.

A **class system** is a less rigid system of social stratification in which social mobility is possible. A class system is a form of *open* stratification in which the position a person has by birth can be changed through their own achievements and/or luck. Individuals born into a class at the bottom of the hierarchy can work their way upward, while individuals born into a class at the top of the hierarchy can slip downward.

While many societies have class systems, the degree of social mobility within a class system varies from society to society. One of the better examples of a class society with relatively low mobility is Great Britain. British society is divided into three main classes: the upper class, which is made up of individuals whose families have had wealth, prestige, and occasionally power for generations; the middle class, whose members are involved in professional, managerial, and clerical occupations; and the working class, whose members earn their living from manual occupations. The middle class is further subdivided into the upper-middle class, whose members are involved in important managerial occupations and the prestigious professions (e.g., lawyers, accountants, stockbrokers, doctors), and the lower-middle class, whose members are involved in clerical work (e.g., bank tellers) and the less prestigious professions (e.g., schoolteachers).

What is significant about the British class system is the extent of divergence between the life chances of members of different classes. The upper and upper-middle classes typically send their children to a select group of private schools, where they do not mix with lower-class children, and where they pick up many of the speech accents and social norms that distinguish them as being from the higher strata of society. These private schools often have close ties with the most prestigious universities, such as Oxford and Cambridge. Indeed, until very recently Oxford and Cambridge reserved a certain number of places for the graduates of these private schools. Having attended prestigious universities, the already favored offspring of the upper and upper-middle classes then have excellent chances of being offered prestigious jobs in companies, banks, brokerage firms, and law firms run by members of the upper and upper-middle classes.

In stark contrast, the members of the British working and lower-middle classes typically go to state schools. The majority of them leave school at age 16, and those who do go on to higher education find it more difficult to get accepted at the best universities. When they do, they find that their lower-class accent and lack of certain social attributes marks them as being from a lower social stratum. Unless they can change this, they will have more difficulty getting access to the most prestigious jobs.

As a result of these factors, the class system in Great Britain tends to perpetuate itself from generation to generation, and mobility is limited. Although upward mobility is possible, it cannot normally be achieved in one generation. While an individual from a working-class background may succeed in establishing an income level that is consistent with membership of the upper-middle class, he or she may not be accepted as such by others of that class due to accent and background. However, by sending his or her offspring to a "right" school, the individual can ensure that his or her children will be accepted.

The class system in the United States is far less rigid than in Great Britain; mobility is much greater. Like Great Britain, the United States has its own upper, middle, and working classes; but class membership is determined more by individual economic achievements than by the class one is born into or the schools attended. Thus, an individual can, by their own economic achievement, move smoothly from the working class to the upper class in their own lifetime. Indeed, in American society successful individuals from humble origins are highly respected, whereas in British society such individuals are regarded as "nouveau riche" and are never quite accepted by their economic peers.

Significance

From a business perspective, the stratification of a society is significant insofar as it impacts upon the operation of business organizations. In American society, the high degree of social mobility and the extreme emphasis upon individualism limits the impact

Figure 3.2
Work Days Lost Due to Strikes per 100,000 Employees (latest available year, in thousands)

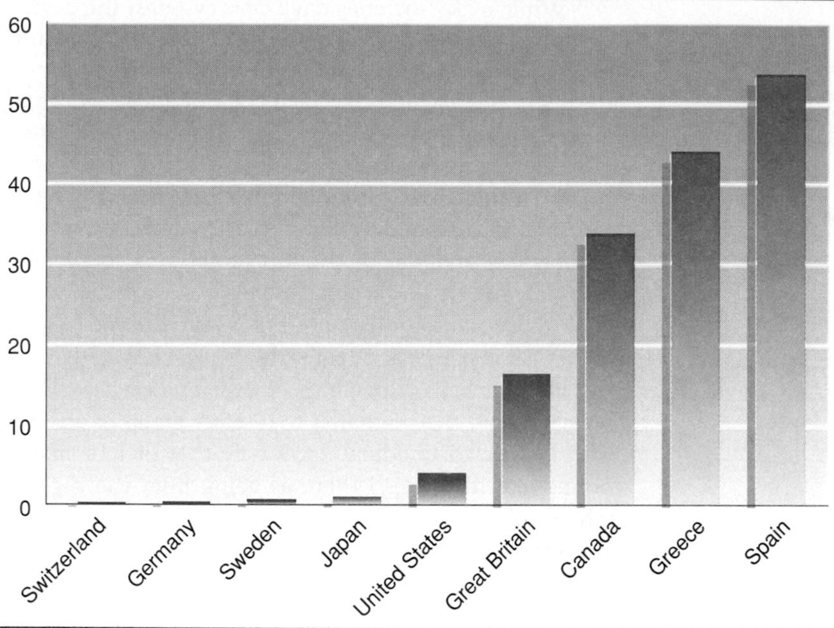

Source: *The Economist*, Book of Vital World Statistics (*New York: Random House, 1990), p. 200.*

of class background on business operations. The same is true in Japan, where the vast majority of the population perceive themselves as of the middle class. In a country like Great Britain, however, the relative lack of class mobility and the striking differences between classes has resulted in the emergence of **class consciousness.** People tend to perceive themselves in terms of their class background, and this shapes their relationships with members of other classes.

One way in which this has been played out in British society is in terms of the traditional hostility between upper-middle-class managers and their working-class employees. Mutual antagonism and lack of respect has made it difficult to achieve cooperation between management and labor in many British companies. Indeed, historically British industry has been racked by a great number of strikes, many of them politically motivated and depicted as "class warfare" between the disadvantaged working classes and the advantaged middle and upper classes. Moreover, politics in Great Britain tends to follow class lines to a much greater degree than in the United States, with the Labor Party representing the interests of the working class and the Conservative Party representing middle- and upper-class interests. Labor Party governments tend to be hostile to business and committed to collectivism (see Chapter 2).

The antagonistic relationship between management and labor in countries such as Great Britain and the resulting lack of cooperation and high level of industrial disruption tends to make the costs of production there higher than they are in such countries as the United States and Japan where there is less class-based conflict. This has made it more difficult for companies based in Great Britain to establish a competitive advantage in the global economy. Bear in mind, however, that Great Britain is not the only country with this problem. Similar problems have emerged in Italy, Spain, Greece, and Australia, to name just four. Indeed, the level of industrial disruption has been significantly higher in these four countries than in Great Britain in recent years (see Figure 3.2).

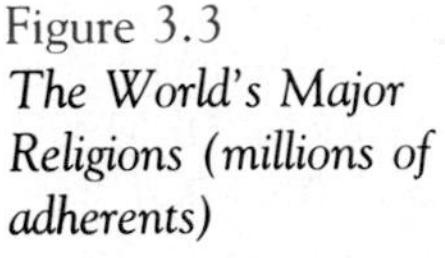

Figure 3.3
The World's Major Religions (millions of adherents)

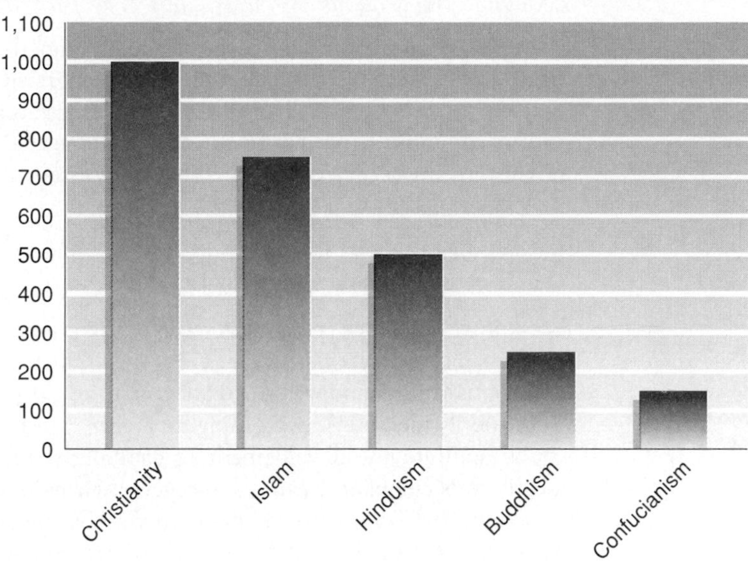

RELIGION

A religion is a system of shared beliefs and rituals concerned with the realm of the sacred.[7] The relationship between religion and society is subtle, complex, and profound. It is likely that religion may be the most powerful shaper of a culture's values and norms. Of the literally thousands of religions in the world today, five dominate: Christianity, Islam, Hinduism, Buddhism, and Confucianism (see Figure 3.3). We shall review each in turn, focusing primarily upon their business implications. Perhaps the most important business implications of religion are the influence of particular religions on attitudes toward work and entrepreneurship and the degree to which the religious ethics of a society increase or decrease the costs of doing business in that country.

Christianity

Christianity is the most widely practiced religion in the world. About one billion people, approximately 20 percent of the world's population, identify themselves as Christians. The vast majority of Christians live in Europe and the Americas, although their numbers are growing rapidly in Africa. Christianity grew out of Judaism. Like Judaism it is a monotheistic (belief in one god) religion. A religious division in the 11th century led to the establishment of two major Christian organizations: the Roman Catholic Church and the Eastern Orthodox Church. Today the Roman Catholic Church accounts for more than half of all Christians, most of them in Southern Europe and Latin America. The Eastern Orthodox Church, while less influential, is of major importance in several countries (e.g., Greece and, increasingly, Russia). In the 16th century the Reformation led to a further split with Rome, resulting in the establishment of Protestantism. The nonconformist nature of Protestantism facilitated the emergence of numerous denominations under the Protestant umbrella (e.g., Baptist, Methodist, Calvinist), which continues even today.

[7] Goodman, *Sociology*.

Economic Implications of Christianity: The Protestant Work Ethic

Many sociologists argue that of the two main branches of Christianity—Catholicism and Protestantism—the latter has the more important economic implications. In 1904 German sociologist Max Weber made a connection between protestant ethics and "the spirit of capitalism" that has since become famous.[8] Pointing out that capitalism emerged in Western Europe, Weber noted that in Western Europe:

> business leaders and owners of capital, as well as the higher grades of skilled labor, and even more the higher technically and commercially trained personnel of modern enterprises, are overwhelmingly Protestant.[9]

According to Weber, there was clearly a relationship between Protestantism and the emergence of modern capitalism. He argued that Protestant ethics emphasize the importance of hard work and wealth creation (for the glory of God) and of frugality (abstinence from worldly pleasures). According to Weber, this was just the kind of value system that would facilitate the development of capitalism. Protestants worked hard and systematically to accumulate wealth. However, their ascetic beliefs suggested that rather than consuming this wealth by indulging in worldly pleasures, they should reinvest it in the expansion of capitalist enterprises. Thus, the combination of hard work and the accumulation of capital that could be used to finance investment and expansion helped pave the way for the development of capitalism in Western Europe and, subsequently, the United States. In contrast, Weber argued that the Catholic promise of salvation in the next world, rather than this world, did not foster the same kind of work ethic among members of that group.

There is also another way in which Protestantism may have encouraged the development of capitalism. By breaking away from the hierarchical domination of religious and social life that characterized the Catholic Church for much of its history, Protestantism gave individuals significantly more freedom to develop their own relationship with God. The right to freedom of form of worship was central to the nonconformist nature of early Protestantism. In turn, the emphasis upon individual religious freedom may have paved the way for the subsequent emphasis on individual economic and political freedoms and for the development of individualism as an economic and political philosophy. As we saw in Chapter 2, such a philosophy is the basis of entrepreneurial free-market capitalism.

Islam

With 750 million adherents, Islam is the second-largest of the world's major religions. Islam dates back to A.D. 610 when the Prophet Muhammad first began spreading the word. Adherents of Islam are referred to as *Muslims.* Muslims constitute a majority in more than 35 countries and inhabit a nearly contiguous stretch of land from the northwest coast of Africa, through the Middle East, to the confines of China and Malaysia in the Far East.

Islam has roots in both Judaism and Christianity. (It views Jesus Christ as one of God's prophets.) Like Christianity and Judaism, Islam is a monotheistic religion. The central principle of Islam is that there is no god whatsoever but the one true omnipotent God. Other major principles of Islam are (1) honoring and respecting parents, (2) respecting the rights of others, (3) being generous but not a squanderer, (4) avoiding

---

[8] M. Weber, *The Protestant Ethic and the Spirit of Capitalism* (New York: Scribner's Sons, 1958, originally 1904–1905. For an excellent review of Weber's work see A. Giddens, *Capitalism and Modern Social Theory* (Cambridge, U.K.: Cambridge University Press, 1971).

[9] Weber, *Protestant Ethic,* p. 35.

killing except for justifiable causes, (5) not committing adultery, (6) dealing justly and equitably with others, (7) being of pure heart and mind, (8) safeguarding the possessions of orphans, and (9) being humble and unpretentious.[10] There are obvious parallels here with many of the central principles of both Judaism and Christianity.

However, to a much greater degree than Christianity, Islam is an all-embracing way of life governing the totality of a Muslim's being. As God's surrogate in this world, a Muslim is not a totally free agent but is circumscribed by religious principles—by a code of conduct for interpersonal relations—in his/her social and economic activities. Religion is paramount in all areas of life. The Muslim lives in a social structure shaped by Islamic values and norms of moral conduct. The ritual nature of everyday life in a Muslim country is perhaps one of the most striking things to a Western visitor. Among other things, Muslim ritual requires prayer five times a day (it is not unusual for business meetings to be suspended while the Muslim participants engage in their prayer ritual), that women be dressed in a certain manner and be subordinate to men, and that neither pig meat nor alcohol be consumed.

The past decade or two has witnessed a surge in Islamic fundamentalism. Fundamentalists demand a rigid commitment to traditional religious beliefs and rituals and they tend to be hostile to the West and to Western businesses, which they see as a corrupting influence. This is not surprising, since many Western values—especially those portrayed in Western movies and television programs—are very different from those espoused in Muslim countries. In several Muslim countries, fundamentalists have gained political power and are trying to make Islamic law (as set down in the Koran, the holy book of Islam) the law of the land. They have been most successful in Iran, where a fundamentalist party holds power, but they have also had considerable influence in many other countries, such as Algeria and Pakistan.

Economic Implications of Islam

Some quite explicit economic principles are set down in the Koran.[11] Many of the economic principles of Islam support free enterprise and are hostile to socialist ideals. The Koran speaks approvingly of free enterprise and of earning legitimate profit through trade and commerce. (The Prophet Muhammad himself was once a trader.) The protection of the rights to private property is also embedded within Islam, although Islam does assert that all property is a favor from Allah (God), who created and so owns everything. In this sense, those who hold property are regarded as trustees who are entitled to receive profits from it, rather than owners in the Western sense of the word. Moreover, those who hold property are admonished to use it in a righteous, socially beneficial, and prudent manner. This reflects Islam's concern with social justice. Islam is critical of those who earn profit through exploiting others. In the Islamic view of the world, man is part of a collective in which the wealthy and successful are obligated to help the disadvantaged. Put simply, in Muslim countries it is fine to earn a profit, so long as that profit is justly earned and not based upon the exploitation of others for one's own advantage. It also helps if those making profits undertake charitable acts to help the poor. Furthermore, Islam stresses the importance of living up to contractual obligations, of keeping one's word, and of abstaining from deception.

---

[10] S. M. Abbasi, K. W. Hollman, and J. H. Murrey, "Islamic Economics: Foundations and Practices," *International Journal of Social Economics* 16, no. 5 (1990), pp. 5–17.

[11] The material in this section is based largely on Abbasi et al., "Islamic Economics."

In general then, Islamic countries are likely to be receptive to international businesses so long as those businesses behave in a manner that is consistent with Islamic ethics. Businesses that are perceived as making unjust profits through exploitation, deception, or breaking contractual obligations are not likely to be welcome in an Islamic state. In addition, in Islamic states where fundamentalism is on the rise, it is also likely that hostility to Western-owned business will increase.

One economic principle of Islam that has received particular attention is the prohibition of the payment or receipt of interest, which is considered usury. The devout Muslim views acceptance of interest payments as a very grave sin. Practitioners of the black art of usury are warned on the pain of hellfire to abstain; the giver and the taker are equally damned. This is not just a matter of theology; in several Islamic states it is also becoming a matter of law. In early 1992, for example, Pakistan's Federal Shariat Court, the highest Islamic lawmaking body in the country, pronounced interest to be un-Islamic and, therefore, illegal and demanded that the government amend all financial laws accordingly.[12]

On the face of it, rigid adherence to this particular Islamic law could wreak havoc with a country's financial and banking system, raising the costs of doing business and scaring away international businesses and international investors. To skirt the ban on interest, Islamic banks have been experimenting with a profit-sharing system. When an Islamic bank lends money to a business, rather than charging that business interest on the loan, it takes a share in the profits that are derived from the investment. Similarly, when a business (or individual) deposits money at an Islamic bank in a saving account, the deposit is treated as an equity investment in whatever activity the bank uses the capital. Thus, the depositor receives a share in the profit from the bank's investment (as opposed to interest payments). Some Muslims claim that this is a more efficient system than the Western banking system, since it encourages both long-term savings and long-term investment. However, there is no hard evidence to this effect, and many believe that an Islamic banking system is less efficient than a conventional Western banking system.

Hinduism

Hinduism has approximately 500 million adherents, most of them living in the Indian subcontinent. Hinduism began in the Indus Valley in India over 4,000 years ago, making it the world's oldest major religion. Unlike Christianity and Islam, its founding is not linked to a particular person, nor does it have an officially sanctioned sacred book. Hindus believe that there is a moral force in society that requires the acceptance of certain responsibilities, called *dharma.* They also believe in reincarnation—rebirth into a different body after death—and in karma, the spiritual progression of each person's soul. A person's karma is affected by the way he or she lives. The moral state of a person's karma determines the challenges the person will face in his or her next life. By perfecting the soul in each new life, Hindus believe that an individual can eventually achieve nirvana, a state of complete spiritual perfection that renders reincarnation no longer necessary. Many Hindus believe that the way to achieve nirvana is to lead a severe ascetic lifestyle of material and physical self-denial, devoting one's life to a spiritual, rather than material quest.

Economic Implications of Hinduism

Whatever its spiritual merit, the ascetic principles embedded in Hinduism do not encourage the kind of hard work in pursuit of wealth creation that we find in Protes-

[12] "Islam's Interest," *The Economist,* January 18, 1992, pp. 33–34.

tantism. Hindus do not value individuals by their material achievements, but by their spiritual achievements. Consequently, there is not the same culturally based incentive for entrepreneurial activity that we find in the Protestant nations of the West. Indeed, the opposite may be the case, since Hindus perceive the pursuit of material well-being as making the attainment of nirvana more difficult.

Hinduism also supports India's rigid caste system. The concept of mobility between castes within an individual's lifetime makes no sense to Hindus, who see mobility between castes as something that is achieved only through spiritual progression and reincarnation. An individual can be reborn into a higher caste in their next life if they achieve spiritual development in this life. Insofar as the caste system limits the opportunities for able individuals to adopt positions of responsibility and influence in society, the economic consequences of this religious belief are bound to be negative. For example, the most able individuals within a business organization may find their route to the higher levels of the organization blocked simply because they come from a lower caste. By the same token, individuals may get promoted to higher positions within a firm as much because of their caste background as because of their ability.

Buddhism

Buddhism was founded in India in the sixth century B.C. by Siddhartha Gautama, an Indian prince who renounced his wealth to pursue an ascetic lifestyle and spiritual perfection. Siddhartha achieved nirvana, but decided to remain on earth to teach his followers how they too could achieve this state of spiritual enlightenment. Siddhartha became known as the *Buddha* ("the awakened one"). Today Buddhism has 250 million followers, most of whom are found in Central and Southeast Asia, China, Korea, and Japan. According to Buddhism, life is suffering. Misery is everywhere and originates in people's desires for pleasure. These desires can be curbed by systematically following the Noble Eightfold Path—right views, right intention, right speech, right action, right livelihood, right effort, right awareness, and right concentration. Unlike Hinduism, Buddhism does not support the caste system. Nor does Buddhism advocate the kind of extreme ascetic behavior that is encouraged by Hinduism. Nevertheless, like Hindus, Buddhists stress the afterlife and spiritual achievement, rather than involvement in this world.

Economic Implications of Buddhism

Because Buddhists, as the Hindus, stress spiritual achievement, rather than involvement in this world, the work ethic and accompanying emphasis upon wealth creation that are embedded in Protestantism are not found in Buddhism. Consequently, in Buddhist societies we do not see the cultural encouragement of entrepreneurial behavior that we see in the Protestant West. This is bound to have negative economic implications. On the other hand, unlike Hinduism, the lack of support for the caste system and extreme ascetic behavior in Buddhism suggests that Buddhism is unlikely to be as severe a brake upon economic growth as Hinduism is.

Confucianism

Confucianism was founded in the fifth century B.C. by K'ung-Fu-tzu, more generally known as Confucius. For more than 2,000 years before the 1949 Communist revolution, Confucianism was the official religion of China. While religious observance has been weakened in China since 1949, more than 150 million people still follow the teachings of Confucius, principally in China, Korea, and Japan. Confucianism teaches the importance of attaining personal salvation through right action. Confucianism is built around a comprehensive ethical code that sets down guidelines for relationships with others. The need for high moral and ethical conduct and loyalty to others are central to Confucianism. Unlike other religions, Confucianism is not concerned with the supernatural and has little to say about the concept of an afterlife. This has led many to argue that Confucianism is not a religion at all, but simply an ethical system. Nonetheless, Confucianism is regarded by many of its adherents as a religion.

Economic Implications of Confucianism

There is a growing realization that Confucianism may have economic implications that are just as profound as those of Protestantism, although they are of a different nature. Indeed, there are those who argue that the influence of Confucian ethics upon the culture of Japan, South Korea, and Taiwan, by lowering the costs of doing business in those countries, may help explain their economic success.[13] In this regard, three values central to the Confucian system of ethics are of particular interest: loyalty, reciprocal obligations, and honesty in dealings with others.

In Confucian thought, loyalty to one's superiors is regarded as a sacred duty—an absolute necessity for religious salvation. In modern organizations based in Confucian cultures, the bonds of loyalty that bind employees to the heads of their organization can be seen as reducing the conflict between management and labor that we find in class-conscious societies such as Great Britain. Put another way, cooperation between management and labor can be achieved at a lower cost in a culture where the virtue of loyalty is emphasized in the value system.

It must be realized, however, that in a Confucian culture loyalty to one's superiors, such as a worker's loyalty to management, is not blind loyalty. The value of reciprocal obligations also comes into play. Confucian ethics stress that superiors are obliged to reward the loyalty of their subordinates by bestowing blessings upon them. If these "blessings" are not forthcoming, then neither will be the loyalty. One way this Confucian ethic exhibits itself in Japanese organizations is in the concept of lifetime employment. The employees of a Japanese company are loyal to the leaders of the organization, and in return the leaders bestow upon them the "blessing" of lifetime employment. The business implications of this particular cultural practice have already been touched upon earlier in the chapter when we discussed the importance of group identification in Japanese society. Specifically, the lack of mobility between companies implied by the lifetime employment system suggests that over the years managers and workers build up knowledge, experience, and a network of interpersonal business contacts. All of these things can help managers and workers perform their jobs more effectively and assist them in achieving cooperation with others in the organization. One result is improved economic performance of the company as a whole.

A third value of Confucian ethics with economic implications is the importance attached to honesty in dealings with others. Confucian thinkers emphasize that although dishonest behavior may yield short-term benefits for the transgressor, in the long run, dishonesty does not pay. The importance attached to honesty in dealings with others has major economic implications. In a society where companies can trust each other not to break contractual obligations, the costs of doing business are lowered. For one thing, there is not the same need to employ expensive lawyers to resolve contract disputes. In addition, in a Confucian society there may be less hesitation to commit substantial resources to cooperative ventures than in societies where honesty is less prevalent. When

---

[13] This is a subject of the author's own research. See C. W. L. Hill, "Transaction Cost Economizing as a Source of Comparative Advantage: The Case of Japan," *Organizational Science*, in press, 1993.

Great Religious Blunders in Business

BOX 3.3

Saudi Arabia nearly restricted a Western airline from initiating flights when the company authorized "normal" newspaper advertisements in Saudi Arabia. One of the ads featured a photograph of attractive hostesses serving champagne to happy airline passengers. Saudi Arabia is an Islamic country in which alcohol is illegal, and unveiled women are not permitted to mix with men. The photo was viewed as an attempt to alter religious customs.

- The typical refrigerator ad for the print media features a photograph of a refrigerator full of delicious-looking food. Because these photos are difficult to take, the photos are generally used in as many places as possible. One company used such a stock photo in one place too many when it used a picture of a refrigerator containing a centrally placed whole ham to promote refrigerators in the Middle East, where Muslims are forbidden to eat ham. Locals considered the advertisement to be insensitive and unappealing.
- A marketer of eyeglasses promoted its spectacles in Thailand, a predominantly Buddhist nation, with television commercials featuring animals wearing glasses. This was unfortunate. In many Buddhist countries, animals are considered a low life form, and it is beneath humans to wear anything worn by an animal.

Source: These examples are taken from David A. Ricks, Big Business Blunders: Mistakes in Multinational Marketing *(Homewood, Ill.: Dow Jones Irwin, 1983).*

companies adhere to Confucian ethics, they can trust each other not to violate the terms of cooperative agreements. Thus, the costs of achieving cooperation between companies may be lower in societies like Japan (relative, that is, to societies such as the U.S. where there is less trust).

For example, it has been argued that the close ties between the automobile companies and their component-part suppliers in Japan are facilitated by a combination of trust and reciprocal obligations. These close ties allow the auto companies and their suppliers to work together on a whole range of issues including inventory reduction, quality control, and design. In turn, it is claimed that the competitive advantage of Japanese auto companies can in part be explained by such factors.[14]

LANGUAGE

One of the most obvious ways countries differ is in their languages. By language, we mean both the spoken and the unspoken means of communication. Language is a defining characteristic of a culture.

Spoken Language

Language obviously enables people to communicate with each other, but it does far more than that. A language also structures the way the world is perceived. The language of a society can direct the attention of its members to certain features of the world rather than to others. The classic illustration of this phenomenon is that whereas the English language has but one word for snow, the language of the Inuit (Eskimos) lacks a general

[14] See, for example, M. Aoki, *Information, Incentives, and Bargaining in the Japanese Economy* (Cambridge, U.K.: Cambridge University Press, 1988); and J. P. Womack, D. T. Jones, and D. Roos, *The Machine that Changed the World* (New York: Rawson Associates, 1990).

Table 3.1
Mother Tongues

Language	Percentage of World Population for Whom This Is First Language
Chinese	20.0
English	6.0
Hindi	4.5
Russian	3.5
Spanish	3.0
Portuguese	2.0
Japanese	2.0
Arabic	2.0
French	1.5
German	1.5
Other	54.0

Source: The Economist Atlas *(London: The Economist Books, 1991), p. 116.*

term for it. Instead, because distinguishing different forms of snow is so important in the lives of the Inuit, they have 24 different words that describe the various types of snow (e.g., powder snow, falling snow, wet snow, drifting snow).[15]

Since language shapes the way people perceive the world, it also serves to define a culture. It follows that in countries with more than one language, one usually finds more than one culture. In Canada, for example, there is an English-speaking culture and a French-speaking culture. Tensions between the two run quite high, with a substantial proportion of the French-speaking minority demanding independence from a Canada "dominated by English speakers." The same phenomenon can be observed in many countries around the world. For example, Belgium is divided into Flemish and French speakers, and tensions between the two groups exist. In Spain a Basque-speaking minority with its own distinctive culture has been agitating for independence from the Spanish-speaking majority for decades. On the island of Cyprus in the Mediterranean, the culturally diverse Greek- and Turkish-speaking populations of the island engaged in open conflict in the 1970s, and the island is now partitioned into two halves. While it does not necessarily follow that language differences create differences in culture and, therefore, separatist pressures (e.g., witness the harmony in Switzerland, where four languages are spoken), there certainly seems to be a tendency in this direction.

Chinese is the "mother tongue" of the largest number of the world's people, followed by English and Hindi (spoken in India), as shown in Table 3.1. However, the most widely spoken language in the world is English, followed by French, Spanish, and Chinese (i.e., many people speak English as a second language). Increasingly, English is the language of international business. When a Japanese businessperson and a German businessperson meet to discuss business, it is almost certain that they will communicate in English. Nonetheless, although English is widely used in the world, there are still considerable advantages for an English-speaking person who learns the local language. For one thing, most people prefer to converse in their own language, and being able to speak the local language can aid in building rapport—which may be very important for a business deal. An additional point is that international businesses that do not understand the local language can make some major translation blunders. Several examples of these are given in Box 3.4. The way to avoid such mistakes, of course, is to ensure that a good bilingual translator is employed by the company.

[15] This hypothesis dates back to two anthropologists, Edward Sapir and Benjamin Lee Whorf. See E. Sapir, "The Status of Linguistics as a Science," *Language* 5(1929):207–214; and B. L. Whorf, *Language, Thought, and Reality* (Cambridge, Mass.: MIT Press, 1956).

BOX 3.4

Embarrassing Language Blunders in International Business

One of the biggest marketing blunders that many international businesses have made is selecting inappropriate names for their products overseas. Consider the following:

- General Motors was troubled by the lack of enthusiasm among Puerto Rican dealers for its newly introduced Chevrolet Nova. When literally translated into Spanish, *Nova* meant "star." However, when spoken it sounded like *no va*, Spanish for "it doesn't go." General Motors subsequently changed the name of the car to *Caribe*.
- Ford introduced a low-cost truck into Latin America called the *Fiera*. Unfortunately, that means "ugly old woman" in Spanish. Not surprisingly, the name did not encourage sales.
- Ford also experienced slow sales when it introduced a car in Mexico under the name of *Caliente*. Only later did Ford discover that *caliente* is slang for "streetwalker" in Mexico.
- The Sunbeam Corporation used the English words for its "Mist-Stick" mist-producing hair-curling iron when it entered the German market, only to discover after an expensive advertising campaign that *mist* means "excrement" in German.

Just as selecting the wrong name can have embarrassing consequences, so can poor translation into a foreign language. Consider the following:

- A department store in Thailand posted a sign that read, "Visit our bargain basement one flight up." Another misguided individual in Thailand tried to attract business with a sign asking, "Would you like to ride on your ass?"
- In Japan, an interesting but misleading translation showed up on a sign in a Japanese garden. The sign read, "Japanese garden is the mental home of Japan."
- A Mexican magazine promotion for a U.S.-brand shirt carried a message exactly the opposite of what was intended. Instead of stating, "When I used this shirt, I felt good," the advertisement read, "Until I used this shirt I felt good."
- When promoting a car in Belgium, General Motors intended the advertisement to state that the car had a "Body by Fisher." (Fisher is GM's auto body pressing operation.) Instead, the phrase was translated into Flemish as "Corpse by Fisher."

Source: These examples are taken from David A. Ricks, Big Business Blunders: Mistakes in Multinational Marketing *(Homewood, Ill.: Dow Jones Irwin, 1983).*

Unspoken Language

Unspoken language refers to nonverbal communications. We all communicate with each other by a host of nonverbal cues. The raising of eyebrows, for example, is a sign of recognition in most cultures, while a smile is a sign of joy. Many nonverbal cues, however, are culturally bound. A failure to understand the nonverbal cues of another culture can lead to a failure of communication. For example, making a circle with the thumb and the forefinger is a friendly gesture in the United States, but a vulgar sexual invitation in Greece and Turkey. Similarly, while most Americans and Europeans use the "thumbs up" gesture to indicate that "it's all right," in Greece the gesture is obscene.

Another aspect of nonverbal communication is "personal space," the comfortable physical distance people tend to maintain when they are talking. The amount of distance regarded as comfortable varies by culture. For example, in the United States, parties in a business discussion seem to be most comfortable when the distance between them is five to eight feet. In Latin America it is three to five feet. Consequently, many North Americans unconsciously feel that Latin Americans are "invading their personal space" and back away from them during a conversation, which a Latin American may perceive as rejection or aloofness. The result can be a regrettable lack of rapport.

EDUCATION

Formal education plays a key role in a society, because it is the means by which individuals acquire the language, conceptual, and mathematical skills that are indispensable in the particular society. Formal education also supplements the family's role in socializing the young into the values and norms of the society. Values and norms are taught both directly and indirectly. Schools generally teach basic facts about the social and political nature of a society and the fundamental obligations of citizenship. Cultural norms are also taught indirectly at school; such things as respect for others, obedience to authority, honesty, neatness, punctuality, and so on, are part of the "hidden curriculum" of schools. The grading system also teaches children the value of personal achievement and competition.[16]

From an international business perspective, one of the most important aspects of education is its role as a determinant of national competitive advantage.[17] The availability of a pool of skilled and educated people seems to be a major determinant of a country's potential economic success. Such a pool is the product of a good national education system. In analyzing the competitive success of Japan since 1945, for example, Michael Porter notes that after the war Japan had almost nothing except a pool of skilled, educated people. To quote:

> With a long tradition of respect for education that borders on reverence, Japan possessed a large pool of literate, educated, and increasingly skilled human resources. . . . Japan has benefited from a large pool of trained engineers. Japanese universities graduate many more engineers per capita than in the United States. . . . A first-rate primary and secondary education system in Japan operates based on high standards and emphasizes math and science. Primary and secondary education is highly competitive. . . . Japanese education provides most students all over Japan with a sound education for later education and training. A Japanese high school graduate knows as much about math as most American college graduates.[18]

Porter's point is that Japan's excellent education system was an important contributor to the country's postwar economic success. Not only does a good education system give a country competitive advantage, it can also guide the location choices of international businesses. For example, it would make little sense to base production facilities that require highly skilled labor in a country where the education system is so poor that a skilled labor pool is not available, no matter how attractive the country might be on other dimensions. On the other hand, it might make sense to base production operations that require unskilled labor in such a country.

---

16 Goodman, *Sociology*.

17 M. E. Porter, *The Competitive Advantage of Nations* (New York: Free Press, 1990).

18 Ibid., pp. 395–97.

The general education level of a country provides an index of the kinds of products that might sell there and of the types of promotional material that should be used. For example, a country such as Pakistan, where 73.8 percent of the population is illiterate, is unlikely to be a good market for popular books. Further, promotional material containing written descriptions of products are unlikely to be effective there. (Pictorial promotions are more appropriate in such circumstances.)

Maps 3.1 and 3.2 provide some important data on education worldwide. Map 3.1 shows the percentage of countries' GNP devoted to education in 1991, and Map 3.2 shows worldwide literacy rates in 1991. Although there is not a direct correspondence between the percentage of a country's GNP devoted to education and the quality of its education, the level of spending would seem to indicate the country's commitment to education. Note that the United States spends more of its GNP on education than many other advanced industrialized nations, including Germany and Japan. Despite this, the quality of U.S. education is often regarded as inferior to that of many other industrialized countries.

IMPLICATIONS FOR BUSINESS

In this chapter we have been examining the cultural differences of countries; that is, their differences in social structure, religion, language, education, economic philosophy, and political philosophy. Two important implications for international business flow from these differences. The first is the need to develop cross-cultural literacy. The second is the need to examine the connection between a country's culture, the costs of doing business there, and its national competitive advantage. As we have pointed out many times, there is clearly a link between a nation's culture and its competitive advantage or lack of it. In this section, we will explore both of these issues in greater detail.

Cross-Cultural Literacy

One of the biggest dangers confronting a company that goes abroad for the first time is the danger of being ill informed. An international business that lacks cross-cultural literacy—sound knowledge about practices in the culture—is unlikely to succeed. Doing business in a different culture requires adaptation to the value systems and norms of that culture. Adaptation can embrace all aspects of a firm's operations in a foreign country. The ways deals are negotiated, appropriate incentive pay systems for salespeople, organizational structure, product names, labor–management relations, the manner in which products are promoted, and so on; all of these are sensitive to cultural differences. What works in one culture might not work in another, and vice versa. Three of the boxes in this chapter and, of course, the opening case illustrate the pitfalls of cross-cultural illiteracy.

To combat the danger of being ill informed, international business should always consider employing local citizens to assist them in the particular culture. They must also ensure that home-country executives are sufficiently cosmopolitan that they understand how differences in culture impact upon the practice of international business. One way to build a cadre of cosmopolitan executives is to transfer executives overseas at regular intervals to give them exposure to different cultures. An international business must also be constantly on guard against the dangers of *ethnocentrism*—the belief that one's own ethnic group or culture is superior. Hand in hand with ethnocentrism goes disregard or even contempt for the culture and people of other countries. Unfortunately, ethnocentrism is all too prevalent; many Americans are guilty of it, as are many French people,

Map 3.1 *Percentage of Gross National Product (GNP) Spent on Education, 1990–91*

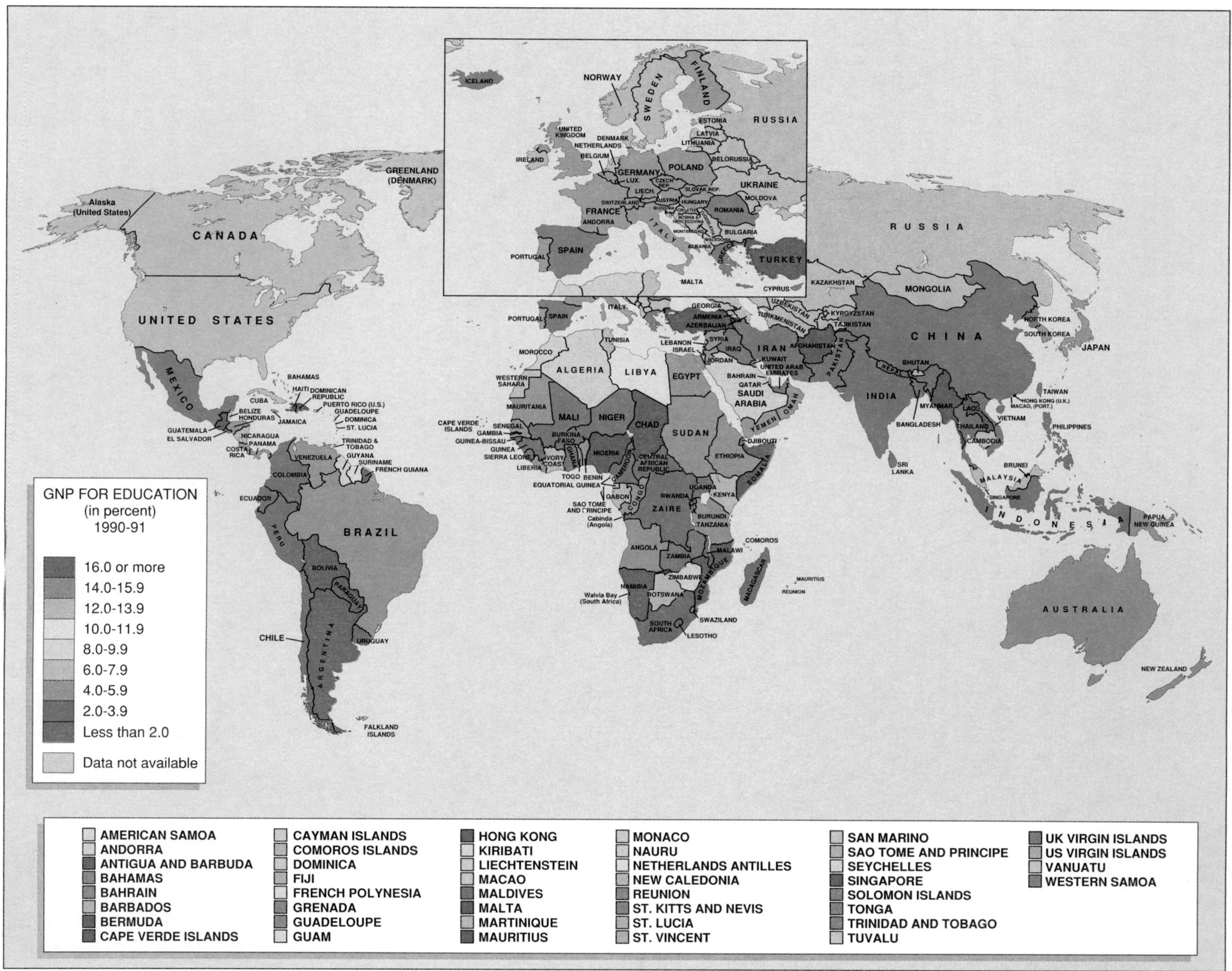

Map 3.2 *Percentage World Literacy Rates, 1990–91*

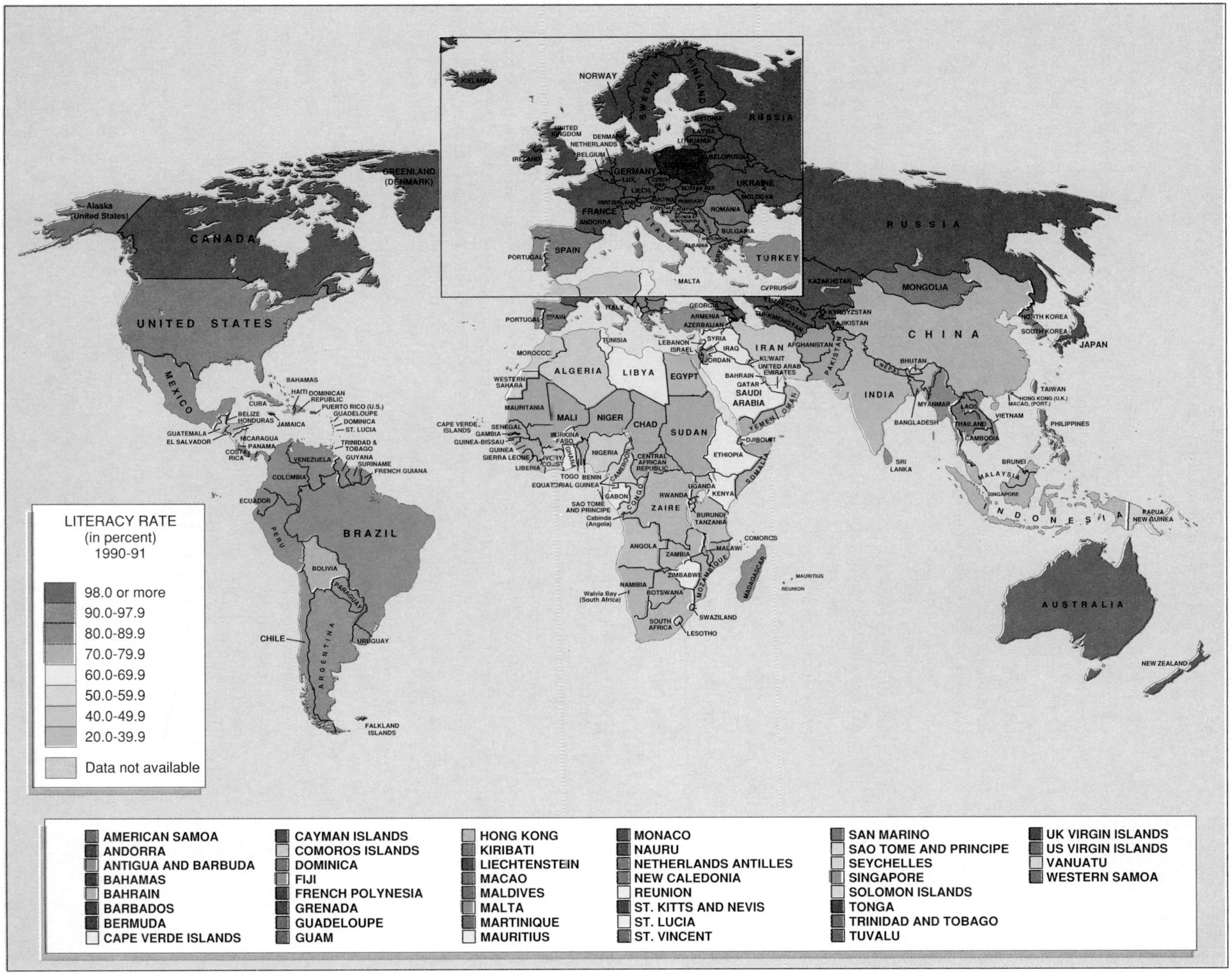

LITERACY RATE
(in percent)
1990-91

- 98.0 or more
- 90.0-97.9
- 80.0-89.9
- 70.0-79.9
- 60.0-69.9
- 50.0-59.9
- 40.0-49.9
- 20.0-39.9
- Data not available

AMERICAN SAMOA
ANDORRA
ANTIGUA AND BARBUDA
BAHAMAS
BAHRAIN
BARBADOS
BERMUDA
CAPE VERDE ISLANDS
CAYMAN ISLANDS
COMOROS ISLANDS
DOMINICA
FIJI
FRENCH POLYNESIA
GRENADA
GUADELOUPE
GUAM
HONG KONG
KIRIBATI
LIECHTENSTEIN
MACAO
MALDIVES
MALTA
MARTINIQUE
MAURITIUS
MONACO
NAURU
NETHERLANDS ANTILLES
NEW CALEDONIA
REUNION
ST. KITTS AND NEVIS
ST. LUCIA
ST. VINCENT
SAN MARINO
SAO TOME AND PRINCIPE
SEYCHELLES
SINGAPORE
SOLOMON ISLANDS
TONGA
TRINIDAD AND TOBAGO
TUVALU
UK VIRGIN ISLANDS
US VIRGIN ISLANDS
VANUATU
WESTERN SAMOA

Source: Map data copyright © 1992 PC Globe, Inc. Tempe, Arizona, USA.

Japanese people, British people, and so on. Ugly as it is, ethnocentrism is a fact of life, but it has no place in international business.

Culture and Competitive Advantage

One theme that has continually surfaced in this chapter is the relationship between culture and national competitive advantage. Put simply, the value systems and norms of a country influence the costs of doing business in that country. The costs of doing business in a country influence the ability of firms based there to establish a competitive advantage in the global marketplace. For example, we have seen how attitudes toward cooperation between management and labor, toward work, and toward the payment of interest are influenced by social structure and religion. It can be argued that the class-based conflict between workers and management in British society, insofar as it leads to industrial disruption, raises the costs of doing business there. This factor will tend to work against British firms, relative to say, firms based in Japan, where the value placed on group identification serves to minimize conflict between management and labor. Similarly, we have seen how the ascetic "other worldly" ethics of Hinduism are not as supportive of capitalism as the ethics embedded in Protestantism and Confucianism. This may well place Indian firms at a disadvantage relative to firms based in Protestant and Confucian nations (e.g., Japan, Korea, the U.S., Germany). We have also raised the possibility that the constraints upon a country's banking system contained in Islamic laws on interest payments may put firms based in Islamic countries at a competitive disadvantage. Put another way, Islamic banking laws may raise the costs of doing business in countries where Islamic fundamentalism is transforming the legal system.

Japan presents a particularly interesting example of how culture can influence competitive advantage. It can be argued that the culture of modern day Japan lowers the costs of doing business in that country, relative to the costs of doing business in most Western nations. We have seen how the Japanese emphases on group affiliation, loyalty, reciprocal obligations, honesty, and education all boost the competitiveness of Japanese companies. The high value placed on group affiliation and loyalty encourages individuals to identify strongly with the companies in which they work. In turn, this tends to foster an ethic of hard work and cooperation between management and labor "for the good of the company." Similarly, the concepts of reciprocal obligations and honesty help foster an atmosphere of trust between companies and their suppliers. In turn, this encourages them to enter into long-term relationships with each other to work on factors such as inventory reduction, quality control, and joint design—all of which have been shown to improve an organization's competitiveness. This level of cooperation is all too often lacking in the West, where the relationship between a company and its suppliers tends to be a short-term one structured around competitive bidding, rather than one based upon long-term mutual commitments. In addition, the availability of a pool of highly skilled labor, particularly engineers, has undoubtedly helped Japanese enterprises develop a number of cost-reducing process innovations that have boosted their productivity.[19] Thus, cultural factors may help explain the competitive advantage enjoyed by many Japanese businesses in the global marketplace. Indeed, the rise of Japan as an economic superpower during the second half of the 20th century may be in part attributed to the economic consequences of its culture.

For the international business, the connection between culture and competitive advantage is important for two reasons. First, the connection suggests which countries are likely to produce the most viable competitors. For example, it is *likely* that U.S.

[19] See Aoki, *Japanese Economy;* Dertouzos et al., *Made in America;* and Porter, *Competitive Advantage,* pp. 395–97.

enterprises are going to see continued growth in aggressive, cost-efficient competitors from those Pacific Rim nations where a combination of free market economics, Confucian ideology, group-orientated social structures, and advanced education system is found (e.g., South Korea, Taiwan, Japan, and increasingly China). By the same reasoning, unless there is some drastic change in culture, it is *unlikely* that the Hindu nation of India, despite its huge population, is going to give rise to major global competitors in the near or even medium-term future.

Second, the connection between culture and competitive advantage has important implications for location decisions. For illustration, consider the hypothetical case of a company that must choose between two countries, A and B, for locating a production facility. Both countries are characterized by low labor costs and good access to world markets. The countries are of roughly the same population size and similar stages of economic development. In Country A the education system is undeveloped, the society is characterized by marked stratification between the upper and lower classes, the dominant religion stresses reincarnation, and there are three major linguistic groups. In Country B the education system is well developed, there is a lack of social stratification, group identification is valued by the culture, the dominant religion stresses the virtue of hard work, and there is only one linguistic group. Which country, A or B, would be the better investment site?

The answer is obvious. Country B would. This is because the culture of Country B is supportive of the capitalist mode of production and social harmony, whereas the culture of Country A is not. In Country A, conflicts between management and labor and between language groups can be expected to lead to social and industrial disruption, which increase the costs of doing business. The lack of a good education system and the dominance of a religion that stresses ascetic behavior as the means of achieving advancement in the next life can also be expected to work against the attainment of business goals.

The same kind of comparison can be useful to an international business in making marketing decisions. That is, for example, should we market our product in Country A or in Country B? Again, Country B would be the logical choice, precisely because cultural factors suggest that in the long run, Country B is likely to achieve the greater level of economic growth. In comparison, the culture of Country A may produce economic stagnation.

SUMMARY OF CHAPTER

This chapter had two main objectives. The first was to explore the relationship between culture, the costs of doing business in a country, and national competitive advantage. The second was to explain how the culture of a country can affect the way in which business is practiced there. The following points have been made in the chapter:

1. Culture is defined as that complex whole which includes knowledge, belief, art, morals, law, custom, and other capabilities acquired by people as members of society.
2. The fundamental building blocks of a culture are its value systems and norms.
3. Values are abstract ideals about what a society believes to be good, right, and desirable.
4. Norms are social rules and guidelines that prescribe appropriate behavior in particular situations.
5. Norms can be subdivided into folkways and mores. Folkways are the routine conventions of everyday life. Mores are norms that are seen as central to the functioning of society.
6. Values and norms are influenced by political and economic philosophy, social structure, religion, language, and education.
7. The social structure of a society is its basic social organization. There are two main dimensions along which social structures differ: the individual-group dimension, and the stratification dimension.
8. In some societies the rights of the individual are para-

mount in the social organization. In these societies individual achievements are encouraged.

9. In some societies the good of the group is the basis of social organization. In these societies group membership and group achievements are encouraged.
10. In societies where the individual is paramount, there is greater cultural admiration of entrepreneurship. In societies where the group is paramount, the costs of achieving cooperation and long-term commitments are lower.
11. All societies are stratified into different classes. The degree of stratification, however, varies. Class-conscious societies are characterized by low social mobility and a high degree of stratification. Societies that are less class-conscious are characterized by high social mobility and a low degree of stratification.
12. In class-conscious societies, a greater degree of conflict between management and labor in likely. This raises the costs of doing business there.
13. Religion may be defined as a system of shared beliefs and rituals concerned with the realm of the sacred. The world's major religions are Christianity, Islam, Hinduism, Buddhism, and Confucianism.
14. According to Weber, there is a close relationship between Protestantism and capitalism. Protestant ethics emphasize the importance of hard work and wealth creation.
15. Many of the economic principles of Islam support free enterprise. However, Islamic laws on the payment of interest may raise the costs of doing business in fundamentalist countries where Islamic law is transforming the legal system.
16. The ethics of Hinduism and Buddhism, however appealing spiritually, seem unlikely to encourage hard work in pursuit of wealth creation encouraged by Protestantism.
17. The economic implications of Confucianism may be just as profound as those of Protestantism, but they are of a different nature. Three values central to the Confucian system of ethics are of particular importance: loyalty, reciprocal obligations, and honesty. Confucianism reduces the costs of business by encouraging loyalty to the group (company), hard work, and dealing honestly with others.
18. Language is a defining characteristic of a culture. It has both a spoken and an unspoken dimension. Most countries with more than one spoken language have more than one culture.
19. Formal education is the medium by which individuals learn skills and are socialized into the values and norms of a society. Education is an important determinant of a country's national competitive advantage or disadvantage.
20. One of the biggest dangers confronting a company that goes abroad for the first time is that of being ill informed. To develop cross-cultural literacy, international businesses need to employ host-country nationals, build a cadre of cosmopolitan executives, and guard against the dangers of ethnocentrism.
21. The value systems and norms of a country influence the costs of doing business in that country.
22. The connection between culture and competitive advantage is important to an international business for two reasons. First, the connection suggests which countries are likely to produce viable competitors. Second, the connection has important implications for location and marketing decisions.

DISCUSSION QUESTIONS

1. Outline why the culture of a country influences the costs of doing business in that country. Illustrate your answer with examples.
2. How are business practices in an Islamic country likely to differ from those in the United States?
3. What are the implications of each of the five dominant religions for international business?
4. Select two countries that appear to be culturally diverse. Compare the cultures of those countries and then explain how you would expect the cultural differences to influence (*a*) the costs of doing business, (*b*) business practices, and (*c*) the likely future economic development for each country.

Arnold Tanner, Western Energy, Inc., and China

CASES

Primarily an oil company, Western Energy, Inc. (WEI), conducted business in more than 100 countries and employed more than 70,000 people in the 1980s. With annual sales of around $10 billion throughout the 1980s, WEI was among the ten largest energy firms in the United States. WEI consisted of one of the world's largest petroleum (oil and gas) operations, a growing chemical business, a coal exploration business, and a nationwide retailing operation in the United States. With a strategy that emphasized foreign production, the firm had production facilities in Argentina, Bolivia, Canada, Ecuador, Malaysia, Pakistan, the Philippines, Syria, and the U.K. North Sea as well as the United States when it entered China in 1980.

Between 1962 and 1990, Arnold Tanner was CEO and then Chairman of the San Francisco–based firm. Tanner had worked for WEI for 25 years in various capacities before becoming CEO, and his leadership made an enormous impact on WEI. He was well respected and a dynamic, charismatic leader in the industry. Moreover, his foresight had led his firm to actively seek opportunities in the Eastern bloc. His legendary achievements included striking one of the first deals between a Western business and the Soviets in the 1930s, supplying the Soviets during World War II, and trading with Eastern Europe since the détente in the 1970s. As a result, he was well known in many quarters of the Eastern bloc. When China instituted its "Open Door" policy in 1979, its leaders naturally looked to Tanner for help.

Tanner responded to the Chinese request with enthusiasm. His first visit to China was in 1979, and he later made many trips to Beijing. As always, his approach was high-profile, and he befriended China's supreme leader, Deng Xiaoping. In the early 1980s, China desperately needed to prove to a suspicious West that its Open Door policy was credible and that direct investment from abroad was genuinely welcome. Well-respected in both the West and the Eastern bloc, Tanner was an ideal candidate for bridging the gap between China and the outside world. Of course, Tanner did not respond to the Chinese interest with goodwill only. WEI's earnings had been flat for several years at that time, and Tanner was seeking new avenues for foreign exploration and production. He sensed that if WEI penetrated China early, it might be able to enjoy some first-mover advantages.[1]

In short, China's new policy and its drive for modernization, Tanner's long-time association with the Eastern bloc, and WEI's desire to expand its global operations made WEI a pioneering U.S. firm in the new China.

POLITICS AND THE TAIBAO COAL MINE

Since the initiation of the Open Door policy in the late 1970s, developing the energy sector to support industrial development had become a priority of the Chinese government. Of its various energy resources, coal is the most important to China; three-quarters of the country's energy demand is met by coal. China's proven coal reserves exceed 900 billion tons, placing it third in the world behind the Soviet Union and the United States.

Source: Mike W. Peng

[1] M. B. Lieberman and D. B. Montgomery, "First Mover Advantages: A Survey," *Strategic Management Journal* 9 (summer special issue), 1988, pp. 41–58.

Total estimated reserves, however, are in the neighborhood of 2 trillion tons. At current production levels, this would supply China's needs for 2,000 years.[2]

Despite the abundance of its coal supply, China's lack of capital and technology to effectively exploit the coal in sufficient amount to meet energy needs led to a national headache in the 1980s. In many parts of the country factories had to shut down for one or two days a month due to energy shortages, and at one point, Shanghai had only two days' worth of coal reserves on hand for power generation. It was evident that without the development of its energy sector, China's goal of modernization would not be realized. Therefore, finding foreign partners that would help to develop its energy resources held very high priority.

In 1980 China opened its premier coal mine, the Taibao mine in Shanxi Province of northern China, to international bidding in search of a foreign partner. One of the largest open-pit coal mines in the world, the Taibao mine was the largest energy project China had ever opened to foreign firms. Eight Western firms participated in the bidding—three from the United States, two from Germany, and one each from France, Japan, and the United Kingdom. Not surprisingly, WEI won the contract.

Politics were instrumental in this process, and China's central leadership was heavily involved in this "pet project." Politically, China desired a major U.S. company as their partner as a means of sending an unambiguous signal to U.S. investors that the Open Door policy was genuine. Unlike European and Japanese companies, which had been doing business with China for years, the United States had had virtually no business with China until 1979, when the two countries normalized their diplomatic relations. Decades of hostility between the two countries had made U.S. investors especially suspicious. However, China sensed that the United States possessed more advanced technologies and more abundant capital than other countries and that courting U.S. investment was strategically important to their Open Door policy.[3] Of the three U.S. firms involved in the bidding, WEI was the most respected and financially the strongest. Moreover, Tanner's assiduous cultivation of *guanxi* ("connections") with Chinese leaders, especially Deng Xiaoping, and his previous contacts throughout the Eastern bloc was an important consideration in China's selection of WEI as their sole foreign partner. (The box explains the Chinese tradition of *guanxi.*)

THE ECONOMICS OF THE TAIBAO JOINT VENTURE

Upon winning the bid, Western Energy, Inc., became the foreign partner in the 50-50 joint venture incorporated as the Taibao Mine Group in China in 1982. A renewable 30-year, joint-venture contract was signed. The Chinese partners were a consortium of Chinese organizations led by China National Coal Corporation, the country's leading coal producer (see Table 1). The venture called for $700 million in capital endowment, with each side contributing $200 million and the remaining $300 million to be syndicated by 39 international banks (see Table 1). It was anticipated that at full capacity, the mine would produce 12 million tons a year and employ 3,000 workers, 20 to 30 of whom would be WEI expatriates.

---

[2] J. P. Huang, "Fueling the Economy," *The China Business Review*, March-April 1991, p. 22.

[3] B. S. Chen, "Economic Development Strategy for China's Coastal Areas and U.S. Investment in China," *Meiguo Yanjiu (Journal of American Studies*, Beijing, China) 2(3), 1988, pp. 7-25.

The Importance of *Guanxi* in China

The Chinese word *guanxi,* meaning "connections," refers to the intricate, pervasive network of personal relationships every Chinese cultivates with energy, subtlety, and imagination. These relationships between people and between organizations contain implicit obligations, assurances, and understandings and they govern Chinese attitudes toward social and business relationships. A *guanxi* relationship of trust and mutual benefit establishes an excellent foundation for a long-term relationship. *Guanxi* ties are especially helpful in dealing with the Chinese bureaucracy, where personal interpretations are often applied in lieu of legal interpretations.

Although *guanxi* networks have mushroomed since the reform in China in 1979,[1] their roots are strong and deeply embedded in the Chinese culture. Traditionally the value of strong family ties has served to emphasize getting things done through *whom you know*. A *guanxi* is neither officially acknowledged nor put into writing. The parties to a *guanxi* network place high value on reciprocity, trust, and implicit understanding between the parties. (I.e., "I give you a favor now, and I believe that you will return a favor to me in the future whenever I need it.")

Due to cultural differences and language barriers, visitors to China cannot cultivate *guanxi* with the depth possible between two Chinese. Nevertheless, good relations can be developed, and things can be accomplished. A foreigner will know he or she has developed *guanxi* with a Chinese when the Chinese person addresses him or her as "old friend." Among U.S. dignitaries who enjoy this "old friend" status are Richard Nixon, Henry Kissinger, and Jimmy Carter, who helped to build a China–U.S. diplomatic relationship in the 1970s.

[1] M. W. Peng, "A Process Model of Governance Transformation for Planned Economics in Transition," working paper, University of Washington, Seattle, 1992.

Table 1
Partners and Financing of the Taibao Mine Venture

United States (50% share)	China (50% share)
Western Energy, Inc. ($200 million initial capital)	China National Coal Corp. China Coal Import/Export Corp. China International Trust & Investment Corp. Province of Shanxi ($200 million initial capital)
$300 million loan syndicated by 39 international banks (each side guaranteeing 50 percent of the loan)	

During the "courtship" period, 1980–82, WEI had responded to Chinese interest with extravagant promises about such things as the scale of the mine, the Chinese workers' salaries, and the amount of coal it could export. It agreed to export 75 percent of the total output and to assume complete responsibility for marketing the coal in the export market. Noted for their preference for "general principles" in the negotiations, the Chinese took these promises seriously, regarding them as the foundation upon which details could be worked out later.

However, by the time the joint venture contract had been signed and the feasibility study began, the economics of the project had become shaky in light of falling world coal prices. WEI was forced to hedge its earlier promises and it began to pressure the Chinese side to grant it various concessions. For example, WEI attempted to force China Coal

Import/Export Corporation, one of the Chinese partners, to buy WEI's share of export coal at prevailing international prices, reneging on its earlier promise to market the coal itself in the international market. The Chinese negotiators were surprised by this, and intense arguments between the two sides occurred. Several times during the negotiations, disputes came close to derailing the project, but Tanner and the Chinese political leadership intervened each time to enforce a solution. Numerous public ceremonies throughout the negotiations bound the prestige of Tanner and the Chinese leadership even more tightly to the consummation of the project. By 1985 WEI had won several concessions from the Chinese side, including the shifting of responsibility for export marketing to China Coal Import/Export Corporation.

OPERATIONAL PROBLEMS: CENTRAL VERSUS LOCAL *GUANXI*

The operational phase of the Taibao venture, which began in 1986, proved to be even more problematic than the negotiation phase. Although getting the mine up and running was undeniably a major achievement, by September 1990, the project still was not certified as "complete." In 1990, its most productive year, it produced only three quarters of its 12-million-ton capacity and suffered a $31 million loss. Exports were probably less than half of the eight to nine million tons WEI originally anticipated.

Four sources of problems contributed to the venture's lackluster performance. First, continuing low world coal prices prevented the venture from earning the foreign exchange necessary to break even. Second, lower-than-expected coal quality—high sulfur content in one seam, high ash content in another—further depressed the coal's international marketability. Technical problems such as defective equipment and the workers' lack of training constituted a third source of problems. To WEI, however, the greatest obstacle was the lack of cooperation between WEI and its local partners, despite its influential *guanxi* with the central leadership.

Tanner was very skillful in cultivating *guanxi* with the central leadership in Beijing and thus was able to get them to grant him concessions. This did not help WEI to develop close *guanxi* relations with the local partners, however. Many WEI managers reported that disputes over production and marketing strategies were common among the partners. For instance, the Americans would want to decrease the production of high-sulfur coal—which could only be sold on the domestic market for local currency—and to increase the production of low-sulfur coal for the export market. However, the Chinese insisted that due to the depressed export market, producing a large amount of low-sulfur coal would result in large inventories and thus aggravate the venture's cash flow problems.

Instead of working together, each side seemed to blame the other for whatever problems occurred. On another occasion, WEI accused the China Coal Import/Export Corporation of failing to market the coal in the export market aggressively. In response, the Chinese managers pointed out that WEI had retreated from its earlier promises to do the marketing themselves. Due to political pressure from China's central leadership, China Coal Import/Export Corporation had reluctantly agreed to assume the exporting functions for the Taibao venture in 1985. Now a depressed world market and the less-than-expected coal quality gave the reluctant Chinese partner an excuse for not living up to its promises. Many WEI officials believed that their Chinese partners deliberately exacerbated these problems to spite the political pressures that forced them to make concessions to WEI in the first place.

STILL MORE POLITICS

In June 1989 the Tiananmen incident in Beijing shocked the world. Foreign businesspeople pulled out of China immediately, and international investors led by the World Bank hesitated to commit further funds to China. The Chinese leadership desperately needed to prove to the world that, despite all the tragedies, the 10-year-old Open Door policy would continue, but the government's credibility had declined to a new low. Once again, the Taibao venture played into the hands of the Chinese leadership. In spite of internal disagreement at WEI, Arnold Tanner went back to China in a "business as usual" fashion in late 1989 to meet with the Chinese leaders, who used this visit by their "old friend" as a photo opportunity to appease the West.

Inside WEI, with the Company's financial situation worsening, discussions of withdrawing from the Taibao venture continued. Similarly to Deng Xiaoping's rule of China, Tanner dismissed such ideas, and urging a long-term perspective. The Chinese leadership, wishing to save political face, wanted to avoid the failure of a flagship project. Therefore, despite huge financial losses that depleted WEI's cash flow, the Taibao venture continued until Tanner's sudden death in August 1990.

EXIT?

Ray Schon was named Tanner's successor as chairman of WEI. Within weeks, Schon had assessed the company's overall strategic position and he concluded that the business climate of the 1990s was vastly different from what it had been in the 1980s. To him, the 1990s climate could be defined by a lack of liquidity in financial markets, recessionary pressure on global economies, increasing volatility in energy prices, and chronic instability in world markets. The year in which Arnold Tanner died, 1990, left the company with a net loss of $1.7 billion. In response, Schon instituted a major restructuring and divestiture program that would build on the company's proven strengths and give it "the operational and financial flexibility to respond in a timely manner to unpredictable markets." Specifically, the program would sell off unprofitable lines to reduce debt—which was $7.4 billion in 1990—and focus WEI's resources on those businesses in which it excelled—oil, natural gas, and chemicals.

The changes in corporate strategy determined the fate of the Taibao venture. In his announcement of the restructuring program, Schon publicly stated his intention to withdraw from the unprofitable project—which may have been Tanner's favorite project but was never part of WEI's core business. To do this, WEI would have to write off $200 million as an unprofitable investment, but it would be relieved of $150 million in loan guarantees. WEI would have only two options: to sell its share to its Chinese partners, or to sell its share to another foreign investor. In either case, Ray Schon knew that his upcoming trip to China would be a stormy one.

DISCUSSION QUESTIONS

1. What were the perceived first-mover advantages for WEI? How did WEI exploit these advantages?
2. Why did Arnold Tanner's connections with the Chinese leadership not lead to successful cooperation between WEI and its Chinese partners?
3. If you were Ray Schon, would you have decided to pull out of the Taibao venture?

American Copier Company in Shanghai

Unlike some Western firms' early-entry, high-profile approach to China (e.g., that of WEI), American Copier Company's China strategy was cautious, low-profile, and aimed at building cooperative relations with local partners. ACC spent about four years (1983–87) negotiating its Shanghai joint venture, and apparently the time was well spent. For ACC, China has proved to be a good match, offering both low-cost design and labor and a growing market for copying machines and products. Formed in late 1987, the $30 million ACC Shanghai had become number-one in China's growing copier market by 1989, and it planned to capture an even greater market share in the future.

ACC AND THE SHANGHAI JOINT VENTURE

With annual sales in the neighborhood of $10 billion throughout the 1980s, ACC is a global company serving worldwide document-processing markets. Its activities encompass developing, manufacturing, marketing, servicing, and financing a wide range of document-processing products and services. Its copiers, duplicators, production publishers, electronic printers, facsimile products, scanners, and computer products are marketed in more than 130 countries. In addition to its worldwide network of dealers and distributors, ACC maintains research and development facilities in Canada, Great Britain, Japan, and the United States. Before joint-venturing with the Chinese, ACC already had substantial experience with joint venture operations in Australia, Brazil, Germany, Great Britain, India, and Japan.

When ACC entered China in the early 1980s through exporting, the copier market in China was dominated by such Japanese makers as Canon, Minolta, Ricoh, and Toshiba. Many of these companies had served the China market for a long time, but ACC was the first copier producer to establish a joint venture in the country. Though it would take ACC significantly longer than its competitors (some of which had technology-transfer agreements with Chinese firms) to show a return on its $15 million investment, the company's dominant position in a restricted-size market undoubtedly reflected greater official support for the joint venture than for its competitors.

ACC's initial exporting to China in the early 1980s was moderately successful. In order to capture a larger share of the growing Chinese market, ACC considered a technology transfer agreement in 1983. It decided to pursue a joint venture instead, however, due to China's underdeveloped intellectual-property-protection regime. Numerous sites were considered for the venture, and all the local authorities who knew of ACC's interest courted ACC for its investment. ACC avoided involvement with local Chinese politics and did not make vague promises or agree to "general principles" in order to gain favor with the Chinese. Eventually ACC decided to locate in Shanghai due to the large concentrations of components suppliers and skilled labor in the area.

ACC's Shanghai venture partners were the Bank of China, which held 5 percent of the venture and provided $10 million investment, and the Shanghai Photo Industry Company, which held 44 percent and contributed existing plants, equipment, and some personnel assessed at $5 million. ACC held the remaining 51 percent of the venture and invested $15 million (see Table 1). Established in 1987 with a 30-year, renewable joint-venture contract, ACC Shanghai has a 10-year renewable technology license to produce desktop copiers and accessories and other copier products. The license gives ACC

Source: Mike W. Peng

Table 1
Partners and Financing of American Copier Company's Shanghai Venture

United States (51% share)	China (49% share)
American Copier Co. ($15 million initial investment)	Shanghai Photo Industry Co. (holding 44% share; contributing plants and labor assessed at $5 million)
	Bank of China (holding 5% share; $10 million investment)

Shanghai the right to use ACC's desktop office copier technology. ACC Shanghai was designed to produce low-end and mid-range copiers suitable for the China market with the capability of switching to produce more advanced designs. At full capacity, anticipated for 1994, ACC Shanghai expected to be capable of producing 40,000 units annually with 900 employees. By September 1992, ACC Shanghai had more than 600 employees, six of whom were expatriates.

LOCALIZING PRODUCTION

Despite the Chinese desire to export a high percentage of the venture's output, the ACC negotiators managed to persuade the Chinese that since the models ACC would produce in China would be mid-range to low-end ones suitable for China, the focus should be on the domestic market. In return, ACC accepted a stipulation that 70 percent of the venture's components would be sourced locally by the end of 1992. In September 1992 ACC managers claimed that they were on schedule to achieving this goal, although the process had been difficult since no local suppliers had initially had the necessary technical expertise or equipment for producing the quality of components needed by ACC Shanghai.

To overcome these obstacles, ACC instituted an intense vendor development program. ACC, through its Shanghai venture, either transferred technology or provided technical support to approximately 60 suppliers, most of them in Shanghai. In addition to training the suppliers how to use the particular technology or equipment that was transferred, ACC also coached them in materials management and handling and in accounting. Moreover, ACC Shanghai developed a close working relationship with the Shanghai Foreign Investment Commission, which provided funding to local companies for upgrading their plants and purchasing the new technology.

ACC estimates that it spent several million dollars in this early period on training, support, and monitoring of Chinese suppliers to ensure consistent quality and delivery. Some of these development costs were charged to the suppliers; the others were absorbed by ACC Shanghai. Although the training has paid off in improved quality of locally supplied components, Chinese components still tend to be produced at above-world-market prices, which increases the final cost of ACC Shanghai copiers. By company estimates, locally sourced components cost 10–20 percent more than imported ones would.

ENSURING QUALITY

ACC has been known throughout the world for its quality products. All components used by ACC Shanghai are subject to ACC quality standards. The parent company instituted its corporate quality-control culture in the venture to ensure that ACC Shanghai's output would be on par with ACC products manufactured in other countries. These efforts were directed at all levels, not just in interaction with the end user. The company's "LUTI" system—*learn, use, teach, inspect*—was instituted, with each management level teaching it to the level below as well as to the new employees.

Monthly meetings of a Customer Satisfaction Review Board were established by ACC Shanghai to help ensure the reputation of its products. Composed of representatives from the marketing, service, distribution, management, engineering, and quality control departments, the board examines complaints and conducts customer surveys to determine where improvement is needed. The first survey, conducted in 1989, one year after the first copier rolled off the production line, indicated 90 percent customer satisfaction with the venture's products. Further proof of ACC Shanghai's success in attaining high quality came from the Shanghai municipal government, which awarded it the Shanghai Quality Award in 1989 and again in 1990, and from the parent company, which awarded the venture an in-house quality award in 1990.

CAPTURING THE MARKET

The first ACC Shanghai 2020 copier was produced in October 1988, little more than a year after the joint-venture contract was signed. A mid-range model, the 2020 did not incorporate the newest technology, but its reliable, sturdy operation was very suitable for the China market at the time.

In order to meet demand outside the Shanghai area for its copiers, ACC Shanghai—with help from its partner, Shanghai Photo Industry Company—established a nationwide distribution, sales, and service network. The network included more than 100 dealers throughout China, all of whom were trained by ACC Shanghai. Three ACC representative offices—in Beijing, Guangzhou, and Shanghai—provided additional dealer support in such areas as training, inventory, and advertising.

A vigorous advertising campaign was launched through television and newspaper media in China to increase the publicity of ACC Shanghai in 1987. Competing against Japanese brands like Canon, Minolta, Ricoh, and Toshiba, ACC Shanghai adroitly named its products *Shang Am* (pronounced *Hu Mei* in Mandarin Chinese), meaning "Shanghai Beauty."[1] U.S. brand names are generally admired among the Chinese, and products from Shanghai historically are renowned for their high quality in China. Thus, the catchy name *Shanghai Beauty,* highlighting the combination of U.S. technology and Shanghai production, created an attractive and trustworthy image among the Chinese. Moreover, despite the higher cost of locally sourced components, ACC Shanghai was able to price its copiers competitively within the range of Japanese offerings.

Vigorous quality standards, extensive dealer networks, an aggressive and skillfully executed advertising campaign, and reasonable prices all helped ACC Shanghai to become the number-one seller of copy machines in China. In 1989 ACC Shanghai held 32 percent of the Chinese desktop copier market, and by late 1990 it held about 45 percent.

PROBLEMS

As expected, the China market was full of problems, some of which were anticipated and some not. The original feasibility study proved to be overly optimistic in its assumptions of production costs and market size. "These miscalculations were perhaps unavoidable," John White, ACC's vice president for international operations, commented, "given the unforeseen nature of some of the factors that have affected ACC Shanghai's performance."

---

[1] *Mei Guo,* the name for America in Mandarin Chinese, China's official language, means "beautiful country."

In addition to the higher costs of locally sourced components, the devaluation of the Chinese yuan against the U.S. dollar in the mid-1980s resulted in higher costs for imported components. Perhaps more important, the introduction of purchase controls as part of the government's austerity policy in 1988 has resulted in a far smaller market than ACC had envisioned. In order to purchase a copier, a prospective buyer must first obtain permission from several government agencies. This market-restricting policy was strengthened by the government's post-Tiananmen austerity program. The system seriously inhibits market forces; ACC estimates the *real* market in China as five times the present market size.

The austerity program has not changed the government's general Open Door policy or its policy of supporting joint-venture companies. Therefore, ACC's joint-venture strategy has paid off in this changed situation, since government agencies are more likely to approve the purchase of a domestically produced, reasonably priced copier like "Shang Am" than the purchase of an imported model, even when the two models are of the same performance and price level. Thus ACC Shanghai receives official support even though it has not deliberately cultivated *guanxi* with the government.

Problems unrelated to the macroeconomic environment have also confronted ACC Shanghai. For instance, its paper-feeder components malfunctioned due to the poor quality of available copy paper in China. ACC Shanghai engineers redesigned the feeders to handle the low-grade paper used in most Chinese offices.

FUTURE PROSPECTS

In September 1992, as ACC Shanghai neared its fifth year of operations, John White envisioned that ACC Shanghai should focus on designing two new products in the immediate future—a low-end model for developing segments in the China market and a high-end model for the more sophisticated segments. ACC Shanghai engineers collaborated with ACC corporate engineers to develop prototypes for the two models, and then total design responsibility was turned over to ACC Shanghai. The first model of the low-end copier, expected to become a major product line in China, was scheduled to enter the China market in 1993. Small volumes of the high-end model were expected to enter the market in 1994.

With the existing 2020 mid-range model, ACC Shanghai will soon be able to offer three models, each targeted at a particular segment of the China market. Whether other new product lines will be manufactured by ACC Shanghai has not been determined. "My inclination is to continue the three-model operations for a few more years," John White commented. "We have built up a vendor base and have spent a long time training people in quality control and other areas. But starting a new product line is very taxing; I wouldn't let our joint ventures in India and Brazil, for example, even contemplate it. While there are advantages to keeping everything in one organization, it could be too much for a young venture like the one we have in Shanghai. I want to make sure that ACC Shanghai continues to operate on a sound financial footing. This venture is already ahead of where our first venture in Japan was at the equivalent time. Eventually, I'd like to see it become like ACC Japan or ACC UK, a stand-alone operation with its own product lines."

On the other hand, White also noted that achievement of ACC Shanghai's ambitious aspirations will depend on two factors. First, the market must be expanded, which will require the abolition or liberalization of the government's purchase-control system. The Chinese government has not seemed willing to liberalize this stringent policy, however, and ACC has had little influence on it. To expand its customer bases (and to project a good corporate image), ACC Shanghai has been giving selected high schools in China a gift package consisting of copiers and accessories. Second, costs must be reduced, which will require further improvements in the local supplier network. Given existing good *guanxi* with the local suppliers built up over the years of cooperative working relations, ACC Shanghai feels confident that the component-cost problems can be overcome and that the costs of locally sourced components can be brought to international levels in a few years.

DISCUSSION QUESTIONS

1. Why did ACC decide to engage in a joint venture with the Chinese? Compare the advantages and disadvantages of the joint venture mode with those of the export mode and the wholly owned subsidiary mode.
2. In light of the obstacles ACC Shanghai faces, what would you recommend as its course of action for achieving its goals?

Multigama

In 1946 Romania regained much of the territory it had lost earlier in World War II, but Bessarabias and Bukovina remained in the hands of the Soviet Union. The Soviet-backed regime, of which King Michael had served as figurehead since 1944, took over firm control. The Romanian government became the most Stalinist of all the regimes in Eastern Europe, which earned it a certain independence. Because the Soviet Union felt more secure with this "hard-line" regime, it withdrew its troops in 1958, much earlier than it did from other Eastern European countries. Thus the Romanian government enjoyed more independence than other Soviet bloc governments in their internal operations and in their contact and trade with the West. When the Soviet Union invaded Czechoslovakia in 1968, President Nicolae Ceauşescu's refusal to support the effort made him extremely popular with the Romanian people. It also made him popular with Western leaders; Ceauşescu was applauded as a champion of democratic reforms. Ceauşescu was actually increasing the internal control during this period, and Romania soon had a more centrally controlled economy than other countries in Eastern Europe except Albania.

Ceauşescu liked to do things on a grand scale. He ordered oil refineries built even though Romania had no oil for them to refine. He constructed massive steel mills that produced products in large quantity but of such low quality that there was little demand for them outside of Romania. He instituted a policy of economic self-sufficiency that resulted in a large central bureaucracy, firms of tremendous size, and production of thousands of products at costs that were prohibitive. In an effort to modernize the country, he destroyed thousands of beautiful old buildings, including whole villages. In most cases the architecture of the buildings that replaced them was nondescript at best. In other cases, wide empty roadways, leading to public buildings, replaced the old

Source: This case was prepared by Associate Professor John Butler as the basis for class discussion, rather than to illustrate either effective or ineffective handling of an administrative situation.

buildings. Agriculture was largely ignored during this period, and the living standard dropped as Ceauşescu attempted to reduce Romania's foreign debt.

In the late 1980s the economy started to collapse. A group in the communist governmental hierarchy, prompted by a popular uprising, overthrew Ceauşescu. After the overthrow, Ion Iliescu, head of the National Salvation Front, was voted into power. Although Iliescu was nominally a communist, his government quickly attempted to portray itself as an important force in the movement toward free markets. This led to the passage of Law Number 15, which provided that all of Romania's state-owned enterprises would be transformed into either joint-stock or limited-liability companies. It provided that Romanian citizens would receive, free of charge, nominal securities representing 30 percent of the nominal share capital of the newly created companies. The law also created the National Agency for Privatization. The Commercial Companies Privatization Law Number 58, enacted in August 1991, specified how this privatization should occur.

Private companies became legal, and small firms began to emerge immediately, especially in Bucharest. Private enterprise was seen initially in the retail sector, but eventually manufacturing firms began to appear in larger numbers. In some cases, such as restaurants, these firms charged much higher prices, but they were also generally perceived as providing better services or better products. By late winter of 1992, the privatization board had completed its initial evaluations on a series of smaller firms and had effectively privatized 50 *very* small state enterprises. Their success with this initial series of privatizations gave the National Agency for Privatization confidence that it could move forward and meet the government's five-year timetable for privatization. In addition, it was meeting with more success interesting foreign firms in joint ventures with some of the larger state-owned enterprises.

INTRODUCTION

Early in March 1992, Dan Banu left his job as the chief of the quality assurance department at Aversa, the largest pump manufacturer in Romania, to join his partners at Multigama on a full-time basis. Dan had joined Aversa in 1979, as a member of a team that designed pumps for the Romanian nuclear power plant being built at Cernavoda. The plant had been funded by a $400 million grant from the Canadian government. Dan and his colleagues' department handled designing, purchasing, and shipping of special pumps for this power plant. The first nuclear pumps were produced in 1984, and by 1987 they were producing pumps that were actually being used in the new plant.

The work group at Aversa was very unusual in that the engineers were in constant contact with the Canadians. At the time, contact between Romanians and Westerners was very restricted, but because this unit needed to be familiar with the ANSII Code requirements for nuclear plants, frequent foreign contact was required. There was some political surveillance of the employees in this unit, but because their conversations with the Canadians were highly technical, the political oversight officials concluded that the contacts did not constitute a political problem. However, the engineers valued these foreign contacts, which were forbidden for most Romanians, and they enjoyed their conversations, which often centered on subjects with little technical relevance.

It was during this time that Dan and his colleagues concluded that the ways things were done at Aversa were not optimal. They could see that the managerial practices lagged far behind those used in other countries, especially Canada. With the overthrow of Nicolae and Elena Ceauşescu in December 1989, the Aversa management was removed. Ion Iliescu, leader of the National Salvation Front, became the head of the interim government. After six weeks in office, Iliescu restored the jobs of the deposed managers as part of of an effort to keep the electorate sufficiently happy to vote for him in the upcoming elections. To further enhance his party's chances in the election, he increased wages for workers and managers across the country, with no strings attached. At this point Dan and seven of his colleagues decided that Aversa could not be changed from within and that they must start their own business.

The first thing they needed was the 100,000 lae that the government required as a business license application fee.[1] They pulled together the money and got the license. However, they didn't have the manufacturing facilities or cash resources needed to produce pumps, so they entered into a business arrangement with a Syrian exchange student who was interested in selling bubble gum, curtains, and shoes. He sent them goods on consignment, which they would then sell. An empty house was used as a warehouse. The founding group of engineers appreciated this contact, because it provided them with some valuable managerial experience. At this time little commercial interest was being directed at Romania. As Dan Banu stated, "Only the Arab and Turkish people had the courage to come to Romania in 1990. They didn't have the best merchandise, but they were not afraid to come." They named the new firm *Syryus.*

The first shipment of consigned goods arrived in October 1990. Orders were solicited and received almost exclusively by telephone. Interestingly, all of the goods were sold to state-owned trade companies, which then resold them to individual consumers. The eight engineers remained at Aversa during this period and worked in the evenings and on weekends at the trading company.[2] As revenues increased, the engineers began to quit their jobs at Aversa so that they could work at Syryus full time. Dan Banu was the last of the founders to quit his job at Aversa, and by the time he did, Syryus had evolved into a new firm, Multigama. After a time, the Syrian student had decided he wanted to do more than just consign goods. It was decided that he would return to Romania and enter into a joint venture with the engineers. This business relationship resulted in company expansion, and sales increased rapidly. This provided the entrepreneur-engineers the cash flow they needed to begin manufacturing pumps.

MULTIGAMA BEGINS

They began with the manufacture of small pumps designed specifically for small farms. The pump they built also proved ideal for smaller buildings, especially those in Bucharest, where the water pressure was notoriously low. In addition, hot water is produced centrally in Bucharest and then distributed to buildings. Additional pumps permit the users to enjoy a more effective distribution, especially if they are on upper floors or have multiple outlets for hot water.

Production runs were kept small in the beginning. The partners purchased 10 motors, some miscellaneous parts, and a total of 20 kg of raw materials. Once the pumps were produced, they were sold quickly, and all of the profit was reinvested. This reinvestment was necessary, because bank credit was not available. At this time Romanian banks required that loans be secured by assets worth at least 130 percent of the value of the loan. The banks had little expertise in evaluating assets, so they tended to be ultraconservative. The legislature was still discussing what to do about land titles, thus the banks were unwilling to accept land as collateral. Even if they had been willing, the existing law limited the rights of property transfer in 1990. After the government

[1] 1 U.S. dollar = 197 lei in 1990 at the official bank exchange rate.

[2] The normal workweek in Romania was Monday through Saturday at this time.

returned the land to the people it feared that farmers would be swindled out of their land by unscrupulous investors, so it prohibited land sales. In many cases the new owners did not have titles; they had pieces of paper that stated they would get title to the land in the future if it was decided that people could have title to the land. Although villagers were able to acquire 6 to 10 hectares, they did not get proper titles either. They received a piece of paper that stated they had acquired the right to acquire the land. Thus, during this period, new businesses were unlikely to look to banks as a source of funds, and there were no other institutional sources.

As the demand for their pumps began to increase, the firm was divided into two divisions, the trading company, *Syryus,* and the pump manufacturing company, *Multigama.* They attempted to find a location in Bucharest for their production facilities. They thought they could get the space they needed if they agreed to pay all the overhead and maintenance costs for an existing facility, since the decrease in demand for Romanian goods had left many firms with excess production space. However, government officials were reluctant to agree to this type of arrangement, and since the government still controlled all the larger firms, Multigama was unable to arrange for any work space in Bucharest. They spent from February to September of 1991 looking for suitable production space and fell far behind schedule. Without their own production facility, they were forced to have existing firms manufacture the components they needed.

A great contrast existed between state-owned firms and the newer private firms. Phrases such as "a warm place" and "an orphanage for older workers" were frequently used to describe the state enterprises. For instance, Dan Banu felt that 2,500 employees could achieve the same output as the 5,000 Aversa employees. He felt that privatization might not be able to solve this problem, because social networks had been the source of new employees for many firms in Romania. This meant that many employees were related or close friends. Lacking established staffing and evaluation criteria, these friendships and family relationships might make professional human-resource practices impossible.

PRODUCTION BEGINS

For these reasons Multigama decided to find a private firm to do their manufacturing. In October 1991 they identified a small firm 100 kilometers from Bucharest that had been purchased by its employees. The firm was currently producing small car trailers, and it had the necessary equipment and employees to produce the small pumps required by Multigama. They entered into a manufacturing agreement with this firm.

The production arrangements were completed just in time for Multigama to attend the International Industrial Product Exhibit held in Bucharest in October 1991. Multigama rented the cheapest display space available. On the first day of the fair a pipe broke, and all water-using facilities, including restrooms, stopped working. Fair officials went to Aversa for help, but they could not do anything. At this point Multigama stepped in and provided one of their pumps. This earned them a lot of free publicity at the fair, as well as the personal gratitude of those exhibiting at and attending the fair. In addition, because theirs was one of the cheapest spaces at the fair, it was near a nonworking drinking fountain. This allowed them to attach one of their pumps to the nonworking fountain, which not only showed how well their pumps worked but also enhanced their space and attracted additional people to their area. This led to their first order for 10 pumps. At the time of the fair they had manufactured only five pumps, so this order was essential to their next production run, which was set at 30 pumps.

After the fair they began to advertise in newspapers, more to inform people that they had pumps than to sell them. Because of supply shortages, it was more important to advise people in Romania where they could find things than to generate new demand. A large number of newspapers had been founded after the overthrow of Nicolae and Elena Ceauşescu, and the great amount of competition kept advertising costs low.

The initial batch of 30 pumps sold quickly. Gradually, production runs were increased to 300 to 500 pumps. Currently Multigama is manufacturing between 500 to 700 pumps each month. Newspaper advertising has been eliminated, because the partners believe their potential customers are aware of them. Management still views advertising as merely a way of informing predisposed buyers as to where they can purchase the goods they need. Also, Multigama is selling all of the pumps it is currently capable of manufacturing, which reduces their interest in advertising.

Product development has also expanded rapidly. The initial selection of three pumps has been expanded to five models, each of which comes in two or three sizes. Currently, the profit margins are lower and the turnaround is slower on the industrial (Multigama) side of the firm. However, management is more interested in this side of the business. It accounts for over 80 percent of the revenue, and management expects this percentage to increase in the future. They have more expertise in this side of the business, too. They have seen that it is easier to get a trading business started, and they expect margins to gradually fall in this area as more competitors emerge.

The organizational structure of Multigama has become more formal as the business has grown. The eight original partners form the General Owner Assembly, from which they elect a president. Once a month an Administrative Board, consisting of the owners and the president, reviews a report from the president. In addition, the president must prepare the General Balance and Financial Report, which is due each March. This report is also required by the government. It is expected that as the government's privatization effort expands, additional financial reporting will be required, and this will impact the firm.

DIVERSIFICATION

Multigama is planning to build a facility for both its own use and to provide rental income. They plan to have apartments on the upper floors and commercial space for their own administrative offices and to rent to other firms on the first floor. The rent will provide needed revenue, while offering them room for expansion as the firm grows. They have found a potential partner/investor, who wants to build a building in the center of Bucharest. The government paperwork has been completed, and a contractor has been hired. The building is expected to take one year to complete. To further test the feasibility of this idea, Multigama ran a newspaper advertisement to announce what they were doing. The response was encouraging; several businesses have already committed to rent some of the first-floor commercial space. They believe demand will be high because there is a housing shortage in Bucharest, and many of the commercial buildings started by Ceauşescu are of poor quality and will probably be demolished rather than completed.

Multigama is also considering the possibility of manufacturing food-processing equipment. They have been developing a relationship with a Lynnwood, Washington, firm headed by a Romanian expatriate. This potential partner has expertise in refrigeration, which Multigama lacks.

It has been very difficult to attract investors because Romania is not viewed as a good place to invest. The EEC, Canada, and the IMF have directed their investments toward energy generation, because there is currently a shortage of energy production capability in Romania. In addition, most foreign credits have been going to state-owned firms, and

Romania's existing communist government status has resulted in its not being considered for some foreign investment programs, especially those with government sponsorship.

However, the best employees have been gradually moving to private firms. In the old days, the large state firms were required to produce an item domestically, even if only one of the items was needed. With privatization, the larger state-owned firms have been left with labor forces geared to this type of response mode. The turn toward free market operations and privatization has led to much speculation about what form of commercial activity is most appropriate for Romania. Dan Banu feels that these factors will combine to produce an environment that is more conducive to investments in new private start-ups.

THE FUTURE

Banu and his partners are doing a lot of thinking and planning. They are trying to determine where the best opportunities for profit exist and how to obtain the necessary cash, or investors, in order to exploit these opportunities. In addition, they are seeking ways to move from a purely domestic mode to one more focused on foreign trade. Labor costs are currently quite low in Romania, which will allow Multigama to price its product competitively, and their pumps seem ideal for use in many less-developed countries. They are also concerned about their lack of managerial experience; all of the founders still consider themselves primarily engineers. The potential effects of privatization are unclear. They are aware that Aversa may find a powerful and efficient foreign partner, which could limit Multigama's potential for growth.

DISCUSSION QUESTIONS

1. As an executive of a MNE, would you consider investing in Multigama? What would be the main issues to consider?
2. What about investing in Aversa? What are the advantages and disadvantages of investing in each?
3. Given the industries in which Romania had invested under the communist regime, how likely are these industries to help lead Romania toward economic prosperity?
4. As an IMF or World Bank official, how would you target lending to assist in the development of Romania?
5. Given their success to date, and the opportunities they have, what advice would you give to Multigama's management?

PART THREE

The Global Trade and Investment Environment

International Trade Theory

CHAPTER 4

A TALE OF TWO NATIONS

In 1970 living standards in Ghana and South Korea were roughly comparable. Ghana's 1970 gross domestic product (GDP) per head was $250, and South Korea's was $260. By 1988 the situation had changed dramatically. South Korea then had a GDP per head of $4,081, while Ghana's was only $369, reflecting vastly different economic growth rates. Between 1965 and 1988 the average annual growth rate in Ghana's GDP was 1.5 percent, while South Korea achieved a rate of over 9 percent per annum. What explains the difference between Ghana and South Korea? There is no simple answer, but there are reasons for believing that the attitudes of both countries toward international trade provide part of the explanation. A study by the World Bank suggests that whereas the South Korean government has had a strong protrade bias, the actions of the Ghanaian government discouraged domestic producers from becoming involved in international trade. • Ghana was the first of Great Britain's West African colonies to become independent, in 1957. Its first president, Kwame Nkrumah, influenced the rest of the continent with his theories of pan-African socialism. For Ghana this meant the imposition of high tariffs on many imports, an import substitution policy aimed at fostering Ghana self-sufficiency in certain manufactured goods, and the adoption of policies that discouraged Ghana's enterprises from engaging in exports. The results were an unmitigated disaster that transformed one of Africa's most prosperous nations into one of the world's poorest. • As an illustration of how Ghana's antitrade policies destroyed the Ghanaian economy, consider the Ghanaian government's involvement in the cocoa trade. A combination of favorable climate, good soils, and ready access to world shipping routes has given Ghana an absolute advantage in cocoa production. Quite simply, it is one of the best places in the world to grow cocoa. As a consequence, Ghana was the world's largest producer and exporter of cocoa in 1957. Then the government of the newly independent nation created a state-controlled cocoa marketing board. The board was given the authority to fix prices for cocoa and was designated the sole buyer of all cocoa grown in Ghana. The board held down the prices that it paid farmers for cocoa, while selling the cocoa that it bought from them on the world market at world prices. Thus it might buy cocoa from farmers at 25 cents a pound and sell it on the world market for the world price of 50 cents a pound. In effect, the board was taxing exports by paying farmers considerably less for their cocoa than it was worth on the world market and putting the difference into government coffers. This money was used to fund the government policy of nationalization and industrialization. • One result of the cocoa policy was that between 1963 and 1979 the price paid by the cocoa marketing board to Ghana's farmers increased by a factor of 6, while the price of consumer goods in Ghana increased by a factor of 22, and while the price of cocoa in neighboring countries increased by a factor of 36! In real terms, the Ghanaian farmers were paid less every year for their cocoa by the cocoa marketing board, while the world price increased significantly. Ghana's farmers responded by switching to the production of subsistence foodstuffs that could be sold within Ghana, and the country's production and exports of cocoa plummeted by more than one third in seven years. At the same time, the Ghanaian government's attempt to build an industrial base through state-run enterprises was a complete failure. The resulting drop in Ghana's export earnings plunged the country into recession, led to a decline in its foreign currency reserves, and severely limited its ability to pay for necessary imports. • In essence, what happened in Ghana is that the inward-oriented trade policy of the Ghanaian government resulted in a shift of that country's resources away from the profitable activity of growing cocoa—where it had an absolute advantage in the world economy—and toward growing subsistence foods and manufacturing, where it had no advantage. This inefficient use of the country's resources severely damaged the Ghanaian economy and held back the country's economic development. • In contrast, consider the trade policy adopted by the South Korean government. The World Bank has characterized the trade policy of South Korea as "strongly outward-oriented." Unlike in Ghana, the policies of the South Korean government emphasized low import barriers on manufactured goods (but not on agricultural goods) and the creation of incentives to encourage South Korean firms to export. Beginning in the late 1950s, the South Korean government progressively reduced import tariffs from an average of 60 percent of the price of an imported good to less than 20 percent in the mid-1980s. Moreover, on most nonagricultural goods, import tariffs were reduced to zero. In addition, the number of imported goods subjected to quotas was reduced from more than 90 percent in the late 1950s to zero by the early 1980s. Over the same period South Korea progressively reduced the subsidies given to South Korean exporters from an average of 80 percent of their sales price in the late 1950s to an average of less than 20 percent of their sales price in 1965, and down to zero in 1984. Put another way, with the exception of the agricultural sector (where a strong farm lobby maintained import controls), South Korea moved progressively toward a free trade stance. • South Korea's outward-looking orientation has been rewarded by a dramatic transformation of its economy. Initially, South Korea's resources shifted from agriculture to the manufacture of labor-intensive goods, especially textiles, clothing, and footwear. An abundant supply of cheap but well-educated labor helped form the basis of South Korea's comparative advantage in labor-intensive manufacturing. More recently, as labor costs have risen, the growth areas in the economy have been in the more capital-intensive manufacturing sectors, especially motor vehicles, aerospace, consumer electronics, and advanced materials. As a result of these developments, South Korea has gone through some dramatic changes. In the late 1950s 77 percent of the country's employment was in the agricultural sector; today the figure is less than 25 percent. Over the same period the percentage of its GDP accounted for by manufacturing increased from less than 10 percent to more than 30 percent, while the overall GDP grew at an annual rate of more than 9 percent. *Sources: "Poor Man's Burden: A Survey of the Third World,"* The Economist, *September 23, 1989; The Economist,* Book of Vital World Statistics *(New York: Random House, 1991); and The Economist,* The Economist World Atlas and Almanac *(London: The Economist Books, 1990).*

INTRODUCTION

The opening case illustrates the gains that can come from international trade. The economic policies of the Ghanaian government discouraged trade with other nations. The result was a shift in Ghana's resources away from productive uses (growing cocoa) and toward unproductive uses (subsistence agriculture). The economic policies of the South Korean government strongly encouraged trade with other nations. The result was a shift in South Korea's resources away from uses where it had no comparative advantage in the world economy (agriculture) and toward more productive uses (labor-intensive manufacturing). As a direct result of their policies toward international trade, Ghana's economy declined while South Korea's grew.

This chapter has two goals that are related to the story of Ghana and South Korea. The first goal is to review a number of theories that explain why it is beneficial for a country to engage in international trade. The second goal is to explain the pattern of international trade that we observe in the world economy. With regard to the pattern of trade, we will be primarily concerned with explaining the pattern of exports and imports of products between countries. We will not be concerned with the pattern of foreign direct investment between countries; that is discussed in Chapter 7.

The Benefits of Trade

We will open this chapter with a discussion of **mercantilism.** Propagated in the 16th and 17th centuries, mercantilism advocated that countries should simultaneously encourage exports and discourage imports. Although mercantilism is an old and largely discredited doctrine, its echoes remain in modern political debate and in the trade policies of many countries. Next we will look at Adam Smith's theory of **absolute advantage.** Proposed in 1776, Smith's theory was the first to explain why unrestricted free trade is beneficial to a country. A policy of unrestricted free trade requires that there be no import controls and no export policies. Smith argued that the invisible hand of the market mechanism, rather than government policy, should determine what a country imports and what it exports. Moreover, his arguments imply that such a **laissez-faire** stance toward trade was in the best interests of a country.

Building on Smith's work are two additional theories that we shall review. One is the theory of **comparative advantage,** advanced by the 19th-century English economist David Ricardo. This theory is the intellectual basis of the modern argument for unrestricted free trade. In the 20th century Ricardo's work was refined by two Swedish economists, Eli Heckscher and Bertil Ohlin, whose theory is known as the **Heckscher-Ohlin theory.**

The great strength of the theories of Smith, Ricardo, and Heckscher-Ohlin is that they identify with precision the specific benefits of international trade. Of course, common sense suggests that some international trade is beneficial. For example, nobody would suggest that Iceland should grow its own oranges. Iceland can benefit from trade by exchanging some of the products that it can produce at a low cost (fish) for some products that it cannot produce at all (oranges). Thus, by engaging in international trade, Icelanders are able to add oranges to their diet of fish. The theories of Smith, Ricardo, and Heckscher-Ohlin go beyond this commonsense notion, however, to show why it is beneficial for a country to engage in trade even for products it is able to produce for itself. This is more difficult for people to grasp. After all, many people believe that the United States should buy U.S. products whenever possible to help save U.S. jobs. However, the theories of Smith, Ricardo, and Heckscher-Ohlin tell us that the U.S. economy as a whole may gain if we buy certain products from overseas that we could produce ourselves. The gains arise because international trade allows the U.S. economy to specialize in the manufacture and export of products that can be produced most efficiently in our country, while importing products that can be produced more efficiently in other countries. For example, it makes sense for the United States to specialize in the production and export of commercial jet aircraft, since the efficient production of commercial jet aircraft requires resources that are abundant here—such as a highly skilled labor force and cutting-edge technological know-how. On the other hand, it makes sense for the United States to import textiles from South Korea, since the efficient production of textiles requires a relatively cheap labor force—and cheap labor is not abundant here.

Of course, this economic argument is difficult for U.S. textile businesses and their employees to accept. As we shall see in Chapter 5, they have responded to the importation of textiles by demanding quotas and tariffs to restrict imports. The point to bear in mind, however, is that although such import controls may benefit particular groups, such as U.S. textile businesses and their employees, the theories of Smith, Ricardo, and Heckscher-Ohlin suggest that the economy as a whole is hurt by such protectionism.

The Pattern of International Trade

The theories of Smith, Ricardo, and Heckscher-Ohlin also help to explain the pattern of international trade that we observe in the world economy. Some aspects of the pattern are easy to understand. Climate and natural-resource endowments explain why Ghana exports cocoa, Brazil exports coffee, and Saudi Arabia exports oil. But much of the observed pattern of international trade is more difficult to explain. For example, why does Japan export automobiles, consumer electronics, and machine tools? Why does Switzerland export chemicals, watches, and jewelry? David Ricardo's **theory of comparative advantage** offers an explanation in terms of international differences in labor productivity. The more sophisticated Heckscher–Ohlin theory emphasizes the interplay between the proportions in which the factors of production (such as land, labor, and capital) are available in different countries and the proportions in which they are needed for producing particular goods. This explanation rests on the assumption that different countries have different endowments of the various factors of production. Tests of this theory, however, suggest that it is a less powerful explanation of real-world trade patterns than once thought.

One early response to the failure of the Heckscher–Ohlin theory to explain the observed pattern of international trade was the **product life-cycle theory.** Proposed by Raymond Vernon, this theory suggests that early in their life cycle, most new products are produced in and exported from the country in which they were developed. As a new product becomes widely accepted internationally, however, production starts up in other countries. As a result, the theory suggests, the product may ultimately be exported back to the country of its original innovation.

In a similar vein, during the 1980s economists such as Paul Krugman of MIT developed what has come to be known as the **new trade theory.** New trade theory stresses that in some cases countries specialize in the production and export of particular products not because of underlying differences in factor endowments, but because in certain industries the world market can support only a limited number of firms. (This is argued to be the case for the commercial aircraft industry.) In such industries, firms that enter the market first are able to build a competitive advantage that is subsequently difficult to challenge. Thus the observed pattern of trade between nations may in part be due to the ability of firms within a given nation to capture first-mover advantages. Put another way, the United States predominates in the export of commercial jet aircraft because U.S. firms such as Boeing were first-movers in the world market. Boeing built a competitive advantage that has subsequently been difficult for firms from countries with equally favorable factor endowments to challenge.

In a work related to the new trade theory, Michael Porter of Harvard Business School has recently developed a theory that attempts to explain why particular nations achieve international success in particular industries. We shall refer to this theory as the **theory of national competitive advantage.** Like the new trade theorists, in addition to factor endowments, Porter points out the importance of country factors such as domestic demand and domestic rivalry in explaining a nation's dominance in the production and export of particular products.

Trade Theory and Government Policy

Before discussing these theories in more detail, we must point out that although all of these theories agree that international trade is beneficial to a country, they lack agreement in their recommendations for government policy. Mercantilism makes a crude case for government involvement in promoting exports and limiting imports. The theories of Smith, Ricardo, and Heckscher–Ohlin form part of the case for unrestricted free trade. This is essentially the policy that the United States government has been committed to, publicly at least, since 1945. The argument for unrestricted free trade is that both import controls and export incentives (such as subsidies) are self-defeating and result in wasted resources. On the other hand, both the new trade theory and Porter's theory of national competitive advantage can be interpreted as justifying some limited and selective government intervention to support the development of certain export-oriented industries. We will discuss the pros and cons of this argument, known as *strategic trade policy,* as well as the pros and cons of the argument for unrestricted free trade, in Chapter 5.

MERCANTILISM

The first theory of international trade emerged in England in the mid-16th century. Referred to as *mercantilism,* its principle assertion was that gold and silver were the mainstays of national wealth and essential to vigorous commerce. At that time, gold and silver were the currency of trade between countries; a country could earn gold and silver by exporting goods. By the same token, importing goods from other countries would result in an outflow of gold and silver to those countries. The basic mercantilist argument was that it was in a country's best interests to maintain a trade surplus, to export more than it imported. By doing so, a country would accumulate gold and silver and, consequently, increase its national wealth and prestige. As the English mercantilist writer Thomas Mun put it in 1630:

> The ordinary means therefore to increase our wealth and treasure is by foreign trade, wherein we must ever observe this rule: to sell more to strangers yearly than we consume of theirs in value.[1]

Consistent with this belief, the mercantilist doctrine advocated government intervention to achieve a surplus in the balance of trade. The mercantilists saw no virtue in a large volume of trade per se. Rather, they recommended policies to maximize exports and minimize imports. In order to achieve this, imports were limited by tariffs and quotas, and exports were subsidized.

An inherent inconsistency in the mercantilist doctrine was pointed out by the classical economist David Hume in 1752. According to Hume, if England had a balance-of-trade surplus with France (it exported more than it imported) the resulting inflow of gold and silver would swell the domestic money supply and generate inflation in England. In France, however, the outflow of gold and silver would have the opposite effect. France's money supply would contract, and its prices would fall. This change in relative prices between France and England would encourage the French to buy fewer English goods (because they were becoming more expensive) and the English to buy more French goods (because they were becoming cheaper). The result would be a deterioration in the English balance of trade and an improvement in France's trade balance, until the English surplus was eliminated. Hence, according to Hume, in the long run no country could sustain a surplus on the balance of trade and so accumulate gold and silver as the mercantilists had envisaged.

Hume's critique apart, the flaw with mercantilism was that it viewed trade as a **zero-sum game.** (A zero-sum game is one in which a gain by one country results in a loss by another.) It was left to Adam Smith and David Ricardo to show the shortsightedness of this approach and to demonstrate that trade is a **positive-sum game** in which all countries can benefit, even if some benefit more than others. We shall discuss the views of Smith next. Before doing so, however, we must note that the mercantilist doctrine is by no means dead. For example, Jarl Hagelstam, a director at the Finnish Ministry of Finance and a participant at the Uruguay Round of negotiations on the General Agreement on

---

[1] H. W. Spiegel, *The Growth of Economic Thought* (Durham, N.C.: Duke University Press, 1991).

Tariffs and Trade (GATT), whose purpose is to create a more open and fair trading system, has observed that:

> The approach of individual negotiating countries, both industrialized and developing, has been to press for trade liberalization in areas where their own comparative competitive advantages are the strongest, and to resist liberalization in areas where they are less competitive and fear that imports would replace domestic production.[2]

Hagelstam attributes this strategy by negotiating countries to a neomercantilist belief held by the politicians of many nations. This belief equates political power with economic power, and economic power with a balance-of-trade surplus. Thus the trade strategy of many nations is designed to simultaneously boost exports and limit imports.

ABSOLUTE ADVANTAGE

In his 1776 landmark book *The Wealth of Nations,* Adam Smith attacked the mercantilist assumption that trade is a zero-sum game. Smith argued that countries differ in their ability to produce goods efficiently. In his time, for example, by virtue of their superior manufacturing processes, the English were the world's most efficient manufacturers of textiles. On the other hand, due to the combination of favorable climate, good soils, and accumulated expertise, the French had the world's most efficient wine industry. Put another way, the English had an **absolute advantage** in the production of textiles, while the French had an absolute advantage in the production of wine. Thus, a country has an absolute advantage in the production of a product when it is more efficient than any other country in producing it.

According to Smith, countries should specialize in the production of goods for which they have an absolute advantage, and then trade these goods for the goods produced by other countries. In Smith's time this suggested that the English should specialize in the production of textiles while the French should specialize in the production of wine. England could get all the wine it needed by selling its textiles to France and buying wine in exchange. Similarly, France could get all the textiles it needed by selling wine to England and buying textiles in exchange. Smith's basic argument, therefore, is that you should never produce goods at home that you can buy at a lower cost from other countries. Moreover, Smith demonstrates that by specializing in the production of goods in which each has an absolute advantage, both countries benefit by engaging in trade.

To see why this is so, let us consider the effects of trade between Ghana and South Korea. The production of any good (output) requires resources (inputs) such as land, labor, and capital. Assume that Ghana and South Korea both have the same amount of resources and that these resources can be used to produce either rice or cocoa. Assume further that 200 units of resources are available in each country. Imagine that in Ghana it takes 10 resources to produce one ton of cocoa and 20 resources to produce one ton of rice. Thus Ghana could produce 20 tons of cocoa and no rice, 10 tons of rice and no cocoa, or some combination of rice and cocoa in between these two extremes. The different combinations that Ghana could produce are represented by the line GG′ in Figure 4.1. This is referred to as Ghana's **production possibility frontier (PPF).** Similarly, imagine that in South Korea it takes 40 resources to produce one ton of cocoa and 10 resources to produce one ton of rice. Thus South Korea could produce 5 tons of cocoa

---

[2] Jarl Hagelstam, "Mercantilism Still Influences Practical Trade Policy at the End of the Twentieth Century," *Journal of World Trade,* 1991, pp. 95–105.

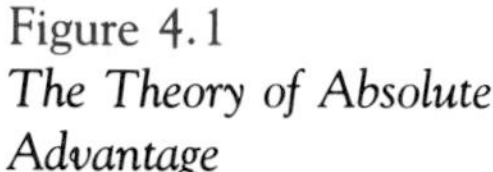

Figure 4.1
The Theory of Absolute Advantage

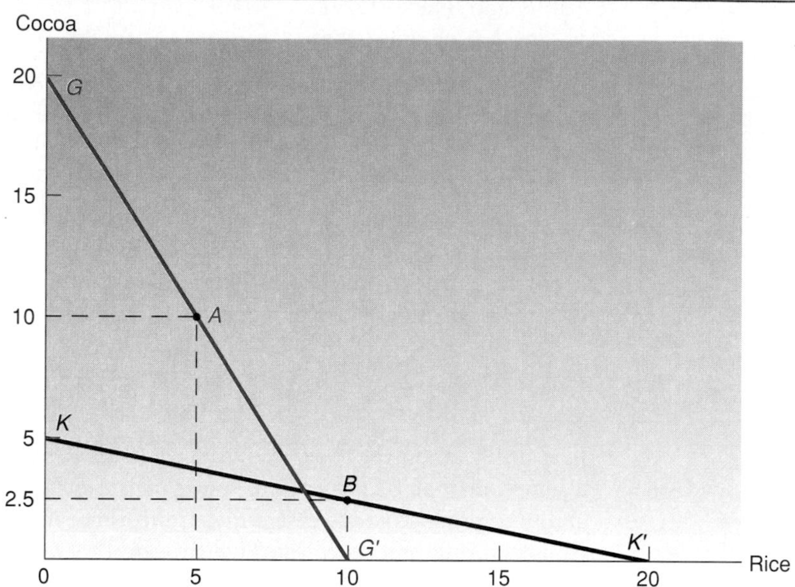

and no rice, 20 tons of rice and no cocoa, or some combination in between these two extremes. The different combinations available to South Korea are represented by the line *KK'* in Figure 4.1, which is South Korea's PPF. Clearly, Ghana has an absolute advantage in the production of cocoa. (More resources are needed to produce a ton of cocoa in South Korea than in Ghana.) By the same token, South Korea has an absolute advantage in the production of rice.

Now consider a situation in which neither country trades with any other. Each country devotes half of its resources to the production of rice and half to the production of cocoa. Each country must also consume what it produces. Ghana would be able to produce 10 tons of cocoa and 5 tons of rice (point *A* in Figure 4.1), while South Korea would be able to produce 10 tons of rice and 2.5 tons of cocoa. Without trade, the combined production of both countries would be 12.5 tons of cocoa (10 tons in Ghana plus 2.5 tons in South Korea) and 15 tons of rice (5 tons in Ghana and 10 tons in South Korea). If each country were to specialize in producing the good for which it had an absolute advantage and then trade with the other for the good it lacks, Ghana could produce 20 tons of cocoa, and South Korea could produce 20 tons of rice. Thus, by specializing, the production of both goods could be increased. Production of cocoa would increase from 12.5 tons to 20 tons, while production of rice would increase from 15 tons to 20 tons. The increase in production that would result from specialization is therefore 7.5 tons of cocoa and 5 tons of rice. These figures are summarized in Table 4.1.

Now by engaging in trade and swapping one ton of cocoa for one ton of rice, producers in both countries could consume more of both cocoa and rice. Imagine that Ghana and South Korea swap cocoa and rice on a one-to-one basis; that is, the price of one ton of cocoa is equal to the price of one ton of rice. If Ghana decided to export 6 tons of cocoa to South Korea and import 6 tons of rice in return, its final consumption after trade would be 14 tons of cocoa and 6 tons of rice. This is 4 tons more cocoa than it could have consumed before specialization and trade, and 1 ton more rice. Similarly, South Korea's final consumption after trade would be 6 tons of cocoa and 14 tons of rice. This is 3.5 tons more cocoa than it could have consumed before specialization and trade, and 4

Table 4.1
Absolute Advantage and the Gains from Trade

	Resources Required to Produce 1 Ton of Cocoa and Rice	
	Cocoa	**Rice**
Ghana	10	20
South Korea	40	10
	Production and Consumption without Trade	
	Cocoa	**Rice**
Ghana	10.0	5.0
South Korea	2.5	10.0
Total production	12.5	15.0
	Production with Specialization	
	Cocoa	**Rice**
Ghana	20.0	0.0
South Korea	0.0	20.0
Total production	20.0	20.0
	Consumption after Ghana Trades 6 Tons of Cocoa for 6 Tons of South Korean Rice	
	Cocoa	**Rice**
Ghana	14.0	6.0
South Korea	6.0	14.0
	Increase in Consumption as a Result of Specialization and Trade	
	Cocoa	**Rice**
Ghana	4.0	1.0
South Korea	3.5	4.0

tons more rice. Thus, as a result of specialization and trade, output of both cocoa and rice would be increased, and consumers in both nations would be able to consume more. Thus we can see that trade is a positive-sum game; it produces net gains for all involved.

COMPARATIVE ADVANTAGE

David Ricardo took Adam Smith's theory one step further by exploring what might happen when one country has an absolute advantage in the production of *all* goods. Smith's theory of absolute advantage suggests that such a country might derive no benefits from international trade. In his 1817 book *Principles of Political Economy,* Ricardo showed that this was not the case. According to Ricardo, it makes sense for such a country to specialize in the production of those goods that it produces most efficiently and to buy the goods that it produces less efficiently from other countries, even if this means buying goods from other countries that it could produce more efficiently itself. While this may initially seem counterintuitive, the logic can be explained with a simple example.

Let us stay with the example of Ghana and South Korea that we used to explain Adam Smith's theory. This time we will assume that Ghana is more efficient in the production of *both* cocoa and rice; that is, that Ghana has an absolute advantage in the

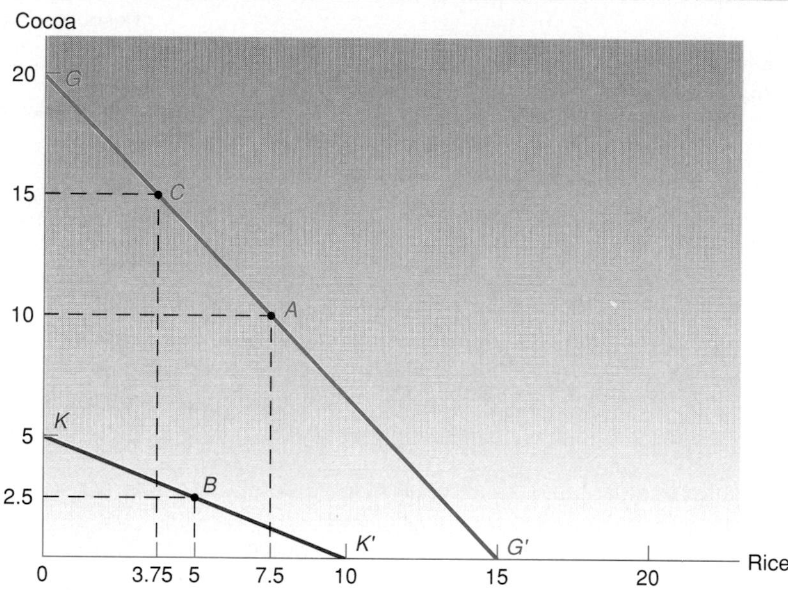

Figure 4.2
The Theory of Comparative Advantage

production of both products. Put another way, assume that productivity in Ghana is greater than in South Korea. In Ghana it takes 10 resources to produce one ton of cocoa and $13^1/_3$ resources to produce one ton of rice. Thus, given its 200 units of resources, Ghana can produce 20 tons of cocoa and no rice, 15 tons of rice and no cocoa, or any combination in between on its PPF (the line GG′ in Figure 4.2). In South Korea it takes 40 resources to produce one ton of cocoa and 20 resources to produce one ton of rice. Thus South Korea can produce 5 tons of cocoa and no rice, 10 tons of rice and no cocoa, or any combination on its PPF (the line *KK*′ in Figure 4.2). Again assume that without trade, each country uses half of its resources to produce rice and half to produce cocoa. Thus without trade, Ghana will produce 10 tons of cocoa and 7.5 tons of rice (point *A* in Figure 4.2), while South Korea will produce 2.5 tons of cocoa and 5 tons of rice (point *B* in Figure 4.2).

The question that now must be answered is, in light of Ghana's absolute advantage in the production of both goods, why should it trade with south Korea? The answer lies in the fact that although Ghana has an absolute advantage in the production of both cocoa and rice, it has a *comparative* advantage only in the production of cocoa: Ghana can produce 4 times as much cocoa as South Korea, but only 1.5 times as much rice. Thus Ghana is comparatively more efficient at producing cocoa than it is at producing rice.

Without trade the combined production of cocoa will be 12.5 tons (10 tons in Ghana and 2.5 in South Korea), and the combined production of rice will also be 12.5 tons (7.5 tons in Ghana and 5 tons in South Korea). Without trade each country must consume what it produces. By engaging in trade, the two countries can increase their combined production of rice and cocoa, and consumers in both nations can consume more of both goods.

The Gains from Trade

Imagine that Ghana exploits its comparative advantage in the production of cocoa to increase its output from 10 tons to 15 tons. This uses up 150 units of resources, leaving the remaining 50 units of resources to use in producing 3.75 tons of rice (point C in Figure 4.2). Meanwhile, South Korea specializes in the production of rice, producing 10

Table 4.2
Comparative Advantage and the Gains from Trade

	Resources Required to Produce 1 Ton of Cocoa and Rice	
	Cocoa	**Rice**
Ghana	10	13.33
South Korea	40	20
	Production and Consumption without Trade	
	Cocoa	**Rice**
Ghana	10.0	7.5
South Korea	2.5	5.0
Total production	12.5	12.5
	Production with Specialization	
	Cocoa	**Rice**
Ghana	15.0	3.75
South Korea	0.0	10.0
Total production	15.0	13.75
	Consumption after Ghana Trades 4 Tons of Cocoa for 4 Tons of South Korean Rice	
	Cocoa	**Rice**
Ghana	11.0	7.75
South Korea	4.0	6.0
	Increase in Consumption as a Result of Specialization and Trade	
	Cocoa	**Rice**
Ghana	1.0	0.25
South Korea	1.5	1.0

tons. The combined output of both cocoa and rice has now increased. Before specialization, the combined output was 12.5 tons of cocoa and 12.5 tons of rice. Now it is 15 tons of cocoa and 13.75 tons of rice (3.75 tons in Ghana and 10 tons in South Korea). The source of the increase in production is summarized in Table 4.2.

Not only is output higher, but also both countries can now benefit from trade. If Ghana and South Korea swap cocoa and rice on a one-to-one basis, with both countries choosing to exchange 4 tons of their export for 4 tons of the import, both countries are able to consume more cocoa and rice than they could before specialization and trade (see Table 4.2). Thus, if Ghana exchanges 4 tons of cocoa with South Korea for 4 tons of rice, it is still left with 11 tons of rice, which is 1 ton more than it had before trade. Moreover, the 4 tons of rice it gets from South Korea in exchange for its 4 tons of cocoa, when added to the 3.75 tons it now produces domestically, leaves it with a total of 7.75 tons of rice, which is .25 of a ton more than it had before trade. Similarly, after swapping 4 tons of rice with Ghana, South Korea still ends up with 6 tons of rice, which is more than it had before trade. In addition, the 4 tons of cocoa it receives in exchange is 1.5 tons more than it produced before trade. Thus, consumption of cocoa and rice can increase in both countries as a result of specialization and trade.

Generalizing from this example, the basic message of the theory of comparative advantage is that potential world production is greater with unrestricted free trade than it is with restricted trade. Moreover, Ricardo's theory suggests that consumers in all nations can consume more if there are no restrictions on trade. This occurs even in the case of countries that lack an absolute advantage in the production of any good. In other words, to an even greater degree than the theory of absolute advantage, the theory of comparative advantage suggests that trade is a positive-sum game in which all gain. As such, this theory provides a strong rationale for encouraging free trade. Indeed, so powerful is Ricardo's theory that it remains a major intellectual weapon for those who argue for free trade.

Qualifications and Assumptions

At this point one might object that the conclusion that free trade is universally beneficial is a rather bold one to draw from such a simple model. There are many unrealistic assumptions inherent in our simple model, including:

1. We have assumed a simple world in which there are only two countries and two goods. In the real world there are many countries and many goods.
2. We have assumed away transportation costs between countries.
3. We have assumed away differences in the prices of resources in different countries. We have said nothing about exchange rates, and instead, simply assumed that cocoa and rice could be swapped on a one-to-one basis.
4. We have assumed that while resources can move freely from the production of one good to another within a country, they are not free to move internationally. In reality, some resources are somewhat internationally mobile. This is true of capital and, to a lesser extent, labor.
5. We have assumed constant returns to scale; that is, that specialization by Ghana or South Korea has no effect on the amount of resources required to produce one ton of cocoa or rice. In reality, both diminishing and increasing returns to specialization exist. The amount of resources required to produce a good might decrease or increase as a nation specializes in production of that good.
6. We have assumed that each country has a fixed stock of resources and that free trade does not change the efficiency with which a country uses its resources. This static assumption makes no allowances for the dynamic changes in a country's stock of resources and in the efficiency with which the country uses its resources that might result from free trade.
7. We have assumed away the effects of trade on income distribution within a country.

Given these assumptions, the question arises as to whether the conclusion that free trade is mutually beneficial can be extended to the real world of many countries, many goods, positive transportation costs, volatile exchange rates, internationally mobile resources, nonconstant returns to specialization, and dynamic changes. Although a detailed extension of the theory of comparative advantage is beyond the scope of this book, economists have shown that the basic result derived from our simple model *can* be generalized to a world composed of many countries producing many different goods, in which case the above assumptions no longer hold.[3] Moreover, despite all of its shortcomings, research suggests that the basic proposition of the Ricardian model—that countries will export the goods that they are most efficient at producing—is born out by the data.[4]

---

[3] For example, R. Dornbusch, S. Fischer, and P. Samuelson, "Comparative Advantage: Trade and Payments in a Ricardian Model with a Continuum of Goods," *American Economic Review* 67 (December 1977), pp. 823–39.

[4] B. Balassa, "An Empirical Demonstration of Classic Comparative Cost Theory," *Review of Economics and Statistics*, 1963, pp. 231–38.

Figure 4.3
Ghana's PPF under Diminishing Returns

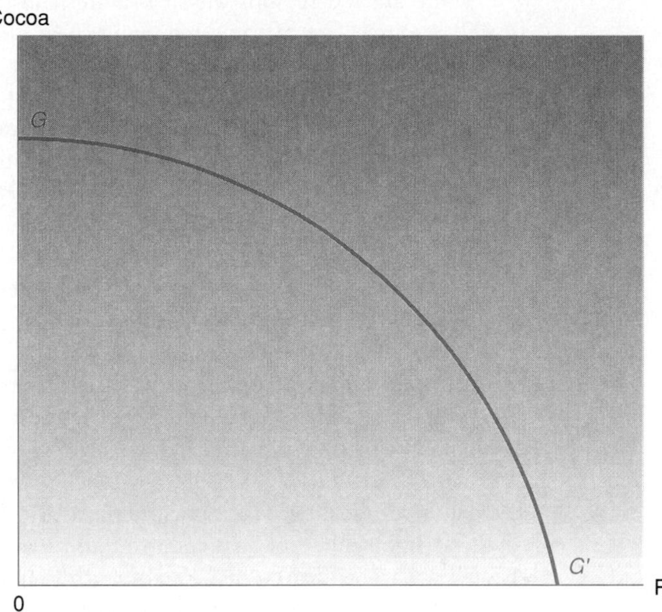

However, once all of the assumptions are dropped, the case for unrestricted free trade, while still positive, has been argued by some economists associated with the "new trade theory" to lose some of its strength.[5] We will return to this issue later in this chapter and in the next.

Some Simple Extensions of the Ricardian Model

Before moving on, let us explore the effect of relaxing two of the assumptions identified above in the simple comparative advantage model. We shall relax the assumption of constant returns to specialization and the static assumption that trade does not change a country's stock of resources or the efficiency with which it utilizes those resources.

Diminishing Returns

The simple comparative advantage model developed in the preceding subsection assumes constant returns to specialization. That is, the units of resources required to produce a good (cocoa or rice) are assumed to remain constant no matter where one is on a country's production possibility frontier (PPF). Thus we assumed that it always took Ghana 10 units of resources to produce one ton of cocoa. However, it is more realistic to assume **diminishing returns** to specialization. The concept of diminishing returns is simply that the more of a good a country produces, the greater the units of resources that will be required to produce each additional item. In the case of Ghana, for example, whereas 10 units of resources may be sufficient to increase output of cocoa from 12 tons to 13 tons, 11 units of resources may be needed to increase output of cocoa from 13 to 14 tons, 12 units of resources to increase output of cocoa from 14 tons to 15 tons, and so on. Diminishing returns implies a convex PPF for Ghana (see Figure 4.3), rather than the straight line depicted in Figure 4.2.

[5] See P. R. Krugman, "Is Free Trade Passé?" *Journal of Economic Perspectives* 1 (Fall 1987), pp. 131–44.

There are two reasons why it is more realistic to assume diminishing returns. First, not all resources are of the same quality. As a country tries to increase its output of a certain good, it is increasingly likely to draw upon more marginal resources whose productivity is not as great as those initially employed. The end result is that it requires ever more resources to produce an equal increase in output. For example, some land is more productive (fertile) than other land. As Ghana tries to expand its output of cocoa, it might have to utilize increasingly marginal land that is less fertile than the land it originally used. As yields per acre decline, Ghana must use ever more land to produce one ton of cocoa.

A second reason for assuming diminishing returns is that different goods typically use resources in different proportions. For example, imagine that growing cocoa uses more land and less labor than growing rice, and that Ghana tries to transfer resources from rice production to cocoa production. The rice industry will release proportionately too much labor and too little land for efficient cocoa production. To absorb the additional resources of labor and land, the cocoa industry will have to shift toward more labor-intensive methods of production. The effect is that the efficiency with which the cocoa industry uses labor will decline; returns will diminish.

The significance of diminishing returns is that it is not feasible for a country to specialize to the degree suggested by the simple Ricardian model outlined earlier. Diminishing returns to specialization suggest that the gains from specialization are likely to be exhausted before specialization is complete. In reality, most countries do not specialize, but instead, produce a range of goods. However, the theory predicts that it is worthwhile to specialize up until that point where the resulting gains from trade are outweighed by diminishing returns. Thus the basic conclusion that unrestricted free trade is beneficial still holds, although due to diminishing returns, the gains may not be as great as suggested in the constant returns case.

Dynamic Effects and Economic Growth

Our simple comparative advantage model assumed that trade does not change a country's stock of resources or the efficiency with which it utilizes those resources. This static assumption makes no allowances for the dynamic changes that might result from trade. If we relax this assumption, it becomes apparent that opening up an economy to trade is likely to generate dynamic gains. These dynamic gains are of two sorts. First, free trade might increase a country's stock of resources as increased supplies of labor and capital from abroad become available for use within the country. This is occurring right now in Eastern Europe, where many Western businesses are investing large amounts of capital in the former Communist bloc countries.

Second, free trade might also increase the efficiency with which a country utilizes its resources. Gains in the efficiency of resource utilization could arise from a number of factors. For example, economies of large-scale production might become available as trade expands the size of the total market available to domestic firms. Trade might make better technology from abroad available to domestic firms. In turn, better technology can increase labor productivity or the productivity of land. (The so-called green revolution had just this effect on agricultural outputs in developing countries.) It is also possible that opening up an economy to foreign competition might stimulate domestic producers to look for ways to increase the efficiency of their operations. Again, this phenomenon is arguably occurring currently in the once protected markets of Eastern Europe, where many former state monopolies are having to increase the efficiency of their operations in order to survive in the competitive world market.

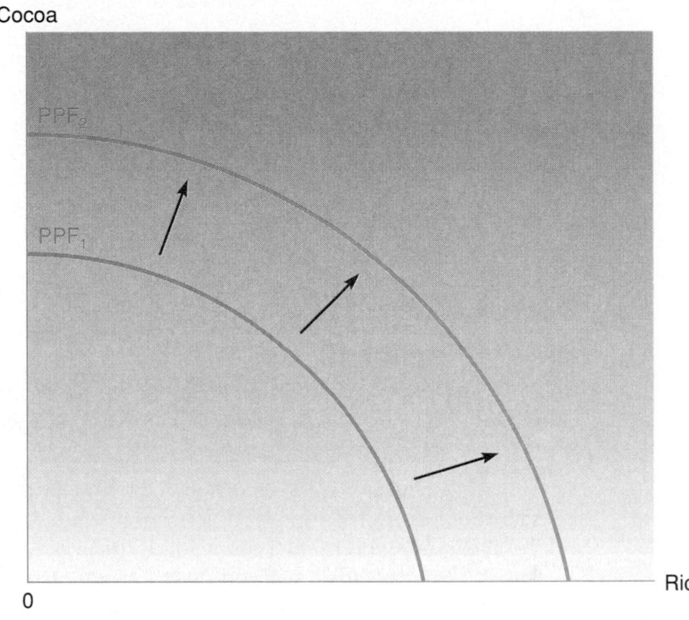

Figure 4.4
The Influence of Free Trade on the PPF

Dynamic gains in both the stock of a country's resources, and the efficiency with which resources are utilized will cause a country's PPF to shift outward. This is illustrated in Figure 4.4, where the shift from PPF_1 to PPF_2 results from the dynamic gains that arise from free trade. As a consequence of this outward shift, the country in Figure 4.4 can produce more of *both* goods than it did before introduction of free trade. Put another way, the theory suggests that opening up an economy to free trade not only results in static gains of the type discussed earlier, but also results in dynamic gains that stimulate economic growth. If this is so, the case for free trade becomes stronger. In point of fact, there is evidence that a free trade stance has beneficial effects on economic growth. Some of the evidence recently compiled by the World Bank is discussed in Box 4.1.

HECKSCHER-OHLIN THEORY

Ricardo's theory stresses that comparative advantage arises from differences in productivity (the efficiency with which a country utilizes its resources to produce outputs). Thus, whether Ghana is more efficient than South Korea in the production of cocoa depends upon how productively it uses its resources. Ricardo himself placed particular stress on labor productivity and argued that differences in labor productivity between nations underlie the notion of comparative advantage. Swedish economists Eli Heckscher (in 1919) and Bertil Ohlin (in 1933) put forward a different explanation of comparative advantage. They argued that comparative advantage arises from differences in national **factor endowments.** By factor endowments they meant the extent to which a country is endowed with such resources as land, labor, and capital. Different nations have different factor endowments, and different factor endowments explain differences in factor costs. The more abundant a factor, the lower its cost. The Heckscher-Ohlin theory predicts that countries will export those goods that make intensive use of those factors that are locally abundant, while importing goods that make intensive use of

The Effect of a Protrade Stance on Economic Growth

In its 1987 World Development Report, the World Bank classified 41 developing countries according to their trade orientation during two periods, 1963–73 and 1973–75. the World Bank used these classifications:

Strongly outward oriented Countries where trade controls are either nonexistent or very low.

Moderately outward oriented Countries where incentives favor production for the domestic rather than export market but the average rate of protection for the home market is relatively low.

Moderately inward oriented Countries where incentives clearly favor production for the domestic market and the average rate of protection for the home market is fairly high.

Strongly inward oriented Countries where incentives strongly favor production for the domestic market and the average rate of protection for the home market is high.

After classifying the countries for both time periods, the World Bank compared the countries in the four groups against two measures of economic growth: (1) the country's average annual percentage growth in real gross domestic product (GDP) and (2) the country's average annual percentage growth in gross national product (GNP) per person. The results of this exercise are summarized in the table and the figure. These results strongly suggest that a protrade stance increased a country's economic growth rate, while an antitrade stance was associated with a lower, and in some cases negative, growth rate.

Trade Orientation and Average Annual Percentage Growth of Real GDP

	Annual Percentage Growth of Real GDP	
Trade Orientation	**1963–73**	**1973–85**
Strongly outward oriented	9.5	7.7
Moderately outward oriented	7.6	4.4
Moderately inward oriented	6.8	4.7
Strongly inward oriented	4.1	2.5

BOX 4.1

Trade Regimes and Economic Growth (real GNP per person, average annual % change)

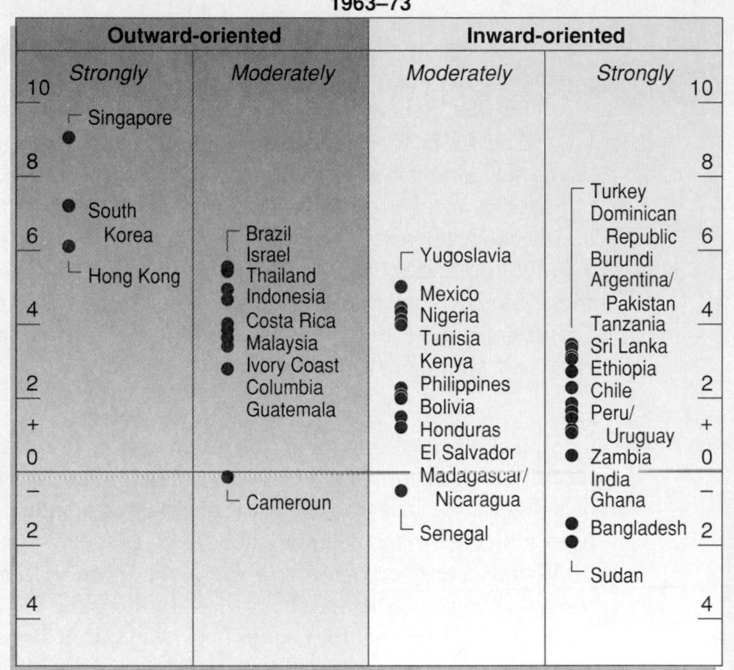

1973–85

Outward-oriented | Inward oriented

Strongly | Moderately | Moderately | Strongly

10
8
6
4
2
+
0
–
2
4

Singapore
Hong Kong
South Korea

Malaysia
Thailand
Tunisia
Brazil
Turkey
Israel/
Uruguay
Chile

Cameroun
Indonesia
Sri Lanka
Pakistan
Yugoslavia
Columbia
Mexico
Philippines
Kenya
Honduras
Senegal
Costa Rica
Guatemala
Ivory Coast
El Salvador
Nicaragua

Bangladesh/
India
Burundi
Dominican
Republic
Ethiopia/Sudan
Peru
Tanzania
Argentina
Zambia
Nigeria
Bolivia
Ghana
Madagascar

Source: "The Gains from Trade," The Economist (Third World Survey), *September 23, 1989, pp. 25–26.*

factors that are locally scarce. Thus the Heckscher–Ohlin theory attempts to explain the pattern of international trade that we observe in the world economy. Like Ricardo's theory, the Heckscher–Ohlin theory argues that free trade is beneficial. Unlike Ricardo's theory, however, the Heckscher–Ohlin theory argues that the pattern of international trade is determined by differences in factor endowments, rather than differences in productivity.

The Heckscher–Ohlin theory also has common-sense appeal. For example, the United States has long been a substantial exporter of agricultural goods, reflecting in part its unusual abundance of large tracts of arable land. In contrast, South Korea has excelled in the export of goods produced in labor-intensive manufacturing industries, such as textiles and footwear. This reflects South Korea's relative abundance of low-cost labor. The United States, which lacks abundant low-cost labor, has been a primary importer of these goods. Note that it is *relative,* not absolute, endowments that are important; a country may have larger absolute amounts of land and labor than another country, but be relatively abundant in one of them.

The Leontief Paradox

The Heckscher–Ohlin theory has been one of the most influential theoretical ideas in international economics. Most economists prefer the Heckscher–Ohlin theory to Ricardo's theory, because it makes fewer simplifying assumptions. Not surprisingly then, it has been subjected to many empirical tests. Beginning with a famous study published in 1953 by Wassily Leontief (winner of the Nobel prize in economics in 1973), many of these tests have raised questions about the validity of the Heckscher–Ohlin theory.[7] Using the Heckscher–Ohlin theory, Leontief postulated that since the United States was relatively abundant in capital compared to other nations, the United States would be an exporter of capital-intensive goods and an importer of labor-intensive goods. To his surprise, however, he found that U.S. exports were less capital intensive than U.S. imports. Since this result was at variance with the predictions of the theory, it has become known as the *Leontief paradox.*

Why then do we observe the Leontief paradox? No one is quite sure. One possible explanation is that the United States has a special advantage in producing new products or goods made with innovative technologies. Such products may well be less capital intensive than products whose technology has had time to mature and become suitable for mass production techniques. Thus the United States may be exporting goods that heavily use skilled labor and innovative entrepreneurship, while importing heavy manufactures that use large amounts of capital. Some more recent empirical studies tend to confirm this.[8] However, recent tests of the Heckscher–Ohlin theory using data for a large number of countries tend to confirm the existence of the Leontief paradox.[9]

This leaves economists in a rather difficult dilemma. They prefer the Heckscher–Ohlin theory, but it is a relatively poor predictor of real-world international trade patterns. On the other hand, the theory they regard as being too limited, Ricardo's theory of comparative advantage, actually predicts trade patterns with greater accuracy. The best solution to this dilemma may be to return to the Ricardian idea that trade patterns are largely driven by international differences in productivity. Thus one might

---

[7] W. Leontief, "Domestic Production and Foreign Trade: The American Capital Position Re-Examined," *Proceedings of the American Philosophical Society* 97 (1953), pp. 331–49.

[8] R. M. Stern and K. Maskus, "Determinants of the Structure of U.S. Foreign Trade," *Journal of International Economics* 11 (1981), pp. 207–44.

[9] For example, H. P. Bowen, E. E. Leamer, and L. Sveikayskas, "Multicountry, Multifactor Tests of the Factor Abundance Theory," *American Economic Review* 77 (1987), pp. 791–809.

argue that the United States exports commercial aircraft and imports automobiles not because its factor endowments are especially suited to aircraft manufacture and not suited to automobile manufacture, but because the United States is more efficient at producing aircraft than automobiles.

THE PRODUCT LIFE-CYCLE THEORY

Raymond Vernon initially proposed the product life-cycle theory in the mid-1960s.[10] Vernon's theory was based on the observation that for most of the 20th century a very large proportion of the world's new products had been developed by U.S. firms and sold first in the U.S. market (e.g., mass-produced automobiles, televisions, instant cameras, photocopiers, personal computers, and semiconductor chips). To explain this, Vernon argued that the wealth and size of the U.S. market gave U.S. firms a strong incentive to develop new consumer products. In addition, the high cost of U.S. labor gave U.S. firms an incentive to develop cost-saving process innovations.

Just because a new product is developed by a U.S. firm and first sold in the U.S. market, it does not follow that the product must be produced in the United States. It could be produced abroad at some low-cost location and then exported back into the United States. However, Vernon argued that most new products were initially produced in the United States. Apparently, the pioneering firms felt that it was better to keep production facilities close to the market and to the firm's center of decision making, given the uncertainty and risks inherent in new-product introduction. Moreover, the demand for most new products tends to be based on nonprice factors. Consequently, firms can charge relatively high prices for new products, which obviates the need to look for low-cost production sites in other countries.

Vernon went on to argue that early in the life cycle of a typical new product, while demand is starting to grow rapidly in the United States, demand in other advanced countries is limited to high-income groups. The limited initial demand in other advanced countries does not make it worthwhile for firms in those countries to start producing the new product, but it does necessitate some exports from the United States to those countries.

Over time, however, demand for the new product starts to grow in other advanced countries (e.g., Great Britain, France, Germany, and Japan). As it does, it becomes worthwhile for foreign producers to begin producing for their home markets. In addition, U.S. firms might set up production facilities in those advanced countries where demand is growing. Consequently, production within other advanced countries begins to limit the potential for exports from the United States.

As the market in the United States and other advanced nations matures, the product becomes more standardized, and price becomes the main competitive weapon. As this occurs, cost considerations start to play a greater role in the competitive process. One result is that producers based in advanced countries where labor costs are lower than in the United States (e.g., Italy, Spain) might now be able to export to the United States.

If cost pressures become intense, the process might not stop there. The cycle by which the United States lost its advantage to other advanced countries might be repeated once more, as developing countries (e.g., South Korea and Thailand) begin to acquire a production advantage over advanced countries. Thus, the locus of global production

---

[10] R. Vernon, "International Investments and International Trade in the Product Life Cycle," *Quarterly Journal of Economics*, May 1966, pp. 190–207; and R. Vernon and L. T. Wells, *The Economic Environment of International Business*, 4th ed. (Englewood Cliffs, N.J.: Prentice Hall, 1986).

initially switches from the United States to other advanced nations, and then from those nations to developing countries.

The consequence of these trends for the pattern of world trade is that over time the United States switches from being an exporter of the product to an importer of the product as production becomes concentrated in lower-cost foreign locations. These dynamics are illustrated in Figure 4.5, which shows the growth of production and consumption over time in the United States, other advanced countries, and developing countries.

Evaluating the Product Life-Cycle Theory

How good an explanation of international trade patterns is the product life-cycle theory? Historically, it is quite accurate. Consider photocopiers; the product was first developed in the early 1960s by Xerox in the United States and sold initially to U.S. users. Originally Xerox exported photocopiers from the United States, primarily to Japan and the advanced countries of Western Europe. As demand began to grow in those countries, Xerox entered into joint ventures to set up production in Japan (Fuji-Xerox) and Great Britain (Rank-Xerox). In addition, once Xerox's patents on the photocopier process expired, other foreign competitors began to enter the market (e.g., Cannon in Japan, Olivetti in Italy). As a consequence, exports from the United States declined, and U.S. users began to buy some of their photocopiers from lower-cost foreign sources—particularly from Japan. More recently, Japanese companies have found that their own country is too expensive a location to manufacture photocopiers, so they have begun to switch production to developing countries such as Singapore and Thailand. As a result, initially the United States, and now several other advanced countries (e.g., Japan and Great Britain) have switched from being exporters of photocopiers to being importers. This evolution in the pattern of international trade in photocopiers is obviously consistent with the predictions of the product life-cycle theory. The product life-cycle theory clearly does go some way toward explaining the migration of mature industries out of the United States and into low-cost assembly locations.

The product life-cycle theory is not without weaknesses, however. Viewed from an Asian or European perspective, Vernon's argument that most new products are developed and introduced in the United States seems ethnocentric. Although it may be true that during the period of U.S. global dominance (1945–75) most new products were introduced in the United States, there have always been important exceptions. In recent years these exceptions appear to have become the rule. Many new products are now first introduced in Japan (e.g., high-definition television or digital audio tapes). More importantly, with the increased globalization and integration of the world economy that we discussed in Chapter 1, a growing number of new products are now introduced simultaneously in the United States, Japan, and the advanced European nations (e.g., laptop computers, compact disks, and electronic cameras). This may be accompanied by globally dispersed production, with particular components of a new product being produced in those locations around the globe where the mix of factor costs and skills is most favorable (as predicted by the theory of comparative advantage).

Consider laptop computers, which were introduced simultaneously into a number of major national markets by Toshiba. Although various components for Toshiba laptop computers are manufactured in Japan (e.g., display screens, memory chips), other components are manufactured in Singapore and Taiwan, and still others (e.g., hard drives and microprocessors) are manufactured in the United States. All of the components are shipped to Singapore for final assembly, and the completed product is then shipped to the major world markets (the United States, Western Europe, and Japan). The pattern of trade associated with this new product is both different from and more

Figure 4.5
The Product Life-Cycle

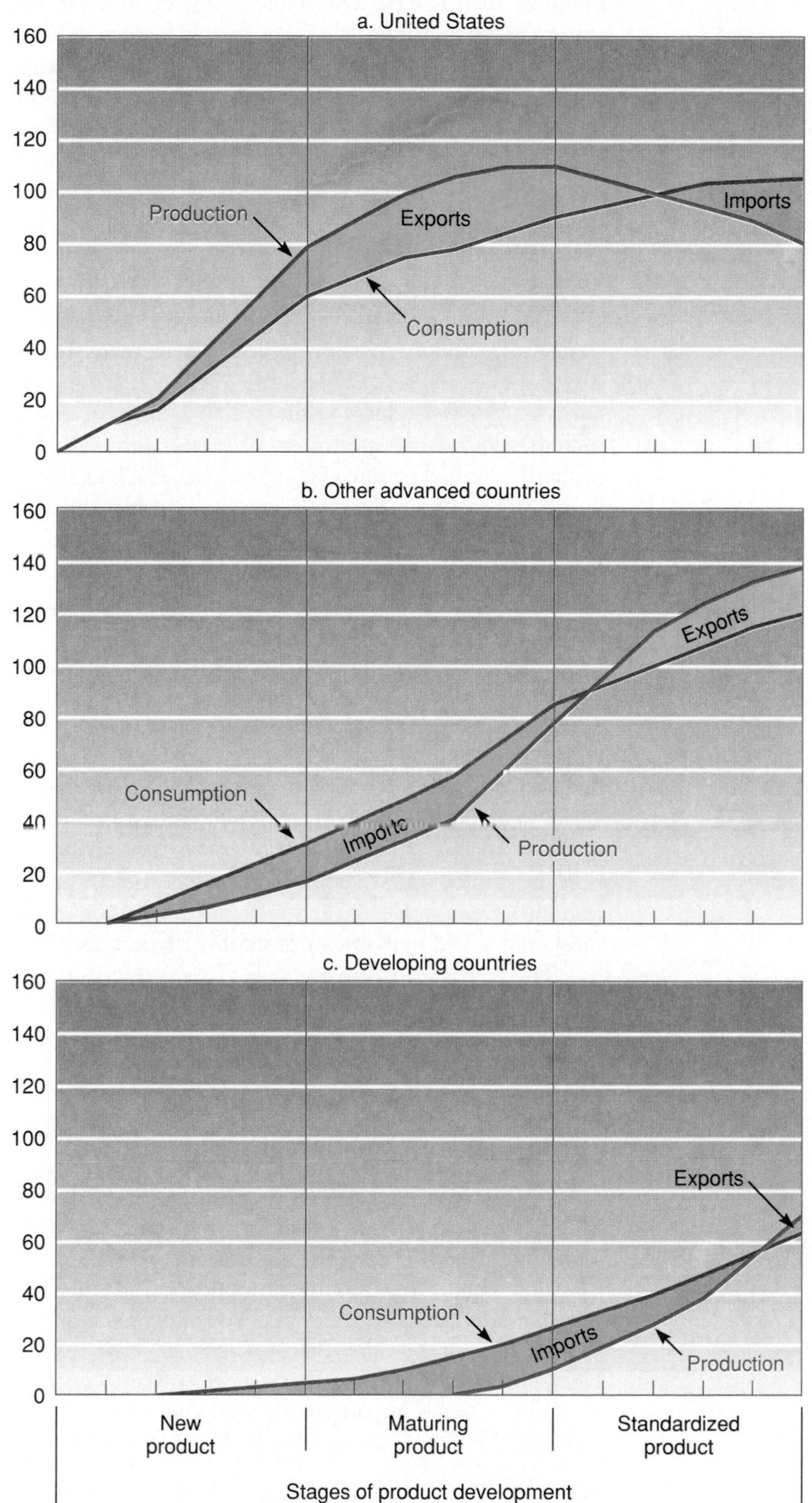

Source: Adapted from R. Vernon and L. T. Wells, The Economic Environment of International Business, *4th ed. (Englewood Cliffs, N.J.: Prentice Hall, 1986).*

complex than the pattern predicted by Vernon's model. Trying to explain this pattern using the product life-cycle theory would be very difficult. Indeed, the theory of comparative advantage might better explain why certain components are produced in certain locations and why the final product is assembled in Singapore. In short, although Vernon's theory may be useful for explaining the pattern of international trade during the brief period of American global dominance, its relevance in the modern world is limited.

THE NEW TRADE THEORY

The new trade theory began to emerge in the 1970s. At that time a number of economists were questioning the assumption of diminishing returns to specialization used in international trade theory.[11] They argued that in many industries, because of the presence of substantial **economies of scale,** there are **increasing returns** to specialization. Put another way, as output expands with specialization, the ability to realize economies of scale increases and so the unit costs of production should decrease. Economies of scale are primarily derived by spreading fixed costs (such as the costs of developing a new product) over a larger output. As an illustration, consider the commercial jet aircraft industry. The fixed costs of developing a new commercial jet airliner are astronomical. It has been estimated that Boeing will have to spend $3 billion to develop its new 777 before it sells a single plane. The company will have to sell at least 300 777s just to recoup these development costs and break even. Thus, due to the high fixed costs of developing a new jet aircraft, the economies of scale in this industry are substantial.

The new trade theorists further argue that due to the presence of substantial scale economies, in many industries world demand will only support a few firms. This is the case in the commercial jet aircraft industry; estimates suggest that, at most, world demand can profitably support only three major manufacturers. For example, the total world demand for 300-seater commercial jet aircraft similar to Boeing's 777 model will probably be only 1,500 aircraft over the 10 years between 1995 and 2005. If we assume that firms must sell at least 500 aircraft to get an acceptable return on their investment (which is reasonable, given the breakeven point of 300 aircraft), we can see that, at most, the world market can profitably support only three firms!

The new trade theorists go on to argue that in those industries where the existence of substantial economies of scale imply that the world market will profitably support only a few firms, countries may export certain products simply because they have a firm that was an early entrant into that industry. Underpinning this argument is the notion of **first-mover advantages.** Because they are able to gain economies of scale, the early entrants into an industry may get a lock on the world market that discourages subsequent entry. In other words, the ability of first-movers to reap economies of scale creates a **barrier to entry.** In the commercial aircraft industry, for example, the fact that Boeing, Airbus, and McDonnell Douglas are already in the industry and have the benefits of economies of scale effectively discourages new entry.

This theory has profound implications. The theory suggests that a country may predominate in the export of a good simply because it was lucky enough to have one or more firms among the first to produce that good. This is at variance with the Heckscher–Ohlin theory, which suggests that a country will predominate in the export of a product when it is particularly well endowed with those factors used intensively in its manufacture. Thus, the new trade theorists argue that the United States leads in exports

[11] For a summary of this literature, see E. Helpman and P. Krugman, *Market Structure and Foreign Trade: Increasing Returns, Imperfect Competition, and the International Economy* (Boston: MIT Press, 1985).

of commercial jet aircraft not because it is better endowed with the factors of production required to manufacture aircraft, but because two of the first movers in the industry, Boeing and McDonnell Douglas, were U.S. firms. It should be noted, however, that the new trade theory is not at variance with the theory of comparative advantage. Since economies of scale result in an increase in the efficiency of resource utilization, and hence in productivity, the new trade theory identifies an important source of comparative advantage.

How useful is this theory in explaining trade patterns? It is perhaps too early to say; the theory is so new that little supporting empirical work has been done. Consistent with the theory, however, a recent study by Harvard business historian Alfred Chandler does suggest that the existence of first-mover advantages is an important factor in explaining the dominance of firms from certain nations in certain industries.[12] Moreover, it is true that the number of firms is very limited in many global industries. This is the case with the commercial aircraft industry, the chemical industry, the heavy construction-equipment industry, the heavy truck industry, the tire industry, the consumer electronics industry, and the jet engine industry, to name but a few examples.

Perhaps the most contentious implication of the new trade theory, however, is the argument that it generates for government intervention and **strategic trade policy.** New trade theorists stress the role of luck, entrepreneurship, and innovation in giving a firm first-mover advantages. According to this argument, the reason why Boeing was the first mover in commercial jet aircraft manufacture—rather than firms like Great Britain's DeHavilland and Hawker Siddely, or Holland's Fokker, all of which could have been—was that Boeing was both lucky and innovative. One way Boeing was lucky is that DeHavilland shot itself in the foot when its Comet jet airliner, introduced two years earlier than Boeing's first jet airliner, the 707, was found to be full of serious technological flaws. Had DeHavilland not made some serious technological mistakes, Great Britain might now be the world's leading exporter of commercial jet aircraft! Boeing's innovativeness was demonstrated by its independent development of the technological know-how required to build a commercial jet airliner. Several new trade theorists have pointed out, however, that Boeing's R&D was largely paid for by the U.S. government; that the 707 was in fact a spinoff from a government-funded military program. Herein lies a rationale for government intervention. By the sophisticated and judicious use of subsidies, might not a government be able to increase the chances of its domestic firms becoming first movers in newly emerging industries, as the U.S. government apparently did with Boeing? If this is possible, and the new trade theory suggests it might be, then we have an economic rationale for a proactive trade policy that is at variance with the free trade prescriptions of the trade theories we have reviewed so far. We will consider the policy implications of this issue in Chapter 5.

NATIONAL COMPETITIVE ADVANTAGE: PORTER'S DIAMOND

In 1990 Michael Porter of Harvard Business School published the results of an intensive research effort that attempted to determine why some nations succeed and others fail in international competition.[13] Porter and his team looked at 100 industries in 10 nations. The book that contains the results of this work, *The Competitive Advantage of Nations,*

[12] A. D Chandler, *Scale and Scope* (New York: Free Press, 1990).

[13] M. E. Porter, *The Competitive Advantage of Nations* (New York: Free Press, 1990). For a good review of this book, see R. M. Grant, "Porter's *Competitive Advantage of Nations:* An Assessment," *Strategic Management Journal* 12 (1991), pp. 535–48.

Figure 4.6
Determinants of National Competitive Advantage: Porter's Diamond

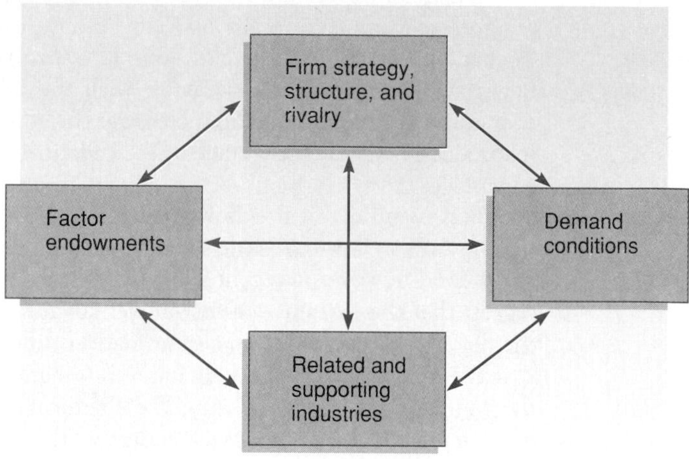

Source: Adapted from M. E. Porter, "The Competitive Advantage of Nations," Harvard Business Review, *March–April 1990, p. 77.*

seems destined to become a modern classic. Like the work of the new trade theorists, Porter's work was driven by a feeling that the existing theories of international trade told only part of the story. For Porter, the essential task was to explain why a nation achieves international success in a particular industry. Why does Japan do so well in the automobile industry? Why does Switzerland excel in the production and export of precision instruments and pharmaceuticals? Why do Germany and the United States do so well in the chemical industry? These questions cannot be answered easily by the Heckscher–Ohlin theory, and the theory of comparative advantage offers only a partial explanation. The theory of comparative advantage would say that Switzerland excels in the production and export of precision instruments because it uses its resources very productively in these industries. Although this may be correct, this does not explain why Switzerland is more productive in this industry than Great Britain, Germany, or Spain. It is this puzzle that Porter tries to solve.

Porter's basic thesis is that four broad attributes of a nation shape the environment in which local firms compete, and that these attributes promote or impede the creation of competitive advantage (see Figure 4.6). These attributes are

Factor endowments A nation's position in factors of production such as skilled labor or the infrastructure necessary to compete in a given industry.

Demand conditions The nature of home demand for the industry's product or service.

Relating and supporting industries The presence or absence in a nation of supplier industries and related industries that are internationally competitive.

Firm strategy, structure, and rivalry The conditions in the nation governing how companies are created, organized, and managed and the nature of domestic rivalry.

Porter speaks of these four attributes as constituting "the diamond." He argues that firms are most likely to succeed in industries or industry segments where "the diamond is most favorable." He also argues that the diamond is a mutually reinforcing system. The effect of one attribute is contingent on the state of others. For example, Porter argues, favorable demand conditions will not result in competitive advantage unless the state of rivalry is sufficient to cause firms to respond to them.

Porter maintains that two additional variables can influence the national diamond in important ways; chance and government. Chance events, such as major innovations, create discontinuities that can unfreeze or reshape industry structure and provide the opportunity for one nation's firms to supplant another's. Government, by its choice of policies, can detract from or improve national advantage. For example, regulation can alter home demand conditions, antitrust policies can influence the intensity of rivalry within an industry, and government investments in education can change factor endowments.

Factor Endowments

We have seen that factor endowments lie at the center of the Heckscher–Ohlin theory. While Porter does not propose anything radically new, he does analyze the characteristics of factors of production in some detail. He recognizes hierarchies among factors, distinguishing between **basic factors** (e.g., natural resources, climate, location, and demographics) and **advanced factors** (e.g., communications infrastructure, sophisticated and skilled labor, research facilities, and technological know-how). He argues that advanced factors are the most significant for competitive advantage. Moreover, unlike basic factors (which are naturally endowed), advanced factors are a product of investment by individuals, companies, and governments. Thus government investments in basic and higher education, by improving the general skill and knowledge level of the population and by stimulating advanced research at higher education institutions, can upgrade a nation's advanced factors.

The relationship between advanced and basic factors is complex. Basic factors can provide an initial advantage that is subsequently reinforced and extended by investment in advanced factors. Conversely, disadvantages in basic factors can create pressures to invest in advanced factors. The most obvious example of this phenomenon is Japan, a country that lacks much in the way of arable land or mineral deposits and yet through investment has built up a substantial endowment of advanced factors. In particular, Porter notes that Japan's large pool of engineers (reflecting a much higher number of engineering graduates per capita than almost any other nation) has been vital to Japan's success in many manufacturing industries.

Demand Conditions

Porter emphasizes the role home demand plays in providing the impetus for "upgrading" competitive advantage. Firms are typically most sensitive to the needs of their closest customers. Thus the characteristics of home demand are particularly important in shaping the attributes of domestically made products and in creating pressures for innovation and quality. Porter argues that a nation's firms gain competitive advantage if their domestic consumers are sophisticated and demanding. Sophisticated and demanding consumers pressure local firms to meet high standards of product quality. He notes that Japan's sophisticated and knowledgeable buyers of cameras helped stimulate the Japanese camera industry to improve product quality and to introduce innovative models.

Related and Supporting Industries

The third broad attribute of national advantage in an industry is the presence in a country of suppliers or related industries that are internationally competitive. The benefits of investments in advanced factors of production by related and supporting industries can spill over into an industry, thereby helping it achieve a strong competitive position internationally. Swedish strength in fabricated steel products (e.g., ball bearings and cutting tools) has drawn on strengths in Sweden's specialty steel industry. Technological leadership in the U.S. semiconductor industry during the period up until the mid-1980s provided the basis for U.S. success in personal computers and several other technically advanced electronic products. Similarly, Switzerland's success in pharmaceuticals is closely related to its previous international success in the technologically related dye industry.

One consequence of this process is that successful industries within a country tend to be grouped into "clusters" of related industries. Indeed, this was one of the most pervasive findings of Porter's study. One such cluster is the German textile and apparel sector, which includes high-quality cotton, wool, synthetic fibers, sewing machine needles, and a wide range of textile machinery.

Firm Strategy, Structure, and Rivalry

The fourth broad attribute of national competitive advantage in Porter's model is the strategy, structure, and rivalry of firms within a nation. Porter makes two important points here. His first is that different nations are characterized by different "management ideologies," which either help them or do not help them to build national competitive advantage. For example, Porter notes the predominance of engineers on the top-management teams of German and Japanese firms. He attributes this to these firms' emphasis on improving manufacturing processes and product design. In contrast, Porter notes a predominance of people with finance backgrounds on the top-management teams of many U.S. firms. He links this to the lack of attention of many U.S. firms to improving manufacturing processes and product design, particularly during the 1970s and 80s. He also argues that the dominance of finance has led to a corresponding over-emphasis on maximizing short-term financial returns. According to Porter, one consequence of these different management ideologies has been a relative loss of U.S. competitiveness in those engineering-based industries where manufacturing processes and product design issues are all-important (e.g., the automobile industry).

Porter's second point is that there is a strong association between vigorous domestic rivalry and the creation and persistence of competitive advantage in an industry. Vigorous domestic rivalry induces firms to look for ways to improve efficiency, which in turn makes them better international competitors. Domestic rivalry creates pressures to innovate, to improve quality, to reduce costs, and to invest in upgrading advanced factors. All of this helps to create world-class competitors. To support this argument, Porter cites the case of Japan:

> Nowhere is the role of domestic rivalry more evident than in Japan, where it is all-out warfare in which many companies fail to achieve profitability. With goals that stress market share, Japanese companies engage in a continuing struggle to outdo each other. Shares fluctuate markedly. The process is prominently covered in the business press. Elaborate rankings measure which companies are most popular with university graduates. The rate of new product and process development is breathtaking.[14]

Evaluating Porter's Theory

Porter's argument, therefore, is that the degree to which a nation is likely to achieve international success in a certain industry is a function of the combined impact of factor endowments, domestic demand conditions, related and supporting industries, and domestic rivalry. He argues that for "this diamond" to positively impact competitive

---

[14] Porter, *Competitive Advantage*, p. 121.

performance usually requires the presence of all four components (although there are some exceptions). Porter also contends that government can influence each of the four components of the diamond either positively or negatively. Factor endowments can be affected by subsidies, policies toward capital markets, policies toward education, and the like. Government can shape domestic demand through local product standards or with regulations that mandate or influence buyer needs. Government policy can influence supporting and related industries through regulation, and influence firm rivalry through such devices as capital market regulation, tax policy, and antitrust laws.

If Porter is correct, we would expect his model to predict the pattern of international trade that we observe in the real world. More precisely, countries should be exporting products from those industries where all four components of the diamond are favorable, while importing in those areas where the components are not favorable. So is he correct? At this point we simply do not know. Porter's theory is so new that it has not yet been subjected to independent empirical testing. There is certainly much about the theory that rings true, but the same can be said for the new trade theory, the theory of comparative advantage, and the Heckscher–Ohlin theory. In reality it may well be that each of these theories explains something about the pattern of international trade. After all, in many respects these theories complement each other.

IMPLICATIONS FOR BUSINESS

Why does all of this matter for business? There are perhaps three main implications of the material discussed in this chapter for international businesses: location implications, first-mover implications, and policy implications.

Location Implications

The first, and perhaps most important, way in which the material discussed in this chapter matters to an international business concerns the link between the theories of international trade and a firm's decision about where to locate its various productive activities. Underlying most of the theories we have discussed is the notion that different countries have particular advantages in different productive activities. Thus, from a profit perspective, it makes sense for a firm to disperse its various productive activities to those countries where, according to the theory of international trade, they can be performed most efficiently. If design can be performed most efficiently in France, that is where design facilities should be located; if the manufacture of basic components can be performed most efficiently in Singapore, that is where they should be manufactured; and if final assembly can be performed most efficiently in China, that is where final assembly should be performed. The end result is a global web of productive activities, with different activities being performed in different locations around the globe depending on considerations of comparative advantage, factor endowments, and the like. Indeed, if the firm does not do this, it may find itself at a competitive disadvantage relative to firms that do.

For an example, consider the process of producing a laptop computer, a process with four major stages: (1) basic research and development of the product design, (2) manufacture of standard electronic components (e.g., integrated circuits), (3) manufacture of advanced components (e.g., flat-top color display screens), and (4) final assembly. Basic R&D and design requires a pool of highly skilled and educated workers with good backgrounds in microelectronics. The two countries with a comparative advantage in basic microelectronics R&D and design are Japan and the United States, so most producers of laptop computers locate their R&D facilities in one, or both, of these

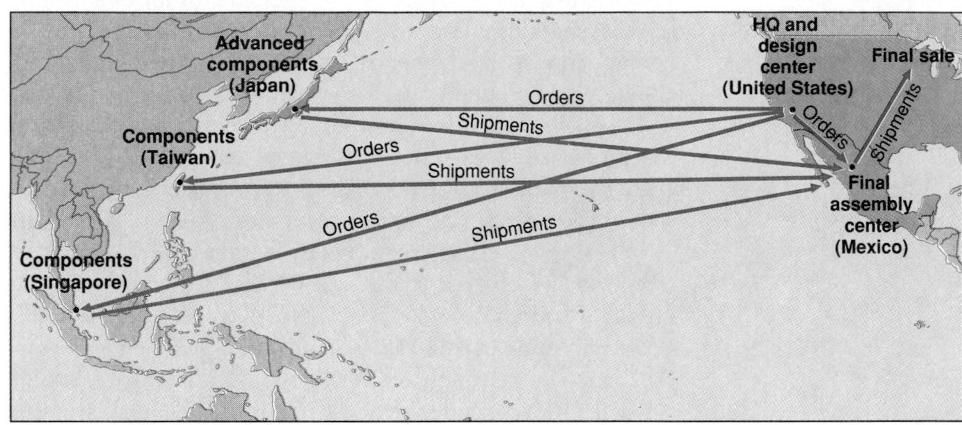

Figure 4.7
Production of a Laptop Computer

countries. (Apple, IBM, Motorola, Texas Instruments, Toshiba, and Sony all have major R&D facilities in both Japan and the United States.)

The manufacture of standard electronic components is a capital-intensive process requiring semiskilled labor, and cost pressures are intense. The best locations for such activities today are places such as Singapore, Taiwan, and Malaysia. These countries have pools of relatively skilled, low-cost labor. Thus, many producers of laptop computers have standard components produced at these locations.

The manufacture of advanced components is a capital-intensive process requiring highly skilled labor, and cost pressures are less intense. Since cost pressures are not so intense at this stage of the process, these components can be—and are—manufactured in countries with high labor costs that also have pools of highly skilled labor (primaily Japan).

Finally, assembly is a relatively labor-intensive process requiring only low-skilled labor, and cost pressures are intense. As a result, final assembly may be carried out in a country such as Mexico, which has an abundance of low-cost, low-skilled labor.

The end result is that when we look at a laptop computer produced by a U.S. manufacturer, we may find that it was designed in California, its standard components were produced in Taiwan and Singapore, its advanced components were produced in Japan, its final assembly took place in Mexico, and the finished product was then sold in the United States or elsewhere in the world (see Figure 4.7). By dispersing production activities to different locations around the globe, the U.S. manufacturer is taking advantage of the difference between countries identified by the various theories of international trade.

First-Mover Implications

The new trade theory suggests the importance to firms of building and exploiting first-mover advantages. According to the new trade theory, firms that establish a first-mover advantage with regard to the production of a particular new product may subsequently dominate global trade in that product. This is particularly true in those industries where the global market can only profitably support a handful of firms (such as the aerospace market). For the individual firm, the clear message is that it pays to invest substantial financial resources in trying to build a first-mover advantage, even if that means several years of substantial losses before a new venture becomes profitable. Although the precise details of how to achieve this are beyond the scope of this book, it should be noted that there is a vast literature on strategies for exploiting first-mover advantages.[15] It should perhaps also be noted that in recent years, Japanese firms, rather than U.S. firms, seem to have been prepared to undertake the vast investments and bear the years of losses required to build a first-mover advantage. This has certainly been true in the production of liquid crystal display (LCD) screens for laptop computers. While firms such as Toshiba and NEC invested heavily in this technology during the 1980s, many large U.S. firms exited the market. As a result, today Japanese firms dominate global trade in LCD screens, even though the technology was invented in the United States.

Policy Implications

The theories of international trade also matter to international businesses because business firms are major players on the international trade scene. Business firms produce exports, and business firms import the products of other countries. Because of their pivotal role in international trade, business firms can and do exert a strong influence on government trade policy. By lobbying government, business firms can help promote free trade, or they can promote trade restrictions. The message for business contained in the theories of international trade is that promoting free trade is generally in the best interests of the United States, although it may not always be in the best interest of an individual firm. Many firms do recognize this and do lobby for open markets.

For example, in 1991 when the U.S. government announced its intention to place a tariff on Japanese imports of liquid crystal display (LCD) screens, IBM and Apple Computer protested strongly. Both IBM and Apple pointed out that (1) Japan was the lowest-cost source of LCD screens, (2) they used these screens in their own laptop computers, and (3) the proposed tariff, by increasing the cost of LCD screens, would increase the cost of laptop computers produced by IBM and Apple, thus making them less competitive in the world market. In other words, the tariff, designed to protect U.S. firms, would be self-defeating. In response to these pressures, the U.S. government is currently rethinking its posture on this issue.

Unlike IBM and Apple, however, businesses do not always lobby for free trade. In the United States, for example, "voluntary" restrictions on imports on automobiles, machine tools, textiles, and steel are the result of direct pressures by U.S. firms in these industries on the government. The government has responded by getting foreign companies to agree to "voluntary" restrictions on their imports, using the implicit threat of more comprehensive formal trade barriers to get them to adhere to these agreements. As predicted by international trade theory, many of these agreements have been self-defeating. Take the voluntary restriction on machine-tool imports agreed to in 1985 as an example. Due to limited import competition from more-efficient foreign suppliers, the prices of machine tools in the United States have risen to higher levels than would have prevailed under a free trade scenario. Since machine tools are used throughout the manufacturing industry, the result has been to increase the costs of U.S. manufacturing in general, and a corresponding loss in world market competitiveness. Moreover, shielded from international competition by import barriers, the U.S. machine tool industry has had no incentive to increase its efficiency. Consequently, it has lost many of its export markets to ever more efficient foreign competitors. Thus the U.S. machine tool industry is now smaller than it was in 1985. For anyone schooled in international trade theory, none of these events are surprising.[16]

---

[15] For example, see M. B. Lieberman and D. B. Montgomery, "First-Mover Advantages," *Strategic Management Journal* 9 (Special issue, Summer 1988), pp. 41–58.

[16] C. A. Hamilton, "Building Better Machine Tools," *The Journal of Commerce*, October 30, 1991, p. 8; and "Manufacturing Trouble," *The Economist*, October 12, 1991, p. 71.

Finally, Porter's theory of national competitive advantage also contains important policy implications. Porter's theory suggests that it is in the best interest of business for a firm to invest in upgrading advanced factors of production; for example, to invest in better training for its employees and to increase its commitment to research and development. It is also in the best interests of business to lobby the government to adopt policies that have a favorable impact on each component of the national "diamond." Thus, according to Porter, businesses should urge government to increase its investment in education, infrastructure, and basic research (since all of these enhance advanced factors) and to adopt policies that promote strong competition within domestic markets (since this makes firms stronger international competitors, according to Porter's findings).

SUMMARY OF CHAPTER

This chapter has reviewed a number of theories that explain why it is beneficial for a country to engage in international trade and has explained the pattern of international trade that we observe in the world economy. We have seen how the theories of Smith, Ricardo, and Heckscher-Ohlin all make strong cases for unrestricted free trade. In contrast, the mercantilist doctrine and, to a much lesser extent, the new trade theory can be interpreted to support government intervention to promote exports through subsidies and to limit imports through tariffs and quotas. Porter's theory occupies more neutral ground. Unlike the mercantilists and some of the new trade theorists, Porter does not believe that governments should intervene directly in trade. Porter believes the role of government should be to create an environment that favorably influences the four components of "the national diamond," thereby stimulating the development of internationally competitive industries. We review the pros and cons of these various positions in more depth in Chapter 5.

With regard to explaining the pattern of international trade, the second objective of this chapter, we have seen that with the exception of mercantilism, which is silent on this issue, the different theories offer largely complementary explanations. Although no one theory may explain the apparent pattern of international trade, taken together, the theory of comparative advantage, the Heckscher-Ohlin theory, the product life-cycle theory, the new trade theory, and Porter's theory of national competitive advantage do suggest which factors are important. Comparative advantage tells us that productivity differences are important; Heckscher-Ohlin tells us that factors endowments matter; the product life-cycle theory tells us that where a new product is introduced is important; the new trade theory tells us that increasing returns to specialization and first-mover advantages matter; and Porter tells us that all of these factors may be important insofar as they impact upon the four components of the national diamond.

More specifically, the following points have been made in this chapter:

1. Mercantilists argued that it was in a country's best interests to run a balance-of-trade surplus.
2. Mercantilism views trade as a zero-sum game, in which one country's gains cause losses for other countries.
3. The theory of absolute advantage suggests that countries differ in their ability to produce goods efficiently. The theory suggests that a country should specialize in producing goods in areas where it has an absolute advantage and import goods in areas where other countries have absolute advantages.
4. The theory of absolute advantage argues that trade is a positive-sum game; it produces net gains for all involved.
5. The theory of comparative advantage suggests that it makes sense for a country to specialize in producing those goods that it can produce most efficiently, while buying goods that it can produce relatively less efficiently from other countries—even if that means buying goods from other countries that it could produce more efficiently itself.
6. The theory of comparative advantage suggests that unrestricted free trade brings about increased world production; that is, that trade is a positive-sum game.
7. The theory of comparative advantage also suggests that opening up a country to free trade stimulates economic growth, which in turn creates dynamic gains from trade.
8. The Heckscher-Ohlin theory argues that the pattern of international trade is determined by differences in factor endowments. It predicts that countries will export those goods that make intensive use of locally abundant factors and will import goods that make intensive use of factors that are locally scarce.
9. The Leontief paradox casts doubt on the accuracy of the Heckscher-Ohlin theory.

10. The product life-cycle theory suggests that trade patterns are influenced by where a new product is introduced.
11. In an increasingly integrated global economy, the product life-cycle theory seems to be less predictive than it was between 1945 and 1975.
12. The new trade theory argues that in those industries where the existence of substantial economies of scale imply that the world market will profitably support only a few firms, countries may predominate in the export of certain products simply because they had a firm that was a first mover in that industry.
13. Some new trade theorists have promoted the idea of strategic trade policy. The argument is that government, by the sophisticated and judicious use of subsidies, might be able to increase the chances of domestic firms becoming first movers in newly emerging industries.
14. Porter's theory of national competitive advantage suggests that the pattern of trade is influenced by four attributes of a nation: (*i*) factor endowments, (*ii*) domestic demand conditions, (*iii*) relating and supporting industries, and (*iv*) firm strategy, structure, and rivalry.
15. Porter notes that some of the most important factors that result in the creation of national competitive advantage in an industry are the presence of advanced factors of production, sophisticated and discerning domestic buyers, efficient related and supporting industries, and intense domestic rivalry.
16. Porter argues that the policies of government and of business firms can enhance or detract from the four attributes that determine national competitive advantage.
17. Theories of international trade are important to an individual business firm primarily because they can help the firm decide where to locate its various production activities.
18. Firms involved in international trade can and do exert a strong influence on government policy toward trade. By lobbying government bodies, business firms can help promote free trade or they can promote trade restrictions.

DISCUSSION QUESTIONS

1. Mercantilism is a bankrupt theory that has no place in the modern world. Discuss.
2. Using the theory of comparative advantage to support your arguments, outline the case for free trade.
3. Using the new trade theory and Porter's theory of national competitive advantage, outline the case for government policies that would build national competitive advantage in a particular industry. What kind of policies would you recommend that the government adopt? Are these policies at variance with the basic free trade philosophy?
4. You are the CEO of a textile firm that designs and manufactures mass-market clothing products in the United States. Your manufacturing process is labor-intensive and does not require highly skilled employees. Currently you have design facilities in Paris and New York and manufacturing facilities in North Carolina. Drawing upon the theory of international trade, decide whether these are optimal locations for these activities.
5. In general, policies designed to promote trade restrictions tend to be self-defeating. Discuss.

The Political Economy of International Trade

CHAPTER 5

THE RISE OF THE JAPANESE SEMICONDUCTOR INDUSTRY

The semiconductor industry was born with the invention of the transistor at Bell Laboratories in 1947. The transistor was commercialized in the 1950s by U.S. firms and it soon became a major component of electronic products. In the 1960s the transistor was replaced by the integrated circuit. Just as the transistor, the integrated circuit was developed and first commercialized by U.S. firms. Today, semiconductors are the main components of numerous electronic products including computers, photocopiers, and telecommunications equipment. In addition, they are increasingly being used in a host of other products from automobiles to machine tools. The total world market for semiconductors, which stood at $30 billion plus in 1988, is predicted to reach $200 billion by the year 2000. • United

States enterprises dominated the world market from the 1950s until the early 1980s. At the height of U.S. success in the mid-1970s U.S. firms held close to 60 percent of the world market. However, by 1988 the market share of U.S. firms had plummeted to around 35 percent, while the share held by Japanese producers had increased to around 50 percent (see Figures 5.1 and 5.2). The United States is now a net importer of semiconductors, and 5 of the 10 largest semiconductor producers are Japanese. More significantly still, by 1988 Japanese firms had captured 80 percent of the world market for the most widely used integrated circuit in digital equipment, the dynamic random access memory (DRAM). Invented by Intel and once produced exclusively by U.S. firms, there are now only two U.S. firms in the DRAM market, Micron Technologies and Texas Instruments—and Texas Instruments manufactures most of its DRAMs in Japan! • Why have the Japanese been so successful? One argument is that the industrial policy of the Japanese government was the driving force behind Japan's success in semiconductors. During the 1960s and 70s the Japanese government, principally through the Ministry of International Trade and Industry (MITI), sought to build a competitive semiconductor industry by limiting foreign competition in the domestic market and acquiring foreign technology and know-how. The foreign investment laws created after World War II (ironically by the U.S. occupation government) required the Japanese government to review for approval all applications for foreign direct investment in Japan. MITI consistently rejected all applications by U.S. semiconductor firms to set up wholly owned subsidiaries in Japan, to set up joint ventures in which the U.S. partner would have a majority stake, or to acquire equity in Japanese semiconductor firms. At the same time, the government limited foreign import penetration of the Japanese market through a combination of high tariffs and restrictive quotas. Import penetration of the Japanese market was also limited by requirements that Japanese companies get permission from MITI before buying advanced integrated circuits from foreign companies. For example, until 1974, integrated circuits that contained more than 200 circuit elements could not be imported without special permission. • Because U.S. producers were denied direct access to the Japanese semiconductor market, they typically sought indirect access by licensing their product and process know-how to Japanese enterprises. This too was regulated closely by MITI. MITI's policy was to insist that if a foreign firm was going to license technology in Japan, that technology had to be licensed to *all* Japanese firms that requested access. In other words, U.S. firms were not able to discriminate between licensees. MITI also conditioned approval of certain deals on the willingness of the involved Japanese firms to diffuse their technological developments, through sublicensing agreements, to other Japanese firms. The net result of these policies was to encourage the rapid diffusion of advanced semiconductor product and process technology throughout the Japanese semiconductor industry. • United States firms went along with this policy because it was their only way to get access to the Japanese market. In addition, licensing was initially a very lucrative arrangement for U.S. firms. By the end of the 1960s, Japanese semiconductor firms were reportedly paying at least 10 percent of their sales revenues as royalties to U.S. firms—2 percent to Western Electric, 4.5 percent to Fairchild, and 3.5 percent to Texas Instruments. The most notable long-run consequence, however, was a transfer of U.S. technological know-how to a number of emerging Japanese competitors. Shielded from foreign competition by import barriers and

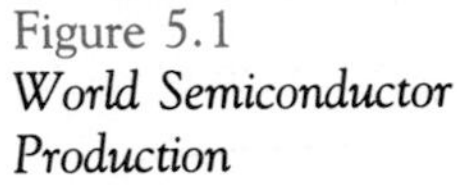

Figure 5.1
World Semiconductor Production

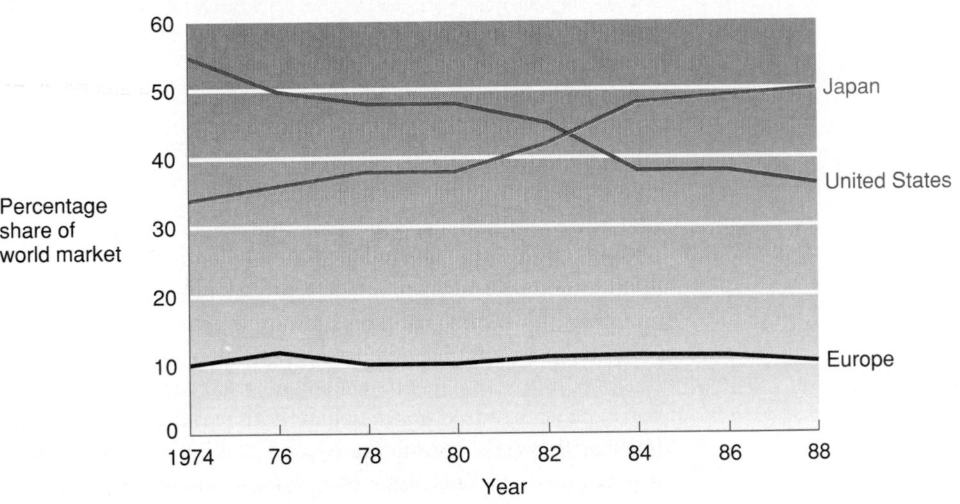

Source: Data from Standard & Poor's industry surveys; Electronics, *various issues.*

Figure 5.2
World DRAM Production

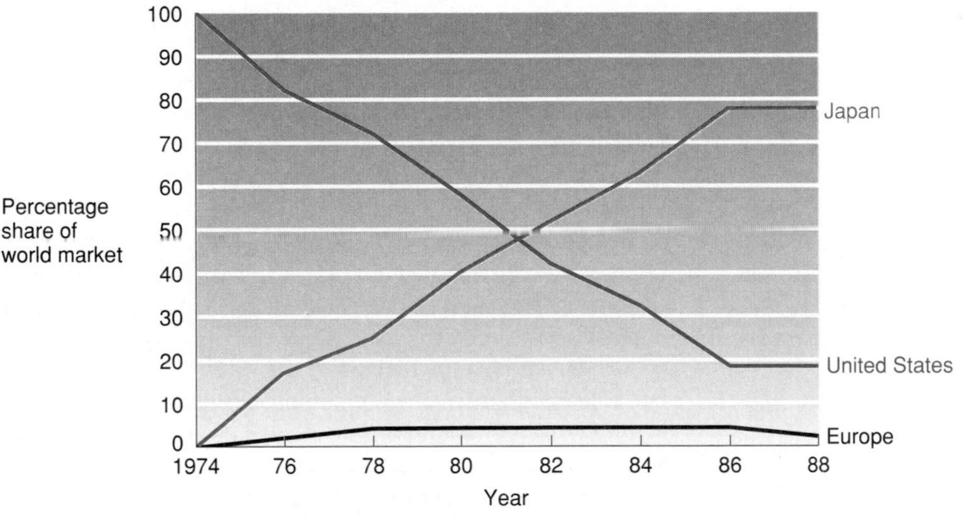

Source: Data from Standard & Poor's industry surveys; Electronics, *various issues.*

restrictions on foreign direct investment, and armed with state-of-the-art technological know-how, the Japanese firms had only each other to compete with for a share of the rapidly growing Japanese semiconductor market. Stimulated by MITI's insistence that technology be shared by all Japanese semiconductor firms, this competition was intense and based primarily on cost (since everyone had the same technology). The end result was that the firms that rose to the top in this tough environment, such as NEC, were by the mid-1970s more than capable of going head to head with U.S. semiconductor firms. ⊕ *Sources: M. Borrus, L. A. Tyson, and J. Zysman, "Creating Advantage: How Government Policies Create Trade in the Semiconductor Industry" and K. Yamamura, "Caveat Emptor: The Industrial Policy of Japan," both in* Strategic Trade Policy and the New International Economics, *ed. P. R. Krugman (Cambridge, Mass: MIT Press, 1986); and M. L. Dertouzos, R. K. Lester, and R. M. Solow,* Made in America: Regaining the Productive Edge *(Cambridge, Mass.: MIT Press, 1989).*

INTRODUCTION

Our review of the classical trade theories of Smith, Ricardo, and Heckscher–Ohlin in Chapter 4 showed us that in a world without trade barriers, trade patterns will be determined by the relative productivity of different factors of production in different countries. Countries will specialize in the production of products that they can produce most efficiently, while importing products that they can produce less efficiently. In Chapter 4 we also noted the argument that free trade is a positive-sum game. The consequences of free trade include both static gains (because free trade supports a higher level of domestic consumption) and dynamic gains (because free trade stimulates economic growth). This argument underlies much of the modern intellectual case for free trade.

This chapter is concerned with the political economy of international trade. **Political economy** is the study of how political factors influence the functioning of an economic system, such as the international trading system. The major objective of this chapter is to describe how political realities have shaped, and continue to shape, the international trading system. What we will see is that trading patterns can be determined as much by political realities as they are by economic realities (such as productivity differences across countries). Moreover, we shall see that progress toward the economic ideal of free trade is often limited by political constraints. While in theory many countries adhere to the free trade ideal, in practice most have been reluctant to engage in unrestricted free trade. Instead, to varying degrees, all countries have used trade policy tools to protect domestic producers from foreign imports. This is true of countries like the United States, Great Britain, and Germany, which, while being publicly committed to promoting free trade, have in practice adopted policies designed to restrict foreign imports and to protect producers in certain sectors of their economies. It is also true of countries like Japan, which since the early 1980s has had very few formal trade barriers but still maintains numerous informal barriers to foreign competition. And it is most definitely true of countries like Argentina, Ghana, India, and Peru, all of which have long histories of restricting imports.

Due to the dominance of the classical theories of international trade, until the 1980s the economic rationale for engaging in protectionism was limited to a few special cases. Protection was usually viewed as the unfortunate outcome of domestic political pressures within the various members of the world community. Thus, despite a public commitment to free trade, successive U.S. governments have supported controls on the importation of textiles, primarily because of the political influence exercised by representatives and senators from the textile-producing regions of the United States. Despite such domestic political pressures, however, there has been a general belief among the advanced industrialized nations that if international institutions could be constructed to promote greater free trade, all would benefit.

Recently there have been some signs of a shift away from this position. Most important, limited protectionism has been given intellectual respectability in some circles by the rise of the new trade theory. As we saw in Chapter 4, new trade theory suggests that in industries where economies of scale are significant and the world market can profitably support only a few firms, first-mover advantages are critical. In such circumstances, government support can have two effects: (*a*) it can help domestic firms achieve first-mover advantages and (*b*) it can help domestic firms compete against foreign firms that have first-mover advantages. This forms the basis of the economic argument for **strategic trade policy**. Strategic trade policy is policy aimed at improving the competitive position of a domestic industry in the world market. The advocates of strategic trade policy often hold up the rise of the Japanese semiconductor industry, detailed in the opening case, as an example of how selective government intervention can benefit national firms and a national economy. However, as we shall see in this chapter, the case for strategic trade policy is far from solid. Most telling, many of those who developed the new trade theory argue that strategic trade policy is in reality unworkable.

With these issues in mind, the rest of this chapter is structured as follows. First, we will look at the evolution of the world trading system, including the roots of the post–World War II movement toward free trade, the formation of the **General Agreement on Tariffs and Trade (GATT)**, and the rise of protectionist pressures in the 1980s. Second, we will review the various instruments of trade policy. Third, we will review the political and economic arguments for government intervention in trade, including the strategic trade policy argument. Fourth, we will reexamine the economic case for free trade in light of the economic arguments for government intervention. Finally, we will discuss the implications of the trade debate for business practice.

DEVELOPMENT OF THE WORLD TRADING SYSTEM

In this section we look at the evolution of the world trading system. Our reason for reviewing some history at this juncture is that history casts a long shadow over the current trade debate. In particular, the post-1945 movement toward greater free trade was shaped by the experiences of the Great Depression of the 1930s.

From Smith to the Great Depression

As we saw in Chapter 4, the intellectual case for free trade goes back to the late 18th century and the work of two economists, Adam Smith and David Ricardo. Free trade as a government policy was first officially embraced by Great Britain in 1846, when the British Parliament repealed the Corn Laws. The Corn Laws placed a high tariff on imports of foreign corn. (A **tariff** is a tax on imports; its effect is to raise the price of imports.) The objectives of the Corn Law tariff were to raise government revenues and to protect British corn producers. There had been annual motions in Parliament in favor of free trade since the 1820s when David Ricardo was a member of Parliament. However, agricultural protection was withdrawn only as a result of a protracted debate when the effects of a harvest failure in Britain were compounded by the imminent threat of famine in Ireland. Faced with considerable hardship and suffering among the populace, Parliament narrowly reversed its long-held position.

During the next 80 years or so, Great Britain, as one of the world's dominant trading powers, pushed the case for trade liberalization; but by and large the British government was a voice in the wilderness. Its policy of unilateral free trade was not reciprocated by its major trading partners. The only reason Great Britain was able to hold on to this policy for so long was that, as the world's largest exporting nation, it had far more to lose from a trade war than did any other country.

By the 1930s, however, the British attempt to stimulate free trade was buried under the economic rubble of the Great Depression. The Great Depression had roots in the failure of the world economy to mount a sustained economic recovery after the end of

World War I in 1918. Things got worse in 1929 with the U.S. stock market collapse and the subsequent run on the U.S. banking system. Economic problems were compounded in 1930 when the U.S. Congress passed the Smoot-Hawley tariff. Aimed at avoiding rising unemployment by protecting domestic industries and diverting consumer demand away from foreign products, the Smoot-Hawley tariff erected an enormous wall of tariff barriers. Captured by special interests in Congress, almost every industry was rewarded with its "made to order" tariff. A particularly odd aspect of the Smoot-Hawley tariff-raising binge was that the United States was running a balance-of-payment surplus at the time and it was the world's largest creditor nation. In any event, the Smoot-Hawley tariff had a damaging effect on employment abroad. Other countries reacted to the U.S. action by raising their own tariff barriers. U.S. exports tumbled in response, and the world slid further into the Great Depression.[1]

GATT, Trade Liberalization, and Economic Growth

The economic damage caused by the beggar-thy-neighbor trade policies that the Smoot-Hawley act ushered in exerted a profound influence on the economic institutions and ideology of the post-World War II world. The United States emerged from the war not only victorious but economically dominant. After the debacle of the Great Depression, opinion in the U.S. Congress had swung strongly in favor of free trade. As a consequence, under U.S. leadership, the General Agreement on Tariffs and Trade (GATT) was established in 1947.

The GATT is a multilateral agreement whose objective is to liberalize trade by eliminating tariffs, subsidies, import quotas, and the like. Since its foundation in 1947, the GATT's membership has grown from 19 to more than 100 nations. The GATT did not attempt to liberalize trade restrictions in one fell swoop; that would have been impossible. Rather, the process of tariff reduction has been spread over eight rounds. (The latest, the Uruguay Round was launched in 1986, and as of June 1993 it still had not been completed.) In these rounds mutual tariff reductions are negotiated among all members, who then commit themselves not to raise import tariffs above negotiated rates. GATT regulations are enforced by a mutual monitoring mechanism. If a country feels that one of its trading partners is violating a GATT regulation, it can ask the Geneva-based bureaucracy that administers the GATT to investigate. If GATT investigators find the complaints to be valid, member countries may be asked to pressure the offending party to change its policies. Up until now, such pressure has always been sufficient to get an offending country to change its policies. If it were not, the offending country could in theory be expelled from the GATT.

In its early years the GATT was by most measures very successful. In the United States, for example, the average tariff declined by nearly 92 percent over the 33 years spanning the Geneva Round of 1947 and the Tokyo Round of 1973-79 (see Figure 5.3). Consistent with the theoretical arguments first advanced by Ricardo and reviewed in Chapter 4, the move toward free trade under the GATT appeared to stimulate economic growth. From 1953 to 1963 world trade grew at an annual rate of 6.1 percent, and world income grew at an annual rate of 4.3 percent. Performance in the period 1963 to 1973 was even better; world trade grew at 8.9 percent per annum, and world income grew at 5.1 percent per annum.[2]

---

[1] Note that the Smoot-Hawley tariff did not cause the Great Depression. However, the beggar-thy-neighbor trade policies that it ushered in certainly made things worse. See J. Bhagwati, *Protectionism* (Cambridge,Mass.: MITT Press, 1989).

[2] Bhagwati, *Protectionism.*

Figure 5.3 *Reductions in Average U.S. Tariff Rates after GATT Rounds*

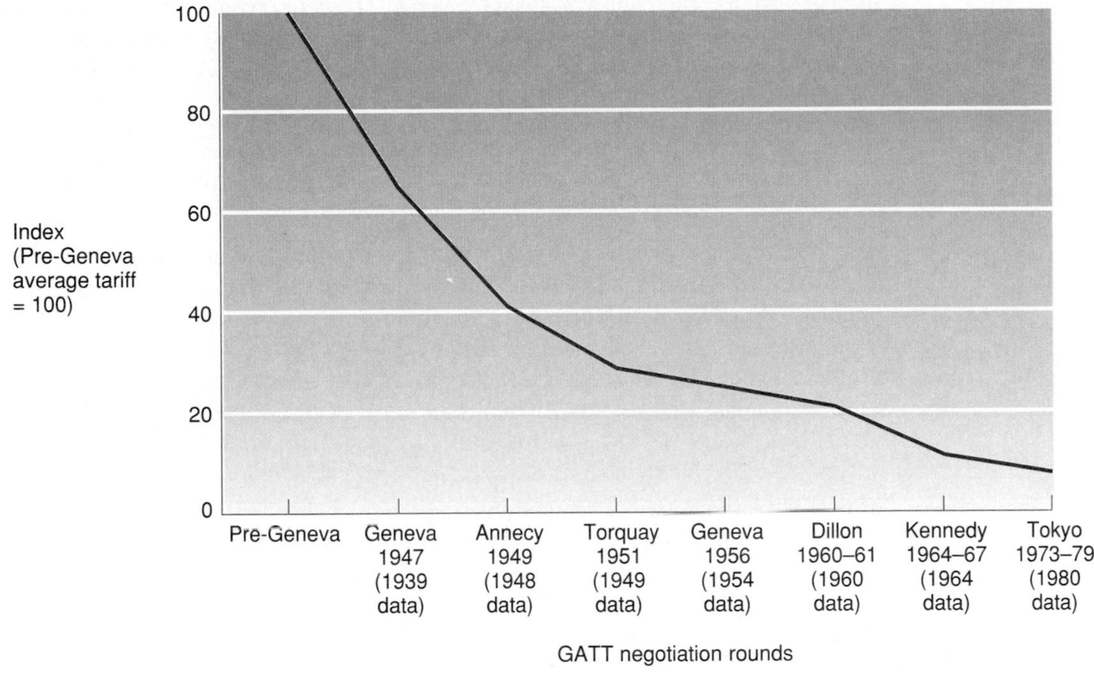

Note: Indexes are calculated from percentage reductions in average weighted tariff rates given in Finger, 1979 (Table 1, p. 425), and World Bank, 1987 (Table 8.1, p. 136). Weighted average U.S. tariff rate after Tokyo Round was 4.6 percent (World Bank, 1987).

Rising Protectionist Pressures

Sometime during the 1970s the tide began to turn against the GATT and free trade. Slowly at first, but gathering strength in the late 1980s, protectionist pressures began to increase in a number of industrialized countries. There seem to be three main reasons for this trend. First, the economic success of Japan has strained the world trading system. Japan was in ruins when the GATT was created; since then it has become the world's second-largest economy and its largest exporter. Japan's success in such industries as automobiles and semiconductors by itself might have been enough to strain the world trading system. Things have been made worse, however, by the widespread perception in the West that despite low tariff rates and subsidies, Japanese markets are effectively closed to imports and foreign investment by **administrative trade barriers** (nontariff barriers to imports; the concept is discussed in detail later in the chapter).

Second, the world trading system has been further strained by the persistent (since the early 1980s) trade deficit in the world's largest economy, the United States. Although the deficit peaked in 1987 at over $170 billion, by the end of 1992 the annual rate was still running at around $80 billion. From a political perspective, the matter is worsened by the fact that in 1992 the United States ran a $45 billion deficit in its trade with Japan—a country perceived as not playing by the rules.

The consequences of the U.S. deficit have included painful adjustments in industries such as automobiles, machine tools, semiconductors, steel, and textiles, where domestic producers have been steadily losing market share to foreign competitors. Resulting unemployment has given rise to renewed protectionist pressures in the U.S. Congress. Consider the case of the automobile industry. In 1991 the big three U.S. companies

(GM, Ford, and Chrysler) posted combined losses of $4.9 billion for the first three quarters of the year. Due to weak demand, their sales dropped by 12.4 percent, while the sales of Japanese companies dropped by only 5.9 percent, resulting in a market-share gain for the Japanese. With this as background, the big three have worked hard to generate support in the Congress for limits on Japanese competition—with some success. Senator Donald Riegle of Michigan, for example, has stated that

> the fact is that Japan has been carrying out an economic invasion of the United States, and it's being largely directed by the government of Japan. . . . The events are different from World War II, but the effects are the same.[3]

Another Michigan senator, Carl Levin, is sponsoring a bill aimed at Japan that would force the U.S. government to retaliate against countries that discriminate against U.S. products. This trend is particularly worrisome for pro-free trade forces in the world community, primarily because from 1947 to the mid-1970s the U.S. government was one of the world's main advocates of free trade. Without the backing of the U.S. government, many feel that the GATT will lose much of its strength.

A third reason for the trend toward greater protectionism is that in response to the pressures created by the Japanese surplus and the U.S. deficit, many countries have found ways to get around GATT regulations. In particular, bilateral voluntary export restraints (VERs), in which one country agrees to "voluntarily" limit its exports to another, circumvent GATT agreements, because neither the importing country nor the exporting country complains to the GATT bureaucracy in Geneva—and without a complaint, the GATT bureaucracy can do nothing. Exporting countries agree to VERs as a way of avoiding far more damaging punitive tariffs. One of the best-known examples is the VER between Japan and the United States, under which Japanese producers promised to limit their auto imports into the United States as a way of defusing growing trade tensions.

According to a World Bank study, 13 percent of the imports of industrialized countries in 1981 were subjected to nontariff trade barriers such as VERs. By 1986 this figure had increased to 16 percent. The most rapid rise was in the United States, where the value of imports affected by nontariff barriers (primarily VERs) increased by 23 percent between 1981 and 1986.[4]

The International Trade Framework in the 1990s

Given these trends, the question arises as to whether the post-war free trade framework can be held together. Some fear that the world might slide into a trade war similar to that experienced in the aftermath of the Smoot-Hawley tariff, with countries adopting beggar-thy-neighbor trade policies. This danger increased in late 1992 when the United States and the European Community (EC) clashed over EC subsidies to European oil seed producers. The United States claimed that the EC subsidies allowed European oil seed farmers to underprice their U.S. competitors on world markets, thereby gaining an unfair competitive advantage. As a way of getting the subsidies reduced, the United States threatened to impose a 300 percent punitive tariff on imports of French wine. The United States targeted French wine because more than another EC country, France has argued for maintaining EC subsidies at their present level. (France has a politically powerful farm lobby.) The French countered with a threat to impose similar tariffs on imports of U.S. goods, and suddenly the possibility of a trade war between the United States and the European Community seemed very real. Having gone to the brink of the

---

[3] "Tensions Mount as Auto Losses Mount Up," *The Seattle Times*, November 3, 1991, p. E1, E4.

[4] World Bank, *World Development Report* (New York: Oxford University Press, 1987).

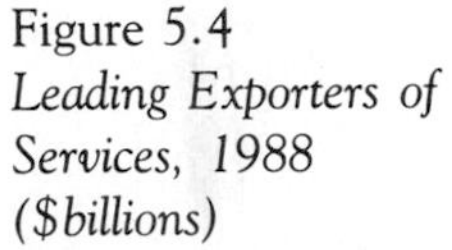

Figure 5.4
Leading Exporters of Services, 1988 ($billions)

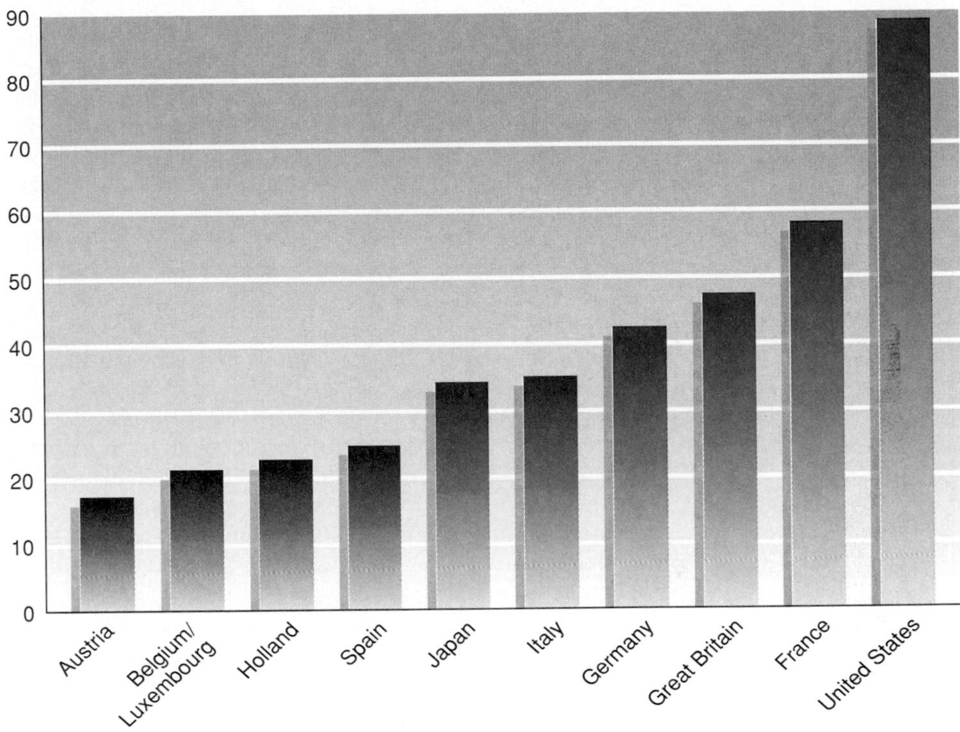

Source: Data from The Economist, *July 1990, p. 70.*

abyss, in November 1992 the European Community and the United States agreed to a compromise in which the European Community would reduce its subsidies somewhat, and the United States would lift the threat of imposing punitive tariffs. At of the time of writing, however, it was still not clear whether the French would go along with the rest of the European Community and support this deal.

Despite such problems, there are promising signs that the world will not slip into a trade war. For one thing, there is the countertrend of the rise of free trade blocs in Europe and North America (which we consider in Chapter 8). There is also a marked trend among developing countries, particularly those of Latin America, away from protectionist policies and toward a free trade regime.

In addition, after stalling for some time, the current Uruguay Round of GATT negotiations seems to be drawing to a close. If successful, they may for the first time extend the GATT accords to include a wide range of services including banking, insurance, transportation, telecommunications, consultancy, construction, and retail. Currently world exports of services amount to $600 billion, and the total is growing fast (see Figure 5.4). The leader is the United States, which in 1988 exported $88.7 billion of services, compared to Japan's exports of $34.2 billion. By extending the GATT to include services, the Uruguay Round could stimulate further growth in world trade and output. Since most commentators agree that the United States has a comparative advantage in the provision of services, this trend could benefit the United States more than most countries, thereby reducing protectionist pressures in the Congress.[5]

[5] "GATT and Services," *The Economist*, July 1990, p. 70.

BOX 5.1

Japan's Distribution System as a Barrier to Trade

Many foreign firms claim that Japan's extremely complex and tightly controlled distribution system is the biggest stumbling block for foreign firms trying to enter the Japanese market. Japan's distribution system is layered with many middlemen between producer and the final point of sale to consumers. Moreover, Japan's retail laws, designed to protect the hundreds of thousands of small retailers in the country, block American-style supermarkets and discount stores. The effect is to increase the price of many imported goods by four or five times. For high-status consumer products the effect can be much worse. For example, the wholesale price of a bottle of Hennessy's VSOP cognac is about $7. By the time it gets to the store shelves, it is priced at $77.50. Or take a women's scarf, purchased by an import agent for $30, as an example. The agent sells it to a wholesaler for $60, who then sells it to a department store for $90, which charges the consumer $160! This kind of markup makes it difficult for a foreign firm to build up significant sales in Japan. It also hurts the Japanese consumer, who must pay far more for many products than his or her Western counterpart. In addition to these problems, just finding someone to distribute a firm's product can be difficult because of long-standing exclusive arrangements between wholesalers and retailers. However, there are signs that this system is beginning to crack. For example, in what may be the beginning of a revolution in Japan's distribution system, after years of lobbying to overcome opposition from small retailers, in December 1991 the U.S. discount toystore chain, Toys R Us, opened its first store in Japan. Others are planned to open in the near future.

Source: L. W. Tuller, Going Global: New Opportunities for Growing Companies to Compete in World Markets *(Homewood, Ill.: Richard D. Irwin, 1991).*

Also encouraging are the signs that the United States and Japan may be beginning to work out some of their differences over trade. In 1990, for example, a joint communiqué issued by Washington and Tokyo announced agreement on mutual changes by the two countries designed to improve trade relations and reduce the Japanese trade surplus with the United States. Among other things, the so-called **Structural Impediments Initiative** aims to open up Japan's restrictive distribution system to foreign imports and foreign investment. If successful, this could go a long way to reducing trade tensions between the two countries. (Box 5.1 provides a description of Japan's restrictive distribution system.) In addition, after years of promoting exports, Japan's government is now reportedly urging its producers to import more products in an attempt to reduce its trade surplus, thereby defusing trade tensions. As a gesture of good faith in this effort, in November 1991 Japan's government approved measures to boost the government's own procurement of foreign products. The government intends to increase its purchases from abroad from ¥70 billion ($550 million) to ¥150 billion.[6]

INSTRUMENTS OF TRADE POLICY

We review six main instruments of trade policy in this section: tariffs, subsidies, import quotas, voluntary export restraints, local content requirements, and administrative policies. Tariffs are the oldest and simplest instrument of trade policy. They are also the instrument that GATT has been most successful in limiting. It is worth emphasizing that

[6] "Japanese Trade: Import or Else, *The Economist*, November 30, 1991, p. 72.

the rise of protectionist pressures in the 1980s has been accompanied by a rise of nontariff barriers; particularly of subsidies, quotas, and voluntary export restraints.

Tariffs

Tariffs are the oldest form of trade policy. Typically placed on imports of foreign products, they fall into two categories. **Specific tariffs** are levied as a fixed charge for each unit of a good imported (for example, $3 per barrel of oil). **Ad valorem tariffs** are levied as a proportion of the value of the imported good. An example of an ad valorem tariff is the 25 percent tariff that the Bush administration placed on imported light trucks (pickup trucks, four-wheel-drive vehicles, minivans, etc.).

The effect of a tariff is to raise the cost of imported products relative to domestic products. Thus the 25 percent tariff on imported light trucks has increased the price of Japanese light truck imports relative to U.S.-produced light trucks, as an attempt to protect the market share of U.S. auto manufacturers. (A cynic might note that, in practice, all that the tariff did was speed up the plans of Japanese automobile companies to build light trucks in the United States.) While the principal objective of most tariffs is to protect domestic producers against foreign competition, they also raise revenue for the government. Until the introduction of the income tax, for example, the U.S. government raised most of its revenues from tariffs.

The important thing to understand about a tariff is who loses and who gains. The government gains, because the tariff increases government revenues. Domestic producers gain, because the tariff affords them some protection against foreign competitors by increasing the cost of imported foreign goods. Consumers lose, on the other hand, since they must pay more for certain imports. Whether the gains to the government and domestic producers exceed the loss to consumers depends on various factors such as the amount of the tariff, the importance of the imported good to domestic consumers, the number of jobs saved in the protected industry, and so on. Detailed consideration of these issues is beyond the scope of this book.[7] However, it is worth emphasizing two conclusions that can be derived from a more advanced analysis. First, tariffs are unambiguously proproducer and anticonsumer. Second, tariffs reduce the overall efficiency of the world economy. They reduce efficiency because a protective tariff encourages domestic firms to produce products at home that, in theory, could be produced more efficiently abroad.

Subsidies

A subsidy is a government payment to a domestic producer. Subsidies take many forms including cash grants, low-interest loans, tax breaks, and government equity participation in domestic firms. By lowering costs, subsidies help domestic producers in two ways: they help them compete against low-cost foreign imports and they help them gain export markets.

According to official national figures, government subsidies to industry in most industrialized countries in 1986 amounted to between 2 percent and 3.5 percent of the value of industrial output. (These figures exclude subsidies to agriculture and public services.) The average rate of subsidy in the United States was 0.5 percent; in Japan it was 1 percent, and in Europe it ranged from just below 2 percent in Great Britain and West Germany to as much as 6 to 7 percent in Sweden and Ireland.[8] These figures, however, almost certainly underestimate the true value of subsidies, since they are based only on cash grants and ignore other kinds of subsidies (e.g., equity participation or low-

---

[7] For a detailed analysis of the effect of a tariff, see P. Krugman and M. Obstfeld, *International Economics, Theory and Policy*, 2nd Ed. (New York: Harper Collins, 1991).

[8] "From the Sublime to the Subsidy," *The Economist*, February 24, 1990, p. 71

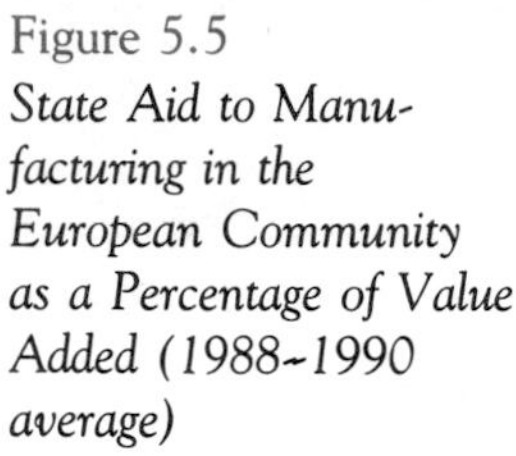

Figure 5.5
State Aid to Manufacturing in the European Community as a Percentage of Value Added (1988–1990 average)

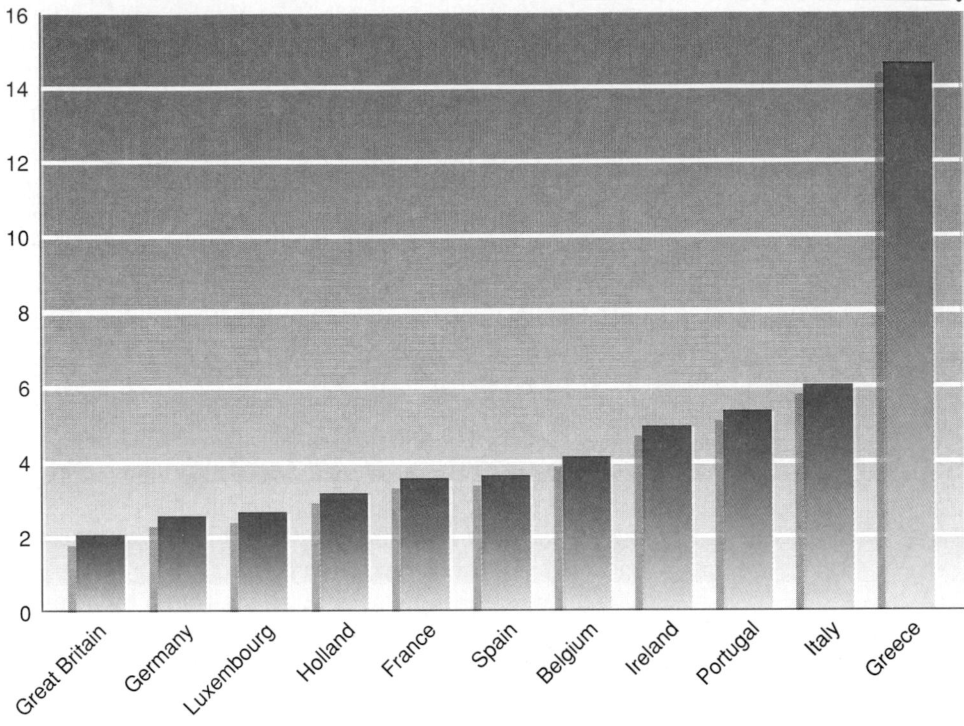

Source: EC Commission.

interest loans). A more detailed study of subsidies within the European Community was undertaken by the EC Commission (see Figure 5.5). This study found that subsidies to manufacturing enterprises in 1990 ranged from a low of 2 percent of total valued added in Great Britain to a high of 14.6 percent in Greece. Among the four largest EC countries, Italy was the worst offender; its subsidies are three times those of Great Britain, twice those of Germany, and 1.5 times those of France.[9]

The main gains from subsidies accrue to domestic producers, whose international competitiveness is increased as a result of them. Advocates of strategic trade policy favor the use of subsidies as a way of helping domestic firms achieve a dominant position in those industries where economies of scale are important and the world market is not large enough to profitably support more than a few firms (e.g., aerospace, semiconductors). According to this argument, subsidies can help a firm achieve a first-mover advantage in an emerging industry (just as U.S. government subsidies, in the form of substantial R&D grants, allegedly helped Boeing). If this is achieved, further gains to the domestic economy arise from the employment and tax revenues that a major global company can generate.

On the other hand, subsidies must be paid for. Typically governments pay for subsidies by taxing individuals. Therefore, whether subsidies generate national benefits that exceed their national costs is debatable. Moreover, in practice many subsidies are not that successful at increasing the international competitiveness of domestic producers. Rather, they tend to protect the inefficient, rather than promoting efficiency.

[9] "Aid Addicts," *The Economist,* August 8, 1992, p. 61.

Import Quotas and Voluntary Export Restraints

An import quota is a direct restriction on the quantity of some good that may be imported into a country. The restriction is normally enforced by issuing import licenses to a group of individuals or firms. For example, the United States has a quota on imports of cheese. The only firms allowed to import cheese are certain trading companies, each of which is allocated the right to import a maximum number of pounds of cheese each year. In some cases the right to sell is given directly to the governments of exporting countries. This is the case for sugar and textile imports in the United States.

A variant on the import quota is the **voluntary export restraint (VER)**. A VER is a quota on trade imposed by the exporting country, typically at the request of the importing country's government. One of the most famous examples is the limitation on auto exports to the United States enforced by Japanese automobile producers in 1981. A response to direct pressure from the U.S. government, this VER limited Japanese imports to no more than 1.68 million vehicles per year. The agreement was revised in 1984 to allow Japanese producers to import 1.85 million vehicles per year. In 1985 the agreement was allowed to lapse, but the Japanese government indicated its intentions at that time to continue to restrict exports to the United States to 1.85 million vehicles per year.

Foreign producers agree to VERs because they fear that if they do not, far more damaging punitive tariffs or import quotas might follow. Agreeing to a VER, therefore, is seen as a way of making the best of a bad situation by appeasing protectionist pressures in a country.

As with tariffs and subsidies, both import quotas and VERs benefit domestic producers by limiting import competition. On the other hand, quotas do not benefit consumers. An import quota or VER always raises the domestic price of an imported good. When imports are limited to a low percentage of the market by a quota or VER, the effect is to bid the price up for that limited foreign supply. In the case of the automobile industry, for example, the VER had the effect of increasing the price for the limited supply of Japanese imports into the United States. As a result, according to a study by the U.S. Federal Trade Commission, the automobile industry VER cost U.S. consumers about $1 billion per year between 1981 and 1985. That $1 billion per year went to Japanese producers in the form of higher prices.[10]

Local Content Requirements

A local content requirement is a requirement that some specific fraction of a good be produced domestically. The requirement can be expressed either in physical terms (e.g., 75 percent of component parts for this product must be produced locally) or in value terms (e.g., 75 percent of the value of this product must be produced locally). Local content regulations have been widely used by developing countries as a device for trying to shift their manufacturing base from the simple assembly of products whose parts are manufactured elsewhere, into the local manufacture of component parts. More recently, the issue of local content has been raised by several developed countries. In the United States, for example, pressure is building to insist that 75 percent of the component parts that go into cars built in the United States by Japanese companies such as Toyota and Honda be manufactured in the United States. Both Toyota and Honda have reacted to such pressures by announcing their intention to buy more American manufactured parts.

From the point of view of a domestic producer of component parts, local content regulations provide protection in the same way an import quota does: by limiting foreign competition. The aggregate economic effects are also the same; domestic producers benefit, but the restrictions on imports raise the prices of imported components. In turn,

---

[10] Quoted in Krugman and Obstfeld, *International Economics*.

higher prices for imported components are passed on to consumers of the final product in the form of higher final prices. So as with all trade policies, local content regulations tend to benefit producers and not consumers.

Administrative Policies

In addition to the formal instruments of trade policy, governments of all types sometimes use a range of informal administrative instruments to restrict imports and boost exports. Some would argue that the Japanese are the masters of this kind of trade policy. In recent years Japan's formal tariff and nontariff barriers have been among the lowest in the world. However, critics charge that their informal administrative barriers to imports more than compensate for this. One example is that of tulip bulbs; the Netherlands exports tulip bulbs to almost every country in the world except Japan. The reason is that Japanese customs inspectors insist on checking every tulip bulb by cutting it vertically down the middle, and even Japanese ingenuity cannot put them back together again! Another example concerns the U.S. express mail operator, Federal Express. Federal Express has had a tough time expanding its global express services into Japan, primarily because Japanese customs inspectors insist on opening a large proportion of express packages to check for pornography—a process that can delay an "express" package for days. However, it would be wrong to think that Japan is the only country that engages in such policies. In yet another example, France required that all imported videotape recorders arrive through a small customs entry point that was both remote and poorly staffed. The resulting delays kept Japanese VCRs out of the French market until a VER agreement was negotiated.[11] As with all instruments of trade policy, administrative instruments benefit producers and hurt consumers, who are denied access to possibly superior foreign products.

THE CASE FOR GOVERNMENT INTERVENTION

This section looks at the case for government intervention in trade policy. There are two types of argument for government intervention, *political and economic*. Political arguments for intervention are typically concerned with protecting the interests of certain groups within a nation (normally producers), often at the expense of other groups (normally consumers). Economic arguments for intervention are typically concerned with boosting the overall wealth of a nation (to the benefit of all, both producers and consumers).

Political Arguments for Intervention

Political arguments for government intervention cover a range of issues including protecting jobs, protecting industries deemed important for national security, and retaliating to unfair foreign competition. A characteristic of political arguments for government intervention is that they are not always based on careful economic reasoning. Thus they tend to be relatively easy for economists to refute.

Protecting Jobs and Industries

Perhaps the most common political argument for government intervention is that it is necessary for protecting jobs and industries from foreign competition. The voluntary export restraints (VERs) that offered some protection to the U.S. automobile, machine tool, and steel industries during the 1980s were motivated by such considerations.

---

[11] Sources: Bhagwati, *Protectionism*; and "Japan to Curb VCR Exports," *The New York Times*, November 21, 1983, p. D5.

BOX 5.2

The European Community's Common Agriculture Policy—An Illustration of the Costs of Government Intervention

The European Community's Common Agricultural Policy (CAP) began in 1957 as an attempt to guarantee high prices to European farmers, who have always been a politically important force in Europe. This is particularly true in France (where the farm vote has the power to influence the outcome of national elections) and to a lesser extent in Germany.

The basic machinery of the CAP works as follows. For each agricultural product, a support price is specified. If prices fall below this price, the European Community (EC) purchases a proportion of the product and takes it off the market. By reducing supply, the European Community pushes prices back up to the support level. To prevent this policy from drawing in imports, it is backed by tariffs that offset the difference between EC and world prices. This policy has basically succeeded in keeping EC food prices high, thereby benefiting inefficient farmers.

The cost to EC consumers, however, has been enormous. In the early 1980s, for example, the EC support price for wheat was 46 percent higher than the world price; for beef it was 90 percent higher, and for butter it was 186 percent higher. To keep prices at support levels, the European Community has been forced to buy and store huge quantities of food. At the end of 1985, for example, it had stored 780,000 tons of beef, 1.2 million tons of butter, and 12 million tons of wheat. By the end of the 1980s the annual cost of buying up surplus food was reckoned to be running at $20 billion. In effect, this represented a subsidy to Europe's inefficient farmers financed by Europe's taxpayers.

The cost to the rest of the world is also nontrivial. Not only are efficient agricultural producers outside of Europe denied free access to the EC market, the CAP has depressed world prices for food. To dispose of their food stockpiles, the European Community has turned to a policy of exporting the surplus at world prices. Much to the annoyance of other major agricultural producers, the flood of subsidized EC agricultural products onto the world market has further depressed world prices, and in the view of many, created unfair competition.

At the time of writing, the CAP is under attack, both from budgetary pressures within the European Community and from the United States and other efficient agricultural producers at the current GATT negotiations. Indeed, the Uruguay Round of GATT talks almost broke down because of a refusal by the EC to reform the CAP to reduce farm subsidies. As of 1993, some limited reform of the CAP looks possible, although whether this will correct the distorting effect it has on world trade is unlikely.

Source: D. Swann, The Economics of the Common Market, *6th ed. (London: Penguin Books, 1990).*

Similarly, Japan's quotas on imports of rice are aimed at protecting jobs in that country's agricultural sector. The same motive underlay the establishment of the Common Agricultural Policy (CAP) by the European Community. The CAP was designed to protect the jobs of Europe's politically powerful farmers by restricting imports and guaranteeing prices. However, as the example in Box 5.2 demonstrates, the higher prices that resulted from the CAP have cost Europe's consumers dearly. Indeed, this is true of most attempts to protect jobs and industries through government intervention. As we saw earlier in the chapter, all that the VER in the automobile industry succeeded in doing was raising the price of Japanese imports, at a cost of $1 billion per year to U.S. consumers. More generally, the International Trade Commission calculated in a recent report that U.S. tariffs designed to protect U.S. jobs and industries from foreign competition are costing U.S. consumers about $15 billion per year.[12]

---

12 "Costs of Protection," *Journal of Commerce*, September 25, 1991, p. 8A.

In addition to the fact that trade controls hurt consumers, there is also evidence that they may sometimes hurt the very producers they are intended to protect. In Chapter 4, for example, we noted how the VER agreement in the U.S. machine tool industry has been self-defeating. By limiting Japanese and Taiwanese machine tool imports, the VER raised the prices of machine tools purchased by U.S. manufacturers to levels above those prevailing in the world market. In turn, this raised the capital costs of the U.S. manufacturing industry in general, thereby decreasing its international competitiveness.

National Security

Countries sometimes argue that it is necessary to protect certain industries because they are important for national security. Defense-related industries often get this kind of attention (e.g., aerospace, advanced electronics, semiconductors, etc.). Although not as common as it used to be, this argument is still made from time to time. Those in favor of protecting the U.S. semiconductor industry from foreign competition, for example, argue that semiconductors are now such important components of defense products that it would be dangerous to rely primarily on foreign producers for them. In 1986 this argument helped convince the federal government to support Sematech, a consortium of 14 U.S. semiconductor companies that accounts for 90 percent of the U.S. industry's revenues. Sematech's mission is to conduct joint research into manufacturing techniques that can be parceled out to members. The U.S. government provides a $100 million per year subsidy to Sematech.

Retaliation

Some argue that governments should use the threat to intervene in trade policy as a bargaining tool to help open up foreign markets and force trading partners to "play by the rules of the game." The Bush administration was among those that adopted this "get tough" approach. If it works, this politically motivated rationale for government intervention may liberalize trade. It is a risky strategy, however, for if it fails, the result can be higher trade barriers all around.

Consider the recent trade dispute between China and the United States. The United States has accused China of violating numerous U.S. copyrights and patents, cheating U.S. firms of $400 million annually in the process. For example, pirated copies of MS-Dos version 5.0, Microsoft's operating system software for personal computers, are manufactured in China and then sold in other countries as the real thing. Microsoft receives not one cent from these sales and is justifiably upset. In addition, China has been accused by the U.S. government of throwing dozens of tariffs and administrative restrictions in the way of U.S. exports to China.

Against this background, in 1991 U.S. trade representative Carla Hills prepared a list of Chinese products that will be subjected to tariffs if China does not change its trade practices. Since China's 1991 trade surplus with the United States was second only to Japan's, the effects of such action on China's economy would be nontrivial. If the Chinese back down, the result will be a victory for free trade. However, it is not clear that the Chinese will back down. As of 1993 the Chinese are threatening to retaliate to U.S. tariffs with trade restrictions of their own. Among the deals at risk are the sales of four dozen Boeing jetliners worth more than $3 billion and already ordered by China. If this worst-case scenario comes to pass, all will lose.[13]

---

[13] "U.S., China Trade Dispute Worsens," *Seattle Times*, October 27, 1991, pp. E1, E4.

Economic Arguments for Intervention

With the development of the new trade theory and strategic trade policy (see Chapter 4), the economic arguments for government intervention have undergone something of a renaissance in recent years. Until the early 1980s, most economists saw little benefit in government intervention and strongly advocated a free trade policy. This position has changed somewhat with the development of strategic trade policy, although as we will see in the next section, there are still strong arguments for sticking to a free trade stance.

The Infant Industry Argument

The infant industry argument is by far the oldest argument for government intervention. It was first proposed by Alexander Hamilton in 1792. According to this argument, many developing countries have a potential comparative advantage in manufacturing, but new manufacturing industries there cannot initially compete with well-established industries in developed countries. In order to allow manufacturing to get a toehold, the argument is that governments should temporarily support new industries (with tariffs, import quotas, and subsidies) until they have grown strong enough to meet international competition.

This argument has had substantial appeal for the governments of developing nations during the last 40 years. Moreover, the infant industry argument has been recognized as a legitimate reason for protectionism by the GATT. Nevertheless, many economists remain very critical of this argument. They make two main points. First, protection of manufacturing from foreign competition does no good unless the protection helps make the industry efficient. In case after case, however, protection seems to have done little more than foster the development of inefficient industries that have little hope of ever competing in the world market. Brazil, for example, built up the world's 10th-largest auto industry behind tariff barriers and quotas. Once those barriers were removed in the late 1980s, however, foreign imports soared and the industry was forced to face up to the fact that after 30 years of protection, the Brazilian industry was one of the world's most inefficient.[14]

A second point is that the infant industry argument relies on an assumption that firms are unable to make efficient long-term investments by borrowing money from the domestic or international capital market. Consequently, governments have been required to subsidize long-term investments. Given the development of global capital markets over the last 20 years, this assumption no longer looks as valid as it once did (see Chapter 11 for details). Today, if a developing country really does have a potential comparative advantage in a manufacturing industry, firms in that country should be able to borrow money from the capital markets to finance the required investments. Moreover, given financial support, firms based in countries with a potential comparative advantage have an incentive to go through the necessary period of initial losses in order to make long-run gains without requiring government protection. After all, this is what many Taiwanese and South Korean firms did in industries such as textiles, semiconductors, machine tools, steel, and shipping. Thus, given efficient global capital markets, the only industries that would require government protection would be those that are not worthwhile.

Strategic Trade Policy

The strategic trade policy argument has been proposed by the new trade theorists.[15] We reviewed the basic argument in Chapter 4 when we considered the new trade theory. To

[14] "Brazil's Auto Industry Struggles to Boost Global Competitiveness," *Journal of Commerce*, October 10, 1991, p. 6A.

[15] For reviews see J. A. Brander, "Rationales for Strategic Trade and Industrial Policy," in *Strategic Trade Policy and the New International Economics*, ed. P. R. Krugman (Cambridge, Mass.: MIT Press, 1986); and P. R. Krugman, "Is Free Trade Passé?" *Journal of Economic Perspectives* 1 (1987), pp. 131–44.

recap, the new trade theory argues that in industries where the existence of substantial scale economies implies that the world market will profitably support only a few firms, countries may predominate in the export of certain products simply because they had firms that, as early entrants into that industry, were able to capture first-mover advantages. The dominance of Boeing in the commercial aircraft industry is attributed to such factors.

Against this background, there are two components to the strategic trade policy argument. First, it is argued that by appropriate actions, a government can help raise national income if it can somehow ensure that the firm or firms to gain first-mover advantages in such an industry are domestic rather than foreign enterprises. Thus, according to the strategic trade policy argument, a government should use subsidies to support promising firms that are active in newly emerging industries. Advocates of this argument point out that the substantial R&D grants that the U.S. government gave Boeing in the 1950s and 60s probably helped tilt the field of competition in the newly emerging market for jet passenger planes in Boeing's favor. (Boeing's 707 jet airliner was derived from a military plane.) Similar arguments are now made with regard to Japan's dominance in the production of liquid crystal display screens (used in lap-top computers). Although these screens were invented in the United States, the Japanese government, in cooperation with major electronics companies, targeted this industry for research support in the late 1970s and early 80s. The result was that Japanese firms, not U.S. firms, subsequently captured the first-mover advantages in this market.

The second component of the strategic trade policy argument is that it might pay government to intervene in an industry if it helps domestic firms overcome the barriers to entry created by foreign firms that have already reaped first-mover advantages. This catch-up argument underlies government support of Airbus Industrie, Boeing's major competitor. Airbus is a consortium of four companies from Great Britain, France, Germany, and Spain. Formed in 1966, when it began production in the mid-1970s it had less than 5 percent of the world commercial aircraft market. By 1990 it had increased its share to over 30 percent and was beginning to threaten Boeing's dominance. How has Airbus achieved this feat? According to the U.S. government, the answer is a $13.5 billion subsidy from the governments of Great Britain, France, Germany, and Spain.[16] Without this subsidy, Airbus would have never been able to break into the world market. In another example, the rise to dominance of the Japanese semiconductor industry, despite the first-mover advantages enjoyed by U.S. firms, is attributed to intervention by the Japanese government. In this case the government did not subsidize the costs of domestic manufacturers. Rather, it protected the Japanese home market while pursuing policies that ensured Japanese companies got access to the necessary manufacturing and product know-how (see the opening case).

If these arguments are correct, they clearly suggest a rationale for government intervention in international trade. Specifically, governments should target technologies that may be important in the future and use subsidies to support development work aimed at commercializing those technologies. Furthermore, government should provide export subsidies until the domestic firms have established first-mover advantages in the world market. Government support may also be justified if it can help domestic firms overcome the first-mover advantages enjoyed by foreign competitors and emerge as viable

---

[16] "Airbus and Boeing: The Jumbo War," *The Economist*, June 15, 1991, p. 65–66.

competitors in the world market (as in the Airbus and semiconductor examples). In this case, a combination of home-market protection and export-promoting subsidies may be called for.

THE REVISED CASE FOR FREE TRADE

As we have just seen, the strategic trade policy arguments of the new trade theorists suggest an economic justification for government intervention in international trade. This justification challenges the rationale for unrestricted free trade found in the work of classic trade theorists such as Adam Smith and David Ricardo. In response to this challenge to economic orthodoxy, a number of economists—including some of those responsible for the development of the new trade theory, such as Paul Krugman of MIT—have been quick to point out that although strategic trade policy looks nice in theory, in practice it may be unworkable. This response to the strategic trade policy argument constitutes the revised case for free trade.[17]

Retaliation and Trade War

Krugman argues that strategic trade policy aimed at establishing domestic firms in a dominant position in a global industry are beggar-thy-neighbor policies that boost national income at the expense of other countries. A country that attempts to use such policies will probably provoke retaliation. In many cases, the resulting trade war between two or more interventionist governments will leave all countries involved worse off than if a hands-off approach had been adopted in the first place. If the U.S. government were to respond to the Airbus subsidy by increasing its own subsidies to Boeing, for example, the result might be that the subsidies would cancel each other out. In the process, both European and U.S. taxpayers would end up supporting an expensive and pointless trade war, and both Europe and the United States would be worse off.

Krugman may be right about the danger of a strategic trade policy leading to a trade war. The problem, however, is how to respond when one's competitors are already being supported by government subsidies; that is, how should Boeing and the United States respond to the subsidization of Airbus? According to Krugman, the answer is probably not to engage in retaliatory action, but to help establish rules of the game that minimize the use of trade distorting subsidies in the first place. This, of course, is what the GATT seeks to do. Since we do not live in a perfect world, the GATT has only been partially successful. However, if the world economy is to avoid repeating the trade war that followed the introduction of the Smoot-Hawley tariff in 1930, Krugman argues that governments would be well advised to continue strengthening the framework of this international institution.

Domestic Politics

Governments do not always act in the national interest when they intervene in the economy. Instead they are influenced by politically important interest groups. The European Community's support for the common agricultural policy, which arose because of the political power of French and German farmers (see Box 5.2), is an example of this. The CAP benefited inefficient farmers and the politicians who relied upon the farm vote, but no one else. Thus, a further reason for not embracing strategic trade policy, according to Krugman, is that such a policy is almost certain to be captured by special interest

[17] For details see Krugman, "Is Free Trade Passé?" and Brander, "Rationales."

groups within the economy, who will distort it to their own ends. Krugman concludes that with regard to the United States;

> To ask the Commerce Department to ignore special-interest politics while formulating detailed policy for many industries is not realistic; to establish a blanket policy of free trade, with exceptions granted only under extreme pressure, may not be the optimal policy according to the theory but may be the best policy that the country is likely to get.[18]

IMPLICATIONS FOR BUSINESS

What are the implications of all of this for business practice? Why should the international manager care about the political economy of free trade; about the relative merits of arguments for free trade and protectionism? There are two answers to this question. The first concerns the impact of trade barriers on a firm's strategy. The second concerns the role that business firms can play in promoting free trade and/or trade barriers.

Trade Barriers and Firm Strategy

To understand how trade barriers impact a firm's strategy, consider first the material we covered in Chapter 4. Drawing on the theories of international trade, we discussed how it may make sense for the firm to disperse its various production activities to those countries around the globe where they can be performed most efficiently. Thus, it may make sense for a firm to design and engineer its product in one country, to manufacture components in another, to perform final assembly operations in yet another country, and then export the finished product to the rest of the world.

Clearly, trade barriers are a constraint upon a firm's ability to disperse its productive activities in such a manner. First, and most obviously, tariff barriers raise the costs of exporting products to a country (or of exporting partly finished products between countries). This may put the firm at a competitive disadvantage vis-à-vis indigenous competitors in that country. In response, the firm may then find it economical to locate production facilities in that country so that it can compete on an even footing with indigenous competitors. Second, voluntary export restraints (VERs) may limit a firm's ability to serve a country from locations outside of that country. Again, the response by the firm might be to set up production facilities in that country—even though it may result in somewhat higher production costs. Such reasoning was one of the factors that underlay the rapid expansion of Japanese automaking capacity in the United States during the 1980s. This followed the establishment of a VER agreement between the United States and Japan that placed limits on U.S. imports of Japanese automobiles.

Third, to conform with local content regulations, a firm may have to locate more production activities in a given market than it would otherwise. Again, from the firm's perspective, the consequence might be to raise costs above the level that could be achieved if each production activity was dispersed to the optimal location for that activity. And fourth, even when trade barriers do not exist, the firm may still want to locate some production activities in a given country to reduce the *threat* of trade barriers being imposed at some future date.

All of the above effects are likely to raise the firm's costs above the level that could be achieved in a world without trade barriers. The higher costs that result need not translate into a significant competitive disadvantage, however, if the countries imposing trade barriers do so to the imported products of all foreign firms, irrespective of their

---

[18] Krugman, "Is Free Trade Passé?"

national origin. On the other hand, when trade barriers are *targeted* at exports from a particular nation, the effect may be to put firms based in that nation at a competitive disadvantage vis-à-vis the firms of other nations. For example, in 1988 the United States placed a 25 percent ad valorem tariff on imports of light trucks from Japan. This tariff placed the Japanese at a competitive disadvantage vis-à-vis other foreign manufacturers of light trucks, whose imports did not face a tariff (to say nothing of U.S.-based manufacturers). One strategy that the firm may adopt to deal with such **targeted trade barriers** is to move production into the country imposing barriers. Another strategy may be to move production to countries whose exports are not targeted by the specific trade barrier. Thus, some Japanese automobile firms considered moving their production of light trucks from Japan to Mexico, since U.S. imports of light trucks from Mexico were not subjected to the 25 percent tariff.

Policy Implications

As noted in Chapter 4, business firms are major players on the international trade scene. Because of their pivotal role in international trade, business firms can and do exert a strong influence on government policy toward trade. This influence can encourage protectionism, or it can encourage the government to support the GATT and push for open markets and freer trade among all nations. Moreover, government policies with regard to international trade obviously can have a direct impact on business.

Consistent with strategic trade policy, examples can be found of government intervention in the form of tariffs, quotas, and subsidies helping firms and industries to establish a competitive advantage in the world economy. The Japanese semiconductor industry discussed in the opening case may be the best such example. In general, however, the arguments contained in this chapter suggest that a policy of government intervention has the three following drawbacks. Intervention can be self-defeating, since in practice it tends to protect the inefficient rather than help firms become efficient global competitors. Intervention is dangerous, since it may invite retaliation and trigger a trade war. Finally, intervention is unlikely to be well executed, given the opportunity for such a policy to be captured by special interest groups. Does this mean, then, that business should simply encourage government to adopt a laissez-faire, free trade policy?

Most economists would probably argue that the best interests of international business are served by a free trade stance, but not a laissez-faire stance. Put differently, it is probably in the best long-run interests of the business community to encourage the government to aggressively promote greater free trade by, for example, strengthening the GATT. In general, business has probably much more to gain from government efforts to open up protected markets to imports and foreign direct investment, than from government efforts to support certain domestic industries in a manner consistent with the recommendations of strategic trade policy.

This conclusion is reinforced by a phenomenon that we first touched on in Chapter 1; the increasing integration of the world economy and internationalization of production that has occurred over the last two decades. We live in a world where many firms of all national origins increasingly depend for their competitive advantage on globally dispersed production systems. Such systems are the result of free trade. Free trade has brought great advantages to firms that have exploited it and to consumers who benefit from the resulting lower prices. Given the danger of retaliatory action, business firms that lobby their governments to engage in protectionism must realize that by doing so they may be denying themselves the opportunity to build a competitive advantage by constructing a globally dispersed production system. Moreover, by encouraging their governments to engage in protectionism, their own activities and sales overseas may be jeopardized if other governments retaliate. This is a nontrivial danger for U.S. firms, who, despite their perceived relative decline, still have enormous economic interests abroad. The United States, after all, is still the world's number-one exporter.

SUMMARY OF CHAPTER

The main objective of this chapter was to describe how the reality of international trade deviates from the theoretical ideal of unrestricted free trade that we reviewed in Chapter 4. Consistent with this objective, in this chapter we have reviewed the various instruments of trade policy, looked at some of the history of trade policy, reviewed the political and economic arguments for government intervention in international trade, and reexamined the economic case for free trade in light of the strategic trade policy argument. The main conclusion reached is that, while a policy of free trade may not always be the theoretically optimal policy (given the arguments of the new trade theorists), in practice it is probably the best policy for a government to pursue. In particular, the long-run interests of business and consumers may be best served by strengthening international institutions such as the GATT. Given the danger that isolated protectionism might escalate into an all-out trade war, business probably has far more to gain from government efforts to open up protected markets to imports and foreign direct investment (though the GATT) than from government efforts to protect domestic industries from foreign competition.

More specifically, in this chapter the following points have been made:

1. The Smoot-Hawley tariff, introduced in 1930, erected an enormous wall of tariff barriers to U.S. imports. Other countries responded by adopting similar tariffs, and the world slid further into the Great Depression
2. The economic damage that followed the beggar-thy-neighbor trade policies that the Smoot-Hawley tariff ushered in helped lay the groundwork for the post-war consensus to promote greater free trade.
3. GATT was a product of the post-war free trade movement. The move toward greater free trade under GATT appeared to stimulate economic growth.
4. Sometime during the late 1970s the tide began to turn against GATT and free trade. Protectionist pressures have been increasing. There are three main reasons for this: (*i*) the rise of Japan and the Japanese trade surplus, (*ii*) the persistent U.S. trade deficit, and (*iii*) the growing popularity of VERs, which are a way of getting around GATT rules.
5. Despite this, there are some promising trends. These include (*i*) the rise of free trade blocs, (*ii*) the trend toward free trade by Latin American countries, (*iii*) the proposed extension of GATT to cover services, and (*iv*) some signs that the United States and Japan may be beginning to work out some of their differences.
6. The effect of a tariff is to raise the cost of imported products. Gains accrue to the government (from revenues) and to producers (who are protected from foreign competitors). Consumers lose, since they must pay more for imports.
7. By lowering costs, subsidies help domestic producers to compete against low-cost foreign imports and to gain export markets. On the other hand, subsidies must be paid for by taxpayers. Moreover, they tend to be captured by special interests who use them to protect the inefficient.
8. An import quota is a direct restriction imposed by an importing country on the quantity of some good that may be imported. A voluntary export restraint (VER) is a quota on trade imposed from the exporting country's side. VERs appease protectionist interests in the importing country. Both import quotas and VERs benefit domestic producers by limiting import competition, but they result in higher prices, which hurts consumers.
9. A local content requirement is a requirement that some specific fraction of a good be produced domestically. Local content requirements benefit the producers of component parts, but they raise prices of imported components, which hurts consumers.
10. An administrative policy is an informal instrument that can be used to restrict imports and boost exports. Administrative instruments benefit producers but hurt consumers, who are denied access to possibly superior foreign products.
11. There are two types of arguments for government intervention: political and economic. Political arguments for intervention are typically concerned with protecting the interests of certain groups, often at the expense of other groups. Economic arguments for intervention are about boosting the overall wealth of a nation.
12. The most common political argument for intervention is that it is necessary to protect jobs. However, there is evidence that such political intervention often hurts consumers and that it can be self-defeating.
13. Countries sometimes argue that it is important to protect certain industries for reasons of national security.
14. Some argue that government should use the threat to intervene in trade policy as a bargaining tool to open up foreign markets. This can be a risky policy, however, for if it fails, the result can be higher trade barriers all round.

15. The infant industry argument for government intervention is that to let manufacturing get a toehold, governments should temporarily support new industries. In practice, however, governments often end up protecting the inefficient.
16. Strategic trade policy suggests that with subsidies, government can help domestic firms gain first-mover advantages in global industries where economies of scale are important. Government subsidies may also help domestic firms overcome barriers to entry into such industries.
17. The problems with strategic trade policy are twofold: (*i*) such a policy may well invite retaliation, in which case all will lose and (*ii*) strategic trade policy may be captured by special interest groups, who will distort it to their own ends.
18. Trade barriers act as a constraint upon a firm's ability to disperse its various production activities to optimal locations around the globe. One response to trade barriers is to establish more production activities in the protected country.
19. Business may have more to gain from government efforts to open up protected markets to imports and foreign direct investment (through GATT), than from government efforts to protect domestic industries from foreign competition.

DISCUSSION QUESTIONS

1. How should the U.S. government respond to Japan's apparently successful attempt to dominate the semiconductor industry (described in the opening case)?
2. Whose interests should be the paramount concern of government trade policy—the interests of producers (businesses and their employees) or those of consumers?
3. Outline the pros and cons of using the threat to impose trade barriers as a bargaining tool to open up foreign markets? Given your arguments, is this a good policy for government to adopt?
4. Given the arguments relating to the new trade theory and strategic trade policy, what kind of trade policy should business be pressuring government to adopt?
5. You are the CEO of a U.S. firm that produces personal computers in Thailand and then exports them to the United States and other countries for sale. The personal computers were originally produced in Thailand to take advantage of relatively low labor costs and a skilled workforce. Other possible locations considered at the time were Malaysia and Hong Kong. The U.S. government decides to impose punitive 100 percent ad valorem tariffs on imports of computers from Thailand. How would you respond? What does this tell you about the use of targeted trade barriers?

Foreign Direct Investment

CHAPTER 6

HONDA IN NORTH AMERICA

One of the most dramatic trends during the 1980s was the surge in Japanese direct investment in the United States. Leading this trend were the Japanese automobile companies, particularly Honda, Mazda, Nissan, and Toyota. Collectively these companies invested $5.3 billion in North American–based automobile assembly plants between 1982 and 1991. The early leader in this trend was Honda, which by 1991 had invested $1.13 billion in three North American auto assembly plants—two major plants in central Ohio and a smaller one in Ontario, Canada. Honda has invested an additional $500 million in an engine plant in Ohio that supplies its Ohio assembly plants. The company has also established major R&D and engineering facilities at its Ohio plants and has purchased an existing au-

tomotive test-center—adjacent to the assembly plants—from the state of Ohio for $31 million. • As a result of these investments, Honda now employs 10,000 workers in its central Ohio plants and pumps a payroll of $7.3 million per week into the local economy. Of the 854,879 cars that Honda sold in the United States during 1990, nearly two thirds were built at its three North American assembly plants—the vast majority of them in Ohio. Moreover, Honda claims that the domestic content of its American-built cars is 75 percent—meaning that three fourths of the final cost of a car is accounted for by North American labor, components, and other costs. The remaining 25 percent of the cost is accounted for by imported parts. • Honda had considered establishing auto assembly operations in North America as early as 1974, but initially ruled out investment due to the high cost of North American labor. In 1977, Honda announced that it had selected a site in the small town of Marysville, Ohio, for a motorcycle assembly plant. Motorcycle production would test the ground for the possible manufacture of automobiles. This experiment was deemed necessary, because Honda's internal feasibility studies still predicted that high labor costs and poor productivity would make North American–based automobile production unprofitable. However, Honda quickly realized that its assumptions about poor productivity of U.S. workers were unfounded, and in 1979 it announced plans to construct an automobile assembly plant adjacent to its Marysville motorcycle plant. Two years later, in November 1982, the first U.S.-built Honda was assembled, and by 1984 the plant was producing 150,000 automobiles per year. • Throughout the 1980s Honda's direct investment in North America produced complementary investments by many of its Japanese suppliers of component parts. By 1989 at least 29 major Japanese supplier companies had established transplant manufacturing facilities in Ohio in order to supply Honda with component parts. In addition, 33 other Japanese firms had invested in the United States in order to supply Honda and several other Japanese and U.S. automobile manufacturers. Honda required many of these companies to build their plants close to its Ohio complex so they could introduce a just-in-time production system, in which parts are delivered to the assembly plants just as they are needed. This technique virtually eliminates the need to hold in-process inventories and is regarded as a major source of cost savings. In addition, Honda wanted major suppliers close by so that they could conveniently collaborate on the design of major components and on techniques for reducing costs and boosting quality. • A number of concerns seem to underlie Honda's decision to invest in North America. First, it is widely assumed that many Japanese firms, including Honda, did this largely to circumvent the threat of protectionist trade legislation, which seemed very real following the rapid increase in Japanese automobile exports to North America during the 1970s and early 80s. The threat of protectionism—especially the 1981 Voluntary Restraint Agreement under which Japanese companies agreed not to further increase their imports into the United States—may well have accelerated Honda's late 1980s investments in Ohio. A second concern was probably the sharp rise in the value of the Japanese yen against the U.S. dollar during 1987. This dramatically increased the cost of exporting both finished automobiles and component parts from Japan to North America. This also may have accelerated Honda's investments in the late 1980s. • However, it is also necessary to consider Honda's investment in North America in the context of its long-term corporate strategy. As a latecomer to automobile production in Japan, Honda had always struggled to remain profitable in the intensely competitive Japanese auto industry. Against this background, Honda's establishment of North American assembly plants can be seen as part of a strategy designed to circumvent Toyota and Nissan and to make major inroads in the U.S. market ahead of its Japanese rivals. Underlying this strategy was Honda's strong belief that products need to be customized to the requirements of local markets. To paraphrase Hideo Sugiura, the former chairman of Honda, there are subtle differences, from country to country and from region to region, in the ways a product is used and what customers expect of it. If a corporation believes that simply because a product has succeeded in a certain market it will sell well throughout the world, it is most likely destined for large and expensive errors or even total failure. To produce products that account for local differences in customer tastes and preferences, Sugiura claimed that a company needed to establish top-to-bottom engineering, design, and production facilities in each major market in which it competed. Thus in the late 1970s Honda made the decision to invest in North America. Its success can be judged by the fact that although it was only the fourth-largest automobile manufacturer in Japan in 1990 (with 9.3 percent of the market, compared to Toyota's 32.5 percent), it was the second-largest Japanese automobile manufacturer in the United States (with 6.14 percent of the market, compared to first-place Toyota's 7.6 percent). ⊕ *Sources: A. Mair, R. Florida, and M. Kenney, "The New Geography of Automobile Production: Japanese Transplants in North America,"* Economic Geography *64 (1988), pp. 352–373; H. Sugiura, "How Honda Localizes Its Global Strategy,"* Sloan Management Review, *Fall 1990, pp. 77–82; S. Toy, N. Gross, and J. B. Treece, "The Americanization of Honda,* Business Week, *April 25, 1988, pp. 90–96; and P. Magnusson, J. B. Treece, and W. C. Symonds, "Honda: Is It an American Car?"* Business Week, *November 18, 1991, pp. 105–9.*

INTRODUCTION

This chapter is concerned with the phenomenon of **foreign direct investment (FDI).** Foreign direct investment may occur when a firm invests directly in new facilities to produce a product in a foreign country, as Honda did in the United States during the 1980s, or it may occur when a firm buys an existing enterprise in a foreign country. Thus, for example, the purchase of two U.S. companies (CBS Records and Columbia Pictures) by Japan's Sony Corporation is considered to be FDI. More generally, foreign direct investment occurs whenever a firm establishes a controlling interest in a business entity based in another country by acquiring ownership of more than 50 percent of that entity's's stock. Once a firm undertakes FDI it becomes a **multinational enterprise** (the meaning of *multinational* here being "more than one country").

Control over a foreign entity distinguishes FDI from **foreign portfolio investment (FPI).** FPI is investment by individuals, firms, or public bodies (e.g., national and local governments) in foreign financial instruments (e.g., government bonds, foreign stocks). FPI does not involve taking a controlling interest in a foreign business entity. FPI is determined by different factors than FDI and raises different issues. Accordingly, we do not consider FPI in this chapter, but we do discuss it in Chapter 11 in our review of the international capital market.

In Chapter 4 we considered several theories that sought to explain the *pattern of trade* between countries. These theories focus on why countries export some products and import others. What none of these theories address is why a firm might decide to invest directly in production facilities in a foreign country, rather than exporting its domestic production to that country. In other words, the theories we reviewed in Chapter 4 do not explain the *pattern of foreign direct investment* between countries. The theories we examine in this chapter seek to do just this.

Our central objective will be to identify the economic rationale that underlies foreign direct investment. The first point that must be made is that firms often view exports and FDI as "substitutes" for each other. In the opening case, for example, we saw how Honda progressively replaced exports of automobiles to the United States with automobiles produced by its wholly owned operations in the United States. Whereas all Honda cars sold in the United States in 1980 were manufactured in Japan, as a result of export substitution more than two thirds of Honda cars sold in the United States by 1990 were manufactured in the United States. One question that this chapter attempts to answer is, Why do firms such as Honda prefer FDI to exporting? The opening case hints at some of the answers (e.g., trade barriers, access to markets, or the need to customize a product to local requirements). Here we will review various theories that attempt to provide a comprehensive explanation for this question.

This is not the only question these theories need to address. They also need to explain why it is preferable for a firm to engage in FDI rather than licensing. **Licensing** occurs when a domestic firm, the *licensor,* licenses the right to produce its product, to use its production processes, or to use its brand name or trademark to a foreign firm, the *licensee.* In return for giving the licensee these rights, the licensor collects a royalty fee on every unit the licensee sells. The great advantage claimed for licensing over FDI is that the licensor does not have to pay for opening up a foreign market; the licensee does that. For example, one might argue that one advantage Honda has over its U.S. competitors (General Motors, Ford, and Chrysler) is that its cars are better designed and engineered. Why then did Honda not allow GM, Ford, or Chrysler, to build its cars under license and collect a royalty fee on each car that that licensee subsequently sold? Why did Honda prefer to bear the substantial risks and costs (of $1.7 billion by 1990) involved in establishing its own production facilities in the United States, when in theory it could have earned a good return by licensing? This is not just a hypothetical example. In the early 1980s Honda did choose a licensing arrangement over FDI to enter the British market; it allowed Great Britain's Rover group to build Honda cars under license. So why in the case of the U.S. market—and by the late 1980s in Great Britain, too—did Honda decide to forgo licensing and opt for FDI? The theories reviewed herein attempt to provide an answer to this puzzle.

The remainder of the chapter is structured as follows. First, we look at the importance of FDI in the world economy. Next we look at the theories that have been used to explain horizontal foreign direct investment. **Horizontal FDI** is FDI in the same industry as a firm operates in at home. Honda's investment in the North American auto industry is an example of horizontal FDI. Having reviewed horizontal FDI, we move on to consider the theories that help to explain vertical foreign direct investment. **Vertical FDI** is FDI in an industry that provides inputs for a firm's domestic operations. Alternatively, it may be FDI in an industry abroad that sells the outputs of a firm's domestic operations. Finally, as always, we review the implications of these theories for business practice.

FOREIGN DIRECT INVESTMENT IN THE WORLD ECONOMY

Over the last 10 to 15 years the nature of foreign direct investment in the world economy has undergone several notable shifts. First, there has been a marked increase in the amount of FDI being undertaken. Second, there has been a significant change in the importance of various countries as sources of FDI outflows. Similarly, there has been a

Table 6.1
FDI Outflows from the Larger Industrialized Countries (annual averages)

	1975–79	1980–84	1985–89	1990	1991
Total Outflows, $ billions	34	40	126	214	157
Percent Distribution					
United States	47	24	19	15	17
Larger EC countries	40	53	48	50	55
Belgium	1	0.3	2	3	0
France	5	8	7	16	15
Germany	9	9	8	11	14
Italy	1	4	3	4	5
Holland	6	7	6	7	7
Spain	0.4	0.6	0.6	1	2
Great Britain	18	24	21	8	12
Australia	0.8	2	3	0.9	0.2
Canada	4	7	4	0.2	3
Japan	6	11	17	22	20
Sweden	2	2	4	7	5
Switzerland	0	0.8	4	3	0

Source: "World Economy Survey," The Economist, *September 19, 1992, p. 17.*

significant shift in the importance of certain countries as recipients of FDI inflows. In particular, the importance of the United States as a source for FDI outflows has declined markedly, while the importance of Japan and certain European countries as sources for FDI outflows has increased. At the same time, the United States has become a major recipient of FDI inflows. Finally, it became apparent during the 1980s that more and more FDI was being undertaken by relatively small firms. It used to be that FDI was primarily the preserve of the large corporation. Today, although large firms still undertake most FDI, more and more medium-sized and small firms are now increasing their investment abroad. We consider these trends in this section.[1]

The Growth of FDI

When discussing foreign direct investment, it is important to distinguish between the flow of FDI and the stock of FDI. The **flow of FDI** refers to the amount of FDI undertaken over a given time period (normally a year). The **stock of FDI** refers to the total accumulated value of foreign-owned assets at a given time. During the 1980s there was a marked acceleration in the flow of FDI in the world economy. The average yearly outflow of FDI from the larger industrialized countries increased from around $40 billion per annum during the 1980–84 period to $126 billion per annum during the 1985–89 period (see Table 6.1). In 1990 the outflow exceeded even this figure, reaching a record $214 billion, and then it fell back to $157 billion in 1991. Not only did the flow of FDI accelerate during the 1980s, it accelerated faster than the growth in world trade. In the five years up until 1989, the flow of new FDI worldwide rose at an annual rate of 29 percent, three times the growth rate in world trade!

At the same time the flow of FDI was accelerating, its composition also was changing. For most of the period after World War II, the United States was by far the largest source country for FDI. Even during the late 1970s the United States was still accounting for about 47 percent of all FDI outflows from industrialized countries, while

[1] Sources: "Foreign Investment and the Triad," *The Economist,* August 24, 1991, p. 57; and R. B. Reich, *The Work of Nations* (New York: Alfred Knopf, 1991).

Table 6.2
Change in the Stock of FDI, 1970–1991 ($ millions)

Year	Stock of U.S. FDI Abroad	Stock of Foreign FDI in the United States
1991	450,196	407,577
1990	424,086	396,702
1989	372,419	368,924
1988	335,893	314,754
1987	314,307	263,394
1986	259,800	220,414
1985	230,250	184,615
1984	211,480	164,583
1983	207,203	137,061
1982	207,725	124,677
1981	228,348	108,714
1980	215,375	83,046
1979	187,858	54,462
1978	162,727	42,471
1977	145,990	34,595
1976	136,809	30,770
1975	124,050	27,662
1974	110,078	25,144
1973	101,313	20,556
1972	89,878	14,868
1971	82,760	13,914
1970	75,480	13,270

Source: U.S. Department of Commerce, Survey of Current Business, *various issues.*

second-placed Great Britain accounted for about 18 percent (see Table 6.1). Indeed, U.S. firms so dominated the growth of FDI in the 1960s and 70s that the words *American* and *multinational* became almost synonymous. As a result, by 1980, 178 of the world's largest 382 multinationals were U.S. firms, and 40 of them were British.[2] By 1990, however, the U.S. share of FDI outflows had slumped to 15 percent. The big gainer had been Japan, whose share of total FDI outflows had increased from around 6 percent during late 1970s to 22 percent in 1990. Several of the larger European countries, particularly France and Germany, also markedly increased their shares in the same period.

Paralleling the decline in U.S. FDI outflows, the United States became a major target country for FDI during the 1980s. This is shown in Table 6.2, which plots the changes in the stock of FDI owned by U.S. firms abroad and by foreign firms in the United States from 1970 through to 1991. As can be seen, in 1970 U.S. firms owned almost six times as many assets abroad as foreign firms owned in the United States. By 1991, however, the ratio was fast approaching 1:1. In that year the stock of U.S.-owned assets abroad was $450 billion, while foreign firms owned assets in the United States worth $407 billion. Other countries that have seen relatively high levels of inward FDI in recent years include Great Britain, France, and Spain—primarily by U.S. and Japanese firms wanting to invest in the European Community. It is notable, however, that despite the surge in Japanese FDI outflows during the 1980s, there has been very little growth in

[2] M. Kidron and R. Segal, *The New State of the World Atlas* (New York: Simon & Schuster, 1987).

Table 6.3
Foreign Direct Investment Inflows into the Larger Industrialized Countries (annual averages)

	1975–79	1980–84	1985–89	1990	1991
Total Inflows, $ billions	33	34	96	156	84
Percent Distribution					
United States	33	53	51	29	14
Larger EC countries	57	38	37	57	66
Belgium	6	3	3	6	0
France	10	7	6	8	18
Germany	7	2	2	2	3
Italy	3	3	3	4	3
Holland	4	3	4	7	5
Spain	4	5	5	9	12
Great Britain	23	15	14	21	25
Australia	6	6	5	4	5
Canada	2	−1	1	5	5
Japan	0.5	0.8	0.4	1	2
Sweden	0.3	0.5	1	1	8
Switzerland	0	0.8	2	3	0

Source: "World Economy Survey," The Economist, *September 19, 1992, p. 17.*

FDI inflows into Japan (see Table 6.3). Although 1991 saw more FDI inflows into Japan than any other year in the country's history, Japan was still the recipient of only 2 percent of total FDI inflows into larger industrialized countries in that year.

A widespread perception is that the majority of FDI inflows into the United States during the 1980s and early 90s were undertaken by Japanese corporations intent on buying up America's industrial base.[3] In reality, however, the two leading investors in the United States for most of the 1970s and 80s were the British and the Dutch.[4] Although it is true that there was a surge in Japanese investment, it peaked in 1989 and has declined since then. This is confirmed by Table 6.4, which shows the stock of FDI in the United States as of 1991, along with the inflow of FDI for 1989, 1990, and 1991. Two facts stand out in Figure 6.4. The first is that as of 1991, the stock of Japanese FDI in the United States was less than one fifth of the stock of British FDI, and one third of the stock of Dutch FDI. The second fact is that even in 1989—the high point for Japanese investment in the United States—the British invested more than the Japanese did. What should also be born in mind by those who believe that FDI by foreigners in the United States should be restricted, is that by 1991 the total value of foreign-owned assets in the United States was still less than the book value of U.S.-owned assets abroad. (The gap has been closing fast, however; see Table 6.2.) Moreover, in terms of accumulated FDI between 1970 and 1990, U.S. firms ranked a clear first, followed by British firms and then Japanese firms.[5]

Four interesting questions arise from the statistics reviewed here. First, why is FDI growing more rapidly than world trade? Second, after decades of being the main source of FDI, why did the United States become a net recipient of FDI in the 1980s? Third, will the growth of FDI into the United States be good or bad for the country? And fourth,

[3] For an example of this viewpoint see M. Tolchin and S. Tolchin, *Buying into America* (New York: Times Books, 1988).

[4] "Foreign Investment in the U.S." *The New York Times,* July 17, 1990, p. D2.

[5] Reich, *Work of Nations;* and "Japan Remains Top Investor," *The New York Times,* December 19, 1991, p. C6.

Table 6.4
Foreign Direct Investment in the United States ($ millions)

Stock of FDI in the United States		Inflow of FDI into the United States		
Country	**1991**	**1989**	**1990**	**1991**
Canada	30,002	1,793	1,414	−1,324
Europe	258,127	43,046	21,439	8,212
Great Britain	106,064	18,939	5,226	4,210
The Netherlands	63,848	7,323	6,397	29
Germany	28,171	3,738	726	1,258
France	22,740	2,744	5,726	3,704
Japan	17,205	18,653	17,355	5,183
Other	407,477	—	—	—
Total	407,477	69,010	46,108	12,619

Source: U.S. Department of Commerce, Survey of Current Business, *vol. 72, no. 8, Table 16, pp. 111–12.*

why has the level of inward FDI in Japan remained so low? The theories we examine in this chapter and the next will help us to answer these questions. However, a few brief observations are called for now.

FDI and World Trade

The reason FDI is growing more rapidly than world trade seems to be twofold. The first reason is a general fear among business firms that protectionist pressures are growing in the world economy. Much like Honda in the mid-1980s, business executives see FDI as a way of circumventing future trade barriers. As we saw in Chapter 5, the fear of rising protectionist pressures is not without foundation. In addition, many companies are now adopting Honda's philosophy (discussed in the opening case) that products need to be customized to local conditions, and they believe that local production in each region or country in which they compete is the best way to achieve this. (This issue is discussed in greater depth in Chapter 13.) By investing in each region in which they do business, these companies are substituting FDI and local production for exports.

FDI in the United States

A number of factors lay behind the inflow of FDI into the United States during the 1980s and early 90s. For a start, as the largest and richest consumer market in the world, the United States was clearly attractive to foreign firms. In addition, during the latter half of the 1980s the value of the dollar on the foreign exchange market fell quite rapidly. At the same time, the value of the Japanese yen, the British pound, and the German mark all rose. (For an explanation of this, see Chapters 8 and 9). This made it expensive for U.S. firms to purchase assets abroad and relatively cheap for British, Japanese, and German firms to purchase U.S. assets. There is no doubt that to some extent this factor lay behind the decline in outward FDI by U.S. firms and the rise of direct investment in the United States by foreign firms (particularly by Japanese and British firms).

In addition to these factors, the rise of FDI in the United States during the 1980s and early 90s seems to have been due to a belief on the part of foreign firms that they could manage U.S. workers and assets more efficiently than U.S. managers and investors could. Put another way, the perceived decline in the competitiveness of many firms during the 1970s and 80s may have been the reason for the rise of FDI by foreigners in the

United States. On the face of it, some evidence suggests that many foreigners have judged correctly. For example, the success of Japanese-owned automobile assembly plants in the United States, such as Honda's Ohio plants, is largely due to Japanese managers' ability to utilize U.S. workers to make a higher-quality car in less time than U.S.-owned auto makers can.[6] Box 6.1 tells how another foreign firm, the British company Hanson PLC, has been able to utilize U.S. assets and workers more efficiently than U.S. managers do. If much FDI is driven by foreigners' belief that they can manage U.S. workers and assets more efficiently than U.S. managers can, the rise of FDI into the United States will come to a halt once U.S. managers succeed in managing workers and assets as efficiently as their foreign competitors do.

The Effects of FDI on the United States

Is the growth of FDI into the United States good or bad for the U.S. economy? We discuss the impact of FDI on a host economy in detail in the next chapter, but for now, note that if one believes that foreigners are in general doing a better job of managing U.S. workers and assets than U.S. managers, the answer is that it is good. It can be argued that foreign know-how is helping to improve U.S. competitiveness as well as providing jobs and investment that otherwise would not be there. On the other hand, critics charge that the United States has a lot to lose and little to gain from the growth of FDI. Japanese FDI tends to be the main target of these critics. They argue that in exchange for a few lower-skilled, lower-paying jobs, U.S. companies are sacrificing their competitiveness to a Japanese strategy that keeps higher-valued, higher-paying jobs in Japan. The United States, they believe, will ultimately be left with "screwdriver" plants, where low-wage U.S. workers assemble Japanese products.[7] We will return to this issue in the next chapter when we review the pros and cons of FDI from the perspective of a host country in more detail. For now, all that should be noted is that this debate is ongoing, and its resolution may well influence future U.S. policy toward FDI.

FDI in Japan

Why is the level of FDI into Japan so low? On the face of it, Japan appears to be wide open; although the government has some power to block foreign investments, that power is rarely used. On the other hand, it is argued that foreign firms face endless informal obstacles when trying to invest in Japan.[8] European and U.S. companies have both found that Japanese companies tend to be more willing to buy from other Japanese companies than from foreign companies. This may reflect the Japanese practice of entering into long-term cooperative relationships with their suppliers. The Japanese seem to believe that foreign companies are less willing to make the same kind of long-term commitments as other Japanese companies, and so they are reluctant to buy from foreign companies. Whatever the reason for the Japanese reluctance to buy from non-Japanese enterprises, this does make FDI in Japan relatively unattractive, hence the low level of FDI. On the other hand, it should be pointed out that many of those Western companies that have been persistent in their efforts to invest in Japan have been rewarded with success.

---

[6] See J. P. Womack, D. T. Jones, and D. Roos, *The Machine that Changed the World* (New York: Rawson Associates, 1990); and Reich, *Work of Nations*.

[7] R. B. Reich and E. D. Mankin, "Joint Ventures with Japan Give Away Our Future," *Harvard Business Review*, March–April 1986, pp. 78–90.

[8] P. Krugman, *The Age of Diminished Expectations* (Cambridge, Mass.: MIT Press, 1990).

BOX 6.1

Hanson PLC's FDI in the United States

In 1973 Gordon White, cofounder of the British conglomerate Hanson Trust PLC, arrived in the United States to start the North American arm of Hanson Trust. Thirteen years later the company he set up, Hanson Industries, was ranked 97th among the Fortune 500 Industrials. Hanson Industries' achievement in joining the elite of U.S. companies capped a 22-year period during which Hanson Trust's pretax profits had grown at an average rate of 45 percent a year. This phenomenal growth was based upon a carefully thought-out acquisition strategy. Between 1974 and 1990 Hanson Industries bought 12 U.S. corporations for a total purchase price of $4.96 billion. Among these acquisitions was the 1984 purchase of US Industries, a conglomerate with 33 operating divisions, for $532 million; the 1986 purchase of SCM Corporation, a typewriter and chemicals conglomerate, for $930 million; and the 1988 purchase of Kidde, a conglomerate with 108 operating divisions, for $1.7 billion.

The basis of the company's strategy has been to acquire businesses cheaply, often against the existing management's will, to liquidate surplus assets, and then to manage what is left in such a way as to increase earnings and generate cash for the next acquisition. When seeking companies to acquire, Hanson looks for fundamentally sound but poorly managed businesses based in mature, low-tech industries. It seems particularly interested in acquiring firms that historically have had good earnings but that are suffering a short-term setback due to poor management or adverse economic conditions.

Once Hanson acquires a company, it typically cuts costs by selling headquarters buildings and eliminating staff jobs or pushing them down into operations. Underperforming divisions in acquired companies are either turned around quickly or sold. The remaining divisions are given substantial operating autonomy but held accountable for their performance through a system of tight financial controls. Strong profit incentives encourage divisional executives to focus on the bottom line. Hanson's objective is to markedly improve the profitability of the companies it acquires.

These factors can produce remarkable results. For example, Hanson Industries paid $930 million for SCM in January 1986, after a bitterly contested takeover battle. By September 1986 it had sold off a number of SCM subsidiaries for more than $1 billion. Hanson held onto the typewriter and chemicals businesses, which, in effect, cost nothing and earned record pretax profits of $165 million in 1987. Since 1987, the chemicals and typewriter businesses have shown further significant improvements in performance.

Consider Smith-Corona, SCM's typewriter business. Under Hanson, Smith-Corona reduced the number of parts in its leading products from 1,400 to 400 and the required time for assembly from 8 hours to 1.5 hours. In addition, employment was cut from 5,200 workers in 1985 to 3,100 by 1988. By such moves, Smith-Corona has been able to establish a cost advantage over its major Japanese competitors. As a consequence, by 1989 Smith-Corona had regained its hold on more than 50 percent of the U.S. typewriter market, after having seen its share sink to as low as 32 percent in 1986.

Sources: H. Lampert, "Britons on the Prowl," The New York Times Magazine, *November 29, 1987, pp. 22–24; and C. W. L. Hill, "Hanson PLC," in* Strategic Management: An Integrated Approach, *2nd ed., ed. C. W. L. Hill and G. R. Jones (Boston: Houghton-Mifflin, 1992).*

Examples include Kodak, IBM, Procter & Gamble, Motorola, and Xerox, all of whom have successful Japanese subsidiaries.

FDI by Medium-Sized and Small Firms

FDI used to be associated almost exclusively with multibillion-dollar multinational corporations. Indeed, most people probably still think that the two are synonymous. In practice, however, the globalization of world markets has been accompanied by the rapid growth of FDI by small and medium-sized firms. In no small part, FDI by such firms has been driven by a need to stay close to major customers who have themselves gone abroad. Although hard statistics detailing the growth of smaller multinationals are hard to come by, some examples will give a feel for what now seems to be occurring.

Consider first the experience of Molex, a Chicago-based company with worldwide sales of about $500 million in 1989. Molex makes some 2,500 varieties of connectors used in such applications as linking the wires in an automobile or in the circuit boards of computers and videorecorders. The company had little choice but to go abroad, because its customers began investing abroad in the early 1970s to take advantage of cheap labor. Molex, which in those days generated revenues of less than $20 million, had to go abroad in order to hold on to this business. Today the company's 46 factories in more than 20 countries employ 6,000 foreign workers. For another example, consider Loctite, a U.S. manufacturer of industrial adhesives that in 1986 generated $267 million of sales worldwide. Loctite has pushed hard overseas since its founding in the 1950s. Today the company does business in more than 80 countries and has factories in Ireland, Brazil, and Japan (where it dominates the industrial market). Of the 3,000 people in the company worldwide, two thirds are employed outside of North America. Finally, as an even smaller example, consider Lubricating Systems, Inc., of Kent, Washington. In 1991 this manufacturer of lubricating fluids for machine tools employed 25 people and generated sales of $6.5 million—hardly an industrial giant. Yet more than $2 million of the company's total sales were generated by exports to a score of countries from Japan to Israel and the United Arab Emirates. Moreover, Lubricating Systems is now investing in a joint venture with a German company to serve the European market.[9] The point is that although large firms still account for the lion's share of FDI, opportunities exist for medium-sized and small firms to profit from investing abroad.

HORIZONTAL FOREIGN DIRECT INVESTMENT

Horizontal FDI is FDI in the same industry abroad as a firm operates in at home. We need to understand why firms go to all of the trouble of acquiring or establishing operations abroad, when the alternatives of exporting and licensing are available to them. Why, for example, did Honda choose FDI in the United States over exporting from Japan, or licensing a U.S. automaker to build its cars in the United States? This puzzle is a very real one given that, *other things being equal,* FDI is expensive and risky compared to exporting or licensing. FDI is expensive because a firm must bear the costs of establishing production facilities in a foreign country, or of acquiring a foreign enterprise. FDI is risky because of the problems associated with doing business in a different culture where the "rules of the game" may be very different. Relative to firms native to the particular culture, there is a greater probability that a firm undertaking FDI in a foreign culture will make costly mistakes due to its ignorance. When a firm exports, it need not bear the costs

[9] R. A. Mosbacher, "Opening Export Doors for Smaller Firms, *Seattle Times,* July 24, 1991, p. A7, and R. A. King, "You Don't Have to Be a Giant to Score Big Overseas," *Business Week,* April 13, 1987, pp. 62–63.

of FDI, and the risks associated with selling abroad can be reduced by using a native sales agent. Similarly, when a firm licenses its know-how it need not bear the costs or risks of FDI, since these are born by the native firm that licenses the know-how. So why do so many firms apparently prefer FDI over either exporting or licensing?

The quick answer is that other things are *not equal!* A number of factors can alter the relative attractiveness of exporting, licensing, and FDI. We will consider these factors: (1) transportation costs, (2) market imperfections, (3) following competitors, and (4) the product life cycle.

Transportation Costs

When transportation costs are added to production costs, it becomes unprofitable to ship some products over a large distance. This is particularly true of products that have a low value-to-weight ratio and which can be produced in almost any location (e.g., cement, soft drinks, etc.). For such products, relative to either FDI or licensing, the attractiveness of exporting decreases. For products with a high value-to-weight ratio, however, transport costs are normally a very minor component of total landed cost (e.g., electronic components, personal computers, medical equipment, computer software, etc.). In such cases, transportation costs have very little impact on the relative attractiveness of exporting, licensing, and FDI.

Market Imperfections

Market imperfections provide a major explanation of why firms may prefer FDI to either exporting or licensing. At this time, it is probably correct to say that the market imperfections explanation of FDI is the one favored by most economists.[10] With regard to horizontal FDI, market imperfections arise in two circumstances: when there are impediments to the free flow of products between nations, and when there are impediments to the sale of know-how. (Licensing is a mechanism for selling know-how.) The existence of impediments to the free flow of products between nations decreases the profitability of exporting, relative to FDI and licensing. The existence of impediments to the sale of know-how increases the profitability of FDI relative to licensing. Thus, the market imperfections explanation predicts that FDI will be preferred whenever there are impediments that make both exporting and the sale of know-how difficult and/or expensive. We will consider each situation in turn.

Impediments to Exporting

Governments are the main source of impediments to the free flow of products between nations. By placing tariffs on imported goods, governments can increase the cost of exporting relative to FDI and licensing. Similarly, by limiting imports through the imposition of quotas, governments increase the attractiveness of FDI and licensing. As mentioned earlier, the current wave of FDI by Japanese auto companies in the United States is being driven by protectionist threats from Congress and by quotas on the importation of Japanese cars. For Japanese auto companies, these factors have decreased the profitability of exporting and increased the profitability of FDI.

---

[10] For example, see S. H. Hymer, *The International Operations of National Firms: A Study of Direct Foreign Investment* (Cambridge, Mass.: MIT Press, 1976); A. M. Rugman, *Inside the Multinationals: The Economics of Internal Markets* (New York: Columbia University Press, 1981); D. J. Teece, "Multinational Enterprise, Internal Governance, and Industrial Organization," *American Economic Review* 75 (May 1983), pp. 233–38; and C. W. L. Hill and W. C. Kim, "Searching for a Dynamic Theory of the Multinational Enterprise: A Transaction Cost Model," *Strategic Management Journal* (special issue) 9 (1988), pp. 93–104.

Impediments to the Sale of Know-How

The competitive advantage that many firms enjoy comes from their technological, marketing, or management know-how. Technological know-how can enable a company to build a better product; for example, Xerox's technological know-how enabled it to build the first photocopier, and IBM's technological know-how still gives it a competitive advantage in the mainframe computer market. Alternatively, technological know-how can enable a company to improve its production process vis-à-vis competitors; for example, many claim that Toyota's competitive advantage comes from its superior production system. Marketing know-how can enable a company to better position its products in the market place vis-à-vis competitors; the competitive advantage of such companies as Kellogg, H. J. Heinz, and Procter & Gamble seems to come from superior marketing know-how. Management know-how with regard to factors such as organizational structure, human relations, control systems, planning systems, and so on, can enable a company to manage its assets more efficiently than competitors; the competitive advantage of Hanson PLC, profiled in Box 6.1, seems to derive from management know-how.

If we view know-how—expertise—as a competitive asset, it follows that the larger the market in which that asset is applied, the greater the profits that can be earned from the asset. Put simply, IBM can earn greater returns on its know-how by selling its mainframe computers worldwide than by selling them only in North America. However, this alone does not explain why IBM undertakes FDI. For IBM to favor FDI, two conditions must hold. First, transportation costs and/or impediments to exporting must rule out exporting as an option. Second, there must be some reason why IBM cannot sell its computer mainframe know-how to foreign producers. Since licensing is the main mechanism by which firms sell their know-how, it follows that there must be some reason why IBM is not willing to license a foreign firm to manufacture and market its mainframe computers. Other things being equal, licensing might look attractive to such a firm, since it would not have to bear the costs and risks associated with FDI yet it could still earn a good return from its know-how in the form of royalty fees.

According to economic theory (and depicted in Figure 6.1), there are three reasons why the market does not always work well as a mechanism for selling know-how, or why licensing is not as attractive as it initially appears. First, licensing may result in a firm's giving away its technological know-how to a potential foreign competitor. For example, back in the 1960s RCA licensed its leading-edge color television technology to a number of Japanese companies, including Matsushita and Sony. At the time RCA saw licensing as a way to earn a good return from its technological know-how in the Japanese market without the costs and risks associated with FDI. However, Matsushita and Sony quickly assimilated RCA's technology and used it to enter the U.S. market to compete directly against RCA. As a result, RCA is now a minor player in its home market, while Matsushita and Sony have a much bigger market share.

Second, licensing does not give a firm the tight control over manufacturing, marketing, and strategy in a foreign country that may be required to profitably exploit its advantage in know-how. With licensing, control over manufacturing, marketing, and strategy is granted to a licensee in return for a royalty fee. However, for both strategic and operational reasons, a firm may want to retain control over these functions. The rationale for wanting control over the *strategy* of a foreign entity is that a firm might want its foreign subsidiary to price and market very aggressively as a way of keeping a foreign competitor in check. Kodak is in fact pursuing this strategy in Japan. The competitive attacks launched by Kodak's Japanese subsidiary are keeping its major global competitor, Fuji, busy defending its competitive position in Japan. Consequently, Fuji has had to pull

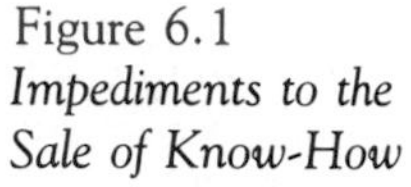

Figure 6.1
Impediments to the Sale of Know-How

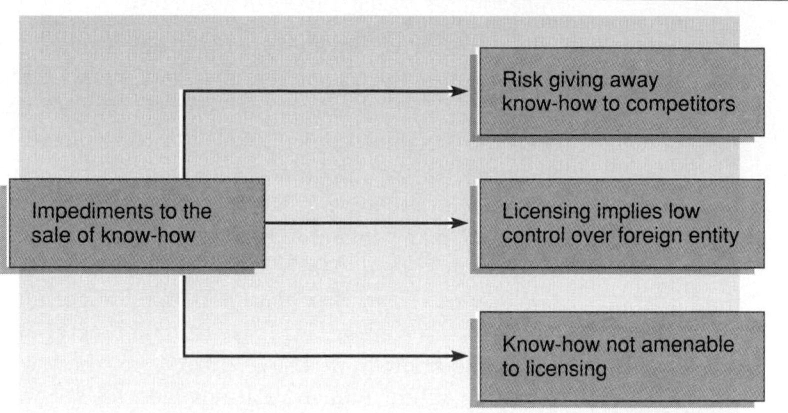

back from its earlier strategy of attacking Kodak aggressively in the United States. Unlike a wholly owned subsidiary, a licensee would be unlikely to accept such an imposition, since the implication of such a strategy is that the licensee would only be allowed to make a low profit, or might have to take a loss.

The rationale for wanting control over the *operations* of a foreign entity is that the firm might wish to take advantage of differences in factor costs across countries, producing only part of its final product in a given country, while importing other parts from elsewhere where they can be produced at lower cost. Again, a licensee would be unlikely to accept such an arrangement, since it would limit the licensee's autonomy. Thus, for these reasons, when tight control over a foreign entity is desirable, horizontal FDI is preferable to licensing.

Third, a firm's know-how may not be amenable to licensing. This is particularly true of management and marketing know-how. It is one thing to license a foreign firm to manufacture a particular product, but quite another to license the way a firm does business—how it manages its process and markets its products. For example, although Honda has certain products and manufacturing processes that can be licensed, its real competitive advantage comes from its superior ability to manage the overall process of designing, engineering, manufacturing, and selling automobiles—that is, from its management know-how. These kinds of managerial skills are difficult to articulate or codify; they certainly cannot be written down in a simple licensing contract. They are organizationwide and they have been developed over the years. They are not embodied in any one individual, but instead are widely dispersed throughout the company. Put another way, Honda's skills are embedded in its organizational culture, and culture is something that cannot be licensed. Thus, as Honda discovered when it allowed Rover of Great Britain to manufacture some of its cars under license, licensing alone is not enough to produce high-quality cars that can gain a large share of the British market and produce high profits for Honda. Honda needs to have its own operations in Great Britain, run according to its own management practices, in order to do that. Hence, Honda abandoned its licensing arrangement with Rover and is now invested directly in Great Britain. (Its first British production plant will start producing in 1994.)

All of this suggests that when one or more of the following conditions holds, markets fail as a mechanism for selling know-how and FDI is more profitable than licensing: (*i*) when the firm has valuable know-how that cannot be adequately protected by a licensing contract, (*ii*) when the firm needs tight control over a foreign entity to maximize its market share and earnings in that country, and (*iii*) when a firm's skills and know-how are not amenable to licensing.

Following Competitors

Another theory used to explain FDI is based on the idea that firms follow their domestic competitors overseas. First expounded by F. T. Knickerbocker, this theory has been developed with regard to **oligopolistic industries.**[11] An oligopoly is an industry composed of a limited number of large firms (e.g., an industry in which four firms control 80 percent of a domestic market). A critical competitive feature of such industries is interdependence of the major players: what one firm does can have an immediate impact on the major competitors, forcing a response in kind. Thus if one firm in an oligopoly cuts prices, this can take market share away from its competitors, forcing them to respond with similar price cuts in order to retain their market share.

This kind of imitative behavior can take many forms in an oligopoly. One firm raises prices, the others follow; someone expands capacity, and the rivals imitate lest they be left in a disadvantageous position in the future. Building on this, Knickerbocker argued that the same kind of imitative behavior characterizes FDI. Consider an oligopoly in the United States in which three firms—A, B, and C—dominate the market. Firm A establishes a subsidiary in France. Firms B and C reflect that if this investment is successful, it may knock out their export business to France and give Firm A a first-mover advantage. Furthermore, Firm A might discover some competitive asset in France that it could repatriate to the United States to torment Firms B and C on their native soil. Given these possibilities, Firms B and C decide to follow Firm A and establish operations in France.

There is some evidence that imitative behavior does lead to FDI. Most of the empirical studies that have been done relate to FDI by U.S. firms during the 1950s and 60s. In general, these studies show that firms based in oliogopolistic industries tended to imitate each other's FDI.[12] More recently, the same phenomenon has been observed with regard to Japanese firms. For example, Toyota and Nissan responded to Honda's FDI in the United States and Europe by undertaking their own FDI in the United States and Europe.

Although Knickerbocker's theory explains imitative behavior by firms in an oligopolistic industry, it does not explain why the first firm in an oligopoly to undertake FDI decides to do so, rather than to export or license. In contrast, the market imperfections explanation addresses this phenomenon. Moreover, the imitative theory does not address the issue of whether FDI is more efficient than exporting or licensing for expanding abroad. Again, the market imperfections approach does address the efficiency issue. For these reasons, most economists favor the market imperfections explanation for FDI, although most would agree that the imitative explanation tells part of the story.

The Product Life Cycle

We considered Raymond Vernon's product life-cycle theory in Chapter 4. What we did not dwell on, however, was Vernon's contention that his theory also explains FDI. Vernon argued that in many cases the establishment of facilities abroad to produce a

---

11 The argument is most often associated with F. T. Knickerbocker, *Oligopolistic Reaction and Multinational Enterprise* (Boston: Harvard Business School Press, 1973).

12 For a review of the evidence, see R. E. Caves, *Multinational Enterprise and Economic Analysis* (Cambridge, U.K.: Cambridge University Press, 1982).

product for consumption in that market, or for export to other markets, is often undertaken by the same firm or firms that first introduced the product into the U.S. market. Thus Xerox originally introduced the photocopier into the U.S. market, and it was Xerox that originally set up production facilities in Japan (Fuji-Xerox) and Great Britain (Rank-Xerox) to serve those markets.

Vernon's view is that firms undertake FDI at particular stages in the life cycle of a product they have pioneered. They invest in other advanced countries when local demand in those countries grows large enough to support local production (as Xerox did). They subsequently invest in developing countries when product standardization and market saturation give rise to price competition and cost pressures. Investment in developing countries, where labor costs are lower, is seen as the best way to reduce costs.

There is, of course, merit to Vernon's theory. Firms do indeed invest in a foreign country when demand in that country will support local production, and they do invest in low-cost locations (e.g., developing countries) when cost pressures become intense. What Vernon's theory fails to explain, however, is why it is profitable for a firm to undertake FDI at such times, rather than continuing to export from its home base, and rather than licensing a foreign firm to produce its product. Just because demand in a foreign country is large enough to support local production, it does not necessarily follow that local production is the most profitable option. It may still be more profitable to produce at home and export to that country (in order to realize the scale economies that arise from serving the global market from one location). Alternatively, it may be more profitable for the firm to license a foreign firm to produce its product for sale in that country. The product life-cycle theory ignores these options and, instead, simply argues that once a foreign market is large enough to support local production, FDI will occur. This limits its explanatory power and its usefulness to business (in that it fails to identify when it is profitable to invest abroad).

VERTICAL FOREIGN DIRECT INVESTMENT

Vertical FDI takes two forms. First, there is **backward vertical FDI** into an industry abroad that provides inputs for a firm's domestic production processes. Historically, most backward vertical FDI has been in extractive industries (e.g., oil extraction, bauxite mining, tin mining, copper mining). The objective has been to provide inputs into a firm's downstream operations (e.g., oil refining, aluminum smelting and fabrication, tin smelting and fabrication). Firms such as Royal Dutch Shell, British Petroleum (BP), RTZ, Consolidated Gold Field, and Alcoa, are among the classic examples of such vertically integrated multinationals.

A second form of vertical FDI is **forward vertical FDI.** Forward vertical FDI is FDI into an industry abroad that sells the outputs of a firm's domestic production processes. Forward vertical FDI is much less common than backward vertical FDI. For example, when Volkswagen first entered the U.S. market, rather than distribute its cars through independent U.S. dealers, at no small expense it acquired a large number of dealers.

With both horizontal and vertical FDI, the question that must be answered is why would a firm go to all the trouble and expense of setting up operations in a foreign country? Why, for example, did petroleum companies like BP and Royal Dutch Shell vertically integrate backward into oil production abroad? Why did they not simply import oil extracted by local producers? And why do companies like Volkswagen feel it is necessary to acquire their own dealers in foreign markets, when in theory it might seem less costly to rely on foreign dealers? There are two basic answers to these kinds of questions. The first is a *market power* argument, and the second draws, once again, upon the *market imperfections* approach.

Market Power

One aspect of the market power argument is that firms undertake vertical FDI to limit competition and strengthen their control over the market. The most common argument is that by vertically integrating backward to gain control over the source of raw-material inputs, a firm can effectively shut new competitors out of an industry. Such a strategy involves FDI only because the raw-material inputs are found abroad. An example occurred in the 1930s, when commercial smelting of aluminum was pioneered by North American firms like Alcoa and Alcan. Aluminum is derived by smelting bauxite. Although bauxite is a common mineral, the percentage of aluminum in bauxite is typically so low that it is not economical to mine and smelt. During the 1930s only one large-scale deposit of bauxite with an economical percentage of aluminum had been discovered, and it was on the Caribbean island of Jamaica. Alcoa and Alcan vertically integrated backward and acquired ownership of the deposit. This action created a *barrier to entry* into the aluminum industry. Potential competitors were deterred because they could not get access to high-grade bauxite—it was all owned by Alcoa and Alcan. Those that did enter the industry had to use lower-grade bauxite than Alcan and Alcoa, and found themselves at a cost disadvantage vis-à-vis these two companies. This situation persisted until the 1950s and 1960s, when new high-grade deposits were discovered in Australia and Indonesia.

However, despite the bauxite example, the opportunities for barring entry through vertical FDI seem far too limited to explain the incidence of vertical FDI among the world's multinationals. In most extractive industries, mineral deposits are not as concentrated as in the case of bauxite in the 1930s, while new deposits are constantly being discovered. Consequently, any attempt to monopolize all viable raw material deposits is bound to prove very expensive if not impossible.

Another strand of the market power explanation of vertical FDI sees such investment not as an attempt to built entry barriers, but as an attempt to circumvent the barriers established by firms already doing business in a country. This may explain Volkswagen's decision to establish its own dealer network when it entered the North American auto market. The market was then dominated by GM, Ford, and Chrysler. Each firm had its own network of independent dealers that carried their cars. Volkswagen felt that the only way to get quick access to the U.S. market was to promote its cars through independent dealerships.

Market Imperfections

As in the case of horizontal FDI, a more general explanation of vertical FDI can be found in the market imperfections approach.[13] The market imperfections approach offers two explanations for vertical FDI. As with horizontal FDI, the first explanation revolves around the idea that there are impediments to the sale of know-how through the market mechanism. The second explanation is based upon the idea that investments in specialized assets expose the investing firm to hazards that can be reduced only through vertical FDI.

Impediments to the Sale of Know-How

Consider the case of oil refining companies such as British Petroleum (BP) and Royal Dutch Shell. Historically these firms pursued backward vertical FDI in order to supply their British and Dutch oil refining facilities with crude oil. At the time when this occurred (the early decades of this century), neither Great Britain nor the Netherlands

[13] See J. F. Hennart, "Upstream Vertical Integration in the Aluminum and Tin Industries," *Journal of Economic Behavior and Organization* 9 (1988), pp. 281–99; and O. E. Williamson, *The Economic Institutions of Capitalism* (New York: Free Press, 1985).

had domestic oil supplies. What must be answered, however, is why these firms pursued backward vertical FDI to provide oil inputs. Why did they not just import oil from firms in oil-rich countries such as Saudi Arabia and Kuwait?

The answer is that originally there were no Saudi Arabian or Kuwaiti firms with the technological expertise for finding and extracting oil. BP and Royal Dutch Shell had to develop this know-how themselves in order to get access to oil. This alone does not explain FDI, however, for once BP and Shell had developed the necessary know-how they could have licensed it to Saudi Arabian or Kuwaiti firms. However, as we saw in the case of horizontal FDI, licensing can be self-defeating as a mechanism for the sale of know-how. If the oil refining firms had licensed their prospecting and extraction know-how to Saudi Arabian or Kuwaiti firms, they would have risked giving away their technological know-how to those firms, creating future competitors in the process. Once they had the know-how, the Saudi and Kuwaiti firms might themselves have gone prospecting for oil in other parts of the world, competing directly against BP and Royal Dutch Shell. Thus it made more sense for these firms to undertake backward vertical FDI and extract the oil themselves, instead of licensing their hard-earned technological expertise to local firms.

Generalizing from this example, the prediction is that backward vertical FDI will occur when a firm has the knowledge and the ability to extract raw materials in another country *and* there is no efficient producer in that country that can supply raw materials to the firm.

Investment in Specialized Assets

Another strand of the market imperfections argument predicts that vertical FDI will occur when a firm must undertake investments in specialized assets whose value is dependent upon inputs provided by a foreign supplier. In this context, a **specialized asset** is an asset designed to perform a specific task, and whose value is significantly reduced in its next-best use. For an example, consider the case of an aluminum refinery, which is designed to refine bauxite ore and produce aluminum. There are several types of bauxite ore; the ores vary in content and chemical composition from deposit to deposit. Each type of ore requires a different type of refinery. Running one type of bauxite through a refinery designed for another type increases production costs by 20 percent to 100 percent.[14] Thus, the value of an investment in an aluminum refinery depends on the availability of the desired kind of bauxite ore.

Imagine that a U.S. aluminum company must decide whether to invest in an aluminum refinery designed to refine a certain type of ore. Assume further that this ore is available only through an Australian mining firm at a single bauxite mine. Using a different type of ore in the refinery would raise production costs by at least 20 percent. Therefore, the value of the U.S. company's investment is dependent on the price it must pay the Australian firm for this bauxite. Recognizing this, once the U.S. company has made the investment in a new refinery, what is to stop the Australian firm from raising bauxite prices? Absolutely nothing; and once it has made the investment, the U.S. firm is locked into its relationship with the Australian supplier. The Australian firm can increase bauxite prices, secure in the knowledge that so long as the increase in the total production costs of the U.S. firms are less than 20 percent, the U.S. firm will continue to buy from it. (It would become economical for the U.S. firm to buy from another supplier only if total production costs increased by more than 20 percent).

[14] Hennart, *Upstream Vertical Integration.*

How can the U.S. firm reduce the risk of the Australian firm opportunistically raising prices in this manner? The answer is by buying out the Australian firm. If the U.S. firm can buy the Australian firm, or its bauxite mine, it need no longer fear that bauxite prices will be increased after it has invested in the refinery. In other words, it would make economic sense for the U.S. firm to engage in vertical FDI. In practice, these kinds of considerations have driven aluminum firms to pursue vertical FDI to such a degree that in 1976 91 percent of the total volume of bauxite was transferred within vertically integrated firms.[15]

IMPLICATIONS FOR BUSINESS

The implications of the theories of horizontal and vertical FDI for business practice are relatively straightforward. Perhaps the most useful theory from a business perspective is the market imperfections approach. With regard to horizontal FDI, this approach is useful because it identifies with some precision how the relative profitabilities of horizontal FDI, exporting, and licensing vary with circumstances. The theory suggests that exporting is preferable to licensing and horizontal FDI so long as transport costs are minor and tariff barriers are trivial. As transport costs and/or tariff barriers increase, exporting becomes unprofitable, and the choice is between horizontal FDI and licensing. Since horizontal FDI is more costly and more risky than licensing, other things being equal, the theory argues that licensing is preferable to horizontal FDI. Other things are seldom equal, however. Although licensing may work, it is not an attractive option when one or more of the following conditions exist: (*a*) the firm has valuable know-how that cannot be adequately protected by a licensing contract, (*b*) the firm needs tight control over a foreign entity in order to maximize its market share and earnings in that country, and (*c*) a firm's skills and know-how are not amenable to licensing. Figure 6.2 presents these considerations as a decision tree.

Firms for which licensing is not a good option tend to be clustered in three types of industries:

1. High-technology industries where protecting firm-specific expertise is of paramount importance and licensing is hazardous.
2. Global oligopolies, where competitive interdependence requires that multinational firms maintain tight control over foreign operations so that they have the ability to launch coordinated attacks against their global competitors (as Kodak has done with Fuji.)
3. Industries where intense cost pressures require that multinational firms maintain tight control over foreign operations (so that they can disperse manufacturing to locations around the globe where factor costs are most favorable in order to minimize costs).

Although empirical evidence is limited, the majority of the evidence seems to support these conjectures.[16]

Firms for which licensing is a good option tend to be in industries whose conditions are opposite to those specified above. That is, licensing tends to be more common (and more profitable) in fragmented, low-technology industries in which globally dispersed manufacturing is not an option. A good example is the fast food industry. McDonald's has expanded globally by using a franchising strategy. Franchising is essentially the

[15] Ibid.

[16] For a discussion of the evidence up until 1982, see Caves, *Multinational Enterprise.*

Figure 6.2
A Decision Framework

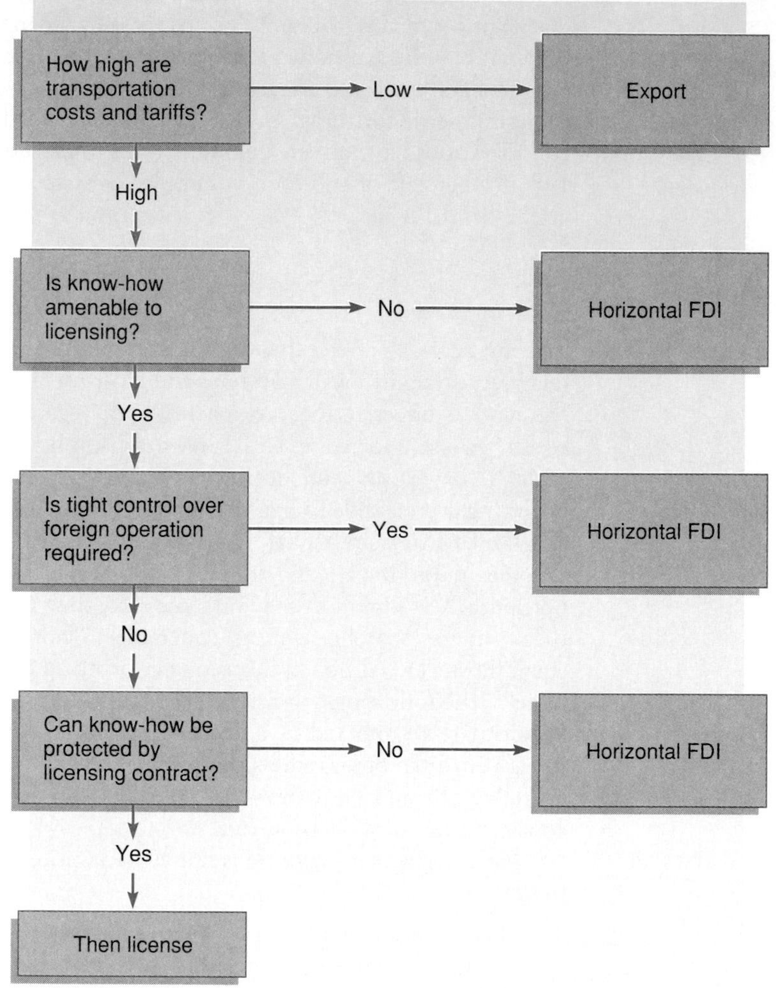

service-industry version of licensing—although it normally involves much longer term commitments than licensing. With franchising, the firm licenses its brand name to a foreign firm in return for a percentage of the franchisee's profits. The franchising contract specifies the conditions that the franchisee must fulfill if it is to use the franchisor's brand name. Thus McDonald's allows foreign firms to use its brand name so long as they agree to run their restaurants on exactly the same lines as McDonald's restaurants elsewhere in the world. This strategy makes sense for McDonald's because (*a*) like many services, fast food cannot be exported, (*b*) franchising economizes the costs and risks associated with opening up foreign markets, (*c*) unlike technological know-how, brand names are relatively easy to protect using a contract, (*d*) there is no compelling reason for McDonald's to have tight control over franchisees, and (*e*) McDonald's know-how, in terms of how to run a fast-food restaurant, is amenable to being specified in a written contract (e.g., the contract specifies the details of how to run a McDonald's restaurant).

In contrast to the market imperfections approach, the product life-cycle theory and Knickerbocker's theory of horizontal FDI tend to be less useful from a business perspective. The problem with these two theories is that they are descriptive rather than analytical. They do a good job of describing the historical evolution of FDI by U.S. firms, but they do a relatively poor job of identifying the factors that influence the relative profitability of FDI, licensing, and exporting. Indeed, the issue of licensing as an alternative to FDI is ignored by both of these theories.

Finally, with regard to vertical FDI, both the market imperfections approach and the market power approach have some useful implications for business practice. The market power approach has the virtue of pointing out that vertical FDI may be a way of building barriers to entry into an industry. The strength of the market imperfections approach is that it points out the conditions under which vertical FDI might be preferable to the alternatives. Most importantly, the market imperfections approach points to the importance of investments in specialized assets and imperfections in the market for know-how as factors that increase the relative attractiveness of vertical FDI.

SUMMARY OF CHAPTER

The principal objective of this chapter was to review theories that attempt to explain the pattern of FDI between countries. This objective takes on added importance in light of growing importance of FDI in the world economy. As we saw early in the chapter, the volume of FDI has grown more rapidly than the volume of world trade in recent years. We also noted that any theory seeking to explain FDI must explain why firms go to all of the trouble of acquiring or establishing operations abroad, when the alternatives of exporting and licensing are available to them.

We reviewed a number of theories that attempt to explain horizontal and vertical FDI. With regard to horizontal FDI, it was argued that the market imperfections approach might have the greatest explanatory power, and therefore be most useful for business practice. This is not to belittle the explanations for horizontal FDI put forward by Vernon and Knickerbocker, since these theories also have value in explaining the pattern of FDI in the world economy. However, both theories seem dated now that the United States no longer dominates the flow of outward FDI. Moreover, both theories are weakened by their failure to explicitly consider the factors that drive the choice between exporting, licensing, and FDI. Finally, with regard to vertical FDI, it was argued that the market power and market imperfections approaches both have a certain amount of explanatory power.

More specifically, in this chapter the following points have been made:

1. Foreign direct investment occurs when a firm invests directly in facilities to produce a product in a foreign country. It also occurs when a firm buys an existing enterprise in a foreign country.
2. Horizontal FDI is FDI in the same industry abroad as a firm operates at home. Vertical FDI is FDI in an industry abroad that provides inputs into a firm's domestic operations.
3. Any theory seeking to explain FDI must explain why firms go to all of the trouble of acquiring or establishing operations abroad, when the alternatives of exporting and licensing are available to them.
4. In recent years the volume of FDI has grown more rapidly than the volume of world trade, while the U.S. share of FDI has declined and the shares taken by Japan and European countries have increased.
5. FDI seems to be growing more rapidly than world trade due to a general rise of protectionist pressures in the world economy during the 1980s. (We discussed this in depth in Chapter 5.)
6. The rise in FDI in the United States seems to be driven by the belief of foreign companies that they can manage U.S. workers and assets more efficiently than U.S. managers can.
7. The low level of FDI in Japan seems to reflect a preference of Japanese companies to buy from other Japanese companies. Through persistence, however, some Western companies have been able to break down this informal barrier and establish profitable operations in Japan.
8. The globalization of world markets has been accompanied by a rapid growth of FDI by small and medium-sized firms.
9. High transportation costs and/or tariffs imposed on imports help explain why many firms prefer horizontal FDI or licensing over exporting.
10. Impediments to the sale of know-how explain why firms prefer horizontal FDI to licensing. These impediments arise in the following circumstances: (*i*) when a firm has valuable know-how that cannot be adequately protected by a licensing contract, (*ii*) when a firm needs tight control over a foreign entity in order to maximize its market share and earnings in that country, and (*iii*) when a firm's skills and know-how are not amenable to licensing.
11. Knickerbocker's theory suggests that much FDI is ex-

plained by imitative behavior by rival firms in an oligopolistic industry. However, this theory does not address the issue of whether FDI is more efficient than exporting or licensing for expanding abroad.

12. Vernon's product life-cycle theory suggests that firms undertake FDI at particular stages in the life cycle of products they have pioneered. However, Vernon's theory does not address the issue of whether FDI is more efficient than exporting or licensing for expanding abroad.
13. Backward vertical FDI may be explained as an attempt to create barriers to entry by gaining control over the source of material inputs into the downstream stage of a production process. Alternatively, forward vertical FDI may be seen as an attempt to circumvent entry barriers and gain access to a national market.
14. The market imperfections approach suggests that vertical FDI is a way of reducing a firm's exposure to the risks that arise from investments in specialized assets.
15. From a business perspective, the most useful theory is probably the market imperfections approach, because it identifies with some precision how the relative profitabilities of horizontal FDI, exporting, and licensing vary with circumstances.

DISCUSSION QUESTIONS

1. In recent years Japanese FDI in the United States has grown far more rapidly than U.S. FDI in Japan. Why do you think this is the case? What are the implications of this trend?
2. Compare and contrast these explanations of horizontal FDI: the market imperfections approach, Vernon's product life-cycle theory, and Knickerbocker's theory of FDI. Which theory do you think offers the best explanation of the historical pattern of horizontal FDI? Why?
3. Compare and contrast these explanations of vertical FDI: the market power approach and the market imperfections approach. Which theory do you think offers the better explanation of the historical pattern of vertical FDI? Why?
4. You are the international manager of a U.S. business that has just developed a revolutionary new personal computer that can perform the same functions as IBM and Apple computers and their clones but costs only half as much to manufacture. Your CEO has asked you to formulate a recommendation for how to expand into the Western European market. Your options are (*i*) to export from the United States, (*ii*) to license a European firm to manufacture and market the computer in Europe, and (*iii*) to set up a wholly owned subsidiary in Europe. Evaluate the pros and cons of each alternative and suggest a course of action to your CEO.

The Political Economy of Foreign Direct Investment

CHAPTER 7

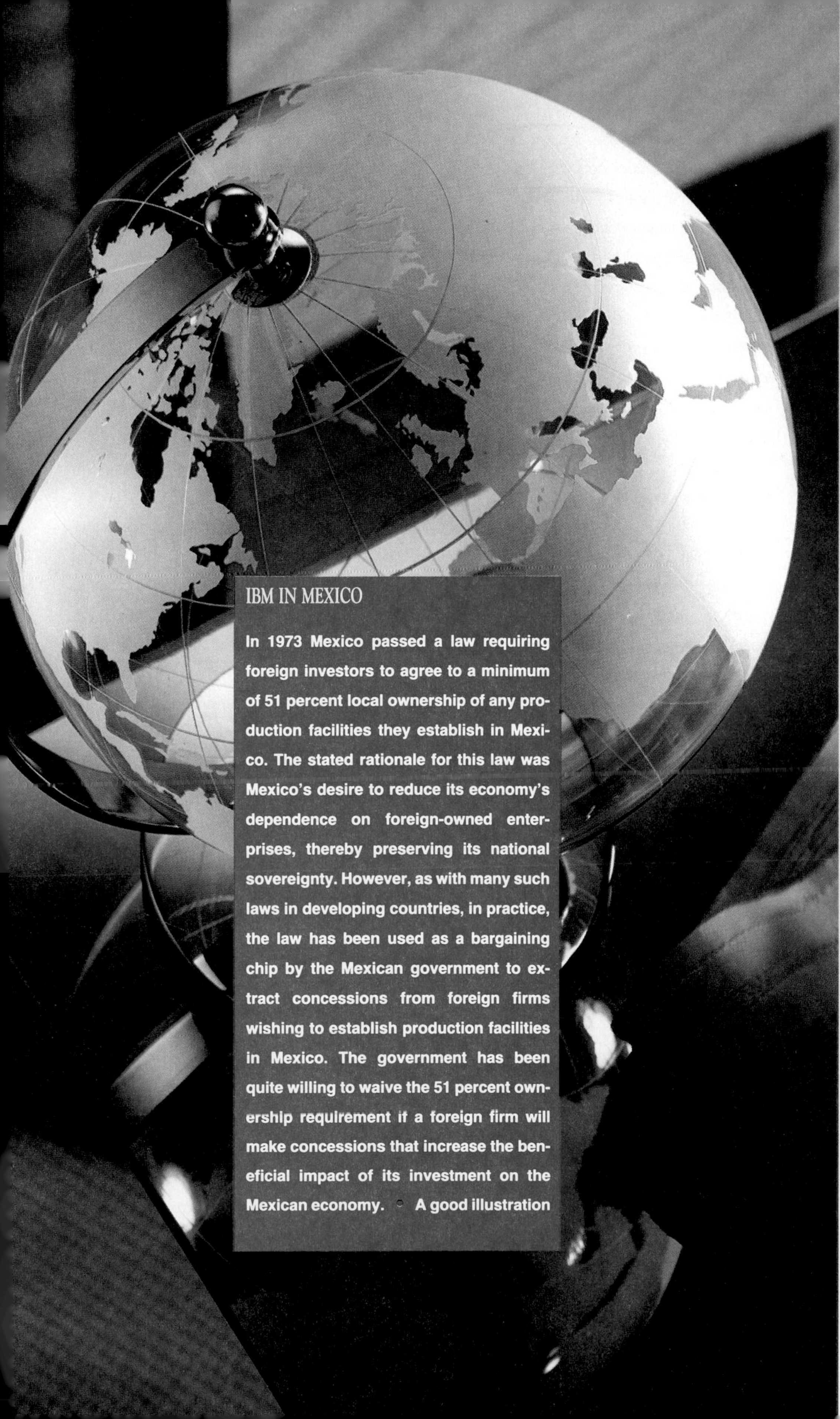

IBM IN MEXICO

In 1973 Mexico passed a law requiring foreign investors to agree to a minimum of 51 percent local ownership of any production facilities they establish in Mexico. The stated rationale for this law was Mexico's desire to reduce its economy's dependence on foreign-owned enterprises, thereby preserving its national sovereignty. However, as with many such laws in developing countries, in practice, the law has been used as a bargaining chip by the Mexican government to extract concessions from foreign firms wishing to establish production facilities in Mexico. The government has been quite willing to waive the 51 percent ownership requirement if a foreign firm will make concessions that increase the beneficial impact of its investment on the Mexican economy. ◦ A good illustration

of how the process works occurred in 1984 and 85 when IBM tried to get permission to establish a facility to manufacture personal computers in Guadalajara, Mexico. IBM proposed to invest about $40 million in a state-of-the-art production facility with the capacity to produce 100,000 PCs per year, 75 percent of which would be exported (primarily to the United States). IBM's strategic objective was to take advantage of Mexico's low labor costs to reduce the costs of manufacturing PCs. Given the proprietary nature of the product and process technology involved in the design and manufacture of PCs, IBM wanted to maintain 100 percent ownership of the Guadalajara facility. IBM clearly felt that if it entered into a joint venture with a Mexican firm to produce PCs, as required under Mexico's 1973 law, it would risk giving away valuable technology to a potential future competitor. • When presenting its case to the Mexican government, IBM stressed the benefits of the proposed investment for the Mexican economy. These included the creation of 80 direct jobs and 800 indirect ones, the transfer of high-technology job skills to Mexico, new direct investment of $7 million (the remaining $33 million required to finance the investment would be raised from the Mexican capital market), and exports of 75,000 personal computers per year. • The Mexican government rejected the proposal on the grounds that IBM did not propose to use sufficient local content in the plant, and would thus be importing too many parts and materials. IBM twice resubmitted its proposal. Maintaining its insistence on 100 percent ownership, with each proposal IBM increased its commitment to purchase local parts, increased the level of its direct investment, and raised its planned level of exports. The Mexican government agreed to the third proposal, which had in effect extracted significant concessions from IBM. • The final agreement required IBM to invest a total of $91 million (up from $40 million). This money was distributed among expansion of the Guadalajara plant ($7 million), investment in local R&D ($35 million), development of local component-part suppliers ($20 million), expansion of its purchasing and distribution network ($13 million), contributions to a Mexican government-sponsored semiconductor technology center ($12 million), and various other minor investments. In addition, IBM agreed to achieve 82 percent local content by the fourth year of operation and to export 92 percent of the PCs produced in Mexico. In exchange, the Mexican government waived its 51 percent local ownership requirement and allowed IBM to maintain 100 percent control. *Sources: J. Behrman and R. E. Grosse,* International Business and Government: Issues and Institutions *(Columbia: University of South Carolina Press, 1990); and S. Weiss, "The Long Path to the IBM–Mexico Agreement: An Analysis of Microcomputer Investment Negotiations, 1983–1986," working paper no. 3 (NYU School of Business, 1989).*

INTRODUCTION

In Chapter 6 we looked at the phenomenon of foreign direct investment (FDI) and reviewed several theories that attempt to explain the economic rationale for FDI. What we did not discuss in Chapter 6, however, is the role of governments in FDI. Through their choice of policies, governments of countries that are the hosts to FDI can both encourage and restrict FDI. Host governments can encourage FDI by providing incentives for foreign firms to invest in their economies, and they can restrict FDI through a variety of laws and policies. In the opening case, for example, we saw how Mexico's law on foreign ownership theoretically limited FDI to minority investments in Mexico.

The government of a source country for FDI (the home government) also can encourage or restrict FDI by domestic firms. In recent years, for example, the Japanese government has pressured many Japanese firms to undertake FDI. The Japanese government sees FDI as a substitute for exporting, and thus as a way of reducing Japan's politically embarrassing balance-of-payments surplus. In contrast, the U.S. government has, for political reasons, from time to time restricted FDI by domestic firms. In 1986, for example, in response to Libyan support for terrorist attacks in Western Europe, U.S. firms were prohibited from investing in or exporting to Libya.

Historically, one of the most important determinants of a government's policy toward FDI has been its political ideology. Accordingly, this chapter opens with a discussion of how political ideology influences government policy. As we shall see, to a greater or lesser degree, the officials of many governments tend to be pragmatic nationalists who weigh the benefits and costs of FDI and tend to vary their stated policy on a case-by-case basis. Mexico falls into this category, and the opening case illustrates how pragmatic Mexico is in practice, despite its apparently restrictive foreign investment laws. (It should be pointed out that since the time of IBM's negotiations reported in the case, Mexico has adopted a much more liberal stance with regard to FDI.) Following the discussion of political ideology, we will turn our attention to a consideration of the benefits and costs of FDI. Then we will look at the various policies home and host governments adopt to encourage and/or restrict FDI. The chapter closes with a detailed discussion of the implications of government policy for the business firm. In this closing section we examine the factors that determine the relative bargaining strengths of a host government and a firm contemplating FDI. We will look at how the negotiations between firm and government are often played out in practice, and at how firms can use this knowledge to their advantage. The opening case, of course, describes the negotiating process between IBM and the Mexican government.

POLITICAL IDEOLOGY AND FOREIGN DIRECT INVESTMENT

Historically, ideology toward FDI has ranged from a dogmatic radical stance that is hostile to all FDI at one extreme to an adherence to the noninterventionist principle of free market economics at the other. In between these two extremes is an approach that might be called pragmatic nationalism. The spectrum is shown in Figure 7.1, and we will review each of these approaches in turn.

The Radical View

The radical view traces its roots back to Marxist political and economic theory. In a nutshell, radical writers argue that the **multinational enterprise (MNE)** is an instrument of imperialist domination. They see the MNE as a tool for exploiting host countries to the exclusive benefit of their capitalist-imperialist home countries. They argue that MNEs extract profits from the host country and take them to their home country, giving nothing of value to the host country in exchange. They note, for example, that key technology is tightly controlled by the MNE, and that important jobs in the foreign subsidiaries of MNEs go to home-country nationals rather than to citizens of the host country. Because of this, according to the radical view, FDI by the MNEs of advanced capitalist nations keeps the less-developed countries of the world relatively backward and dependent on advanced capitalist nations for investment, jobs, and technology. Thus, according to the extreme version of this view, no country under any circumstances should ever permit foreign corporations to undertake FDI, since they can never be instruments of

Figure 7.1
The Spectrum of Political Ideology toward FDI

Radical view	Pragmatic nationalism	Free market

economic development, only of economic domination. Moreover, where MNEs do already exist in a country, they should be immediately nationalized.[1]

From 1945 until the 1980s the radical view was very influential in the world economy. Until the collapse of communism between 1989 and 1991, the countries of Eastern Europe were by and large opposed to any FDI. Similarly, communist countries elsewhere, such as China, Cambodia, and Cuba, were all opposed in principal to FDI (although in practice the Chinese started to allow FDI in mainland China in the 1970s). The radical position was also embraced by many socialist countries, particularly in Africa where one of the first actions of many newly independent states was to nationalize foreign-owned enterprises. The radical position was further embraced by countries whose political ideology was more nationalistic than socialistic. This was true in Iran and India, for example, both of which adopted tough policies restricting FDI and nationalized many foreign-owned enterprises. Iran is a particularly interesting case because its Islamic government, while rejecting Marxist theory, has essentially embraced the radical view that FDI by MNEs is an instrument of imperialism.

By the end of the 1980s, however, the radical position was in retreat almost everywhere. There seem to be three reasons for this:

1. The collapse of communism in Eastern Europe.
2. The generally abysmal economic performance of those countries that embraced the radical position, and a growing belief by many of these countries that, contrary to the radical position, FDI can be an important source of technology and jobs and can stimulate economic growth.
3. The strong economic performance of those developing countries that embraced capitalism rather than radical ideology (e.g., Singapore, Hong Kong, South Korea, and Taiwan).

The Free Market View

The free market view traces its roots back to classical economics and the international trade theories of Adam Smith and David Ricardo (see Chapter 4). The intellectual case for this view has been strengthened by the market imperfections explanation of horizontal and vertical FDI that we reviewed in Chapter 6. The free market view argues that international production should be distributed among countries according to the theory of comparative advantage. That is, countries should specialize in the production of those goods and services that they can produce most efficiently. Within this framework, the MNE is seen as an instrument for dispersing the production of goods and services to those locations around the globe where they can be produced most efficiently. Viewed this way, FDI by the MNE is a way to increase the overall efficiency of the world economy.

For example, IBM's decision to produce PCs in Mexico, rather than in the United States, can be seen as increasing the overall efficiency of resource utilization in the world economy. Mexico, due to its low labor costs, has a comparative advantage in the

[1] For elaboration see S. Hood and S. Young, *The Economics of the Multinational Enterprise* (London: Longman, 1979); and P. M. Sweezy and H. Magdoff, *The Dynamics of U.S. Capitalism* (New York: Monthly Review Press, 1972).

assembly of PCs. According to the free market view, by moving the production of PCs from the United States to Mexico, IBM frees up U.S. resources for use in activities in which the U.S. has a comparative advantage (e.g., the design of computer software or basic R&D). Moreover, U.S. consumers benefit because the PCs they want now cost less than they would if they were produced domestically. In addition, Mexico gains from the technology, skills, and capital that IBM transfers with its FDI. Contrary to the radical view, the free market view stresses that such resource transfers *benefit* the host country and stimulate its economic growth. Thus, the free market view argues that FDI is a benefit to both the source country and the host country.

The free market view has been embraced in principle by a number of advanced and developing nations, including the United States, Great Britain, Chile, Switzerland, Singapore, Hong Kong, the Netherlands, and Denmark. In addition, the free market view has been embraced by many of the former communist countries of Eastern Europe—particularly Poland, the new Czech state, and Hungary, which currently are aggressively seeking foreign capital and investment. In practice, however, no country has adopted the free market view in its pure form (just as no country has adopted the radical view in its pure form). Countries such as Great Britain and the United States are among the most open to FDI, but the governments of both countries have demonstrated a tendency to intervene. Great Britain does so formally by reserving the right to block foreign takeovers of domestic firms if the takeovers are seen as "contrary to national security interests" or if they have the potential for "reducing competition." (In practice this right is rarely exercised.) U.S. controls on FDI are more limited still and largely informal. As noted earlier for political reasons the United States will occasionally restrict U.S. firms from undertaking FDI in certain countries (e.g., Cuba and Libya). In addition, there are some limited restrictions on inward FDI. For example, foreigners are currently prohibited from purchasing more than 25 percent of any U.S. airline. Moreover, since 1989 the government has had the right to review foreign investment on the grounds of "national security." It is of note, however, that the rise of FDI into the United States in recent years (discussed in Chapter 6) has created pressures to pass stricter laws limiting it. In 1991, for example, there were 24 bills before Congress aimed at restricting FDI in the United States. Although none of these bills passed, the fact that so many were introduced indicates the mood in the Congress. The trend toward restricting foreign investment in the United States is discussed in more detail in Box 7.1.

Pragmatic Nationalism

Most countries have adopted neither a radical policy nor a free market policy toward FDI, but instead a policy that can best be described as pragmatic nationalism. The pragmatic nationalist view is that FDI has both benefits and costs. FDI can benefit a host country by bringing capital, skills, technology, and jobs, but those benefits often come at a cost. When products resulting from an investment are produced by a foreign company rather than a domestic company, the profits from that investment go abroad. Many countries are also concerned that a foreign-owned manufacturing plant may import many components from its home country, which has negative implications for the host country's balance-of-payments position.

Recognizing this, countries adopting a pragmatic stance pursue policies designed to maximize the national benefits and minimize the national costs. According to this view, FDI should be allowed only if the benefits outweigh the costs. Mexico's demands that IBM meet a number of conditions before it be allowed to set up a 100-percent-owned subsidiary in Guadalajara provide a good example of such a pragmatic national policy. By making such demands, Mexico was essentially trying to maximize the benefits and minimize the costs that IBM's investment might have for the Mexican economy.

Popular Arguments for and against FDI in the U.S. Economy

As a result of a surge in FDI, foreigners owned more than 13 percent of all manufacturing assets in the United States by 1990, up from 5 percent in 1977. This surge in investment has created a backlash, and pressures are now growing to limit FDI into the United States. The flavor of popular arguments for and against restrictions on FDI into the United States might best be understood by examining some of the arguments for and against restrictions.

Arguments against FDI in the United States

The following are excerpts from Martin Tolchin and Susan Tolchin, *Buying into America: How Foreign Money Is Changing the Face of Our Nation* (New York: Times Books, 1988).

The Reagan administration's enthusiasm over foreign investment was expressed in a 1983 statement: "We believe that there are only winners, no losers, and all participants gain from it."

But others are less sanguine. They warn that the United States is becoming addicted to foreign capital. They fear that this overdependence has made us vulnerable to the vagaries of foreign investment and that the withdrawal of foreign investment could wreak havoc on the economy. They lament the loss of profits that are taken out of the country and say that some foreign investors treat their American hirelings with the tenderness that imperialist powers reserved for the colonies. Mostly they fear that the surge of foreign investment is eroding the nation's independence, both political and economic. They warn that major decisions affecting the lives of Americans and, possibly, the security of the nation, are now being made in Tokyo, London, Riyadh, and other foreign capitals (p. 5).

There is persuasive evidence that some foreign investors, notably the Japanese, have purchased U.S. companies to acquire their technology and ultimately eliminate U.S. competition in key industries. In this area especially, foreign investment takes on aggressive overtones: a clear attempt to acquire advanced technology in order to dominate industrial markets (p. 11).

There is little recognition that some of these foreign businessmen have hidden agendas, including the destruction of American competitors and the acquisition of American technology. Many of these foreign investors have been motivated by a desire to avoid protective tariffs and view foreign investment as part of their nation's export strategy, to increase their market share (p. 15).

Japan offers a much more extreme version of pragmatic nationalism than Mexico. Until the 1980s Japan's policy was probably one of the most restrictive among countries adopting a pragmatic nationalist stance. This was due to Japan's perception that direct entry of foreign (especially U.S.) firms with ample managerial resources into the Japanese markets could be detrimental to the development and growth of their own industry and technology.[2] This belief led Japan to block the majority of applications by foreign firms to invest in Japan (e.g., see the opening case in Chapter 6 on the Japanese semiconductor

[2] M. Itoh and K. Kiyono, "Foreign Trade and Direct Investment," in R. Komiya, M. Okuno, and K. Suzumura, *Industrial Policy of Japan*, ed. (Tokyo: Academic Press, 1988).

BOX 7.1

Arguments in Favor of Permitting FDI into the United States

The following is an excerpt from "Of State and Industry," *The Economist,* June 8, 1991, p. 15.

More sought-after today are measures to control foreign investment. Here is industry policy at its daftest. Concern over the ownership of assets, rather than their location, is absurd. Inward foreign investment is, after all, investment, and often the especially valuable sort that brings in new products and skills. The charge that foreign owners "hollow out" whatever they buy by closing research and development facilities and so on is, on the evidence, simply false. The charge that they take some of their profits home is true, but puzzling: those who fear foreign ownership ought surely to prefer this to seeing those profits ploughed back into even more investment. Most foreign owners, and especially Japanese ones, are good corporate citizens.

The following are excerpts from Robert B. Reich, *The Work of Nations: Preparing Ourselves for the 21st Century* (New York: Alfred A. Knopf, 1991).

Canadians have long fretted over the dominance of corporations owned and controlled by foreigners—in particular, by citizens of the United States. Western Europeans have been similarly upset by the power of the American-owned multinational. But now, as the Japanese, West Germans, and others appear to be "buying up" America, we are experiencing similar trepidation.

Such concerns, however, are the product of outmoded thinking. . . . As corporations of all nations are transformed into global webs, the important question—from the standpoint of national wealth—is not which nation's citizens own what, but which nation's citizens learn to do what, so that they are capable of adding more value to the world economy and therefore increasing their own personal wealth (p. 137).

Just as empty is the concern that foreign-owned companies might leave the United States stranded by suddenly abandoning their American operations. The typical argument suggests that foreign-owned firms might withdraw because of profit or foreign policy considerations. But either way, the bricks and mortar would remain in the United States, as would the equipment. So would the accumulated learning gained by the firm's American employees. Under such circumstances, capital from another source would surely rush in to finance these attractive assets (p. 144).

The main reason why foreigners bring their money and strategic brokering skills to the United States is the same reason Americans invest their money and strategic brokering skills abroad: because they think they can utilize the other nation's assets and its workers better than the nation's investors and managers can—rendering the assets and workers more productive than before (p. 146).

industry). However, there were always exceptions to this policy. In particular, firms that had important technology were often able to get permission to undertake FDI if they insisted that they would neither license their technology to a Japanese firm nor enter into a joint venture with a Japanese enterprise. IBM and Texas Instruments were among the firms that were able to set up wholly owned subsidiaries in Japan by adopting this negotiating position. From the perspective of the Japanese government, the benefits of FDI in such cases—the stimulus that these firms might impart to the Japanese economy—outweighed the perceived costs.

Another aspect of pragmatic nationalism is the tendency to aggressively court FDI seen to be in the national interest by, for example, offering subsidies to foreign MNEs in the form of tax breaks or grants. This is currently being seen within the 12 countries of

Table 7.1
Political Ideology toward FDI

Ideology	Characteristics	Host-Government Policy Implications
Radical	Marxist roots Views the MNE as an instrument of imperialist domination	Prohibit FDI Nationalize subsidaries of foreign-owned MNEs
Free market	Classical economic roots (Smith) Views the MNE as an instrument for allocating production to most efficient locations	No restrictions on FDI
Pragmatic nationalism	Views FDI as having both benefits and costs	Restrict FDI where costs outweigh benefits Bargain for greater benefits and fewer costs Aggressively court beneficial FDI by offering incentives

the European Community, as they seem to be competing with each other to attract U.S. and Japanese FDI by offering large tax breaks and subsidies. Among these countries, Great Britain has been the most successful at attracting Japanese investment in the automobile industry. Toyota, Honda, and Nissan are all now building major assembly plants in Great Britain, and it seems that they may use this country as their base for serving the rest of Europe—with obvious employment and balance-of-payments benefits for Great Britain.

Summary

The three main ideological positions with regard to FDI are summarized in Table 7.1. From a practical perspective, it is important to note that recent years have seen a marked decline in the number of countries that adhere to a radical ideology. Moreover, although no countries have adopted a pure free market policy stance, an increasing number of countries are gravitating toward the free market end of the spectrum. This includes many countries that only a few years ago were firmly in the radical camp (e.g., the former communist countries of Eastern Europe and many of the socialist countries of Africa) and several countries that until recently could best be described as pragmatic nationalists with regard to FDI (e.g., Japan, South Korea, Italy, Spain, and most Latin American countries). Ironically, at the same time that most of the world seems to be moving toward more of a free market stance with regard to FDI, domestic political pressures within the United States—for a long time the strongest defender of the free market position—are trying to shift U.S. policy toward a more pragmatic nationalist position.

THE BENEFITS OF FDI TO HOST COUNTRIES

To a greater or lesser degree, most of the world's countries are now pragmatic nationalists with regard to FDI. For these countries, the main issue is to weigh the relative benefits against the cost of FDI. Accordingly, in this section we explore the three main benefits of FDI for a host country: the resource-transfer effect, the employment effect, and the balance-of-payments effect. Then in the following section we will explore the costs of FDI to host countries. It should be noted that economists who favor the free market view argue that the benefits of FDI to a host country so outweigh the costs that pragmatic nationalism is itself a misguided policy. According to the free market view, in a perfect world the best policy would be for all countries to forgo intervening in the investment decisions of MNEs.[3]

Resource-Transfer Effects

Foreign direct investment can make a positive contribution to a host economy by supplying capital, technology, and management resources that would otherwise not be available. If capital, technology, or management skills are scarce in a country, the provision of these skills by an MNE (through FDI) may boost that country's economic growth rate. The opening case suggests that the Mexican government understood the importance of resource-transfer effects. When negotiating with IBM, the Mexican government insisted that IBM transfer more capital and technology to Mexico than originally proposed.

Capital

The basic argument with regard to capital is that many MNEs, by virtue of their large size and financial strength, have access to financial resources not available to host-country firms. These funds may be available from internal company sources, or, because of their reputation, large MNEs may find it easier to borrow money from capital markets than host-country firms would. IBM, for example, by virtue of its reputation, size, and experience, may find it much easier to borrow money from capital markets to finance investments in Mexico than a small Mexican start-up that has never borrowed money before and has no track record.

Technology

The crucial role played by technology in the process of economic growth is now widely accepted. Technology is a catalyst that can stimulate economic development and industrialization. Technology can take two forms, both of which are valuable. It can be incorporated in a production process (e.g., the technology for manufacturing personal computers) or it can be incorporated in a product (e.g., the personal computers themselves). However, many countries lack the research and development resources and skills required to develop their own indigenous product and process technology. This is particularly true of the world's less-developed nations. Such countries must rely on advanced industrialized nations for much of the technology required to stimulate economic growth, and FDI can provide it. Mexico, for example, probably lacked the technological know-how required to develop its own personal computer industry. However, FDI and the associated technological transfer by MNEs such as IBM and Apple Computer have created a viable personal computer industry in Mexico and have probably had a beneficial effect on the economic well-being of Mexico as a whole.

It should be noted, however, that FDI is not the only way to access advanced technology. Another option is to license that technology from foreign MNEs. The Japanese government, in particular, has favored this strategy. (The opening case in Chapter 6 on the Japanese semiconductor industry provides an example of this.) The belief of the Japanese government has been that, in the case of FDI, the technology is still ultimately controlled by the foreign MNE. Consequently, it is difficult for indigenous Japanese firms to develop their own, possibly better, technology, since they are denied

[3] Most of the material for this section is drawn from Hood and Young, *Economics of the Multinational Enterprise.*

access to the basic technology. With this in mind, the Japanese government has insisted in the past that technology be transferred to Japan through licensing agreements, rather than through FDI. The advantage of licensing is that in return for royalty payments, host-country firms are given *direct access* to valuable technology. The licensing option is generally less attractive to the MNE, however. By licensing its technology to foreign companies, an MNE risks creating a future competitor—as many U.S. firms have learned at great cost in Japan. (The opening case in Chapter 5 provides an example.) Given this tension, the mode for transferring technology—licensing or FDI—can be a major negotiating point between an MNE and a host government. Whether the MNE gets its way or not depends on the relative bargaining powers of the MNE and the host government. In the case of Japan, for example, such was the bargaining power of IBM that it was able to get around Japan's preference for licensing arrangements and establish a wholly owned subsidiary in Japan.

Management

The provision of foreign management skills through FDI may also produce important benefits for the host country. Particularly valuable may be the spin-off effects. Beneficial spin-off effects arise when local personnel who are trained to occupy managerial, financial, and technical posts in the subsidiary of a foreign MNE subsequently leave the firm and help to establish indigenous firms. Similar benefits may arise if the superior management skills of a foreign MNE stimulate local suppliers, distributors, and competitors to improve their own management skills.

On the other hand, the beneficial effects may be considerably reduced if most management and highly skilled jobs in the subsidiaries of foreign firms are reserved for home-country nationals. In such cases, citizens of the host country do not receive the benefits of training by the MNE. This may limit the spin-off effect. Consequently, the percentage of management and skilled jobs that go to citizens of the host country can be a major negotiating point between an MNE wishing to undertake FDI and a potential host government. In recent years most MNEs have responded to host-government pressures on this issue by agreeing to reserve a large proportion of management and highly skilled jobs for citizens of the host country.

Employment Effects

The beneficial employment effect claimed for FDI is that FDI brings jobs to a host country that would otherwise not be created there. Employment effects are both direct and indirect. Direct effects arise when a foreign MNE directly employs a number of host-country citizens. Indirect effects arise when jobs are created in local suppliers as a result of the investment and when jobs are created because of the increased spending in the local economy resulting from employees of the MNE. As a rule, the indirect employment effects are greater than the direct effects. The opening case, for example, mentions IBM's estimate that its investment in Mexico would directly create 80 new jobs and indirectly create 800 new jobs. Similarly, it has been estimated that FDI by Japanese automobile companies in the United States during the 1980s directly created 20,000 new jobs and indirectly created another 200,000.

On the other hand, cynics note that not all of the "new jobs" created by FDI represent net additions in employment. In the case of FDI by Japanese auto companies in the United States, for example, some argue that the jobs created by this investment have been more than offset by the jobs lost in U.S.-owned auto companies, who have lost market share to their Japanese competitors. As a consequence of such substitution effects, the *net* number of new jobs created by FDI may not be as great as initially claimed by an

MNE. Not surprisingly, then, the issue of the likely net gain in employment may be a major negotiating point between an MNE wishing to undertake FDI and the host government.

Balance-of-Payments Effects

The effect of FDI on a country's **balance-of-payments accounts** is an important policy issue for most host governments. To understand this concern we must first familiarize ourselves with balance-of-payments accounting. Having done this, we will examine the link between FDI and the balance-of-payments accounts.

Balance-of-Payments Accounts

A country's balance-of-payments accounts keep track of both its payments to and its receipts from other countries. Any transaction resulting in a payment to other countries is entered in the balance-of-payments accounts as a debit and given a negative (−) sign. Any transaction resulting in a receipt from other countries is entered as a credit and given a positive (+) sign.

Balance-of-payments accounts are divided into two main sections: the current account and the capital account. The **current account** records transactions that involve the export or import of goods and services. Thus, when a U.S. consumer purchases a car made in Japan, the purchase is recorded as debit on the current account. A **current account deficit,** or **trade deficit** as it is often called, is said to occur when a country imports more goods and services than it exports. A **current account surplus (trade surplus)** occurs when a country exports more goods and services than it imports. (In recent years the United States has run a persistent trade deficit.) The **capital account** records transactions that involve the purchase or sale of assets. Thus, when a Japanese firm purchases stock of a U.S. company, the transaction enters the U.S. balance of payments as a credit on the capital account. This is because capital is flowing into the country. When capital flows out of the United States, it enters the U.S. capital account as a debit.

A basic principle of balance-of-payments accounting is **double-entry bookkeeping.** Specifically, *every international transaction automatically enters the balance of payments twice—once as a credit and once as a debit.* As an explanation of why this is so, imagine that you purchase a car produced in Japan by Toyota for $12,000. Since your purchase represents a payment to another country for goods, it will enter the balance of payments as a debit on the current account. Toyota now has the $12,000 and must do something with it. If Toyota deposits the money at a U.S. bank, Toyota has purchased a U.S. asset—a bank deposit worth $12,000—and the transaction will show up as a $12,000 credit on the capital account. Alternatively, Toyota might deposit the cash in a Japanese bank in return for Japanese yen. Now the Japanese bank must decide what to do with the $12,000. Any action that it takes will ultimately result in a credit for the U.S. balance of payments. For example, if the bank lends the $12,000 to a Japanese firm that uses it to import personal computers from the United States, then the $12,000 must be credited to the U.S. balance-of-payments current account. Alternatively, the Japanese bank might use the $12,000 to purchase U.S. government bonds, in which case it will show up as a credit on the U.S. balance-of-payments capital account.

Thus, any international transaction automatically gives rise to two offsetting entries in the balance of payments. Because of this, the current account balance and the capital account balance should always add up to zero. (In practice, this does not always occur due to the existence of statistical discrepancies that need not concern us here.)

Governments normally are concerned when their country is running a deficit *on the current account* of their balance of payments (i.e., when there is a trade deficit).[4] When a country runs a current-account deficit, the money that flows to other countries is typically then used by those countries to purchase assets in the deficit country. Thus, when the United States runs a trade deficit with Japan, the Japanese use the money that they receive from U.S. consumers to purchase U.S. assets such as stocks, bonds, and the like. Put another way, a deficit on the current account is financed by selling assets to other countries; that is, by a surplus on the capital account. Thus, for example, the U.S. current-account deficit during the 1980s was financed by a steady sale of U.S. assets (stocks, bonds, real estate, and increasingly, whole corporations) to other countries. In effect, countries that run current-account deficits become net debtors.

What is wrong with this? The main problem is that debtor nations owe people money. As a result of financing its current account deficit through asset sales, for example, from now on, the United States will be obliged to deliver a stream of interest payments to foreign bondholders, rents to foreign landowners, and dividends to foreign stockholders. Such payments to foreigners drain resources from a country and limit the amount of funds available for investment within the country. Since investment within a country is necessary to stimulate economic growth, a persistent current-account deficit can choke off a country's future economic growth.

FDI and the Balance of Payments

Given the concern about current-account deficits, the balance-of-payments effects of FDI can be an important consideration for a host government. From a balance-of-payments perspective, there are three potential consequences of FDI. First, when an MNE establishes a foreign subsidiary, the capital account of the host country benefits from the initial capital inflow. (A debit will be recorded in the capital account of the home country, since capital is flowing out of the home country.) Thus, when IBM agreed to invest $91 million in Mexico (see opening case), Mexico's capital account improved by $91 million. However, this is a one-time-only effect. Set against this must be the outflow of earnings to the foreign parent company—which will be recorded as a debit on the capital account of the host country.

Second, if the FDI is a substitute for imports of goods or services, the effect can be to improve the current account of the host country's balance of payments. Much of the FDI by Japanese automobile companies in the United States, for example, can be seen as substituting for imports from Japan. Thus, the current account of the U.S. balance of payments has improved somewhat, because many Japanese companies are now supplying the U.S. market from production facilities in the United States, as opposed to facilities in Japan. Insofar as this has reduced the need to finance a current-account deficit by asset sales to foreigners, the United States has clearly benefited from this.

A third potential benefit to the host country's balance-of-payments position arises when the MNE uses a foreign subsidiary to export goods and services to other countries. As outlined in the opening case, one of the benefits to Mexico of IBM's investment was that IBM committed itself to export 92 percent of the PCs produced in Mexico—which would have a commensurate favorable impact on the current account of Mexico's balance of payments.

---

[4] The section is based on P. Krugman, *The Age of Diminished Expectations* (Cambridge, Mass.: MIT Press, 1990).

THE COSTS OF FDI TO HOST COUNTRIES

Three costs of FDI concern host countries. They arise from possible adverse effects on competition within the host nation, adverse effects on the balance of payments, and the perceived loss of national sovereignty and autonomy.

Adverse Effects on Competition

Host governments sometimes worry that the subsidiaries of foreign MNEs operating in their country may have greater economic power than indigenous competitors. This arises from the fact that they may be part of a larger international organization than the indigenous firms. As such, the foreign MNE may be able to draw on funds generated elsewhere to subsidize its costs in the host market, which could drive indigenous companies out of business and allow the firm to monopolize the market. (Once the market was monopolized, the foreign MNE could raise prices above those that would prevail in competitive markets, with harmful effects on the economic welfare of the host nation.) This concern tends to be greater in countries that have few large firms of their own that are able to compete effectively with the subsidiaries of foreign MNEs (generally less-developed countries). It tends to be a relatively minor concern in most advanced industrialized nations.

Another variant of the competition argument is related to the **infant industry** concern that we first discussed in Chapter 6. We explained there that import controls may be motivated by a desire to let a local industry develop to a stage where it is capable of competing in world markets. The same logic suggests that FDI should be restricted. If a country with a potential comparative advantage in a particular industry allows FDI in that industry, indigenous firms may never have a chance to develop.

It should be noted that in practice the above arguments are often used by inefficient indigenous competitors when lobbying their government to restrict direct investment by foreign MNEs. Although a host government may state publicly in such cases that its restrictions on inward FDI are designed to protect indigenous competitors from the market power of foreign MNEs, they may have been enacted to protect inefficient but politically powerful indigenous competitors from foreign competition.

Adverse Effects on the Balance of Payments

The possible adverse effects of FDI on a host country's balance-of-payments position have been hinted at earlier. In general, there are two main areas of concern with regard to the balance of payments. First, as mentioned earlier, set against the initial capital inflow that comes with FDI must be the subsequent outflow of earnings from the foreign subsidiary to its parent company. Such outflows show up as a debit on the capital account. Some governments have responded to such outflows by placing restrictions on the amount of earnings that can be repatriated to a foreign subsidiary's home country.

A second concern arises when a foreign subsidiary imports a substantial number of its inputs from abroad—which results in a debit on the current account of the host country's balance of payments. One of the criticisms leveled against Japanese-owned auto assembly operations in the United States, for example, is that they tend to import a large number of component parts from Japan. Due to such effects, the favorable impact of this FDI on the current account of the U.S. balance-of-payments position may not be as great as initially supposed. The Japanese auto companies have responded to these criticisms by pledging to purchase 75 percent of their component parts from U.S.-based manufacturers (but not necessarily U.S.-owned manufacturers). In the case of IBM's investment in Mexico, the Mexican government dealt with this concern by getting IBM to agree that 82 percent of the parts going into PCs manufactured in Mexico should be made in Mexico.

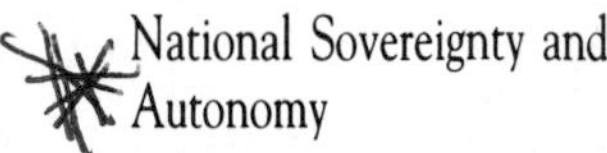

National Sovereignty and Autonomy

Many host governments worry that FDI is accompanied by some loss of economic independence. The concern is that key decisions that can affect the host country's economy will be made by a foreign parent that has no real commitment to the host country, and over which the host country's government has no real control. Twenty years ago this concern was expressed by several European countries, who feared that FDI by U.S. MNEs was threatening their national sovereignty. Ironically, the same concerns are now surfacing in the United States with regard to European and Japanese FDI. The main fear seems to be that if foreigners own assets in the United States, they can somehow "hold the country to economic ransom." Twenty years ago when officials in the French government were making similar complaints about U.S. investments in France, many U.S. politicians dismissed the charge as silly. Now that the shoe is on the other foot, many U.S. politicians no longer think the notion is silly. However, most economists dismiss such concerns as groundless and irrational. (For a selection of such views, see Box 7.1.) Economist Robert Reich recently spoke of such concerns as the product of outmoded thinking, because they fail to account for the growing interdependence of the world economy.[5] In a world where firms from all advanced nations are increasingly investing in each other's markets, it is not possible for one country to hold another to "economic ransom" without hurting itself in the process.

THE BENEFITS AND COSTS OF FDI TO HOME COUNTRIES

Although the cost and benefits of FDI for a host country have received most attention, there are also costs and benefits to the home (or source) country that warrant attention. Does the U.S. economy benefit or lose from IBM's investment in Mexico? Does the Japanese economy lose or gain from Toyota's investment in the United States? Some would argue that FDI is not always in the home country's national interest and should, therefore, be restricted. Others argue that the benefits far outweigh the costs, and that any restrictions would be contrary to national interests. To understand why people take these positions, let us look at the benefits and costs of FDI to the home (source) country.

Benefits of FDI to the Home Country

The benefits of FDI to the home country arise from three sources. First, and perhaps most important, the capital account of the home country's *balance-of-payments* benefits from the inward flow of foreign earnings. Thus, one benefit to the United States from IBM's investment in Mexico are the earnings that are subsequently repatriated to the United States from Mexico. FDI can also have a beneficial impact on the current account of the home country's balance of payments if the foreign subsidiary creates demands for home-country exports of capital equipment, intermediate goods, complementary products, and the like.

Second, benefits to the home country from outward FDI arise from *employment effects.* As with the balance of payments, positive employment effects arise when the foreign subsidiary creates demand for home-country exports of capital equipment, intermediate goods, complementary products, and the like. Thus, Toyota's investment in auto assembly operations in the United States has had a beneficial effect on both the Japanese balance-of-payments position and employment in Japan, because Toyota imports many component parts for its U.S.-based auto assembly operations directly from Japan. (In response to U.S. government pressures, this is now changing.)

---

[5] Robert B. Reich, *The Work of Nations: Preparing Ourselves for the 21st Century* (New York: Alfred A. Knopf, 1991).

Third, benefits arise when the home-country MNE learns valuable skills from its exposure to foreign markets that can subsequently be transferred back to the home country. This amounts to a **reverse resource-transfer effect.** Through its exposure to a foreign market, an MNE can learn about superior management techniques and superior product and process technologies. These resources can then be transferred back to the home country, with a commensurate beneficial effect on the home country's economic growth rate.[6] For example, one purpose behind the investment by General Motors and Ford in Japanese automobile companies (GM owns part of Isuzu, and Ford owns part of Mazda) has been for GM and Ford to learn about those Japanese companies' apparently superior management techniques and production processes. If GM and Ford are successful in transferring this know-how back to their U.S. operations, the result may be a net gain for the U.S. economy.

Costs of FDI to the Home Country

Against these benefits must be set the apparent costs of FDI for the home (source) country. The most important concerns center around the balance-of-payments and employment effects of outward FDI. The home country's *balance of payments* may suffer in three ways. First, the capital account of the balance of payments suffers from the initial capital outflow required to finance the FDI. This effect, however, is usually more than offset by the subsequent inflow of foreign earnings. Second, the current account of the balance of payments suffers if the purpose of the foreign investment is to serve the home market from a low-cost production location. This certainly was the case with IBM's investment in Mexico, the purpose of which was to build PCs for sale in the U.S. market. Third, the current account of the balance of payments suffers if the FDI is a substitute for direct exports. Thus, insofar as Toyota's assembly operations in the United States are intended to substitute for direct exports from Japan, the current-account position of Japan will deteriorate.

With regard to *employment effects*, the most serious concerns arise when FDI is seen as a substitute for domestic production. This was the case with IBM's investment in Mexico and with Toyota's investment in the United States. One obvious result of such FDI is reduced home-country employment. If the labor market in the home country is already very tight, with little unemployment (as was the case in both Japan and the United States during the 1980s), this concern may not be that great. However, if the home country is suffering from unemployment, concern about the "export of jobs" may rise to the fore. For example, one objection frequently raised by U.S. labor leaders to the free trade pact between the United States, Mexico, and Canada (see next chapter) is that the United States will lose hundreds of thousands of jobs as U.S. firms invest in Mexico to take advantage of cheaper labor and then export back to the U.S. market.[7]

International Trade Theory and Offshore Production

When assessing the costs and benefits of FDI to the home country, it is as well to keep in mind the lessons of international trade theory (see Chapter 4). International trade theory tells us that home-country concerns about the negative economic effects of "offshore production" may be misplaced. The term *offshore production* refers to FDI undertaken to serve the home market—such as IBM's investment in Mexico to produce PCs for the U.S. market. Far from reducing home-country employment, by freeing up home-country

---

[6] This idea has recently been articulated, although not quite in this form, by C. A. Bartlett and S. Ghoshal, *Managing across Borders: The Transnational Solution* (Boston: Harvard Business School Press, 1989).

[7] See P. Magnusson, "The Mexico Pact: Worth the Price?" *Business Week*, May 27, 1991, pp. 32–35.

resources to concentrate on activities where the home country has a comparative advantage, such FDI may actually stimulate economic growth (and hence employment) in the home country. In addition, bear in mind that home-country consumers benefit if the price of the particular product falls as a result of the FDI. Thus U.S. consumers arguably benefited from IBM's decision to produce personal computers in Mexico for export to the U.S., primarily because IBM was able to reduce the price of its PCs as a result.

Also bear in mind that if a company such as IBM were prohibited from making such investments on the grounds of negative employment effects while its international competitors were able to reap the benefits of low-cost production locations, IBM would undoubtedly lose market share to its international competitors. Under such a scenario, the adverse long-run economic effects for the U.S. economy would probably far outweigh the relatively minor balance-of-payments and employment effects associated with off-shore production.

GOVERNMENT POLICY INSTRUMENTS AND FDI

We have now reviewed the costs and benefits of FDI from the perspective of both home country and host country. Before tackling the important issue of bargaining between the MNE and the host government, we need to discuss the policy instruments that governments use to regulate FDI activity by MNEs. Both home (source) countries and host countries have a range of policy instruments that they can use. We will look at each in turn.

Home-Country Policies

By their choice of policies, home countries can both encourage and restrict FDI by local firms. We look at policies designed to encourage outward FDI first. These include foreign risk insurance, capital assistance, tax incentives, and political pressure. Then we will look at policies designed to restrict outward FDI.

Encouraging Outward FDI

Many investor nations now have government-backed insurance programs to cover major types of foreign investment risk. The types of risks insurable through these programs include the risks of expropriation (nationalization), war losses, and the inability to transfer profits back home. Such programs are particularly useful in encouraging firms to undertake investments in politically unstable countries.[8] In addition, several advanced countries also have special funds or banks that make government loans to firms wishing to invest in developing countries. As a further incentive to encourage domestic firms to undertake FDI, many countries have taken steps to eliminate double taxation of foreign income (i.e., taxation of income in both the host country and the home country). Last, and perhaps most significant, a number of investor countries (particularly the United States) have used their political influence to persuade host countries to relax their restrictions on inbound FDI. For example, in response to direct U.S. pressure, Japan relaxed many of its formal restrictions on inward FDI in the early 1980s. Now, in response to further U.S. pressure, Japan is beginning to move toward relaxing its informal

[8] See C. Johnston, "Political Risk Insurance" in *Assessing Corporate Political Risk,* ed. D. M. Raddock (Totowa, N.J.: Rowan & Littlefield, 1986).

barriers to inward FDI. One of the most recent beneficiaries of this trend is Toys-R-Us, which, after five years of intensive lobbying by company and U.S. government officials, was able to open up its first retail stores in Japan in December 1991.

Restricting Outward FDI

Virtually all investor countries, including the United States, have exercised some control over outward FDI from time to time. One of the most common policies has been to limit capital outflows out of concern for the country's balance of payments. From the early 1960s until 1979, for example, Great Britain had exchange-control regulations that effectively limited the amount of capital a firm could take out of the country. Although the main intent of such policies was to improve the British balance of payments, an important secondary intent was to make it more difficult for British firms to undertake FDI.

In addition, countries have occasionally manipulated tax rules to try to encourage their firms to invest at home. The objective behind such policies is to create jobs at home rather than in other nations. These policies also have been adopted by Great Britain. The British advanced corporation tax system taxes British companies' foreign earnings at a higher rate than their domestic earnings. This tax code creates an incentive for British companies to invest at home.

Finally, countries sometimes prohibit national firms from investing in certain countries for political reasons. Such restrictions can be formal or informal. For example, formal U.S. rules have prohibited U.S. firms from investing in countries such as Cuba, Libya, and Iran, whose political ideology and actions are judged to be contrary to U.S. interests. Similarly, informal pressure has been applied to dissuade U.S. firms from investing in South Africa. In this case, the objective was to put pressure on South Africa to change its apartheid laws. (The policy appears to have succeeded.)

Host-Country Policies

Host countries adopt policies designed both to restrict and to encourage inward FDI. As noted earlier in this chapter, political ideology has determined the type and scope of these policies in the past. In the last decade of the 20th century, we seem to be moving quickly away from a situation where many countries adhered to some version of the radical stance and prohibited much FDI, and toward a situation where a combination of free market objectives and pragmatic nationalism seems to be taking hold.

Encouraging Inward FDI

It is increasingly common for governments to offer incentives to foreign firms to invest in their countries. Such incentives take many forms, but the most common are tax concessions, low-interest loans, and outright grants or subsidies. Incentives are motivated by a desire to gain from the resource-transfer and employment effects of FDI. They are also motivated by a desire to capture FDI away from other potential host countries. In the mid-1980s, for example, the governments of Great Britain and Spain competed with each other on the size of the incentives they offered Japanese automobile companies considering investment in Europe. Great Britain won, and the size of the tax concessions granted to the Japanese companies was no small factor in the final decision. Not only do countries compete with each other to attract FDI; regions of countries do as well. In the United States, for example, state governments often compete with each other to attract FDI. In one case, it has been estimated that in attempting to persuade Toyota to build its

U.S. automobile assembly plants in Kentucky, rather than elsewhere in the United States, the state offered Toyota an incentive package worth $112 million. The package included tax breaks, new state spending on infrastructure, and low-interest loans.[9]

Restricting Inward FDI

Host governments use a wide range of controls to restrict FDI in one way or another. The two most common, however, are ownership restraints and performance requirements. **Ownership restraints** can themselves take on several forms. In some countries foreign companies are excluded from specific business fields altogether. For example, they are excluded from tobacco and mining in Sweden; from the development of certain natural resources in Brazil, Finland, and Morocco; from iron and steel, most mining, and oil, in India. In other industries, foreign ownership may be permitted, although there may be a requirement that a significant proportion of the equity of a subsidiary of a foreign MNE be owned by local investors. For example, foreign ownership is restricted to 40 percent or less of a company in India, except in some high-technology industries, where foreign ownership levels of between 51 percent and 100 percent are permitted.

The rationale underlying ownership restraints seems to be twofold. First, foreign firms are often excluded from certain sectors on the grounds of national security or competition. Particularly in less-developed countries, the feeling seems to be that local firms might not be able to develop unless foreign competition is restricted by a combination of import tariffs and controls on FDI. This is really a variant of the infant industry argument that we discussed in Chapter 5. Thus, taking India as an example, the logic for banning foreign ownership in the oil industry is that the Indian government believes that if foreign firms are allowed to invest in this industry, indigenous Indian firms will not be able to develop.

Second, ownership restraints seem to be based on a belief that local owners can help to maximize the resource-transfer and employment benefits of FDI for the host country. Consistent with this belief, until the early 1980s the Japanese government prohibited most FDI but was prepared to allow joint ventures between Japanese firms and foreign MNEs if the MNE had a particularly valuable technology. The Japanese government clearly felt that such an arrangement would help speed up the subsequent diffusion of the MNE's valuable technology throughout the Japanese economy.

As for **performance requirements,** these too can take several forms. Performance requirements are controls over the behavior of the local subsidiary of an MNE. If we go back to the opening case, Mexico's insistence that IBM's PC subsidiary achieve 82 percent local content and export 92 percent of its output are performance requirements. The most common performance requirements are related to local content, exports, technology transfer, and local participation in top management. As with certain ownership restrictions, the logic underlying performance requirements is that such rules help to maximize the benefits and minimize the costs of FDI for the host country. Virtually all countries employ some form of performance requirement when it suits their objectives. However, performance requirements tend to be more common in less-developed coun-

---

[9] Martin Tolchin and Susan Tolchin, *Buying into America: How Foreign Money Is Changing the Face of Our Nation* (New York: Times Books, 1988).

tries than in advanced industrialized nations. For example, one study found that some 30 percent of the affiliates of U.S. MNEs in less-developed countries were subject to performance requirements, while only 6 percent of the affiliates in advanced countries were faced with such requirements.[10]

IMPLICATIONS FOR BUSINESS

There are a number of fairly obvious implications for business inherent in the material discussed in this chapter. For a start, a host government's attitude toward FDI should be an important variable in decisions about where to locate foreign production facilities and where to make a foreign direct investment. Other things being equal, investing in countries that have permissive policies toward FDI is clearly preferable to investing in countries that restrict FDI.

Generally, however, the issue is not this straightforward. Most countries have a rather pragmatic stance toward FDI, and a firm considering FDI in a country usually must negotiate the specific terms of the investment with the country's government. Such negotiations center on two broad issues. If the host government is trying to attract FDI, the central issue is likely to be the kind of incentives the host government is prepared to offer to the MNE and what the firm will commit in exchange. If the host government is uncertain about the benefits of FDI and might choose to restrict access, the central issue is likely to be the concessions that the firm must make in order to be allowed to go forward with a proposed investment. Given this, in the remainder of this section we will focus our attention on the issue of negotiating with a host government.

The Nature of Negotiation

The objective of any negotiation is to reach an agreement that benefits both parties. The process of negotiation is both an "art" and a "science." The "science" of it requires systematically analyzing the relative bargaining strengths of each party and the different strategic options available to each party and assessing how the other party might respond to various bargaining ploys.[11] The "art" of negotiation incorporates "interpersonal skills, the ability to convince and be convinced, the ability to employ a basketful of bargaining ploys, and the wisdom to know when and how to use them."[12] In the context of international business, it might be added that the "art" of negotiation also includes understanding the influence of national norms, value systems, and culture on the approach and likely negotiating tactics of the other party as well as sensitivity to such factors in shaping a firm's approach to negotiations with a foreign government. For example, negotiating with the Japanese government for access is likely to be very different from negotiating with the British government. Consequently, it requires different interpersonal skills and bargaining ploys. We discussed the importance of national differences in society and culture in Chapter 3. It would be well to keep these differences in mind at this juncture.

---

[10] J. Behrman and R. E. Grosse, *International Business and Government: Issues and Institutions* (Columbia: University of South Carolina Press, 1990).

[11] This is the stuff of game theory. For a good introduction for the general reader, see A. Dixit and B. Nalebuff, *Thinking Strategically: The Competitive Edge in Business, Politics, and Everyday Life* (New York: W. W. Norton, 1991).

[12] H. Raiffa, *The Art and Science of Negotiation* (Cambridge, Mass.: Harvard University Press, 1982).

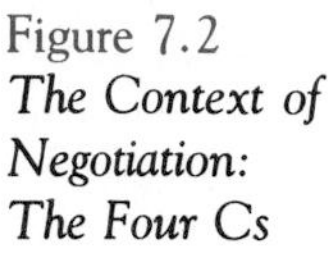

Figure 7.2
The Context of Negotiation: The Four Cs

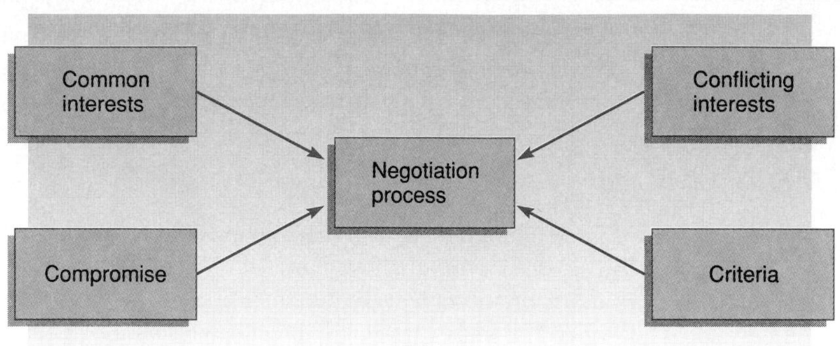

The negotiation process has been characterized as occurring within the context of "the four Cs": common interests, conflicting interests, compromise, and criteria (see figure 7.2).[13] In the IBM and Mexico example (the opening case), the *common interest* of both IBM and Mexico is in establishing a new enterprise in Mexico. *Conflicting interests* arise from such issues as the proportion of component parts that will be procured locally rather than imported, the total amount of investment, the total number of jobs created, and the proportion of output that will be exported. *Compromise* involves reaching a decision that brings benefits to both parties, even though neither will get all of what they want. IBM's *criteria* or objectives are to achieve satisfactory profits and to maintain 100 percent ownership. Mexico's criteria are to achieve satisfactory net benefits from the resource-transfer, employment, and balance-of-payments effects of the investment.

Bargaining Power

To a large degree, the outcome of any negotiated agreement depends on the relative **bargaining power** of both parties. Each side's bargaining power depends on three factors (see Table 7.2):

- The value each side places on what the other has to offer.
- The number of comparable alternatives available to each side.
- Each party's time horizon.

From the perspective of a firm negotiating the terms of an investment with a host government, the firm's bargaining power is high when the host government places a high value on what the firm has to offer, the number of comparable alternatives open to the firm is greater, and the firm has a long time in which to complete the negotiations. The converse also holds. The firm's bargaining power is low when the host government places a low value on what the firm has to offer, the number of comparable alternatives open to the firm is fewer, and the firm has a short time in which to complete the negotiations.

[13] J. Fayerweather and A. Kapoor, *Strategy and Negotiation for the International Corporation* (Cambridge, Mass.: Ballinger, 1976).

Table 7.2
Determinants of a Firm's Bargaining Power

	Bargaining Power of Firm	
	High	**Low**
Firm's time horizon	Long	Short
Comparable alternatives open to firm	Many	Few
Value placed by host government on investment	High	Low

To see how this plays out in practice, consider the case of IBM and Mexico (the opening case). First, note that IBM was in a fairly strong bargaining position, primarily because Mexico was suffering from a flight of capital out of the country at the time (1985 and 86), which made the government eager to attract new foreign investment. On the other hand, IBM's bargaining power was moderated somewhat by three things. First, symbolic importance apart, the size of the proposed investment was unlikely to have more than a marginal impact on the Mexican economy, so the economic value placed by Mexico on the investment was not that great. Second, IBM was looking for a low-labor-cost, politically stable location close to the U.S. market. Mexico was obviously the most desirable location given these criteria. Greater distance and higher transportation costs made alternative low-labor-cost locations, such as Taiwan or Singapore, relatively less attractive, while other potential locations in Central America were ruled out by political instability. Third, given the profusion of low-cost competitors moving into the U.S. personal computer market during the mid-1980s, IBM probably felt it needed to move quickly to establish its own low-cost production facilities. On the other hand, symbolism apart, there was no compelling reason for Mexico to close a deal quickly. Due to all of these factors, the Mexican government also held a degree of bargaining power in the negotiations and thus was able to extract some concessions from IBM. On the other hand, IBM's basically strong position allowed it to insist that it maintain 100 percent ownership of its Mexican subsidiary. This represented a significant concession from the Mexican government; IBM was the first major company for which Mexico waived its prohibition of majority ownership.

In a similar case during the 1960s, by using its bargaining power, IBM was one of the few firms able to get the Japanese government to waive the restriction on FDI that would allow it to establish a 100-percent-owned subsidiary in Japan. IBM was able to do this because it was the only major source of mainframe computer technology at that time, and numerous Japanese companies needed that technology for data processing. The lack of comparable alternatives available to the Japanese enabled IBM to pry open the Japanese market. Similarly, during the 1980s Toyota was able to extract significant concessions from the state of Kentucky in the form of tax breaks, low-interest loans, and grants, and Honda was able to extract similar concessions from the state of Ohio, when both companies undertook investment in U.S.-based auto assembly operations. At that time both of these states were suffering from high unemployment, and the proposed investments promised to have a substantial impact on employment. Moreover, both companies had a number of states from which to choose. Thus, the high value placed by state governments on the proposed investment and the number of comparable alternatives open to each company considerably strengthened the bargaining power of both companies relative to that of the state governments.

SUMMARY OF CHAPTER

The main objective of this chapter has been to examine the influence of governments on firms' decisions to invest in foreign countries. By their choice of policies, both host-country and home-country governments encourage and restrict FDI. A second objective has been to explore the factors that influence negotiations between a host-country government and a firm contemplating FDI. In particular, the following points have been made:

1. One of the most important determinants of government policy toward FDI is political ideology. Political ideology ranges from a radical stance that is hostile to FDI to a noninterventionist, free market stance. Between the two extremes is an approach best described as pragmatic nationalism.
2. The radical view sees the MNE as an imperialist tool for exploiting host countries. According to this view, no country should allow FDI. Due to the collapse of communism, the radical view was in retreat everywhere by the end of the 1980s.
3. The free market view sees the MNE as an instrument for increasing the overall efficiency of resource utilization in the world economy. FDI can be viewed as a way of dispersing the production of goods and services to those locations around the globe where they can be produced most efficiently. This view is embraced in principle by a number of nations; in practice, however, most are pragmatic nationalists.
4. Pragmatic nationalism views FDI as having both benefits and costs. Countries adopting a pragmatic stance pursue policies designed to maximize the benefits and minimize the costs of FDI.
5. The benefits of FDI to a host country arise from resource-transfer effects, employment effects, and balance-of-payments effects.
6. FDI can make a positive contribution to a host economy by supplying capital, technology, and management resources that would otherwise not be available. Such resource transfers can stimulate the economic growth of the host economy.
7. Employment effects arise from the direct and indirect creation of jobs by FDI.
8. Balance-of-payments effects arise from the initial capital inflow to finance FDI, from import substitution effects, and from subsequent exports by the new enterprise.
9. The costs of FDI to a host country include adverse effects on competition and balance of payments and a perceived loss of national sovereignty.
10. Host governments are concerned that foreign MNEs may have greater economic power than indigenous companies and that they may be able to monopolize the market.
11. Adverse effects on the balance of payments arise from the outflow of a foreign subsidiary's earnings and from the import of inputs from abroad.
12. With regard to national sovereignty, the concern is that with FDI, key decisions that affect the host country will be made by a foreign parent that has no real commitment to the host country and that the host government will have no control over them.
13. The benefits of FDI to the home (source) country include improvement in the balance of payments as a result of the inward flow of foreign earnings, positive employment effects when the foreign subsidiary creates demand for home-country exports, and benefits from a reverse resource-transfer effect. A reverse resource-transfer effect arises when the foreign subsidiary learns valuable skills abroad that can be transferred back to the home country.
14. The costs of FDI to the home country include adverse balance-of-payments effects that arise from the initial capital outflow and from the export substitution effects of FDI. Costs also arise when FDI exports jobs abroad.
15. Home countries can adopt policies designed to both encourage and restrict FDI. Host countries try to attract FDI by offering incentives and try to restrict FDI by dictating ownership restraints and requiring that foreign MNEs meet specific performance requirements.
16. A firm considering FDI usually must negotiate the terms of the investment with the host government. The object of any negotiation is to reach an agreement that benefits both parties. Negotiation inevitably involves compromise.
17. The outcome of negotiation is typically determined by the relative bargaining powers of the foreign MNE and the host government. Bargaining power depends on the value each side places on what the other has to offer, the number of comparable alternatives available to each side, and each party's time horizon.

DISCUSSION QUESTIONS

1. Explain how the political ideology of a host government might influence the process of negotiating access between the host government and a foreign MNE.
2. Under what circumstances is an MNE in a powerful negotiating position vis-à-vis a host government? What kind of concessions is a firm likely to win in such situations?
3. Under what circumstances is an MNE in a weak negotiating position vis-à-vis a host government? What kind of concessions is a host government likely to win in such situations?
4. Inward FDI is bad for the U.S. economy and should be subjected to stricter controls! Discuss.
5. U.S. firms should not be investing abroad when there is a need for investment to create jobs at home! Discuss.

Regional Economic Integration

CHAPTER 8

MARTIN'S TEXTILES

August 12, 1992, was a really bad day for John Martin. That was the day Canada, Mexico, and the United States announced an agreement in principle to form the North American Free Trade Association (NAFTA). Under the plan, all tariffs between the three countries would be eliminated within the next 10 to 15 years, with most being cut in five years. What disturbed John most was the plan's provision that all tariffs on trade of textiles among the three countries are to be removed within 10 years. Under the proposed agreement, Mexico and Canada would also be allowed to ship a specific amount of clothing and textiles made from foreign materials to the United States each year, and this quota would rise slightly over the first five years of the agreement. "My God!" thought John.

"Now I'm going to *have* to decide about moving my plants to Mexico." • John is the CEO of a New York-based textile company, Martin's Textiles. The company has been in the Martin family for four generations, having been founded by his great-grandfather in 1910. Today the company employs 1,500 people in three New York plants that produce cotton-based clothes, primarily underwear. All production employees are union members, and the company has a long history of good labor relations. The company has never had a labor dispute, and John, like his father, grandfather, and great-grandfather before him, regards the work force as part of the "Martin family." Indeed, John prides himself not only on knowing many of the employees by name, but also on knowing a great deal about the family circumstances of many of the long-time employees. • Over the last 20 years the company has experienced increasingly tough competition, both from overseas and at home. The mid-1980s was particularly difficult. The strength of the dollar on the foreign exchange market during that period enabled Asian producers to enter the U.S. market with very low prices. Since then, although the dollar has weakened against many major currencies, the Asian producers have not raised their prices in response to the falling dollar. In a low-skilled, labor-intensive business such as clothing manufacture, costs are driven by wage rates and labor productivity. Not surprisingly, most of John's competitors in the northeastern United States responded to the intense cost competition by moving production south, first to states such as South Carolina and Mississippi, where nonunion labor could be hired for significantly less than in the unionized Northeast, and then to Mexico, where labor costs for textile workers were less than $2 per hour. In contrast, wage rates are $12.50 per hour at John's New York plant and $8 to $10 per hour at nonunion textile plants in the southeastern United States. • The last three years have been particularly tough at Martin's Textiles. The company has registered a small loss each year, and John knows the company cannot go on like this. His major customers, while praising the quality of Martin's products, have warned him that his prices are getting too high and that they may not be able to continue to do business with him. His long time banker has told him that he must get his labor costs down. John agrees, but he knows of only one surefire way to do that, to move production south—way south, to Mexico. He has always been reluctant to do that, but now he seems to have little choice. He fears that in five years the U.S. market will be flooded with cheap imports from Asian, U.S., and Mexican companies, all producing in Mexico. It looks like the only way for Martin's Textiles to survive is to close down the New York plants and move production to Mexico. All that would be left in the United States would be the sales force. • John's mind was spinning. How could something that throws good honest people out of work be good for the country? The politicians said it would be good for trade, good for economic growth, good for the three countries. John could not see it that way. What about Mary Morgan, who has worked for Martin's for 30 years. She is now 54 years old. How on earth will she and others like her ever find another job? What about his moral obligation to his workers? What about the loyalty his workers have shown his family over the years? Is this a good way to repay it? How would he break the news to his employees, many of whom have worked for the company 10 to 20 years? And what about the Mexican workers; could they be as loyal and productive as his present employees? From other U.S. textile companies that had set up production in Mexico he had heard stories of low productivity, poor workmanship, high turnover, and high absenteeism. Is this true; if so, how could he ever cope with that? John has always felt that the success of Martin's Textiles is partly due to the family atmosphere, which encourages worker loyalty, productivity, and attention to quality, an atmosphere that has been built up over four generations. How could he replicate that in Mexico with a bunch of foreign workers who speak a language that he doesn't even understand? *This is a disguised case of a U.S.-based textile manufacturer.*

INTRODUCTION

One of the most notable trends in the global economy since 1945 has been the movement toward regional economic integration. Nowhere has this been more successful than in Western Europe, where the 12 members of the European Community (EC) seem to be moving, albeit with some reservations, toward an ever-closer economic—and perhaps political—union. If the EC succeeds in achieving its objectives, by the end of the century it will be a single market in which all significant barriers to trade and investment among the 12 countries have been removed and in which there is a common currency. Similar experiments have been tried, with far less success to date, in Latin America, Asia, and Africa. Stimulated by the success of the EC, there are signs that some of these failed attempts at integration are being revived—particularly in Latin America. Moreover, as discussed in the opening case, it is now likely that Canada, Mexico, and the United States will enter into some form of North American Free Trade Agreement (NAFTA).

In most cases, the idealistic goal underlying regional economic integration has been to create a free trade zone in which barriers to trade among member-countries are removed. Consistent with the predictions of international trade theory, and particularly the theory of comparative advantage (see Chapter 4), the belief has been that a free trade zone will produce nontrivial gains from trade for all member-countries. Not all attempts at regional integration, however, have been based on free-market economics. Most important, for 50 years the now-defunct USSR achieved regional economic integration between itself and the then-communist nations of Eastern Europe under an agreement known as COMECON. The ideology guiding COMECON was not free-market economics but rather Soviet-style central planning. Since COMECON to all intents and purposes collapsed in 1990 and is now little more than historical curiosity, we will discuss it no further.

As the opening case demonstrates, the move toward economic integration is not without pain. As a result, it has aroused substantial opposition from those whose interests are threatened. In addition, there are fears that the world is moving toward a situation in which a number of regional trade blocs compete against each other. In this scenario of the future, free trade will exist within each bloc, but each bloc will protect its market from outside competition with high tariffs. The specter of the EC and NAFTA turning into "economic fortresses" that shut out foreign producers with high tariff barriers is particularly worrisome to those who believe in the value of unrestricted free trade. If such a scenario were to materialize, the resulting decline in trade between blocs could more than offset the gains from free trade within blocs.

With these issues in mind, the main objectives of this chapter are as follows: (1) to explore the economic and political debate surrounding regional economic integration. In doing this we will pay particular attention to the economic and political benefits and costs of integration, (2) to review progress toward regional economic integration in Europe, North and South America, and elsewhere, and (3) to map the important implications of regional economic integration for the practice of international business. Before tackling these objectives, however, we first need to examine the levels of integration that are theoretically possible.

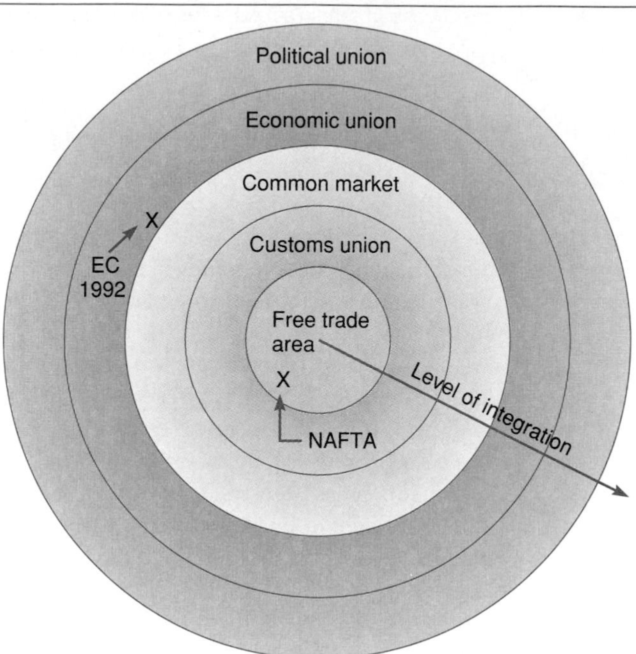

Figure 8.1
Levels of Economic Integration

LEVELS OF ECONOMIC INTEGRATION

Several levels of economic integration are possible in theory (see Figure 8.1). From least integrated to most integrated, they are a free trade area, a customs union, a common market, an economic union, and, finally, a full political union.

Free Trade Area

In a free trade area all barriers to the trade of goods and services among member-countries are removed. In the theoretically ideal free trade area, no discriminatory tariffs, quotas, subsidies, or administrative impediments are allowed to distort trade between member-countries. Each country, however, is allowed to determine its own trade policies with regard to nonmembers. Thus, for example, the tariffs placed on the products of nonmember countries may well vary from member-country to member-country.

The most enduring free trade area in the world is the European Free Trade Association (EFTA). Established in January 1960, EFTA currently joins six countries: Finland, Austria, Norway, Sweden, Iceland, and Switzerland. EFTA was founded by those Western European countries that initially decided not to be part of the European Community. Its original members included Great Britain and Denmark, both of whom subsequently joined the EC. The emphasis of EFTA has been on free trade in industrial goods. In the main, agriculture was left out of the arrangement, each member being allowed to determine its own level of support. Members were also left free to determine the level of protection applied to goods coming from outside EFTA. Other free trade areas include the U.S.–Canadian free trade area, established in 1989, and the North American Free Trade Agreement.

Customs Union

The customs union is one step further along the road to full economic and political integration. A customs union eliminates trade barriers between member-countries and adopts a common external trade policy. Establishment of a common external trade policy necessitates significant administrative machinery to oversee trade relations with non-members. Most countries that enter into a customs union desire even greater economic integration down the road. The EC began as a customs union and has moved beyond this stage. Other customs unions around the world include the current version of the Andean Pact (between Bolivia, Columbia, Ecuador, and Peru). The aims of the Andean Pact are to establish free trade between member-countries and to impose a common tariff, of 5 to 20 percent, on products imported from outside.[1]

Common Market

Like a customs union, the theoretically ideal common market has no barriers to trade between member-countries and a common external trade policy. Unlike in a customs union, in a common market factors of production also are allowed to move freely between member-countries. Thus labor and capital are free to move, as there are no restrictions on immigration, emigration, or cross-border flows of capital between member-countries. Hence, a much closer union is envisaged in a common market than in a customs union. The EC is currently a common market, although its goal is full economic union. The EC apart, however, no successful common market has ever been established, although several regional groupings have aspired to this goal. One reason for this lack of success is that establishing a common market demands a significant degree of harmony and cooperation on fiscal, monetary, and employment policies. Achieving this degree of cooperation has proven very difficult.

Economic Union

An economic union entails even closer economic integration and cooperation than a common market. Like the common market, an economic union involves the free flow of products and factors of production between member-countries and the adoption of a common external trade policy. Unlike a common market, a full economic union also requires a common currency, harmonization of the member-countries tax rates, and a common monetary and fiscal policy. Such a high degree of integration demands a coordinating bureaucracy and that member-countries sacrifice significant amounts of their national sovereignties to that bureaucracy. There are no true economic unions in the world today, but the EC aims to establish itself as one by the end of the century.

Political Union

The move toward economic union raises the issue of how to make a coordinating bureaucracy accountable to the citizens of member-nations. The answer is through political union. The EC is already on the road toward political union. The European Parliment, which is playing an ever more important role in the EC, has been directly elected by citizens of the EC countries since the late 1970s. In addition, the Council of Ministers (the controlling, decision-making body of the EC) is composed of government ministers from each EC member-country. Canada and the United States provide examples of even closer degrees of political union; in each country independent states were effectively combined into a single nation. Ultimately, the EC may move toward a similar federal structure.

---

[1] The Andean Pact has been through a number of changes since its original inception. The latest version was established in 1991, and the details are still being worked out. See "Free-Trade Free for All," *The Economist*, January 4, 1991, p. 63.

THE CASE FOR REGIONAL INTEGRATION

The case for regional integration is both economic and political. The case for integration is typically not accepted by many groups within a country, which explains why in practice most attempts to achieve regional economic integration have been contentious and halting. In this section we examine the economic and political cases for integration and two impediments to integration. In the next section we look at the case against integration.

The Economic Case for Integration

The economic case for regional integration is relatively straightforward. We saw in Chapter 4 how economic theories of international trade predict that unrestricted free trade will allow countries to specialize in the production of goods and services that they can produce most efficiently. The result is greater world production than would be possible with trade restrictions. We also saw in that chapter how opening up a country to free trade stimulates economic growth in the country, which in turn creates dynamic gains from trade. Further, we saw in Chapter 6 how foreign direct investment (FDI) can transfer technological, marketing, and managerial know-how to host nations. Given the central role of knowledge in stimulating economic growth, opening up a country to FDI also is likely to stimulate economic growth. In sum, economic theories suggest that free trade and investment is a positive-sum game, in which all participating countries stand to gain.

Given this, the theoretical ideal is a total absence of barriers to the free flow of goods, services, and factors of production among nations. However, as we saw in Chapters 5 and 7, a case can be made for government intervention in international trade and FDI. Because many governments have accepted part or all of the case for intervention, unrestricted free trade and FDI have proved to be only an ideal. Although international agreements such as the General Agreements on Trade and Tariffs (GATT) have been aimed at moving the world toward a free trade regime, success has been less than total. One of the problems is that in a world of many nations and many political ideologies, it is very difficult to get all countries to agree to a common set of rules.

Against this background, regional economic integration can be seen as an attempt to achieve additional gains from the free flow of trade and investment between countries beyond those attainable under international agreements such as GATT. Undoubtedly, it is easier to establish a free trade and investment regime among a limited number of adjacent countries than among the world community as a whole. Problems of coordination and policy harmonization are largely a function of the number of countries that seek agreement. The greater the number of countries involved, the greater the number of different perspectives that must be reconciled, and the harder it will be to reach agreement. Thus, attempts at regional economic integration are motivated by a desire to exploit the gains from free trade and investment.

The Political Case for Integration

The political case for regional economic integration has also loomed large in most attempts to establish free trade areas, customs unions, and the like. By linking neighboring economies and making them increasingly dependent on each other, incentives are created for political cooperation between the neighboring states. In turn, the potential for violent conflict between the states is reduced. In addition, by grouping their economies together, the countries can enhance their political weight in the world.

These considerations certainly underlay the establishment of the EC in 1957. Europe had suffered two devastating wars in the first half of the century, both arising out of the unbridled ambitions of nation-states. Those who have sought a united Europe have always had at the forefront of their minds the desire to prevent another outbreak of war in Europe, to make it unthinkable. Many Europeans also felt that after World War II the European nation-states were no longer large enough to hold their own in world markets and world politics. The need for a united Europe to deal with the United States and the politically alien USSR certainly loomed large in the minds of many of the EC's founders.[2]

Impediments to Integration

Despite the strong economic and political arguments for integration, it has never been easy to achieve or sustain. There are two main reasons for this. First, although economic integration benefits the majority, it has its costs. Although a nation as a whole may benefit significantly as a result of entering into a regional free trade agreement, certain groups may lose. Moving to a free trade regime inevitably involves some painful adjustments. We saw this in the opening case on Martin's Textiles. If the proposed NAFTA between Canada, Mexico, and the United States becomes a reality, some Canadian and U.S. workers in such industries as textiles, which employ low-cost, low-skilled labor, will certainly lose their jobs as Canadian and U.S. firms move production to Mexico. The promise of significant net benefits to the Canadian and U.S. economies as a whole is little comfort to those who will lose as a result of the NAFTA. Understandably, such groups will use political influence to attempt to water down or stop it.

A second impediment to integration arises from concerns over national sovereignty. For example, Mexico's concerns about maintaining control of its oil interests are likely to result in an agreement with Canada and the U.S. to exempt the Mexican oil industry from any liberalization of foreign investment regulations achieved under the NAFTA. More generally, concerns about national sovereignty arise because close economic integration demands that countries give up some degree of their control over such key policy issues as monetary policy, fiscal policy (e.g., tax policy), and trade policy. This has been a major stumbling block in the EC. To achieve full economic union, the EC is trying to reach agreement on a common currency to be controlled by a central EC bank. With 11 of the 12 member-states agreeing in principle, Great Britain is the holdout. A politically important segment of public opinion in Great Britain opposes a common currency on the grounds that it would require relinquishing control of their country's monetary policy to the EC—which many British perceive as bureaucracy run by foreigners. In 1992 the British won the right to opt out of any single currency agreement.

THE CASE AGAINST REGIONAL INTEGRATION

Although the tide has been running strongly in favor of regional free trade agreements in recent years, some economists have expressed concern that the benefits of regional integration have been oversold, while the costs have often been ignored.[3] They point out that the benefits of regional integration to the participants are determined by the extent of *trade creation*, as opposed to *trade diversion*. **Trade creation** occurs when high-cost domestic producers are replaced by low-cost producers within the free trade area. **Trade diversion** occurs when lower-cost external suppliers are replaced by higher-cost suppliers within the free trade area. A regional free trade agreement will benefit the world only if the amount of trade it creates exceeds the amount it diverts.

---

[2] D. Swann, *The Economics of the Common Market,* 6th ed. (London: Penguin Books, 1990).

[3] See J. Bhagwati, "Regionalism and Multilateralism: An Overview," Columbia University Discussion Paper 603 (Department of Economics, Columbia University, New York); and Augusto de la Torre and Margaret Kelly, "Regional Trade Arrangements," Occasional Paper 93 (Washington D.C.: International Monetary Fund, March 1992).

As an example, suppose the United States and Mexico imposed tariffs on imports from all countries, and then they set up a free trade area, scrapping all trade barriers between them but maintaining tariffs on imports from the rest of the world. If the United States began to import textiles from Mexico, would this change be for the better? If the United States previously produced all of its own textiles at a higher cost than Mexico, then the free trade agreement has shifted production to the cheaper source. According to the theory of comparative advantage, trade has been *created* within the regional grouping, and there would be no decrease in trade with the rest of the world. Clearly, the change would be for the better. If, however, the United States previously imported textiles from South Korea, which produced them more cheaply than either Mexico or the United States, then trade has been *diverted* from a low-cost source—a change for the worse.

In theory, GATT rules should ensure that a free trade agreement does not result in trade diversion. The GATT's rules allow free trade areas to be formed only if the members set tariffs that are not higher or more restrictive to outsiders than the ones previously in effect. However, as we saw in Chapter 5, in recent years there has been a proliferation of nontariff barriers not covered by the GATT (e.g., voluntary export restraints, VERs). As a result, fear is growing that regional trade blocs could emerge whose markets are protected from outside competition by high nontariff barriers. In such cases, the trade diversion effects might well outweigh the trade creation effects. The only way to guard against this possibility, according to those concerned about this potential, is to increase the GATT's scope so that it covers nontariff barriers to trade such as VERs. There is no sign that this is going to occur anytime soon, however, so the risk remains that regional economic integration will result in trade diversion.

REGIONAL ECONOMIC INTEGRATION IN EUROPE

There are now two main trade blocs in Europe; the European Community (EC) and the European Free Trade Association (EFTA). Of the two, the EC is by far the more significant, not just in terms of membership (the EC has 12 members, and EFTA has 6; see Map 8.1), but also in terms of economic and political influence in the world economy. Indeed, many now see the EC as an emerging economic and political superpower of the same order as the United States and Japan. Accordingly, we will concentrate our attention on the EC.[4]

Background of the EC

The EC was the product of two political factors; first, the devastation of two world wars on Western Europe and the desire for a lasting peace, and second, the European nations' desire to hold their own on the world's political and economic stage. In addition, many Europeans were aware of the potential economic benefits of closer economic integration of the countries.

The forerunner of the EC, the European Coal and Steel Community, was formed in 1951 by Belgium, France, West Germany, Italy, Luxembourg, and the Netherlands. Its objective was to remove barriers to intragroup shipments of coal, iron, steel, and scrap metal. With the signing of the Treaty of Rome in 1957, the EC was formally established, being referred to as the *European Economic Community* or *EEC* at the time.

---

[4] Sources for the material in this section: N. Colchester and D. Buchan, *Europower: The Essential Guide to Europe's Economic Transformation in 1992* (London: The Economist Books, 1990); and Swann, *Common Market.*

Map 8.1
The EC and EFTA, 1992

"A Survey of the European Community," The Economist, *July 11, 1992, p. 5.*

The Treaty of Rome provided for the creation of a common market. This is apparent in Article 3 of the treaty, which laid down the key objectives of the new community. Article 3 calls for the elimination of internal trade barriers and the creation of a common external tariff and requires member-states to abolish obstacles to the free movement of factors of prodution among the member-states. To facilitate the free movement of goods, services, and factors of production, the treaty provides for any necessary harmonization of the member-states' laws. Furthermore, the treaty commits the EC to establish common policies in agriculture and transportation.

The first enlargement of the community occurred in 1973, when Great Britain, Ireland, and Denmark joined. These three were followed in 1981 by Greece, and in 1986 by Spain and Portugal, bringing the total membership to the current 12. (East Germany became part of the EC after the reunification of Germany in 1990.) These enlargements made the EC a potential global superpower in 1990:

- The total population of the community was 320 million, 60 million more than the United States.
- Its gross domestic product was more than that of the United States.
- Its gross domestic product per head was 270 percent of the world average.
- Its exports accounted for 33 percent of total world exports.

The Single European Act and 1992

Two revolutions occurred in Europe in the late 1980s. The first was the dramatic collapse of communism in Eastern Europe. The second revolution was much quieter, but its impact on Europe and the world may have been just as profound as the first. It was the adoption of the Single European Act by the 12 member-nations of the EC in 1987. This act committed the EC countries to work toward the establishment of a single market by December 31, 1992.

The Stimulus for the Single European Act

The Single European Act was born of a frustration among EC member-countries that the community was not living up to its promise. By the early 1980s it was clear to all that the EC had fallen some considerable way short of its objectives of removing barriers to the free flow of trade and investment between member-countries and to harmonizing the wide range of technical and legal standards for doing business. At the end of 1982 the European Commission found itself inundated with 770 cases of intra-EC protectionism to investigate. In addition, some 20 EC directives setting common technical standards for a variety of products ranging from cars to thermometers were deadlocked.

As far as many businesspeople were concerned, the main problem with the EC was the disharmony of the member-countries' technical, legal, regulatory, and tax standards. The "rules of the game" differed substantially from country to country, which effectively stalled the creation of a true single internal market.

As an example, consider the EC's automobile industry. In the mid-1980s there was no single EC-wide automobile market analogous to the U.S. automobile market. Instead, the EC market remained fragmented into 12 national markets. There were four main reasons for this:

1. Different technical standards in different countries required cars to be customized to national requirements (e.g., the headlights and sidelights of cars sold in Great Britain must be wired in a significantly different way than those of cars sold in Italy, and the standards for car windscreens in France are very different from those in Germany).
2. Different tax regimes in the countries created price differentials across countries that would not be found in a single market.
3. An agreement to allow automobile companies to sell cars through exclusive dealer networks allowed auto companies and their dealers to adapt their model ranges and prices on a country-by-country basis with little fear that these differences would be undermined by competing retailers.
4. In violation of Article 3 of the Treaty of Rome, each country had adopted its own trade policy with regard to automobile imports (e.g., whereas Japanese imports were not restricted at all in Belgium, they were limited to 11 percent of the car market in Great Britain and to less than 2 percent in France and Italy). The net result of these divisions was substantial price differentials between countries. For example, in 1989 the prices of the same model of car were, on average,

31 percent higher in Great Britain and 11 percent higher in Germany than in Belgium.[5]

Numerous other administrative barriers to intra-EC trade and investment had become apparent by the mid-1980s. French buildings were uninsurable unless tiled with French-standard tiles. Government procurement policies typically favored local companies. Local banking rules effectively inhibited the creation of a single EC banking industry. The French had persistently refused to abolish exchange controls, thereby limiting French companies' ability to invest in other EC countries and other EC countries' companies' ability to repatriate profits to their home countries. Truck drivers traveling between EC countries had to carry some 35 documents for import–export declarations and community transit forms. Simply dealing with the paperwork could make a journey take three to five times longer than it would have needed to take, and the costs of the paperwork accounted for more than 3 percent of the value of the sales involved.[6]

In addition to the profusion of barriers to intra-EC trade, many member-countries were subsidizing national firms, thereby distorting competition. For example, in 1990 the French government decided to pump FFr 6 billion into Groupe Bull, a state-owned computer maker, and Thompson, a defense and electronics group. This bought protests from ICL, a British computer maker, on the grounds that such a subsidy would allow Groupe Bull to capture more of the EC computer market.[7] As can be seen from Figure 8.2, the worst offender with regard to subsidies was Italy.

Against this background, in the early 1980s many of the EC's prominent businesspeople mounted an energetic campaign to end the EC's economic divisions. Under the leadership of industrialists such as Wisse Dekker, CEO of the Dutch company Philips, the Roundtable of European Industrialists was established in 1983. Roundtable participants were chairmen, CEOs, and managing directors of large corporations with important manufacturing and technological commitments in the EC. Its principal objective was to foster the creation of a single market by encouraging the EC to harmonize the rules of the game and by encouraging the member-countries to remove their administrative barriers to trade within the EC. The Roundtable members believed that a single EC market was absolutely essential if European firms were to be competitive with their U.S. and Asian rivals.

The EC responded to this stimulus by creating the Delors Commission. Under the chairmanship of Jacques Delors, the former French finance minister and president of the EC Commission (which essentially heads the EC's bureaucracy), the commission produced a discussion paper in 1985. The discussion paper proposed that all impediments to the formation of a single market be eliminated by December 31, 1992. Two more years passed before the EC persuaded all member-countries to accept the proposals contained in the discussion paper. The result was the Single European Act, which was independently ratified by the parliaments of each member-country and became EC law in 1987.

The Objectives of the Act

The purpose of the Single European Act was to have a single market in place by December 31, 1992. The changes the act proposed include the following.[8]

---

[5] Colchester and Buchan, *Europower.*

[6] Nan Stone, "The Globalization of Europe: An Interview with Wisse Dekker," *Harvard Business Review,* May–June 1989, pp. 90–95.

[7] "The Aid Plague: Business in Europe, A Survey," *The Economist,* June 8, 1991, pp. 12–18.

[8] "One Europe, One Economy," *The Economist,* November 30, 1991, pp. 53–54; and "Market Failure: A Survey of Business in Europe," *The Economist,* June 8, 1991, pp. 6–10.

Figure 8.2
State Aid to Manufacturing in the EC, 1986–1988

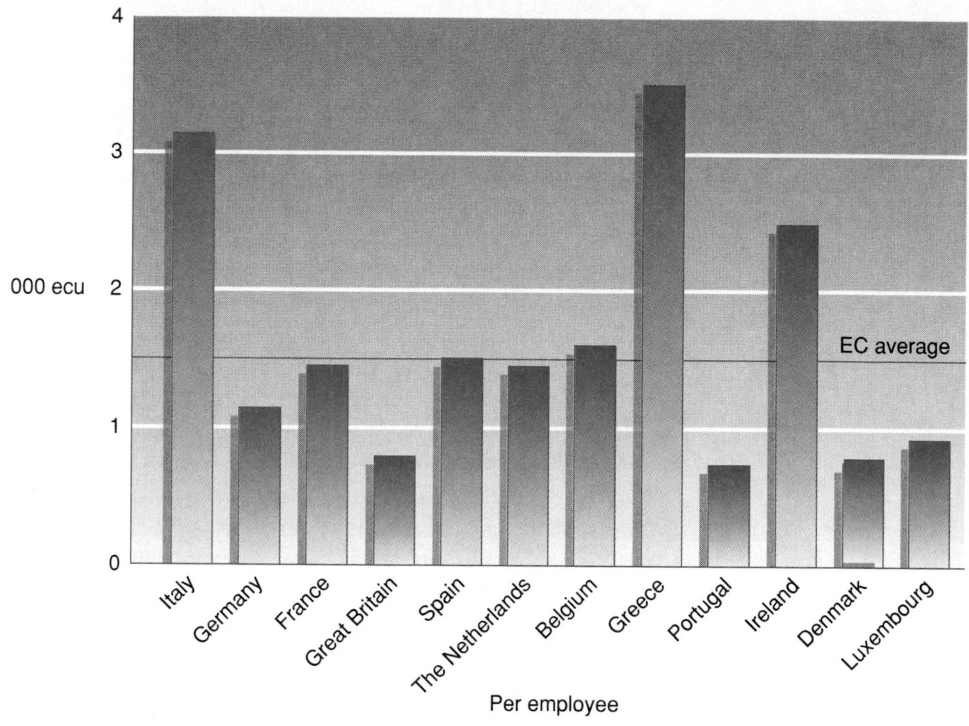

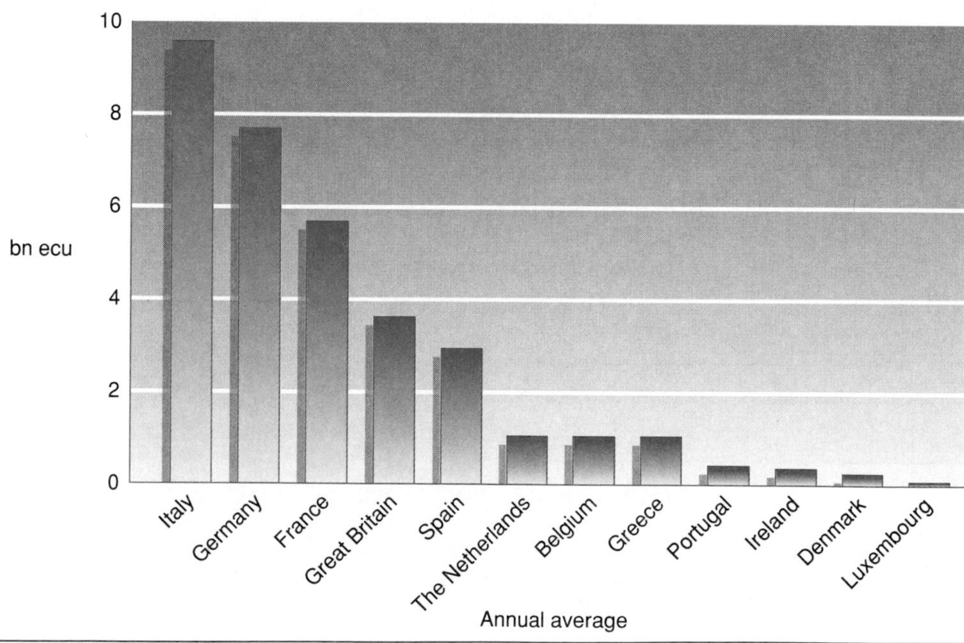

Source: European Commision.

1. *Frontier controls*—remove all frontier controls between EC countries, thereby abolishing delays and reducing the resources required for complying with trade bureaucracy.

2. *Mutual recognition of standards*—to harmonize the product standards of different EC members would be a huge task. Germany alone has some 20,000 standards, France 8,000, and Great Britain 12,000. Instead, the EC will apply the principle of "mutual recognition," which is that a standard developed in one EC country should be accepted in another, provided it meets basic requirements in such matters as health and safety.

3. *Public procurement*—open up procurement to nonnational suppliers. This should reduce costs directly by allowing lower-cost suppliers into national economies, and indirectly by forcing national suppliers to compete.

4. *Financial services*—the EC's retail banking and insurance businesses was split into national markets. The Act proposed lifting barriers to competition which should drive down the costs of financial services, including borrowing, throughout the EC.

5. *Exchange controls*—remove all restrictions on foreign exchange transactions between member-countries by the end of 1992.

6. *Freight transport*—abolish restrictions on *cabotage*—the right of foreign truckers to pick up and deliver goods within another member-state's borders—by the end of 1992. This could reduce the cost of haulage within the EC by 10 to 15 percent.

7. *Supply-side effects*—all of those changes should lower the costs of doing business in the EC, but the single-market program is also expected to have more complicated supply-side effects. For example, the expanded market should give EC firms greater opportunities to exploit economies of scale. In addition, the increase in competitive intensity brought about by removing internal barriers to trade and investment should force EC firms to become more efficient.

Implications

Although it is not yet clear how successful the EC will be in attaining the act's objectives,[9] the implications of the act are potentially enormous. We discuss the implications for business practice in more detail in the Implications for Business section at the end of the chapter. For now it should be noted that, as long as the EC is successful in establishing a single market, the member-countries can expect significant gains from the free flow of trade and investment. These gains may be greater than those predicted by standard trade theory that accrue when regions specialize in producing those goods and services that they produce most efficiently. The lower costs of doing business implied by the Single European Act will benefit EC firms, as will the potential economies of scale inherent in serving a single market of 320 million consumers. On the other hand, many EC firms will face increased competitive pressure. Countries such as France and Italy have long used administrative trade barriers and subsidies to protect their home markets from foreign competition. Removing these barriers will undoubtedly increase competition, and some firms may well go out of business. Ultimately, however, both consumers and EC firms will benefit from this. Consumers will benefit from the lower prices implied by a more competitive market. EC firms will benefit if the increased competitive pressure

---

[9] For example, plans to remove frontier passport checks for citizens of member-countries, which were to take effect on January 1, 1993, were postponed because of opposition from Great Britain and Denmark.

forces them to become more efficient, thereby transforming them into more effective international competitors capable of going head-to-head with U.S. and Asian rivals in the world marketplace.

The Treaty of Maastricht and Its Aftermath

In December 1991 leaders of the 12 EC member-states met in Maastricht, the Netherlands, to discuss the next steps for the EC. The results of the Maastricht meeting surprised both Europe and the rest of the world. For months the countries of the EC had been fighting over the issue of a common currency. Although many economists believed a common currency was required to "cement" a closer economic union, deadlock had been predicted. The British in particular had opposed any attempt to establish a common currency. Instead, the 12 members signed a treaty that not only committed them to adopting a common EC currency by January 1, 1999, but also paved the way for closer political cooperations and the possible creation of a European superstate.

The details of key decisions reached at Maastricht are summarized in Box 8.1. Proponents of a federal Europe insist that the treaty lays down the main elements, if only in embryo, of a future European government: a single currency, a common foreign and defense policy, a common citizenship, and an EC parliament with teeth. It is just a matter of waiting, they believe, for history to take its course. Of more immediate interest are the implications for business of the plans to establish a single currency by 1999.

As with many of the provisions of the Single European Act, the move to a single currency should significantly lower the costs of doing business in the EC. The gains come from reduced *exchange costs* and *reduced risk.*[10] Let us consider exchange costs first. The EC has calculated that EC businesses convert roughly $8 trillion from one EC currency to another every year, which necessitates about $12 billion in exchange costs. A single currency would avoid these costs and help firms in other ways, as fewer resources would be required for accounting, treasury management, and the like. As for reduced risk, a single currency would reduce the risks that arise from currency fluctuations. The values of currencies fluctuate against each other continually. As we will see in Chapter 9, this introduces risks into international transactions. For example, if a British firm builds a factory in Greece, and the value of the Greek currency subsequently declines against the British pound, the value of the British firm's Greek assets will also decline. A single currency would eliminate such risks. In turn, eliminating these risks would reduce the cost of capital. Interest rates would fall, and investment and output would increase as a consequence.

The drawback, for some, of a single currency is that national authorities would lose control over monetary policy. Thus it is crucial to ensure that the EC's monetary policy is well managed. The Maastricht treaty calls for an independent EC central bank, similar to the U.S. Federal Reserve, with a clear mandate to manage monetary policy so as to ensure price stability. The British, in particular, are concerned about the effectiveness of such an arrangement and the implied loss of national sovereignty. Accordingly, Great Britain won the right from the other 11 EC members to stay out of the monetary union if it should so choose. Although this has pleased the elements of the British public that are hostile to the EC, if the British do opt out, the result would probably be the rapid demise of London as the financial capital of Europe.

To become law, the treaty of Maastricht must be ratified by all 12 member-states. As of early 1993 it was unclear if this was going to occur. Danish voters were the first to cast their verdict on the treaty. Worried about a loss of Danish sovereignty to an EC

---

[10] "One Europe," *Economist.*

BOX 8.1

Key Elements of the Treaty of Maastricht

Uniting Europe: Key decisions regarding European unification announced by the 12 European Community leaders. They are to take effect after ratification by the national legislatures in all 12 EC states.

▶ Agreements ▷ Stumbling blocks

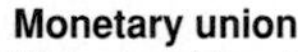

Monetary union

▶ European Monetary Institute to be created on January 1, 1994, and start operating on January 1, 1997, at the earliest.

▶ A single currency issued any day after January 1, 1999. It is hoped at least seven EC nations — all with low inflation and modest budget deficits — will abandon their national moneys and adopt the EC currency union in 1997.

▷ Great Britain was allowed to stay out of the EC currency union until an unspecified date. It opposes monetary union for ideological reasons.

▷ Denmark was also allowed to opt out pending a referendum on the issue, a constitutional requirement. The Danish government backs monetary union.

Political union

▶ EC jurisdiction in areas includig industrial affairs, health, education, trade, environment, energy, culture, tourism, and consumer and civil protection. Member-states vote to implement decisions.

▶ Increased political cooperation under a new name — European Union. Permanent diplomatic network of senior political officials created in the EC capitals.

▷ Great Britain rejected EC-imposed labor legislation, forcing the removal of the so-called social chapter from the treaty. It will be implemented separately by the other 11 members, officials said.

Federalism

▶ EC leaders dropped reference to an EC " with a federal goal." Instead, the political union accord describes the community as "an ever-closer union in which political decisions have to be taken as near to the people as possible."

▷ Great Britain rejected the "federalism" as the embodiment of what it feels would be an encroaching EC superstate.

Foreign affairs

▶ EC states move toward a joint foreign policy with most decisions requiring unanimity.

▷ Great Britain wanted the ability to opt out of any joint decisions. How this provision will be interpreted by the various sides is yet to be seen.

Defense

▶ The Western European Union, a long-dormant group of nine EC states, will be revived to act as the EC's defense body, but linked to the NATO alliance.

▷ France and Germany had supported a greater military role for the union, but Great Britain, Italy and others did not want to see NATO's influence diluted.

European parliament

▶ The 518-member EC assembly gets a modest say in shaping some EC legislation. Its new powers fall short of what the assembly had sought (i.e., an equitable sharing of the right to make EC laws with the EC governments).

▷ Great Britain and Denmark refused to grant the assembly broader powers.

Rich–poor gap

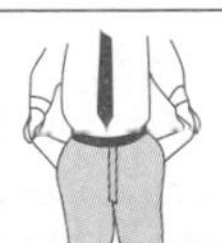

▶ Spain got a formal commitment from its richer partners for more money for itself, Ireland, Greece, and Portugal. The EC will review its bookkeeping methods and take more account of the relative wealth of EC members.

Source: Seattle Times, *December 11, 1991, p. A3.*

superstate, on June 2, 1992, in a stunning setback for their political leaders, the Danes rejected the treaty by a narrow margin. In September 1992, French voters supported it but only by a narrow margin that did little to bolster waning enthusiasm for the accord across Europe. Also in September 1992, the European exchange rate mechanism (ERM), which is intended to maintain currency stability and to help pave the way for the introduction of a common currency, was hit by a wave of speculative pressure. This nearly caused the system to collapse and resulted in the withdrawal of Great Britain and Italy from the mechanism. (For details see Chapter 9 and the case "Chaos in the Currency Markets.") Thus, by early 1993 the goals so boldly articulated in the Maastricht treaty seemed to be receding into the distance. Ultimately, a modified form of the treaty will probably be put into effect. Right now, however, Maastricht seems to be one of those rare cases in history where politicians moved too fast for the people.

The EC and EFTA

The European Free Trade Association (EFTA) currently consists of six members—Austria, Finland, Iceland, Norway, Sweden, and Switzerland. Originally set up by those Western European countries that did not sign the Treaty of Rome, EFTA is a loosely constituted free trade area. The move toward closer integration within the EC has worried EFTA, whose member-countries have close trading links with many EC countries. The EFTA countries fear being shut out of the EC by a possible increase in tariff barriers after 1992. As a consequence, in 1990 EFTA entered into negotiations with the EC to set up a free trade area. After 14 months of negotiations, EFTA and the EC agreed to set up a European Economic Area (EEA) in 1993. If ratified by the EC parliament and by all 18 countries, the EEA will be the world's largest free trade area with 380 million consumers and 46 percent of world trade.[11]

The proposed EEA is to be a free trade area, not a customs union or a common market. As with all free trade areas, potential benefits to all parties arise from the free flow of trade and investment that will be possible within the EEA. In addition, the EEA will guarantee EFTA and EC countries access to each other's markets. The opening up of EFTA markets to EC competition will also increase competitive intensity in many industries within EFTA countries, thereby producing benefits for EFTA consumers in the form of lower prices, and forcing EFTA firms to become more efficient international competitors. Furthermore, the EEA will also allow EFTA firms to compete on equal terms with EC firms for public-sector contracts, which are to be opened up to EEA competition.

Whether the EEA will be ratified and whether it will develop beyond a mere free trade area remain to be seen. It is worth noting, however, that several EFTA countries see the EEA as the first step toward the six countries' eventual full membership in the EC. If this does occur, the economic and political importance of the EC in world affairs will be enhanced.

Fortress Europe?

One of the main concerns of U.S. and Asian countries is that the EC that emerges after 1992 will impose new barriers on imports from outside the EC. The fear is that EC 1992 could increase external protection as weaker member-states attempt to offset their loss of protection against other EC countries by arguing for limitations on outside competition.

---

11 "Let a Fortress Arise, *The Economist,* October 26, 1991, pp. 81–82.

This fear was certainly part of the reason for EFTA's push to establish a free trade area with the EC.

In theory, given the free-market philosophy of the 1992 plans, this should not occur. In October 1988, the European Commission debated external trading policy and published a detailed statement of the EC's trading intentions in the post-1992 era.[12] The commission stressed the EC's interests in vigorous external trade. It noted that exports by EC countries to non-EC countries are equivalent to 20 percent of total world exports, as against 15 percent of the United States and 9 percent for Japan. These external exports are equivalent to 9 percent of its own GDP, compared to 6.7 percent for the United States and 9.7 percent for Japan. In short, it is not in the EC's interests to adopt a protectionist stance, given the EC's reliance on external trade. The commission has also promised loyalty to GATT rules on international trade. As for the types of trade not covered by GATT, the EC states that it will push for reciprocal access. The EC stated that in certain cases it might replace individual national trade barriers with EC protection against imports, but it also promised that the overall level of protection would not rise.

Despite such reassurances, there is no guarantee that the EC will not adopt a protectionist stance toward external trade, and there are indications that this is already occurring in two industries, agriculture and automobiles. In agriculture, the EC appears likely to continue the Common Market Agricultural Policy, which effectively blocks many food imports. (Box 5.2 provides some details of the CAP.) In autos, the EC has reached an agreement with the Japanese to limit the Japanese market share of the EC auto market. Starting in 1993, those countries that still have quotas on Japanese car imports will lift them gradually until the end of 1998, when they are scheduled to be abolished. Meanwhile, Japanese producers will voluntarily restrain sales so that by the end of the century they hold no more than 17 percent of the European market. After that time, all restrictions are to be abolished.

REGIONAL ECONOMIC INTEGRATION IN THE AMERICAS

No other attempt at regional economic integration comes close to the EC in its boldness or its potential implications for the world economy. Nevertheless, there are signs that attempts at regional economic integration are on the rise again, particularly in the Americas. The most significant attempt is the proposed North American Free Trade Area (NAFTA). In addition to NAFTA, four other trade blocs are in the offing in the Americas (see Map 8.2), the most significant and enduring of which has been the Andean Pact.

The North American Free Trade Agreement

In 1988 the governments of the United States and Canada agreed to enter into a free trade agreement (FTA), which went into effect January 1, 1989. The FTA aims to eliminate all tariffs on bilateral trade between Canada and the United States by 1998. This was followed in 1991 by talks between the United States, Canada, and Mexico aimed at establishing a North American Free Trade Area (NAFTA) in the three countries. The talks concluded in August 1992 with an agreement to establish a NAFTA. For NAFTA to become a reality, each country must ratify it.

---

12 "What Are They Building? Survey of Europe's Internal Market," *The Economist,* July 8, 1989, pp. 5–7; and Colchester and Buchan, *Europower.*

Map 8.2
Trade Agreements in the Americas

If this does occur, the result will be the creation of the world's largest free market with 360 million consumers and a total output of $6 trillion, 25 percent larger than that of the European Community (see Table 8.1). However, this proposal has generated a heated debate between those who favor it and those who oppose it. The controversy stems from the very nature of the proposed pact. Never before have advanced industrialized countries considered such a massive free trade area with a Third World neighbor, much less one with 90 million people, half of whom are under 16 years of age and many of whom are desperately poor. Let us examine some of the arguments surrounding the NAFTA proposal.

Table 8.1
Comparison of NAFTA Countries

	United States	Canada	Mexico
Gross domestic product (billions)	$5,673	$593	$283
Population (millions)	252	27	88
GDP per person	$22,420	$21,961	$3,222
Hourly pay, benefits			
Steel	$21.67	$21.53	$3.22
Autos	$21.93	$19.23	$2.75
Textiles	$10.31	$11.91	$1.94
Exports (billions)	$417	$128	$27
Imports (billions)	$490	$120	$38

Source: Journal of Commerce, *August 13, 1992, p. 1A.*

Arguments for NAFTA

Proponents argue that NAFTA should be viewed as an opportunity to create an enlarged and more efficient productive base for the entire region. The most likely immediate effect of NAFTA would be that many U.S. and Canadian firms would move some of their production to Mexico to take advantage of lower labor costs. In 1989 the average hourly labor costs in Mexico were $2.32, compared with $14.31 in the United States and $14.71 in Canada. Movement of production to Mexico is most likely to occur in low-skilled, labor-intensive manufacturing industries where Mexico might have a comparative advantage (e.g., textiles). Many will benefit from such a trend. Mexico benefits because it gets much needed investment and employment. The United States and Canada should benefit because the increased incomes of the Mexicans will allow them to import more U.S. and Canadian goods, therby recycling demand and making up for the jobs lost in industries that moved production to Mexico. U.S. and Canadian consumers will benefit from the lower costs, and hence prices, of products produced in Mexico. In addition, the international competitiveness of U.S. and Canadian firms that move production to Mexico to take advantage of lower labor costs will be enhanced, enabling them to better compete with Asian and European rivals.

Arguments against NAFTA

U.S. and Canadian critics of NAFTA argue that the promised benefits do not stand up to realistic assessment in light of U.S. and Canadian economic needs. They note that no free trade agreement exists between a large, low-wage developing country and an advanced high-wage, industrialized one. They fear that the proposed pact will have a negative impact on income distribution and wage levels in the United States and Canada. Labor leaders argue that hundreds of thousands of U.S. and Canadian workers will lose jobs as plants move to cheap-labor havens in Mexico. Furthermore, they note that the U.S. and Canadian workers who will lose jobs are the same ones who have taken major cuts in real weekly earnings and family income since the late 1970s. They also claim that free trade will draw thousands of Mexico's desperate jobless north, driving down U.S. and Canadian wage rates in the process.

Environmentalists also voice concerns about NAFTA. They point to the sludge in the Rio Grande River and the smog in the air over Mexico City and warn that Mexico could degrade clean air and toxic-waste standards across the continent. Already, they claim, the lower Rio Grande is the most polluted river in the United States, increasing in chemical waste and sewage along its course from El Paso, Texas, to the Gulf of Mexico. Nor is the consternation limited to environmentalists and labor leaders. Farmers fear that cheap fruits and vegetables, some of them contaminated with pesticides banned in the United States, will stream over the boarder if NAFTA is implemented.

There is also opposition in Mexico to NAFTA from those who fear a loss of national sovereignty. Mexican critics argue that their entire country will be dominated by U.S. firms that will not really contribute to Mexico's economic growth, but instead will use Mexico as a low-cost assembly site, while keeping their high-paying, high-skilled jobs north of the border.

Government Responses

With all of the political heat being generated over NAFTA, the three governments involved are being careful to allay fears. As of 1993, it looks as if any final agreement will be hedged with qualifications to protect the interests of various groups. For example, on the issue of tariff reductions, various measures might be adopted to guard against a sudden surge in imports of fruits, vegetables, cement, and other goods from Mexico into the United States and Canada. Phasing out tariffs over 10 years or more is one possibility being discussed. With regard to the environment, U.S. officials in the Clinton administration insist that Mexico will have to commit to stronger enforcement of existing environmental regulations along the border before any agreement can be signed. Also, U.S. companies might be required to submit environmental assessments of their plants in Mexico. As for jobs in the United States, President Clinton has promised retraining and extended unemployment benefits for U.S. workers who lose their jobs because of imports or plant relocations, even though no such provision will be in the pact. U.S. officials have also tried to calm the labor unions' biggest fears by ruling out so-called labor exports—allowing Mexico to export its surplus labor along with its goods by opening up the borders to totally free immigration. And in a bow to Mexican sensitivities, the United States and Canada have agreed not to push for direct foreign investment in Mexico's nationalized oil industries.[13]

The Andean Pact

The Andean Pact was formed in 1969 when Bolivia, Chile, Ecuador, Columbia, and Peru signed the Cartagena Agreement. The Andean Pact was largely based on the EC model, but it has been far less successful at achieving its stated goals. The integration steps begun in 1969 included an internal tariff reduction program, the creation of a common external tariff, a transportation policy, a common industrial policy, and special concessions for the smallest members, Bolivia and Ecuador.

By the mid-1980s the Andean Pact had all but collapsed. The pact had manifestly failed to achieve any of its stated objectives. There was no tariff-free trade between member-countries, no common external tariff, and no harmonization of economic policies. The attempt to achieve cooperation between member-countries seems to have been substantially hindered by political and economic problems. The countries of the Andean Pact have had to deal with low economic growth, hyperinflation, high unem-

---

[13] Sources: P. Magnusson, "The Mexico Pact: Worth the Price?" *Business Week,* May 27, 1991, pp. 32–35; R. Villarreal, "The Supply-Side Case for Free Trade with Mexico," *International Economic Insights,* March/April 1991, pp. 17–19; and B. Turner, "Measuring the Costs of an FTA with Mexico," *International Economic Insights,* March/April 1991, pp. 19–20.

ployment, political unrest, and crushing burdens of debt. All of these problems have made it extremely difficult to achieve cooperation. In addition, the dominant political ideology in many of the Andean countries during this period tended toward the radical/socialist end of the political spectrum. Since such an ideology is hostile to the free-market economic principle on which the Andean Pact was based, progress toward closer integration could not be expected.

The tide began to turn in the late 1980s when, after years of economic decline, the governments of Latin America began to adopt free-market economic policies. In 1990 the heads of the five current members of the Andean Pact—Bolivia, Ecuador, Peru, Colombia, and Venezuela—met in the Galápagos Islands. The resulting Galápagos Declaration effectively relaunched the Andean Pact. The declaration's objectives include the establishment of a free trade area by 1992, a common external tariff by 1994, and a full common market by 1995.

Although it remains to be seen how successful this attempt at integration will be, there are some grounds for cautious optimism. For the first time, the controlling political ideology of the Andean countries is at least consistent with the free-market principles underlying a common market. In addition, since the Galápagos Declaration, internal tariff levels have been reduced by all five members. On the other hand, significant differences between member-countries still exist that may make harmonization of policies and close integration difficult. For example, Venezuela's GNP per person is four times that of Bolivia's, and Ecuador's tiny production-line industries can hardly compete with Columbia and Venezuela's more advanced industries. Such differences are a recipe for disagreement and suggest that many of the adjustments required to achieve a true common market will be painful—even though the net benefits will probably outweigh the costs.[14]

Other Trade Blocs in the Americas

Three other trade blocs are currently in the offing in Latin America. The largest is MERCOSUR, an agreement between Argentina, Brazil, Paraguay, and Uruguay. MERCOSUR originated in 1988 as a free trade pact between Brazil and Argentina. The modest reductions in tariffs and quotas accompanying this pact reportedly helped bring about an 80 percent increase in trade between the two countries in the late 1980s.[15] Encouraged by this success, the pact was expanded in March 1990 to include Paraguay and Uruguay. The aim of the MERCOSUR pact is to establish a full free trade area by the end of 1994 and a common market sometime thereafter. The four countries of MERCOSUR have a combined population of 200 million. With a market of this size, MERCOSUR could have a significant impact on the economic growth rate of the four economies. On the other hand, it could just as easily fall victim to economic mismanagement in Brazil and Argentina.

The countries of Central America are trying to revive their trade pact. In the early 1960s, Costa Rica, El Salvador, Guatemala, Honduras, and Nicaragua attempted to set up a Central American common market. It collapsed in 1969 when war broke out between Honduras and El Salvador after a riot at a soccer match between teams from the two countries. Now the five countries are trying to revive their agreement, although no definite progress had been made by early 1993.

---

[14] J. Sweeney, "First Latin American Customs Union Looms over Venezuela," *Journal of Commerce*, September 26, 1991, p. 5A; and "The Business of the American Hemisphere," *The Economist*, August 24, 1991, pp. 37–38.

[15] "Business of the American Hemisphere," *The Economist*.

Finally, there is the customs union that was to have been created in 1991 between the English-speaking Caribbean countries under the auspices of the Caribbean Community. Referred to as CARICOM, it was originally established in 1973. However, it has repeatedly failed to progress toward economic integration. A formal commitment to economic and monetary union was adopted by CARICOM's member-states in 1984, but since then little progress has been made. In October 1991 the CARICOM governments failed, for the third consecutive time, to meet a deadline for establishing a common external tariff.

REGIONAL ECONOMIC INTEGRATION ELSEWHERE

Outside of Western Europe and the Americas, there have been few significant attempts at regional integration. For a number of years the most notable regional economic grouping was COMECON, the association of Eastern European communist states headed by the USSR, but it is now defunct. The most significant group outside of Europe and the Americas today is the Association of Southeast Asian Nations (ASEAN). Formed in 1967, ASEAN currently includes Brunei, Indonesia, Malaysia, the Philippines, Singapore, and Thailand. The ASEAN countries are characterized by an abundance of natural resources (with the exception of the city-state of Singapore), large international trade sectors, and an emphasis on free-market economic policies. Singapore and Thailand are two of Southeast Asia's most successful economies. Thus, the potential exists for a vibrant free trade area.

The basic objectives of ASEAN are to foster freer trade between member-countries and to achieve some cooperation in their industrial policies. Progress has been very limited, however. For example, although some progress has been made in tariff reduction between ASEAN countries, only 5 percent of intra-ASEAN trade currently consists of goods whose tariffs have been reduced through ASEAN preferential trade arrangement.

In addition to ASEAN, several attempts have been made to achieve some kind of economic integration between African countries. Currently, however, most of these associations exist in name only and are of little practical significance in the world economic and political stage.

IMPLICATIONS FOR BUSINESS

The most significant developments in regional economic integration are occurring in Europe and North America. Although some of the Latin American trade blocs may have greater economic significance in the future, at present the events in Europe and North America have far more profound and immediate implications for business practice. Accordingly, in this section we will concentrate on the business implications of the EC and NAFTA. Similar conclusions, however, could be drawn with regard to the creation of a single market anywhere else in the world.

Opportunities

The creation of a single market offers significant opportunities, because markets that were formally protected from foreign competition are opened. For example, in Europe before 1992 the large French and Italian markets were among the most protected. These markets are now much more open to foreign competition in the form of both exports and direct investment. Nonetheless, the specter of "Fortress Europe" suggests that to fully exploit such opportunities, it will pay non-EC firms to set up EC subsidiaries. Many major U.S. firms have long had subsidiaries in Europe. Those that do not would be well advised to consider establishing them now, lest they run the risk of being shut out of the EC by tariff barriers, quotas, and the like. In fact, non-EC firms have rapidly increased their direct investment in the EC in recent years in anticipation of the creation of a single market. During the 1985–89 period, for example, approximately 37 percent of the FDI inflows into industrialized countries was directed at the EC. By 1991 this figure had risen to 66 percent.[16]

Additional opportunities arise from the inherent lower costs of doing business in a single market—as opposed to 12 national markets in the case of the EC or 3 national markets in the case of NAFTA. Free movement of goods across borders, harmonized product standards, and simplified tax regimes make it possible for firms based in the EC and the NAFTA countries to realize potentially enormous cost economies by centralizing production in those EC and NAFTA locations where the mix of factor costs and skills is optimal. At the extreme, rather than producing a product in each of the 12 EC countries or the 3 NAFTA countries, a firm may be able to serve the whole EC or North American market from a single location. This location must be chosen carefully, of course, with an eye on local factor costs and skills.

For example, in response to the challenges created by EC in 1992, the Minneapolis company 3M has been consolidating its European manufacturing and distribution facilities to take advantage of economies of scale. Thus, a plant in Great Britain now produces 3M's printing products and a German factory its reflective traffic control materials for all of the EC. In each case, 3M chose a location for centralized production after carefully considering the likely production costs in alternative locations within the EC. The ultimate goal of 3M is to dispense with national distinctions altogether, directing R&D, manufacturing, distribution, and marketing for each product group from an EC headquarters.[17] Similarly, Unilever, one of Europe's largest companies, was busy rationalizing its production in advance of 1992. Unilever concentrated its production of dishwashing powder for the EC in one plant, toilet soap in another, and so on.[18]

Threats

Just as the emergence of single markets in the EC and North America creates opportunities for business, so it also presents a number of threats. For one thing, the business environment within both groups will become more competitive. The lowering of barriers to trade and investment between countries will be followed by increased price competition throughout the EC and North America. For example, prior to 1992 a Volkswagen Golf cost 55 percent more in Great Britain than in Denmark and 29 percent more in Ireland than in Greece.[19] Such price differentials will vanish in a single market. This is a direct threat to any firm doing business in the EC or the NAFTA countries. To survive in the tougher single-market environment, firms must take advantage of the opportunities offered by the creation of a single market to rationalize their production and reduce their costs. Otherwise, they will be severely disadvantaged.

A further threat to non-EC and/or non-North American firms arises from the likely long-term improvement in the competitive position of many European and North American firms. This is particularly relevant in the EC, where many firms are currently limited in their ability to compete globally with North American and Asian firms by a

[16] "World Economic Survey," *The Economist,* September 19, 1992, p. 17.

[17] P. Davis, "A European Campaign: Local Companies Rush for a Share of EC Market while Barriers Are Down," *Minneapolis–St. Paul City Business,* January 8, 1990, p. 1.

[18] "The Business of Europe," *The Economist,* December 7, 1991, pp. 63–64.

[19] E. G. Friberg, "1992: Moves Europeans Are Making," *Harvard Business Review,* May–June 1989, pp. 85–89.

high cost structure. The creation of a single market and the resulting increased competition in the EC can be expected to result in serious attempts by many EC firms to reduce their cost structure by rationalizing production. This could transform many EC companies into efficient global competitors. The message for non-EC businesses is that they need to prepare for the emergence of more capable European competitors by reducing their own cost structures.

A final threat to non-EC and/or non-North American firms inherent in the creation of a single market has already been alluded to. This is the threat of being shut out of the single market by the creation of "Fortress Europe" or "Fortress North America." As noted earlier in the chapter, although the free trade philosophy underpinning the EC theoretically argues against the creation of any "fortress" in Europe, there are signs that the EC may raise barriers to imports and investment in certain areas, such as autos. Non-EC firms might be well advised, therefore, to set up their own EC operations as quickly as possible. This could also occur in the NAFTA countries, but it seems less likely.

SUMMARY OF CHAPTER

Three main objectives have been pursued in this chapter. They were to examine the economic and political debate surrounding regional economic integration; to review the progress toward regional economic integration in Europe, the Americas, and elsewhere; and to distinguish the important implications of regional economic integration for the practice of international business. The following points have been made in the chapter.

1. A number of levels of economic integration are possible in theory. In order of increasing integration, they include a free trade area, a customs union, a common market, an economic union, and full political union.
2. In a free trade area, barriers to trade between member-countries are removed, but each country determines its own external trade policy. In a customs union, internal barriers to trade are removed and a common external trade policy is adopted. A common market is similar to a customs union, except that in a common market factors of production also are allowed to move freely between countries. An economic union involves even closer integration, including the establishment of a common currency and the harmonization of tax rates. A political union is the logical culmination of attempts to achieve ever-closer economic integration.
3. Regional economic integration is an attempt to achieve economic gains from the free flow of trade and investment between neighboring countries.
4. Economic integration can also create incentives for political cooperation between neighboring states and thereby reduce the potential for violent conflict.
5. In practice, integration is not easily achieved or sustained. Although integration brings benefits to the majority, it is never without costs for the minority. Furthermore, concerns over national sovereignty often slow down or stop integration attempts.
6. Regional integration will not increase economic welfare if the trade creation effects in the free trade area are outweighed by the trade diversion effects.
7. The Single European Act grew out of frustration that the EC was not living up to its promise due to the failure to standardize the rules of the game between countries. A profusion of administrative barriers to intra-EC trade and widespread use of subsidies to promote national firms appeared to be jeopardizing the achievement of a single market.
8. The Single European Act sought to create a true single market by abolishing administrative barriers to the free flow of trade and investment between EC countries.
9. If ratified, the treaty of Maastricht promises to take the EC even further along the road to economic union by establishing a common currency. The economic gains from a common currency come from reduced exchange costs and reduced risk associated with currency fluctuations.
10. If ratified by the EC parliament and by all 18 countries of the EC and the EFTA, the EEA will be the world's largest free trade area with 380 million consumers and 46 percent of world trade.
11. A major concern has been that after 1992 the EC would become a fortress of protectionism. In theory, this should not occur, given the free market philosophy of the EC. There is no guarantee that the EC will not adopt a protectionist stance toward external trade.
12. Although no other attempt at regional economic integration comes close to the EC in terms of potential economic and political significance, various other attempts are being made in the world. The most notable include NAFTA in North America, the Andean Pact and MERCOSUR in Latin America, and ASEAN in Southeast Asia.

13. The creation of single markets in the EC and North America means that many markets that were formerly protected from foreign competition are now more open. This creates major investment and export opportunities for firms within and outside these regions.
14. The free movement of goods across borders, the harmonization of product standards, and the simplification of tax regimes make it possible for firms based in the EC and North America to realize potentially enormous cost economies by centralizing production in those locations in the EC and NAFTA countries where the mix of factor costs and skills is optimal.
15. The lowering of barriers to trade and investment between countries will be followed by increased price competition throughout the EC and North America.
16. A threat to non-EC business arises from the likely long-term improvement in the competitive position of many European firms following the creation of a single market.

DISCUSSION QUESTIONS

1. The proposed NAFTA is likely to produce net benefits for the U.S. economy. Discuss.
2. What are the economic and political arguments for regional economic integration? Given these arguments, why don't we see more integration in the world economy?
3. What is the likely effect of EC 1992 on competition wthin the EC? Why?
4. How should a U.S. firm that currently exports only to Western Europe respond to the creation of a single market?
5. How should a firm with self-sufficient production facilities in several EC countries respond to the creation of a single market?

The Commercial Aircraft Industry

Airbus Industrie, Boeing, and McDonnell Douglas

For years the commercial aircraft industry has been an American success story. Until 1980 U.S. manufacturers held a virtual monopoly. Even today, despite the rise of the Europe-based Airbus Industrie, two U.S. firms, Boeing and McDonnell Douglas, account for two thirds of world market share (see Figure 1). The U.S. industry is routinely the largest net contributor to the U.S. balance of trade, and Boeing, the dominant manufacturer in the industry, is the largest U.S. exporter. In the late 1980s and early 90s, the U.S. industry regularly ran a substantial positive trade balance with the rest of the world of 12 to 15 billion dollars per year. The impact of the industry on U.S. employment is also enormous. Boeing directly employs more than 100,000 people in the Seattle area and indirectly probably supports another 300,000 in subcontractors and through its payroll.

In recent years, however, U.S. dominance has been threatened by the rise of Airbus Industrie, a consortium of four European aircraft manufacturers—one British, one French, one German, and one Spanish. Founded in 1970, Airbus was initially a marginal competitor and was regarded as unlikely to challenge U.S. dominance. Since 1981, however, Airbus has confounded its critics and emerged as the world's second-largest aircraft manufacturer. In 1991 Airbus held 24 percent of all new orders for commercial aircraft, up from 14 percent in 1981 (see Figure 1).

In response, the U.S. industry has been crying foul, claiming that Airbus is heavily subsidized by the governments of Great Britain, France, Germany, and Spain. Airbus has responded in kind, pointing out that both Boeing and McDonnell Douglas have benefited for years from hidden U.S. government subsidies. In this case we examine the debate between the two sides in this trade dispute. First, however, let us look at the competitive structure of the commercial aircraft industry.

INDUSTRY COMPETITIVE STRUCTURE

The commercial aircraft industry has a unique set of characteristics.

1. *The costs of developing a new airliner are enormous.* For example, McDonnell Douglas spent $1.5 billion developing and tooling its MD-11 wide-bodied jetliner, introduced in the late 1980s, and it calculates that its development costs for the proposed MD-12—to compete with Boeing's 747—will be around $5 billion.
2. *Given such enormous development costs, a company must capture a significant share of world demand in order to break even.* In the case of the MD-11, for example, McDonnell Douglas will have to sell more than 200 aircraft to break even, a figure that represents 13 percent of predicted industry sales between 1990 and 2000. For an aircraft such as the MD-12, 400 to 500 units may be required to break even. Given this, it can take 10 to 14 years of production for an aircraft to reach its break-even point—and this on top of the 5 to 6 years of negative cash flows during development.

Source: Charles Hill and Maria Gonzalez.

Figure 1

a. Year-end 1991 percentage of market share

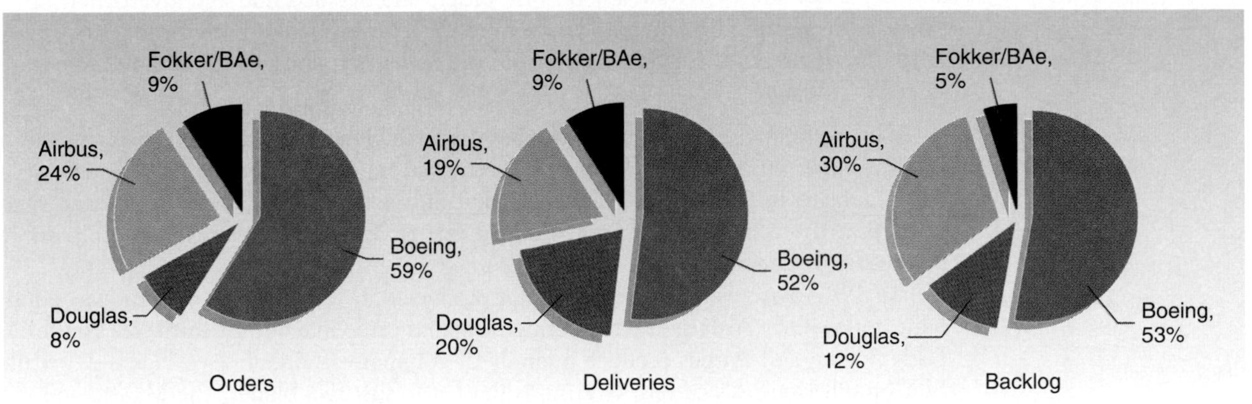

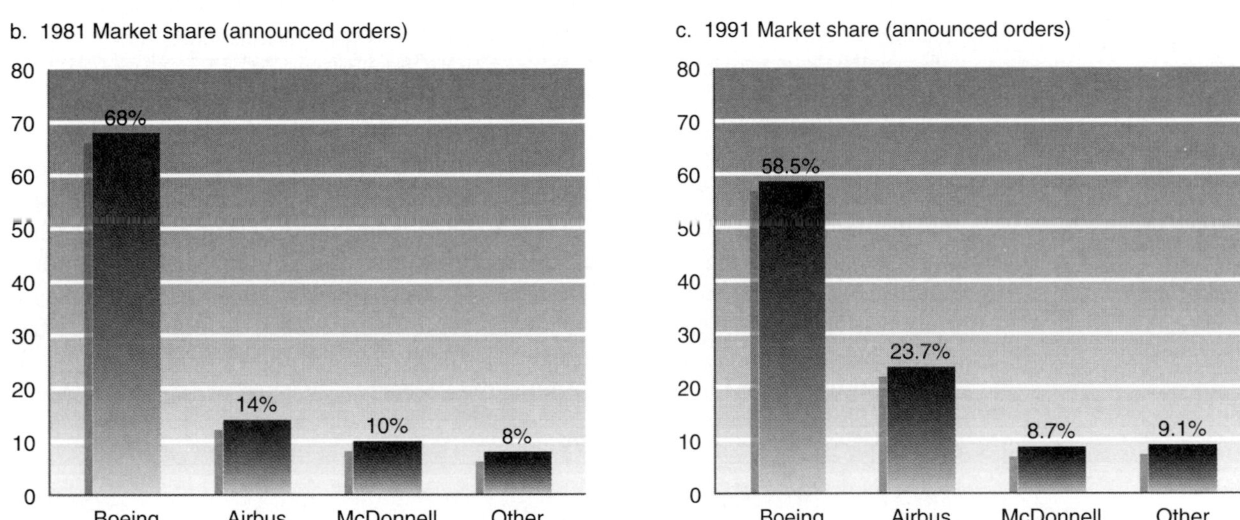

Source: Data provided by Boeing Commercial Airplane Group.

3. *Worldwide consensus is that a significant "experience curve" exists in aircraft production.* Due to learning effects, on average, unit cost falls by about 20 percent with each doubling of accumulated output. An implication of this is that companies that fail to move along the experience curve face a significant unit-cost disadvantage. A company that achieves only half of the market share required to break even will suffer a 20 percent unit-cost disadvantage.

4. *Demand for aircraft is highly volatile.* This fact makes long-run planning difficult and raises the risks involved in producing aircraft. The commercial airline business is prone to boom-and-bust cycles. During the early 1990s many major airlines ex-

perienced financial trouble. Pan Am, Continental, Eastern, Braniff, and TWA were all either in Chapter 11 or had recently folded. Many other airlines were losing money. In response, airlines slowed down their ordering of new aircraft, pushed back delivery dates for aircraft already on firm order, and decided not to convert their options on future aircraft deliveries to firm orders. Thus although both Boeing and Airbus had entered the 1990s with record orders, the troubles in the airline business spread to them.

The combination of high development costs, break-even levels that constitute a significant percentage of world demand, substantial experience-curve effects, and volatile demand makes for an industry that can support only a few major players. Analysts seem to agree that the commercial aircraft industry can *profitably support* only two, or possibly three, major producers.

In 1991 there were only three major producers in the industry. Boeing was dominant, followed by Airbus, and McDonnell Douglas came in a distant third (see Figure 1). Both Boeing and Airbus produce a family of commercial aircraft (see Figure 2), while McDonnell Douglas's current offering is limited to just two planes, the MD-80 and the MD-11. Both Boeing and Airbus are currently profitable. In 1991 Boeing had profits of $1.6 billion on sales of $29.3 billion. Although Airbus does not publish its accounts, estimates suggest that it made $250 million on sales of $8.5 billion in 1991. McDonnell Douglas is currently losing money on its commercial aircraft operations. It laid off 10,000 employees during 1990 and 1991 and has plans to lay off thousands more. The company also cut back its projections of future production for both the MD-80 and the MD-11. Without outside financing, it is unlikely that McDonnell Douglas will be able to go ahead and build the MD-12. The company's future in the industry is clearly in jeopardy.

As a final point, Airbus has recently made some notable inroads into Boeing's customer base. Almost 45 percent of all commerical aircraft are sold to U.S. carriers, and Boeing has long had the inside track with most of them. In July 1992, however, United Airlines, one of Boeing's most loyal customers, announced that it had signed a $3 billion contract with Airbus to lease 50 A320s and to take options on 50 more. In announcing the decision, United cited the A320's range, speed, comfort, technology, and fuel efficiency. In addition, the deal guarantee's that Airbus will train United's pilots to fly the A320 and allows United to back out of the lease with just 11 months' notice—which reduces United's financial liability

THE TRADE DISPUTE

Both Boeing and McDonnell Douglas have argued that Airbus has an unfair competitive advantage due to the level of subsidy it receives from the governments of Great Britain, France, Germany, and Spain. They argue that the subsidies allow Airbus to set unrealistically low prices, to offer concessions and attractive financing terms to airlines, to write off development costs, and to use state-owned airlines to obtain orders. In making these claims, Boeing and McDonnell Douglas have had the support of the U.S. government. According to a study by the Department of Commerce, Airbus received more than $13.5 billion in government subsidies between 1970 and 1990 ($25.9 billion if commercial interest rates are applied). Most of these subsidies were in the forms of loans at below-market interest rates and tax breaks. The subsidies financed research and development and provided attractive financing terms for Airbus's customers. For most of its customers, Airbus is believed to have financed 80 percent of the cost of aircraft for a term of 8 to 10 years at an annual interest rate of approximately 7 percent. In contrast, the U.S. Export-

Figure 2

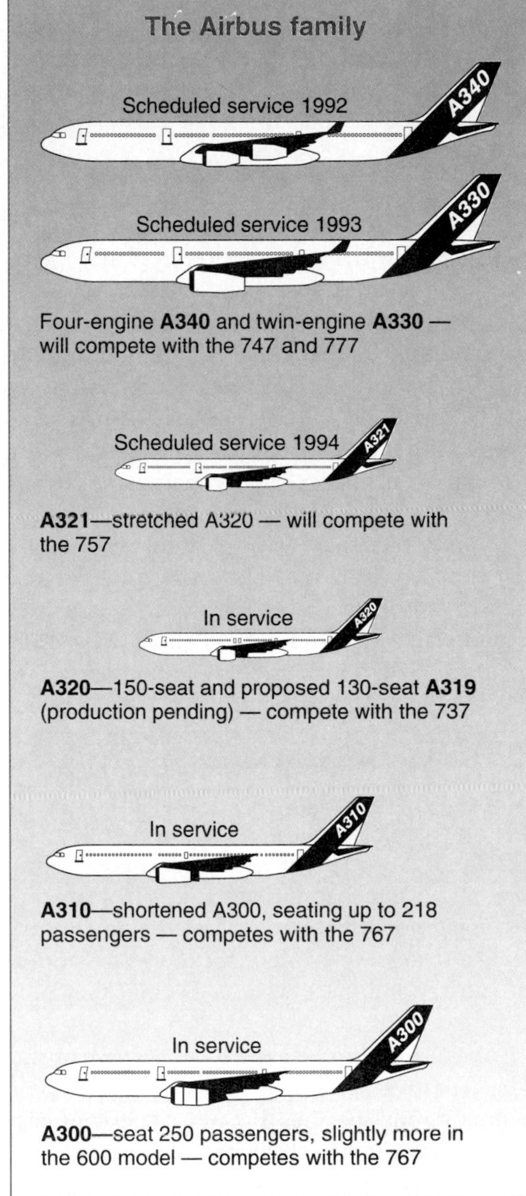

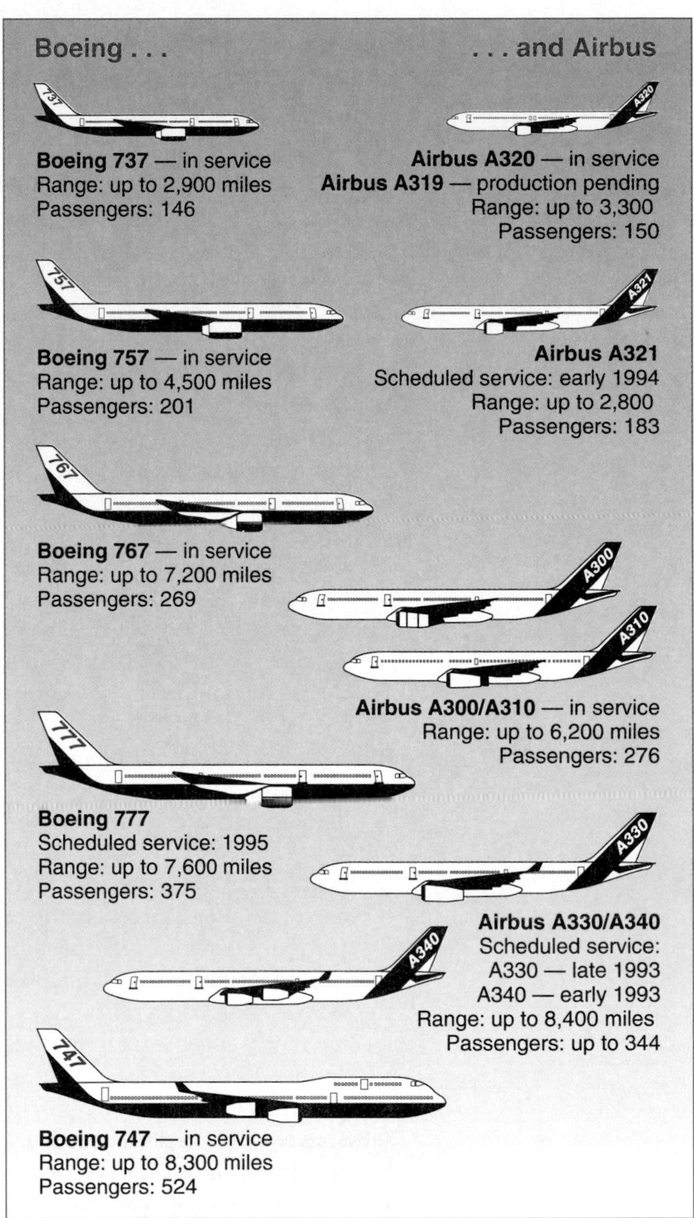

Source: Adapted from a chart designed by Sheila Raymond from data supplied by Boeing Commercial Airplane Group. Range and passenger data based on two-class configuration.

Import Bank required 20 percent down payments from Boeing and McDonnell Douglas customers, financed only 40 percent of the cost of an aircraft directly, and guaranteed the financing of the remaining 40 percent by private banks at an average interest rate of 8.4 percent to 8.5 percent for a period of 10 years.

Airbus's response to these charges has been to point out that its success is not due to subsidies at all but to a good product and a good strategy. Most observers agree that Airbus's aircraft incorporate state-of-the-art technology—particularly in materials applications, systems for flight control and safety, and aerodynamics. Airbus gained ground initially by targeting market segments not served by new aircraft or not served at all. Thus Airbus has taken the initiative in targeting two segments of the market with wide-bodied twin-engined aircraft, then in developing a new generation of aircraft for the 150-seat market, and most recently in going after the market below the 747 for a long, thin airliner.

Airbus has also argued that both Boeing and McDonnell Douglas have benefited from U.S. government aid for a long time and that the aid *it* has received has merely leveled the playing field. In the United States, planes were built under government contract during World War I, and the construction of mail planes was subsidized between the world wars. Almost all production was subsidized during World War II, and subsidies continued at a high level after the war. The Boeing 707, for example, is a derivative of a military transport program that was subsidized by the U.S. government. Boeing's subsidized programs include the B-17, B-29, B-47, B-52, and K-135, just to name a few. Its nonairline programs have included the Minuteman missile, Apollo-Saturn, and space station programs.

More recently, a 1991 European Commission study attempted to estimate the amount of subsidies currently received by the U.S. industry. The study contends that Boeing and McDonnell Douglas received $18 billion to $22 billion in indirect government aid between 1976 and 1990. The report claims that commercial aircraft operations benefited through defense department contracts by as much as $6.34 billion during the 1976–90 period. In addition, the report claims that NASA has pumped at least $8 billion into commercial aircraft production over the same period, and that tax exemptions have given an additional $1.7 billion to Boeing and $1.4 billion to McDonnell Douglas.

Boeing rejects the claims of the European Commission report. The company points out that the report's assumption that Boeing receives direct government grants in the form of an additional 5 percent for commercial work with every military or space contract it receives is false. Moreover, the company points out that during the last 10 years only 3 percent of Boeing's R&D spending has come from Department of Defense funding and only 4 percent from NASA funding. Boeing also argues that since the four companies in the Airbus consortium do twice as much military and space work as Boeing, they must receive much larger indirect subsidies.

In mid-1992 the United States and Airbus seemed to be close to an agreement that could end the long-standing dispute. The tentative agreement limits direct European subsidies to 33 percent of new development costs and specifies that future subsidies must be repaid with interest. The agreement also limits indirect subsidies, such as military research that has applications to commercial aircraft, to 5 percent of development costs for commercial aircraft. Although Airbus officials say the controversy has been resolved, Boeing officials say that they will be competing for years against subsidized products.

DISCUSSION QUESTIONS

1. Do you believe Airbus could have become a viable competitor without subsidies?
2. Why do you think the four European governments agreed to subsidize the establishment of Airbus.
3. Is Airbus's position with regard to the dispute over subsidies reasonable?

4. What additional action (if any) should the U.S. government take with respect to Airbus?

SOURCES

1. Coleman, B. "GATT to Rule Against German Aid to Airbus." *The Wall Street Journal,* January 16, 1992, p. 5.
2. Core, O. C. "Airbus Arrives." *The Seattle Times,* July 21, 1992, C1–C3.
3. Dertouzos, M. L.; R. K. Lester; and R. M. Solow. *Made in America.* Cambridge, Mass.: MIT Press, 1989.
4. "Dissecting Airbus." *The Economist,* February 16, 191, pp. 51–52.
5. "The Jumbo War." *The Economist,* June 15, 1991, pp. 65–66.
6. Klepper, G. "Entry into the Market for Large Transport Aircraft." *European Economic Review,* 34 (1990), pp. 775–803.
7. Lane, P. "Study Complains of Alleged Subsidies." *Seattle Times,* December 4, 1991, p. G2.
8. Stroud, M. "Worries over a Technology Shift Follow McDonnell-Taiwan Accord." *Investor's Business Daily,* November 21, 1991, p. 36.
9. Toy, S., et al. "Zoom! Airbus Comes On Strong." *Business Week,* April 22, 1991, pp. 48–50.

Active Matrix Liquid Crystal Displays

The active-matrix liquid crystal display screen (AM-LCD) is seen as a technology of the future. These flat display screens offer several advantages over the monochromatic, passive-matrix liquid crystal display screens (PM-LCD) used in laptop computer and digital watches. Compared to PM-LCDs, AM-LCDs are light, use little electricity, do not emit radiation, are easy on the eyes, and respond quickly to electrical inputs. These features make high-quality color, text, graphic, and video possible when the screens are integrated into laptop computers. In addition to computer displays, the screens are also critical components in camcorders, medical instruments, high-definition television, auto dashboards, aerospace instruments, factory control devices, and instrumentation for the military. Although production is just getting off the ground—sales were $250 million worldwide in 1990—forecasts suggest worldwide sales of $1 billion in 1994 and $10 billion plus by 2000.

THE MARKET

The technology was pioneered in the United States during the 1960s. In recent years, however, the Japanese have emerged as the major producers of AM-LCDs and now account for 95 percent of worldwide production. Sharp, NEC, and Toshiba dominate the market. Unlike their major U.S. competitors, these Japanese firms made massive investments in AM-LCD research and production facilities during the 1980s. Sharp alone reportedly spent more than $1 billion on developing the technology during the 1980s and planned to spend $640 million more in the 1991–95 period.

Source: Charles Hill and Maria Gonzalez.

Although a number of small U.S. companies are involved in this business, they tend to focus on highly specialized niches (e.g., supplying the Defense Department) and have made investments only to support their limited production. With the exception of IBM, which has a joint venture with Toshiba in Japan to manufacture AM-LCDs, no major U.S. company has a presence in the industry, and no U.S. company is capable of mass production. There are a number of reasons for this. First, the massive capital expenditures required to produce AM-LCD screens have deterred many U.S. firms, as have the high risks involved. The risks are judged to be particularly acute, given the Japanese lead in the technology and the long payback period for any investments. (Japanese executives regard five or six years of losses as the cost of entering this business.) Few American companies are willing to invest in an industry where Japanese companies are already well ahead. In addition, the production process is particularly difficult to master, since even the smallest contaminant in the production process (such as dust) can cause damage to a display. It is estimated that 80 percent of AM-LCDs coming off Japanese production lines are defective and must be scrapped. Thus, the combination of high capital costs, high risks, and a difficult production process have deterred many major U.S. firms from entering the market.

THE IMPOSITION OF ANTIDUMPING DUTIES

Against this background, in July 1990 a group of small U.S. manufacturers of AM-LCDs filed an "antidumping" action with the U.S. Department of Commerce. They claimed that the Japanese suppliers of AM-LCDs were selling their screens below market value and at less than half of their production cost—in other words, *dumping* them—in the United States. The International Trade Commission (ITC), a branch of the Department of Commerce, investigated the charges. In August 1991, the ITC reported that the Japanese producers had indeed been selling AM-LCDs below cost and imposed a 62.67 percent duty on AM-LCDs imported from Japan in an effort to shelter small U.S. manufacturers from unfair foreign competition. The ITC acknowledged that the Japanese competition was killing small U.S. companies, but it warned that the duties would not guarantee the U.S. industry's success. U.S. success would require significant investments by U.S. firms—investments that the government, with its long-standing opposition to industrial policy, was not prepared to subsidize.

The decision to impose an antidumping tariff on AM-LCD screens imported from Japan follows a 1987 U.S. government decision to impose a 100 percent tariff on laptop computers imported from Japan. Note that both of these tariffs are country specific; they target imports from only Japan.

THE RESPONSE OF U.S. COMPUTER MAKERS

The response by American computer manufacturers to the imposition of duties took the Department of Commerce by surprise. Most U.S. manufacturers of laptop computers were already importing LCD screens from Japanese suppliers. IBM, for example, was importing screens made in Japan by its joint venture with Toshiba. AM-LCD screens are the most costly component for laptops, accounting for 50 percent of their total cost. Thus, the duty increased the cost of manufacturing a laptop computer in the United States by about 30 percent. Not surprisingly, U.S. computer companies felt that this placed them at a significant competitive disadvantage vis-à-vis companies that manufactured laptops in other countries.

The response of U.S. computer manufacturers was twofold. First, they lodged formal protests with the U.S. government for imposing the duties and filed appeals with the Court of International Trade for a reversal of the decision. IBM, Apple, Compaq, and Tandy all argued that the government's decision to protect small AM-LCD makers via antidumping duties was only possible at their expense. Second, they began to move their assembly of laptop computers out of the United States. Apple abandoned its plans to manufacture its new "notebook" computers in Colorado and decided to move production to Ireland; Compaq announced plans to produce laptops in Scotland. Their logic was that these third countries do not levy tariffs on imports of AM-LCDs from Japan and that the United States does not levy tariffs on imports of finished laptops from these countries. By pursuing such a strategy, the likes of Apple and Compaq could maintain their competitive cost structure—but only at the cost of lost jobs in the United States.

THE JAPANESE REACTION

Some analysts believe that behind the antidumping duty was a cynical attempt by the commerce department to encourage Japanese manufacturers to move their production of AM-LCDs to the United States, which would benefit the United States with job creation and technology transfer. If this is true, the commerce department badly miscalculated. At present few if any Japanese companies would seem to have any intention of switching AM-LCD production to the United States. Mass production of AM-LCDs has barely begun in Japan, and it will be years before the capital costs of their investments are recouped, so additional investments in the United States are unlikely. Instead, seven Japanese manufacturers, including Sharp, Toshiba, and Hitachi, have joined the U.S. computer manufacturers in lodging appeals with the Court of International Trade. They have charged that the decision to impose duties was illogical, because there were virtually no U.S. manufacturers capable of producing AM-LCDs commercially. Moreover, they note that the charge of dumping is misplaced. While it is true that no Japanese manufacturers are currently making profits on AM-LCDs, they contend that this is due to the enormous capital expenditure required to start up production. They argue that production costs will decline and profits will follow once the production process is perfected, output builds, and scale economies are realized. Japan's Ministry of International Trade and Industry is also investigating the possibility the Department of Commerce's decision violates the General Agreement on Tariffs and Trade (GATT).

CAN THE U.S. INDUSTRY BE SAVED?

Many people believe that the decision to impose antidumping duties came too late to save the U.S. LCD industry. They point out that Japanese companies have been investing heavily in AM-LCD technology for years now and that U.S. companies lack the capacity to sell commercially. Instead, U.S. manufacturers sell most of their screens to the Pentagon. It is believed that a minimum investment of $300 million would be required to set up a commercial manufacturing operation—a figure that is probably beyond the reach of most U.S. firms currently in the industry. In addition, U.S. firms would have to support five to six years of losses in order to enter the market and would have to solve the substantial production problems that currently bedevil AM-LCD production in Japan, the world capital of precision manufacturing.

While all of this seems unlikely, some government experts remain convinced that the United States is still capable of catching up with Japan. Having toured AM-LCD plants in Japan, these experts believe that U.S. companies can obtain enough government and private funds not only to reproduce AM-LCD technology, but also to improve on the manufacturing processes currently in use. Against this background, the U.S. Air Force has proposed to fund AM-LCD production. The air force is interested because it uses large numbers of AM-LCD screens for cockpit instrumentation and flight-simulation devices. The U.S. Army also needs the screens for its battle tanks, and the U.S. Navy uses them in its shipboard command centers. The Pentagon says that the AM-LCD project meets its criteria for the "selective production" program. This program allows the Pentagon to commit funds for purchasing critical defense materials from selected contractors when projects meet certain standards. Firms obtaining contracts for AM-LCD production would be expected to find commercial buyers for the screens to keep their manufacturing cost effective and to avoid high-priced products. A Pentagon commitment to AM-LCD production may be enough to encourage other U.S. investors to finance AM-LCD production to cultivate a customer base for the screens.

DISCUSSION QUESTIONS

1. Evaluate the commerce department's decision to impose duties on Japanese-manufactured AM-LCDs. On balance, has this decision helped or harmed U.S. industry? What is the likely impact on the U.S. consumer?
2. What, if anything, could the U.S. government do to keep U.S. computer manufacturers from moving their manufacturing operations offshore? Should the government take such action?
3. What criteria should the U.S. government apply in targeting industries for anti-dumping protection?
4. If you were the CEO of a small U.S. firm interested in AM-LCD manufacturing, what factors would be important in your decision to enter the AM-LCD market? Under what conditions might you enter the market?
5. Should the U.S. government urge the Pentagon to support production of AM-LCDs? Explain the reasoning behind your answer.

SOURCES

1. Department of Commerce, International Trade Administration. *High Information Content of Flat Panel Displays and Display Glass Therefor from Japan: Anti-Dumping Duty Orders.* September 4, 1992.
2. "Flat Out in Japan." *The Economist,* February 1, 1992, pp. 79–80.
3. "Imported Japanese Flat Panel Displays Injure U.S. Industry, ITC Says." *International Trade Reporter,* August 21, 1991.

4. Johnson, R. "Flat Out for Profits." *Far Eastern Economic Review,* April 19, 1990.
5. "Flat Screens Come to Life." *Far Eastern Economic Review,* August 15, 1991, p. 58.
6. "LCD Makers Appeal against U.S. Anti-Dumping Ruling." *Kyodo News Service,* October 9, 1991.
7. Magnusson, P. "Did Washington Lose Sight of the Big Picture?" *Business Week,* December 2, 1991.
8. Nomura, H. "IBM, Apple Fight LCD Screen Tariffs: U.S. Decision Forcing Assembly Offshore." *The Nikkei Weekly,* October 26, 1992.
9. Tanzer, A. "The New Improved Color Computer." *Forbes,* July 23, 1990, pp. 276–280.

PART FOUR

The Global Monetary System

The Foreign Exchange Market

CHAPTER 9

HOW TO LOSE $269 MILLION

Businesses that trade internationally face foreign exchange risk every day. Consider the case of the British food and drink manufacturer Allied-Lyons, which exports many products to the United States. When Allied-Lyons enters into a contract to supply a U.S. supermarket chain with food products, the contract typically specifies that the chain will pay for the products two to three months after the shipment date. Giving the buyer two to three months' credit is normal business practice; it allows the buyer time to sell the product and generate the cash necessary to pay for the purchase. When foreign exchange fluctuations are introduced into the picture, however, the seller can experience a problem. For illustration, let us assume Allied-Lyons enters into a contract on January 2 to supply Safeway Stores with a shipment of food products for which Safeway agrees to pay $10 million. Assume further that the rate at which British pounds are converted into U.S. dollars on January 2 is £1 = $2. At this exchange rate, Allied-Lyons can earn £5 million from the deal. If it costs Allied-Lyons £4.5 million to produce and ship the products to the United States, the company will realize a healthy gross profit of £0.5 million. • Imagine now that Safeway does not have to pay for the shipment until April 2, and that in the intervening period there is a crisis of confidence in the ability of the U.S. government to control inflation. Foreign exchange dealers react by selling U.S. dollars, and the pound/dollar exchange rate falls from £1 = $2 to £1 = $2.5. Safeway still pays $10 million for its shipment, but by April 2 this is worth only £4 million. Instead of making its anticipated profit of £0.5 million, Allied-Lyons experiences a loss of £0.5 million! • This illustrates foreign exchange risk. The problem that Allied-Lyons and other firms that do business internationally must resolve is to determine a means for ensuring that future movements in relative exchange rates do not make seemingly profitable deals unprofitable. • Fortunately, there are a variety of ways to insure against foreign exchange risk. The most common is to **buy forward**. By this means Allied-Lyons could have contracted with a foreign exchange dealer on the day the deal was signed (January 2) to sell the $10 million it was to receive from Safeway on April 2 at a fixed exchange rate. The three-month forward exchange rate quoted Allied-Lyons by the dealer might have been £1 = $2.1. At this rate Allied-Lyons would receive £4.76 from the deal, giving it a profit of £0.26 million. Although this would not be as great as the profit it would receive if exchange rates did not change, Allied-Lyons might consider it worthwhile to settle for a guaranteed profit of £0.26 million. • In our example, Allied-Lyons would have been wise to buy forward. The shift could have been in the other direction, however, with the British pound collapsing rather than the dollar. If this had occurred, Allied-Lyons could have made even more profit by *not* buying forward. The decision of whether to buy forward, therefore, must depend on a company's predictions about likely future exchange rates. • The uncertainty surrounding future exchange rates opens the door to speculation. Foreign exchange dealers buy and sell currencies in the hope that their values relative to other currencies will change in a positive direction so that they can sell them at a profit at some future date. For example, if on January 2 a U.S. foreign exchange dealer believes that a collapse in the value of the dollar against the pound is imminent, the dealer might sell dollars and buy pounds. Imagine that the dealer sells $10 million and gets £5 million in exchange (at the exchange rate of £1 = $2). Three months later the exchange rate has shifted to £1 = $2.5. Now the dealer sells the £5 million, getting $12.5 million in exchange. By speculating in currencies, the dealer has made a profit of $2.5 million in just three months on an initial investment of $10 million! But think what might have happened if the dealer was wrong, and the value of the dollar rose against the pound, say to £1 = $1.5. In that case the dealer could have lost $2.5 million. Speculation is always risky business. • Let us return to the case of Allied-Lyons. Like many others, this company traditionally operated with a conservative policy of buying forward, staying well clear of the risky (but potentially very profitable) business of speculation. This changed in 1986, when former Eurobond trader Clifford Hatch became its finance director. Hatch believed a company that engages in major foreign exchange transactions on a daily basis should pursue an aggressive foreign exchange policy. By moving away from its conservative attitude toward the management of foreign exchange risk, Hatch believed the company's five-member foreign exchange team could have a major impact on Allied-Lyon's bottom line. Hatch began to write currency options. A currency option contract gives its holder the right to receive and to pay for an amount of foreign currency at a fixed date in the future (a *call option*) or to deliver and to receive payment for an amount of foreign currency at a fixed date in the future (a *put option*). The writer of an option (e.g., Allied-Lyons) has, in theory, an unlimited risk. Although the writer of an option can earn enormous profits if the market moves in his favor, he may also have to give currency at a horrifying level of cost or have to accept currency that has become worthless if the market moves adversely. Put simply, writing currency options is a very speculative exercise. The writer can win big, or he can lose his proverbial shirt. • Hatch and Allied-Lyons lost the proverbial shirt. At first things looked good. In 1988 Allied-Lyons made a profit of £3 million on foreign exchange transactions. This increased to £5 million in 1989 and to a healthy £9 million in 1990—not a bad return for a five-member team. Encouraged by their success, Hatch and his team began to take bigger and bigger risks. In early 1991 they bet that the value of the British pound would rise against that of the U.S. dollar, and they wrote call options that would pay handsomely if this occurred. It didn't! Between February 11 and April 1 the value of the pound against the dollar fell precipitously. On February 11 one pound bought \$2; by April 1 it bought less than \$1.75, and Allied-Lyons had to pay out currency for the options it had written at an enormous loss. The total loss amounted to \$269 million, more than the company was projected to earn from all of its food and drink activities in 1991! *Sources: "Allied-Lyons' Deadly Game,"* Euromoney, *April 1991, pp. 22–28; and C. Forman, "Allied-Lyons to Post \$269 Million Loss from Foreign Exchange as Dollar Soars,"* The Wall Street Journal, *March 20, 1991, p. A17.*

INTRODUCTION

This chapter has three main objectives. The first is to explain how the foreign exchange market works. The second is to examine the forces that determine exchange rates and to discuss the degree to which it is possible to predict future exchange rate movements. The third objective is to map the implications for international business of exchange rate movements and the foreign exchange market. This chapter is the first of three that deal with the international monetary system and its relationship to international business. In the next chapter (Chapter 10) we will explore the institutional structure of the international monetary system. The institutional structure is the context within which the foreign exchange market functions. As we shall see, changes in the institutional structure of the international monetary system can exert a profound influence on the development of foreign exchange markets. In Chapter 11 we will look at the recent evolution of global capital markets and discuss the implications of this development for international businesses.

The **foreign exchange market** is a market for converting the currency of one country into that of another country. An **exchange rate** is simply the rate at which one currency is converted into another. We saw in the opening case how Allied-Lyons used the foreign exchange market to convert U.S. dollars into British pounds. Without the foreign exchange market, international trade and international investment on the scale that we see today would be impossible; companies would have to resort to barter. The foreign exchange market is the lubricant that enables companies based in countries that use different currencies to trade with each other.

We know from earlier chapters that international trade and investment have their risks. As the opening case illustrates, some of these risks exist because future exchange rates cannot be perfectly predicted. The rate at which one currency is converted into another typically changes over time. One function of the foreign exchange market is to provide some insurance against the risks that arise from changes in exchange rates, commonly referred to as **foreign exchange risk**. Although the foreign exchange market offers some insurance against foreign exchange risk, it cannot provide complete insurance. Allied-Lyons's loss of $269 million on foreign exchange transactions is an extreme example of what can happen, but it is not at all unusual for international businesses to suffer losses because of unrestricted changes in exchange rates. Currency fluctuations can make seemingly profitable trade and investment deals unprofitable, and vice versa. The opening case contains an example of this as it relates to *trade*. As an example that deals with *investment*, consider the case of Mexico. Between 1976 and 1987, the value of the Mexican peso dropped from 22/U.S. dollar to 1,500/U.S. dollar. As a result of this, a U.S. company with an investment in Mexico that yielded an income of 100 million pesos per year would have seen the dollar value of that income shrink from $4.55 million in 1976 to $66,666 by 1987!

In addition to altering the value of trade deals and foreign investments, currency movements can also open up or shut down export opportunities and alter the attractiveness of imports. In 1984, for example, the U.S. dollar was trading at an all-time high against most other currencies. At that time one dollar could buy one British pound or 550 Japanese yen, compared to 0.55 of a British pound and about 120 yen in early 1992. In the 1984 U.S. presidential campaign, President Reagan boasted about how good the strong dollar was for the United States. Many U.S. companies did not see it that way. Companies like Caterpillar that earned their living by exporting to other countries were being priced out of foreign markets by the strong dollar. In 1980 when the dollar-to-pound exchange rate was $1 = £0.63, a $100,000 Caterpillar earthmover cost a British buyer £63,000. In 1984, with the exchange rate at $1 = £0.99, it cost close to £99,000—a 60 percent increase in four years! At that exchange rate Caterpillar's products were overpriced in comparison to those of its foreign competitors, such as Japan's Komatsu. At the same time, the strong dollar reduced the price of the earthmovers Komatsu imported into the United States, which allowed the Japanese company to take U.S. market share away from Caterpillar.

Thus, as we can see, while the existence of foreign exchange markets is a necessary precondition for large-scale international trade and investment, the movement of exchange rates over time introduces many risks into international trade and investment. Some of these risks can be insured against by using some of the instruments offered by the foreign exchange market; others cannot be.

In this chapter we will examine these issues. We begin by looking at the functions and the form of the foreign exchange market. This includes distinguishing among spot exchanges, forward exchanges, and currency swaps. Then we will consider the factors that determine exchange rates. We will also look at how foreign trade is conducted when a country's currency cannot be exchanged for other currencies; that is, when its currency is not convertible. The chapter closes with a discussion of these things in terms of their implications for business.

THE FUNCTIONS OF THE FOREIGN EXCHANGE MARKET

The foreign exchange market serves two main functions. The first is to convert the currency of one country into the currency of another. The second is to provide some insurance against foreign exchange risk; that is, against the adverse consequences of unpredictable changes in exchange rates. We consider each function in turn.[1]

Currency Conversion

Each country has a currency in which the prices of goods and services are quoted. In the United States it is the dollar ($); in Great Britain, the pound (£); in France, the French franc (FFr); in Germany, the deutsche mark (DM); in Japan, the yen (¥); and so on. In general, within the borders of a particular country one must use the national currency. A U.S. tourist cannot walk into a store in Edinburgh, Scotland, and use U.S. dollars to buy a bottle of Scotch whisky. Dollars are not recognized as legal tender in Scotland; the tourist must use British pounds. Fortunately, the tourist can go to a bank and exchange her dollars for pounds. Then she can buy the whisky.

When a tourist exchanges one currency into another, she is participating in the **foreign exchange market**. The **exchange rate** is at the rate at which the market converts one currency into another. For example, an exchange rate of $1 = ¥120 specifies that 1 U.S. dollar has the equivalent value of 120 Japanese yen. The exchange rate allows us to compare the relative prices of goods and services in different countries. Returning to our example of the U.S. tourist wishing to buy a bottle of Scotch whisky in Edinburgh, she may find that she must pay £25 for the bottle, knowing that the same bottle costs $40 in the United States. So is this a good deal? Imagine the current dollar/pound exchange rate is $1 = £0.50. Our intrepid tourist takes out her calculator and converts £25 into dollars. (The calculation is 25/0.50.) What she finds is that the bottle of Scotch costs the equivalent of $50. She is indeed surprised that a bottle of Scotch whisky could cost less in the United States than in Scotland. (This is actually true; alcohol is taxed heavily in Great Britain.)

Tourists are minor participants in the foreign exchange market; companies engaged in international trade and investment are major ones. There are four main uses of foreign exchange markets to international businesses.

1. The payments a company receives for its exports, the income it receives from foreign investments, or the income it receives from licensing agreements with foreign firms may be in foreign currencies. To use those funds in its home country, the company must convert them to its home country's currency. Consider the Scotch distillery that exports its whisky to the United States. The distillery is paid in dollars, but since those dollars cannot be spent in Great Britain, they must be converted into British pounds.
2. International businesses use foreign exchange markets when they must pay a foreign company for its products or services in its country's currency. For example, our friend Michael runs a company called NST, a large British travel service for school groups. Each year Michael's company arranges vacations for thousands of British school children and their teachers in France. French hotel proprietors demand payment in francs, so Michael must convert large sums of money from pounds into francs in order to pay them.
3. International businesses use foreign exchange markets when they have spare cash that they wish to invest for short terms in money markets. For example, consider a U.S. company that has $10 million it wants to invest for three months. The best

[1] For a good general introduction to the foreign exchange market, see R. Weisweiller, *How the Foreign Exchange Market Works* (New York: New York Institute of Finance, 1990). A detailed description of the economics of foreign exchange markets can be found in P. R. Krugman, and M. Obstfeld, *International Economics: Theory and Policy* (New York: Harper Collins, 1991).

interest rate it can earn on these funds in the United States may be 8 percent. Investing in a French money market account, however, it may be able to earn 12 percent. Thus, the company may change its $10 million into francs and invest it in France. Note, however, that the rate of return it earns on this investment depends not only on the French interest rate; it also depends on the changes in the value of the franc against the dollar in intervening period.

4. Currency speculation is another use of foreign exchange markets. This is the short-term movement of funds from one currency to another in the hopes of profiting from shifts in exchange rates. For illustration, consider again the U.S. company with $10 million to invest for three months. Suppose the company suspects that the U.S. dollar is overvalued against the French franc. That is, the company expects the value of the dollar to *depreciate* against that of the franc. Imagine the current dollar/franc exchange rate is $1 = FFr 6. The company exchanges its $10 million into francs, receiving FFr 60 million. Over the next three months the value of the dollar depreciates until $1 = FFr 5. Now the company exchanges its FFr 60 million back into dollars and finds that it has $12 million. The company has made a $2 million profit on currency speculation in three months on an initial investment of $10 million.

The problem with speculation is that the company cannot know for sure what will happen to exchange rates. Its guess may be correct (the dollar may depreciate against the franc), but it is also possible that the dollar will *appreciate* against the franc. If that happens, the company will lose money. Speculation is a risky game, perhaps one that should be left to professional dealers and bankers. When companies get into speculation, their inexperience can result in some major losses, as illustrated by the opening case.

Insuring against Foreign Exchange Risk

A second function of the foreign exchange market is to provide insurance to protect against the possible adverse consequences of unpredictable changes in exchange rates (foreign exchange risk). To explain how the market performs this function, we must first distinguish among spot exchange rates, forward exchange rates, and currency swaps.

Spot Exchange Rates

When two parties agree to exchange currency and execute the deal immediately, the transaction is referred to as a **spot exchange.** Exchange rates governing such "on the spot" trades are referred to as *spot exchange rates.* The **spot exchange rate** is the rate at which a foreign exchange dealer converts one currency into another currency on a particular day. Thus when our U.S. tourist in Edinburgh goes to a bank to convert her dollars into pounds, the exchange rate is the spot rate for that day.

Although it is necessary to use a spot rate to execute a transaction immediately, it may not be the most attractive rate. To understand why this is so, it is necessary to realize that exchange rates can change constantly. The value of a currency is determined by the interaction between the demand and supply of that currency relative to the demand and supply of other currencies. For example, if lots of people want U.S. dollars and dollars are in short supply, and few people want French francs and francs are in plentiful supply, it is a sure bet that the spot exchange rate for converting dollars into francs will change. The dollar is likely to appreciate against the franc (or, conversely the franc will depreciate against the dollar). As an illustration, imagine the spot exchange rate is $1 = FFr 5 when the market opens. As the day progresses, dealers demand more dollars and fewer francs. By the end of the day the spot exchange rate might be $1 = FFr 5.3. The dollar has appreciated, and the franc has depreciated.

Forward Exchange Rates

The fact that spot exchange rates change daily as determined by the relative demand and supply for different currencies can be problematic for an international business. One example was given in the opening case; here is another. A U.S. company that imports laptop computers from Japan knows that in 30 days it must pay yen to a Japanese supplier when a shipment arrives. The company will pay the Japanese supplier ¥200,000 for each laptop computer, and the current dollar/yen spot exchange rate is $1 = ¥120. At this rate, each computer costs the importer $1,667 (i.e., 1667 = 200,000/120). The importer knows she can sell the computers the day they arrive for $2,000 each, which yields a gross profit of $333 on each computer ($2,000 − $1667). However, the importer will not have the funds to pay the Japanese supplier until the computers have been sold. If over the next 30 days the dollar unexpectedly depreciates against the yen, say to $1 = ¥95, the importer will still have to pay the Japanese company ¥200,000 per computer, but in dollar terms that would be equivalent $2,105 per computer—which is more than she can sell the computers for. In other words, a depreciation in the value of the dollar against the yen from $1 = ¥120 to $1 = ¥95 would transform a profitable deal into an unprofitable one.

To avoid the risk of this occurring, the U.S. importer might want to engage in a forward exchange. A **forward exchange** occurs when two parties agree to exchange currency and execute the deal at some specific date in the future. Exchange rates governing such future transactions are referred to as **forward exchange rates.** For most major currencies, forward exchange rates are quoted for 30 days, 90 days, and 180 days into the future. (An example of exchange rate quotations appears in Table 9.1.) In some cases, it is possible to get forward exchange rates for several years into the future. Returning to our example let us assume the 30-day forward exchange rate for converting dollars into yen is $1 = ¥110. The importer enters into a 30-day forward exchange transaction with a foreign exchange dealer at this rate and is guaranteed that she will have to pay no more than $1,818 for each computer (1,818 = 200,000/110). This guarantees her a profit of $182 per computer ($2,000 − $1,818). Moreover, she insures herself against the possibility that an unanticipated change in the dollar/yen exchange rate will turn a profitable deal into an unprofitable one.

In this example the spot exchange rate ($1 = ¥120) and the 30-day forward rate ($1 = ¥110) differ. Such differences are normal; they reflect the expectations of the foreign exchange market about future currency movements. In our example, the fact that $1 bought more yen with a spot exchange than with a 30-day forward exchange indicates that foreign exchange dealers expected the dollar to depreciate against the yen in the next 30 days. When this occurs we say the dollar is selling at a **discount** on the 30-day forward market (i.e., it is worth less than on the spot market). Of course, the opposite can also occur. If the 30-day forward exchange rate were $1 = ¥130, for example, $1 would buy more yen with a forward exchange than with a spot exchange. In such a case, we say the dollar is selling at a **premium** on the 30-day forward market. This reflects the foreign exchange dealers' expectations that the dollar will appreciate against the yen over the next 30 days.

Table 9.1
Foreign Exchange Quotations

EXCHANGE RATES

Monday, January 11, 1993

The New York foreign exchange selling rates below apply to trading among banks in amounts of $1 million and more, as quoted at 3 p.m. Eastern time by Bankers Trust Co., Telerate and other sources. Retail transactions provide fewer units of foreign currency per dollar.

	U.S. $ equiv.		**Currency per U.S. $**	
Country	**Mon.**	**Fri.**	**Mon.**	**Fri.**
Argentina (Peso)	1.01	1.01	.99	.99
Australia (Dollar)	.6735	.6728	1.4848	1.4863
Austria (Schilling)	.08709	.08640	11.48	11.57
Bahrain (Dinar)	2.6522	2.6522	.3771	.3771
Belgium (Franc)	.02977	.02955	33.59	33.84
Brazil (Cruzeiro)	.0000693	.0000795	14435.01	12584.01
Britain (Pound)	1.5555	1.5325	.6429	.6525
30-Day Forward	1.5495	1.5272	.6454	.6548
90-Day Forward	1.5409	1.5181	.6490	.6587
180-Day Forward	1.5298	1.5075	.6537	.6633
Canada (Dollar)	.7828	.7798	1.2775	1.2823
30-Day Forward	.7803	.7774	1.2816	1.2864
90-Day Forward	.7761	.7729	1.2885	1.2938
180-Day Forward	.7703	.7620	1.2982	1.3123
Czechoslovakia (Koruna)				
Commercial rate	.0349650	.0350754	28.6000	28.5100
Chile (Peso)	.002688	.002689	372.08	371.82
China (Renminbi)	.171233	.171233	5.8400	5.8400
Colombia (Peso)	.001607	.001612	622.20	620.50
Denmark (Krone)	.1586	.1573	6.3054	6.3563
Ecuador (Sucre)				
Floating rate	.000552	.000554	1812.02	1806.00
Finland (Markka)	.18399	.18214	5.4352	5.4902
France (Franc)	.18041	.17873	5.5430	5.5950
30-Day Forward	.17892	.17742	5.5892	5.6365
90-Day Forward	.17667	.17510	5.6602	5.7110
180-Day Forward	.17417	.17279	5.7415	5.7875
Germany (Mark)	.6130	.6079	1.6312	1.6450
30-Day Forward	.6099	.6051	1.6397	1.6526
90-Day Forward	.6054	.6004	1.6518	1.6656
180-Day Forward	.5994	.5948	1.6683	1.6813
Greece (Drachma)	.004579	.004551	218.40	219.75
Hong Kong (Dollar)	.12919	.12916	7.7406	7.7425
Hungary (Forint)	.0120351	.0120700	83.0900	82.8500
India (Rupee)	.03484	.03482	28.70	28.72
Indonesia (Rupiah)	.0004854	.0004843	2060.03	2065.00
Ireland (Punt)	1.6230	1.5970	.6161	.6262
Israel (Shekel)	.3577	.3659	2.7960	2.7328
Italy (Lira)	.0006752	.0006626	1481.13	1509.30

Currency Swaps

The above discussion of spot and forward exchange rates might lead you to conclude that the option to buy forward is very important to companies engaged in international trade—and you would be right. But take a look at Figure 9.1, which shows the nature of foreign exchange transactions in April 1992 for a sample of U.S. banks surveyed by the Federal Reserve Board. What we see is that the majority (49 percent) of foreign exchange transactions were spot exchanges, followed by "swaps" (30 percent). Forward exchanges accounted for only 7 percent of all foreign exchange transactions that month. Does this

Country	U.S. $ equiv. Mon.	Fri.	Currency per U.S. $ Mon.	Fri.
Japan (Yen)	.007993	.007974	125.11	125.40
30-Day Forward	.007989	.007971	125.18	125.46
90-Day Forward	.007987	.007968	125.21	125.49
180-Day Forward	.007990	.007974	125.16	125.41
Jordan (Dinar)	1.4810	1.4789	.6752	.6762
Kuwait (Dinar)	3.2857	3.2927	.3044	.3037
Lebanon (Pound)	.000547	.000544	1828.00	1838.00
Malaysia (Ringgit)	.3855	.3851	2.5937	2.5970
Malta (Lira)	2.6918	2.6525	.3715	.3770
Mexico (Peso)				
Floating rate	.3211819	.3206156	3.11	3.12
Netherland (Guilder)	.5454	.5410	1.8335	1.8486
New Zealand (Dollar)	.5132	.5103	1.9486	1.9596
Norway (Krone)	.1432	.1422	6.9840	7.0299
Pakistan (Rupee)	.0388	.0390	25.75	25.62
Peru (New Sol)	.6216	.6235	1.61	1.60
Philippines (Peso)	.04057	.04082	24.65	24.50
Poland (Zloty)	.00006546	.00006550	15276.00	15268.01
Portugal (Escudo)	.006842	.006770	146.16	147.72
Saudi Arabia (Riyal)	.26663	.26665	3.7505	3.7503
Singapore (Dollar)	.6028	.6015	1.6588	1.6625
South Africa (Rand)				
Commercial rate	.3259	.3235	3.0688	3.0913
Financial rate	.2058	.2045	4.8600	4.8900
South Korea (Won)	.0012618	.0012628	792.50	791.90
Spain (Peseta)	.008628	.008561	115.90	116.81
Sweden (Krona)	.1355	.1345	7.3812	7.4354
Switzerland (Franc)	.6714	.6667	1.4895	1.5000
30-Day Forward	.6698	.6652	1.4930	1.5032
90-Day Forward	.6674	.6627	1.4984	1.5090
180-Day Forward	.6648	.6603	1.5042	1.5145
Taiwan (Dollar)	.039321	.039746	25.43	25.16
Thailand (Baht)	.03914	.03917	25.55	25.53
Turkey (Lira)	.0001162	.0001157	8606.00	8645.06
United Arab (Dirham)	.2723	.2723	3.6725	3.6725
Uruguay (New Peso)				
Financial	.000277	.000277	3604.01	3611.00
Venezuela (Bolivar)				
Floating rate	.01267	.01269	78.90	78.78
SDR	1.37260	1.36664	.72854	.73172
ECU	1.20600	1.19180	....	....

Special Drawing Rights (SDR) are based on exchange rates for the U.S., German, British, French and Japanese currencies. Source: International Monetary Fund.

European Currency Unit (ECU) is based on a basket of community currencies.

Source: The Wall Street Journal, *January 12, 1993, p. C16.*

mean forward exchanges are not very important? Actually it does not, because swaps are a sophisticated kind of forward exchange.

A **swap** is the simultaneous purchase and sale of a given amount of foreign exchange for two different value dates. Swaps are transacted between international businesses and their banks, between banks, and between governments when it is desirable to move out of one currency into another for a limited period without incurring foreign exchange risk. A common kind of swap is **spot against forward.** As an illustration of how this works, consider a company such as Apple Computer. Apple assembles laptop computers in the

Figure 9.1
Foreign Exchange Transactions, April 1992

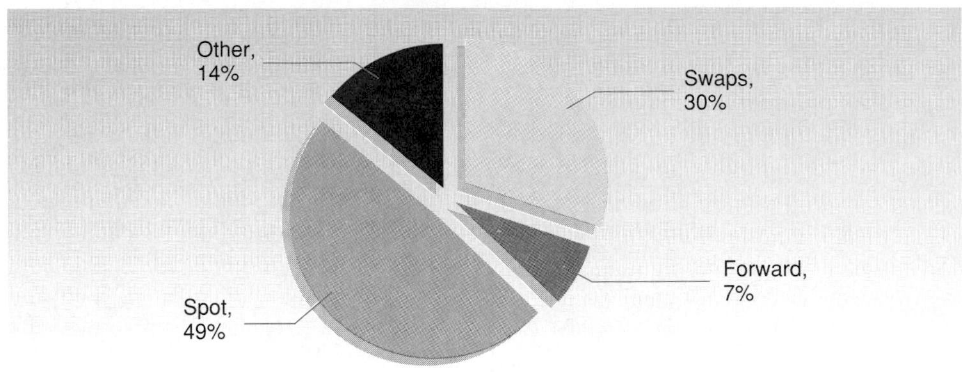

Source: Summary of Results of U.S. Foreign Exchange Market Survey conducted April 1992 (New York: Federal Reserve Bank of New York, 1992).

United States, the screens for which are made in Japan. Apple also sells some of the finished laptops in Japan. So, like many companies, Apple both buys from and sells to Japan. Imagine Apple needs to change $1 million into yen in order to pay its supplier of laptop screens today. Apple knows that in 90 days it will be paid ¥120 million by the Japanese importer that buys its finished laptops. It will want to convert these yen into dollars for use in the United States. Let us say today's spot exchange rate is $1 = ¥120 and the 90-day forward exchange rate is $1 = ¥110. Apple sells $1 million to its bank in return for ¥120 million. Now Apple can pay its Japanese supplier. At the same time, Apple enters into a 90-day forward exchange deal with its bank for converting ¥120 million into dollars. Thus, in 90 days Apple will receive $1.09 million (¥120 million/110 = $1.09 million). Since the yen is trading at a premium on the 90-day forward market, Apple ends up with more dollars than it started with (although the opposite could just as well occur). In any event, the swap deal is just like a conventional forward deal in one important respect: it enables Apple to insure itself against foreign exchange risk. By engaging in a swap, Apple knows today that the ¥120 million payment it will receive in 90 days will yield $1.09 million.

THE NATURE OF THE FOREIGN EXCHANGE MARKET

So far we have dealt with the foreign exchange market only as an abstract concept. It is now time to take a closer look at the nature of this market. The first point to note is that the foreign exchange market is not located in any one place. Rather, it is a global network of banks, brokers, and foreign exchange dealers connected by electronic communications systems. When companies wish to convert currencies, they typically go through their own banks rather than entering the market directly themselves. In recent years the foreign exchange market has been growing at a rapid pace, reflecting a general growth in the volume of cross-border trade and investment (see Chapter 1). In March 1986, for example, the average total value of global foreign exchange trading was in the neighborhood of $200 billion per day. By April 1989 it had soared to over $650 billion per day, and by April 1992 it was close to $1,000 billion per day.[2] The most important trading

[2] *Summary of Results of U.S. Foreign Exchange Market Turnover Survey Conducted April 1989* (New York: Federal Reserve Bank of New York, 1989); and A. Meyerson, "Currency Markets Resisting Power of Central Banks," *The New York Times*, September 25, 1992, pp. Al, C15.

Figure 9.2
Share of Global Foreign Exchange Trading accounted for by London, New York, and Tokyo

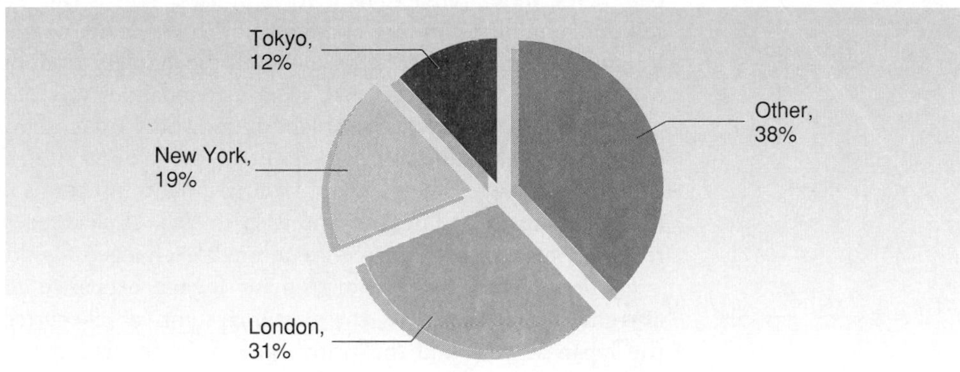

Source: Summary of Results of U.S. Foreign Exchange Market Survey Conducted April 1992 (New York: Federal Reserve Bank of New York, 1992).

centers are London, New York, and Tokyo. In April 1992, $303 billion was traded through London each day, $192 billion through New York, and $128 billion through Tokyo (see Figure 9.2). Important secondary trading centers are Zurich, Frankfurt, Paris, Hong Kong, Singapore, San Francisco, and Sydney.

London's dominance in the foreign exchange market is due to both history and geography. As the capital of the world's first major industrial trading nation, London had become the world's largest center for international banking by the end of the last century, a position it has retained. Today London also has an advantageous location; its central position between Tokyo to the east and New York to the west has made it the critical link between the Tokyo and New York markets. Due to the particular differences in time zones, London opens as Tokyo shuts down for the night and is still open for the first few hours of trading in New York.

Two features of the foreign exchange market are of particular note. The first is that the market never sleeps. There are only 3 hours out of every 24 that Tokyo, London, and New York are all shut down. During these three hours, trading continues in a number of minor centers, particularly San Francisco and Sydney, Australia.

The second feature of the market is the extent of integration of the various trading centers. Direct telephone lines, fax, and computer linkages between trading centers around the globe have effectively created a single market. The integration of financial centers implies there can be no significant difference in exchange rates quoted in the trading centers. For example, if the dollar/franc exchange rate quoted in London at 3 P.M. is $1 = FFr 5.0, the dollar/franc exchange rate quoted in New York at the same time (9 A.M. New York time) will be identical. If the New York dollar/franc exchange rate were $1 = FFr 5.5, a dealer could make a profit through **arbitrage,** the process of buying a currency low and selling it high. For example, if the prices differed in London and New York as given, a dealer could purchase FFr 550,000 for $100,000 in New York and immediately sell them in London for $110,000, making a quick profit of $10,000. If all dealers tried to cash in on the opportunity, however, the demand for francs in New York would result in an appreciation of the franc against the dollar, while the increase in the supply of francs in London would result in their depreciation there. Very quickly, the discrepancy in the New York and London exchange rates would disappear. Since foreign exchange dealers are continually watching their computer screens for arbitrage opportunities, the few that arise tend to be small, and they disappear in minutes.

Another feature of the foreign exchange market is the important role played by the U.S. dollar. Although a foreign exchange transaction can in theory involve any two currencies, most transactions involve dollars. This is true even when a dealer wants to sell one nondollar currency and buy another. A dealer wishing to sell Dutch guilders for Italian lira, for example, will usually sell the guilders for dollars and then use the dollars to buy lira. Although this may seem a roundabout way of doing things, it is actually cheaper than trying to find a holder of lira who wants to buy guilders. The advantage of trading through the dollar is a result of the United States' importance in the world economy. Because the volume of international transactions involving dollars is so great, it is not hard to find dealers who wish to trade dollars for guilders or lira. In contrast, relatively few transactions require a direct exchange of guilders for lira.

Due to its central role in so many foreign exchange deals, the dollar is a **vehicle currency.** After the dollar, the most important vehicle currencies are the German mark, the Japanese yen, and the British pound—reflecting the importance of these trading nations in the world economy. The British pound used to be second in importance to the dollar as a vehicle currency, but its importance has diminished in recent years.

ECONOMIC THEORIES OF EXCHANGE RATE DETERMINATION

At the most basic level, exchange rates are determined by the demand and supply of one currency relative to the demand and supply of another. For example, if the demand for dollars outstrips the supply of them and if the supply of German deutsche marks is greater than the demand for them, the dollar/mark exchange rate will change. More precisely, the dollar will appreciate against the mark (or, alternatively, the mark will depreciate against the dollar). However, while differences in relative demand and supply explain the determination of exchange rates, they do so only in a superficial sense. This simple explanation does not tell us what factors underlie the demand for and supply of a currency. Nor does it tell us when the demand for dollars will exceed the supply (and vice versa) or when the supply of German marks will exceed demand for them (and vice versa). Neither does it tell us under what conditions a currency is in demand or under what conditions it is not demanded. In this section we will review economic theory's answers to these questions. This will give us a deeper understanding of how exchange rates are determined.

If we understand how exchange rates are determined, we may be able to forecast exchange rate movements. Since future exchange rate movements influence export opportunities, the profitability of international trade and investment deals, and the price competitiveness of foreign imports, this is valuable information for an international business to have. Unfortunately, there is no simple explanation here. The forces that determine exchange rates are complex, and no theoretical consensus exists, even among academic economists who study the phenomenon every day. Nonetheless, most economic theories of exchange rate movements seem to agree that two things are important predictors of future exchange rate movements in a country's currency: the country's price inflation and its interest rate.

Prices and Exchange Rates

To understand how prices are related to exchange rate movements, we first need to discuss an economic proposition known as the *law of one price.* Then we will discuss the theory of purchasing power parity (PPP), which links changes in the exchange rate between two countries' currencies to changes in the countries' price levels.

The Law of One Price

The **law of one price** states that in competitive markets *free of transportation costs and barriers to trade* (such as tariffs), identical products sold in different countries must sell for the same price when their price is expressed in terms of the same currency.[3] For example, if the exchange rate between the dollar and the French franc is $1 = FFr 5, a jacket that retails for $50 in New York should retail for FFr 250 (50 × 5) in Paris. To see why this must be so, consider what would happen if the jacket cost FFr 300 in Paris ($60 in U.S. currency). At this price, it would pay a company to buy jackets in New York and sell them in Paris (an example of arbitrage). Initially the company could make a profit of $10 on each jacket by purchasing them for $50 in New York and selling them for FFr 300 in Paris. (Remember we are assuming away transportation costs and trade barriers.) However, the increased demand for jackets in New York would raise their price in New York, and the increased supply of jackets in Paris would lower their price there. This would continue until prices were equalized. Thus prices might equalize when the jacket cost $55 in New York and FFr 275 in Paris (assuming no change in the exchange rate of $1 = FFr 5).

Purchasing Power Parity

If the law of one price were true for all goods and services, the **purchasing power parity (PPP)** exchange rate could be found from any individual set of prices. By comparing the prices of identical products in different currencies, it would be possible to determine the "real" or PPP exchange rate that would exist if markets were efficient. (An "efficient" market has no impediments to the free flow of goods and services—such as trade barriers.) The "hamburger standard," as christened by *The Economist*, illustrates the law of one price and PPP exchange rates (see Box 9.1).

A less extreme version of the PPP theory states that given "relatively efficient" markets (markets in which few impediments to international trade and investment exist), the price of a "basket of goods" should be roughly equivalent in each country. To express the PPP theory in symbols, let $P_\$$ be the U.S. dollar price of a basket of particular goods and P_{DM} be the price of the same basket of goods in German deutsche marks. The PPP theory predicts that the dollar/DM exchange rate should be equivalent to:

$$\$/\text{DM exchange rate} = P_\$/P_{DM}$$

Thus if a basket of goods costs $200 in the United States and DM 600 in Germany, PPP theory predicts that the dollar/DM exchange rate should be $0.33 per DM (i.e., $1 = DM 3).

The next step in the PPP theory is to argue that the exchange rate will change if relative prices change. For example, imagine there is no price inflation in the United States, while prices in Germany are increasing by 20 percent a year. At the beginning of the year, a basket of goods costs $200 in the United States and DM 600 in Germany, so the dollar/DM exchange rate, according to PPP theory, should be $0.33 = DM 1. At the end of the year, the basket of goods still costs $200 in the United States, but it costs DM 720 in Germany. PPP theory predicts that the exchange rate should change as a result. More precisely, by the end of the year, $0.27 = DM 1 (i.e., $1 = DM 3.6). Due to the effects of price inflation, the DM has depreciated against the dollar. One dollar should buy more marks at the end of the year than at the beginning.

Money Supply and Price Inflation

PPP theory predicts that changes in relative prices will result in a change in exchange rates. Theoretically, a country in which price inflation is running wild should expect to

[3] P. R. Krugman and M. Obstfeld, *International Economics: Theory and Policy* (New York: HarperCollins, 1991), p. 380.

The Hamburger Standard

The Economist's Big Mac index was first launched in 1986 as a ready reckoner to whether currencies are at their "correct" exchange rate. It is time for our annual update.

The case for munching our way around the globe on Big Macs is based on the theory of purchasing power parity. This argues that the exchange rate between two currencies is in equilibrium when it equalizes the prices of an identical basket of goods and services in both countries. Advocates of PPP argue that in the long run currencies tend to move toward their PPP.

Our basket is simply a Big Mac, one of the few products that is produced locally in a great many countries. Many of our readers ask why we do not simply derive our PPP from different cover prices of *The Economist*. But because the magazine is not printed in every country, local prices would be distorted by transport and distribution costs.

The Big Mac PPP is the exchange rate that leaves hamburgers costing the same in each country. Comparing the current exchange rate with its PPP gives a measure of whether a currency is under- or overvalued.

For example, the average price of a Big Mac in four American cities is $2.19. In Japan our Big Mac watcher had to fork out ¥380 ($2.86) for the same gastronomic delight. Dividing the yen price by the dollar price gives a Big Mac PPP of $1 = ¥174. On April 10th the actual dollar exchange rate was ¥133, which implies that on PPP grounds the dollar is 24 percent undervalued against the yen.

On similar sums, the dollar is 20 percent undervalued against the D-mark, with an estimated PPP of DM 2.05. The dollar has moved further away from its PPP over the past year: in April 1991 it was undervalued by only 13 percent. How can the dollar have become more undervalued when its actual exchange rate has barely budged? The answer lies in price movements. Big Mac prices have fallen by an average of 3 percent in America over the past 12 months; in Germany they have risen by 5 percent.

As the table shows, the dollar seems to be undervalued against most currencies. The exceptions are the currencies of countries where Big Macs cost less in dollars than in America: the Australian dollar, the Brazilian cruzeiro, the Chinese yuan, the Hong Kong dollar, the Hungarian forint, and last, but by no means least, the

The Dollar: Trade-Weighted Exchange Rate

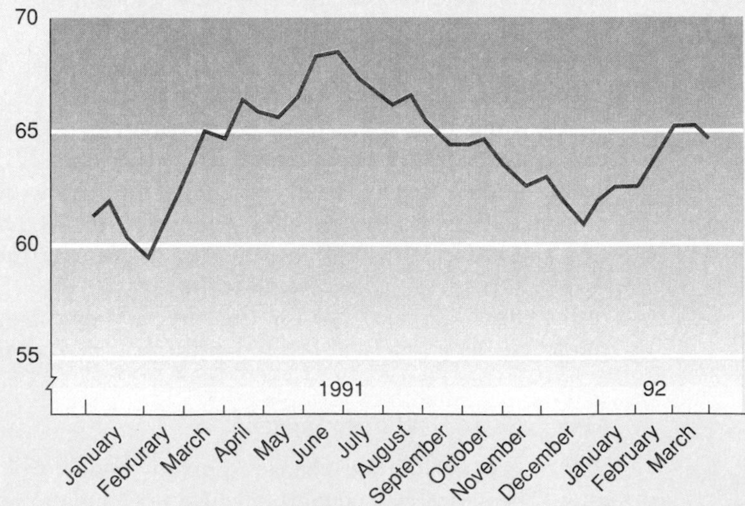

Big Mac Prices Country	Prices* in Local Currency	Implied ppp† of the Dollar	Actual Exchange Rate 10/4/92	% over(+) or Under(−) Valuation of Dollar
Argentina	Peso3.30	1.51	0.99	−34
Australia	A$2.54	1.16	1.31	+13
Belgium	BFr108	49.32	33.55	−32
Brazil	Cr3,800	1,735	2,153	+24
Britain	£1.74	0.79	0.57	−28
Canada	C$2.76	1.26	1.19	−6
China	Yuan6.30	2.88	5.44	+89
Denmark	DKr27.25	12.44	6.32	−49
France	FFr18.10	8.26	5.55	−33
Germany	DM4.50	2.05	1.64	−20
Holland	Fl5.35	2.44	1.84	−24
Hong Kong	HK$8.90	4.06	7.73	+91
Hungary	Forint133	60.73	79.70	+31
Ireland	I£1.45	0.66	0.61	−8
Italy	Lire4,100	1872	1,233	−34
Japan	¥380	174	133	−24
Russia	Ruble58	26.48	98.95‡	+273
Singapore	S$4.75	2.17	1.65	−24
S.Korea	Won2,300	1,050	778	−26
Spain	Ptas315	144	102	−29
Sweden	SKr25.50	11.64	5.93	−49
United States	$2.19	—	—	—
Venezuela	Bs170	77.63	60.63	−22

*Source: McDonald's * prices may vary locally, † Purchasing power parity: local price divided by dollar price, ‡ Market rate, New York, Chicago, San Francisco, and Atlanta.*

ruble. Moscow is the best place for burger-bargain hunters: a Big Mac costs only 59 cents at the market exchange rate. In other words, the ruble is undervalued by 73 percent against the dollar.

The message, therefore, is that the greenback should rise in the future. But when? Exchange rates can deviate significantly from PPP for long periods.

Yet other economic fundamentals now seem to point in the same direction. Most currency watchers expect interest rates to rise in America over the next 12 months as the economy picks up steam. Germany's interest rates may fall as its economy continues to stall. If so, interest rate differentials will move in favor of the dollar, and the greenback will rise. It has already gained almost 10 percent against the yen and the D-mark since January, and most forecasters are betting it will climb further this year.

The snag is that forecasters used the same arguments about relative interest rates a year ago, and that expectation helped to push the dollar up by 27 percent against the D-mark in the five months to July. As America's recovery faltered, the Fed cut interest rates again, and inflation fears caused Germany's Bundesbank to raise its rates further. The dollar slid, to end the year little higher than it began.

Forecasts of a firmer dollar are therefore only as firm as forecasts of economic recovery. Wise investors will not hold their breath—and will grab those cut-price Big Macs while they can.

Source: The Economist, *April 18, 1992, p. 81.*

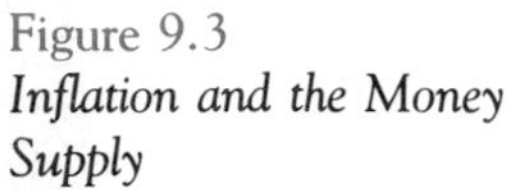

Figure 9.3
Inflation and the Money Supply

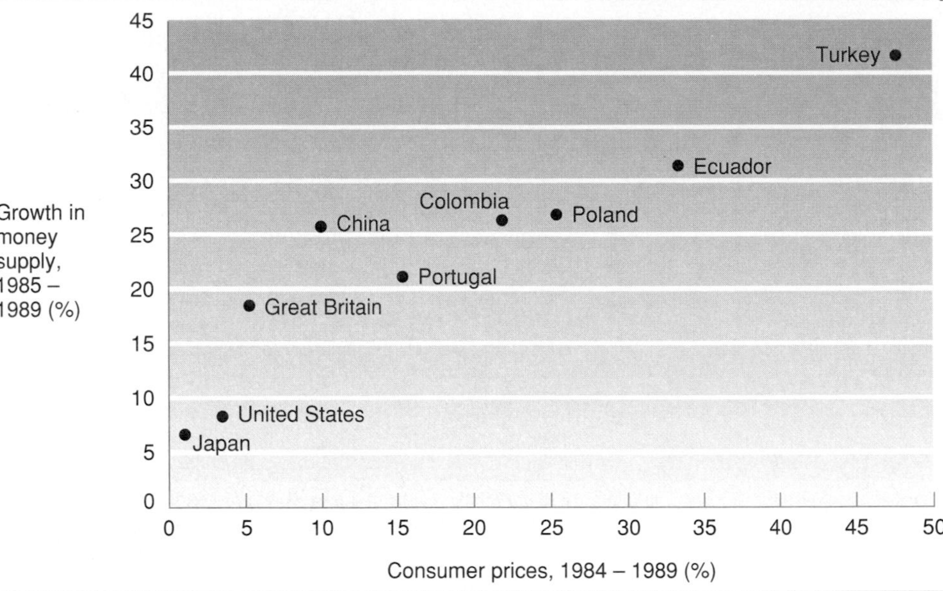

Source: The Economist Book of Vital World Statistics (*New York: Random House, 1990*).

see its currency depreciate against that of countries in which inflation rates are lower. This is all well and good, but unless we can predict the likely future inflation rates of different countries, it may be of little use in forecasting exchange rate movements. As it turns out, however, there is a way to predict a country's likely inflation rate. Specifically, the growth rate of a country's money supply and its inflation rate are closely correlated.[4] Inflation is a monetary phenomenon. Inflation occurs when the quantity of money in circulation rises faster than the stock of goods and services; that is, when the money supply increases faster than output increases. The reason for this is relatively straightforward. Imagine what would happen if everyone in the country was suddenly given $10,000 by the government. Many people would rush out to spend their extra money on those things they had always wanted—new cars, new furniture, better clothes, and so on. There would be a surge in demand for goods and services. How would car dealers, department stores, and other providers of goods and services respond to this upsurge in demand? They would do what any sensible businessperson would do—raise prices. The result would be price inflation.

A government increasing the money supply is analogous to giving people more money. An increase in the money supply makes it easier for banks to borrow from the government and for individuals and companies to borrow from banks. The resulting increase in credit causes increases in demand for goods and services. Unless the output of goods and services is growing at a rate similar to that of the money supply, the result will be inflation. This relationship has been observed time after time in country after country. Figure 9.3 for example, shows the relationship between the growth in money supply and the rate of inflation in consumer prices between 1984 and 1989 for a sample of countries. Although there is not a perfect one-to-one relationship, it is clear from Figure 9.3 that countries with higher rates of growth in money supply had higher inflation rates.

So now we have a connection between the growth in a country's money supply, price inflation, and exchange rate movements. Put simply, when the growth in a country's

[4] M. Friedman, *Studies in the Quantity Theory of Money* (Chicago: University of Chicago Press, 1956). For an accessible explanation, see M. Friedman and R. Friedman, *Free to Choose* (London: Penguin Books, 1979), chap. 9.

BOX 9.2

Money Supply Growth, Inflation, and Exchange Rates in Bolivia

In the mid-1980s Bolivia experienced hyperinflation—an explosive and seemingly uncontrollable price inflation in which money loses value very rapidly. The table presents data on Bolivia's money supply, inflation rate, and its peso's exchange rate with the U.S. dollar during the period of hyperinflation. The exchange rate is actually the "black market" exchange rate, as the Bolivian government prohibited converting the peso to other currencies during the period. The data shows that the growth in money supply, the rate of price inflation, and the depreciation of the peso against the dollar all moved in step with each other. This is just what PPP theory and monetary economics predict. Between April 1984 and July 1985, Bolivia's money supply increased by 17,433 percent, prices increased by 22,908 percent, and the value of the peso against the dollar fell by 24,662 percent! In October 1985 the Bolivian government instituted a dramatic stabilization plan—which included the introduction of a new currency and tight control of the money supply—and by 1987 the country's inflation rate was down to 16 percent per annum.

Macroeconomic Data for Bolivia, April 1984–October 1985

Month	Money Supply (billions of pesos)	Price Level relative to 1982 (average = 1)	Exchange Rate (pesos per dollar)
1984			
April	270	21.1	3,576
May	330	31.1	3,512
June	440	32.3	3,342
July	599	34.0	3,570
August	718	39.1	7,038
September	889	53.7	13,685
October	1,194	85.5	15,205
November	1,495	112.4	18,469
December	3,296	180.9	24,515
1985			
January	4,630	305.3	73,016
February	6,455	863.3	141,101
March	9,089	1,078.6	128,137
April	12,885	1,205.7	167,428
May	21,309	1,635.7	272,375
June	27,778	2,919.1	481,756
July	47,341	4,854.6	885,476
August	74,306	8,081.0	1,182,300
September	103,272	12,647.6	1,087,440
October	132,550	12,411.8	1,120,210

Source: Juan-Antino Morales, "Inflation Stabilization in Bolivia," in Inflation Stabilization: The Experience of Israel, Argentina, Brazil, Bolivia, and Mexico, *ed. Michael Bruno et al. (Cambridge, Mass.: MIT Press, 1988).*

money supply is faster than the growth in its output, price inflation is fueled. In turn, the PPP theory tells us that a country with a high inflation rate will see a depreciation in its currency exchange rate. A detailed example of how this can play out in practice is given in Box 9.2.

Another way of looking at the same phenomenon is that an increase in a country's money supply—which increases the amount of currency available—changes the relative demand and supply conditions in the foreign exchange market. If the U.S. money supply is growing more rapidly than U.S. output, dollars will be relatively more plentiful than the currencies of countries where monetary growth is closer to output growth. As a result of this relative increase in supply of dollars, the dollar will depreciate on the foreign exchange market against the currencies of countries with slower monetary growth.

The only remaining question is, what determines whether the rate of growth in a country's money supply is greater than the rate of growth in output? The answer is government policy. Governments generally have significant control over the money supply. A government can increase the money supply simply by telling the country's central bank to print more money. Governments tend to do this to finance public expenditure (building roads, paying government workers, paying for defense, etc.). Of course, a government could finance public expenditure by raising taxes, but since nobody likes paying more taxes and since politicians do not like to be unpopular, they have a natural preference for printing money. Unfortunately, there is no magic money tree. The inevitable result of excessive growth in money supply is price inflation. However, this has not stopped governments around the world from printing money, with predictable results. In short, if an international business is attempting to predict future movements in the value of a country's currency on the foreign exchange market, it should examine that country's government's policy toward monetary growth. If the government seems committed to controlling the rate of growth in money supply, the country's future inflation rate may be low (even if the current rate is high) and its currency should not depreciate too much on the foreign exchange market. On the other hand, if the country's government seems to lack the political will to control the rate of growth in money supply, the future inflation rate may be high, which is likely to cause its currency to depreciate. Historically, many Latin American governments have fallen into this latter category, including Argentina, Bolivia, and Brazil. (The case of Bolivia is discussed in Box 9.2.) More recently, there are signs that many of the newly democratic states of Eastern Europe might be making the same mistake.

Empirical Tests of PPP Theory

PPP theory predicts that changes in relative prices will result in a change in exchange rates. A country in which price inflation is running wild should expect to see its currency depreciate against that of countries with lower inflation rates. This is intuitively appealing, but is it true in practice? There are certainly several good examples of the connection between a country's price inflation and exchange rate position (see Box 9.2). Some evidence of this connection can be seen in Figure 9.4. This figure compares a country's average annual inflation rate between 1984 and 1989 against the percentage decline in the rate at which its currency could be converted into dollars over the same time period. The figure clearly shows that currencies of countries with much higher inflation rates than the United States (e.g., Mexico, Uruguay, Colombia) depreciated sharply against the U.S. dollar. This corroborates the predictions of PPP theory. On the other hand, the figure also suggests that the relationship between inflation rates and exchange rates is not absolute. Italy, for example, had marginally higher inflation than the United States for the period, and yet its currency *appreciated* against the dollar by close to 60 percent! According to PPP theory, its currency should have depreciated.

There has been extensive empirical testing of the PPP theory, and in general, the tests have not shown it to be completely accurate in estimating exchange rate changes.[5]

---

[5] For a review see L. H. Officer, "The Purchasing Parity Theory of Exchange Rates: A Review Article," *International Monetary Fund Staff Papers,* March 1976, pp. 1–60.

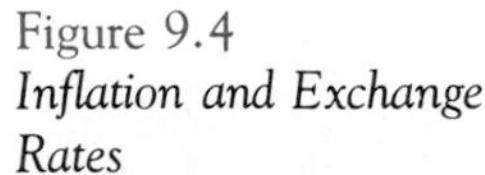

Figure 9.4
Inflation and Exchange Rates

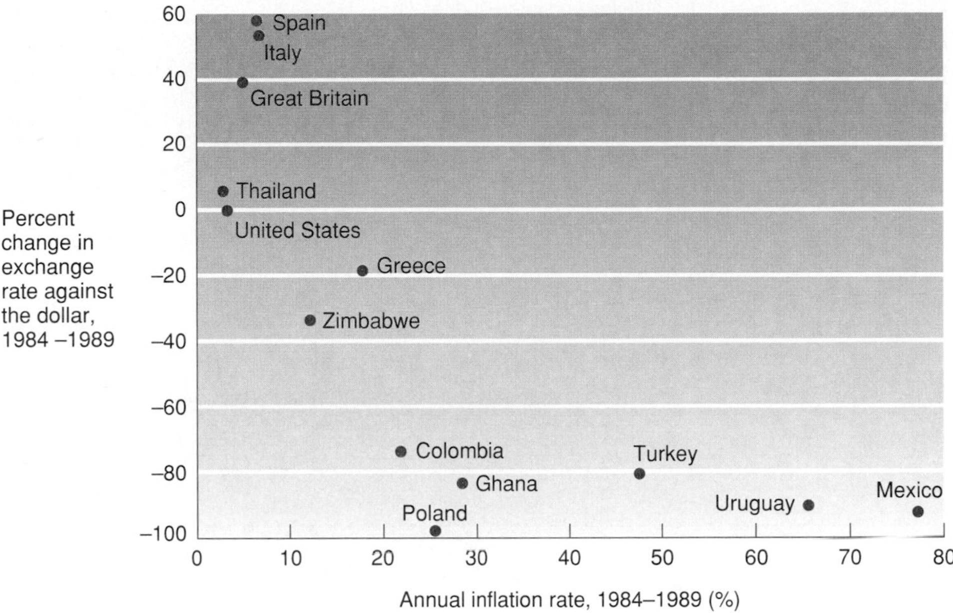

While the PPP theory seems to yield relatively accurate predictions in the *long run* (i.e., over several years), it does not hold up in the short run. Moreover, the theory seems to best predict exchange rate changes for countries with very high rates of inflation and underdeveloped capital markets (e.g., Colombia, Poland, and Mexico; again see Figure 9.4). As suggested by Figure 9.4, PPP theory is less useful in predicting exchange rate movements between the currencies of advanced industrialized nations that have relatively small differentials in inflation rates (e.g., the United States and Italy).

Several things may explain the failure of PPP theory to predict exchange rates more accurately. The PPP theory assumes away transportation costs and barriers to trade and investment. In practice, these factors are significant and they tend to create price differentials between countries. As we saw in Chapters 5 and 7, governments routinely intervene in international trade and investment. Such intervention, by violating the assumption of efficient markets, weakens the link between relative price changes and changes in exchange rates predicted by PPP theory. Another factor of some importance is that governments also intervene in the foreign exchange market in attempting to influence the value of their currencies. We will look at why and how they do this in Chapter 10. For now, the important thing to note is that governments regularly intervene in the foreign exchange market, and this further weakens the link between price changes and changes in exchange rates.

Interest Rates and Exchange Rates

Economic theory tells us that interest rates reflect expectations about likely future inflation rates. In countries where inflation is expected to be high, interest rates also will be high, because investors want compensation for the decline in the value of their money. This relationship was first formalized by economist Irvin Fisher and is thus referred to as the **Fisher effect.** The Fisher effect states that a country's "nominal" interest rate (i) is the sum of the required "real" rate of interest (r) and the *expected* rate of inflation over the period of time for which the funds are to be lent (I). More formally,

$$i = r + I$$

Figure 9.5
Inflation and Interest Rates in Switzerland, the United States, and Italy, 1965–1989

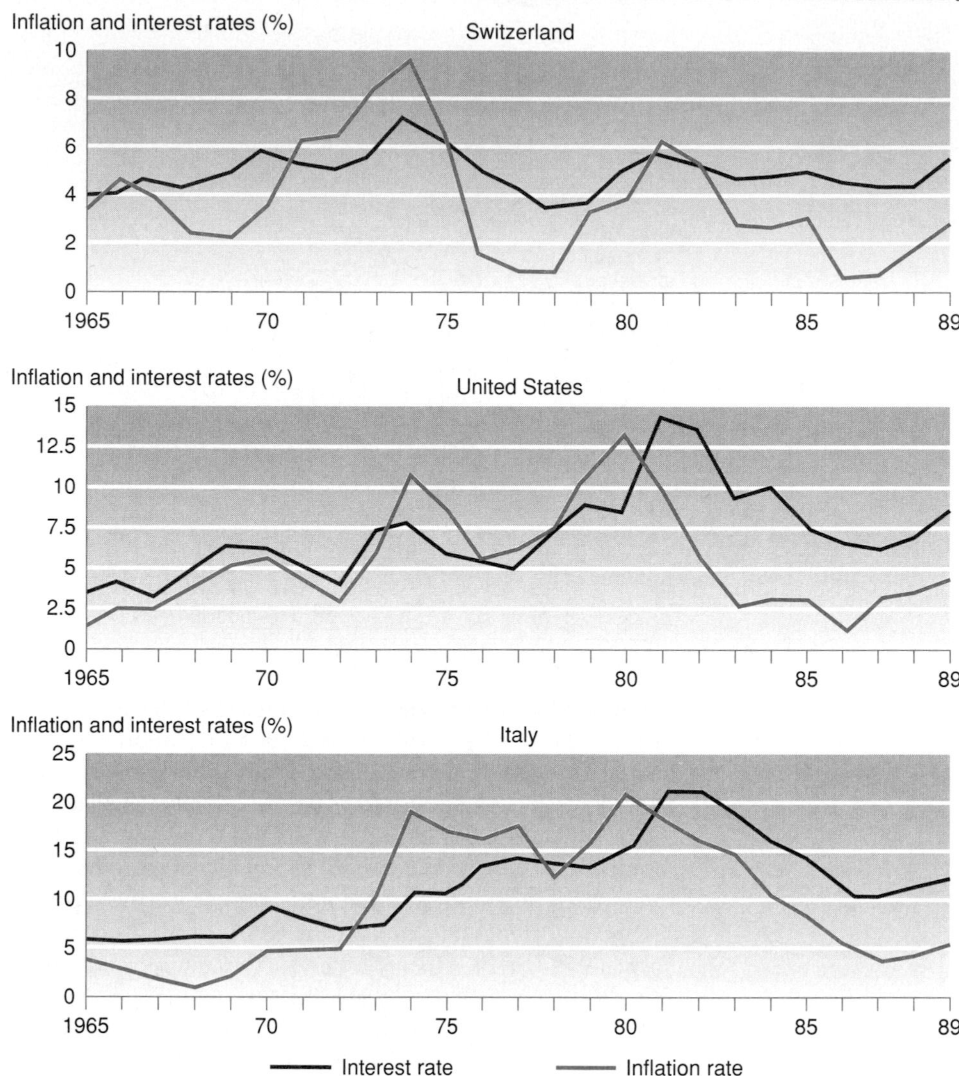

Source: OECD, Main Economic Indicators.
Note: Inflation rates are year-to-year percentage changes in consumer price indexes. Interest rates: Switzerland, yield of confederation bonds; United States, 3-month Treasury bill rate; Italy, bond yields of credit institutions; all measured at end of second quarter.

For example, if the real rate of interest in a country is 5 percent and annual inflation is expected to be 10 percent, the nominal interest rate will be 15 percent. As predicted by the Fisher effect, a strong relationship does seem to exist between inflation rates and interest rates. (Figure 9.5 provides some examples.)

We can take this one step further and consider how it applies in a world of many countries and unrestricted capital flows. The first point to note is that when investors are free to transfer capital between countries, real interest rates will be the same in every country. If differences in real interest rates did emerge between countries, arbitrage would soon equalize them. For example, if the real interest rate in Germany was 10 percent and only 6 percent in the United States, it would pay investors to borrow money in the Unites States and invest it in Germany. The resulting increase in the demand for money in the United States would raise the real interest rate there, while the increase in the supply of foreign money in Germany would lower the real interest rate there. This would continue until the two sets of real interest rates were equalized. (In practice, differences in real interest rates may persist due to government controls on capital flows; investors are not always free to transfer capital between countries.)

It follows from the Fisher effect that if the real interest rate is the same worldwide, any difference in interest rates between countries reflects differing expectations about inflation rates. Thus if the expected rate of inflation in the United States is greater than that in Germany, U.S. nominal interest rates will be greater than German nominal interest rates.

Since we know from PPP theory that there is a link (in theory at least) between inflation and exchange rates, and since interest rates reflect expectations about inflation, it follows that there must also be a link between interest rates and exchange rates. This link is known as the **International Fisher Effect (IFE).** The International Fisher Effect states that for any two countries, the spot exchange rate should change in an equal amount but in the *opposite direction* to the difference in nominal interest rates between two countries. Stated more formally,

$$(S_1 - S_2)/S_2 \times 100 = i^{\$} - i^{DM}$$

where $i^{\$}$ and i^{DM} are the respective nominal interest rates in the United States and Germany (for the sake of example), S_1 is the spot exchange rate at the beginning of the period, and S_2 is the spot exchange rate at the end of the period.

In essence, if the U.S. nominal interest rate is higher than Germany's, reflecting greater expected inflation rates, the value of the dollar against the deutsche mark should fall by that interest rate differential in the future. So if the interest rate in the United States is 10 percent, and in Germany it is 6 percent, reflecting 4 percent higher expected inflation in the United States, we would expect the value of the dollar to depreciate by 4 percent against the mark.

So do interest rate differentials help predict future currency movements? As with so much in economics, the evidence is mixed. As in the case of PPP theory, in the long run there does seem to be a relationship between interest rate differentials and subsequent changes in spot exchange rates. However, considerable short-run deviations occur. The International Fisher Effect is not a good predictor of short-run changes in spot exchange rates.[6]

Summary

In this section we have seen that relative monetary growth, relative inflation rates, and nominal interest rate differentials are all moderately good predictors of *long-run* changes in exchange rates (i.e., for periods longer than one year). They are poor predictors of short-run changes in exchange rates, however. This information is useful for an international business. Insofar as the long-term profitability of foreign investments, export opportunities, and the price competitiveness of foreign imports are all influenced by long-term movements in exchange rates, international businesses would be well advised to pay attention to countries' differing monetary growth, inflation, and interest rates. On the other hand, international businesses that engage in foreign exchange transactions on a day-to-day basis could benefit by knowing some predictors of short-term foreign exchange rate movements. Unfortunately, short-term exchange rate movements are difficult to predict.

---

6 See R. E. Cumby and M. Obstfeld, "A Note on Exchange Rate Expectations and Nominal Interest Differentials: A Test of the Fisher Hypothesis," *Journal of Finance,* June 1981, pp. 697–703.

EXCHANGE RATE FORECASTING

A company's need to predict future exchange rate variations raises the issue of whether it is worthwhile for the company to invest in exchange rate forecasting services to aid decision making. Two schools of thought address this issue. One school, the *efficient market school,* argues that forward exchange rates do the best possible job of forecasting future spot exchange rates, and, therefore, investing in forecasting services would be a waste of money. The other school of thought, the *inefficient market school,* argues that companies can improve the foreign exchange market's estimate of future exchange rates (as contained in the forward rate) by investing in forecasting services. In other words, this school of thought does not believe the forward exchange rates are the best possible predictors of future spot exchange rates.

The Efficient Market School

Forward exchange rates represent market participants' collective predictions of likely spot exchange rates at specified future dates. If forward exchange rates are the best possible predictor of future spot rates, it would make no sense for companies to spend additional money trying to forecast short run exchange rate movements. Many economists believe the foreign exchange market is efficient at setting forward rates.[7] An **efficient market** is one in which prices reflect all available information. (If forward rates reflect all available information about likely future changes in exchange rates, it follows that there is no way a company can beat the market by investing in forecasting services).

If the foreign exchange market is efficient, forward exchange rates should be *unbiased* predictors of future spot rates. This does not mean the predictions will be accurate in any specific situation; it means inaccuracies will not be consistently above or below future spot rates—that they will be random. There have been a large number of empirical tests of the efficient market hypothesis. Although most of the early work seems to confirm the hypothesis (suggesting that companies should not waste their money on forecasting services), more recent studies have challenged it.[8] Most significant, there is increasing evidence that forward rates are *not* unbiased predictors of future spot rates, and that more accurate predictions of future spot rates can be calculated from publicly available information.[9]

The Inefficient Market School

Citing evidence against the efficient market hypothesis, some economists believe the foreign exchange market is inefficient. An **inefficient market** is one in which prices do not reflect all available information. In an inefficient market, forward exchange rates will not be the best possible predictors of future spot exchange rates.

If this is true, it may be worthwhile for international businesses to invest in forecasting services (as many, in fact, do). The belief is that professional exchange rate forecasts might be able to provide better predictions of future spot rates than forward exchange rates do. It should be pointed out, however, that the track record of professional forecasting services is not that good. For example, an analysis of the forecasts of 12 major forecasting services over the 1978–82 period concluded that the forecasters in general did not provide better forecasts than the forward exchange rates.[10]

---

[7] For example, see E. Fama, "Forward Rates as Predictors of Future Spot Rates," *Journal of Financial Economics,* October 1976, pp. 361–77.

[8] For a review see R. M. Levich, "The Efficiency of Markets for Foreign Exchange," in *International Finance,* ed. G. D. Gay and R. W. Kold (Richmond, Va.: Robert F. Dane, Inc., 1983).

[9] See J. Williamson, *The Exchange Rate System* (Washington D.C.: Institute for International Economics, 1983).

[10] R. M. Levich "Currency Forecasters Lose Their Way," *Euromoney,* August 1983, p. 140.

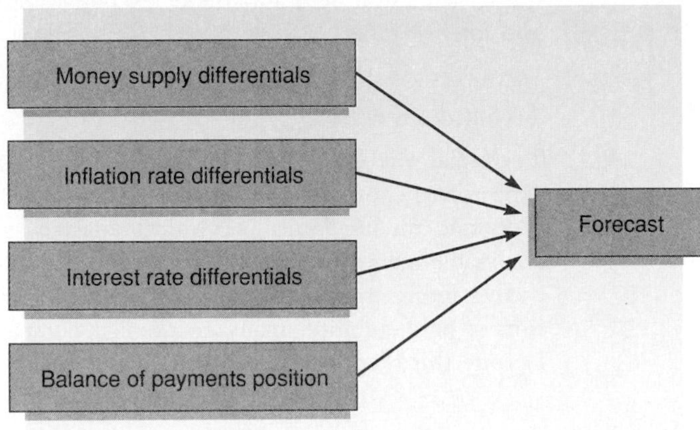

Figure 9.6
Variables used to Forecast Future Exchange Rate Movements

Approaches to Forecasting

Assuming the inefficient market school is correct that the foreign exchange market's estimate of future spot rates can be improved, on what basis should forecasts be prepared? Here again, there are two schools of thought. One adheres to fundamental analysis, while the other uses technical analysis.

Fundamental Analysis

Fundamental analysis draws on economic theory to construct sophisticated econometric models for predicting exchange rate movements. The variables contained in these models typically include those we have discussed—such as relative money supply growth rates, inflation rates, and interest rates. In addition, they may include variables related to countries' balance-of-payments positions. (See Figure 9.6.)

The logic for including balance-of-payments data in exchange rate forecasts is that if a country is running a deficit on its balance-of-payments current account (it is importing more goods and services than it is exporting), pressures are created that result in the depreciation of its currency on the foreign exchange market. (For background on the balance of payments, see Chapter 7.) As an illustration, consider what might happen if the United States was running a persistent current account balance-of-payments deficit. Since the United States would be importing more than it was exporting, people in other countries would be increasing their holdings of U.S. dollars. If these people were willing to hold their dollars, the dollar's exchange rate would not be influenced. However, if these people converted their dollars into other currencies, the supply of dollars in the foreign exchange market would increase (as would demand for the other currencies). This shift in demand and supply conditions would create pressures that could lead to the depreciation of the dollar against other currencies.

The problem with this argument is that it hinges on whether people in other countries are willing to hold dollars. This in turn depends on such factors as U.S. interest rates and inflation rates. So, in a sense, the balance-of-payments position *is not* a fundamental predictor of future exchange rate movements. For example, during the 1981–85 period, the U.S. dollar appreciated against most major currencies despite a growing balance-of-payments deficit. The reason was that relatively high real interest rates in the United States made the dollar very attractive to foreigners, so they did not convert their dollars into other currencies. Given this, we are back to the argument that the fundamental determinants of exchange rates are monetary growth, inflation rates, and interest rates.

Technical Analysis

Technical analysis uses price and volume data to determine past trends, which are expected to continue into the future. This approach does not rely on a consideration of economic fundamentals. Technical analysis is based on the premise that there are analyzable market trends and waves and that previous trends and waves can be used to predict future trends and waves. Since there is no theoretical rationale for this assumption of predictability, many economists compare technical analysis to fortune telling. Despite this skepticism, technical analysis has gained favor in recent years.[11]

CURRENCY CONVERTIBILITY

Until this point we have assumed that the currencies of various countries are freely convertible into other currencies. This assumption is invalid. As we shall see, in many countries the ability of residents and nonresidents to convert the local currency into a foreign currency is restricted. The result is that international trade and investment are more difficult in those countries. Many international businesses have used "countertrade" practices to circumvent problems that arise when a currency is not freely convertible.

Convertibility and Government Policy

Due to government restrictions, a significant number of currencies are not freely convertible into other currencies. A country's currency is said to be *freely convertible* when the country's government allows both residents and nonresidents to purchase unlimited amounts of a foreign currency with it. A currency is said to be *externally convertible* when only nonresidents may convert it into a foreign currency without any limitations. A currency is *nonconvertible* when neither residents nor nonresidents are allowed to convert it into a foreign currency.

Free convertibility is the exception rather than the rule. Many countries place some restrictions on their residents' ability to convert the domestic currency into a foreign currency (a policy of external convertibility). Restrictions on convertibility for residents range from the relatively minor (such as restricting the amount of foreign currency they may take with them out of the country on trips) to the major (such as restricting domestic businesses' ability to take foreign currency out of the country). External convertibility restrictions can limit domestic companies' ability to invest abroad, but they present few problems for foreign companies wishing to do business in that country. For example, even if the German government placed tight controls on the ability of its residents to convert the mark into U.S. dollars, all U.S. businesses with deposits in German banks may at any time convert all of their marks into dollars and take them out of the country. Thus, a U.S. company with a subsidiary in Germany is assured that it will be able to convert the profits from its German operation into dollars and take them out of the country.

Serious problems arise, however, when a policy of nonconvertibility is in force. This was the practice of the former Soviet Union, and it continues to be the practice in Russia. When strictly applied, nonconvertibility means that although a U.S. company doing business in a country like Russia may be able to generate significant ruble profits, it

---

[11] See C. Engel and J. D. Hamilton, "Long Swings in the Dollar: Are They in the Data and Do Markets Know It?" *American Economic Review*, September 1990, pp. 689–713.

may not convert those rubles into dollars and take them out of the country. Obviously this is not a particularly desirable situation for international business.

The main reason governments limit convertibility is to preserve their foreign exchange reserves. A country needs an adequate supply of these reserves to service its international debt commitments and to purchase imports. Governments typically impose convertibility restrictions on their currency when they fear that free convertibility will lead to a run on their foreign exchange reserves. This occurs when residents and nonresidents rush to convert their holdings of domestic currency into a foreign currency—a phenomenon generally referred to as **capital flight**. Capital flight is most likely to occur when the value of the domestic currency is depreciating rapidly because of hyperinflation, or when a country's economic prospects are shaky in other respects. Under such circumstances, both residents and nonresidents tend to feel that their money is more likely to hold its value if it is converted into a foreign currency and invested abroad. Not only will a run on foreign exchange reserves limit the country's ability to service its international debt and pay for imports, it will also lead to a precipitous depreciation in the exchange rate as residents and nonresidents alike unload their holdings of domestic currency on the foreign exchange markets (thereby increasing the market supply of the country's currency). Governments fear that the rise in import prices resulting from currency depreciation will lead to further increases in inflation. This fear provides another rationale for limiting convertibility.

Due to a combination of these reasons, in 1989 more than 80 countries had placed major restrictions on conversions of their currency. Another 32 countries had imposed minor restrictions, and only 31 countries' currencies were considered freely convertible.[12] Countries with major restrictions on currency convertibility include many of the former communist states of Eastern Europe, most of Africa, China, many of the Middle Eastern countries, and several Latin American nations.

Countertrade

So how can a company deal with the nonconvertibility problem? By engaging in countertrade. Countertrade is discussed in detail in Chapter 15. Accordingly, we will not go into detail at this stage but will merely introduce the concept.

Countertrade refers to a whole range of barterlike agreements by which goods and services can be traded for other goods and services. Countertrade can make sense when a country's currency is nonconvertible. For example, consider the deal that General Electric struck with the Romanian government in 1984, when that country's currency was nonconvertible. When General Electric won a contract for a $150 million generator project in Romania, it agreed to take payment in the form of Romanian goods that could be sold for $150 million on international markets. In a similar case, the Venezuelan government negotiated a contract with Caterpillar in 1986 under which Venezuela would trade 350,000 tons of iron ore for Caterpillar heavy construction equipment. Caterpillar subsequently traded the iron ore to Romania in exchange for Romanian farm products, which it then sold on international markets for dollars.[13]

How important is countertrade? One estimate is that 20 to 30 percent of world trade in 1985 involved some form of countertrade agreements. Other estimates are that by 1990 more than 40 percent of world trade by volume involved countertrade.[14] Although

---

[12] *Exchange Agreements and Exchange Restrictions* (Washington, D.C.: International Monetary Fund, 1989).

[13] J. R. Carter and J. Gagne, "The Do's and Don'ts of International Countertrade," *Sloan Management Review*, Spring 1988, pp. 31–37.

[14] L. W. Tuller, *Going Global: New Opportunities for Growing Companies to Compete in World Markets* (Homewood, Ill.: Business One Irwin, 1991).

these estimates might seem very high—and they are difficult to verify because of the lack of hard data—they are perhaps not that far off, given the large number of countries whose currencies remain nonconvertible. Since countertrade is apparently so important, we discuss it again in Chapter 15.

IMPLICATIONS FOR BUSINESS

A number of clear implications for business are contained in this chapter. First, it is absolutely critical that international businesses understand the influence of exchange rates on the profitability of trade and investment deals. Adverse changes in exchange rates can make apparently profitable deals unprofitable. The risk introduced into international business transactions by changes in exchange rates is referred to as *foreign exchange risk.* Means of hedging against foreign exchange risk are available. Most significant, forward exchange rates and currency swaps allow companies to insure against this risk.

International businesses must also understand the forces that determine exchange rates. This is particularly true in light of the increasing evidence that forward exchange rates are not unbiased predictors. If a company wants to know how the value of a particular currency is likely to change over the long term on the foreign exchange market, it should take a close look at those economic fundamentals that appear to predict long-run exchange rate movements—i.e., the growth in a country's money supply, its inflation rate, and its nominal interest rates. For example, an international business should be very cautious about trading with or investing in a country with a recent history of rapid growth in its domestic money supply. The upsurge in inflation that is likely to follow such rapid monetary growth could well lead to a sharp drop in the value of the country's currency on the foreign exchange market, which could transform a profitable deal into an unprofitable one. This is not to say that an international business should not trade with or invest in such a country. Rather, it means an international business should take some precautions before doing so—such as buying currency forward on the foreign exchange market or structuring the deal around a countertrade arrangement.

Complicating this picture is the whole issue of currency convertibility. The proclivity that many governments seem to have to restrict currency convertibility suggests that the foreign exchange market does not always provide the lubricant necessary to make international trade and investment possible. Given this, international businesses need to explore alternative mechanisms for facilitating international trade and investment that do not involve currency conversion. Countertrade seems the obvious mechanism. We return to the topic of countertrade and discuss it in depth in Chapter 15.

SUMMARY OF CHAPTER

The objectives of this chapter were to explain how the foreign exchange market works, to examine the forces that determine exchange rates, and then to discuss the implications of these factors for international business. Given that changes in exchange rates can dramatically alter the profitability of foreign trade and investment deals, this is an area of major interest to international business. These points have been made in the chapter:

1. One function of the foreign exchange market is to convert the currency of one country into the currency of another. The exchange rate is the ratio at which the market converts one currency into another. The exchange rate allows comparison of the relative prices of goods and services in different countries.
2. International businesses participate in the foreign exchange market to facilitate international trade and investment, to invest spare cash in short-term money market accounts abroad, and to engage in currency speculation.
3. A second function of the foreign exchange market is to provide insurance against foreign exchange risk.
4. The spot exchange rate is the exchange rate at which a dealer converts one currency into another currency on a particular day. Spot exchange rates change continu-

ously in response to relative demand-and-supply conditions. This can be problematic for international businesses, since changes in the spot exchange rate can alter the profitability of foreign trade and investment deals. The risk of this occurring is referred to as foreign exchange risk.

5. Foreign exchange risk can be reduced by using forward exchange rates. A forward exchange rate is an exchange rate governing future transactions.
6. Foreign exchange risk can also be reduced by engaging in currency swaps. A swap is the simultaneous purchase and sale of a given amount of foreign exchange for two different value dates.
7. The foreign exchange market is a global network of banks, brokers, and dealers linked by electronic communications systems. This market has been growing at a rapid pace in recent years, reflecting the growth in international trade and investment. The main trading centers are London, New York, and Tokyo, and the market operates 24 hours per day. Due to the high degree of integration within the market, arbitrage is limited.
8. Exchange rates are determined by the demand and supply of one currency relative to the demand and supply of another. The principal determinants of a currency's demand and supply seem to be its country's price inflation and money supply growth.
9. The law of one price is that in competitive markets that are free of transportation costs and barriers to trade (such as tariffs), identical products sold in different countries must sell for the same price when their price is expressed in the same currency.
10. The purchasing power parity (PPP) theory is that given relatively efficient markets, the price of a basket of particular goods should be roughly equivalent in each country. The PPP theory predicts that the exchange rate will change if relative prices change.
11. The rate of change in countries' relative prices depends on their relative inflation rates. A country's inflation rate seems to be a function of the growth in its money supply, which reflects government policy. Inflation will occur when the growth in money supply outstrips the growth in output.
12. The PPP theory of exchange rate changes yields relatively accurate predictions of long-term trends in exchange rates, but not of short-term movements. The failure of PPP theory to predict exchange rate changes more accurately may be due to the existence of transportation costs, barriers to trade and investment, and other market imperfections.
13. Interest rates reflect expectations about inflation. In countries where inflation is expected to be high, interest rates also will be high.
14. The International Fisher Effect (IFE) states that for any two countries, the spot exchange rate should change in an equal amount but in the opposite direction to the difference in nominal interest rates. The IFE seems to be a good predictor of long-run exchange rate changes but not of short-term changes.
15. An efficient market is one in which prices reflect all available information. In an efficient market, forward exchange rates will reflect all that can be known about future spot exchange rates. Any additional forecasting efforts are unnecessary.
16. In an inefficient market, prices do *not* reflect all available information, and market forward exchange rates will not represent the best possible prediction of future spot exchange rates. Thus, it may be worthwhile for a company to engage the services of professional forecasters.
17. The most common approach to exchange rate forecasting is fundamental analysis. This relies on variables such as money supply growth, inflation rates, nominal interest rates, and balance-of-payments positions to predict future changes in exchange rates.
18. In many countries, the ability of residents and nonresidents to convert local currency into a foreign currency is restricted by government policy. A government restricts the convertibility of its currency in attempting to protect the country's foreign exchange reserves and to halt any capital flight.
19. Particularly bothersome for international business is a policy on nonconvertibility, which prohibits residents and nonresidents from exchanging local currency for foreign currency. A policy of nonconvertibility makes it very difficult to engage in international trade and investment in the country.
20. One way of coping with the nonconvertibility problem is to engage in countertrade—to trade goods and services for other goods and services.

DISCUSSION QUESTIONS

1. The interest rate on German government securities with one-year maturity is 4 percent, and the expected inflation rate for the coming year is 2 percent. The interest rate on U.S. government securities with one-year maturity is 7 percent, and the expected rate of inflation is 5 percent. The current spot exchange rate for German marks is $1 = DM 1.4. Forecast the spot exchange rate one year from today. Explain the logic of your answer.
2. Two countries, France and the United States, produce just one good: beef. Suppose the price of beef in the United States is $2.80 per pound and in France it is FFr 3.70 per pound.
   a. According to PPP theory, what should the $/FFr spot exchange rate be?
   b. Suppose the price of beef is expected to rise to $3.10 in the United States, and to FFr 4.65 in France. What should the one-year forward $/FFr exchange rate be?
   c. Given your answers to parts *a* and *b*, and given that the current interest rate in the Unites States is 10 percent, what would you expect the current interest rate to be in France?
3. You manufacture wine goblets. In mid-June you receive an order for 10,000 goblets from Germany. Payment of DM 400,000 is due in mid-December. You expect the deutsche mark to rise from its present rate of $1 = DM 1.5 to $1 = DM 1.4 by December. You can borrow marks at 6 percent per annum. What should you do?

The International Monetary System

CHAPTER 10

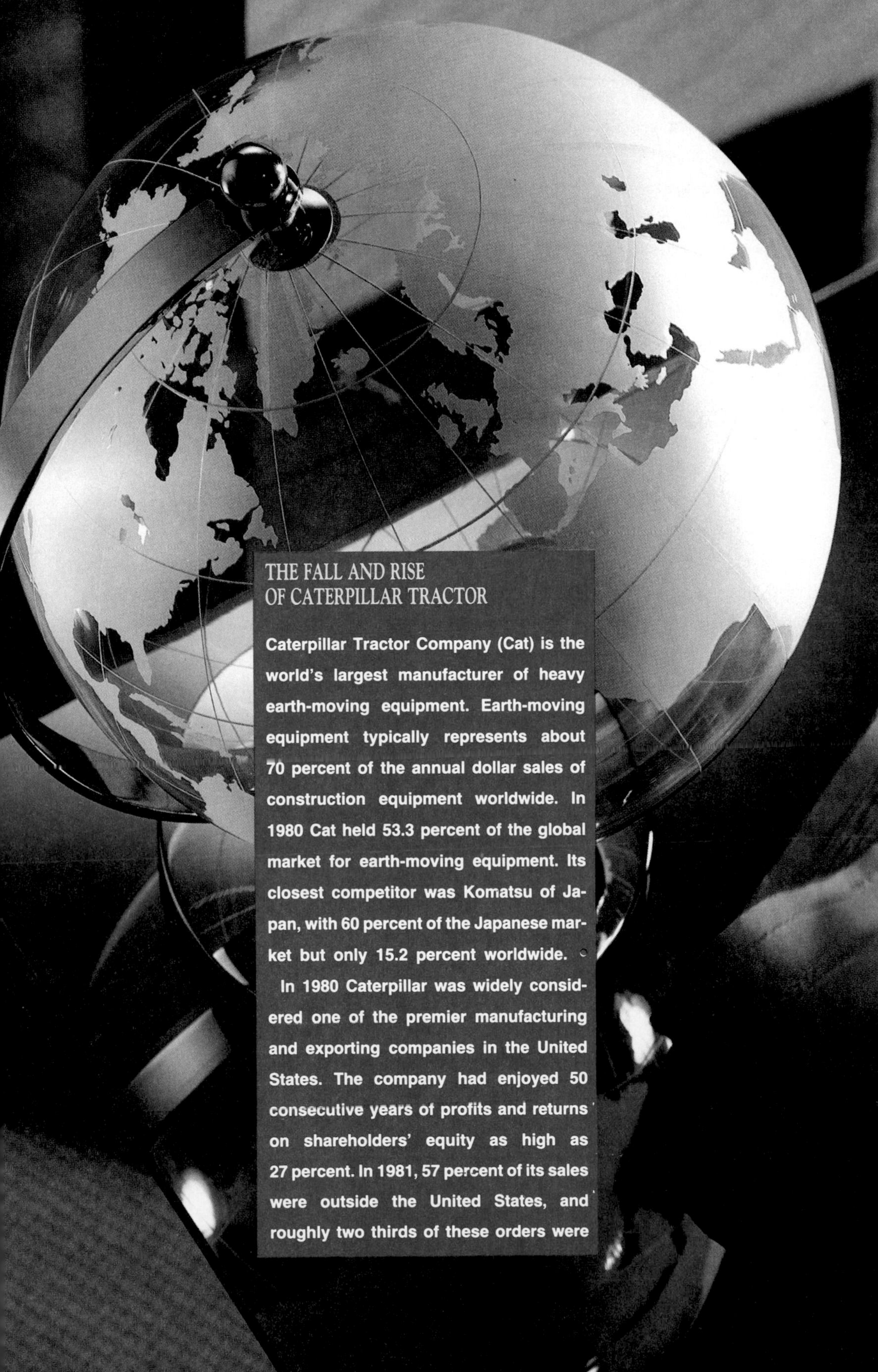

THE FALL AND RISE OF CATERPILLAR TRACTOR

Caterpillar Tractor Company (Cat) is the world's largest manufacturer of heavy earth-moving equipment. Earth-moving equipment typically represents about 70 percent of the annual dollar sales of construction equipment worldwide. In 1980 Cat held 53.3 percent of the global market for earth-moving equipment. Its closest competitor was Komatsu of Japan, with 60 percent of the Japanese market but only 15.2 percent worldwide.

In 1980 Caterpillar was widely considered one of the premier manufacturing and exporting companies in the United States. The company had enjoyed 50 consecutive years of profits and returns on shareholders' equity as high as 27 percent. In 1981, 57 percent of its sales were outside the United States, and roughly two thirds of these orders were filled by exports. Indeed, Cat was the third-largest U.S. exporter. Reflecting this underlying strength, in 1981 Cat recorded record pretax profits of $579 million. However, the next three years were disastrous. Caterpillar lost a total of $1 billion and saw its market share slip to as low as 40 percent in 1985, while Komatsu increased its share to 25 percent. Three factors explain this startling turn of events: the higher productivity of Komatsu, the rise in the value of the dollar, and the Third World debt crisis. • In retrospect, Komatsu had been creeping up on Cat for a long time. In the 1960s the company had a minuscule presence outside of Japan. By 1974 it had managed to increase its global market share of heavy earth-moving equipment to 9 percent, and by 1980 it was over 15 percent. Part of Komatsu's growth was due to its superior labor productivity; throughout the 1970s it had been able to price its machines 10 to 15 percent below Caterpillar's. However, Komatsu lacked an extensive dealer network outside of Japan, and Cat's worldwide dealer network and superior after-sale service and support functions were seen as justifying a price premium for Cat machines. For these reasons, many industry observers believed Komatsu would not increase its share much beyond its 1980 level. • What changed the picture was an unprecedented rise in the value of the dollar against most major world currencies. Between 1980 and 1987, the dollar rose an average of 87 percent against the currencies of 10 other industrialized countries. The dollar was driven up by strong economic growth in the United States, which attracted heavy inflows of capital from foreign investors seeking high returns on capital assets. Moreover, high real interest rates attracted foreign investors seeking high returns on financial assets. At the same time, political turmoil in other parts of the world and relatively slow economic growth in Europe helped create the view that the United States was a good place in which to invest. These inflows of capital increased the demand for dollars in the foreign exchange market, which pushed the value of the dollar upward against other currencies. • Obviously the strong dollar substantially increased the dollar price of Cat's machines. At the same time, the dollar price of Komatsu products imported into the United States fell. Indeed, due to the shift in the relative values of the dollar and the yen, by 1985 Komatsu was able to price its machines as much as 40 percent below Caterpillar's prices. In light of this enormous price difference, many consumers chose to forgo Caterpillar's superior after-sale service and support and bought Komatsu machines. • The third factor, the Third World debt crisis, became apparent in 1982. During the early 1970s the oil-exporting nations of OPEC quadrupled the price of oil, which resulted in a massive flow of funds into these nations. Commercial banks borrowed this money from the OPEC countries and loaned it to the governments of many Third World Nations to finance massive construction projects—which led to a global boom in demand for heavy earth-moving equipment. Caterpillar benefited richly from this development. By 1982, however, it became apparent that the commercial banks had loaned far too much money to risky and unproductive investments, and the governments of several countries (including Mexico, Brazil, and Argentina) threatened to suspend debt payments. At this point the International Monetary Fund stepped in and arranged for new loans to indebted Third World countries, but on the condition that they adopt deflationary macroeconomic policies. For Cat, the party was over; orders for heavy earth-moving equipment dried up almost overnight, and those that were placed went to the lowest bidder—which all too often was Komatsu. • As a result of these factors, Caterpillar was in deep trouble by late 1982. The company responded quickly and between 1982 and 1985 cut costs by more than 20 percent. This was achieved by a 40 percent reduction in work force, the closure of nine plants, and a $1.8 billion investment in flexible manufacturing technologies designed to boost quality and lower cost. At the same time the company launched a campaign of pressing the government to lower the value of the dollar on foreign exchange markets. By 1984 Cat was a leading voice among U.S. exporters in their efforts to get the Reagan administration to intervene in the foreign exchange market. • In early 1985 things began to go Caterpillar's way. Prompted by Cat and other exporters, representatives of the U.S. government met with representatives of Japan, Germany, France, and Great Britain at the Plaza Hotel in New York. In the resulting communique—known as the *Plaza Accord*—the five governments acknowledged that the dollar was overvalued and pledged to take actions that would drive down its price on the foreign exchange market. In practical terms this called for the central bank of each country to intervene in the foreign exchange market, selling dollars and buying other currencies (including its own). The dollar had already begun to fall in early 1985 in response to a string of record U.S. trade deficits. The Plaza Accord accelerated this trend, and over the next three years the dollar fell back to its 1980 level. • The effect for Caterpillar was almost immediate. Like any major exporter, Caterpillar had its own foreign exchange unit. Suspecting that an adjustment in the dollar would come soon, Cat had increased its holdings of foreign currencies in early 1985, using the strong dollar to purchase them. As the dollar fell, the company was able to convert these currencies back into dollars for a healthy profit. In 1985 Cat had pretax profits of $32 million; without foreign exchange gains of $89 million, it would have lost money. In 1986, foreign exchange gains of $100 million accounted for nearly two thirds of its pretax profits of $159 million. • More significant for Cat's long-term position, by 1988 the fall in the dollar against the yen and Caterpillar's cost-cutting efforts had helped to eradicate the 40 percent cost advantage that Komatsu had enjoyed over Caterpillar four years earlier. Indeed, after trying to hold its prices down, Komatsu had to raise its prices that year by 18 percent, while Cat was able to hold its price increase to 3 percent. With the terms of trade no longer handicapping Caterpillar, the company was able to regain some of its lost market share. By 1989 it reportedly held 47 percent of the world market for heavy earth-moving equipment, up from a low of 40 percent three years earlier, while Komatsu's share had slipped to below 20 percent. *Sources: R. S. Eckley, "Caterpillar's Ordeal: Foreign Competition in Capital Goods,"* Business Horizons, *March–April, 1989, pp. 80–86; H. S. Byrne, "Track of the Cat: Caterpillar Is Bulldozing Its Way Back to Higher Profits,"* Barron's, *April 6, 1987, pp. 13, 70–71; R. Henkoff, "This Cat Is Acting like a Tiger,"* Fortune, *December 19, 1988, pp. 71–76; and "Caterpillar and Komatsu," in* Transnational Management: Text, Cases, and Readings in Cross-Boarded Management, *ed. C. A. Bartlett and S. Ghoshal (Homewood, Ill. Richard D. Irwin, 1992).*

INTRODUCTION

Although we discussed the workings of the foreign exchange market in some depth in Chapter 9, at no point did we mention the international monetary system's role in determining exchange rates. Rather, we implicitly assumed that currencies were free to "float" against each other; that is, that a currency's relative value on the foreign exchange market is determined primarily by the impersonal market forces of demand and supply. In turn, we explained, the demand and supply of currencies is influenced by their

Table 10.1 *Currency Arrangements, December 3, 1990**

Currency Pegged to				
U.S. Dollar	**French Franc**	**Other Currency**	**SDR**	**Other Composite†**
Afghanistan	Benin	Bhutan (Indian rupee)	Burundi	Algeria
Angola	Burkina Faso	Kiribati (Australian dollar)	Iran, I. R. of	Austria
Antigua and Barbuda	Cameroon	Lesotho (South African rand)	Libya	Bangladesh
Bahamas	Central African Republic	Swaziland (South African rand)	Myanmar	Botswana
Barbados	Chad	Tonga (Australian dollar)	Rwanda	Bulgaria
Belize	Comoros	Yugoslavia (deutsche mark)	Seychelles	Cape Verde
Djibouti	Congo			Cyprus
Dominica	Côte d'Ivoire			Czechoslovakia
Dominican Republic	Equatorial Guinea			Fiji
Ethiopia	Gabon			Finland
Grenada	Mali			Hungary
Guyana	Niger			Iceland
Haiti	Senegal			Israel
Iraq	Togo			Jordan
Liberia				Kenya
Oman				Kuwait
Panama				Malawi
St. Kitts and Nevis				Malta
St. Lucia				Mauritius
St. Vincent and the Grenadines				Morocco
Sudan				Nepal
Suriname				Norway
Syrian Arab Republic				Papua New Guinea
Trinidad and Tobago				Poland
Yemen, Republic of				Romania
				Sao Tome and Principe
				Solomon Islands
				Sweden
				Tanzania
				Thailand
				Uganda
				Vanuatu
				Western Samoa
				Zimbabwe

* Excluding the currency of Democratic Kampuchea, for which no current information is available. For members with dual or multiple exchange markets, the arrangement shown is that in the major market.

† Comprises currencies pegged to various "baskets" of currencies of the members' own choice, as distinct from the SDR basket.

‡ Exchange rates of all currencies have shown limited flexibility in terms of the U.S. dollar.

¶ Refers to the cooperative arrangement maintained under the European Monetary System.

§ Includes exchange arrangements, under which the exchange rate is adjusted at relatively frequent intervals, on the basis of indicators determined by the respective member countries.

Source: International Monetary Fund, *International Financial Statistics*, March 1991, p. 22.

Flexibility Limited in Terms of a Single Currency or Group of Currencies		More Flexible		
Single Currency‡	**Cooperative Arrangements¶**	**Adjusted According to a Set of Indicators§**	**Other Managed Floating**	**Independently Floating**
Bahrain	Belgium	Chile	China, P.R.	Argentina
Qatar	Denmark	Colombia	Costa Rica	Australia
Saudi Arabia	France	Madagascar	Ecuador	Bolivia
United Arab Emirates	Germany	Mozambique	Egypt	Brazil
	Ireland	Zambia	Greece	Canada
	Italy		Guinea	El Salvador
	Luxembourg		Guinea-Bissau	Gambia
	Netherlands		Honduras	Ghana
	Spain		India	Guatemala
	United Kingdom		Indonesia	Jamaica
			Korea	Japan
			Lao P.D. Rep	Lebanon
			Mauritania	Maldives
			Mexico	Namibia
			Nicaragua	New Zealand
			Pakistan	Nigeria
			Portugal	Paraguay
			Singapore	Peru
			Somalia	Phillipines
			Sri Lanka	Sierra Leone
			Tunisia	South Africa
			Turkey	United States
			Vietnam	Uruguay
				Venezuela
				Zaïre

respective countries' relative inflation rates and interest rates. Only at the end of the chapter in our discussion of currency convertibility did we begin to admit the possibility that the foreign exchange market might not work as we had initially depicted.

We must now admit that our explanation of how exchange rates are determined in Chapter 9 is oversimplified. Contrary to our implicit assumption, many currencies are *not* free to float against each other. Rather, exchange rates are determined within the context of an international monetary system in which many currencies' ability to float against other currencies is limited by their respective governments or by intergovernmental arrangements. As of December 1990, for example, only 25 of the world's 118 viable currencies were freely floating (see Table 10.1). The exchange rates of 85 minor currencies were "pegged to" the exchange rates of particular major currencies—

particularly the U.S. dollar and the French franc—or to "baskets" of other currencies. Thus the exchange rates of 25 currencies (including those of Angola, Barbados, Ethiopia, and Panama) were pegged to the U.S. dollar's exchange rate. By this means, the value of the Ethiopian currency against major currencies, such as the Japanese yen, was determined by the value of the U.S. dollar against the yen. As the dollar appreciated against the yen in the early 1980s, so did the Ethiopian currency; and as the dollar depreciated against the yen in the late 1980s, so did the Ethiopian currency. Other countries have cooperative arrangements that link the values of their currencies. The best known of these is the European Monetary System (EMS) of the European Community (EC).

Against this background, the objective of this chapter is to explain how the international monetary system works and to point out its implications for international business. To understand how the international monetary system works, we must acquire the historical perspective of the system's evolution. Accordingly, we will begin with a discussion of the gold standard and its breakup during the 1930s. Then we will discuss the 1944 Bretton Woods conference, which established the basic framework for the post–World War II international monetary system. The Bretton Woods system called for *fixed exchange rates* against the U.S. dollar. Under this system the U.S. dollar's exchange rate was fixed for long periods of time and allowed to change only under a specific set of circumstances. The Bretton Woods conference also created two major international institutions: the International Monetary Fund (IMF) and the World Bank. The IMF's task was to maintain order in the international monetary system; the World Bank's was to promote development. Since both of these institutions continue to play a major role in the world economy, we discuss them in some detail.

The Bretton Woods system of fixed exchange rates collapsed in 1973. Since then the world has operated with a *managed-float system* in which some currencies are allowed to float freely, but the majority are either managed in some way by government intervention or pegged to another currency. We will explain the reasons for the failure of the Bretton Woods system as well as the nature of the present managed-float system. We will also spend some time discussing the European Monetary System (EMS) because of the importance of the European Community in the global economy.

Two decades after the breakdown of the Bretton Woods system, the debate over what kind of exchange rate regime is best for the world continues. Some economists advocate a system in which major currencies are allowed to float against each other. Others argue for a return to a fixed exchange rate regime similar to the one established at Bretton Woods. This debate is intense and important, and we will examine the arguments of both sides.

Finally, we will discuss the implications of all of this for international business. The opening case on Caterpillar Tractor illustrates some implications of the international monetary system for business. Caterpillar has both benefited and suffered from the present managed-float system. The rise of the dollar against the yen and most other major currencies during the early 1980s contributed to the decline in Caterpillar's global market share during that period and to the rise in Komatsu's. Similarly, the dollar's fall against most major currencies—particularly the yen—during the latter half of the 1980s helped Caterpillar regain market share from Komatsu. So, under a regime of floating exchange rates, for better and for worse, a company's competitive position can be influenced by exchange rate fluctuations. Under a system of fixed exchange rates, volatile fluctuations of the kind experienced by Caterpillar should not occur, which should make the competitive playing field more predictable. Some economists believe the greater certainty that exists in a fixed exchange rate regime is more attractive to international business and more conducive to international trade.

THE GOLD STANDARD

The gold standard had its origin in the use of gold coins as a medium of exchange, unit of account, and store of value—a practice that stretches back to ancient times. In the days when international trade was limited in volume, payment for goods purchased from another country was typically made in gold or silver. However, as the volume of international trade expanded in the wake of the industrial revolutions, a more convenient means of financing international trade was needed. Shipping large quantities of gold and silver around the world to finance international trade seemed impractical. The solution adopted was to arrange for payment in paper currency and for governments to agree to convert the paper currency into gold on demand at a fixed rate.

Nature of the Gold Standard

The practice of pegging currencies to gold and guaranteeing convertibility is known as the **gold standard**. By 1880 most of the world's major trading nations—including Great Britain, Germany, Japan, and the United States—had adopted the gold standard. Given a common gold standard, the value of any currency in units of any other currency (the exchange rate) was easy to determine.

For example, under the gold standard one U.S. dollar was defined as equivalent to 23.22 grains of "fine" (pure) gold. Thus one could, in theory, demand that the U.S. government covert that one dollar into 23.22 grains of gold. Since there are 480 grains in an ounce, one ounce of gold cost $20.67 (480/23.22). The amount of a currency needed to purchase one ounce of gold was referred to as the **gold par value**. The British pound was defined as containing 113 grains of fine gold. In other words, one ounce of gold cost £4.25 (480/113). From the gold par values of pounds and dollars, we can calculate what the exchange rate was for converting pounds into dollars; it was £1 = $4.87 (i.e., $20.67/£4.25).

The Strength of the Gold Standard

The great strength claimed for the gold standard was that it contained a powerful mechanism for simultaneously achieving **balance-of-trade equilibrium** by all countries.[1] A country is said to be in balance-of-trade equilibrium when the income its residents earn from exports is equal to the money its residents pay to people in other countries for imports (i.e, the current account of its balance of payments is in balance).

For illustration, suppose there are only two countries in the world, Japan and the United States. Imagine Japan's trade balance is in surplus because it exports more to the United States than it imports from the United States. Japanese exporters are paid in U.S. dollars, which they exchange for Japanese yen at a Japanese bank. In turn, the Japanese bank submits the dollars to the U.S. government and demands payment of gold in return. (This is a simplification of what actually would occur, but it will suffice to make our point.)

It follows that under the gold standard, when Japan has a trade surplus there will be a net flow of gold from the United States to Japan. These gold flows automatically reduce the U.S. money supply and swell Japan's money supply. As we saw in Chapter 9, there is a close connection between money supply growth and price inflation. An increase in money supply will raise prices in Japan, while a decrease in the U.S. money supply will push U.S. prices downward. The rise in the price of Japanese goods will decrease demand

[1] The argument goes back to 18th-century philosopher David Hume. See D. Hume, "On the Balance of Trade," reprinted in *The Gold Standard in Theory and in History*, ed. B. Eichengreen (London: Methuen, 1985).

for these goods, while the fall in the price of U.S. goods will increase demand for these goods. Thus Japan will start to buy more from the United States, and the United States will buy less from Japan, until a balance-of-trade equilibrium is achieved.

This adjustment mechanism seems to simple and attractive that even today, more half a century after the final collapse of the gold standard, there are people who believe the world should return to a gold standard. Indeed, during the 1980s a series of conferences in the United States hosted by prominent politicians called for a return to the gold standard. The probability of this occurring seems remote.

The Period between the Wars, 1918–39

The gold standard worked reasonably well from the 1870s until the start of World War I in 1914, when it was abandoned. During the war several governments financed part of their massive military expenditures by printing money. This resulted in inflation, and by the war's end in 1918, price levels were higher everywhere. The United States returned to the gold standard in 1919, Great Britain in 1925, and France 1928.

Great Britain returned to the gold standard by pegging the pound to gold at the prewar gold parity level of £4.25 per ounce, despite substantial inflation between 1914 and 1925. This priced British goods out of foreign markets, which pushed the country into a deep depression. When foreign holders of pounds lost confidence in Great Britain's commitment to maintaining its currency's value, they began converting their holdings of pounds into gold. The British government saw that it could not satisfy the demand for gold without seriously depleting its gold reserves, so it suspended convertibility in 1931.

The United States followed suit and left the gold standard in 1933 but returned to it in 1934, raising the dollar price of gold from $20.67 per ounce to $35 per ounce. Since more dollars were needed to buy an ounce of gold than before, the implication was that the dollar was worth less. This effectively amounted to a **devaluation** of the dollar relative to other currencies. Thus, whereas before the devaluation the pound/dollar exchange rate was £1 = $4.87, after the devaluation it was £1 = $8.24. By reducing the price of U.S. exports and increasing the price of U.S. imports, the government was trying to create employment in the United States by boosting output. However, a number of other countries adopted a similar tactic, and in the cycle of competitive devaluations that soon emerged, no country could win.

The net result was the shattering of any remaining confidence in the system. With countries devaluing their currencies at will, one could no longer be certain how much gold a currency could buy. Instead of holding onto another country's currency, people often tried to change it into gold immediately, lest the country devalue its currency in the intervening period. This put pressure on the gold reserves of various countries, forcing them to suspend gold convertibility. As a result, by the start of World War II in 1939, the gold standard was dead.

THE BRETTON WOODS SYSTEM

In 1944, at the height of World War II, representatives from 44 countries met at Bretton Woods, New Hampshire, to design a new international monetary system. With the collapse of the gold standard and the Great Depression of the 1930s fresh in their minds, these statesmen were determined to build an enduring economic order that would facilitate postwar economic growth. There was general consensus that fixed exchange rates were desirable. In addition, the conference participants wanted to avoid the senseless competitive devaluations of the 1930s, and they recognized that the gold standard would not assure this. The major problem with the gold standard as previously constituted was that there was no multinational institution that could stop countries from engaging in competitive devaluations.

The agreement reached at Bretton Woods established two multinational institutions—the International Monetary Fund (IMF) and the World Bank. The task of the IMF would be to maintain order in the international monetary system, and that of the World Bank would be to promote general economic development. The Bretton Woods agreement also called for a system of fixed exchange rates that would be policed by the IMF. Under the agreement, all countries were to fix the value of their currency in terms of gold but were not required to exchange their currencies for gold. Only the dollar remained convertible into gold—at a price of $35 per ounce. Each other country decided what it wanted its exchange rate to be vis-à-vis the dollar and then calculated the gold par value of their currency based on that selected dollar exchange rate. All participating countries agreed to try to maintain the value of their currencies within 1 percent of the par value by buying or selling currencies (or gold) as needed. For example, if foreign exchange dealers were selling more of a country's currency than they demanded, the government of that country would intervene in the foreign exchange markets, buying its currency in an attempt to increase demand and maintain its gold par value.

Another aspect of the Bretton Woods agreement was a commitment *not* to use devaluation as a weapon of competitive trade policy. However, if a currency became too weak to defend, a devaluation of up to 10 percent would be allowed without any formal approval by the IMF. Larger devaluations required IMF approval.

The Role of the IMF

The IMF Articles of Agreement were heavily influenced by the inter-war experience of worldwide financial collapse, competitive devaluations, trade wars, high unemployment, hyperinflation in Germany and elsewhere, and general economic disintegration. The aim of the Bretton Woods agreement, of which the IMF was the main custodian, was to try to avoid a repetition of the chaos that occurred between the wars through a combination of discipline and flexibility.

Discipline

A fixed exchange rate regime imposes discipline in two ways. First, the need to maintain a fixed exchange rate puts a brake on the practice of competitive devaluations and brings stability to the world trade environment. Second, a fixed exchange rate regime imposes monetary discipline on countries, thereby curtailing price inflation. For example, consider what would happen under a fixed exchange rate regime if Great Britain rapidly increased its money supply by printing pounds. As explained in Chapter 9, the increase in money supply would lead to price inflation. In turn, given fixed exchange rates, inflation would make British goods uncompetitive in world markets, while the prices of imports would become more attractive in Great Britain. The result would be a widening trade deficit in Great Britain, with the country importing more than it exports. To correct this trade imbalance under a fixed exchange rate regime, Great Britain would be required to restrict the rate of growth in its money supply to bring price inflation back under control. Thus, fixed exchange rates are seen as a mechanism for controlling inflation and imposing economic discipline on countries.

Flexibility

Although monetary discipline was a central objective of the Bretton Woods agreement, it was recognized that a rigid policy of fixed exchange rates would be too inflexible. It would probably break down just as the gold standard had. Moreover, in some cases a country's attempts to reduce its money supply growth and correct a persistent balance-of-payments deficit could force the country into recession and create high unemployment. The architects of the Bretton Woods agreement wanted to avoid high unemployment, so they built some limited flexibility into the system. Two major features of the IMF Articles of Agreement fostered this flexibility: IMF lending facilities and adjustable parities.

With regard to lending facilities, the IMF stood ready to lend foreign currencies to members to tide them over during short periods of balance-of-payments deficit, when a rapid tightening of monetary or fiscal policy would have an adverse effect on domestic employment. A pool of gold and currencies contributed by IMF members provided the resources for these lending operations. A persistent balance-of-payments deficit can lead to a depletion of a country's reserves of foreign currency, forcing it to devalue its currency. By providing deficit countries with short-term foreign currency loans, IMF funds would buy countries time in which to bring down their inflation rates and reduce their balance-of-payments deficit. The belief was that such loans would reduce pressures for devaluation and allow for a more orderly and less painful adjustment.

Countries were to be allowed to borrow a limited amount from the IMF without adhering to any specific agreements. However, extensive drawings from IMF funds would require a country to agree to increasingly stringent IMF supervision of its macroeconomic policies. In other words, heavy borrowers from the IMF must agree to conditions concerning monetary and fiscal policy set down by the IMF—which typically include IMF-mandated targets on domestic money supply growth, exchange rate policy, tax policy, government spending, and so on.

The system of adjustable parities allows for the devaluation of a country's currency by more than 10 percent if the IMF agrees that the country's balance of payments is in "fundamental disequilibrium." The term *fundamental disequilibrium* was not actually defined in the IMF's Articles of Agreement, but it was intended to apply to countries that have suffered permanent adverse shifts in the demand for their products. Without a devaluation, such a country would experience high unemployment and a persistent trade deficit until the domestic price level had fallen far enough to restore a balance-of-payments equilibrium. The belief was that devaluation could help sidestep a painful adjustment process in such circumstances.

The Role of the World Bank

The official name for the World Bank is the *International Bank for Reconstruction and Development (IBRD)*. When the Bretton Woods participants established the World Bank, the need to reconstruct the war-torn economies of Europe was foremost in their minds. The bank's initial mission was to help finance the building of Europe's economy by providing low-interest loans. As it turned out, the World Bank was entirely overshadowed in this role by the Marshall Plan, under which the United States loaned money directly to European nations to help them rebuild. So the bank soon turned its attention to the problem of "development" and began lending money to the less-developed nations of the Third World. In the 1950s the bank concentrated its efforts on public-sector projects. Power station projects, road building, and other transportation investments were much in favor at this time. During the 1960s the bank also began to lend heavily in support of agriculture, education, population control, and urban development.

The bank lends money under two schemes. Under the *IBRD scheme,* money is raised through bond sales in the international capital market. Borrowers pay what the bank calls a market rate of interest—the bank's cost of funds plus a margin for expenses. In fact, this "market" rate is lower than commercial banks' market rate. Essentially, under the IBRD scheme the bank offers low-interest loans to risky customers whose credit rating is often poor.

A second scheme is overseen by the International Development Agency (IDA), an arm of the bank created in 1960. Resources to fund IDA loans are raised through subscriptions from wealthy members such as the United States, Japan, and Germany. IDA loans go only to the poorest countries. (In 1991 those were defined as countries with annual incomes per capita of less than $580.) Borrowers have 50 years to repay at an interest rate of 1 percent a year.

THE COLLAPSE OF THE FIXED EXCHANGE RATE SYSTEM

The system of fixed exchange rates established at Bretton Woods worked well until the late 1960s, when it began to show signs of strain. The system finally collapsed in 1973, and since then we have had a managed-float system. To understand why the system collapsed, one must appreciate the special role of the U.S. dollar in the system. As the only currency that could be converted into gold, and as the currency that served as the reference point for all others, the dollar occupied a central place in the system. It followed that any pressure on the dollar to devalue could wreak havoc with the system, and that is precisely what occurred.

Most economists trace the breakup of the fixed exchange rate system to the U.S. macroeconomic policy package of 1965–68.[2] To finance both the Vietnam conflict and his welfare programs, President Johnson backed an increase in U.S. government spending that was not financed by an increase in taxes. Instead, it was financed by an increase in the money supply—which, in turn, led to a rise in price inflation from less than 4 percent in 1966 to close to 9 percent by 1968 (see Figure 10.1). At the same time, the rise in government spending had stimulated the economy. With more money in their pockets, people spent more—particularly on imports—and the U.S. trade balance began to deteriorate rapidly.

The rise in inflation and the worsening of the U.S. foreign trade position gave rise to speculation in the foreign exchange market that the dollar would be devalued. Things came to a head in spring 1971 when U.S. trade figures were released, which showed that for the first time since 1945, the United States was importing more than it was exporting. This set off massive purchases of deutsche marks in the foreign exchange market by speculators who guessed that the DM would be revalued against the dollar. On a single day, May 4, 1971, the Bundesbank (Germany's central bank) had to buy $1 billion to hold the dollar/DM exchange rate at its fixed exchange rate given the great demand for DMs. On the morning of May 5, the Bundesbank purchased another $1 billion during the first hour of foreign exchange trading! At that point, the Bundesbank faced the inevitable and allowed its currency to float.

In the weeks following the decision to float the DM, the foreign exchange market became increasingly convinced that the dollar would have to be devalued. However, devaluation of the dollar was no easy matter. Under the Bretton Woods provisions, any other country could change its exchange rates against all currencies simply by fixing its dollar rate at a new level. But as the key currency in the system, the dollar could be devalued only if all countries agreed to simultaneously revalue against the dollar. And

[2] For details see R. Solomon, *The International Monetary System, 1945–1981* (New York: Harper & Row, 1982).

Figure 10.1 *U.S. Macroeconomic Data, 1964–1972*

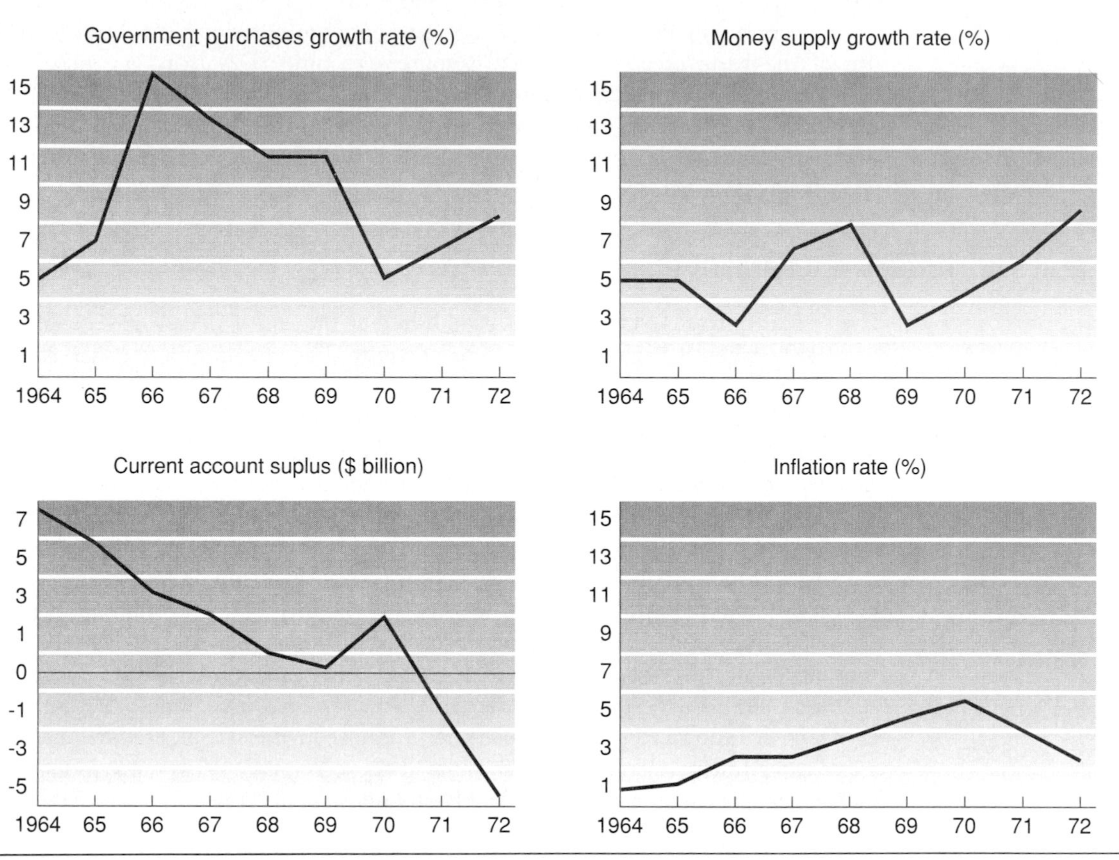

Source: Economic Report of the President, 1985. *Money-supply growth rate is the December-to-December percentage increase in M1. Inflation rate is the percentage increase in each year's average consumer price index over the average consumer price index for the previous year.*

many countries did not want this, since it would make their products more expensive relative to U.S. products.

To force the issue, in August 1971 President Nixon announced that the dollar was no longer convertible into gold. He also announced that a new 10 percent tax on imports would remain in effect until the U.S.'s trading partners agreed to revalue their currencies against the dollar. This brought the trading partners to the bargaining table, and in December 1971 an agreement was reached to devalue the dollar by about 8 percent against foreign currencies. The import tax was then removed.

The problem was not solved, however. The U.S. balance-of-payments position continued to deteriorate throughout 1972, while the U.S. money supply continued to expand at an inflationary rate (see Figure 10.1). Given this, speculation continued to grow that the dollar was still overvalued and that a second devaluation would be necessary. In anticipation, foreign exchange dealers began converting dollars to deutsche marks and other currencies. After a massive wave of speculation in February, which culminated with European central banks spending $3.6 billion on March 1 to try to prevent their currencies from appreciating against the dollar, the foreign exchange market was closed down. When the foreign exchange market reopened on March 19, the currencies of Japan and most European countries were floating against the dollar—although many developing countries continued to peg their currency to the dollar, and many still do to this day. At that time, the switch to a floating system was viewed as a temporary response to unmanageable speculation in the foreign exchange market. But it is now more than 20 years since the Bretton Woods system of fixed exchange rates collapsed, and the temporary solution is beginning to look permanent.

In sum, it is clear that the Bretton Woods system had an Achilles' heel: the system could not work if its key currency, the U.S. dollar, was under speculative attack. The Bretton Woods system could work only as long as the U.S. inflation rate remained low and the United States did not run a balance-of-payments deficit. Once these things occurred, the system soon became strained to the breaking point.

THE FLOATING EXCHANGE RATE REGIME

The floating exchange rate regime that followed the collapse of the fixed exchange rate system was formalized in January 1976 when IMF members met in Jamaica and agreed to the rules for the international monetary system that are in place today. We will discuss the Jamaica agreement before looking at how the floating exchange rate regime has operated in practice.

The Jamaica Agreement

The purpose of the Jamaica meeting was to revise the IMF's Articles of Agreement to reflect the new reality of floating exchange rates. The main elements of the Jamaica agreement include the following:

1. Floating rates were declared acceptable. IMF members were permitted to enter the foreign exchange market to even out "unwarranted" speculative fluctuations.
2. Gold was abandoned as a reserve asset. The IMF returned its gold reserves to members at the current market price, placing the proceeds in a trust fund to help poor nations. IMF members were permitted to sell their own gold reserves at the

3. Total annual IMF quotas—the amount member-countries contribute to the IMF—were increased to $41 billion. Since then they have been increased to $180 billion. Non-oil-exporting, less-developed countries were given greater access to IMF funds.

After Jamaica, the IMF continued its role of helping countries cope with macroeconomic and exchange rate problems, albeit within the context of a radically different exchange rate regime. However, as we shall see, the IMF's role has expanded over the last 20 years, and this has led to a debate about the future of the twin pillars of Bretton Woods—the IMF and the World Bank.

Exchange Rates since 1973

Since March 1973 exchange rates have become much more volatile and far less predictable than they were between 1945 and 1973. This volatility has been partly due to a number of unexpected shocks to the world monetary system, including:

1. The oil crisis in 1971, when OPEC quadrupled the price of oil. The harmful effect of this on the U.S. inflation rate and trade position resulted in a further decline in the value of the dollar.
2. The loss of confidence in the dollar that followed the rise of U.S. inflation in 1977 and 1978.

3. The oil crisis of 1979, when OPEC once again increased the price of oil dramatically—this time it was doubled.
4. The unexpected rise in the dollar between 1980 and 1985, despite a worsening balance-of-payments picture.
5. The rapid fall of the U.S. dollar between 1985 and 1987.

Figure 10.2 summarizes the volatility of the U.S. dollar in the 1973–90 period. The Morgan Guaranty Index, the basis for Figure 10.2, represents the exchange rate of the U.S. dollar against a weighted basket of the currencies of 15 other industrial countries. As can be seen, the index was as low as 85 (in 1989) and as high as 138 (in 1985) in the 1973–90 period.

Two of the most interesting phenomena in Figure 10.2 are the rapid rise in the value of the dollar between 1980 and 1985 and its even more rapid fall between 1985 and 1988. We will spend some time discussing these phenomena, since they tell us something about how the international monetary system has operated in recent years.[3]

The rise in the value of the dollar between 1980 and 1985 is particularly interesting, because it occurred at a time when the United States was running a large and growing trade deficit, importing substantially more than it exported. Conventional wisdom would suggest that the increased supply of dollars in the foreign exchange market as a result of the deficit should lead to a reduction in the value of the dollar, but it *increased* in value. Why? The answer is that a number of favorable factors temporarily overcame the unfavorable effect of a trade deficit. Strong economic growth in the United States attracted heavy inflows of capital from foreign investors seeking high returns on capital assets. Moreover, high real interest rates attracted foreign investors seeking high returns on financial assets. At the same time, political turmoil in other parts of the world, along with relatively slow economic growth in the developed countries of Europe, helped create the view that the United States was a good place to invest. These inflows of capital increased the demand for dollars in the foreign exchange market, which pushed the value of the dollar upward against other currencies.

The fall in the value of the dollar between 1985 and 1988 was caused by a combination of government intervention and market forces. The rise in the dollar, which priced U.S. goods out of foreign markets and made imports relatively cheap, had contributed to a dismal trade picture (as illustrated by Caterpillar's experience in the opening-case). In 1985 the United States posted a record-high trade deficit of over $160 billion. This led to a growth of protectionist pressure in the United States. Against this background, in September 1985 the finance ministers and central bank governors of the so-called Group of Five major industrial countries (Great Britain, France, Japan, Germany, and the United States) met at the Plaza Hotel in New York and reached what was later referred to as the *Plaza Accord.* They announced that it would be desirable for most major currencies to appreciate vis-à-vis the U.S. dollar and pledged to intervene in the foreign exchange markets, selling dollars, to encourage this objective. The dollar had already begun to weaken in the summer of 1985, and this announcement further accelerated the decline.

The dollar continued to decline until early 1987. In fact, the governments of the Group of Five began to worry that the dollar might decline too far. In response, in February 1987 the finance ministers of the Group of Five met again, in Paris, and reached

---

[3] For an extended discussion of the dollar exchange rate in the 1980s, see B. D. Pauls, "U.S. Exchange Rate Policy: Bretton Woods to the Present," *Federal Reserve Bulletin,* November 1990, pp. 891–908.

Figure 10.2
U.S. Dollar Movements, 1970–90

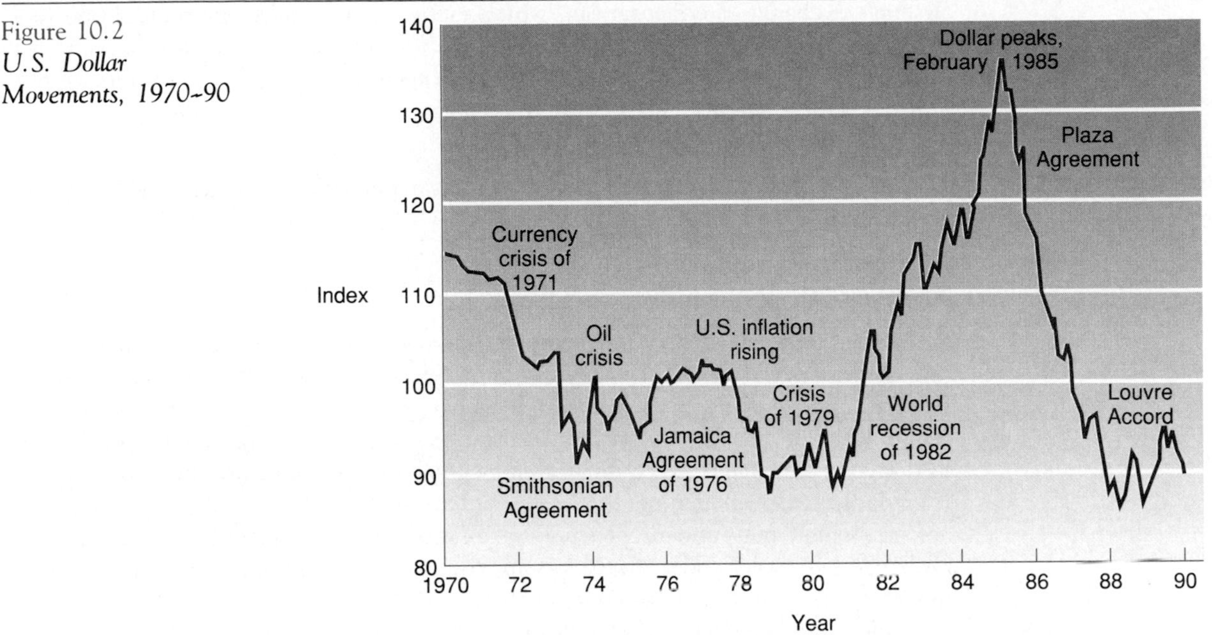

Source: 15-country nominal exchange rate index of the U.S. dollar. Morgan Guaranty, World Financial Markets, *various issues. 1980–1982 = 100.*

a new agreement known as the *Louvre Accord.* They agreed that exchange rates had been realigned sufficiently and pledged to support the stability of exchange rates around their current levels by intervening in the foreign exchange markets when necessary to buy and sell currency. Although the dollar continued to decline for a few months after the Louvre Accord, the rate of decline slowed, and by early 1988 the decline had ended. Except for a brief speculative flurry around the time of the Persian Gulf War in 1991, the dollar has been relatively stable since then.

Thus, we see that in recent history the value of the dollar has been determined by both market forces and government intervention. Under a floating exchange rate regime, the working out of market forces has produced a very volatile dollar exchange rate. Governments have responded by intervening in the market—buying and selling dollars —in attempting to limit the market's volatility and to correct what they see as overvaluation (in 1985) or potential undervaluation (in 1987) of the dollar. The frequency of government intervention in the foreign exchange markets explains why the current system is variously referred to as a *managed-float system* or a *dirty float system.*

FIXED VERSUS FLOATING EXCHANGE RATES

The breakdown of the Bretton Woods system has not stopped the debate about the relative merits of fixed versus floating exchange rate regimes. Indeed, disappointment with the system of floating rates in recent years has led to renewed debate about the merits of a fixed exchange rate system. In this section we review the arguments for fixed and floating exchange rate regimes.[4] In the next we will discuss the European Monetary

[4] For a feel for the issues contained in this debate, see P. Krugman, "Has the Adjustment Process Worked?" Institute for International Economics, 1991; "Time to Tether Currencies, *The Economist,* January 6, 1990, pp. 15–16; and P. R. Krugman and M. Obstfeld, *International Economics: Theory and Policy* (New York: Harper Collins, 1991).

System's exchange rate mechanism, which many see as a prototype for a future fixed exchange rate system. We will discuss the case for floating rates before discussing why many commentators are disappointed with the experience under floating exchange rates and yearn for a reform to a system of fixed rates.

The Case for Floating Exchange Rates

The case for floating exchange rates has two main elements: monetary policy autonomy and automatic trade balance adjustments.

Monetary Policy Autonomy

It is argued that a floating exchange rate regime gives countries monetary policy autonomy. Under a fixed system, a country's ability to expand or contract its money supply as it sees fit is limited by the need to maintain exchange rate parity. Monetary expansion can lead to inflation, which puts downward pressure on a fixed exchange rate (as predicted by PPP theory; see Chapter 9). Similarly, monetary contraction requires high interest rates (to reduce the demand for money). Higher interest rates lead to an inflow of money from abroad, which puts upward pressure on a fixed exchange rate. Thus, to maintain exchange rate parity under a fixed system, countries were limited in their ability to use monetary policy to expand or contract their economies.

Advocates of a floating exchange rate regime argue that removal of the obligation to maintain exchange rate parity would restore monetary control to a government. If a government faced with unemployment wanted to increase its money supply to stimulate domestic demand and reduce unemployment, it could do so unencumbered by the need to maintain its exchange rate. While monetary expansion might lead to inflation, this in turn would lead to a depreciation in the country's currency. If PPP theory is correct, the resulting currency depreciation on the foreign exchange markets should offset the effects of inflation. Put another way, although under a floating exchange rate regime domestic inflation would have an impact on the exchange rate, it should have no impact on the country's businesses' international cost competitiveness due to exchange rate depreciation. The rise in domestic costs should be exactly offset by the fall in the value of the country's currency on the foreign exchange markets. Similarly, a government could use monetary policy to contract the economy without worrying about the need to maintain parity.

Trade Balance Adjustments

Under the Bretton Woods system, if a country developed a permanent deficit in its balance of trade (importing more than it exported) that could not be corrected by domestic policy, this would require the IMF to agree to a currency devaluation. Critics of this system argue that the adjustment mechanism works much more smoothly under a floating exchange rate regime. They argue that if a country is running a trade deficit, the imbalance between the supply and demand of that country's currency in the foreign exchange markets (supply exceeding demand) will lead to depreciation in its exchange rate. In turn, by making its exports cheaper and its imports more expensive, an exchange rate depreciation should ultimately correct the trade deficit.

The Case for Fixed Exchange Rates

The case for fixed exchange rates rests on arguments about monetary discipline, speculation, uncertainty, and the lack of connection between the trade balance and exchange rates.

Monetary Discipline

We have already discussed the nature of monetary discipline inherent in a fixed rate system when we discussed the form of the Bretton Woods system. The impo. point to remember is that the need to maintain a fixed exchange rate parity ensures that governments do not expand their money supplies at inflationary rates. While advocates of floating rates argue that each country should be allowed to choose its own inflation rate (the monetary autonomy argument), advocates of fixed rates argue that governments all too often give in to political pressures and expand the monetary supply far too rapidly, causing unacceptably high price inflation. A fixed exchange rate regime will ensure that this does not occur.

Speculation

Critics of a floating exchange rate regime also argue that speculation can cause fluctuations in exchange rates. They point to the dollar's rapid rise and fall during the 1980s, which they claim had nothing to do with comparative inflation rates and the U.S. trade deficit, but everything to do with speculation. They argue that if foreign exchange dealers see a currency depreciating, they tend to sell the currency in the expectation of future depreciation regardless of the currency's longer-term prospects. As more traders jump on the bandwagon, the expectations of depreciation are realized. Such destabilizing speculation tends to accentuate the fluctuations around the exchange rate's long-run value. It can be very damaging to a country's economy by distorting export and import prices. (For example, in 1985 U.S. exports may have been overpriced and imported goods underpriced due to the very high value of the dollar.) Thus, advocates of a fixed exchange rate regime argue that such a system will limit the destabilizing effects of speculation.

Uncertainty

Speculation also adds to the uncertainty surrounding future currency movements that characterizes floating exchange rate regimes. The unpredictability of exchange rate movements in the post-Bretton Woods era has made business planning difficult and it makes exporting, importing, and foreign investment risky activities. Given a volatile exchange rate, international businesses do not know how to react to the changes—and often they do not react. Why change plans for exporting, importing, or foreign investment after a 6 percent fall in the dollar this month, when the dollar may rise 6 percent next month? This uncertainty, according to the critics, puts a damper on the growth of international trade and investment. They argue that a fixed exchange rate, by eliminating such uncertainty, promotes the growth of international trade and investment. Advocates of a floating system reply that the forward exchange market does a good job of insuring against the risks associated with exchange rate fluctuations (see Chapter 9). Accordingly, the adverse impact of uncertainty on the growth of international trade and investment have been overstated.

Trade Balance Adjustments

Those in favor of floating exchange rates argue that floating rates help adjust trade imbalances. Critics question the closeness of the link between the exchange rate and the trade balance. They claim trade deficits are determined by the balance between savings and investment in a country, not by the external value of its currency.[5] Moreover, they argue that a depreciation in a currency will lead to inflation (due to the resulting increase in import prices). This inflation will wipe out any apparent gains in cost competitiveness that come from currency depreciation. In other words, a depreciating exchange rate will not boost exports and reduce imports, as advocates of floating rates claim; it will simply boost price inflation. In support of this argument, those who favor floating rates point out that the 40 percent drop in the value of the dollar between 1985 and 1988 did not seem to correct the U.S. trade deficit. In reply, advocates of a floating exchange rate regime argue that between 1985 and 1992, the U.S. trade deficit fell from over $160 billion to around $70 billion, and they attribute this in part to the decline in the value of the dollar.

Who Is Right?

So what we see today is a vigorous debate between those who favor a fixed exchange rate regime and those who favor a floating exchange rate regime. Which side is right? At this point we don't know. From a business perspective, this is unfortunate, since as a major player on the international trade and investment scene, business has a large stake in the resolution of the debate. Would international business be better off under a fixed regime, or are flexible rates better? The evidence is not yet in.

We do, however, know that a fixed exchange rate regime modeled along the lines of the Bretton Woods system will not work. Indeed, it is telling that speculation ultimately broke the system—a phenomenon that advocates of fixed rate regimes claim is associated with *floating* exchange rates! Nevertheless, it is quite possible that a different kind of fixed exchange rate system might be more enduring and might foster the kind of stability that would facilitate more rapid growth in international trade and investment. In the next section we look at a potential model for such a system, the exchange rate mechanism of the European Monetary System.

THE EUROPEAN MONETARY SYSTEM

In our discussion of the European Community (EC) in Chapter 8, we noted that the EC is currently committed to establishing a single currency by January 1, 1999 (although the feasibility of this is now in doubt, as we pointed out). A formal commitment to a common currency dates back only to the Treaty of Maastricht in December 1991, but it has been an underlying theme in the EC and a subject of debate for some time. If the EC is ever going to have a common currency, it must first achieve convergence between the inflation rates and interest rates of its 12 member-states. The European Monetary System (EMS) is viewed as a major mechanism for attaining this goal.[6] As we will see, however, in late 1992 the EMS was strained to a breaking point by waves of speculative pressure that cast doubt over the future of the system.

When the EMS was formally created in March 1979, it was entrusted with three main objectives:

1. To create a zone of monetary stability in Europe (by reducing exchange rate volatility and converging national interest rates).

---

[5] The argument is made by several prominent economists, particularly Stanford's Robert McKinnon. See R. McKinnon, "An International Standard for Monetary Stabilization," *Policy Analyses in International Economics* 8 (Washington, D.C.: Institute for International Economics, 1984). The details of this argument are beyond the scope of this book. For a relatively accessible exposition, see P. Krugman, *The Age of Diminished Expectations* (Cambridge, Mass.: MIT Press, 1990).

[6] See N. Colchester and D. Buchan, *Europower* (New York: Random House, 1990); and D. Swann, *The Economics of the Common Market* (London: Penguin Books, 1990).

Figure 10.3 *The Composition of an ecu*

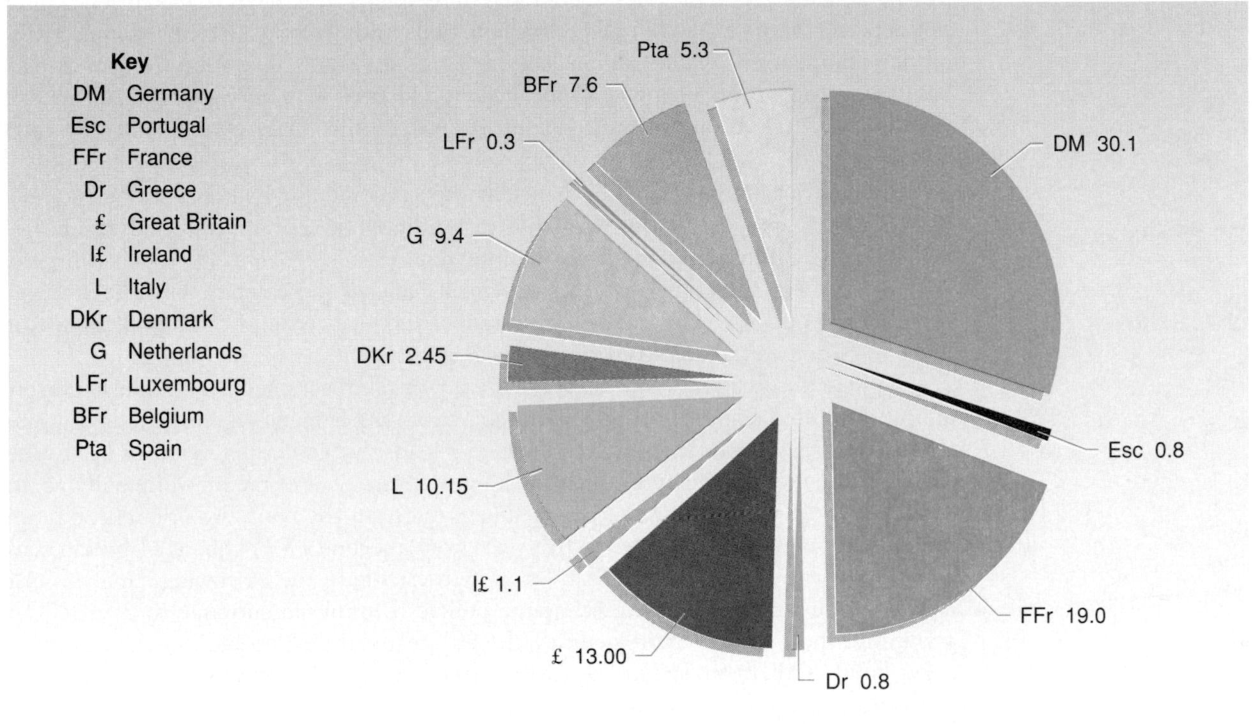

2. To control inflation through the imposition of monetary discipline.
3. To coordinate exchange rate policies versus non-EC currencies such as the U.S. dollar and the yen.

To these objectives can now be added the objective of paving the way for introduction of a common currency in 1999. Two instruments are being used to achieve these objectives, the European currency unit (ecu) and the exchange rate mechanism (ERM).

The ecu and the ERM

The **ecu** is a "basket" of the EC currencies that serves as the unit of account for the EMS. One ecu comprises defined percentages of national currencies. Figure 10.3 shows the composition of the ecu agreed to by EC finance ministers in September 1989. The share of each country's currency in the ecu is to depend on the country's relative economic weight within the EC. Thus, for example, 30.1 percent of the ecu's value was established by the value of the German deutsche mark in 1989, because that was the estimate of Germany's relative strength and size within the EC economy at the time.

The exchange rate mechanism (ERM) works as follows: Each national currency in the EC is given a "central rate" vis-à-vis the ecu. For example, in September 1989 one ecu was equal to DM 2.05853, to FFr 6.90404, or to £0.739615. This central rate can only be changed by a commonly agreed realignment (which has occurred 11 times since the inception of the system). From these central rates flow a series of bilateral rates—the French franc against the Italian lira, the German deutsche mark against the British pound, and so on. For example, the given figures vis-à-vis the ecu indicate that the bilateral rate for exchanging deutsche marks into francs was DM 1 = FFr 2.9586 (i.e., FFr 6.90404/DM 2.05853). The bilateral rates form a cat's cradle known as the *ERM parity grid,* which is the system's operational component. The rule is that a currency must not depart by more than 2.25 percent from its bilateral central rate with another ERM-participating currency. The only exceptions allowed to date have been for the Spanish peseta and the British pound. As more recent additions to the ERM, those currencies were allowed to fluctuate by up to 6 percent against other ERM currencies in the early 1990s.

Intervention in the foreign exchange markets is compulsory whenever one currency hits its outer margin of fluctuation relative to another. The central banks of the countries issuing both currencies are supposed to intervene to keep their currencies within the 2.25 percent (or 6 percent) band. The central bank of the country with the stronger currency is supposed to buy the weaker currency, and vice versa. In practice, however, it tends to be left to the country with the weaker currency to take action.

To defend its currency against speculative pressure, each member-state may borrow almost unlimited amounts of foreign currency from other members for periods of up to three months. A second line of defense includes loans that can be extended for up to nine months, but the total amount available is limited to a pool of credit—originally about 14 billion ecus—and the size of the member's quota in the pool. Additional funds are available for maturities from two to five years from a second pool of about 11 billion ecus (originally). However, as a condition of using these funds, the borrowing member must commit itself to correcting the economic policies causing its currency to deviate. To administer these various credit facilities, the EC created the European Monetary Cooperation Fund (EMCF) in 1982. The EMCF issued an initial supply of ecus to member-countries, each of which deposited 20 percent of their gold and dollar reserves with the EMCF in return for a corresponding amount of ecus.

The Performance of the System and Its Future

Underlying the ERM are all the standard beliefs about the virtues of fixed rate regimes that we have discussed. EC members believe the system imposes monetary discipline, removes uncertainty, limits speculation, and promotes international trade and investment within the EC. For most of the EMS's existence, its ability to achieve these objectives has been fairly good. When the ERM was first established, wide variations in national interest rates and inflation rates made its prospects seem shaky. For example, in early 1979 inflation was running at 2.7 percent in Germany and 12.1 percent in Italy. Since then, however, both inflation rates and interest rates have converged somewhat. As this occurred, the need for intervention and realignments declined, and the system appeared to become more stable.

However, there had long been concern within the EC about the dominance of the German deutsche mark within the ERM and about the vulnerability of a fixed system to speculative pressures. Many of these concerns were realized dramatically in September 1992, when two of the major EMS currencies—the British pound and the Italian lira—were hit by waves of speculative pressure. Dealers in the foreign exchange market, believing a realignment of the pound and the lira within the ERM was imminent, started to sell pounds and lira and to purchase German deutsche marks. This led to a fall in the value of the pound and the lira against the mark on the foreign exchange markets. Although the central banks of Great Britain and Italy tried to defend their currencies by raising interest rates and buying back pounds and lira, they were unable to keep the values of their currencies within their respective ERM bands. As a consequence, first

Great Britain and then Italy pulled out of the ERM, leaving the EMS teetering on the brink of collapse.

Since September 1992 the ERM has restabilized. As of early 1993, however, there were few signs that either Great Britain or Italy would reenter the EMS anytime soon. This near collapse of the EMS in September 1992 does not bode well for the planned adoption of a common currency by 1999. In addition, the ability of speculative pressure to bring the system to its knees demonstrates once again a limitation of a fixed exchange rate regime—its vulnerability to breakdown under speculative pressure on the foreign exchange market. (For further details on what happened in September 1992, see the case "Chaos in the Currency Markets," which follows Chapter 11).

THE IMF AND WORLD BANK AFTER BRETTON WOODS

The collapse of the Bretton Woods system left the IMF with a diminished role in the international monetary system. Recall that the IMF's original function was to provide a pool of money from which members could borrow, short term, to adjust their balance-of-payments position and maintain their exchange rate. Under a floating exchange rate regime, the demand for short-term loans was considerably diminished. A trade deficit would presumably lead to a decline in a country's exchange rate, which in turn would help reduce imports and boost exports. No temporary IMF adjustment loan would be needed. Consistent with this, most industrialized countries developed a tendency to let the foreign exchange market determine exchange rates in response to demand and supply. Indeed, no major industrial country has borrowed funds from the IMF since the mid-1970s, when Great Britain and Italy did. Moreover since the early 1970s the rapid development of global capital markets has allowed developed countries such as Great Britain and the United States to finance their deficits by borrowing private money, as opposed to drawing on IMF funds.

In response to these changes, the IMF has done what any bureaucracy interested in self-preservation might do; it found a new mission. This new mission was inspired by the OPEC oil price hikes of 1973 and 1979 and the resulting Third World debt crisis.

The Third World Debt Crisis[7]

The OPEC oil price increases in 1973 and 1979 resulted in massive flows of funds from the major oil-importing nations (e.g., Germany, Japan, and the United States) to the oil-producing nations of OPEC. Never slow to spot a profit opportunity, commercial banks quickly stepped in to recycle this money—borrowing from OPEC countries and lending to governments and businesses around the world. Much of the recycled money—too much, as it turned out—ended up in the form of loans to the governments of various Latin American and African nations. These loans were made on the basis of optimistic assessments about these nations' short- and medium-term growth prospects, which did not materialize. Rather, Third World economic growth was choked off in the early 1980s by a combination of factors, including:

- Rising short-term interest rates worldwide (which increased the costs of debt).
- Poor macroeconomic management in a number of Third World countries—in particular, inflationary growth policies.

[7] For details see A. J. Schwartz, "International Debt: What's Fact and What's Fiction," *Economic Inquiry* 27 (January 1989), pp. 1–19; and "What Happens to the IMF when a Whole Nation Calls on It?" *The Economist*, December 11, 1982, pp. 69–80.

- Poor use of the funds borrowed by Third World governments (all too often to finance consumption rather than investment).
- A slowdown in the growth rate of the industrialized West, the main markets for Third World products.

The consequence was a Third World debt crisis of massive proportions. At one point it was calculated that commercial banks had over $1 trillion of bad debts on their books, debts that the debtor nations had no hope of paying off. If any major country had defaulted at this time, the shock waves would have shaken the world financial system. Many feared that if this were to occur, the resulting bank failures in the advanced nations would turn the widespread recession of the 1980s into a deep depression.

Against this background, Mexico, long thought to be the most creditworthy of the major Third World debtor countries, announced in 1982 that it could no longer service its $80 billion in international debt without an immediate new loan of $3 billion. Brazil quickly followed, revealing that it could not meet the required payments on its borrowed $87 billion. Then Argentina and several dozen other countries of lesser credit standings followed suit. The international monetary system was facing a crisis of enormous dimensions.

From the IMF Solution to the Brady Plan

Into the breach stepped the IMF. Together with several Western governments, particularly that of the United States, the IMF emerged as the key player in resolving the debt crisis. The deal with Mexico involved three elements:

1. Rescheduling of Mexico's old debt.
2. New loans to Mexico from the IMF, the World Bank, and commercial banks.
3. The Mexican government's agreement to abide by a set of IMF-dictated macroeconomic prescriptions for its economy, including tight control over the growth of the money supply and major cuts in government spending.

Among other things, orchestrating this agreement required the IMF to persuade approximately 1,600 commercial banks that had already loaned money to Mexico to increase the amount of their loans by 8 percent. The IMF's success in pulling this off, first for Mexico and later for other debt-ridden Third World countries, was no small achievement.

However, the IMF's solution to the debt crisis contained a major weakness: it depended on the rapid resumption of growth in the debtor nations. If this occurred, their capacity to repay debt would grow faster than their debt itself, and the crisis would be resolved. By the mid-1980s, clearly this was not going to happen. True, the IMF-imposed macroeconomic policies did succeed in bringing the trade deficits and inflation rates of many debtor nations under control, but it was at the price of sharp contractions in their economic growth rates.

By 1989 it was clear that the debt problem was not going to be solved merely by rescheduling debt. In April of that year, the IMF endorsed a new approach that had first been proposed by Nicholas Brady, the U.S. Treasury secretary. The *Brady Plan,* as it became known, stated that debt reduction—as distinguished from debt rescheduling—was a necessary part of the solution and that the IMF and World Bank would assume roles in financing it. The essence of the plan was that the IMF, the World Bank, and the Japanese government would each contribute $10 billion to the task of debt reduction. To gain access to these funds, a debtor nation would once again have to submit to a set of imposed conditions for macroeconomic policy management and debt repayment. The first application of the Brady Plan was the Mexican debt reduction of 1989. The deal, which reduced Mexico's 1989 debt of $107 billion by about $15 billion, has been widely regarded as a success.[8]

The Future of the IMF and the World Bank

One consequence of the IMF's involvement in resolving the Third World debt crisis is the blurring of the line between it and the World Bank. Under the original Bretton Woods agreement, the IMF was to provide short-term loans, and the World Bank was to provide long-term loans. Since the 1970s, however, the IMF has been increasingly involved in providing long-term loans to debt-ridden nations. According to one estimate, some 20 of these countries have been continuous users of IMF credit for more than 12 years.

The evolution of the IMF into a long-term lending and development agency looks set to continue. The collapse of communism in Eastern Europe and the subsequent breakup of the Soviet Union has resulted in a flood of applications for IMF membership from the newly democratic nations there, including a much debated one from Russia. No doubt, given the problems associated with transforming their centrally planned economies into market economies, many of these potential new members will be calling on the IMF for long-term loans.

Not only is the IMF moving closer to the World Bank, the World Bank has also been moving closer to the IMF since the 1970s. During the 1970s the bank noticed that many of its specific loan projects—such as those for irrigation, energy, and transportation projects—were failing to produce the kind of long-term economic gains for the borrowing countries that the bank's officials had predicted. On closer examination, the bank found that many of its specific projects were undermined not by defects in their design but by the broader policy environment of the particular country. More precisely, the bank found that the returns on its loan projects were much lower in countries where growth was limited by a poor macroeconomic policy. A good project in a bad economy was likely to be a bad project. It was obvious that loan conditions needed to extend beyond the project to the economy as a whole.

In response, the World Bank has devised a new type of loan. In addition to providing funds to support specific projects, the bank will now also provide loans for the government of a nation to use as it sees fit in return for promises on macroeconomic policy. This is essentially the same approach as the IMF's in recent years. As we have seen, the IMF has loaned money to debtor nations in return for promises about macroeconomic policy. Now the World Bank is doing the same thing.

The convergence between the World Bank and the IMF points to the possibility of a merger between the IMF and the bank sometime in the future. Since these two institutions are now doing each other's jobs, the argument for merging them is compelling. Although this may occur in the future, at present both institutions are so busy with their new commitments in Eastern Europe that they would not have the time to effect a merger. As one commentator put it, "This is not the time to sap the institutions' energies with grandiose schemes of reform. But a merger makes sense, and in time it will happen."[9]

The evolution of global capital markets has also raised questions about the role of the IMF and the World Bank. In 1944 the global capital market hardly existed. As we shall

---

[8] For a summary of the arguments for debt reductions, see "And Forgive Us Our Debts: A Survey of the IMF and the World Bank," *The Economist,* October 12, 1991, pp. 23–33; and Krugman, *Diminished Expectations.*

[9] "Prelude to Testing Time: A Survey of the IMF and the World Bank," *The Economist,* October 12, 1991, p. 48.

see in Chapter 11, by 1990 it was channeling immense flows of money around the world every day. Before the emergence of a global capital market there was arguably a strong need for lending institutions such as the World Bank and the IMF to channel funds to poorer nations. Now critics argue that with the exception of emergencies such as a debt crisis, the capital market should perhaps decide which governments are worth lending to and which are not. Put another way, do we need the IMF and the World Bank? At this time, there is significant debate over this issue.[10]

IMPLICATIONS FOR BUSINESS

The implications of the material discussed in this chapter for international businesses fall into three main areas: currency management, business strategy, and corporate-government relations.

Currency Management

An obvious implication with regard to currency management is that companies must recognize that the foreign exchange market does not work quite as depicted in Chapter 9. The current system is a *managed-float system* in which government intervention can help drive the foreign exchange market (e.g., as in the cases of the Plaza Accord and the Louvre Accord). Companies engaged in significant foreign exchange activities need to be aware of this and to adjust their foreign exchange transactions accordingly. For example, the currency management unit of Caterpillar Tractor claims that it made millions of dollars in the hours following the announcement of the Plaza Accord by selling dollars and buying currencies that it expected to appreciate on the foreign exchange market following government intervention (see the opening case).

A second message contained in this chapter is that under the present system, speculative buying and selling of currencies can create very volatile movements in exchange rates (as exhibited by the rise and fall of the dollar during the 1980s). Moreover, contrary to the predictions of the purchasing power parity theory (see Chapter 9), we have seen that exchange rate movements during the 1980s, at least with regard to the dollar, did not seem to be strongly influenced by relative inflation rates. Insofar as volatile exchange rates increase foreign exchange risk, this is not good news for business. On the other hand, as we saw in Chapter 9, the foreign exchange market has developed a number of instruments, such as the forward market and swaps, that can help to insure against foreign exchange risk. Not surprisingly, use of these instruments has increased markedly since the breakdown of the Bretton Woods system in 1973.

Business Strategy

One thing illustrated by the opening case is that the present international monetary system presents both opportunities and threats. As an example of threats, Caterpillar Tractor's problems during the early 1980s were partly due to the volatility of a floating exchange rate regime in which speculative pressure drove up the value of the dollar and partly due to the tough macroeconomic discipline enforced on Third World debtor nations by the IMF (which led to a contraction of Cat's market). As for opportunities, the rise in the value of the dollar clearly created an opportunity for Komatsu to gain market share from Cat.

Firms respond to opportunities and threats by their choice of strategy. The volatility of the present floating exchange rate regime suggests that one response might be to build

[10] "Back It or Scrap It, *Euromoney*, September 1990, pp. 29–36.

strategic flexibility. Faced with uncertainty about the future value of currencies, firms can utilize the forward exchange market. However, the forward market is far from perfect as a predictor of future exchange rates (see Chapter 9). Moreover, it is difficult if not impossible to get adequate insurance coverage for exchange rate changes that might occur several years in the future. The forward market tends to offer coverage for exchange rate changes a few months—not years—ahead. Given this, it makes sense to pursue strategies that will increase the company's strategic flexibility in the face of unpredictable exchange rate movements.

Maintaining strategic flexibility can take the form of dispersing production to different locations around the globe as a hedge against currency fluctuations. Ingersoll-Rand has taken this approach, increasing its overseas capacity and reducing its dependence on U.S. exports in an attempt to protect itself against any future speculative upsurges in the value of the dollar. Similarly, the move by Japanese automobile companies to expand their productive capacity in the United States and Europe can be seen in the context of the increase in the value of the yen since 1985, which has increased the price of Japanese exports. For the Japanese companies, building production capacity overseas is a hedge against continued appreciation of the yen (as well as against trade barriers).

Another way of building strategic flexibility involves contracting out manufacturing. This allows a company to shift suppliers from country to country in response to shifts in relative costs brought about by exchange rate movements. However, this kind of strategy only works for low-value-added manufacturing (e.g., textiles), in which the individual manufacturers have few if any firm-specific skills that contribute to the value of the product. It is completely inappropriate in the case of **high-value-added** manufacturing, in which firm-specific technology and skills add significant value to the product (e.g., the heavy equipment industry) and in which switching costs are correspondingly high. Put another way, in the case of high-value-added manufacturing, switching suppliers will lead to a reduction in the value that is added, which may offset any cost gains arising from exchange rate fluctuations.

The role of the IMF and the World Bank in the present international monetary system also has implications for business strategy. Increasingly, the IMF and World Bank are acting as macroeconomic policemen, insisting that countries coming to them for significant borrowings adopt IMF- or World Bank-mandated macroeconomic policies. These policies typically include antiinflationary monetary policy and reductions in government spending. In the short run, such policies usually result in a sharp contraction of demand. International businesses selling or producing in such countries need to be aware of this and plan accordingly (e.g., witness what IMF policies did to Caterpillar's international markets in the early 1980s). On the other hand, in the long run, the kind of policies imposed by the IMF and World Bank can promote economic growth and an expansion of demand, which create opportunities for international business.

Corporate-Government Relations

As major players in the international trade and investment environment, businesses can influence government policy toward the international monetary system. For example, intense government lobbying by Caterpillar and other U.S. exporters helped persuade the U.S. government that intervention in the foreign exchange market was necessary. Similarly, much of the impetus behind the establishment of the exchange rate mechanism of the European Monetary System came from European businesspeople, who understood very well the costs of volatile exchange rates.

With this in mind, business can and should use its influence to promote an international monetary system that facilitates the growth of international trade and investment. Whether a fixed or floating regime is optimal is a subject for debate. What does seem probable, however, is that exchange rate volatility such as the world experienced during the 1980s creates an environment less conducive to international trade and investment than one with more stable exchange rates. Therefore, it would seem to be in the interests of international business to promote an international monetary system that minimizes volatile exchange rate movements, particularly when those movements are unrelated to long-run economic fundamentals.

SUMMARY OF CHAPTER

The objectives of this chapter were to explain the workings of the international monetary systems and to point out its implications for international business. Specific points we have made include the following:

1. The gold standard is a monetary standard that pegs currencies to gold and guarantees convertibility to gold.
2. It was thought that the gold standard contained an automatic mechanism that contributed to the simultaneous achievement of a balance-of-payments equilibrium by all countries.
3. The gold standard broke down during the 1930s as countries engaged in competitive devaluations.
4. The Bretton Woods system of fixed exchange rates was established in 1944. The U.S. dollar was the central currency of this system; the value of every other currency was pegged to its value. Significant exchange rate devaluations were allowed only with the permission of the IMF.
5. The role of the IMF was to maintain order in the international monetary system (*i*) to avoid a repetition of the competitive devaluations of the 1930s and (*ii*) to control price inflation by imposing monetary discipline on countries.
6. To build flexibility into the system, the IMF stood ready to lend countries funds to help protect their currency on the foreign exchange market in the face of speculative pressure, and to assist countries in correcting a fundamental disequilibrium in their balance-of-payments position.
7. The fixed exchange rate system collapsed in 1973, primarily due to speculative pressure on the dollar following a rise in U.S. inflation and a growing U.S. balance-of-trade deficit.
8. Since 1973 the world has operated with a floating exchange rate regime, and exchange rates have become more volatile and far less predictable. For example, the value of the dollar rose rapidly on the foreign exchange market between 1980 and 1985 and then fell rapidly between 1985 and 1988.
9. Volatile exchange rate movements have helped reopen the debate over the merits of fixed and floating systems.
10. The case for a floating exchange rate regime claims: (*i*) that such a system gives countries autonomy regarding their monetary policy and (*ii*) that floating exchange rates facilitate smooth adjustment of trade imbalances.
11. The case for a fixed exchange rate regime claims: (*i*) that the need to maintain a fixed exchange rate imposes monetary discipline on a country, (*ii*) that floating exchange rate regimes are vulnerable to speculative pressure, (*iii*) that the uncertainty that accompanies floating exchange rates puts a damper on the growth of international trade and investment, and (*iv*) that far from correcting trade imbalances, depreciating a currency on the foreign exchange market tends to cause price inflation.
12. The objectives of the European Monetary System (EMS) are to (*i*) create a zone of monetary stability in Europe, (*ii*) control inflation, and (*iii*) coordinate exchange rate policies with non-EC currencies.
13. The ecu is a "basket" of currencies that serves as the unit of account for the EMS. Each national currency in the EMS is given a central rate vis-à-vis the ecu. Bilateral rates are calculated from these central rates. Currencies are not allowed to depart by more than 2.25 percent from their bilateral rate with another EMS currency. A country may borrow from another country to defend its currency against speculative pressure.
14. The collapse of the Bretton Woods system left the IMF and World Bank with diminished roles in the international monetary system. In response, both the IMF and the World Bank have developed into global macroeconomic policemen. Today they lend money to countries with balance-of-payments, debt, or development problems, extracting promises to adopt specific macroeconomic policies as a condition.
15. Given the convergence of roles, the IMF and the World Bank may merge in the future.
16. The present managed-float system of exchange rate de-

termination has increased the importance of currency management in international businesses.

17. The volatility of exchange rates under the present managed-float system creates both opportunities and threats. One way of responding to this volatility is for companies to build strategic flexibility by dispersing production to different locations around the globe by contracting out manufacturing (in the case of low-value-added manufacturing), and other means.

DISCUSSION QUESTIONS

1. Why did the gold standard collapse? Is there a case for returning to some type of gold standard? What is it?
2. What opportunities might IMF lending policies to Third World nations create for international businesses? What threats might they create?
3. Debate the relative merits of fixed and floating exchange rate regimes. From the perspective of an international business, what are the most important criteria in a choice between the systems? Which system is the more desirable for an international business?
4. Imagine that Canada, the United States, and Mexico decide to adopt a fixed exchange rate system similar to the ERM of the European Monetary System. What would be the likely consequences of such a system for (*a*) international businesses and (*b*) the flow of trade and investment among the three countries.

The Global Capital Market

CHAPTER 11

BIOMEDEX

Biomedex is a medium-sized Belgian pharmaceutical firm. The company began exploratory biotechnology research in the early 1970s and by the latter half of that decade had developed some enzymes that seemed to have industrial applications. Production of a commercially viable biotechnology product would take several years, however. To proceed further, Biomedex would need to raise large sums of capital to fund an extensive research and product development phase. The most obvious thing for Biomedex to do would have been to arrange for a new issue of shares on the Belgian stock market. Unfortunately, Belgium's stock market was small, lacked liquidity, and was segmented from international markets. As a consequence, it would have been very difficult for Biomedex to successfully float a new equity issue of the size it needed. Moreover, even if an equity issue of the required size could have been floated successfully, the rate of return demanded by Belgian stockholders would have made Biomedex's cost of capital significantly higher than its international competitors'. In other words, the limited liquidity and conservative nature of Belgium's capital market would have made it very costly for Biomedex to raise the capital in its own country. • Faced with this dilemma, Biomedex contacted Morgan Grenfell, a London-based commercial bank with major international banking operations. Morgan Grenfell advised Biomedex to issue Eurobonds to foreign investors. In 1979 Morgan Grenfell successfully organized a syndicate to underwrite and sell an issue of convertible Eurobonds that would raise $35 million for Biomedex. Also, Morgan Grenfell arranged for Biomedex to list its shares on the London Stock Exchange to facilitate conversion and gain visibility. • At this time biotechnology was attracting the interest of the U.S. investment community. Stock issues by a number of U.S. start-up firms such as Genentech and Cetus had been oversubscribed. Biomedex, needing additional funds, decided to explore the potential for a U.S. stock offering and listing of its shares on the New York Stock Exchange (NYSE). As a first step, it decided to have its shares quoted on the U.S. over-the-counter market (NASDAQ) for the purpose of increasing its visibility in the U.S. investment community. Having done this, with the assistance of Morgan Grenfell and Goldman Sachs, a major U.S. stockbroker, Biomedex prepared a prospectus for Securities Exchange Commission (SEC) registration of its U.S. stock offering and listing on the NYSE. To comply with the SEC's regulations, Biomedex had to prepare financial statements consistent with U.S. accounting principles. This was no small task, since its existing accounting systems—tailored to Belgian law—did not supply data in the form required by the SEC. • By June 1981 Biomedex was ready to announce its new share issue, which would increase the number of Biomedex shares outstanding by 20 percent. Immediately following the announcement, Biomedex's shares lost 15 percent of their value on the Belgian stock exchange. This reaction is typical in an illiquid, conservative stock market. Many Belgian investors, worried about the dilution effect of the new share issue, dumped the stock. When the market opened in the United States six hours later, however, Biomedex's shares quickly rose to above their previous value. The demand for Biomedex stock in the United States reflected the U.S. investors' belief that a greater supply of Biomedex stock following the new issue would create a more liquid market for the stock. This attracted many institutional investors that had previously held off buying out of fear that they may not be able to subsequently sell the stock without depressing the price. The broader market in Biomedex stock that would exist after the new issue made this less likely—hence the upsurge in U.S. demand for Biomedex stock. As it turned out, the new issue was a huge success, raising an additional $50 million for Biomedex. *Biomedex is a fictitious company. The case is based on information contained in a case on a Danish firm, Nova, that faced similar problems. See A. Stonehill and K. B. Dullum,* Internationalizing the Cost of Capital in Theory and in Practice: The Nova Experience and National Policy Implications *(New York: Wiley, 1983).*

INTRODUCTION

Biomedex overcame the limits to its growth imposed by an illiquid, conservative domestic capital market by tapping the international capital market. This kind of financial strategy would not have been possible in the early 1960s. At that time most capital markets were purely domestic. The barriers to the flow of funds across borders made it difficult for companies to raise money through international bond issues or by floating stock on international equity markets. The intervening 30 or so years have seen enormous growth in the international capital market. Due to deregulation of domestic financial markets during the 1980s and the advent of modern communications and data processing technology, such cities as New York, London, and Tokyo have become hubs of an international capital market in which billions of dollars flow across national borders each day.

To get a feel for how dramatic this development has been, consider these statistics:[1]

- In 1980 the stock of "international bank lending" (i.e., cross-border lending plus domestic lending denominated in foreign currency) was $324 billion. By 1991 it had risen to $7.5 trillion.
- In 1982 the total of international bonds outstanding was $259 million; by 1991 it was $1.65 trillion.
- In 1970 U.S. securities transactions with foreigners (purchases and sales of bonds and equities involving a resident and a nonresident) amounted to the equivalent of 3 percent of the U.S. gross domestic product (GDP). In 1980 the figure was 9 percent, and in 1990 it was 93 percent. The corresponding figures for West Germany were 3 percent, 8 percent, and 58 percent. For Japan they were 2 percent, 7 percent, and 119 percent. Due to the dominant position of London in the world's financial markets, Great Britain's cross-border securities transactions were equivalent to 368 percent of GDP even in 1985. By 1990 this figure had increased to 690 percent.
- Between 1980 and 1990 the volume of worldwide cross-border transactions in equities grew at a compound rate of 28 percent per year, from $120 billion to $1.4 trillion per year.

The dramatic rate of growth in the international capital market revealed by these figures has led some to comment that when an economic history of the 20th century is written, the 1980s will not be remembered for the international debt crisis, the dollar's rise and fall, the U.S. budget deficit, or Reaganomics. Rather, it will be remembered as the decade in which many of the boundaries between national capital markets dissolved and a truly global capital market emerged. The implications of this transformation in the global financial environment are only starting to become apparent.

To service this global market we have seen the rapid internationalization of the financial services industry. Banks that only 20 years ago confined themselves primarily to their domestic markets—banks such as Sumitomo Bank (Japan), Citicorp (United States), Banque Nationale de Paris (France), National Westminster Bank (Great Britain), Deutsche Bank (Germany), and the Union Bank of Switzerland—now have offices in all of the world's important financial centers.

In this environment the financial strategy pursued by Biomedex has become commonplace. Nor is international borrowing limited to firms such as Biomedex that are

---

[1] Data drawn from "Fear of Finance: Survey of the World Economy," *The Economist*, September 19, 1992, pp. 5–9.

based in countries with illiquid domestic capital markets. As the listed statistics suggest, it is now quite normal for companies of all nations to raise funds on the international capital market. For example, in 1989 the Dai-Ichi Kangyo Bank of Japan, then the world's largest bank, helped Dow Chemical, the largest U.S. chemical company, to raise funds in the Japanese credit market by issuing yen-denominated bonds.[2]

In a related development, it is no longer unusual for investors to diversify their portfolios by investing in foreign equity or bond markets. In 1989, for example, cross-border equity investing amounted to about 14.5 percent of world stock turnover. One transaction out of seven involved a foreign investor, and more than 7 percent of the aggregate value of the world's major stock markets was held by nonresident (foreign) investors.[3]

Against this background, the objective of this chapter is to explain the functions and form of the international capital market and to map out the implications for international business practice. We begin by examining the international capital market, the reasons for its recent growth, and the major players in the market. The international capital market comprises three submarkets: the Eurocurrency market, the international bond market, and the international equity market. Accordingly, we will review each of these in turn. As usual, we close the chapter by pointing out some of the implications of the chapter material for the practice of international business.

THE NATURE OF THE INTERNATIONAL CAPITAL MARKET

Although this section is about the international capital market, we open it by discussing the functions of a generic capital market. Then we will look at the limitations of domestic capital markets, which help explain why an increasing number of companies are using the international capital market to raise funds. Having done this, we will look at the forces responsible for the enormous growth of international capital markets in the last 20 years. Then we will examine the geography of the international capital market and distinguish some of its key players.

The Functions of a Generic Capital Market

Starting with an elementary question, Why do we *have* capital markets? What is their function? In simplest terms, a capital market brings together those who want to invest money and those who want to borrow money (see Figure 11.1). Those who want to invest money are corporations with surplus cash, individuals, and nonbank financial institutions (e.g., pension funds, insurance companies). Those who want to borrow money are individuals, companies, and governments. In between these two groups are the market makers. **Market makers** are the financial service companies that connect investors and borrowers, either directly or indirectly. They include commercial banks (e.g., Citibank, U.S. Bank) and investment banks (e.g., Merrill Lynch, Goldman Sachs).

Commercial banks perform an indirect connection function. They take deposits from corporations and individuals and pay them a rate of interest in return. They then loan that money to borrowers at a higher rate of interest, making a profit from the difference in interest rates. **Investment banks** perform a direct connection function. They bring investors and borrowers together and charge commissions for doing so. For example, Merrill Lynch may act as a stockbroker for an individual who wants to invest some money. Its personnel will advise her as to the most attractive purchases, buy stock on her behalf, and charge her a fee for the service.

---

2 R. J. Maturi, "Foreign Bankers No Longer Bit Players," *Industry Week*, July 17, 1989, pp. 62–63.

3 R. Reich, *The Work of Nations* (New York: Alfred A. Knopf, 1991).

Figure 11.1
The Main Players in a Generic Capital Market

Investors:		Market makers:		Borrowers:
Companies	→	Commercial bankers	→	Individuals
Individuals		Investment bankers		Companies
Institutions				Governments

The Distinction between Debt and Equity

Capital market loans to corporations are either equity loans or debt loans. An **equity loan** is made when a corporation sells stock to investors. The money the corporation receives in return for its stock can be used to purchase plants and equipment, fund R&D projects, pay wages, and so on. A share of stock gives its holder a claim to a firm's profit stream. The corporation honors this claim by paying out dividends to the stockholders. The amount of the dividends is not fixed in advance. Rather, it is determined by management on the basis of how much profit the corporation is making.

A **debt loan** requires the corporation to repay a predetermined portion of the loan amount (the sum of the principal plus the specified interest) at regular intervals regardless of how much profit it is making. Unlike equity loans, management has no discretion as to the amount it will pay investors. Debt loans include cash loans from banks and funds raised from the sale of corporate bonds to investors. When an investor purchases a corporate bond, she purchases the right to receive a specified fixed stream of income from the corporation for a specified number of years (i.e., until the bond maturity date).

Attractions of the International Capital Market

At this point one might ask, Why do we *need* international capital markets? Why are domestic capital markets not sufficient? An international capital market benefits both borrowers and investors. It benefits borrowers by increasing the supply of funds available for borrowing and by lowering the cost of capital. It benefits investors by providing a wider range of investment opportunities, thereby allowing them to build portfolios of international investments that diversify their risks.

The Borrower's Perspective: A Lower Cost of Capital

In a purely domestic capital market, the pool of investors is limited to residents of the country. This places an upper limit on the supply of funds available to borrowers. In other words, the liquidity of the market is limited. (Biomedex faced this problem in the opening case.) It follows that an international capital market, with its much larger pool of investors, provides a larger supply of funds for borrowers to draw on.

Perhaps the most important drawback of the limited liquidity of a purely domestic capital market is that the cost of capital tends to be higher than it is in an international market. The **cost of capital** is the rate of return that borrowers must pay investors (the price of borrowing money). This is the interest rate on debt loans and the dividend yield on equity loans. In a purely domestic market, the limited pool of investors implies that borrowers must pay more to persuade investors to loan them their money. The larger pool of investors in an international market implies that borrowers will be able to pay less.

The argument is illustrated in Figure 11.2, using the Biomedex example. The vertical axis in the figure is the cost of capital, and the horizontal axis, the amount of money available at varying interest rates. *DD* is Biomedex's demand curve for borrow-

Figure 11.2
Market Liquidity and the Cost of Capital

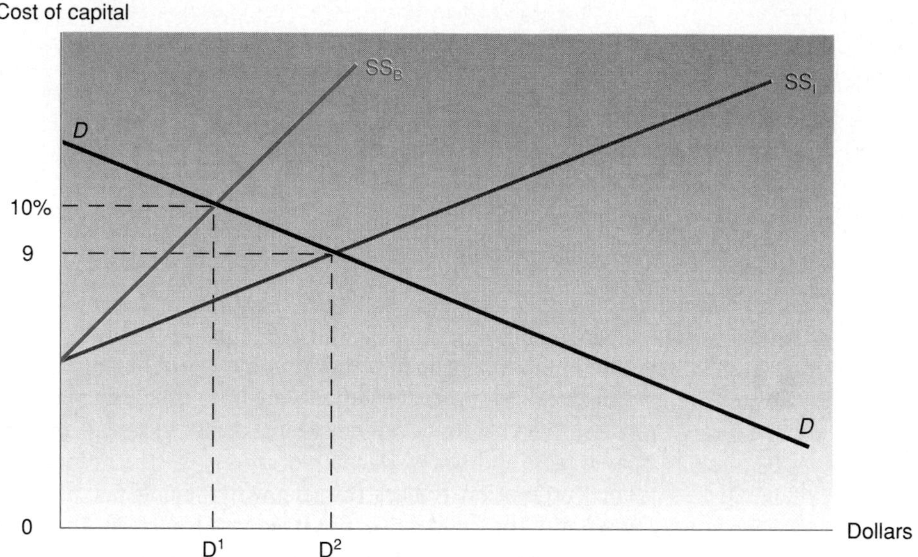

ings. Note that Biomedex's demand for funds varies with the cost of capital; the lower the cost of capital, the more money Biomedex will borrow. (Money is just like anything else; the lower its price, the more of it people can afford.) SS_B is the supply curve of funds available in the Belgian capital market, and SS_I represents the funds available in the international capital market. Note that Biomedex can borrow more funds more cheaply on the international capital market. As Figure 11.2 illustrates, the greater pool of resources in the international capital market both lowers the cost of capital and increases the amount Biomedex can borrow. Thus, the advantage of an international capital market to borrowers is that it lowers the cost of capital.

The Investor's Perspective: Portfolio Diversification

From the perspective of an investor, the set of investment opportunities is limited in a purely domestic capital market. In contrast, by utilizing the international capital market, the investor has a much wider range of investment opportunities. The most significant consequence of this choice is that the investor can diversify her portfolio of holdings internationally, thereby reducing her risk to below what could be achieved by portfolio diversification in a purely domestic capital market.

Consider an investor who buys stock in a biotech firm, such as Biomedex, that has not yet produced a new product. Imagine the price of the stock is very volatile—investors are buying and selling the stock in large numbers in response to information about the firm's prospects. Such stocks are risky investments; the investor may win big if the firm produces a marketable product, but the investor may also lose all her money if the firm fails to come up with a product that sells. The investor can guard against the risk associated with holding this stock by buying other firms' stocks—particularly those weakly or negatively correlated with the biotech stock. The investment strategy here is that of acquiring a **diversified portfolio** of stock holdings. By holding a variety of stocks, the losses incurred when some stocks fail to live up to their promises are offset by the gains enjoyed when other stocks exceed their promise.

Figure 11.3
Risk Reduction through Portfolio Diversification

(*a*) Risk reduction through domestic diversification

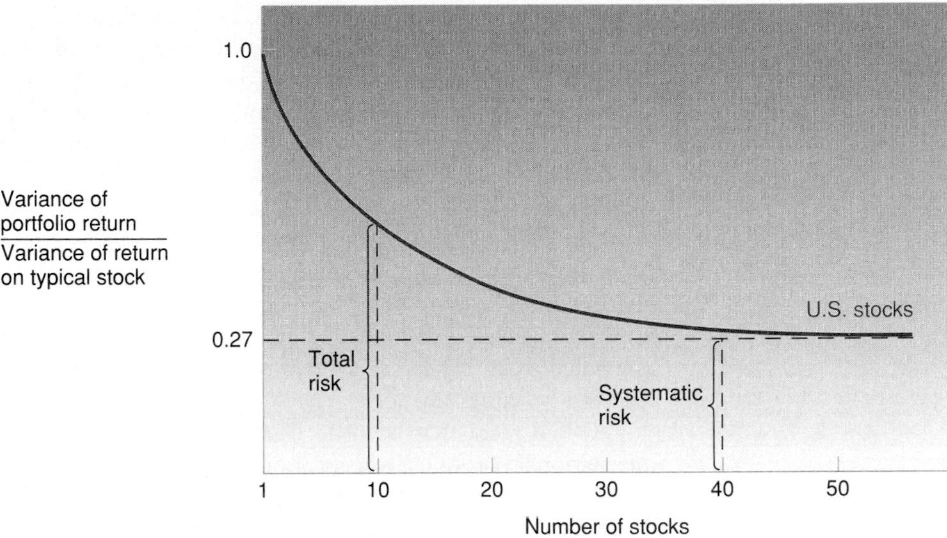

(*b*) Risk reduction through domestic and international diversification

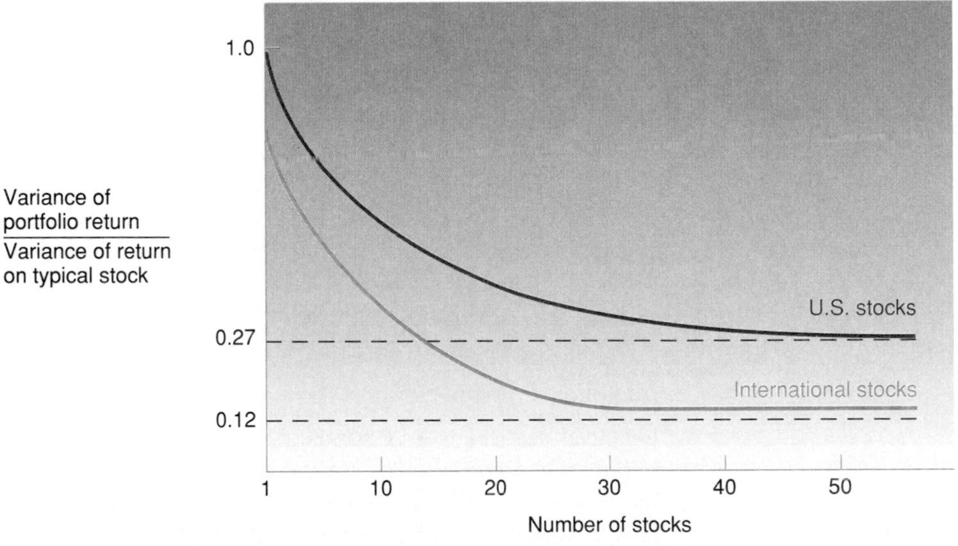

Source: B. Solnik, "Why Not Diversify Internationally Rather than Domestically?" Financial Analysts Journal, *July 1974, p. 17.*

Due to this effect, as an investor increases the number of stocks in her portfolio, the portfolio's risk declines. At first this decline is rapid. Soon, however, the rate of decline falls off and asymptotically approaches the **systematic risk** of the market. Systematic risk refers to movements in a stock portfolio's value that are attributable to macroeconomic forces affecting all firms in an economy, rather than factors specific to an individual firm. The systematic risk is the level of nondiversifiable risk in an economy. Figure 11.3a illustrates this relationship for the United States. It suggests that a fully diversified U.S. portfolio is only about 27 percent as risky as a typical individual stock.

By diversifying her portfolio internationally, an investor can reduce the level of risk even further. This is because the movement in stock market prices across countries is not strongly correlated. For example, between 1973 and 1982 the correlation of returns for all U.S. stocks was 0.439. However, for all U.S. and British stocks it was only 0.279, while for all U.S. and German stocks it was only 0.170.[4] Among other things, the lower international correlations reflect countries' differing macroeconomic policies and conditions. The implication is that by diversifying a portfolio to include non-U.S. stocks, a U.S. investor can reduce the level of risk still further.

Figure 11.3b illustrates this relationship. According to the figure, a fully diversified portfolio that contains stocks from many countries is less than half as risky as a fully diversified portfolio that contains only U.S. stocks. A fully diversified portfolio of international stocks is only about 12 percent as risky as a typical individual stock, whereas a fully diversified portfolio of U.S. stocks is about 27 percent as risky as a typical individual stock. The case for investing internationally as a means of diversifying risk seems to be rather strong.[5]

A final point that needs to be emphasized here is that the risk-reducing effects of international portfolio diversification would be even greater were it not for the volatile exchange rates associated with the current floating exchange rate regime. Floating exchange rates introduce an additional element of risk into investing in foreign assets. As we have said repeatedly, adverse exchange rate movements can transform otherwise profitable investments into unprofitable investments. Indeed, the uncertainty engendered by volatile exchange rates may be acting as a brake on the otherwise fairly rapid growth of the international capital market.

Growth of the International Capital Market

The preceding subsection established the fact that an international capital market benefits both investors and borrowers, since it allows investors to diversify their risk and allows borrowers to lower their cost of capital. Given this, it may seem surprising that the international capital market did not emerge until the 1960s and did not really come to life until the 1980s. Prior to the 1960s the world was divided into a series of relatively isolated domestic capital markets. What changed to allow the international capital market to bloom in the 1980s? There seem to be two answers—advances in information technology and deregulation by governments.

Information Technology

Financial services is an information-intensive industry. It draws on large volumes of information about markets, risks, exchange rates, interest rates, creditworthiness, and so on. It uses this information to make decisions about what to invest where, how much to charge borrowers, how much interest to pay to depositors, and about the value and riskiness of a whole range of financial assets including corporate bonds, stocks, government securities, and currencies.

As a consequence of this information intensity, the financial services industry has been revolutionized more than any other industry by advances in information technology since the 1960s. The growth of international communications technology has facilitated instantaneous communication between any two points on the globe. At the same time,

---

[4] For evidence see C. Eun and B. Resnick, "Estimating the Correlation Structure of International Share Prices," *Journal of Finance*, December 1984, pp. 1314–25.

[5] The data is from B. Solnik, "Why Not Diversify Internationally Rather than Domestically," *Financial Analysts Journal*, July 1974, p. 17.

Figure 11.4 *Trading Hours of the World's Major Financial Centers*

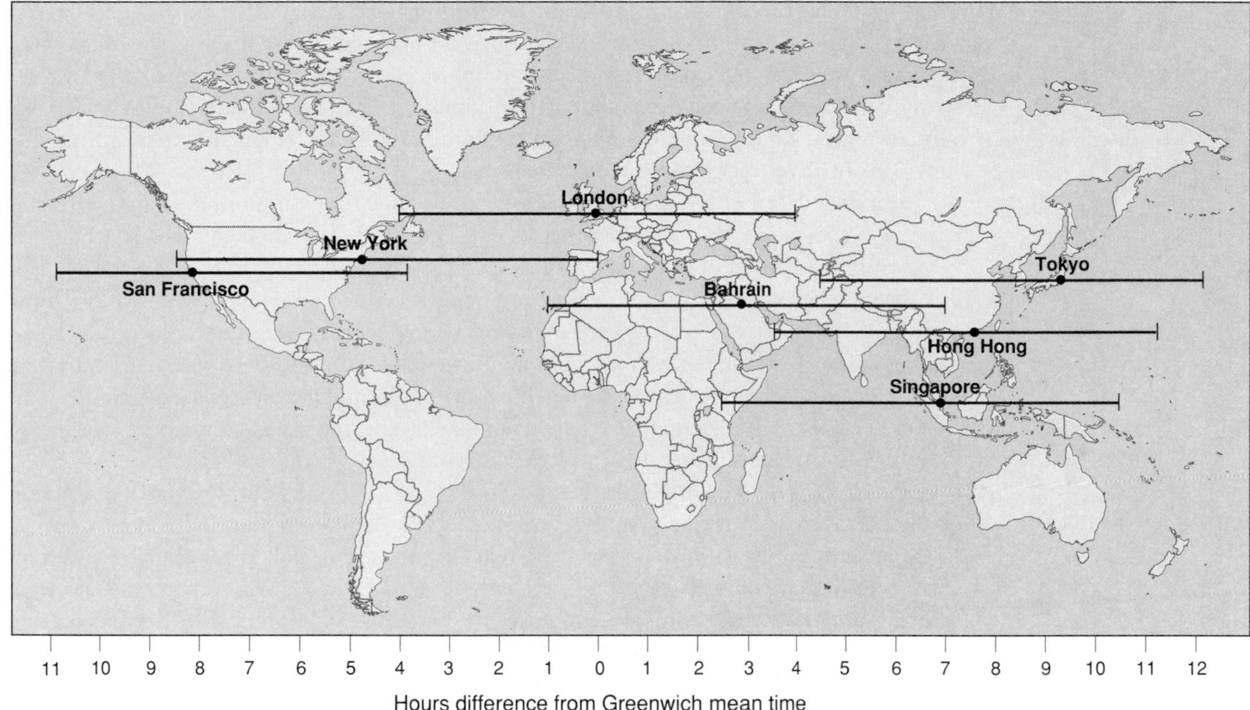

rapid advances in computers' data processing capabilities have allowed market makers to absorb and process large volumes of information from around the world. According to one study, a consequence of these technological developments is that the real cost of recording, transmitting, and processing information has fallen by 95 percent since 1964.[6]

Clearly such developments have facilitated the emergence of an integrated international capital market. It is now technologically possible for financial services companies to engage in 24-hour-a-day trading, whether it be in stocks, bonds, foreign exchange, or any other financial asset. Figure 11.4 shows how the trading hours of the world's major financial centers overlap. Due to advances in communications and data processing technology, the international capital market never sleeps. (There is a one hour time difference between San Francisco closing and Tokyo opening. During this period trading continues in New Zealand.)

Before moving on, we should point out that the integration facilitated by technology has a dark side. "Shocks" that occur in one financial center now spread around the globe very quickly. The collapse of U.S. stock prices on the notorious Black Monday of October 19, 1987, immediately triggered similar collapses in all of the world's major stock markets, wiping billions of dollars off the value of corporate stocks worldwide. Such events apart, however, most market participants would argue that the benefits of an integrated global capital market far outweigh any potential costs.

---

[6] T. F. Huertas, "U.S. Multinational Banking: History and Prospects," in *Banks as Multinationals*, ed. G. Jones (London: Routledge, 1990).

Deregulation

In country after country, financial services have probably been the most tightly regulated of all industries. Governments around the world have traditionally kept other countries' financial service firms from entering their capital markets. In some cases they have also restricted the overseas expansion of their domestic financial services firms. In addition, many countries' laws have segmented the domestic financial services industry. In the United States, for example, commercial banks are prohibited by law from performing the functions of investment banks, and vice versa.

Since the late 1970s many of these restrictions have been crumbling. In part, this has been a response to the development of the Eurocurrency market, which from the beginning was outside of national control. (This is explained later in the chapter.) It has also been a response to pressure from financial services companies, which have long wanted to operate in a less regulated environment. Increasing acceptance of the free-market ideology associated with an individualistic political philosophy also has a lot to do with the global trend toward the deregulation of financial markets (see Chapter 2). Whatever the reason, deregulation in a number of key countries around the world has undoubtedly facilitated the growth of the international capital market.

The trend began in the United States in the late 1970s and early 80s with a series of changes that allowed foreign banks to enter the U.S. capital market and domestic banks to expand their operations overseas. In Great Britain, the so-called Big Bang of October 1986 removed barriers that had existed between banks and stockbrokers and allowed foreign financial service companies to enter the British stock market. Restrictions on the entry of foreign securities houses have been relaxed (though not removed) in Japan, and Japanese banks are now allowed to open international banking facilities. In France, the "Little Bang" of 1987 is gradually opening up the French stock market to outsiders and to foreign and domestic banks. And in Germany, foreign banks are now allowed to lend and manage foreign DM issues, subject to reciprocity agreements.[7] All of this has allowed financial service companies to transform themselves from primarily domestic companies into international operations with major offices around the world—a prerequisite for the development of a truly international capital market.

Geography of the International Capital Market

Figure 11.5 presents a hierarchy of the world's 25 largest financial centers identified in a 1989 study.[8] The larger the size of the dot on the map, the more important the city is as a center for international financial transactions. As can be seen, there are three tiers: tier 1 contains London and New York; tier 2, Tokyo, Amsterdam, Paris, Zurich, and Frankfurt; and tier 3, the remaining cities. Note that Tokyo placed in the second tier in the study, although the global financial system is increasingly geared around the New York–London–Tokyo axis. The explanation for this is that Tokyo's importance rests primarily on the strength of the Japanese economy. Tokyo is distinguished from New York and London in that a relatively small number of foreign financial service companies operate there. In 1985 there were only 76 foreign banking institutions in Tokyo, in contrast to well over 400 in London and about 350 in New York. However, this situation could change rapidly in the 1990s.[9]

---

[7] P. Dicken, *Global Shift: The Internationalization of Economic Activity* (London: The Guilford Press, 1992).

[8] H. C. Reed, "Financial Center Hegemony, Interest Rates, and the Global Political Economy," *International Banking and Financial Centers,* ed. Y. S. Park and N. Essayyad (Boston: Kluwer Academic, 1989).

[9] Dicken, *Global Shift.*

Figure 11.5 *The Hierarchy of International Financial Centers, 1989*

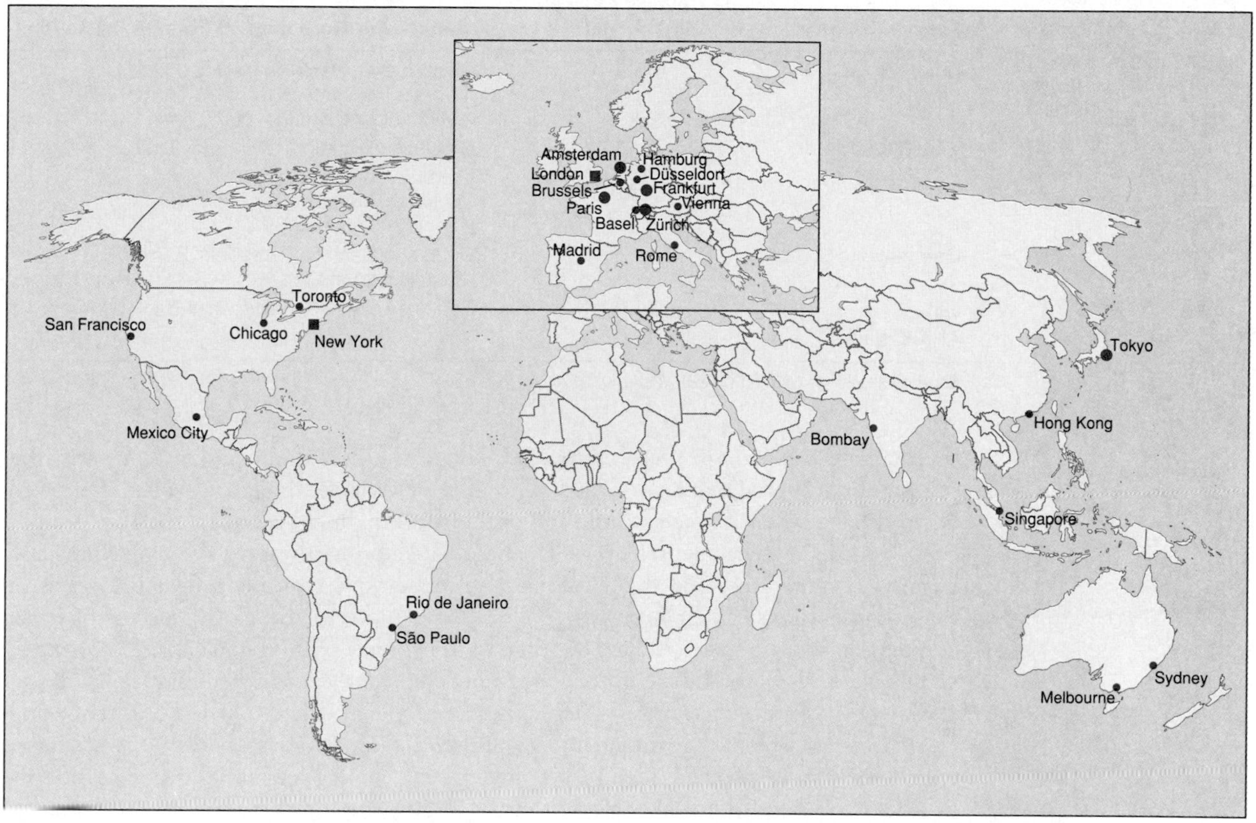

Note: *Size of dots (squares) indicates cities' relative importance.*

London, New York, and (increasingly) Tokyo can be seen as the nerve centers of the international capital market. This is not to say that the other centers are unimportant. However, none of the second-tier centers have the scale or scope of operations found in the big three centers. As for the third-tier cities, these serve mainly as regional financial centers. The third-tier center most likely to grow would seem to be Hong Kong. Indeed, if China continues its move toward a free market economy (see Chapter 2), Hong Kong will undoubtedly emerge as the financial linchpin of the Chinese economy, and the city could develop to rival Tokyo for regional dominance in financial services by the early years of the next century.

The Market Makers

The market makers in the international capital market are those financial service companies that act as intermediaries between investors and borrowers. In the main, these are commercial banks and investment banks. One trend that has commanded much attention in recent years is the rise of a number of Japanese banks to the top of the world league of commercial banks. In 1990, for example, 7 of the world's top 10 commercial banks measured by asset value were Japanese banks.[10] This has led many commentators

[10] *Euromoney*, June 1990, p. 119.

Table 11.1
Foreign Networks of Leading Commercial Banks, 1987

Source Country	Average Number of Foreign Operations by Country's Banks in Top 100	Banks with More than 50 Foreign Operations
United States	58.9	Citicorp 240, Bank America Corp 184, Chase Manhattan 107, J. P. Morgan 85, Manufacturers Hanover 67
United Kingdom	50.8	Barclays 187, Midland 69
France	76.4	Crédit Lyonnais 102, Banque Nationale de Paris 128, Société Générale 89
Germany	26.3	Deutsche Bank 67, Dresdner Bank 83, Commerzbank 58
Japan	26.0	Bank of Tokyo 101, Mitsubishi Bank 53
All 100 banks	46.6	

Source: Based on UNCTC (1988), Table VII.2, Annex Table B.2.

to conclude erroneously that Japanese banks are the dominant market makers in the international capital market. As large as their asset value is, the Japanese banks are well down the list when it comes to the size of their international network and the international nature of their clientele. The Japanese banks primarily serve the major Japanese business corporations, and their international operations typically reflect the needs of those corporations. Their huge asset value is due more to the global success of these corporations during the 1970s and 80s than to the volume of their non-Japanese business.

Table 11.1 shows the size of the foreign networks of the leading commercial banks in 1987, the most recent year for which data is available. Notice that U.S., British, and French banks all have far more foreign affiliates than Japanese banks do. A similar conclusion can be reached if we look at investment banks (i.e., banks dealing primarily in stocks and bonds). In the later half of the 1980s, the top three investment banks in terms of assets were the U.S. trio of American Express, Salmon Inc., and Merrill Lynch. The largest Japanese investment bank, Nomura Securities Company, was number 14 on the list. Moreover, while the U.S. trio had 122, 54, and 48 foreign affiliates, respectively, Nomura had only 21.[11] Of course, all of this might change in the future, but for now it seems safe to conclude that the "threat" of a Japanese takeover of the international financial services industry has been much overstated.

THE EUROCURRENCY MARKET

A **Eurocurrency** is any currency banked outside of its country of origin. **Eurodollars,** which account for about two thirds of all Eurocurrencies, are dollars banked outside of the United States. Other important Eurocurrencies include the Euro-yen, the Euro-deutsche mark, the Euro-franc, and the Euro-pound. The term *Eurocurrency* is actually a misnomer, since a Eurocurrency can be created anywhere in the world; the persistent *euro-* prefix reflects the European origin of the market. As we shall see, the significance of the Eurocurrency market is that it is an important, relatively low-cost source of funds for international businesses. From small beginnings, this market has mushroomed. In 1982 Eurocurrency deposits amounted to around $2 trillion (U.S.). By 1988 they amounted to more than $4.5 trillion, and the market looks set to continue growing through the 1990s.

[11] Data from UNCTC, *Transnational Corporations in World Development: Trends and Prospects* (New York: United Nations, 1988).

Genesis and Growth of the Market

The Eurocurrency market was born in the mid-1950s when Eastern European holders of dollars, including the former Soviet Union, were afraid to deposit their holdings of dollars in the United States lest they be seized by the U.S. government to settle U.S. residents' claims against business losses resulting from the communist takeover of Eastern Europe. So these countries deposited many of their dollar holdings in Europe, particularly in London. Additional dollar deposits came from various Western European central banks and from companies that earned dollars by exporting to the United States. These two groups deposited their dollars in London banks, rather than U.S. banks, because they were able to earn a higher rate of interest (a fact that will be explained).

The Eurocurrency market received a major push in 1957 when the British government prohibited British banks from lending British pounds to finance non-British trade, a business that had been very profitable for British banks. To not lose the business, British banks began financing the same trade by attracting dollar deposits and lending dollars to companies engaged in international trade and investment. As a consequence of this historical event, London became (and has since remained) the leading center of Eurocurrency trading.

The market received another push in the 1960s when the U.S. government enacted regulations that discouraged U.S. banks from lending to non-U.S. residents. Would-be dollar borrowers outside the United States found it increasingly difficult to borrow dollars in the United States to finance international trade, so they turned to the Eurodollar market to obtain the necessary dollar funds.

The U.S. government changed its policies in the aftermath of the 1973 collapse of the Bretton Woods system (see Chapter 10), removing an important impetus to the growth of the Eurocurrency market that had existed since the mid-1960s. However, another political event, the oil price increases engineered by OPEC in the 1973–74 and 1979–80 periods, gave the market another big shove. As a result of the oil price increases, the Arab members of OPEC accumulated huge amounts of dollars, oil being priced in dollars. They were afraid to place their money in U.S. banks or their European branches, lest the U.S. government attempt to confiscate them. (Iranian assets in U.S. banks and their European branches had been frozen by President Carter in 1979 after the taking of hostages at the U.S. embassy in Tehran; their fear was not unfounded.) Instead, these countries deposited their dollars with banks in London, further increasing the supply of Eurodollars.

Although these various political events undoubtedly contributed to the growth of the Eurocurrency market, they alone were not responsible for it. On the contrary, the market grew because it offered real financial advantages—initially to those who wanted to deposit dollars or borrow dollars, and later to those who wanted to deposit and borrow other currencies. We now look at the source of these financial advantages.

Attractions of the Eurocurrency Market

The main factor that makes the Eurocurrency market so attractive to both depositors and borrowers is its lack of government regulation. This allows banks to offer higher interest rates on Eurocurrency deposits than on deposits made in the home currency—making Eurocurrency deposits attractive to those who have cash to deposit. The lack of regulation also allows banks to charge borrowers a lower interest rate for Eurocurrency borrowings than for borrowings in the home currency—making Eurocurrency loans attractive for those who want to borrow money. In other words, the **spread** between the Eurocurrency deposit rate and the Eurocurrency lending rate is less than the spread between the domestic deposit and lending rates (see Figure 11.6). To understand why this is so, we must examine how government regulations raise the costs of domestic banking.

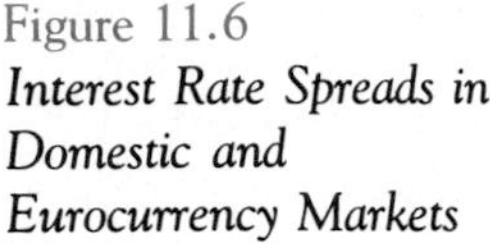

Figure 11.6
Interest Rate Spreads in Domestic and Eurocurrency Markets

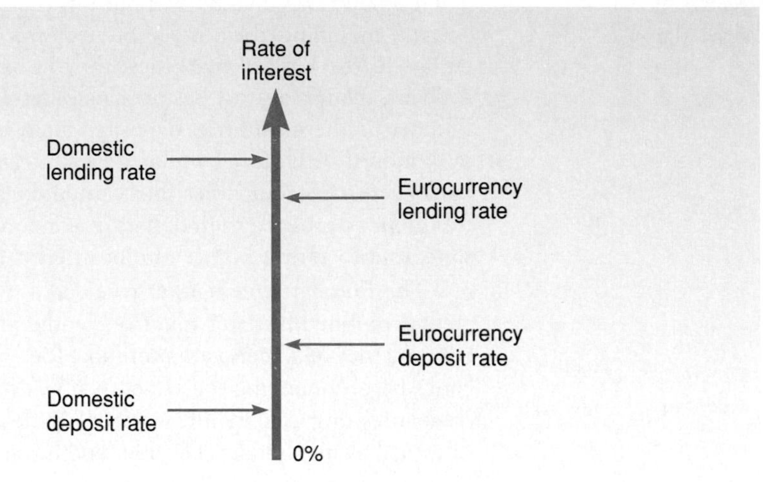

Domestic currency deposits are regulated in all industrialized countries. Such regulations ensure that banks have enough liquid funds to satisfy demand if large numbers of domestic depositors should suddenly decide to withdraw their money. Most important, all countries operate with certain **reserve requirements.** For example, each time a U.S. bank accepts a deposit in dollars, it must place some fraction of that deposit in a non-interest-bearing account at a Federal Reserve bank as part of its required reserves. Similarly, each time a British bank accepts a deposit in pounds sterling, it must place a certain fraction of that deposit with the Bank of England.

Banks are given much more freedom in their dealings in foreign currencies, however. For example, the British government does *not* impose reserve requirement restrictions on deposits of foreign currencies within its borders. Nor are the London branches of U.S. banks subject to U.S. reserve requirement regulations, provided those deposits are payable only outside the United States. This gives Eurobanks a competitive advantage.

For example, suppose a bank based in New York faces a 10 percent reserve requirement. According to this requirement, if the bank receives a $100 deposit, it can lend out no more than $90 of that and it must place the remaining $10 in a non-interest-bearing account at a Federal Reserve bank. Suppose the bank has annual operating costs of $1 per $100 of deposits and that it charges 10 percent interest on loans. The highest interest the New York bank can offer its depositors and still cover its costs is 8 percent per year. Thus the bank pays the owner of the $100 deposit (0.08) × ($100) = $8, earns (0.10) × ($90) = $9 on the fraction of the deposit it is allowed to lend, and just covers its operating costs.

In contrast, a Eurobank can offer a higher interest rate on dollar deposits and still cover its costs. The Eurobank, with no reserve requirements regarding dollar deposits, can lend out *all* of a $100 deposit. Therefore, it can earn (0.10) × ($100) = $10 at a loan rate of 10 percent. If the Eurobank has the same operating costs as the New York bank ($1 per $100 deposit), it can pay its depositors an interest rate of 9 percent, a full percentage point higher than that paid by the New York bank, and still cover its costs. That is, it can pay out (0.09) × ($100) = $9 to its depositor, receive $10 from the borrower, and be left with $1 to cover operating costs. Alternatively, the Eurobank might pay the depositor 8.5 percent (which is still above the rate paid by the New York bank), charge borrowers 9.5 percent (still less than the New York bank charges), and cover its operating costs even better. Thus, the Eurobank has a competitive advantage vis-à-vis the New York bank in both its deposit rate and its loan rate.

Clearly, there are very strong financial motivations for companies to utilize the Eurocurrency market. By doing so they receive a higher interest rate on deposits and can pay less for loans. Given this, the surprising thing is not that the Euromarket has grown so fast in recent years but that it hasn't grown even faster. For that matter why do any depositors hold deposits in their home currency when they could get better yields in the Eurocurrency market?

Drawbacks of the Eurocurrency Market

The Eurocurrency market has two drawbacks. First, when depositors use a regulated banking system, they know that the probability of a bank failure that would cause them to lose their deposits is very low. After all, regulation maintains the liquidity of the banking system. In an unregulated system such as the Eurocurrency market, the probability of a bank failure that would cause depositors to lose their money is greater (although in absolute terms, still low). Thus, the lower interest rate received on home country deposits reflects the costs of insuring against bank failure. Some depositors are more comfortable with the security of such a system and are willing to pay the price.

Second, borrowing funds internationally can expose a company to foreign exchange risk. For example, consider a U.S. company that uses the Eurocurrency market to borrow Euro-pounds—perhaps because it can pay a lower interest rate on Euro-pound loans than on dollar loans. Imagine, however, that the British pound subsequently appreciates against the dollar. This would increase the dollar cost of repaying the Euro-pound loan and thus the company's cost of capital. Of course (as we saw in Chapter 9), this possibility can be insured against by using the forward exchange market, but the forward exchange market does not offer perfect insurance. Consequently, many companies choose to borrow funds in their domestic currency to avoid foreign exchange risk, even though the Eurocurrency markets may offer more attractive interest rates.

THE INTERNATIONAL BOND MARKET

Bonds are an important means of financing for many companies. The most common kind of bond is a **fixed rate bond.** The investor who purchases a fixed rate bond receives a fixed set of cash payoffs. Each year until the bond matures, the investor gets an interest payment and then at maturity he gets back the face value of the bond.

International bonds are of two types: foreign bonds and Eurobonds. **Foreign bonds** are sold outside of the borrower's country and are denominated in the currency of the country in which they are issued. Thus when Dow Chemical issues bonds in Japanese yen and sells them in Japan, it is issuing foreign bonds. Many foreign bonds have nicknames; foreign bonds sold in the United States are called *Yankee bonds,* foreign bonds sold in Japan are *Samurai bonds,* and foreign bonds sold in Great Britain are *bulldogs.*

Eurobonds are normally underwritten by an international syndicate of banks and placed in countries other than the one in whose currency the bond is denominated. For example, a bond may be issued by a German corporation, dominated in U.S. dollars, and sold to investors outside of the United States by an international syndicate of banks. Eurobonds are routinely issued by multinational corporations, large domestic corporations, sovereign governments, and international institutions. They are usually offered simultaneously in several national capital markets—but not in the capital market of the country, nor to residents of the country, in whose currency they are denominated. Eurobonds account for the lion's share of international bond issues. In 1987, for example,

$177.3 million in Eurobonds were issued, in contrast to only $38.4 in million foreign bonds.[12]

Scale and Scope of the Market

Like the Eurocurrency market, the international bond market grew rapidly during the 1980s. Whereas $177 billion in international bonds were issued in 1987, by 1989 the figure was $258.7 billion. Estimates suggest that international bonds accounted for almost 10 percent of all bonds outstanding worldwide by the end of 1988. In addition, by 1988 international bonds accounted for 10.5 percent of all bonds issued in U.S. dollars, 21.3 percent of the bonds issued in British pounds, 14.2 percent of the bonds issued in German marks, 5 percent of the bonds issued in Japanese yen, and 49.2 percent of the bonds issued in Swiss francs.[13]

In recent years the biggest issuers of international bonds have been the Japanese. In 1989 Japanese issuers accounted for $96.7 billion of international bond issues, up from $31.8 billion in 1986. The next most important group in 1989 were the British, who accounted for $23.0 billion of international bond issues, followed by U.S. issuers, who accounted for $16.4 billion. The importance of the Japanese in the international bond market can be attributed to the high cost of issuing bonds in Japan. Japanese Ministry of Finance regulations and the high fees charged by the underwriting oligopoly of the four largest Japanese securities firms raise the cost of issuing bonds in Japan significantly above the costs of issuing Eurobonds.

Attractions of the Eurobond Market

Why has the Eurobond market grown so rapidly in recent years? Part of the answer has already been alluded to in our explanation of how the high cost of issuing bonds in Japan has facilitated the growth of the Eurobond market. In addition, three features of the market make it an appealing alternative to most major domestic bond markets; specifically,

- An absence of regulatory interference.
- Less-stringent disclosure requirements than in most domestic bond markets.
- A favorable tax status.

Regulatory Interference

National governments often impose tight controls on domestic and foreign issuers of bonds dominated in the local currency and sold within their national boundaries. These controls tend to raise the cost of issuing bonds. However, government limitations are generally less stringent for securities dominated in foreign currencies and sold within their market to holders of those foreign currencies. Put another way, Eurobonds fall outside of the regulatory domain of any single nation. As such, they can often be issued at a lower cost to the issuer.

Disclosure Requirements

Eurobond market disclosure requirements tend to be less stringent than those of several national governments. For example, if a firm wishes to issue dollar-denominated bonds

---

[12] R. C. Smith, "Investment Banks and Merchant Banks," in *The Handbook of International Financial Management,* ed. R. Z. Aliber (Homewood, Ill.: Dow Jones Irwin, 1989).

[13] C. Pavel and D. McElravey, *Globalization in the Financial Services Industry* (Chicago: Federal Reserve Bank of Chicago, 1990), pp. 3–18.

within the United States, it must first comply with SEC disclosure requirements. By these, the firm must disclose detailed information about its activities, the salaries and other compensation of its senior executives, stock trades by its senior executives, and the like. In addition, the issuing firm must submit financial accounts that conform to U.S. accounting standards. For non-U.S. firms, redoing their accounts to make them consistent with U.S. standards can be very time consuming and expensive. Therefore, many firms have found it cheaper to issue Eurobonds, including those denominated in dollars, than to issue dollar-denominated bonds within the United States.

Favorable Tax Status

Before 1984, U.S. corporations issuing Eurobonds were required to withhold up to 30 percent of each interest payment to foreigners for U.S. income tax. Not surprisingly, this did not encourage foreigners to hold bonds issued by U.S. corporations. Similar tax laws were at that time operational in a large number of countries. The effect of these tax laws was to limit market demand for Eurobonds. In 1984, however, U.S. laws were revised to exempt foreign holders of bonds issued by U.S. corporations from any withholding tax. As a result, U.S. corporations found it feasible for the first time to sell Eurobonds directly to foreigners. Repeal of the U.S. laws caused other governments—including those of France, Germany, and Japan—to liberalize their tax laws likewise to avoid outflows of capital from their markets. The consequence was an upsurge in demand for Eurobonds from investors who wanted to take advantage of their tax benefits.

The Rise of ecu Bonds

In Chapter 10 we introduced the ecu, the basket of European Community (EC) currencies that serves as the unit of account for the European Monetary System. As we have said, the EC hopes to establish the ecu as its common currency by 1999. With this goal in mind, governments, corporations, and international institutions have been issuing bonds denominated in ecus. Currently, ecu-denominated bonds account for only a small percentage of all bonds issued, but the percentage seems to be growing rapidly. Between 1980 and 1990 the outstanding amount of ecu bonds grew from ecu 250 million to ecu 70 billion. Almost 8 percent of all new international bond issues in 1990 were denominated in ecus, up from 3.8 percent in 1986, and in the first half of 1991, ecu issues accounted for more than 12 percent of all new bond issues. Given the trend toward European integration, the size of this market seems set to grow.[14]

THE INTERNATIONAL EQUITY MARKET

There is no international *equity* market in the sense that there are international currency and bond markets. Rather, many countries have their own domestic equity markets in which corporate stock is traded. The largest of these domestic equity markets, in order of value traded, are the Japanese, U.S., and British markets. In 1990 the stock exchanges in these three countries accounted for a major portion of world equity value. Japan's stock exchanges accounted for more than 44 percent of all world equity value, followed by the United States with more than 28 percent and Great Britain with 9 percent. The fourth-place country was Germany, whose stock exchanges accounted for only 3 percent of world equity value in 1990.

[14] T. Corrigan, "European Governments Help Transformation," *Financial Times Survey: International Capital Markets,* July 22, 1991, p. 2.

Figure 11.7
Gross Cross-Border Equity Flows, 1989 ($ billions)

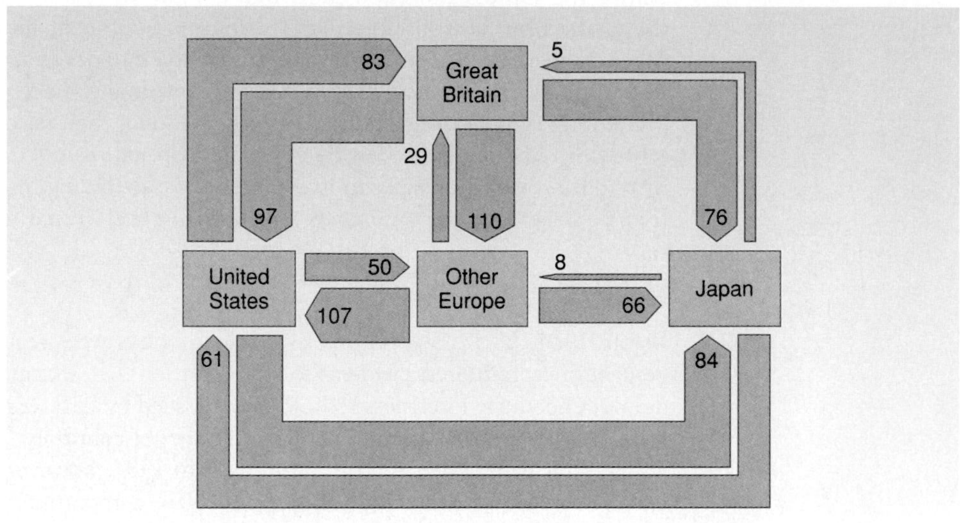

Source: "Survey of International Capital Markets," The Economist, *July 21, 1990, p. 7.*

Although each domestic equity market is still dominated by investors who are citizens of that country and companies incorporated in that country, developments are internationalizing the world equity market. For one thing, foreign investors are investing heavily in domestic equity markets as a means of diversifying their portfolios. Facilitated by deregulation and advances in information technology, this trend seems to be here to stay. Figure 11.7 presents data on the size and direction of recent cross-border equity flows.

An interesting consequence of the trend toward international equity investment is the internationalization of corporate ownership. Today it is still generally possible to talk about "U.S. corporations," "British corporations," and "Japanese corporations," primarily because the majority of stockholders (owners) of these corporations are of the respective nationality. However, this is changing. Increasingly, U.S. citizens are buying stock in companies incorporated abroad, and foreigners are buying stock in companies incorporated in the United States. Looking into the future, Robert Reich has mused about "the coming irrelevance of corporate nationality."[15] If the "stateless corporation" does become a reality, it will indeed be meaningless to talk about "U.S. corporations" or "Japanese corporations."

A second development internationalizing the world equity market is that companies with historic roots in one nation are broadening their stock ownership by listing their stock in the equity markets of other nations. The reasons are primarily financial. Most important, listing stock on a foreign market is often a prelude to issuing stock in that market to raise capital. (Remember that in the opening case Biomedex arranged to get listed on the NASDAQ exchange as a prelude to offering its stock on the NYSE.) The idea is to tap into the liquidity of foreign markets, thereby increasing the funds available for investment and lowering the firm's cost of capital. (The relationship between liquidity and the cost of capital was discussed earlier in the chapter.)

---

[15] R. Reich, *The Work of Nations* (New York: Alfred A. Knopf, 1991).

In addition to liquidity and cost-of-capital benefits, firms often list their stock on foreign equity markets to facilitate future acquisitions of foreign companies. As an example, consider Hanson Plc, a large British conglomerate that specializes in acquiring and turning around poorly managed companies. Hanson has long had a NYSE listing, and a significant proportion of its outstanding shares are traded on the NYSE. This enables Hanson to acquire companies owned by U.S. residents by offering those companies' stockholders Hanson shares in exchange for their shares. The ability to swap shares in making acquisitions relieves Hanson of the pressure to come up with cash each time it wants to acquire a U.S. company. Other reasons for listing a company's stock on a foreign equity market are that the company's stock and stock options can be used to compensate local management and employees, it satisfies the desire for local ownership, and it increases the company's visibility with local employees, customers, suppliers, and bankers.

Data from the late 1980s indicates that at that time, Great Britain had the greatest number of foreign firms listed on its exchange. In 1989 24 percent of the 2,700 or so companies listed on the London exchange were foreign firms. In contrast, less than 5 percent of the 1,550 firms listed on the NYSE were non-U.S. enterprises, and only a handful of the 1,450 firms listed on the Tokyo exchange were non-Japanese firms. Indeed, the relatively small Dutch and Swiss stock markets were the most international. Foreign firms accounted for 50 percent of the approximately 500 listings on the Amsterdam market and 60 percent of the 284 listings on the Zurich exchange in 1989.[16]

FOREIGN EXCHANGE RISK AND THE COST OF CAPITAL

Until now we have emphasized repeatedly that a firm can borrow funds at a lower cost on the international capital market than on the domestic capital market. However, we have also mentioned that under a floating exchange rate regime, foreign exchange risk clearly complicates this picture. This point needs to be emphasized.

As an illustration, consider a U.S. company that wants to borrow money for one year to fund U.S. investments. The interest rate on dollar loans from a U.S. bank is 10 percent. Alternatively, the firm can borrow deutsche marks on the international market for a year at 6 percent. It may seem that the logical thing to do is to borrow the deutsche marks. However, consider what will occur if the DM appreciates against the dollar by 8 percent during the year. Since the DM loan would have to be repaid in deutsche marks, the appreciation of the DM would increase the dollar cost of the loan. More precisely, the true cost of capital to the firm would be the 6 percent interest rate on its DM Loan *plus* the increase in the dollar cost of interest and principal on the loan deriving from the appreciation of the DM. The formula for calculating the true cost of capital in such a circumstance is

		Interest on DM loan		Additional interest due to exchange rate change		Additional principal due to exchange rate change	
Cost of capital	=	6%	×	1.08	+	8%	= 14.48%

[16] "One Market or Many," *The Economist*, December 16, 1989, pp. 24–26.

In other words, as a result of the DM's appreciation, the company's cost of capital would be 14.48 percent, not 6 percent. With the benefit of this hypothetical foresight, it would obviously be less expensive for the company to borrow dollars from a U.S. bank at 10 percent. Of course, the U.S. company could insure against such an adverse change in exchange rates by using the forward exchange market (see Chapter 9). However, if the forward exchange market predicts an appreciation of the DM, this would also raise the cost of borrowing DMs.

Perhaps more important, the forward exchange market is not geared to provide coverage for long-term borrowings (see Chapter 9). To their cost, many international businesses have found that borrowing foreign currency over a long term creates *considerable* exposure to foreign exchange risk. For example, consider the case of TRW, a U.S. multinational that in October 1969 issued DM-denominated foreign bonds. The bonds were scheduled to reach maturity in October 1989. At the time of issue, the cost of the DM funds was 7.82 percent per annum. The cost of bonds denominated in U.S. dollars at that time was 8.7 percent, so this looked like a good deal. However, over the next few years the Bretton Woods system of fixed exchange rates broke down, and the dollar depreciated against the DM (see Chapter 10). As a result, by the time the bonds matured the effective cost of capital for TRW, adjusted for exchange rate changes, was not 7.82 percent per annum, but 14.75 percent per annum! Clearly, TRW would have been better off issuing dollar-denominated bonds.[17]

The central message, then, is that when a firm borrows funds from the international capital market, it must weigh the benefits of a lower interest rate against the risks of an increase in the real cost of capital due to adverse exchange rate movements. Although using forward exchange markets may lower foreign exchange risk with short-term borrowings, it cannot remove the risk altogether. Moreover, the forward exchange market does not provide adequate coverage for long-term borrowings.

IMPLICATIONS FOR BUSINESS

The implications of the material discussed in this chapter for international business are quite straightforward but no less important for being obvious. The growth of the international capital market has created opportunities for international businesses that wish to borrow and/or invest money. On the borrowing side, by using the international capital market, firms can often borrow funds at a lower cost than is possible in a purely domestic capital market. This conclusion holds no matter what form a firm's borrowings take—equity, bonds, or cash loans. The lower cost of capital on the international market reflects their greater liquidity and the general absence of government regulation. As we have observed, government regulation tends to raise the cost of capital in most domestic capital markets. The international market, being transnational, escapes regulation. Balanced against this, however, is the foreign exchange risk associated with borrowing in a foreign currency.

On the investment side, we have seen how the growth of the international capital market is providing opportunities for firms, institutions, and individuals to better diversify their investments in financial assets to limit risk. By holding a diverse portfolio of stocks and bonds in different nations, an investor can reduce total risk to a lower level

[17] D. K. Eiteman, A. I. Stonehill, and M. H. Moffett, *Multinational Business Finance* (Reading, Mass.: Addison-Wesley, 1992).

than can be achieved in a purely domestic setting. Once again, however, foreign exchange risk is a complicating factor.

As for the future, the trends noted in this chapter seem likely to continue, with the international capital market continuing to increase in both importance and degree of integration over the next decade. Perhaps the most significant development will be the emergence of a unified capital market and common currency within the EC by the end of the decade as that grouping of countries continues toward economic and monetary union. Since Europe's capital markets are currently rather fragmented and relatively introspective (with the major exception of Great Britain's capital market), such a development could pave the way for even more rapid internationalization of the capital market in the early years of the next century. If this occurs, the implications for business are likely to be positive.

SUMMARY OF CHAPTER

The objective of this chapter was to explain the functions and form of the international capital market and to define the implications of this for international business practice. In this chapter we have made the following points:

1. The function of a capital market is to bring those who want to invest money together with those who want to borrow money. This connection function is performed by market makers (e.g., commercial banks and investment banks).
2. Relative to a domestic capital market, the international capital market has a greater supply of funds available for borrowing, and this makes for a lower cost of capital for borrowers.
3. Relative to a domestic capital market, the international capital market allows investors to diversify portfolios of holdings internationally, thereby reducing the risk.
4. The growth of the international capital market during the 1970s and 80s can be attributed to advances in information technology and to deregulation of financial services in several major industrialized countries.
5. The international capital market is focused on the New York–London–Tokyo axis.
6. A Eurocurrency is any currency banked outside its country of origin. The lack of government regulations makes the Eurocurrency market attractive to both depositors and borrowers. Due to the absence of regulation, the spread between the Eurocurrency deposit and lending rates is less than the spread between the domestic deposit and lending rates. This gives Eurobanks a competitive advantage.
7. The international bond market has two classifications: the foreign bond market and the Eurobond market. Foreign bonds are sold outside of the borrower's country and are denominated in the currency of the country in which they are issued. A Eurobond issue is normally underwritten by an international syndicate of banks and placed in countries other than the one in whose currency the bond is denominated. Eurobonds account for the lion's share of international bond issues.
8. The Eurobond market is an attractive way for companies to raise funds due to the absence of regulatory interference, less-stringent disclosure requirements, and Eurobonds' favorable tax status.
9. The world's largest equity markets are in Japan, the United States, and Great Britain.
10. Foreign investors are investing in other countries' equity markets to reduce risk by diversifying their stock holdings among nations.
11. Many companies are now listing their stock in the equity markets of other nations, primarily as a prelude to issuing stock in those markets to raise additional capital. Other reasons for listing stock in another country's exchange are to facilitate future stock swaps, to enable the company to use its stock and stock options for compensating local holdings' management and employees, to satisfy local ownership desires, and to increase the company's visibility among its local employees, customers, suppliers, and bankers.
12. When borrowing funds from the international capital market, companies must weigh the benefits of a lower interest rate against the risks of greater real costs of capital due to adverse exchange rate movements.
13. One major implication of the international capital market for international business is that companies can often borrow funds at a lower cost in the international capital markets than they can in a domestic capital market.
14. Furthermore, the international capital market provides greater opportunities for businesses and individuals to build a truly diversified portfolio of international investments in financial assets, which lowers risk.

DISCUSSION QUESTIONS

1. Why has the international capital market grown so rapidly in recent decades? Do you think this growth will continue throughout the 1990s? Why?
2. A firm based in Mexico has found that its growth is limited by the limited liquidity of the Mexican capital market. List the firm's options for raising money on the international capital market. Discuss the pros and cons of each option, and make a recommendation. How might your recommended options be affected if the Mexican peso depreciates significantly on the foreign exchange markets over the next two years?
3. Happy Company wants to raise $2 million in U.S. dollars with debt financing. The funds are needed to finance working capital, and the firm will repay them with interest in one year. Happy Company's treasurer is considering three options:

   a. Borrowing U.S. dollars from Security Pacific Bank at 8 percent.

   b. Borrowing British pounds from Midland Bank at 14 percent.

   c. Borrowing Japanese yen from Sanwa bank at 5 percent.

   If Happy borrows foreign currency, it will not cover it, that is, it will simply change foreign currency for dollars at today's spot rate and buy the same foreign currency a year later at the spot rate then in effect. Happy Company estimates that the pound will depreciate by 5 percent relative to the dollar and that the yen will appreciate 3 percent relative to the dollar in the next year. From which bank should Happy Company borrow?

Chaos in the Currency Markets

Ever since the breakup of the Bretton Woods system of fixed exchange rates in 1971 there has been talk about the possibility of returning to a fixed rate system. Advocates of a fixed exchange rate regime have long maintained that the system has several distinct advantages over the current "managed-float" system. They argue that a fixed exchange rate regime imposes monetary discipline on the nations that participate in it (which, in turn, limits inflation), removes the uncertainty and risk due to fluctuations in exchange rates, limits speculation, and, consequently, promotes international trade and investment.

In contrast, the advocates of floating exchange rates make two points. First, they claim that a floating exchange rate regime gives countries monetary policy autonomy. Under a fixed system, a country's ability to expand or contract its money supply is limited by the need to maintain exchange rate parity. Under a floating system, national governments maintain sovereignty over their monetary policy. Second, these advocates argue that if a country is running a trade deficit, the imbalance between the supply and demand of its currency in the foreign exchange markets will lead to a depreciation of its exchange rate. In turn, by making its exports cheaper and its imports more expensive, an exchange rate depreciation should ultimately correct the trade deficit. Under a fixed regime, in contrast, the adjustment process is nowhere near as smooth, and a formal currency devaluation is required to achieve the same end.

Although this issue has been debated actively in the years since the breakdown of Bretton Woods, it has never been resolved. However, since the early 1980s those who support a return to a fixed rate regime have had a powerful argument on their side: the success of the European Monetary System (EMS). Established in 1979, at the heart of the EMS is a system of fixed exchange rates between the currencies of the 12 member-countries of the European Community (EC). This system has been widely credited with closing the inflation rate differentials among the member-countries during the 1980s. Many saw the EMS as paving the way for the eventual establishment of a common currency for the EC. Then in the space of a few days in September 1992, the EMS was exposed to a gale of speculative pressure that nearly shattered the system and renewed concerns about the viability of fixed exchange rate regimes. This case describes what occurred during those few days. We begin with a brief discussion of the EMS. Then we look at the exchange rate crisis and its aftermath.

THE EMS

The EMS is composed of two instruments: the exchange rate mechanism (ERM) and the European currency unit (ecu). The ecu is a basket of the EC currencies that serves as the unit of account for the EMS. The share of each country's currency in the ecu depends on that country's relative economic weight within the EC. In 1989, 30.1 percent of the ecu's

Source: Charles W. L. Hill.

value (the largest percentage) was determined by the value of the German deutsche mark, primarily because Germany is viewed as the strongest and largest economy within the EC.

The ERM works as follows: Each national currency in the EC is given a *central rate* vis-à-vis the ecu. For example, in September 1989 one ecu was equal to DM 2.05853, FFr 6.90404, and £0.739615. This central rate can only be changed by a commonly agreed on realignment. From these central rates flow a series of *bilateral rates*—the French franc against the Italian lira, the German deutsche mark against the British pound, and so on. For example, the above figures via-à-vis the ecu indicate that the bilateral rate for exchanging deutsche marks into francs was DM 1 = FFr 2.9586 (i.e., FFr 6.90404/DM2.05853). The bilateral rates form a cat's cradle known as the *ERM parity grid,* the operational part of the system. The rule for most currencies is that they may not depart by more than 2.25 percent from their bilateral ECU-determined rate with another ERM-participating currency. The only exceptions are the Spanish peseta and the British pound, which as recent additions to the ERM are allowed to fluctuate by up to 6 percent against other ERM currencies.

Intervention in the foreign exchange markets is compulsory whenever one currency hits its outer margin of fluctuation relative to another. The central banks of the countries issuing both currencies are supposed to intervene to keep their currencies within the 2.25 percent (or 6 percent) band. The central bank of the country with the stronger currency is supposed to buy the weaker currency, and vice versa. To defend its currency against speculative pressure, each member-state can borrow almost unlimited amounts of foreign currency from other members for periods of up to three months. A second line of defense includes loans that can be extended for up to nine months, but the total amount available is limited to a pool of credit—originally about 14 billion ecus—and the size of the member's quota in the pool. Additional funds are available for two to five years from a second pool of (originally) about 11 billion ecus.

SEPTEMBER 1992

The roots of the European currency crisis of September 1992 can be traced back to the fall of the Berlin Wall in 1989 and the subsequent reunification of West and East Germany. In an attempt to reduce the economic pain of reunification on its poorer eastern neighbor, the West German government agreed to a 1-for-1 swap of the East German deutsche mark for the West German deutsche mark after reunification. The Bundesbank, West Germany's (and now Germany's) central bank, objected to this policy, pointing out that a 1-to-12 swap made more sense, but to no avail. The result was a surge in the German money supply after reunification and a subsequent rise in inflation. The government's budget deficit also expanded, adding to the Bundesbank's alarm. In an attempt to control inflation and rein back monetary growth, the Bundesbank began to raise interest rates.

Meanwhile on the other side of the Atlantic, the U.S. economy was mired in its most persistent recession since World War II. After repeated prodding, the U.S. Federal Reserve Board had cut U.S. interest rates several times since late 1991. As a consequence, by August 1992 a significant interest rate differential had opened up between Germany and the United States. For example, on August 25 the interest rate on three-month certificates of deposit was 9.9 percent in Germany and 3.6 percent in the United States. The result? Foreign exchange dealers, financial institutions, and corporations switched their cash balances from dollars to DMs. This drove up the price of DMs relative to the dollar. In April 1992 one dollar bought 1.63 DMs, and by late August it bought only 1.40 DMs.

While the pressure on the dollar was beginning to raise concerns in the United States, its consequences for the EMS were also becoming apparent. The ERM required EC currencies to maintain their value against the DM. Germany's high interest rates were already causing pain in many other EC countries. Great Britain, for example, was suffering its worst recession since 1945 and wanted to cut its interest rates to ease the economic pressure and stimulate domestic demand. However, it had had to keep its base rate at 10 percent to match German interest rates and maintain the value of the pound against the DM. Despite these high interest rates, as demand for the DM rose, so did its value on the foreign exchange markets. This began to put pressure on the weaker EC currencies—particularly on the British pound, the Italian lira, and the Spanish peseta. The governments of these countries faced the prospect of having to raise their already high interest rates even further to avoid devaluation within the ERM.

At this point, speculators in the foreign exchange market began to bet on devaluation of several key European currencies against the DM. The basic strategy was simple: buy the currency expected to appreciate (DMs) and sell the ones expected to depreciate. If the speculators bet correctly, they could make large profits in the event of a realignment within the ERM (but losses could also be huge if they bet incorrectly). The first currency to feel the pressure was the Italian lira. Italy had the weakest economy among the major EC countries and a budget deficit amounting to 11.3 percent of its gross domestic product. As foreign exchange dealers dumped the lira, its value plummeted against the DM, forcing the Italian government to raise interest rates to 15 percent. Then, on September 9, the Italian government announced a tough economic package designed to curb the Italian budget deficit. Foreign exchange dealers were unimpressed, and the pressure on the lira continued.

The continued pressure on the lira prompted a top-level meeting of EC finance ministers and central bankers. Under pressure, the Bundesbank agreed to cut its interest rates on September 14 by one half of a percentage point—the first reduction in five years—in exchange for a 7 percent devaluation in the Italian lira. This was meant to calm the foreign exchange markets and stabilize the ERM, but it did no such thing. Fresh from their victory against the lira, foreign exchange dealers turned their attention to the British pound and the Swedish krona. Although Sweden is not part of the EC, it had linked its currency to the ERM in anticipation of joining the EC sometime during the 1990s. Foreign exchange dealers were undoubtedly encouraged in their belief that further devaluations were likely by statements made by Helmet Schlesinger, Bundesbank president. On September 15, clearly annoyed at being pressured to cut German interest rates, Schlesinger suggested to a German newspaper that the deal of September 14 had not gone far enough toward resolving Europe's currency crisis and that only a broad realignment of EC currencies against the DM would stabilize the EMS. Within minutes this statement was transmitted around the world by wire services. In response, the foreign exchange markets were hit by an explosion of speculative pressure.

Attention now concentrated on the British pound. On September 16 the pound was dipping below its permitted floor against the DM of 2.778. To protect the pound, Great Britain's government was forced to raise interest rates, initially from 10 percent to 12 percent, and then later the same day to 15 percent. Moreover, estimates suggest that the British government reportedly spent \$15 billion to \$20 billion, up to half of its total foreign exchange reserves, to support the pound on September 16. All of this was to no avail; the pound remained below its floor in the ERM. That evening, Great Britain admitted defeat. Finance Minister Norman Lamont, who only a few days earlier had stated that the pound would not be devalued, announced that Great Britain would withdraw from the ERM and that the pound would be allowed to float freely. The rise in interest rates from 12 percent to 15 percent was canceled, and a day later rates were cut back to 10 percent.

Also on September 16, the Swedish krona was hit by speculative pressure. Sweden responded by raising its overnight interest rates, first to 30 percent and then to a staggering 500 percent. At least in the short run, this move seemed to scare off speculators—although at enormous cost to Sweden.

On September 17 attention switched once more to the lira. Foreign exchange dealers clearly felt the 7 percent devaluation of the lira announced on September 14 did not go far enough and that a further devaluation was likely. The Italian government responded to the renewed wave of speculative pressure by following Great Britain's lead and pulling the lira out of the ERM. Although the Italian government announced its intention to get back into the ERM at the first opportunity, many doubted this would be anytime soon.

By this point the EMS was teetering on the brink of collapse. Two of the four largest EC countries, Great Britain and Italy, had quit the ERM. Speculators now turned their attention to the French franc. Although the franc was a much stronger currency than either the pound or the lira, on September 20 France was due to hold a national referendum on the Maastricht Treaty. This treaty would open the way for closer economic and political union within the EC, including the establishment of a common currency by 1999. If the French rejected the treaty, and it looked as if the vote was going to be close, the EMS was likely to be a major victim. The French voted yes, but only by a narrow margin, and speculative pressure increased.

However, the franc was to prove a tougher nut to crack. In marked contrast to its earlier stance with regard to Great Britain and Italy, the German Bundesbank joined forces with the Bank of France to defend the franc against speculative pressure. On September 23 the Bank of France raised interest rates from 10.5 percent to 13 percent. At the same time, central banks and finance ministers from France and Germany issued a rare joint statement stressing that there was no need for a change in the EMS parity between the DM and the franc and stating that France and Germany would fight any speculative pressure. This statement was followed by heavy intervention by both central banks. The Bundesbank openly intervened to support the franc, the first time it had acted this way since the ERM had been instituted in 1979. Estimates suggest that on September 22 and 23 the Bundesbank spent between DM 10 billion and DM 30 billion ($6.7 billion to $20 billion) defending the franc, while the Bank of France spent more than FFr 50 billion ($10 billion). By September 26 the foreign exchange dealers recognized that the franc was not going to go the way of the lira and British pound, and speculative pressure eased. For the time being the EMS and ERM remained intact—but only *just.*

AFTERWORD

Figures released by central banks on September 24 showed that foreign exchange trading had grown by about 50 percent between 1989 and 1992 to an estimated $1 trillion (U.S.) each day. At the same time, the amount of money that the central banks have stockpiled for buying their own currencies when they are weak and carrying out other transactions has grown more slowly. Foreign exchange reserves held by the world's central banks amounted to $1 trillion in 1992, no more than the average daily volume of currency trading. Some economists now doubt that central banks, whatever the size of their reserves, can successfully defend their currencies in the long term.

DISCUSSION QUESTIONS

1. What does the crisis of September tell you about the relative abilities of currency markets and national governments to influence exchange rates?
2. What does the crisis of September 1992 tell you about the weaknesses of fixed exchange rate regimes?
3. Assess the impact of the events of September 1992 on the EC's ability to establish a common currency by 1999.
4. The crisis of September 1992 occurred because the ERM system was too inflexible. Discuss.
5. If you were an executive for a company that engages in substantial intra-EC trade, how would you react to the events of September 1992?

REFERENCES

Brittan, S. "Anatomy of the UK Defeat." *Financial Times,* September 24, 1992, p. 2.

________, "Devaluation Threat: How 92 Differs." *Financial Times,* September 19, 1992, p. 17.

"France and Germany Unite to Defend Franc." *Financial Times,* September 24, 1992, p. 1.

"A Ghastly Game of Dominoes." *The Economist,* September 19, 1992, pp. 89–90.

Greising, D.; John Templeman; R. Melcher; and Stewart Toy. "The Buck Stops Where?" *Business Week,* September 7, 1992, pp. 26–28.

Javetski, B.; J. Templeman; and R. Melcher. "Europe's Money Mess." *Business Week,* September 28, 1992, pp. 30–31.

"Mayhem." *The Economist,* September 19, 1992, pp. 15–16.

"Meltdown." *The Economist,* September 19, 1992, p. 69.

Meyerson, A. "Currency Markets Resisting Power of Central Banks." *The New York Times,* September 25, 1992, pp. A1, C15.

Norman, P.; W. Dawkins; and J. Blitz. "French Franc Proves a Tough Nut to Crack." *Financial Times,* September 24, 1992, p. 2.

Sesit, M. R. and D. R. Sease. "Mark Continues to Gain in Uncertain Market." *The Wall Street Journal,* September 18, 1992, pp. C1, C5.

Stephens, P. "Sterling Plummets after U.K. Suspends ERM Membership." *Financial Times,* September 17, 1992, p. 1.

"Torn beyond Repair?" *The Economist,* September 26, 1992, pp. 89–90.

PART FIVE

The Strategy and Structure of International Business

The Strategy of International Business

CHAPTER 12

SWAN OPTICAL CORPORATION

When most people think of multinational enterprises they think of large, complex firms such as General Electric, General Motors, and Procter & Gamble. Actually, however, many small and medium-size companies have become multinational companies in recent decades. Swan Optical Corporation is one of them. Started in the 1960s by Alan Glassman, this manufacturer and distributor of eyewear was generating annual gross revenues of more than $20 million by the end of the 1980s. Not exactly small, but no corporate giant either, Swan Optical was by that time a multinational company with production facilities on three continents and customers around the world.

Swan began its move toward becoming a multinational in the 1970s. The strong dollar at that time made U.S.-based manufacturing very expensive. Low-priced imports were taking an ever-larger share of the U.S. eyewear market, and Swan realized it could not survive unless it also began to import. Initially the company bought from independent overseas manufacturers, primarily in Hong Kong. However, the company became dissatisfied with these suppliers' products' quality and delivery. As Swan's volume of imports increased, Glassman decided the best way to guarantee quality and delivery was to set up Swan's own manufacturing operation overseas. Accordingly, Swan found a Chinese partner, and together they opened a manufacturing facility in Hong Kong, with Swan being the majority shareholder. • Choice of the Hong Kong location was influenced by its combination of low labor costs, a skilled work force, and tax breaks given by the Hong Kong government. By 1986, however, the increasing industrialization of Hong Kong and a growing labor shortage had pushed up wage rates to the extent that it was no longer a "low-cost" location. In response, Glassman and his Chinese partner moved part of their manufacturing to a plant in mainland China to take advantage of the lower wage rates there. The parts for eyewear frames manufactured at this plant are shipped to the Hong Kong factory for final assembly and then distributed to markets in North and South America. The Hong Kong factory now employs 80 people and the China plant between 300 and 400. • Also in the mid-1960s, Swan had begun to look for opportunities to invest in foreign eyewear companies with reputations for fashionable design and high quality. Its objective in this case was not to reduce manufacturing costs but to launch a line of high-quality, "designer" eyewear. Swan did not have the design capability in-house to support such a line, but Glassman knew that certain foreign manufacturers had the capability. As a result, Swan invested in factories in Japan, France, and Italy, taking a minority shareholding in each case. These factories now supply eyewear for Swan's Status Eye division, which markets high-priced designer eyewear. 🌐 *Source: C. S. Trager, "Enter the Mini-Multinational,"* Northeast International Business, *March 1989, pp. 13–14.*

INTRODUCTION

When most people think of international businesses they visualize large, complex, billion-dollar corporations such as Procter & Gamble, Unilever, Toyota, Sony, 3M, and IBM. Even 20 years ago this was largely accurate, as most companies involved in international business were very large. Today, however, medium-sized and even small companies are just as likely to participate in international business as the giants such as IBM. According to a recent United Nations report, 23 percent of Japanese multinationals employed fewer than 300 people in 1984, while 78 percent of British firms with direct investments abroad employed fewer than 500 people.[1] The opening case explains that a small U.S. company, Swan Optical, was forced to go international to survive. Many other such cases exist, some of which we consider in this chapter.

The reason for the growing number of international businesses, particularly smaller firms, is quite straightforward. Forty years of gradual decline in barriers to international trade and investment under successive GATT rounds have opened up market after market around the world to greater international competition (see Chapter 5). This has created both opportunities and threats for businesses of all sizes. On the one hand, the

[1] "Come Back Multinationals," *The Economist,* November 26, 1988, p. 73.

decline in barriers to trade and investment has made it increasingly possible for large and small businesses to exploit profitable opportunities abroad. For example, in recent years Swan Optical has been able to take advantage of lower import barriers in many Latin American countries to expand its market presence there. Similarly, had it not been for a liberal foreign investment environment, Swan would never have been able to invest in factories in Hong Kong, China, France, Italy, and Japan. Another small U.S. company that has exploited foreign market opportunities is Lixi, Inc., which manufactures industrial X-ray equipment. In 1991 fully 70 percent of Lixi's $4.5 million revenues came from exports to Japan.[2] For a more familiar example, consider Toys R Us, the $6 billion U.S. toy retailer. After sustained pressure from the U.S. government, Japan agreed in 1990 to make it easier for foreign retailers to set up shop in Japan. One of the first beneficiaries of this was Toys R Us, which opened its first Japanese store in January 1992. Toys R Us plans to have about 100 outlets in Japan by the year 2000.[3]

On the other hand, the decline in barriers to trade and investment has also increased the number of foreign competitors in industry after industry. In the case of the United States, foreign competitors more often than not offer cost advantages that make it more difficult for U.S.-based companies to survive. Swan Optical and many other U.S. firms have found that the only way to match the cost advantage enjoyed by foreign competitors is to shift their production facilities abroad. Thus, adverse circumstances have *forced* them to become international businesses. Zenith Electronics Corporation announced in 1991 that it was shifting its last U.S. television assembly operation to Mexico to reduce its labor costs.[4] Zenith had found that the cost of producing televisions in the United States put the company at a cost disadvantage vis-à-vis its international competitors, most of whom already had assembly operations in such low-cost locations as Taiwan, South Korea, Mexico, and China.

Against this background, the objective of this chapter is to take a close look at the strategies of international business. We will see how a strategy of expanding internationally can help a firm lower its costs, increase its quality, or simply earn better returns from its existing strengths. Throughout we will emphasize that international business strategies have implications for large, small, and medium-sized companies. Before discussing any of these, however, we must first discuss the concept of strategy and how it relates to the firm.

STRATEGY AND THE FIRM

The fundamental purpose of any business firm is to make a profit. A firm makes a profit if the price it can charge for its output is greater than its costs of producing that output. To do this, a company must produce a product that is valued by consumers. Thus we say that business firms engage in the activity of **value creation.** The price consumers are prepared to pay for a product indicates the value of the product to consumers.

Firms can increase their profits in two ways: by adding value to a product so that consumers are willing to pay more for it and by lowering the costs of value creation (i.e., the costs of production). A firm adds value to a product when it improves the product's quality, provides a service to the consumer, or customizes the product to consumer needs in such a way that consumers will pay more for it. For example, consumers will pay more

---

2 "Small Companies Learn How to Sell to the Japanese," *Seattle Times*, March 19, 1992.

3 "Toy Joy," *The Economist*, January 4, 1992, p. 62.

4 J. Boyd, "Japanese Onslaught Forces Zenith to Mexico," *Journal of Commerce*, October 31, 1991, p. 3A.

for a Mercedes Benz car than a Hyundai car because they value the superior quality of the Mercedes. Firms lower the costs of value creation when they find ways to perform value creation activities more economically.

The Firm as a Value Chain

It is useful to think of the firm as a value chain composed of a series of distinct **value creation activities** including production, marketing, materials management, R&D, human resources, information systems, and the company infrastructure. We can categorize these value creation activities as primary activities and support activities (see Figure 12.1).[5]

Primary Activities The primary activities of a firm have to do with creating the product, marketing and delivering the product to buyers, and providing support and after-sale service to the buyers of the product. Here we consider the activities involved in the physical creation of the product as **production** and those involved in marketing, delivery, and after-sale service as **marketing.** Efficient production can reduce the costs of creating value (e.g., by realizing scale economies) *and* can add value by increasing product quality (e.g., by reducing the number of defective products), which facilitates premium pricing. Efficient marketing also can help the firm reduce its costs creating value (e.g., by generating the volume sales necessary to realize scale economies) and can add value by helping the firm customize its product to consumer needs and differentiate its product from competitors' products—both of which facilitate premium pricing.

Support Activities Support activities provide the inputs that allow the primary activities of production and marketing to occur. The materials management function controls the transmission of physical materials through the value chain—from procurement through production and into distribution. The efficiency with which this is carried out can significantly reduce the cost of creating value. In addition, an effective materials management function can monitor the quality of inputs into the production process. This results in improved quality of the company's outputs, which adds value and thus facilitates premium pricing.

The R&D function develops new product and process technologies. Technological developments can reduce production costs and can result in the creation of more useful and more attractive products that can demand a premium price. Thus R&D can affect primary production and marketing activities and, through them, value creation.

An effective human resource function ensures that the firm has an optimal mix of people to perform its primary production and marketing activities and that the staffing requirements of the support activities are met. The information systems function makes certain that management has the information it needs to maximize the efficiency of its value chain and to exploit information-based competitive advantages in the marketplace. Company infrastructure—consisting of such factors as organizational structure, general management, planning, finance, and legal and government affairs—embraces all other activities of the company and establishes the context for them. An efficient infrastructure thus helps both to create value and to reduce the costs of creating value.

The Role of Strategy

As we have pointed out many times, markets are now extremely competitive due to the liberalization of the world trade and investment environment. In industry after industry,

[5] See M. E. Porter, *Competitive Advantage* (New York: Free Press, 1985).

Figure 12.1
The Firm as a Value Chain

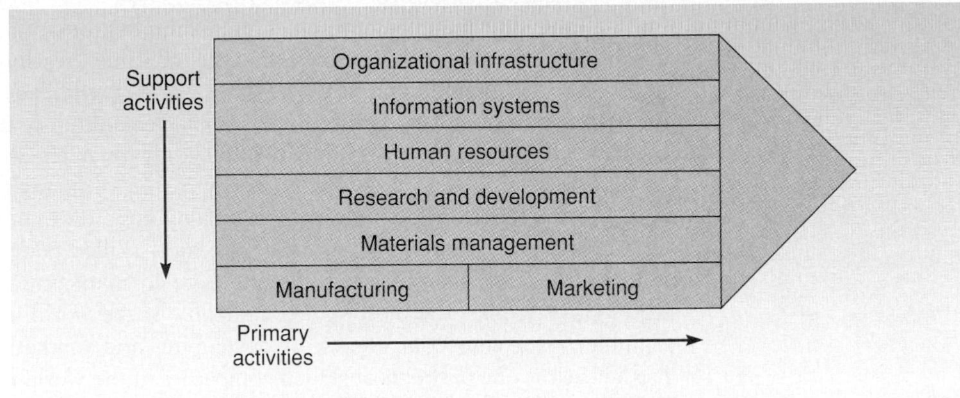

a large number of capable competitors confront each other around the globe. To survive in such an environment, a firm must pay continual attention to both reducing the costs of value creation and performing value creation activities in such ways that consumers are willing to pay more for the product than it costs to produce it. A firm's *strategy* can be defined as the steps it takes to ensure that these two things occur. Strategy is about identifying and taking actions that will reduce the costs of value creation and/or will add value by better serving consumer needs.

To fully understand this, consider again the case of Swan Optical. Confronted with low-cost foreign competitors, Swan adopted a strategy intended to reduce its costs of value creation: shifting its production from a high-cost location, the United States, to a low-cost location, Hong Kong. Later Swan adopted a strategy intended to add value to its basic product so it could charge a premium price. Reasoning that premium pricing in eyewear depended on superior design, its strategy involved investing capital in French, Italian, and Japanese factories that had reputations for superior design. In sum, Swan's strategies included some actions intended to reduce its costs of creating value and other actions intended to add value to its product.

PROFITING FROM GLOBAL EXPANSION

Expanding globally allows firms large and small to increase their profitability in ways not available to purely domestic enterprises. Firms that operate internationally are able to:

1. Earn a greater return from their distinctive skills, or core competencies.
2. Realize location economies by dispersing particular value creation activities to those locations where they can be performed most efficiently.
3. Realize greater experience curve economies, which reduce the costs of value creation.

As we will see, however, a firm's ability to increase its profitability by pursuing these strategies is constrained by the need to customize its product offering, marketing strategy, and business strategy to differing national conditions.

Transferring Core Competencies

The term **core competence** refers to skills within the firm that competitors cannot easily match or imitate. These skills may exist in any of the firm's value creation activities—production, marketing, R&D, human resources, general management, and so on. Such skills are typically expressed in product offerings that other firms find difficult to match or imitate, and thus the core competencies are the bedrock of a firm's competitive advantage. They enable a firm to reduce the costs of value creation and/or to create value in such a way that premium pricing is possible. For example, Toyota has a core competence in the production of cars. Quite simply, it is able to produce high-quality, well-designed cars at a lower delivered cost than any other company in the world. The skills that enable Toyota to do this seem to reside primarily in the company's production and materials management functions.[6] Similarly, McDonald's has a core competence in managing fast-food operations (it seems to be one of the most skilled companies in the world in this industry); Toys R Us has a core competence in managing high-volume, discount toy stores (it is perhaps the most skilled company in the world in this business); Procter & Gamble has a core competence in developing and marketing name brand consumer products (it is one of the most skilled companies in the world in this business); and so on.

For such companies, global expansion is a way of further exploiting the value creation potential of their skills and product offerings by applying those skills and products in a larger market. The potential for creating value from such a strategy is greatest when the skills and products of the firm are most unique, when the value placed on them by consumers is great, and when there are very few capable competitors with similar skills and/or products in foreign markets. Firms with unique and valuable skills can often realize enormous returns by applying those skills, and the products they produce, to foreign markets where indigenous competitors lack similar skills and products.

For example, McDonald's has expanded rapidly overseas in recent years. Its skills in managing fast-food operations have proven to be just as valuable in countries as diverse as France, Russia, China, Germany, and Brazil as they have been in the United States. Prior to McDonald's entry, none of these countries had American-style fast-food chains, so McDonald's brought a unique product as well as unique skills to each country. The lack of indigenous competitors with similar skills and products, and the implied lack of competition, has greatly enhanced the profitability of this strategy for McDonald's.

Similarly, in earlier eras U.S. firms such as Kellogg, Coca-Cola, H. J. Heinz, and Procter & Gamble expanded overseas to exploit their skills in developing and marketing name brand consumer products. These skills and the resulting products—which were developed in the U.S. market during the 1950s and 60s—yielded enormous returns when applied to European markets, where most indigenous competitors lacked similar marketing skills and products. Their near-monopoly on consumer marketing skills allowed these U.S. firms to dominate many European consumer product markets during the 1960s and 70s. Today many Japanese firms are expanding globally to exploit their skills in production, materials management, and new product development—skills that many of their indigenous North Americans and European competitors seem to lack.

Realizing Location Economies

We know from Chapters 2, 3, and 4 that countries differ along a whole range of dimensions, including the economic, political, legal, and cultural. In Chapter 2 we discussed how the benefits, costs, and risks of doing business in a country are influenced by economic and political factors. In Chapter 3 we saw how the culture of a country, as defined by its norms and value systems, can raise or lower the costs of doing business

[6] For evidence to this effect, see J. P. Womack, D. T. Jones, and D. Roos, *The Machine that Changed the World* (New York: Rawson Associates, 1990).

Toys R Us Goes International

BOX 12.1

In the last decade Toys R Us has revolutionized the market for toys in the United States. The company's discounting strategy has allowed it to offer prices 20 to 30 percent below those of competing retailers. To support these low prices, it has developed a policy of dealing directly with manufacturers to get deep discounts on volume purchases of toys. In addition, it runs large, warehouselike suburban stores crammed to the rafters with some 18,000 items and surrounded by large parking areas. The company feels that people will buy more if they're heading straight back to their cars rather than to another store. These tactics helped Toys R Us build a nationwide network of 497 stores that had given it a 25 percent share of the U.S. toy market by 1991.

Toys R Us began expanding internationally in 1984, when it opened stores in Great Britain, Canada, Hong Kong, and Singapore. By 1991 it had 126 outlets abroad, with additional stores in France, Germany, and Japan. The company tries to maintain the same basic format internationally that has proven so successful in the United States, and its international stores are virtual clones of those in the United States. Moreover, some 80 percent of the merchandise sold in the international stores is identical to that in the U.S. stores. The ability to market toys worldwide gives the company added leverage with toy manufacturers in negotiating prices, which in turn enables the company to keep its prices below those of the competition.

The company makes concessions to local tastes. In Great Britain, for example, shoppers find cricket bats right alongside Louisville Sluggers. This works both ways, too. For example, in preparing to open stores in Germany, the company found a number of local products it believed were so good that it is introducing them in the U.S. stores. The chain has also adopted apparel merchandising methods it first used in Great Britain. Instead of hanging clothing on long racks against the wall, U.S. stores now hang each style on a separate bar that juts out toward the aisle, British-style, making it easier to see the merchandise.

Perhaps the most problematic aspect of the company's international expansion so far has been its operation in Japan. Japan's Large-Scale Retail Store Law, designed to protect small shopkeepers (traditionally the supporters of the ruling Liberal Democratic Party), allowed local retailers to block the opening of new stores in their neighborhoods for 10 years or more. Under pressure from Japan's foreign trading partners, particularly from the United States, the law was changed in May 1990. Now local officials and shopkeepers can delay an opening for only 18 months. This has given foreign retailers an opportunity to enter the Japanese market, and Toys R Us was one of the first to do so. It opened its first store in January 1992 to a capacity crowd, and it plans to have about 100 more stores in Japan within a decade.

To ease its entry into Japan, Toys R Us allied itself with Den Fujita, the president of McDonald's in Japan and one of Japan's most skilled retailers. McDonald's has a 20 percent stake in the Japanese operation of Toys R Us, and Fujita is helping the company find new store sites. Fujita's strategy is to build minimalls surrounded by huge parking lots along main roads all over Japan. In addition to a Toys R Us outlet, each mall will contain a McDonald's restaurant, an outlet of the U.S. video-rental giant Blockbuster Entertainment, and other stores.

Despite Fujita's help, however, the company has encountered many obstacles to its discounting strategy in Japan. The Japanese stores are selling toys for only 10 to 20 percent below the prices of smaller retailers, rather than their usual 30 to 40 percent. The reason: Toys R Us has so far failed to persuade many Japanese toy manufacturers to sell directly to it and thus circumvent the layers of distribution that make prices so high in Japan. Many Japanese manufacturers are tempted to make such deals but remain nervous about upsetting their long-standing customers, the hierarchy of distributors and other retailers.

Sources: Mark Maremont, Dori Yang, and Amy Dunkin, "Toys R Us Goes Overseas," Business Week, *January 26, 1987, pp. 71–72; and "Toy Joy,"* The Economist, *January 4, 1992, pp. 62–63.*

there. In Chapters 2 and 3 we argued that all of these factors influence the attractiveness of a country as both a market and an investment site.

In Chapter 4 we discussed a number of theories that point to the importance of differences in factor costs in determining the distribution of world trade. These theories all suggest that due to differences in factor costs, certain countries have a comparative advantage in the production of certain products. For example, Japan excels in the production of automobiles and consumer electronics. The United States excels in the production of chemicals, pharmaceuticals, biotechnology products, and financial services. Switzerland excels in the production of precision instruments and pharmaceuticals.

Creating a Global Web

What does all this mean for a company that is trying to survive in a competitive global market? In brief, it means that, trade barriers and transportation costs permitting, the firm will benefit by basing each value creation activity it performs at that location where economic, political, and cultural conditions, including relative factor costs, are most conducive to the performance of that activity. Thus if the best designers for a product live in France, a firm should base its design operations in France. If the most productive labor force for assembly operations is in Mexico, assembly operations should be based in Mexico. If the best marketers are in the United States, the marketing strategy should be formulated in the United States. And so on. This strategy is focused on achieving **location economies.**

The result of this kind of thinking is the creation of a "global web" in which the various value creation activities of the value chain are dispersed to those locations around the world that either maximize the value added or minimize the costs of creating value. Consider, as an example, the case of General Motor's (GM) Pontiac Le Mans cited in Robert Reich's *The Work of Nations.*[7] Marketed primarily in the United States, the car was designed in Germany; key components were manufactured in Japan, Taiwan, and Singapore; the assembly operation was performed in South Korea; and the advertising strategy was formulated in Great Britain. The car was designed in Germany, because GM believed the designers in its German subsidiary had the skills most suited to the job at hand. (They were the most capable of producing a design that added value.) Components were manufactured in Japan, Taiwan, and Singapore, because favorable factor conditions there—relatively low cost, skilled labor—suggested that those locations had a comparative advantage in the production of components (which helped reduce the costs of value creation). The car was assembled in South Korea, because GM believed that due to its low labor costs, the costs of assembly could be minimized there (also helping to minimize the costs of value creation). Finally, the advertising strategy was formulated in Great Britain, because GM believed a particular advertising agency there was the most able to produce an advertising campaign that would help sell the car. (This decision was consistent with GM's desire to maximize the value added.)

In theory, a firm that realizes location economies by dispersing each of its value creation activities to its optimal location should have a competitive advantage vis-à-vis a firm that bases all of its value creation activities at a single location. It should be able to add more value *and* to create value at lower costs than its single-location competitor. In a world where competitive pressures are increasing, such a strategy may well become an imperative for survival (as it seems to have been for Swan Optical).

---

[7] The example was quoted in R. B. Reich, *The Work of Nations* (New York: Alfred A. Knopf, 1991).

Some Caveats

Introducing transportation costs and trade barriers complicates this picture somewhat. Due to favorable factor endowments, New Zealand may have a comparative advantage for automobile assembly operations, but high transportation costs would make it an uneconomical location for them. Closer to home, a consideration of transportation costs and trade barriers helps explain why many firms are now shifting their production from Asia to Mexico. Mexico has three distinct advantages over many Asian countries as a location for value creation activities. First, low labor costs make it a good location for labor-intensive production processes. In recent years wage rates have increased significantly in Japan, Taiwan, and Hong Kong, but they have remained low in Mexico. Second, Mexico's proximity to the large U.S. market reduces transportation costs. This is particularly important in the case of products with high weight-to-value ratios (e.g., automobiles). And third, the proposed North American Free Trade Agreement (see Chapter 8) would remove most trade barriers between Mexico, the United States, and Canada, increasing Mexico's attractiveness as a production site for the North American market.[8] The point is that although value added and the costs of value creation are important, transportation costs and trade barriers also must be considered in location decisions.

Another caveat concerns the importance of assessing political risks when making location decisions. Even if a country looks very attractive as a production location when measured against all the standard criteria, if its government is unstable or totalitarian, the firm might be well advised not to base production there. (Political risk is discussed in Chapter 2.)

Realizing Experience Curve Economies

The **experience curve** refers to the systematic reductions in production costs that have been observed to occur over the life of a product.[9] A number of studies have observed that a product's production costs decline by some characteristic about each time accumulated output doubles. The relationship was first observed in the aircraft industry, where each time accumulated output of airframes was doubled, unit costs typically declined to 80 percent of their previous level.[10] Thus, production cost for the fourth airframe would be 80 percent of production cost for the second airframe, the eighth airframe's production costs 80 percent of the fourth's, the sixteenth's 80 percent of the eighth's, and so on. This experience curve relationship between production costs and output is illustrated in Figure 12.2. Two things explain this: learning effects and economies of scale.

Learning Effects

Learning effects refer to cost savings that come from learning by doing. Labor, for example, learns by repetition how to carry out a task such as assembling airframes most efficiently. In other words, labor productivity increases over time as individuals learn the most efficient ways to perform particular tasks. Equally important, it has been observed that in new production facilities, management typically learns how to manage the new operation more efficiently over time. Hence, production costs eventually decline due to increasing labor productivity and management efficiency.

---

[8] S. Baker and D. Lee, "Assembly Lines Start Migrating from Asia to Mexico," *Business Week*, July 1, 1991, p. 43.

[9] G. Hall and S. Howell, "The Experience Curve from an Economist's Perspective," *Strategic Management Journal* 6 (1985), pp. 197–212.

[10] A. A. Alchain, "Reliability of Progress Curves in Airframe Production," *Econometrica* 31 (1963), pp. 697–93.

Figure 12.2
The Experience Curve

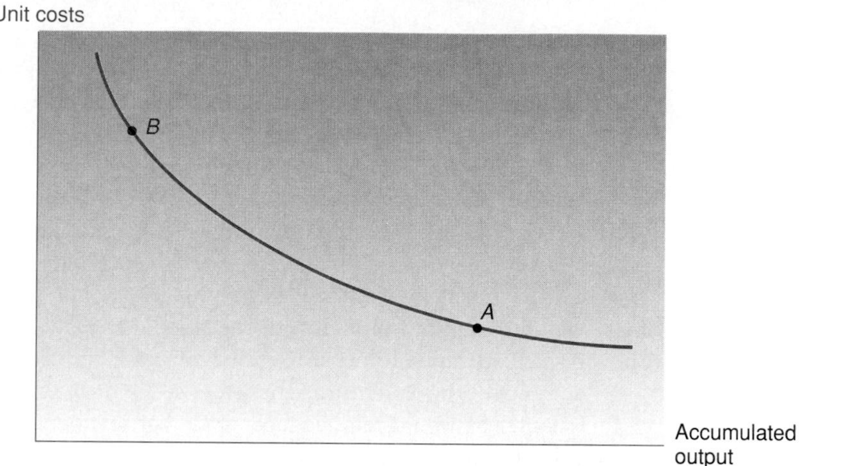

Learning effects tend to be more significant when a technologically complex task is repeated, since there is more that *can be learned* about the task. Thus learning effects will be more significant in an assembly process involving 1,000 complex steps than in one of only 100 simple steps. No matter how complex the task, however, learning effects typically die out after a period of time. Indeed, it has been suggested that they are really important only during the start-up period of a new process and that they cease after two or three years.[11] Any decline in the experience curve after such a point is due to economies of scale.

Economies of Scale

Scale economies are the reductions in unit cost achieved by producing a large volume of a product. They have a number of sources, the most important of which seems to be the ability to spread fixed costs over a large volume. Fixed costs are the costs required to set up a production facility, develop a new product, and the like, and they can be substantial. For example, establishing a new production line to manufacture semiconductor chips costs about $150 million. Or take pharmaceuticals. According to one estimate, developing a new drug costs about $250 million and takes about 12 years.[12] The only way to recoup such high fixed costs is to sell the product worldwide, which reduces unit costs by spreading them over a larger volume. Moreover, the more rapidly that cumulative sales volume is built up, the more rapidly fixed costs can be amortized, and the more rapidly unit costs fall. Hence, in addition to learning effects, economies of scale underlie the experience curve.

Strategic Significance

The strategic significance of the experience curve is clear. Moving down the experience curve allows a firm to reduce its cost of creating value. The firm that moves down the experience curve most rapidly will have a cost advantage vis-à-vis its competitors. Thus

[11] Hall and Howell, "Experience Curve."

[12] J. Main, "How to Go Global—and Why," *Fortune,* August 28, 1989, pp. 70–76.

Firm A in Figure 12.2, because it is further down the experience curve, has a clear cost advantage over Firm B.

Note that many of the underlying sources of experience-based cost economies are plant based. This is true for most learning effects as well as for the economies of scale derived by spreading the fixed costs of building productive capacity over a large output. Thus the key to progressing downward on the experience curve as rapidly as possible is to increase the volume *produced by a single plant* as rapidly as possible. Since global markets are larger than domestic markets, a firm that serves a global market from a single location is likely to build up accumulated volume more quickly than a firm that serves only its home market, or that serves multiple markets from multiple production locations. Thus, serving a global market from a single location is consistent with moving down the experience curve and establishing a low-cost position. In addition, to get down the experience curve rapidly, a firm must price and market very aggressively so demand will expand rapidly. It will also need to build sufficient production capacity for serving a global market. Another point to bear in mind is that the cost advantages of serving the world market from a single location will be all the more significant if that location is the optimal one for performing the particular value creation activity.

Once a firm has established a low-cost position, it can act as a barrier to new competition. Specifically, an established firm that is well down the experience curve—such as Firm A in Figure 12.2—can price so that it is still making a profit while new entrants—which are further up the curve, such as Firm B in the figure—are suffering losses.

One firm that has excelled in the pursuit of such a strategy is Matsushita. Along with Sony and Philips, Matsushita was in the race to develop a commercially viable VCR in the 1970s. Although Matsushita initially lagged behind Philips and Sony, it was able to get its VHS format accepted as the world standard and to reap enormous experience-curve-based cost economies in the process. This cost advantage subsequently constituted a formidable barrier to new competition. Matsushita's strategy was to build global volume as rapidly as possible. To ensure it could accommodate worldwide demand, the company increased its production capacity 33-fold from 205,000 units in 1977 to 6.8 million units by 1984. By serving the world market from a single location in Japan, Matsushita was able to realize significant learning effects and economies of scale. These allowed Matsushita to drop its prices 50 percent within five years of selling its first VHS-formatted VCR. As a result, Matsushita was the world's major VCR producer by 1983, accounting for approximately 45 percent of world production and enjoying a significant cost advantage over its competitors. The next-largest company, Hitachi, accounted for only 11.1 percent of world production in 1983.[13]

The Need for Local Responsiveness

Until this point we have ignored the extent to which national differences constrain a firm's ability to increase its profitability by expanding globally. In practice, this constraint is very important, and we discuss it later in the chapter. For now, let us note that consumer tastes and preferences, business practices, distribution channels, competitive conditions, and government policies differ significantly from nation to nation. Due to these differences, a firm may have to customize its product offering, its marketing strategy, and its business strategy to local conditions in order to succeed there.

The significance of this is as follows. First, we have implicitly assumed that the skills and products associated with a firm's core competencies *can* be transferred wholesale from

[13] "Matsushita Electrical Industrial in 1987," in *Transnational Management*, ed. C. A. Bartlett and S. Ghoshal (Homewood, Ill.: Richard D. Irwin, 1992).

BOX 12.2

McDonald's Goes Global

In the mid-1970s, McDonald's faced a problem: after three decades of rapid growth, the U.S. fast-food market was beginning to show signs of maturity. McDonald's response to the slowdown was to expand abroad rapidly. By 1980, 28 percent of the chain's new store openings were abroad; in 1986 the figure was 40 percent, and in 1990 it was closer to 60 percent. By the late 1980s the company had operations in 44 other countries, which were generating almost one fourth of its revenues, and it had no plans to slow down its global expansion.

The key to the company's international strategy is the export of the management skills that spurred its growth in the United States—not just its fast-food products. McDonald's U.S. success was built on a formula of close relations with suppliers, nationwide marketing might, tight control over store-level operating procedures, and a franchising system that encourages entrepreneurial individual franchisees.

Although this system has worked flawlessly in the United States, some modifications must be made in other countries. One of the company's biggest challenges had been to infuse each store with the same gung ho culture and standardized operating procedures that have been the hallmark of its success in the United States. To aid in this task, in many countries McDonald's has enlisted the help of large partners through joint venture arrangements. The partners play a key role in learning and transplanting the organization's values.

Foreign partners have also played a key role in helping McDonald's adapt its marketing methods and menu to local conditions. Although U.S.-style fast food remains the staple fare on the menu, local products have been added. In Brazil, for example, McDonald's sells a soft drink made from the *guarana,* an Amazonian berry. Patrons of McDonald's in Malaysia, Singapore, and Thailand savor milk shakes flavored with *durian,* a foul-smelling (to U.S. tastes, at least) fruit considered an aphrodisiac by the locals. In addition to their help in product adaptation, these partners can steer the company away from potentially expensive marketing pitfalls. In Japan, for example, Den Fujita, president of McDonald's in Japan, avoided the suburban locations typical in the United States and stressed urban sites that consumers could walk to.

McDonald's biggest problem, however, has been to replicate its U.S. supply chain in other countries. U.S. suppliers are fiercely loyal to McDonald's; they must be, because their fortunes are closely linked to those of McDonald's. McDonald's maintains very rigorous specifications for all the raw ingredients it uses—the key to its consistency and quality control. Outside of the United States, however, McDonald's has found suppliers far less willing to make the investments required to meet its specifications. In Great Britain, for example, McDonald's had problems getting local bakeries to produce the hamburger bun. After experiencing quality problems with two local bakeries, McDonald's built its own bakery to supply its stores there. In a more extreme case, when McDonald's decided to open a store in Russia, it found that local suppliers lacked the capability to produce goods of the quality it demanded. The company was forced to vertically integrate through the local food industry on a heroic scale, importing potato seeds and bull semen and indirectly managing dairy farms, cattle ranches, and vegetable plots. It also had to construct the world's largest food-processing plant, at a cost of $40 million. The restaurant itself cost only $4.5 million.

Sources: Kathleen Deveny et al., "McWorld?" Business Week, *October 13, 1986, pp. 78–86; and "Slow Food,"* The Economist, *February 3, 1990, p. 64.*

one nation to another. In practice, this is not the case; companies often must adapt to local conditions. (Box 12.2 describes some of McDonald's adaptations in various national markets.)

Second, we have implicitly assumed it is *possible* to serve the global marketplace from a single production site, producing a globally standardized product, and marketing it worldwide to achieve experience curve cost economies. In practice, the need to customize the product offering to local conditions may work against the implementation of such a strategy. Automobile firms, for example, have found that Japanese, American, and European consumers demand different kinds of cars, and that this necessitates producing products customized for local markets. In response, companies such as Honda, Ford, and Toyota are pursuing a strategy of establishing top-to-bottom production facilities in each of these regions so they can better serve local demands. Although such customization obviously brings benefits, it also limits a firm's ability to realize significant experience curve and location economies.

Third, we have assumed it is *possible* to realize location economies by dispersing various value creation activities (e.g., marketing, production, R&D) to those locations where the economic, political, and cultural conditions (including relative factor costs) are optimal. This implies that, in practice, worldwide marketing should be coordinated from a single location, production should be performed at a single location, all R&D should be performed at a single location, and so on. Such a strategy is obviously inconsistent with strong demands for local customization, which *may* require that marketing, production, R&D, and the like all be oriented toward satisfying local demands and hence must be based in each nation in which the firm does business.

Thus demands for local responsiveness act as a constraint on a firm's ability to transfer its core competencies, to realize experience curve economies by serving the global marketplace from a single location, and to realize location economies by dispersing its various value creation activities to the optimal location for each activity.

THREE TRADITIONAL STRATEGIES

According to a study by Christopher Bartlett and Sumantra Ghoshal, firms that have expanded overseas in the past can be categorized into three types (see Figure 12.3): firms that pursue a "global" strategy, those that pursue an "international" strategy, and those that pursue a "multidomestic" strategy.[14]

Global Strategy

Firms that pursue a **global strategy** attempt to increase their profitability by reaping the cost reductions that come from experience curve and location economies. As might be expected, these firms' production, marketing, and R&D activities tend to be concentrated in a few favorable locations. Global firms tend not to customize their product offering and marketing strategy to local conditions because customization raises costs. Instead, they prefer to market a standardized product worldwide so they can reap the maximum benefits from experience curve economies. They also tend to use their cost advantage to support aggressive pricing in world markets.

This group includes firms such as Matsushita, which served the global market for VCRs from a single favorable location. Indeed, until relatively recently a large number of Japanese firms—including Toyota, Koa, NEC, and Sony pursued this strategy. The

---

[14] This section is based on C. A. Bartlett and S. Ghoshal, *Managing across Borders* (Boston, Mass.: Harvard Business School Press, 1989).

Figure 12.3
Advantages and Disadvantages of the Three Traditional Strategies

	Advantages	Disadvantages
Global strategy	Location economies Experience curve economies	Lack of local responsiveness
International strategy	Transferring core skills and products	Limited local responsiveness Limited experience and location economies
Multidomestic strategy	Local responsiveness	Limited transfer of skills and products Limited experience and location economies

resulting cost advantages these firms enjoyed enabled them to make large inroads against their competitors during much of the 1970s and 80s.

International Strategy

Firms pursuing an **international strategy** try to increase their profits by transferring valuable skills and products (derived from core competencies) to markets where indigenous competitors lack those skills and products. Most international firms create value by transferring product offerings developed at home to new markets overseas. Accordingly, they tend to centralize their product development functions (e.g., R&D) at home. However, they tend to establish production and marketing functions in each major country in which they do business. Although they may undertake some local customization of product offering and marketing strategy, it tends to be rather limited in scope, since in most of these firms the head office retains tight control over marketing and product strategy.

International firms include the likes of Toys R Us, McDonald's, IBM, Kellogg, and Procter & Gamble. Indeed, most of the U.S. companies that expanded abroad in the 1950s and 60s fall into this category. As an example, consider Procter & Gamble. P&G has long had production facilities in all of its major markets outside the United States, including Great Britain, Germany, and Japan. These facilities, however, manufacture products developed by the U.S. parent company and often marketed using the marketing message developed in the United States. Historically at least, there has been some local responsiveness by P&G, but it has been rather limited in scope.

Multidomestic Strategy

Firms pursuing a **multidomestic strategy** orient themselves toward local responsiveness. They include many of the older European multinational enterprises, particularly those British and Dutch firms whose origins can be traced back to the pre-World War II colonial empires. Unilever and Philips are the two most notable examples of such firms.

Like international firms, most multidomestic firms expanded to other countries by transferring skills and products developed at home to foreign markets. Unlike international firms, multidomestic firms have extensively customized both their product offering and their marketing strategy to specific national conditions. Consistent with this, they have also tended to establish a complete set of value creation activities—including production, marketing, and R&D—in each major national market where they do business. As a result, they are generally unable to realize value from experience curve and location economies. Moreover, many multidomestic firms have developed into decentralized federations in which each national subsidiary functions quite autonomously. Consequently, after a time they lose the ability to transfer the skills and products derived from core competencies to their various national subsidiaries around the world. One well-known case illustrates the problems this can cause. Philips' chances of establishing its V2000 VCR format as the dominant design in the VCR industry—as opposed to Matsushita's VHS format—were effectively thwarted by its U.S. subsidiary's refusal to adopt the V2000 format. Instead, the subsidiary bought VCRs produced by Matsushita and put its own label on them!

Some Trade-offs

As can be seen from Figure 12.3, although each strategic type is able to increase value, each suffers from a disadvantage. Firms pursuing a global strategy can increase their profitability by exploiting experience curve and location economies, but they suffer from a lack of local responsiveness. Firms pursuing an international strategy can increase their profitability by transferring skills and products derived from their core competencies to foreign markets and by responding to local conditions in a limited way. However, they suffer from a lack of more extensive local responsiveness (when it is called for) and from an inability to exploit experience curve and location economies. Firms pursuing a multidomestic strategy can increase value (and profitability) by customizing their product offering, marketing strategy, and business strategy to national conditions, but they suffer from an inability to exploit experience curve and location economies and, in many cases, from an increasing inability to transfer skills and products between countries.

The fact that each strategy has advantages and disadvantages poses an interesting dilemma for a firm. Specifically, what is the best strategy for the firm to pursue given conditions in the industry in which it competes? In the next section we attempt to answer this question.

COST PRESSURES AND LOCAL RESPONSIVENESS

In any given industry, the appropriateness of the three strategies we have discussed is partly determined by the relative intensities of pressures for cost reductions and pressures for local responsiveness. This is illustrated by Figure 12.4. When pressures for cost reduction are high and pressures for local responsiveness are low (cell 1), firms pursuing a global strategy may have a competitive advantage, since this strategy minimizes the costs of value creation. When pressures for cost reduction are low and pressures for local responsiveness are high (cell 4), firms pursuing a multidomestic strategy may have a competitive advantage, since this strategy maximizes local responsiveness. When both cost pressures and pressures for local responsiveness are low (cell 3), firms that pursue an international strategy may have a competitive advantage, since these firms may have more to offer (i.e., unique products and/or skills) than their global or multidomestic competitors.

To fully appreciate these arguments, in this section we review the factors that determine the pressures for cost reductions and for local responsiveness. Before doing so, however, it should be noted that the author has not overlooked the empty cell in Figure 12.4, cell 2. Firms in this cell face high pressures for cost reductions and for local responsiveness. The discussion of the appropriate strategy for these firms is deferred until the end of the section.

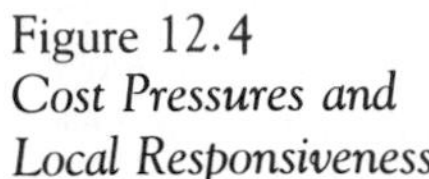

Figure 12.4
Cost Pressures and Local Responsiveness

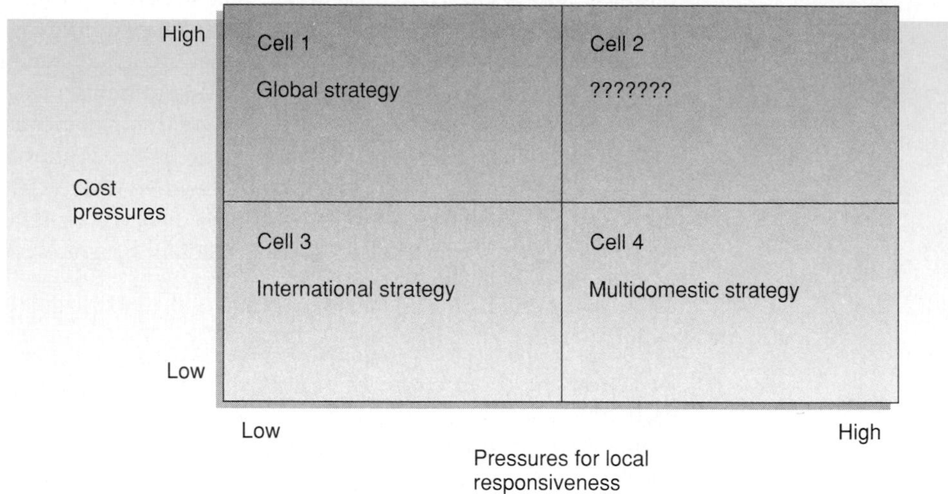

Pressures for Cost Reductions

Pressures for cost reductions can be particularly intense in industries that produce commodity-type products, where meaningful differentiation on nonprice factors is difficult and price is the main competitive weapon. This tends to be the case for products that serve universal needs. **Universal needs** exist when the tastes and preferences of consumers in different nations are very similar if not identical. It is obviously the case for conventional commodities such as bulk chemicals, petroleum, steel, and sugar. It also tends to be the case for many industrial and consumer products (e.g., hand-held calculators, semiconductor chips, and personal computers). Pressures for cost reductions are also intense in industries where major competitors are based in low-cost locations, where there is persistent excess capacity, and where consumers are powerful and switching costs are low.

Conditions similar to this have prevailed in the tire industry in recent years. Tires are essentially a commodity product; differentiation is difficult, and price is the main competitive weapon. The major buyers of tires, automobile companies, are powerful, and their switching costs are low. Hence, it is not surprising that they have been playing tire companies off against each other in an attempt to get lower prices. The decline in global demand for automobiles in the early 1990s created a serious excess capacity problem in the tire industry—as much as 25 percent of world capacity may be standing idle. The result has been a worldwide price war, with almost all tire companies suffering heavy losses in the early 1990s. In response to the cost pressures, most tire companies are now trying to rationalize their operations in a manner consistent with a global strategy.[15]

Many commentators have argued that the liberalization of the world trade and investment environment in recent decades, by fostering greater international competition, has generally increased cost pressures.[16] In response, an increasing number of companies are switching to global strategies. For example, Great Britain's Imperial Chemical Industries, one of the world's largest chemical firms, switched from a multidomestic strategy to a global strategy in 1983 in direct response to cost pressures arising from a severe recession in the chemical industry worldwide.

---

15 "The Tire Industry's Costly Obsession with Size," *The Economist*, June 8, 1992, pp. 65–66.

16 C. K. Prahalad and Yves L. Doz, *The Multinational Mission: Balancing Local Demands and Global Vision* (New York: Free Press, 1987). Prahalad and Doz actually talk about local responsiveness, rather than local customization.

BOX 12.3

The Game of Global Chess

In addition to pressures for cost reduction, a firm may be forced to switch to a more global stance if its main competitors are playing what is often referred to as *global chess*. Large multinational firms sometimes use profits generated in one market to subsidize prices in others to gain market share. This enables them to move down the experience curve, to realize greater cost economies, and, therefore, to increase their long-run profits. Canon, Hitachi, and Seiko are notable for building global market share by this means. Reacting to such threats calls for global strategic coordination and thus creates pressures to centralize decisions regarding the competitive strategy of a firm's national subsidiaries at corporate headquarters. Thus, once one multinational company in an industry adopts global strategic coordination, its competitors may be forced to respond in kind.

This phenomenon occurred in the tire industry in the 1970s. At that time the world tire market was dominated by three multinationals: Michelin Tire Corporation, Goodyear, and Firestone Tire & Rubber Company. Each of these companies pursued a multidomestic strategy, decentralizing manufacturing, marketing, and competitive strategy to various national subsidiaries around the globe. Then, in the early 70s, Michelin used its strong European profits to attack Goodyear's North American home market. Goodyear could have retaliated by cutting its North American prices, but because Michelin would only expose a small amount of its worldwide business in North America, Michelin had little to lose from a North American price war. Goodyear, on the other hand, would sacrifice profits in its largest market. Therefore, Goodyear struck back by cutting prices and expanding its operations in Europe. The action forced Michelin to slow down its attack on Goodyear's North American market and to think again about the costs of taking market share away from Goodyear. In other words, Michelin's decision to engage in global strategic coordination forced Goodyear to respond in kind. The result was an increase in pressure for global integration in the tire industry.

Pressures for Local Responsiveness

Pressures for local responsiveness arise from (1) differences in consumer tastes and preferences, (2) differences in infrastructure and traditional practices, (3) differences in distribution channels, and (4) host-government demands.

Differences in Consumer Tastes and Preferences

Strong pressures for local responsiveness exist when consumer tastes and preferences differ significantly between countries—as they may for historic or cultural reasons. In such cases, products and marketing messages must be customized to appeal to local tastes and preferences, which may, in turn, necessitate delegating production and marketing functions to national subsidiaries—a multidomestic strategy.

In the automobile industry, for example, there is strong demand in North America for pickup trucks, particularly in the South, West, and Midwest. Individuals and families buy them, use them, and love them. In Europe, on the other hand, pickups are regarded as utility vehicles and are purchased primarily by companies. Consequently, marketing messages for pickups must differ in North America and Europe.

Also in the automobile industry, Nissan has developed "lead country" models—products carefully tailored to the dominant, distinctive needs of individual national markets. In the United States, for example, Nissan saw that it needed a sporty Z model and a four-wheel-drive family vehicle to serve strong consumer preferences, neither of which are in great demand in Japan or Europe. Nissan now sells about 5,000 Z cars a month in the United States, and only 500 a month in Japan.[17]

As a counterpoint, Theodore Levitt has argued that consumer demands for local customization are declining in the world.[18] According to Levitt, modern communications and transport technologies have served to converge world tastes and preferences, creating enormous global markets for standardized consumer products. Levitt cites worldwide acceptance of McDonald's hamburgers, Coca-Cola soft drinks, Levi's jeans, and Sony television sets as evidence of the increasing homogeneity of the global marketplace.

Many regard Levitt's argument as extreme. Christopher Bartlett and Sumantra Ghoshal, for example, have observed that in the consumer electronics industry, consumers have rejected standardized global products and are showing a renewed preference for differentiated products.[19] They note that Amstrad, the fast-growing British computer and electronics firm, got its start by recognizing that a good share of the British audio market did not want the standardized, inexpensive music centers marketed by global firms such as Sony and Matsushita. Amstrad encased its product in teak, rather than metal, and tailored a control panel to appeal to British consumers' preferences. In response, Matsushita reversed its earlier bias toward standardized global design and began to customize to local markets. The company increased its portable audio product line from 15 models to 30 in 1985.

Differences in Infrastructure and Traditions

Some pressures for local responsiveness exist because of countries' differences in infrastructure and/or traditions. If a firm is to do business in certain countries, it may have to delegate manufacturing and production functions to foreign subsidiaries. For example, in North America consumer electrical systems are based on 110 volts, whereas 240-volt systems are standard in many European countries. Domestic electrical appliances must be customized for these markets. National traditions also can serve to demand customization. For example, in Great Britain people drive on the left side of the road, which necessitates right-hand-drive cars. In neighboring France, people drive on the right side of the road, necessitating left-hand-drive cars. Obviously automobiles must be customized to accommodate these differences in traditional practices.

Differences in Distribution Channels

Differences in countries' distribution channels may necessitate delegating marketing functions to national subsidiaries. In Germany, for example, five retail chains control 65 percent of the laundry detergent market, whereas no chain controls more than 2 percent of the market in neighboring Italy. This gives retail chains considerable buying power in Germany but relatively little in Italy. These differences require different marketing approaches for detergent companies. Similarly, the marketing of pharmaceuticals in Japan must be responsive to the Japanese distribution system, which radically differs from the U.S. system. Japanese doctors do not accept or respond favorably to an

---

[17] K. Ohmae, "Managing in a Borderless World," *Harvard Business Review*, May–June 1989, pp. 152–61.

[18] T. Levitt, "The Globalization of Markets," *Harvard Business Review*, May–June 1983, pp. 92–102.

[19] Bartlett and Ghoshal, *Managing across Borders*.

American-style, high-pressure sales force. Thus pharmaceutical companies must use different marketing practices in Japan than in the United States (soft sell versus hard sell).

Host-Government Demands

Economic and political demands imposed by host-country governments may necessitate local responsiveness. For example, the world politics of health care require pharmaceutical companies to manufacture in multiple locations. Pharmaceutical companies are subject to local clinical testing, registration procedures, and pricing restrictions that serve to ensure that a drug's manufacture and marketing meet local requirements. Moreover, since government agencies control significant portions of most countries' health-care budgets, governments can demand a high level of local responsiveness. More generally, local sentiments for protectionism and nationalism and local content rules (which require a certain percentage of a product to be manufactured locally) all serve to dictate that international businesses manufacture locally. Note that protectionist, nationalistic feelings exist in the United States as well. Part of the Japanese auto companies' motivation for setting up U.S. production operations, for example, is to counter the threat of protectionism that seems to be growing in Congress.

Choosing a Strategy

If a firm can identify the relative strengths of the pressures for cost reductions and for local responsiveness, determining the appropriate strategy—by referring to Figure 12.4—would seem relatively easy. For example, to survive in an environment where pressures for cost reductions are high and pressures for local responsiveness are low, a firm should attempt to reduce costs by assuming a global strategy. However, this simple picture is complicated by some additional considerations.

First, the pressures for cost reductions and local responsiveness may change over time, often as a result of individual firms' actions. In the television industry, for example, the advent of low-cost global manufacturers such as Matsushita and Sony in the 1970s increased the importance of global integration for other companies in the industry (see Figure 12.5). To compete on a cost basis with Matsushita and Sony, companies such as Philips were forced to switch from a multidomestic strategy to a global strategy.

It would be wrong to generalize from the television industry to all industries, however. In some industries, pressures for local responsiveness have increased in recent years. Amstrad's success in focusing on local needs in the British audio market increased industry pressures for local responsiveness (see Figure 12.6). In attempting to regain market share from the likes of Amstrad, Matsushita and others have moved away from a pure global strategy and are now incorporating more multidomestic elements in their strategic postures.

More problematic still is the fact that many firms face strong pressures for both cost reductions and local responsiveness. One example is Caterpillar Tractor. Its need to compete with such low-cost competitors as Komatsu of Japan forced it to seek greater cost economies. At the same time, variations in construction practices and government regulations across countries demand that Caterpillar be responsive to local needs (see Figure 12.7).

Such firms must create solutions that go beyond the three traditional strategies. In Caterpillar's case, the company has succeeded by combining elements of the global and multidomestic strategies. To deal with cost pressures, Caterpillar redesigned its products to use many identical components and invested in some large-scale component-manufac-

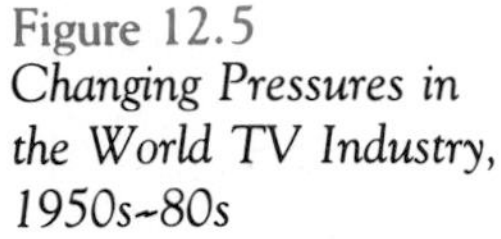

Figure 12.5
Changing Pressures in the World TV Industry, 1950s–80s

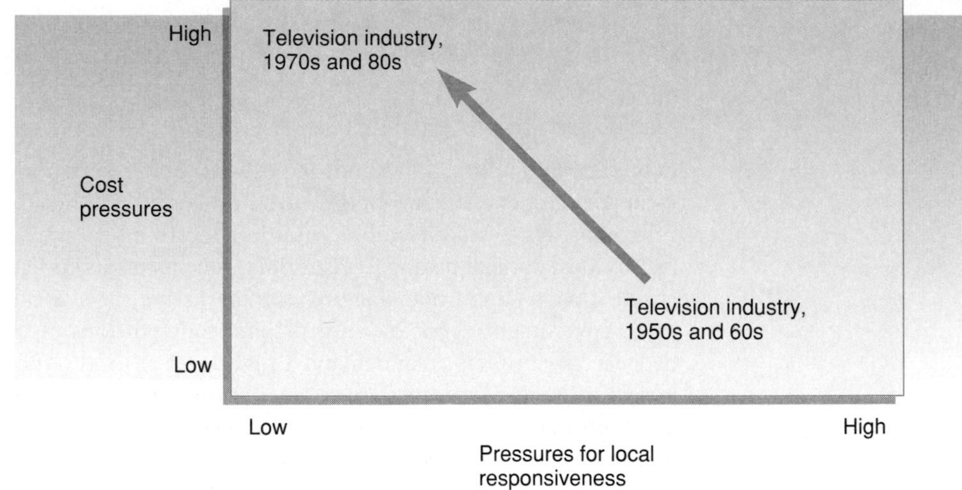

Figure 12.6
Changing Pressures in the World Audio Player Industry, 1970s–80s

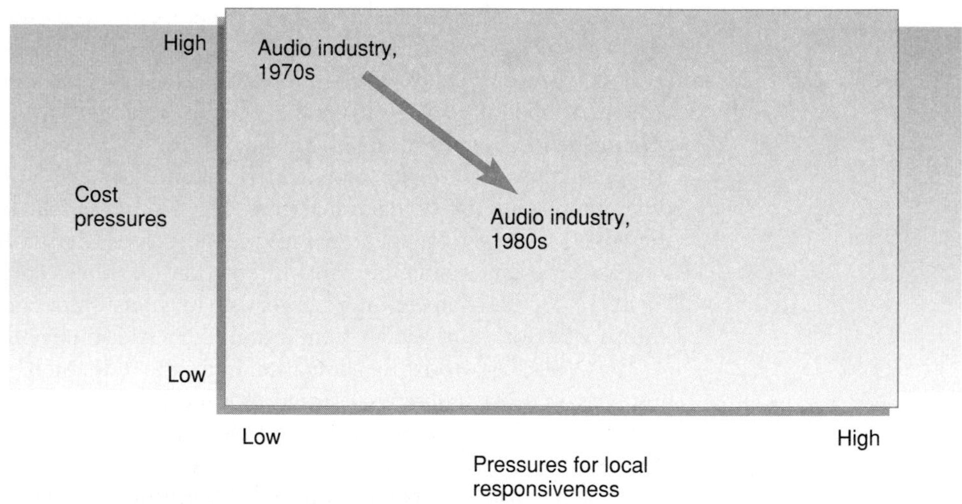

turing facilities, sited at favorable locations, to meet global demand and realize scale economics. The company augments its centralized manufacture of components with assembly plants in each of its major global markets. At these plants, Caterpillar adds features that tailor its products to local needs. Thus, Caterpillar is able to realize many of the benefits of global manufacturing and at the same time to respond to pressures for local accommodation by differentiating its products for various national markets.[20]

[20] T. Hout, M. E. Porter, and E. Rudden, "How Global Companies Win Out," *Harvard Business Review*, September–October 1982, pp. 98–108.

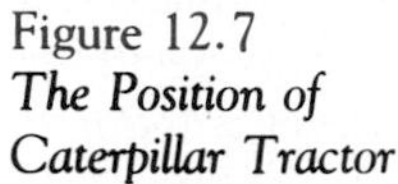
Figure 12.7
The Position of Caterpillar Tractor

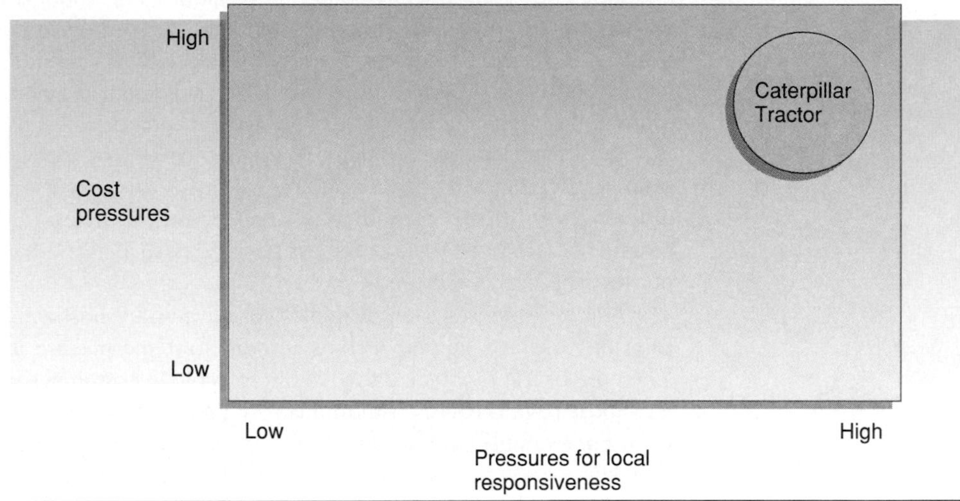

THE TRANSNATIONAL CORPORATION

Christopher Bartlett and Sumantra Ghoshal have taken the arguments developed in the previous two sections one step further.[21] They point out that competitive conditions are now so intense that, to survive, firms *must* exploit experience-based and location economies, they *must* transfer core competencies within the firm, and they must do all of this while paying attention to pressures for local responsiveness. Moreover, they note that in the modern multinational firm, core competencies do not just reside in the home country; they can develop in any of the firm's worldwide operations. Thus, they maintain, skills and product offerings should flow from the home company to its foreign subsidiaries, from the foreign subsidiaries to the home country, *and* from the foreign subsidiaries to other foreign subsidiaries. They refer to this process as **global learning** and to companies that attempt to achieve all of these objectives simultaneously as **transnational corporations.**

Certainly, plenty of examples suggest Bartlett and Ghoshal have a good point. Consider Procter & Gamble (P&G), for example. Once the classic international company, P&G made a virtue of pushing products developed in the U.S. market into foreign markets with U.S.-style marketing and advertising. This did not always work, however. In Japan, for example, after losing more than $200 million between its entry in 1971 and 1987, P&G finally realized that Japanese consumers were not like American consumers, and that if it was going to succeed in Japan it would have to allow its Japanese subsidiary to customize the product offering and marketing strategy to the local market.[22]

Unilever's experience provides a similar example. Once a classic multidomestic company, Unilever has had to shift toward a more global strategy. An increase in low-cost competition, which increased cost pressures, forced Unilever to look for ways to rationalize its laundry detergent business. During the 1980s Unilever had 17 largely self-

[21] Bartlett and Ghoshal, *Managing across Borders.*

[22] Z. Schiller, "P&G Goes Global by Acting like a Local," *Business Week,* August 28, 1989, p. 58.

contained detergent operations in Europe alone. The duplication of assets and marketing was enormous. Moreover, because Unilever was so fragmented, the company needed as long as four years to introduce a new product across Europe. Now Unilever is trying to weld its European operation together into a single entity, by manufacturing detergents in a handful of cost-efficient plants and using standard packaging and advertising for all of Europe. According to company estimates, these changes could result in annual cost savings of more than $200 million. At the same time, however, due to national differences in distribution channels and brand awareness, Unilever recognizes it must remain locally responsive, even while it tries to realize economies from consolidating production and marketing.[23]

Notwithstanding such examples, Bartlett and Ghoshal admit that building an organization that can support a transnational strategic posture is a complex, difficult task. The core of the problem is that trying to achieve cost effectiveness, worldwide learning, and local responsiveness simultaneously places contradictory demands on an organization. For example, the need to realize location and experience-based economies suggests that key value creation activities should be concentrated in the optimal locations, and that the world market should be served from these locations. Demands for local responsiveness, however, can necessitate placing these activities in each of the company's major national markets. Balancing such conflicting demands is no easy task.

Similarly, the need to transfer core competencies from the home country to foreign subsidiaries and from foreign subsidiaries to the home country implies that foreign subsidiaries are given a major role in shaping the future direction of the corporation. That notion, however, is also inconsistent with the idea that value creation activities (e.g., production, marketing, and R&D) should be concentrated in optimal locations and centrally directed. It is also inconsistent with the long-standing practice in most international companies that products and skills are developed at home and then "exported" abroad.

Exactly how a company can deal with the dilemmas posed by such difficult organizational issues is a topic we shall return to and discuss in more detail in Chapter 13 when we look at the organization of international business. For now, it is important to note that the organizational problems associated with pursuing what are essentially conflicting objectives constitute major impediments to the pursuit of a transnational strategy. As we will see in Chapter 13, firms attempting to pursue a transnational strategy *can* become bogged down in an organizational morass that leads to inefficiencies.

It might also be noted at this point that Bartlett and Ghoshal may be overstating the case for the transnational strategy. Returning to the framework introduced in Figure 12.4, transnational firms clearly fall into cell 2. Although no one doubts that in some industries the firm that can adopt a transnational strategy will have a competitive advantage, in other industries global, multidomestic, and international strategies remain viable. In the global chemicals industry, for example, pressures for local customization are minimal and competition is purely a cost game, in which case a global strategy, not a transnational strategy, is optimal. Indeed, this is the case in many industrial goods markets where the product serves universal needs. On the other hand, a case can be made that to compete in certain consumer goods markets, such as the consumer electronics industry, a firm must try to adopt a transnational strategy.

[23] Guy de Jonquieres, "Unilever Adopts a Clean Sheet Approach," *Financial Times*, October 21, 1991, p. 13.

SUMMARY OF CHAPTER

For various reasons, the world is becoming more competitive, and if businesses are to survive, they must look for ways to maximize their profitability. This entails reducing the costs of creating value and/or performing value creation activities in such a way that consumers are willing to pay more for the firm's output. In this chapter we have seen that the pursuit of profit can drive firms, both small and large, to expand internationally. International expansion can help firms increase their profits by increasing the returns they earn from their core competencies and by realizing experience curve and location economies. However, we have also seen how the need to customize products, marketing strategy, and business strategy to local conditions acts as a constraint on a firm's ability to achieve these objectives.

With these factors in mind, we reviewed the three different strategies firms have traditionally used when expanding internationally—global, international, and multidomestic strategies. We observed that each strategy has advantages and drawbacks. Noting this, Bartlett and Ghoshal have introduced the transnational corporation as a solution. We have pointed out that this strategy also may have drawbacks. We will discuss this issue further in the next chapter when we examine the structure of international business.

The following points were made in this chapter:

1. Medium-sized and small firms are just as likely to be involved in international business as large firms.
2. The fundamental purpose of the business firm is to make profits. To survive in competitive markets, firms must maximize their profitability. They do this either by lowering the costs of value creation or by performing value creation activities in such a way that a premium price can be charged. A firm's strategy is the path it takes to ensure that one of these occurs.
3. The firm can be thought of as a value chain composed of a series of distinct value creation activities—such as production, marketing, R&D, materials management, information systems, human resource management, and the firm's infrastructure.
4. For some companies, international expansion is a way to earn greater returns by transferring the skills and product offerings derived from their core competencies to markets where indigenous competitors lack those skills.
5. Due to national differences, it pays a firm to base each value creation activity at that location where economic, political, and cultural conditions, including relative factor costs, are most conducive to performing that activity (transportation costs and trade barriers permitting). This strategy is focused on the attainment of location economies.
6. By building sales volume more rapidly, international expansion can help a firm to move down the experience curve. By reducing the costs of value creation, experience economies can help a firm to build barriers to new competition.
7. Differences between nations require the firm's product offering, marketing strategy, and business strategy to be customized to local conditions. The need to be locally responsive can act as a constraint on a firm's ability to increase its profits by transferring core competencies or by realizing location and/or experience curve economies.
8. Historically, firms that have expanded abroad have pursued a global strategy, an international strategy, or a multidomestic strategy.
9. Firms pursing a global strategy focus on reaping the cost reductions that come from experience curve and location economies. However, they may suffer from a lack of local responsiveness.
10. Firms pursing an international strategy transfer the skills and products derived from core competencies to foreign markets, while undertaking some limited local customization. However, they may suffer from insufficient local responsiveness and from an inability to exploit experience curve and location economies.
11. Firms pursuing a multidomestic strategy customize their product offering, marketing strategy, and business strategy to national conditions. However, they may suffer from an inability to transfer skills and products between countries and from an inability to exploit experience curve and location economies.
12. Given these trade-offs, the best strategy for a firm to pursue may depend in part on a consideration of the pressures for cost reductions and for local responsiveness.
13. Pressures for cost reductions are greatest in industries that produce commodity-type products, where price is the main competitive weapon.
14. Pressures for local responsiveness arise from differences in consumer tastes and preferences, differences in national infrastructure and traditional practices, differences in distribution channels, and host-government demands.
15. When pressures for cost reductions are high and pressures for local responsiveness are low, a global strategy is appropriate. When pressures for cost reductions are low and pressures for local responsiveness are high, a multidomestic strategy is appropriate. When pressures for cost reductions and for local responsiveness are

moderate, firms pursuing an international strategy may have a competitive advantage.

16. In some cases, firms face high pressures for both cost reductions and local responsiveness. Coping with such conflicting demands requires creative solutions.
17. Bartlett and Ghoshal argue that many industries are now so competitive that companies must adopt a transnational strategy. This involves simultaneous focus on reducing costs, transferring skills and products, and local responsiveness. Implementing such a strategy, however, may not be easy.

DISCUSSION QUESTIONS

1. In a world of zero transportation costs, no trade barriers, and large differences between nations in factor endowments, firms must expand internationally if they are to survive. Discuss.
2. Plot the position of these companies on Figure 12.4: Procter & Gamble, IBM, Coca-Cola, Dow Chemical, U.S. Steel, and McDonald's. In each case, justify your answer.
3. Due to modern transportation and communication technologies, differences between nations are disappearing. Discuss the implications of this for the strategy of a specific international business.
4. Are these industries global or multidomestic? Bulk chemicals; pharmaceuticals; brand name food products; movies; television sets; personal computers; airline travel.

The Organization of International Business

CHAPTER 13

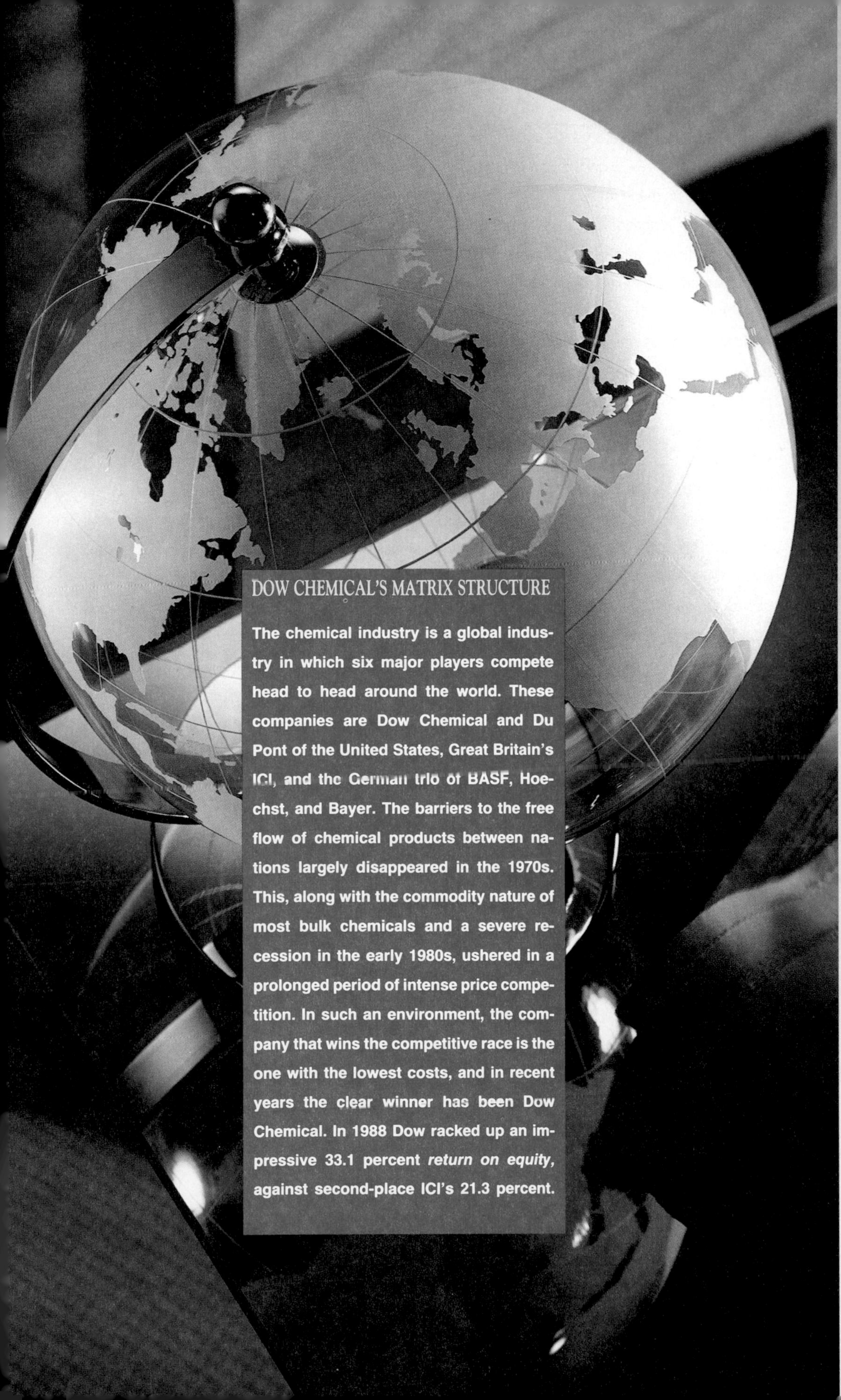

DOW CHEMICAL'S MATRIX STRUCTURE

The chemical industry is a global industry in which six major players compete head to head around the world. These companies are Dow Chemical and Du Pont of the United States, Great Britain's ICI, and the German trio of BASF, Hoechst, and Bayer. The barriers to the free flow of chemical products between nations largely disappeared in the 1970s. This, along with the commodity nature of most bulk chemicals and a severe recession in the early 1980s, ushered in a prolonged period of intense price competition. In such an environment, the company that wins the competitive race is the one with the lowest costs, and in recent years the clear winner has been Dow Chemical. In 1988 Dow racked up an impressive 33.1 percent *return on equity*, against second-place ICI's 21.3 percent.

Moreover, Dow generated $300,600 of *sales per employee* in 1988, in contrast with second-place BASF's $183,400. • How did Dow do it? Dow's managers insist that part of the credit must be placed at the feet of its much maligned "matrix" organization. Dow's organizational matrix has three interacting elements: *functions* (e.g., R&D, manufacturing, marketing), *businesses* (e.g., ethylene, plastics, pharmaceuticals), and *geography* (e.g., Spain, Germany, Brazil). Managers' job titles incorporate all three elements—for example, plastics marketing manager for Spain—and most managers report to at least two bosses. Thus the plastics marketing manager in Spain might report to both the head of the worldwide plastics business and the head of the Spanish operations. The intent of the matrix was to make Dow operations responsive to both local market needs and corporate objectives. Thus the plastics business might be charged with minimizing Dow's global plastics production costs, while the Spanish operation might be charged with determining how best to sell plastics in the Spanish market. • When Dow introduced this structure, the results were less than promising; multiple reporting channels led to confusion and conflict. The large number of bosses' made for an unwieldy bureaucracy. The overlapping responsibilities resulted in turf battles and a lack of accountability. Area managers disagreed with managers overseeing business sectors about which plants should be built and where. In short, the structure didn't work. Instead of abandoning the structure, however, Dow decided to see if it could be made more flexible. • Dow's decision to keep its matrix structure was prompted by its move into the pharmaceuticals industry. The company realized that the pharmaceutical business is very different from the bulk chemicals business. In bulk chemicals, the big returns come from achieving economies of scale in production. This dictates establishing large plants in key locations from which regional or global markets can be served. In pharmaceuticals, on the other hand, regulatory and marketing requirements for drugs vary so much from country to country that local needs are far more important than reducing manufacturing costs through scale economies. A high degree of local responsiveness is essential for this. Dow realized its pharmaceutical business would never thrive if it were managed by the same priorities as its mainstream chemical operations. • Accordingly, instead of abandoning its matrix, Dow decided to make it more flexible so it could better accommodate the different businesses, each with its own priorities, within a single management system. A small team of senior executives at headquarters now helps set the priorities for each type of business. After priorities are identified for each business sector, one of the three elements of the matrix—function, business, or geographical area—is given primary authority in decision making. Which element takes the lead varies according to the type of decision and the market or location in which the company is competing. Such flexibility requires that all employees understand what is occurring in the rest of the matrix so they can be co-opted into it, rather than acting individually. Although this may seem confusing, Dow claims this flexible system works well and credits much of its recent success to the quality of the decisions it facilitates. ⊕ *"Dow Draws Its Matrix Again, and Again, and Again,"* The Economist, *August 5, 1989, pp. 55–56.*

INTRODUCTION

The objective of this chapter is to identify the organizational structures and internal control mechanisms international businesses use to manage and direct their global operations. We will be concerned not just with formal structures and control mechanisms but also with informal structures and control mechanisms such as corporate culture and companywide networks. The basic theme of the chapter is that to succeed, an international business must have appropriate formal *and* informal organizational structure and control mechanisms. A further theme is that what is "appropriate" is determined by the strategy of the firm. In the language of the last chapter, firms pursuing a global strategy require different structures and control mechanisms than firms pursuing a multidomestic or a transnational strategy. To succeed, a firm's structure and control systems must match its strategy in discriminating ways.

The opening case illustrates this. Dow Chemical attributes much of its recent success to its modified matrix organization. According to Dow, this organization embodies appropriate structure and control systems, both formal and informal, for achieving both global cost efficiencies and local responsiveness. (In this respect, Dow is truly a transnational.) As a counterexample, consider the recent sorry history of Philips NV. One of the largest industrial companies in the world (with operations in more than 60 countries), this Dutch company has long been a dominant force in the global electronics, consumer appliances, and lighting industries. However, its performance has been slipping since the 1970s. In the early 1990s Philips suffered a string of record financial losses. During the 1970s and 80s, Philips' markets were attacked by Japanese companies such as Matsushita and Sony. These companies were pursuing a global strategy, using their resulting low costs to undercut Philips. To compete on an equal footing with Matsushita and Sony, Philips must be able to realize experience curve and location economies (see Chapter 12). Unfortunately, its attempts to do this are hindered by an organization more suited to a multidomestic strategy. Most of Philips' foreign subsidiaries are self-contained operations with their own production facilities. Philips desperately needs to consolidate production in a few facilities to realize location and experience curve economies, but it has been hindered in its efforts to do so by resistance from its national operations and by the sheer scale of the needed reorganization. As a consequence of this misfit of structure to strategy, Philips has suffered a decade of financial trouble.[1]

To come to grips with issues of structure and control in international business, in the next four sections we consider the basic dimensions of structure and control: vertical differentiation, horizontal differentiation, integration, and control systems. **Vertical differentiation** is the distribution of decision-making authority within a hierarchy (i.e., centralized versus decentralized). **Horizontal differentiation** is the division of an organization into subunits (e.g., into functions, divisions, or subsidiaries). **Integration** refers to the body of mechanisms that coordinate and integrate the subunits. These mechanisms are formal and informal. **Control systems** are the systems that top management uses to direct and control subunits, and these also are formal and informal. Throughout these sections we will focus attention on the implications of the four dimensions for the international firm. Having done this, we will then look at all of this material together and attempt to determine the optimal structures and controls for multidomestic, global, international, and transnational firms.

VERTICAL DIFFERENTIATION

A firm's vertical differentiation determines where in its hierarchy the decision-making power is concentrated.[2] For example, are production and marketing decisions centralized

[1] See F. J. Aguilar and M. Y. Yoshino, *The Philips Group: 1987,* Harvard Business School Case, 388-050, 1987; and "Philips Fights the Flab," *The Economist,* April 7, 1990, pp. 73–74.

[2] The material in this section draws on John Child, *Organizations* (London: Harper & Row, 1984).

in the offices of upper-level managers, or are they decentralized to lower-level managers? Where does the responsibility for R&D decisions lie? Are strategic and financial control responsibilities pushed down to operating units, or are they concentrated in the hands of top management? And so on. There are arguments for centralization and other arguments for decentralization. Let us examine them.

Arguments for Centralization

There are four main arguments for centralization. First, centralization can facilitate coordination. For example, consider a firm that has a component-manufacturing operation in Taiwan and an assembly operation in Mexico. There may be a need to coordinate the activities of these two operations to ensure a smooth flow of products from the component operation to the assembly operation. This might be achieved by centralizing production scheduling decisions at the firm's head office. Second, centralization can help ensure that decisions are consistent with organizational objectives. When decisions are decentralized to lower-level managers, those managers may make decisions at variance with top management's goals. Centralization of important decisions minimizes the chance of this occurring.

Third, by concentrating power and authority in one individual or a top-management team, centralization can give top-level managers the means to bring about needed major organizational changes. Fourth, centralization can avoid the duplication of activities that occurs when similar activities are carried on by various subunits within the organization. For example, many international firms centralize their R&D functions at one or two locations to ensure that R&D work is not duplicated. Similarly, production activities may be centralized at key locations for the same reason.

Arguments for Decentralization

There are five main arguments for decentralization. First, top management can become overburdened when decision-making authority is centralized, and this can result in poor decisions. Decentralization gives top management the time to focus on critical issues by delegating more routine issues to lower-level managers. Second, motivational research favors decentralization. Behavioral scientists have long argued that people are willing to give more to their jobs when they have a greater degree of individual freedom and control over their work. Third, decentralization permits greater flexibility—more rapid response to environmental changes—because decisions do not have to be "referred up the hierarchy" unless they are exceptional in nature. Fourth, decentralization can result in better decisions, since decisions are made closer to the spot by individuals who (presumably) have better information than managers several levels up in a hierarchy. Fifth, decentralization can serve to increase control. Decentralization can be used to establish relatively autonomous, self-contained subunits within an organization. Subunit managers can then be held accountable for subunit performance. The more responsibility subunit managers have for decisions that impact subunit performance, the fewer alibis they have for poor performance.

The Role of International Strategy

The choice between centralization and decentralization is not absolute. Frequently it makes sense to centralize some decisions and to decentralize others, depending on the type of decision and the firm's strategy. Decisions regarding overall firm strategy, major financial expenditures, financial objectives, and the like are typically centralized at the firm's headquarters. However, operating decisions—such as those relating to production, marketing, R&D, and human resource management—may or may not be centralized depending on the firm's international strategy.

Consider firms pursuing a global strategy. They must decide how to disperse the various value creation activities around the globe so location and experience economies can be realized. The head office must make the decisions about where to locate R&D, production, marketing, and so on. In addition, the globally dispersed web of value creation activities that facilitates a global strategy must be coordinated. All of this creates pressures for centralizing some operating decisions.

In contrast, the emphasis on local responsiveness in multidomestic firms creates strong pressures for decentralizing operating decision to foreign subsidiaries. Thus in the classic multidomestic firm, foreign subsidiaries have autonomy in most production and marketing decisions. International firms tend to maintain centralized control over their core competency and to decentralize other decisions to foreign subsidiaries. This typically centralizes control over R&D and/or marketing in the home country and decentralizes operating decisions to the foreign subsidiaries. Microsoft Corporation, for example, which fits the international mode, currently centralizes its product development activities (where its core competencies lie) at its Redmond, Washington, headquarters and decentralizes marketing activity to various foreign subsidiaries. Thus, while products are developed at home, managers in the various foreign subsidiaries have considerable latitude for formulating strategies to market those products in their particular settings.

The situation in transnational firms is more complex. The need to realize location and experience curve economies requires some degree of centralized control over global production centers (as it does in global firms). However, the need for local responsiveness dictates the decentralization of many operating decisions, particularly for marketing, to foreign subsidiaries. Thus in transnational firms, some operating decisions are relatively centralized, while others are relatively decentralized.

HORIZONTAL DIFFERENTIATION

Horizontal differentiation is basically concerned with how the firm decides to divide itself into subunits.[3] The decision is typically made on the basis of function, type of business, or geographical area. In many firms just one of these criteria predominates, but in others more complex solutions are adopted. This is particularly likely in the case of international firms, where the conflicting demands to organize the company around different products (to realize location and experience curve economies) and different national markets (to remain locally responsive) must be reconciled. One solution to this dilemma is to adopt some kind of matrix structure that divides the organization on the basis of both products and national markets. Dow Chemical is one company that has adopted such a solution (see the opening case). Philips NV is another. Philips is currently organized along matrix lines by which both its worldwide product divisions and its various foreign subsidiaries report to the company's headquarters. In this section we look at some different ways firms have chosen to divide themselves into subunits.

The Structure of Domestic Firms

Most firms begin with no formal structure and as they grow, the demands of management become too great for one individual to handle. At this point the organization is typically split up into functions reflecting the firm's value creation activities (e.g., finance, production, marketing, R&D). These functions are typically coordinated and controlled by a top-management team (see Figure 13.1). By its very nature, decision making in this **functional structure** tends to be relatively centralized.

---

[3] For more detail see S. M. Davis, "Managing and Organizing Multinational Corporations," 1979, reprinted in C. A. Bartlett and S. Ghoshal, *Transnational Management* (Homewood, Ill.: Richard D. Irwin, 1992).

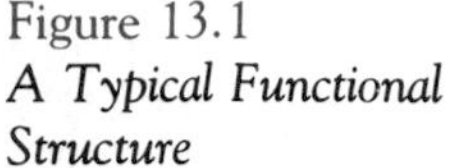
Figure 13.1
A Typical Functional Structure

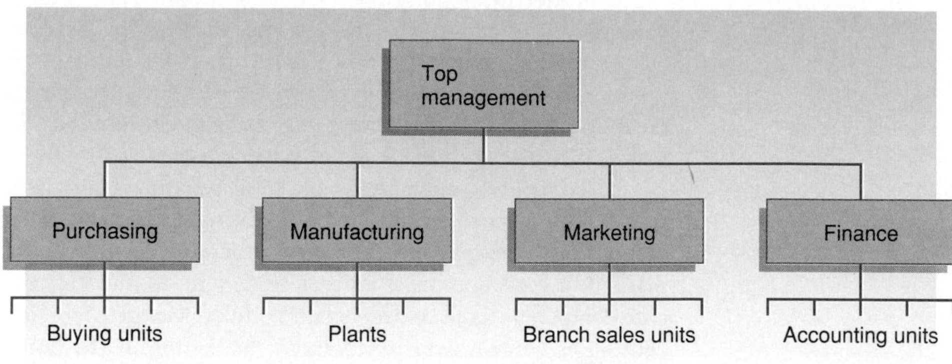

Further horizontal differentiation may be required if the firm significantly diversifies its product offering, which takes the firm into different business areas. Take Philips NV as an example. Although the firm started out as a lighting company, it now also has activities in consumer electronics (e.g., visual and audio equipment), industrial electronics (integrated circuits and other electronic components), and medical systems (CT scanners). In such circumstances a functional structure can be too clumsy. Problems of coordination and control arise when different business areas are managed within the framework of a functional structure.[4] For one thing, it becomes difficult to identify the profitability of each distinct business area. For another, it is difficult to run a functional department—such as production or marketing—if it is supervising the value creation activities of several business areas.

To solve the problems of coordination and control, at this stage most firms switch to a **product division structure** (see Figure 13.2). With a product division structure, each division is responsible for a distinct product line (business area). Thus Philips has divisions for lighting, consumer electronics, industrial electronics, and medical systems. Each product division is set up as a self-contained, largely autonomous entity with its own functions. The responsibility for operating decisions is typically decentralized to product divisions, which are then held accountable for their performance. Headquarters is responsible for the overall strategic development of the firm and for the financial control of the various divisions.

The International Division

Historically, when firms have expanded abroad they have typically grouped all their international activities into an international division. This has tended to be the case for firms organized on the basis of functions and for firms organized on the basis of product divisions. Regardless of the firm's domestic structure, its international division tends to be organized on geography. This is illustrated in Figure 13.3 for a firm whose domestic organization is based on product divisions.

Many manufacturing firms expanded internationally by exporting the product manufactured at home to foreign subsidiaries to sell. Thus, in the firm illustrated in Figure 13.3, the subsidiaries in Countries 1 and 2 would sell the products manufactured by Divisions A, B, and C. In time, however, it might prove viable to manufacture the product in each country, and so production facilities would be added on a country-by-

[4] A. D. Chandler, *Strategy and Structure: Chapters in the History of the Industrial Enterprise* (Cambridge, Mass.: MIT Press, 1962).

Figure 13.2
A Typical Product Division Structure

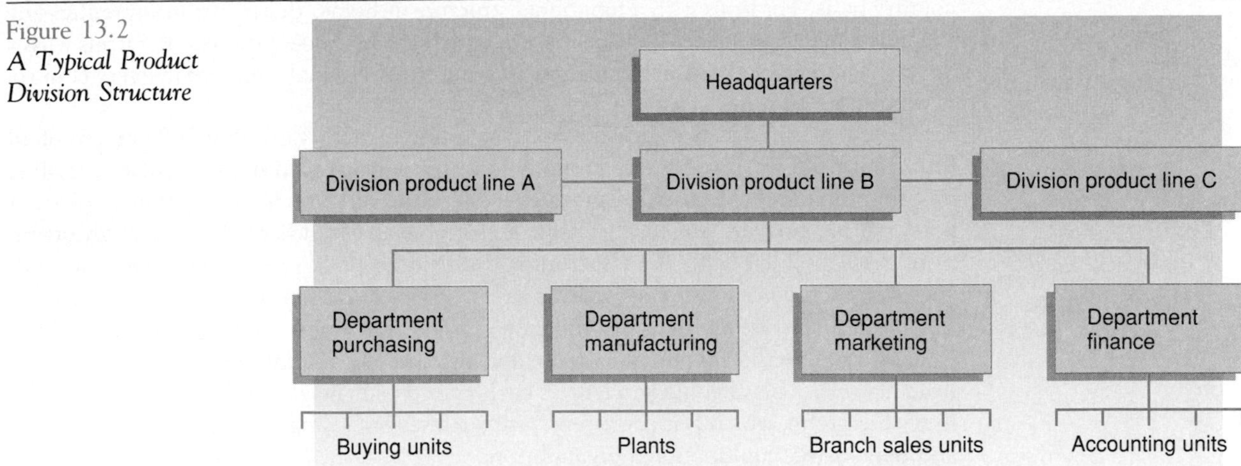

Figure 13.3 *One Company's International Division Structure*

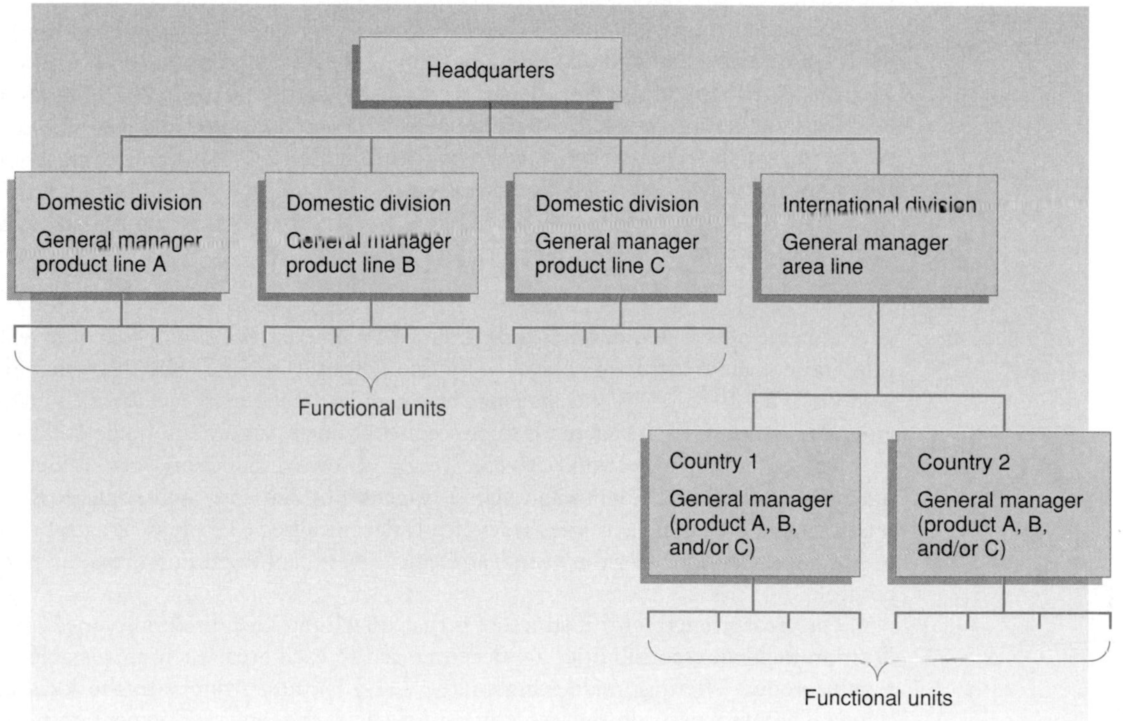

country basis. For firms with a functional structure at home, this might mean replicating the functional structure in every country in which the firm does business. For firms with a divisional structure, this might mean replicating the divisional structure in every country in which the firm does business.

This structure has been widely used; according to a Harvard study, 60 percent of all firms that have expanded internationally have initially adopted it. Nonetheless, it gives rise to problems.[5] Most significant, the dual structure it creates contains inherent potential for conflict and coordination problems between domestic and foreign operations. One problem with the structure is that the heads of foreign subsidiaries are not given as much voice in the organization as the heads of domestic functions (in the case of functional firms) or divisions (in the case of divisional firms). Rather, the head of the international division is presumed to be able to represent the interests of all countries to headquarters. This effectively relegates each country's manager to the second tier of the firm's hierarchy, which is inconsistent with a strategy of trying to expand internationally and build a true multinational organization.

Another problem is the implied lack of coordination between domestic operations and foreign operations, which are isolated from each other in separate parts of the structural hierarchy. Among other things, this can inhibit the worldwide introduction of new products, the transfer of core competencies between domestic and foreign operations, and the consolidation of global production at key locations so as to realize location and experience curve economies.

As a result of such problems, most firms that continue to expand internationally abandon this structure and adopt one of the worldwide structures we discuss next. The two initial choices are a **worldwide product division structure,** which tends to be adopted by diversified firms that have domestic product divisions, and a **worldwide area structure,** which tends to be adopted by undiversified firms whose domestic structures are based on functions. These two alternative paths of development are illustrated in Figure 13.4. The model in the figure is referred to as the **international structural stages model** and it was developed by John Stopford and Louis Wells.[6]

Worldwide Area Structure

A worldwide area structure tends to be favored by firms with a low degree of diversification and a domestic structure based on function (see Figure 13.5). By this structure, the world is divided into areas. An area may be a country (if the market is large enough) or a group of countries. Each area tends to be a self-contained, largely autonomous entity with its own set of value creation activities (e.g., its own production, marketing, R&D, human resources, and finance functions). Operations authority and strategic decisions relating to each of these activities are typically decentralized to each area, with headquarters retaining authority for the overall strategic direction of the firm and overall financial control.

The great strength of this structure is that it facilitates local responsiveness. Because decision-making responsibilities are decentralized to each area, each area is able to customize product offerings, marketing strategy, and business strategy to the local conditions. The weakness of the structure is that it encourages fragmentation of the organization into highly autonomous entities. This can make it difficult to transfer core

---

[5] Davis, "Multinational Corporations."

[6] J. M. Stopford and L. T. Wells, *Strategy and Structure of Multinational Enterprise* (New York: Basic Books, 1972).

Figure 13.4
The International Structural Stages Model

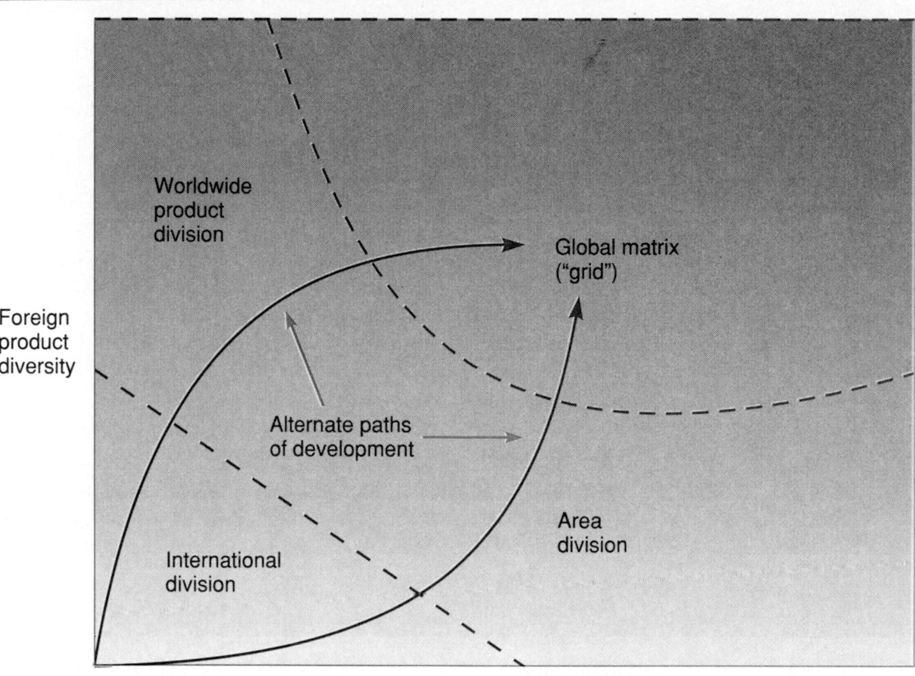

Source: Adapted from John M. Stopford and Louis T. Wells, Strategy and Structure of the Multinational Enterprise *(New York: Basic Books, 1972).*

Figure 13.5
A Worldwide Area Structure

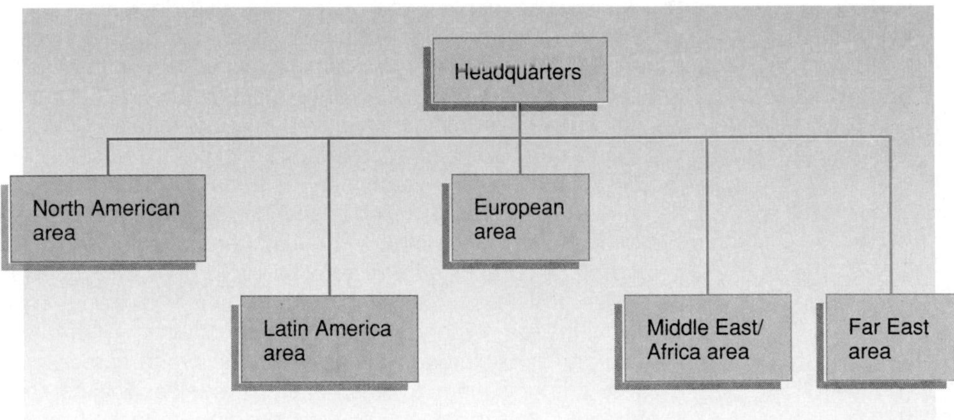

competencies between areas and to undertake the rationalization in value creation activities required for realizing location and experience curve economies. In other words, the structure is consistent with a multidomestic strategy but with little else. Thus, firms structured on this basis may encounter significant problems if local responsiveness is less critical than reducing costs or transferring core competencies for establishing a competitive advantage in their industry. For an example of the nature of such problems, see Box 13.1 on Unilever.

Unilever Becomes a Transnational

BOX 13.1

Unilever is a very old multinational with worldwide operations in the detergent and food industries. For decades Unilever managed its worldwide detergents activities in an arm's-length manner. A subsidiary was set up in each major national market and allowed to operate largely autonomously, with each subsidiary carrying out the full range of value creation activities. As a result, the company had 17 autonomous national operations in Europe alone by the mid-1980s.

In the early 1990s Unilever began to transform its worldwide detergents activities from a loose confederation into a tightly managed business with a global strategy. The shift was prompted by Unilever's realization that its traditional way of doing business was no longer effective in an arena where it had become essential to realize substantial cost economies, to innovate, and to respond quickly to changing market trends.

The point was driven home in the 1980s when the company's archrival, Procter & Gamble, repeatedly stole the lead in bringing new products to market. Within Unilever, "persuading" the 17 European operations to adopt new products could take four to five years. In addition, Unilever was handicapped by its high cost structure resulting from the duplication of manufacturing facilities. The company's high costs ruled out its use of competitive pricing.

To change this situation, Unilever established product divisions to coordinate regional operations. In Europe, "Lever Europe" was set up to do this, and the 17 European companies now report directly to Lever Europe. Using its newfound organizational clout, Lever Europe will consolidate the production of detergents in Europe in a few key locations to reduce costs and speed up new product introduction. Implicit in this new approach is a bargain: the 17 companies are relinquishing autonomy in their traditional markets in exchange for opportunities to help develop and execute a unified pan-European strategy.

As a consequence of these changes, manufacturing is now being rationalized, with detergent production for the European market concentrated in a few key locations. The number of European plants manufacturing soap has been cut from 10 to 2, and some new products will be manufactured at only one site. Product sizing and packaging are being harmonized to cut purchasing costs and to pave the way for unified pan-European advertising. By taking these steps, Unilever may save as much as $400 million a year in its European operations.

Lever Europe is attempting to speed up its development of new products and to synchronize the launch of new products throughout Europe. Its efforts seem to be paying off: a concentrated dishwasher detergent introduced in Germany in early 1991 was available across Europe a year later—a distinct improvement.

Nonetheless, history still imposes constraints. Whereas Procter & Gamble's leading laundry detergent carries the same brand name across Europe, Unilever sells its product under a wide variety of names. The company has no plans to change this. Having spent 100 years building up these brand names, it believes it would be foolish to scrap them in the interest of pan-European standardization.

Source: Guy de Jonguieres, "Unilever Adopts a Clean Sheet Approach," Financial Times, *October 21, 1991, p. 13.*

Worldwide Product Division Structure

A worldwide product division structure tends to be adopted by firms that are reasonably diversified and, accordingly, originally had domestic structures based on product divisions. As with the domestic product division structure, the basic idea is that each division is a self-contained, largely autonomous entity with full responsibility for its own value creation activities. The headquarters retains responsibility for the overall strategic development and financial control of the firm (see Figure 13.6).

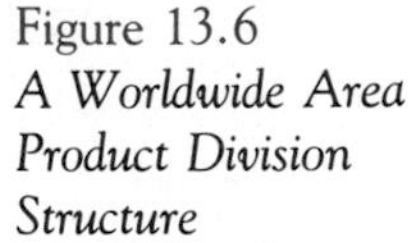
Figure 13.6
A Worldwide Area Product Division Structure

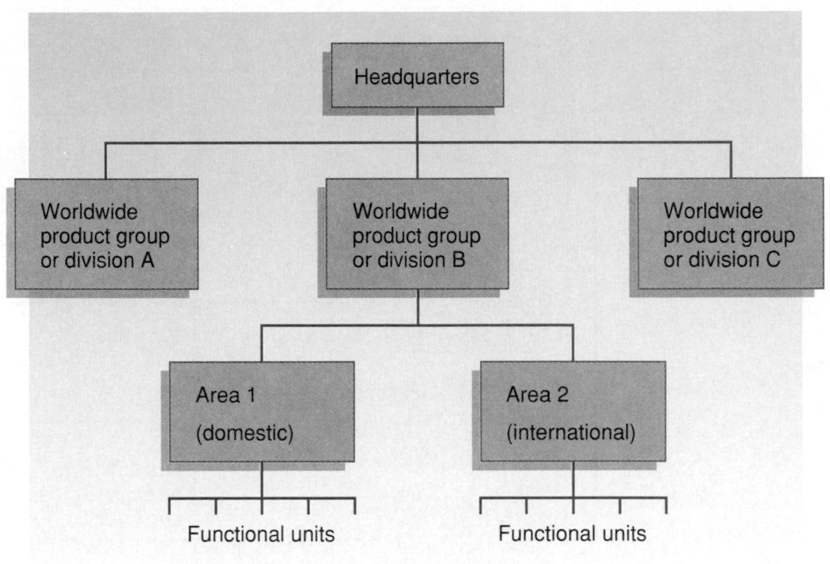

Underpinning the organization is a belief that the various value creation activities of each product division should be coordinated by that division worldwide. Thus, the worldwide product division structure is designed to help overcome the problems of coordination that arise with the international division and worldwide area structures. The great strength of this structure is that it provides an organizational context in which it is easier to pursue the consolidation of value creation activities at key locations necessary for realizing location and experience curve economies. It also facilitates the transfer of core competencies within a division's worldwide operations. The main problem with the structure is the limited voice it gives to area or country managers, since they are seen as subservient to product division managers. The result can be a lack of local responsiveness, which, as we saw in Chapter 12, can be a fatal flaw.

Global Matrix Structure

Both the worldwide area structure and the worldwide product division structure have strengths and weaknesses. The worldwide area structure facilitates local responsiveness, but it can inhibit the realization of location and experience curve economies and the transfer of core competencies between areas. The worldwide product division structure provides a better framework for pursuing location and experience curve economies and for transferring core competencies, but it is weak in local responsiveness. Other things being equal, this suggests that a worldwide area structure is more appropriate if the firm's strategy is multidomestic, whereas a worldwide product division structure is more appropriate for firms pursuing global or international strategies. However, as we saw in Chapter 12, other things are not equal; most important, as Bartlett and Ghoshal have argued, to survive in some industries, firms must adopt a transnational strategy. That is, they must focus simultaneously on realizing location and experience curve economies, on local responsiveness, and on the internal transfer of core competencies (worldwide learning).[7]

[7] C. A. Bartlett and S. Ghoshal, *Managing across Borders* (Boston, Mass.: Harvard Business School Press, 1989).

Figure 13.7
A Global Matrix Structure

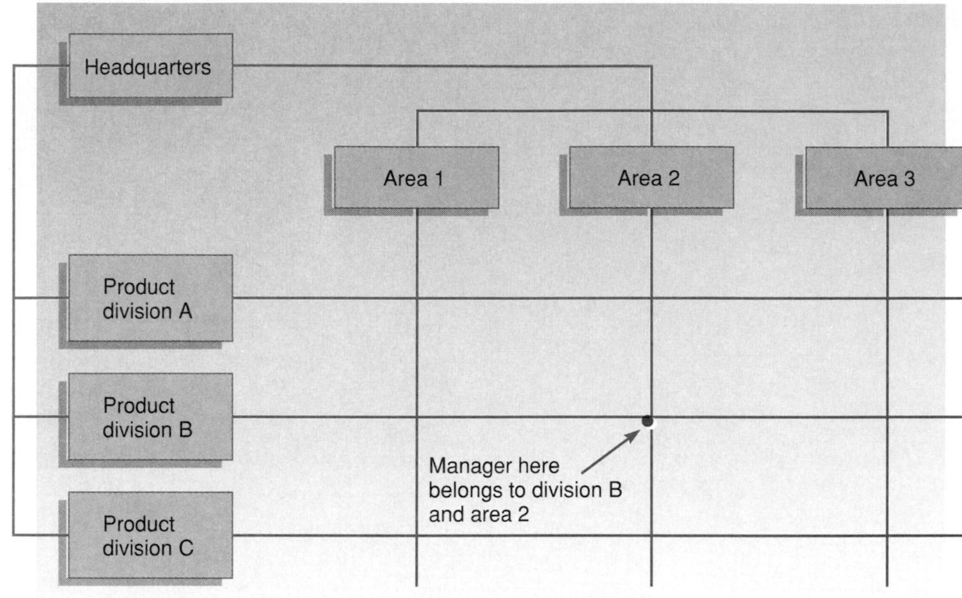

Many firms have attempted to cope with the conflicting demands of a transnational strategy by using a matrix structure. In the classic global matrix structure, horizontal differentiation proceeds along two dimensions: product division and geographical area (see Figure 13.7). The basic philosophy is that responsibility for operating decisions pertaining to a particular product should be shared by the product division and the various areas of the firm. Thus, the nature of the product offering, the marketing strategy, and the business strategy to be pursued in Area 1 for the products produced by Division A are determined by conciliation between Division A and Area 1 management. It is believed that this dual decision-making responsibility should enable the firm to simultaneously achieve its particular objectives. In most classic matrix structures, the idea of dual responsibility is reinforced by giving product divisions and geographical areas equal status within the organization. Individual managers thus belong to two hierarchies (a divisional hierarchy and an area hierarchy) and have two bosses (a divisional boss and an area boss).

The reality of the global matrix structure was that it did not work anywhere near as well as the theory had predicted. In practice, the matrix has turned out to be clumsy and bureaucratic. It necessitated so many meetings that it was difficult to get any work done. All too often, the need to get an area and a product division to reach a decision slowed down decision making and produced an inflexible organization unable to respond quickly to market shifts or to innovate. The dual-hierarchy structure led to conflict and perpetual power struggles between the areas and the product divisions, catching many managers in the middle. To make matters worse, it proved difficult to ascertain accountability in this structure. When all critical decisions are the product of negotiation between divisions and areas, one side can always blame the other when things go wrong. As a manager in one global matrix structure, reflecting on a failed product launch, said to the author, "Had we been able to do things our way, instead of having to accommodate those guys from the product division, this would never have happened." (A manager in the product division expressed similar sentiments.) The result of such finger pointing can be that accountability is compromised, conflict is enhanced, and headquarters loses control over the organization.

In light of these problems, many transnational firms are now trying to build "flexible" matrix structures based more on firmwide networks and a shared culture and vision than on a rigid hierarchical arrangement. Dow Chemical (recall the opening case) is one such firm. Within such companies the informal structure plays a greater role than the formal structure. We discuss this issue when we consider informal integrating mechanisms in the next section.

INTEGRATING MECHANISMS

In the previous section we explained that firms divide themselves into subunits. Now we need to examine some means of coordinating those subunits. As we have seen, one way of achieving coordination is through centralization. If the coordination task is complex, however, centralization may not be very effective. The problem is that the higher-level managers responsible for achieving coordination can soon become overwhelmed by the volume of work required to coordinate the activities of various subunits—particularly if the subunits are large, diverse, and/or geographically dispersed. When this is the case, firms look toward integrating mechanisms, both formal and informal, to help achieve coordination. In this section we introduce the various integrating mechanisms that international businesses can use. Before doing so, however, let us explore the need for coordination in international firms and some impediments to coordination.

International Strategy and Coordination

The need for coordination between subunits varies systematically with the international strategy of the firm. The need for coordination is lowest in multidomestic companies, is higher in international companies, higher still in global companies, and highest of all in the transnational. Multidomestic firms are primarily concerned with local responsiveness. Such firms are likely to operate with a worldwide area structure in which each area has considerable autonomy and its own set of value creation functions. Since each area is established as a stand-alone entity, the need for coordination between areas is minimized.

The need for coordination is greater in firms pursuing an international strategy and trying to profit from the transfer of core competencies between the home country and foreign operations. Coordination is necessary to support the transfer of skills and product offerings from home to foreign operations. The need for coordination is greater still in firms trying to profit from location and experience curve economies; that is, in firms pursuing global strategies. Achieving location and experience economies involves dispersing value creation activities to various locations around the globe. The resulting global web of activities must be coordinated to ensure the smooth flow of inputs into the value chain, the smooth flow of semifinished products through the value chain, and the smooth flow of finished products to markets around the world.

The need for coordination is greatest in transnational firms. Recall that these firms simultaneously pursue location and experience curve economies, local responsiveness, and the *multidirectional* transfer of core competencies among all of the firm's subunits (this is referred to as *global learning*). As in global companies, coordination is required to ensure the smooth flow of products through the global value chain. As in international companies, coordination is required for ensuring the transfer of core competencies to subunits. However, the transnational goal of achieving multidirectional transfer of competencies requires much greater coordination than in international firms. In addition, transnationals require coordination between foreign subunits and the firm's globally dispersed value creation activities (e.g., production, R&D, marketing) to ensure that any product offering and marketing strategy is sufficiently customized to local conditions.

Impediments to Coordination

Managers of the various subunits have different orientations, partly because they have different tasks. For example, production managers are typically concerned with production issues such as capacity utilization, cost control, and quality control, whereas marketing managers are concerned with marketing issues such as pricing, promotions, distribution, and market share. These differences can inhibit communication between the managers. Quite simply, these managers often do not even "speak the same language." There may also be a lack of respect between subunits (e.g., marketing managers "looking down on" production managers, and vice versa), which further inhibits the communication required to achieve cooperation and coordination.

Differences in subunits' orientations also arise from their differing goals. For example, worldwide product divisions of a multinational firm may be committed to cost goals that require global production of a standardized product, whereas a foreign subsidiary may be committed to increasing its market share in its country, which will require a nonstandard product. In this case, these different goals can lead to conflict.

Such impediments to coordination are not unusual in any firm, but they can be particularly problematic in the multinational enterprise with its profusion of subunits at home and abroad. Moreover, differences in subunit orientation are often reinforced in multinationals by the separations of time zone, distance, and nationality between managers of the subunits.

For example, the Dutch company Philips has an organization comprising worldwide product divisions and largely autonomous national organizations. The company has long had problems getting its product divisions and national organizations to cooperate on such things as new product introductions. Indeed, so difficult has this problem proved to be that when Philips developed a VCR format, the V2000 system, it could not get its North American subsidiary to introduce the product. Rather, the North American unit adopted the rival VHS format produced by Philip's global competitor, Matsushita. Unilever has experienced a similar problem in its detergents business. Unilever has found that the need to resolve disputes between its many national organizations and its product divisions can extend the time necessary for introducing a new product across Europe to four years. This denies Unilever the first-mover advantage crucial to building a strong market position. (Box 13.1 provides some details.)[8]

Formal Integrating Mechanisms

The formal mechanisms used to integrate subunits vary in complexity from simple direct contact and liaison roles, to teams, to a matrix structure (see Figure 13.8). In general, the greater the need for coordination, the more complex the formal integrating mechanisms need to be.[9]

Direct contact between subunit managers is the simplest integrating mechanism. By this "mechanism," managers of the various subunits simply contact each other whenever they have a common concern. Direct contact may not be effective if the managers have differing orientations that act to impede coordination, as pointed out in the previous subsection.

---

[8] Guy de Jonquieres, "Unilever Adopts a Clean Sheet Approach," *Financial Times*, October 21, 1991, p. 13.

[9] See J. R. Galbraith, *Designing Complex Organizations* (Reading, Mass.: Addison-Wesley, 1977).

Figure 13.8
Formal Integrating Mechanisms

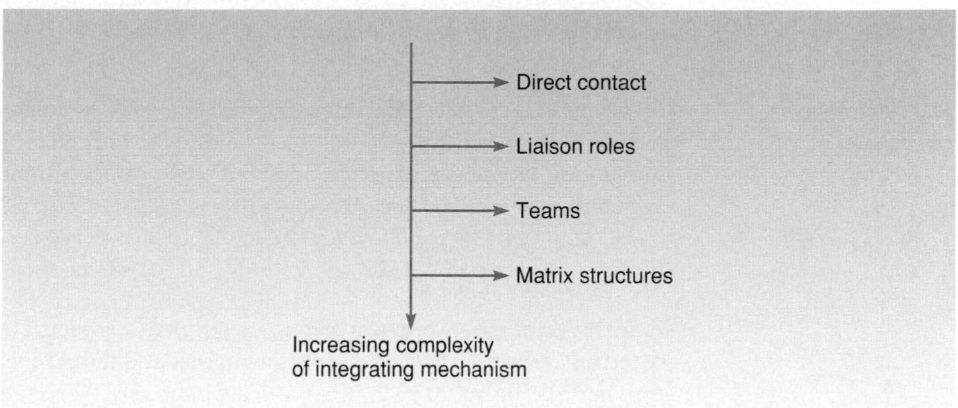

Liaison roles are a bit more complex. When the volume of contacts between subunits increases, coordination can be improved by giving a person in each subunit responsibility for coordinating with another subunit on a regular basis. The idea is that through these roles, a permanent relationship is established between the people involved, which helps attenuate the impediments to coordination discussed in the previous subsection.

When the need for coordination is greater still, firms tend to use temporary or permanent *teams* composed of individuals from the subunits that need to achieve coordination. They are typically used to coordinate new product development and introduction, but they are useful when any aspect of operations or strategy requires the cooperation of two or more subunits. New product development and introduction teams are typically composed of personnel from R&D, production, and marketing. The resulting coordination aids the development of products that are tailored to consumer needs and that can be produced at a reasonable cost (design for manufacturing).

When the need for integration is very high, firms may institute some kind of *matrix structure,* in which all roles are viewed as integrating roles. The structure is designed to facilitate maximum integration among subunits. As explained earlier, the most common matrix in multinational firms is based on geographical areas and worldwide product divisions. This achieves a high level of integration between the product divisions and the areas so that, in theory, the firm can pay close attention to both local responsiveness and the pursuit of location and experience curve economies.

In some multinationals the matrix is more complex still, structuring the firm into geographical areas, worldwide product divisions, and functions, all of which report directly to headquarters. Thus, within a company such as Dow Chemical (see the opening case) each manager belongs to three hierarchies (e.g., a plastics marketing manager in Spain is a member of the Spanish subsidiary, the plastics product division, and the marketing function). In addition to facilitating local responsiveness and location and experience curve economies, such a matrix fosters the transfer of core competencies within the organization. This occurs because core competencies tend to reside in functions (e.g., R&D, marketing). A structure such as Dow's facilitates the transfer of competencies existing in functions from division to division and from area to area.

However, as discussed earlier, such matrix solutions to the problems of coordination in multinational enterprises can quickly become bogged down in a bureaucratic tangle that creates as many problems as it solves. Matrix structures tend to be bureaucratic, inflexible, and characterized by conflict rather than the hoped-for cooperation. As in the case of Dow Chemical, for such a structure to work it needs to be somewhat flexible and to be supported by informal integrating mechanisms.

Informal Integrating Mechanisms

In attempting to alleviate or avoid the problems associated with formal integrating mechanisms in general, and matrix structures in particular, firms with a high need for integration have been experimenting with two informal integrating mechanisms: management networks and organization culture.[10]

Management Networks

A **management network** is a system of informal contacts between managers within an enterprise.[11] For a network to exist, managers at different locations within the organization must be linked to each other at least indirectly. For example, consider Figure 13.9, which shows the simple network relationships between seven managers within a multinational firm. Managers A, B, and C all know each other personally, as do Managers D, E, and F. Although Manager B does not know Manager F personally, they are linked through common acquaintances (Managers C and D). Thus we can say that Managers A through F are all part of the network, and also that Manager G is not.

Imagine Manager B is a marketing manager in Spain and needs to know the solution to a technical problem to better serve an important European customer. Imagine further that Manager F, an R&D manager in the United States, has the solution to Manager B's problem. Manager B mentions her problem to all of her contacts, including Manager C, and asks them if they know of anyone who might be able to provide a solution. Manager C asks Manager D, who tells Manager F, who then calls Manager B with the solution. In this way, coordination is achieved informally through the network, rather than by formal integrating mechanisms such as teams or a matrix structure.

For such a network to function effectively, however, it must embrace as many managers within the organization as possible. For example, if Manager G had a problem similar to manager B's, he would not be able to utilize the informal network to find a solution; he would have to resort to more formal mechanisms. Establishing firmwide networks is difficult, and although network enthusiasts speak of networks as the "glue" that binds multinational companies together, it is far from clear how successful firms have been at building companywide networks. Two techniques firms have been experimenting with in their efforts to establish firmwide networks are information systems and management development policies.

Firms are using their computer and telecommunications networks to provide the physical foundation for informal information systems networks. Electronic mail, teleconferencing, and high-speed data systems make it much easier for managers scattered over the globe to get to know each other. Without an existing network of personal contacts, however, worldwide information systems are unlikely to meet a firm's need for integration. Firms are using their management development programs to build informal networks. Tactics include rotating managers through various subunits on a regular basis so they build up their own informal network and using management education programs to bring managers of subunits together in a single location so they can become acquainted.

---

[10] See Bartlett and Ghoshal, *Managing across Borders;* and F. V. Guterl, "Goodbye, Old Matrix," *Business Month,* February 1989, pp. 32–38.

[11] See M. S. Granovetter, "The Strength of Weak Ties," *American Journal of Sociology* 78 (1973), pp. 1360–80.

Figure 13.9
A Simple Management Network

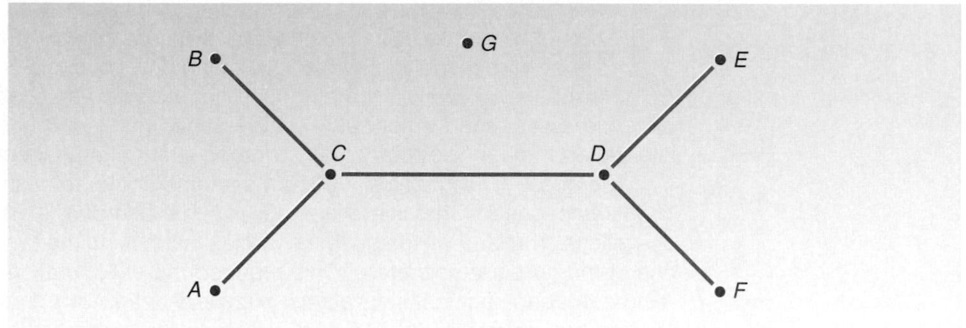

Organization Culture

Management networks by themselves may not be sufficient to achieve coordination if subunit managers persist in pursuing subgoals that are at variance with firmwide goals. For a management network to function properly—and, indeed, for a formal matrix structure to work, also—managers must share a strong commitment to the same goals. To appreciate the nature of the problem, consider again the case of Manager B and Manager F. As before, Manager F hears about Manager B's problem through the network. However, solving Manager B's problem would require Manager F to devote considerable time to the task. Insofar as this would divert Manager F away from his own regular tasks—and the pursuit of subgoals that differ from those of Manager B—he may be unwilling to do it. Thus Manager F may not call Manager B, and the informal network would fail to provide a solution to Manager B's problem.

To eliminate this flaw, it is crucial that the organization's managers adhere to a common set of norms and values; that is, that the firm's culture override differing subunit orientations.[12] When this is the case, a manager is willing and able to set aside the interests of his own subunit when doing so benefits the firm as a whole. If Manager B and Manager F are committed to the same organizational norms and value systems, and if these organizational norms and values place the interests of the firm as a whole above the interests of any individual subunit, Manager F should be willing to cooperate with Manager B on solving her subunit's problems.

The critical question then becomes, How can a firm build a common culture? The ability to establish a common vision for the company seems to be critical here. Top management needs to determine the mission of the firm and how this should be reflected in the organization's norms and values. These determinations then need to be disseminated throughout the organization. As with building informal networks, this can be achieved in part through management education programs that serve to "socialize" managers into the firm's norms and value system. Leadership by example is another important tool for building a common culture. Human relations policies also seem to play a critical role. There is a need to select managers who are team players. There is also a need to devise reward and incentive policies that encourage managers to cooperate for the good of the firm. Put simply, Manager F is more likely to cooperate with Manager B if he gets credit for doing so than if he is made to suffer in some way for spending time on problems not directly related to his immediate task.

---

[12] W. G. Ouchi, "Markets, Bureaucracies, and Clans," *Administrative Science Quarterly* 25 (1980) pp. 129–44.

Network Contacts at IBM

BOX 13.2

IBM has long operated with a matrix-type structure by which functions and product divisions share responsibility for developing new products on a worldwide basis. More recently, however, the company has been de-emphasizing this structure, because it has found it rigid and cumbersome. Instead, it has been encouraging integration through temporary teams and an informal management network.

The latest version of IBM's 9370 mainframe computer, introduced in the fall of 1988, was one of the first offsprings of the company's shift to network-style operations. The idea was to get the complex machine to market quickly with minimal use of the corporate hierarchy. This required the collaboration of people from IBM research labs, manufacturing plants, suppliers, marketing groups, and distribution centers around the world. The participants in this temporary team were linked by electronic mail, teleconferencing, and other communications channels and were forged into working relationships through ad hoc project teams, multidisciplinary conferences, and the like. Some of the worldwide relationships needed to develop the 9370 are shown in the figure.

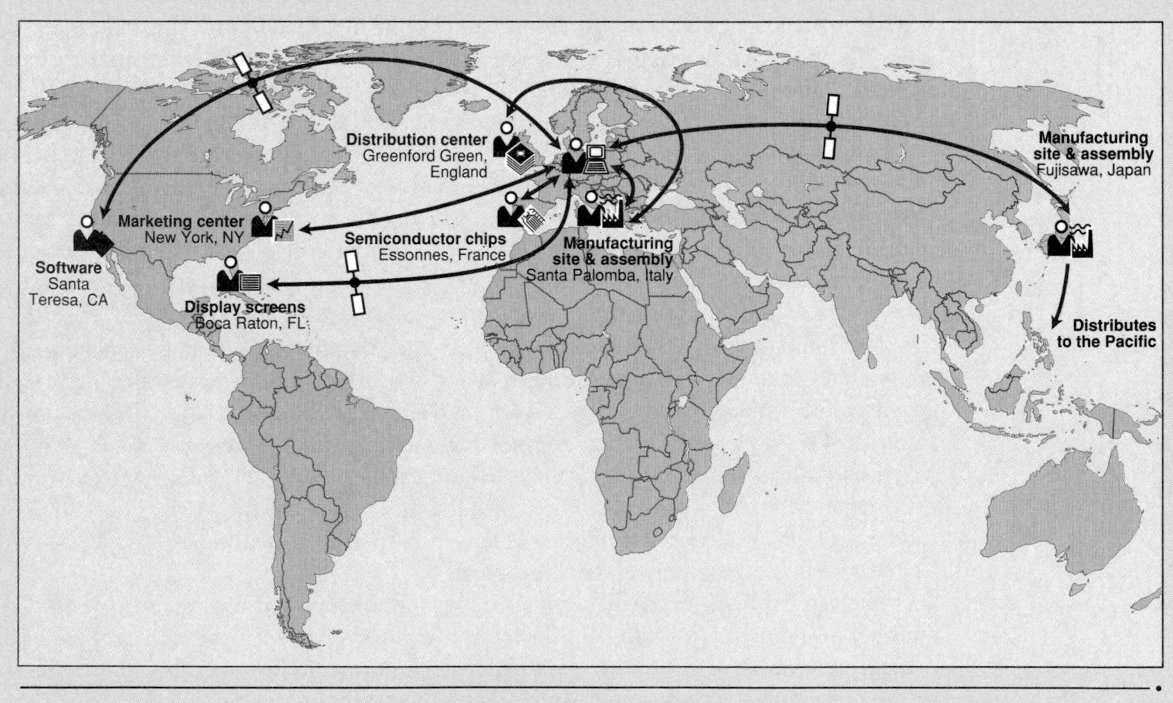

Source: Fred V. Guterl, "Goodbye, Old Matrix," Business Month, *February 1989, pp. 32–38.*

Summary

The message contained in this section is crucial to understanding the problems of managing the multinational firm. Multinationals need integration—particularly if they are pursuing global, international, or transnational strategies—but it can be difficult to achieve due to the impediments to coordination we discussed. Traditionally firms have tried to achieve coordination by adopting formal integrating mechanisms. These do not always work, however, since they tend to be bureaucratic and do not necessarily address the problems that arise from differing subunit orientations. This is particularly likely with a complex matrix structure, and yet, a complex matrix structure is required for simultaneously achieving location and experience curve economies, local responsiveness, and the multidirectional transfer of core competencies within the organization.

The solution to this dilemma seems twofold. First, the firm must try to establish an informal management network that can do much of the work previously undertaken by a formal matrix structure. Second, the firm must build a common culture. Neither of these partial solutions, however, is easy to achieve. For an example of a firm that has an informal management network, IBM, see Box 13.2.

CONTROL SYSTEMS

A major task of a firm's leadership is to control the various subunits of the firm—whether they be defined on the basis of function, product division, or geographical area—to ensure their actions are consistent with the firm's overall strategic and financial objectives. Firms achieve this with various control systems. In this section we first review the various types of control systems firms use to control their subunits. Then we will see that appropriate control systems vary according to firms' international strategies.

Types of Control Systems

Four main types of control systems are used in multinational firms: personal controls, bureaucratic controls, output controls, and cultural controls. In most firms, all four are used, but their relative emphasis tends to vary with the strategy of the firm.

Personal Controls

Personal control is control by personal contact with subordinates. This type of control tends to be most widely used in small firms, where it is seen in the direct supervision of subordinates' actions. However, it also structures the relationships between high-level managers in large multinational enterprises. In fact, the CEO may use a great deal of personal control to influence the behavior of his or her immediate subordinates, such as the heads of worldwide product divisions or major geographical areas. In turn, these heads may use personal control to influence the behavior of their subordinates, and so on down through the organization. For example, Jack Welsh, CEO of General Electric, has regular one-on-one meetings with the heads of all of GE's major businesses (most of which are international). He uses these meetings to "probe" the managers about the strategy, structure, and financial performance of their operations. In doing so, he is essentially exercising personal control over these managers and, undoubtedly, over the strategies that they favor.

Bureaucratic Controls

Bureaucratic control is control through a system of rules and procedures that direct the actions of subunits. The most important bureaucratic controls in subunits within multinational firms are budgets and capital spending rules.

Budgets are essentially a set of rules for allocating a firm's financial resources. A subunit's budget specifies with some precision how much the subunit may spend. By means of such rules, headquarters uses budgets to influence the behavior of subunits. For example, the R&D budget normally specifies how much cash the R&D unit may spend on new product development. R&D managers know that if they spend too much on one project, they will have less to spend on other projects. Hence they modify their behavior to stay within the budget. Most budgets are set by negotiation between headquarters management and subunit management. Headquarters management can encourage the growth of certain subunits and restrict the growth of others by manipulating their budgets.

Capital spending rules require headquarters management to approve any capital expenditure by a subunit that exceeds a certain amount (at GE, $50,000). A budget allows headquarters to specify the amount a subunit can spend in a given year, and capital spending rules give headquarters additional control—control over how the money is spent. They can be expected to deny approval for capital spending requests that are at variance with overall firm objectives and to approve those that are congruent with firm objectives.

Output Controls

Output controls involve setting goals for subunits to achieve; expressing those goals in terms of relatively objective criteria such as profitability, productivity, growth, market share, and quality; and then judging the performance of subunit management by their ability to achieve the goals. The kinds of goals subunits are given depends on their role in the firm. Self-contained product divisions or national subsidiaries are typically given goals for profitability, sales growth, and market share. Functions are more likely to be given goals related to their particular activity. Thus R&D will be given new product development goals, production will be given productivity and quality goals, marketing will be given market share goals, and so on.

As with budgets, goals are normally established through negotiation between subunits and headquarters. Generally, headquarters tries to set goals that are challenging but yet realistic, so subunit managers are forced to look for ways to improve their operations but are not so pressured that they will resort to dysfunctional activities to do so (such as short-run profit maximization). Output controls foster a system of "management by exception," in that so long as subunits meet their goals, they are left alone. If a subunit fails to attain its goals, however, headquarters management is likely to ask some tough questions. If they don't get satisfactory answers, they are likely to intervene proactively in a subunit, replacing its top management and looking for ways to improve its efficiency.

Output controls are typically reinforced by linking management reward and incentive schemes to their attainment. For example, if a worldwide product division achieves its profitability goals, its managers may receive a significant pay bonus. Moreover, the size of the bonus might reflect the extent to which a subunit exceeds its goal so that subunit management has an incentive to *optimize* performance.

Cultural Controls

We touched on the issue of cultural controls in the previous section when we discussed organization culture as a means of facilitating cooperation. Cultural controls exist when employees "buy into" the norms and value systems of the firm. When this occurs, employees tend to control their own behavior, which reduces the need for direct management supervision. In other words, in a firm with a strong culture, *self-control* can reduce the need for other control systems.

McDonald's is a good example of a firm that actively promotes organizational norms and values. McDonald's refers to its franchisees and suppliers as *partners* and emphasizes its long-term commitment to them. This commitment is not just a public relations exercise; it is backed up by actions, including a willingness to help suppliers and franchisees improve their operations by providing capital and/or management assistance when needed. In response, McDonald's franchisees and suppliers are integrated into the firm's culture and thus become committed to helping McDonald's succeed. One result is that McDonald's can devote less time than would otherwise be necessary to controlling its franchisees and suppliers.

The problem with cultural control is that it is very difficult to build. Substantial investments of time and money are required to cultivate organizationwide norms and value systems. As we saw earlier, this involves defining and clarifying the company mission or vision, disseminating the desired norms and value systems through management education programs, leading by example, and adopting appropriate human relations policies. Even with all of these devices in place it may take years more to establish a common, cohesive culture in an organization.

International Strategy and Control Systems

The key to understanding the relationship between international strategy and control systems is the concept of performance ambiguity.

Performance Ambiguity

Performance ambiguity exists when the causes of a subunit's poor performance are ambiguous. This is not uncommon when a subunit's performance is partly dependent on the performance of other subunits; that is, when there is a high degree of interdependence between subunits within the organization.

For purposes of illustration, consider the case of a French subsidiary of a U.S. firm that depends on another subsidiary, a manufacturer based in Italy, for the products it sells. The French subsidiary is failing to achieve its sales goals, and the U.S. management asks the managers to explain. They reply that they are receiving poor-quality goods from the Italian subsidiary. So the U.S. management asks the managers of the Italian operation what the problem is. They reply that their product quality is excellent—the best in the industry, in fact—and that the French simply don't know how to sell a good product. Who is right, the French or the Italians? Without more information, top management cannot tell. Because they are dependent on the Italians for their product, the French have an "alibi" for poor performance. It may be that the French are correct or that the Italians are correct. The point, however, is that the U.S. management needs to have more information to determine who is correct. Collecting this information will be expensive and time consuming and it will divert top-management attention away from other issues. In other words, performance ambiguity raises the costs of control.

Consider further how different things would be if the French operation were entirely self-contained, with its own manufacturing, marketing, and R&D facilities. In that case, the French operation would lack a convenient alibi for its poor performance; the French managers would stand or fall on their own merits. They could not blame the Italians for their poor sales. The *level* of performance ambiguity, therefore, is a function of the extent of interdependence of subunits in an organization.

Strategy, Interdependence, and Ambiguity

Now let us consider the relationship among international strategy, interdependence, and performance ambiguity. In multidomestic firms, each national operation is a stand-alone entity and can thus be judged on its own merits. The level of performance ambiguity is low. In an international firm, the level of interdependence is somewhat higher. Integration is required to facilitate the transfer of core competencies. Since the success of a foreign operation is partly dependent on the quality of the competency transferred from the home country, performance ambiguity can exist.

In global firms, the situation is still more complex. Recall that in a pure global firm the pursuit of location and experience curve economies leads to the development of a global web of value creation activities. Many of the activities in a global firm are interdependent. A French subsidiary's ability to sell a product does indeed depend on how well other operations in other countries perform their value creation activities. Thus the levels of interdependence and performance ambiguity are high in global companies.

The level of performance ambiguity is highest of all in transnational firms. Transnational firms suffer from the same performance ambiguity problems that global firms do. In addition, since they emphasize the multidirectional transfer of core competencies, they also suffer from the problems characteristic of firms pursuing an international strategy. The extremely high level of integration within transnational firms implies a high degree of joint decision making, and the resulting interdependencies create plenty of alibis for poor performance. There is lots of room for finger pointing in transnational firms.

Implications for Control

The arguments of the previous section, along with the implications for the costs of control, are summarized in Table 13.1. The costs of control might be defined as the amount of time top management must devote to monitoring and evaluating subunits' performance. This will be greater when the amount of performance ambiguity is greater. When performance ambiguity is low, management can use output controls and a system of management by exception; when it is high, they have no such luxury. Output controls do not provide totally unambiguous signals of a subunit's efficiency when the performance of that subunit is dependent upon the performance of another subunit within the organization. Thus, management must devote time to resolving the problems that arise from performance ambiguity, with a corresponding rise in the costs of control.

Table 13.1 reveals a paradox. We saw in Chapter 12 that a transnational strategy is desirable because it gives a firm more ways to profit from international expansion than do multidomestic, international, and global strategies. But now we see that due to the high level of interdependence, the costs of controlling transnational firms are higher than the costs of controlling firms that pursue other strategies. It follows that unless there is some way of reducing these costs, the higher profitability associated with a transnational strategy could be canceled out by the higher costs of control. The same point, although to a lesser extent, can be made with regard to global firms. Although firms pursuing a global strategy can reap the cost benefits of location and experience curve economies, they must cope with a higher level of performance ambiguity, and this raises the costs of control (in comparison with firms pursuing an international or multidomestic strategy).

This is where the issue of control systems comes in. When we survey the control systems that corporations use to control their subunits, we find that irrespective of their strategy, multinational firms all use output and bureaucratic controls. However, in firms pursuing either global or transnational strategies, the usefulness of output controls is limited by substantial performance ambiguities. As a result, we find, these firms place greater emphasis on cultural controls. Cultural control—by encouraging managers to want to assume the organization's norms and value systems—gives managers of interdependent subunits an incentive to look for ways to work out problems that arise between them. The result is a reduction in finger pointing and, accordingly, in the costs of control. It follows that the development of cultural controls may be a precondition for the successful pursuit of a transnational strategy, and perhaps of a global strategy as well.

Table 13.1
Interdependence, Performance Ambiguity, and the Costs of Control for the Four International Business Strategies

Strategy	Interdependence	Performance Ambiguity	Costs of Control
Multidomestic	Low	Low	Low
International	Moderate	Moderate	Moderate
Global	High	High	High
Transnational	Very high	Very high	Very high

SYNTHESIS: STRATEGY AND STRUCTURE

In Chapter 12 we identified four international business strategies: multidomestic, international, global, and transnational strategies. So far in this chapter we have looked at four aspects of organizational structure—vertical differentiation, horizontal differentiation, integration, and control systems—and we have discussed the interrelationships between these dimensions and strategies. Now it is time to synthesize this material. Our synthesis is summarized in Table 13.2.

Multidomestic Firms

Firms pursuing a multidomestic strategy focus on local responsiveness. Referring to Table 13.2, we can see that multidomestic firms tend to operate with worldwide area structures, within which operating decisions are decentralized to functionally self-contained foreign subsidiaries. The need for coordination between subunits (areas) is low, so multidomestic firms operate with few interarea integrating mechanisms, either formal or informal. The lack of interdependence implies that the level of performance ambiguity in multidomestic concerns is low, as (by extension) are the costs of control. Thus headquarters can manage foreign operations by relying primarily on output and bureaucratic controls and a policy of management by exception. The need for cultural controls is low. Were it not for the fact that these firms are unable to profit from the realization of location and experience curve economies, or from the transfer of core competencies, their organizational simplicity would make this a very attractive strategy.

International Firms

Firms pursuing an international strategy attempt to create value by transferring core competencies from home to foreign. If they are diverse, as most of them are, these firms operate with a worldwide product division structure. Headquarters typically maintains centralized control over the source of the firm's core competency, which is most typically found in the R&D and/or marketing functions of the firm. All other operating decisions are decentralized within the firm to national operations (which in diverse firms report to worldwide product divisions). The need for coordination is moderate in such firms, reflecting the need to transfer core competencies. Thus, although such firms operate with some integrating mechanisms, they are not that extensive. The relatively low level of interdependence that results translates into a relatively low level of performance ambiguity. Thus these firms can generally get by with output and bureaucratic controls. Overall, although the organization of international firms is more complex than that of multidomestic firms, the increase in the level of complexity is not that great.

Table 13.2
Synthesis of Strategy, Structure, and Control Systems

Structure and Controls	International Strategy			
	Multidomestic	**International**	**Global**	**Transnational**
Vertical differentiation	Decentralized	Core competency centralized; rest decentralized	Some centralized	Mixed centralized and decentralized
Horizontal differentiation	Worldwide area structure	Worldwide product division	Worldwide product division	Informal Matrix
Need for coordination	Low	Moderate	High	Very high
Integrating mechanisms	None	Few	Many	Very many
Performance ambiguity	Low	Moderate	High	Very high
Need for cultural controls	Low	Moderate	High	Very high

Global Firms

Firms pursuing a global strategy focus on the realization of location and experience curve economies. If they are diverse, as most of them are, these firms operate with a worldwide product division structure. To coordinate the firm's globally dispersed web of value creation activities, headquarters typically maintains ultimate control over most operating decisions. In general, then, global firms are more centralized than most multinational enterprises. Reflecting the great need for coordination of the various stages of the firms' globally dispersed value chains, the need for integration in these firms also is high. Thus, these firms tend to operate with an array of formal and informal integrating mechanisms. The resulting interdependencies can lead to significant performance ambiguities. As a result, in addition to output and bureaucratic controls, global firms tend to stress cultural controls. On average, the organization of global firms is more complex than that of multidomestic and transnational firms.

Transnational Firms

Firms pursuing a transnational strategy focus on the simultaneous attainment of location and experience curve economies, local responsiveness, and global learning (the multidirectional transfer of core competencies). These firms tend to operate with matrix-type structures in which both product divisions and areas have significant influence. The needs to coordinate a globally dispersed value chain and to transfer core competencies create pressures for centralizing some operating decisions (particularly production and R&D). At the same time, the need to be locally responsive creates pressures for decentralizing other operating decisions to national operations (particularly marketing). Consequently, these firms tend to mix relatively high degrees of centralization for some operating decisions with relative high degrees of decentralization for other operating decisions.

The need for coordination is particularly high in transnational firms. This is reflected in the use of a wide array of formal and informal integrating mechanisms, including formal matrix structures and informal management networks. The high level of interdependence of subunits implied by such integration can result in significant performance ambiguities, which raise the costs of control. To reduce these, in addition to output and bureaucratic controls, transnational firms need to cultivate cultural controls.

Environment, Strategy, Structure, and Performance

Underlying the scheme outlined in Table 13.2 is the notion that a "fit" between strategy and structure is necessary for a firm to achieve high performance. For a firm to succeed, two conditions must be fulfilled. First, the firm's strategy must be consistent with the environment in which the firm operates. We discussed this issue in Chapter 12 and noted that in some industries a global strategy is most viable, in others an international or transnational strategy may be most viable, and in still others a multidomestic strategy may be most viable (although the number of multidomestic industries is on the decline). Second, the firm's organizational structure and control systems must be consistent with its strategy.

If the strategy does not fit the environment, the firm is likely to experience significant performance problems. If the structure does not fit the strategy, the firm is also likely to experience performance problems. Therefore, to survive, a firm must strive to achieve a *fit* of its environment, its strategy, its organizational structure, and its control systems.

Philips NV, the Dutch electronics firm, provides us with a good illustration of the need for this fit. For reasons rooted in the history of the firm, Philips operated until recently with an organization typical of a multidomestic enterprise. Most significant, operating decisions were decentralized to largely autonomous foreign subsidiaries. The problem was that the industry in which Philips competed had been revolutionized by technological change and the emergence of low-cost Japanese competitors who utilized a global strategy. To survive, Philips needed to become a transnational. The firm recognized this and tried to adopt a transnational posture, but it did little to change its organizational structure. The firm nominally adopted a matrix structure based on worldwide product divisions and national areas. In reality, however, the national areas continued to dominate the organization, and the product divisions had little more than an advisory role. Moreover, Philips lacked the informal management networks and strong unifying culture that transnationals need to succeed. As a result, Philips' structure did not fit the strategy that the firm had to pursue to survive, and by the early 1990s Philips was losing money.[13]

SUMMARY OF CHAPTER

The purpose of this chapter was to identify the organizational structures and internal control mechanisms, both formal and informal, that international businesses use to manage and direct their global operations. A central theme of the chapter was that different strategies require different structures and control systems. To succeed, a firm must match its structure and controls to its strategy in discriminating ways. Firms whose structure and controls do not fit their strategic requirements will experience performance problems. More specifically, the following points were made in the chapter:

1. There are four main dimensions of organizational structure: vertical differentiation, horizontal differentiation, integration, and control systems.
2. Vertical differentiation is the centralization versus decentralization of decision-making responsibilities.

[13] Aguilar and Yoshino, *Philips Group;* and "Philips Fights Flab."

3. Operating decisions are generally decentralized in multidomestic firms, somewhat centralized in international firms, and more centralized still in global firms. The situation in transnational firms is more complex.
4. Horizontal differentiation refers to how the firm is divided into subunits.
5. Undiversified domestic firms are typically divided into subunits on the basis of functions. Diversified domestic firms typically adopt a product divisional structure.
6. When firms expand abroad they often begin with an international division. However, this structure rarely serves satisfactorily very long due to its inherent potential for conflict and coordination problems between domestic and foreign operations.
7. Firms then switch to one of two structures: a worldwide area structure (undiversified firms) or a worldwide product division structure (diversified firms).
8. Since neither of these structures achieves a balance between local responsiveness and achievement of location and experience curve economies, many multinationals adopt matrix-type structures. However, global matrix structures have typically failed to work well, primarily due to bureaucratic problems.
9. Firms use integrating mechanisms to help achieve coordination between subunits.
10. The need for coordination (and hence integrating mechanisms) varies systematically with firm strategy. This need is lowest in multidomestic firms, higher in international firms, higher still in global firms, and highest of all in transnational firms.
11. Integration is inhibited by a number of impediments to coordination, particularly by differing subunit orientations.
12. Integration can be achieved through formal integrating mechanisms. These vary in complexity from direct contact and simple liaison roles, to teams, to a matrix structure. A drawback of formal integrating mechanisms is that they can become bureaucratic.
13. To overcome the bureaucracy associated with formal integrating mechanisms, firms often use informal mechanisms, which include management networks and organization culture.
14. For a network to function effectively, it must embrace as many managers within the organization as possible. Information systems and management development policies (including job rotation and management education programs) can be used to establish firmwide networks.
15. For a network to function properly, subunit managers must be committed to the same goals. One way of achieving this is to foster the development of a common organization culture. Leadership by example, management development programs, and human relations policies are all important in building a common culture.
16. A major task of a firm's headquarters is to control the various subunits of the firm to ensure consistency with strategic goals. Headquarters can achieve this through control systems.
17. There are four main types of controls: personal, bureaucratic, output, and cultural (which foster self-control).
18. The key to understanding the relationship between international strategy and control systems is the concept of performance ambiguity. Performance ambiguity is a function of the degree of interdependence of subunits and it raises the costs of control.
19. The degree of subunit interdependence—and, hence, performance ambiguity and the costs of control—is a function of the firm's strategy. It is lowest in multidomestic firms, higher in international firms, higher still in global firms, and highest of all in transnationals.
20. It follows that to reduce the high costs of control, firms with a high degree of interdependence between subunits (e.g., transnationals) must develop cultural controls.

DISCUSSION QUESTIONS

1. "The choice of strategy for a multinational firm to pursue must depend on a comparison of the benefits of that strategy (in terms of value creation) with the costs of implementing it (as defined by organizational requirements necessary for implementation). On this basis, it may be logical for some firms to pursue a multidomestic strategy, others a global or international strategy, and still others a transnational strategy." Is this statement correct?
2. Discuss this statement: "An understanding of the causes and consequences of performance ambiguity is central to the issue of organizational design in multinational firms."
3. Describe the organizational solutions a transnational firm might adopt to reduce the costs of control.
4. What actions must a firm take to establish a viable organizationwide management network?

Mode of Entry and Strategic Alliances

CHAPTER 14

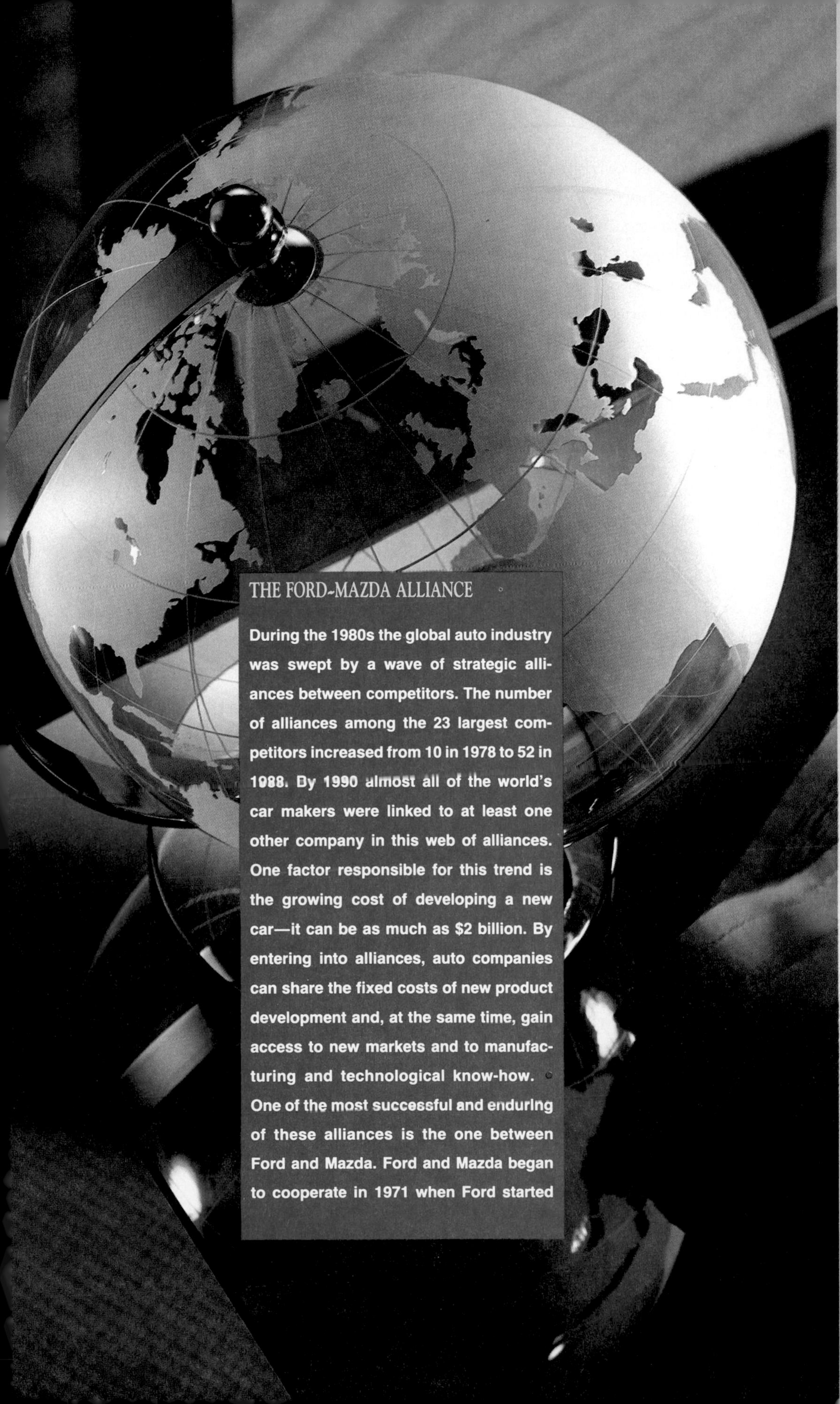

THE FORD-MAZDA ALLIANCE

During the 1980s the global auto industry was swept by a wave of strategic alliances between competitors. The number of alliances among the 23 largest competitors increased from 10 in 1978 to 52 in 1988. By 1990 almost all of the world's car makers were linked to at least one other company in this web of alliances. One factor responsible for this trend is the growing cost of developing a new car—it can be as much as $2 billion. By entering into alliances, auto companies can share the fixed costs of new product development and, at the same time, gain access to new markets and to manufacturing and technological know-how. One of the most successful and enduring of these alliances is the one between Ford and Mazda. Ford and Mazda began to cooperate in 1971 when Ford started purchasing Mazda trucks for sale in Asia. That same year Henry Ford II approached Mazda about buying a stake in the company but was rebuffed. Then came the oil crisis of 1973. At that time Mazda was using a gas-hungry rotary engine in most of its cars, and its sales slumped. Throughout the 1970s Mazda struggled to recover. Reeling under a string of financial losses, Mazda approached Ford in 1977 to see if the U.S. company was still interested in a relationship. Ford was not, but the two companies kept talking. Then in 1979 the second oil crisis hit, and Ford saw Mazda as an attractive partner because Mazda was manufacturing the type of small, fuel-efficient cars that were likely to sell well in a high-oil-price environment—so Ford purchased a 25 percent stake in the Japanese company for $130 million. In 1991 this stake earned Ford dividends of $14.3 million. However, the benefits of the alliance far exceed this return on Ford's initial investment. • For Ford some of the benefits of the alliance have been in the form of sales in Japan. Ford is now the most popular foreign nameplate in Japan; the company sells more than 72,000 cars and trucks a year through a dealer network it owns jointly with Mazda. Ford also benefits from access to Mazda's manufacturing and engineering skills and by being able to share the costs of developing new models with Mazda. When Ford built an assembly plant in Hermosillo, Mexico, in the mid-1980s, it used Mazda's superefficient Hofu (Japan) factory as the blueprint. The Hermosillo plant has become one of Ford's top-ranking plants for quality and productivity and is now serving as a model in the renovation of many of Ford's older European and U.S. facilities. As for new product development, Ford and Mazda have worked together on 10 new models, usually with Ford doing most of the styling and Mazda making many key engineering contributions. For Ford these cars include the Escort, the Mercury Tracer, the Festiva, the Probe, the Mercury Capri, and the Explorer. The Ford-aided Mazda models are the MX-6, the 323, the Protege, and the Navajo. • From Mazda's perspective, in addition to the initial injection of cash, the benefits of the alliance include access to the North American market through Ford's dealer network, access to Ford styling and marketing skills, and a partner with whom to share the costs of developing new car models. • Both partners view the alliance as a success, but it has not been all smooth sailing. Differences in national and corporate cultures have often stood in the path of harmonious relationships and communications. To reduce the possibility of conflicts arising out of misunderstandings, Ford and Mazda have held a series of meetings between the two companies' top and middle-level managers. The purposes of those meetings have been to coordinate activities and also to help facilitate the growth of enduring interpersonal relationships between Ford and Mazda managers. • Nevertheless, at times the competitive squabbles have been fierce. Ford wanted Mazda's rotary engine for use in a sports car, but Mazda refused to share the design. On another occasion, Ford refused to let Mazda copy an innovative window design in one of its models. More recently, Mazda wanted access to the design of the four-door Ford Explorer, which Mazda intended to use as a blueprint for a four-door Navajo, but Ford refused. Mazda, too, likes to keep certain models for itself. For example, Mazda refuses to allow Ford to produce its own version of Mazda's best-selling sports car, the Miata. • Over the years, however, disagreements and conflict have become increasingly rare. Initially the top management at Mazda and Ford were continually having to arbitrate disagreements between their middle managers. The need for such arbitration is less common now, and the companies are able to assist each other in many ways. For example, seeing how Mazda benefited from many small ideas contributed by its workers, Ford instituted a similar employee suggestion program. At its Hermosillo plant, Ford followed Mazda's practice of building a stamping plant nearby. This facilitated the introduction of a just-in-time inventory system and helped Ford boost quality control. • The ideas have also flowed the other way. Ford gave Mazda access to some sophisticated computer programs for measuring noise and vibrations and some electronic systems for helping control engine emissions. Mazda also hopes to profit from Ford's marketing know-how. While working together on the Navajo/Explorer, Mazda got a close look at the customer surveys Ford had collected on the old Bronco II, the Explorer's predecessor. The surveys showed Ford engineers which components and vehicle systems are most important to consumers. Mazda came away so impressed that it adopted Ford's system wholesale. *Sources: J. B. Treece, K. Miller, and R. A. Melcher, "The Partners,"* Business Week, *February 10, 1992, pp. 102–7; C. Rapoport, "Mazda's Bold New Global Strategy,"* Fortune, *December 17, 1990, pp. 109–13; "Car Industry Joint Ventures: Spot the Difference,"* The Economist, *February 24, 1990, p. 74; and J. P. Womack, D. T. Jones, and D. Roos,* The Machine that Changed the World *(New York: Rawson Associates, 1990).*

INTRODUCTION

This chapter is concerned with two closely related topics: entry modes and strategic alliances. Entry modes serving foreign markets include exporting, licensing or franchising to host-country firms, joint venturing with a host-country firm, and setting up a wholly owned subsidiary in a host country to serve its market. Each of these options has advantages and disadvantages. It will be shown that the magnitude of the advantages and disadvantages associated with each entry mode are determined by a number of factors, including transport costs, trade barriers, political risks, economic risks, and firm strategy. The optimal entry mode varies from situation to situation depending on these various factors. Thus, whereas some firms may best serve a given market by exporting, other firms may better serve the market by setting up a wholly owned subsidiary or by using some other entry mode.

You may recall that we touched on the topic of entry modes when we examined foreign direct investment (FDI) in Chapter 6. There we related economic theory to exporting, licensing, and foreign direct investment as means of entering foreign markets. Here we integrate that material with the material we discussed in Chapter 12 on firm strategy to present a comprehensive picture of the factors that determine the optimal entry mode. We consider a wider range of modes in this chapter as well as mixed entry modes. (For example, joint venturing and setting up a wholly owned subsidiary in another country are both FDI, but we did not make a distinction in Chapter 6.)

The second topic of this chapter is that of strategic alliances. **Strategic alliances** are agreements between actual or potential competitors to cooperate. The term *strategic alliances* is often used loosely to embrace a wide range of arrangements between firms, including cross-shareholding deals, licensing arrangements, formal joint ventures, and informal cooperative arrangements. The motives for entering strategic alliances are varied, but they often include market access; hence the overlap with the topic of entry mode. We saw this in the Ford–Mazda alliance in the opening case. Since the alliance helped Ford and Mazda enter each other's markets, we can see that strategic alliances are yet another entry mode. Indeed, in many respects, the entry modes of licensing, franchising, and joint ventures are strategic alliances. However, strategic alliances tend to involve much more than market access. As seen in the Ford-Mazda alliance, strategic alliances can also involve sharing the fixed costs of new product development, skills, and technology.

We will see that strategic alliances have advantages and disadvantages and that a firm must weigh these carefully before deciding whether to ally itself with an actual or potential competitor. Perhaps the biggest danger is that the firm will give away more to its ally than it receives. As we will see, firms can reduce this risk by how they structure their strategic alliances. We will also see how firms can build alliances that benefit both partners, as the Ford-Mazda alliance seems to be doing.

The rest of this chapter is structured as follows. First, we will review the options available to firms wishing to enter a foreign market, discussing the advantages and disadvantages of each option. Second, we will consider the factors that determine a firm's optimal entry mode. Third, we will look at the advantages and disadvantages of engaging in strategic alliances with competitors. Fourth, we will consider how a firm should select an ally, structure the alliance, and manage it to maximize the advantages and minimize the disadvantages associated with alliances.

ENTRY MODES

When a firm is considering entering a foreign market, the question arises as to the best means of achieving it. There are basically six different ways to enter a foreign market: exporting, turnkey projects, licensing, franchising, joint venturing with a host-country firm, and setting up a wholly owned subsidiary in the host country. Each entry mode has advantages and disadvantages. Managers need to consider these carefully when deciding which entry mode to use.[1]

Exporting

Most manufacturing firms begin their global expansion as exporters and only later switch to another mode for serving a foreign market.

Advantages

Exporting has two distinct advantages. The first is that it avoids the costs of establishing manufacturing operations in the host country, which are often substantial. Second, exporting may help a firm achieve experience curve and location economies (see Chapter 12). By manufacturing the product in a centralized location and exporting it to other national markets, the firm may be able to realize substantial scale economies from its global sales volume. This, after all, is how Sony came to dominate the global TV market, how Matsushita came to dominate the VCR market, and how many Japanese auto firms made inroads into the U.S. auto market.

[1] This section draws on two studies: C. W. L. Hill, P. Hwang, and W. C. Kim, "An Eclectic Theory of the Choice of International Entry Mode," *Strategic Management Journal* 11, (1990), pp. 117-28; and C. W. L. Hill and W. C. Kim, "Searching for a Dynamic Theory of the Multinational Enterprise: A Transaction Cost Model," *Strategic Management Journal* 9 (Special Issue on Strategy Content; 1988), pp. 93-104. See also E. Anderson and H. Gatignon, "Modes of Foreign Entry: A Transaction Cost Analysis and Propositions," *Journal of International Business Studies* 17 (1986), pp. 1-26; and F. R. Root, *Entry Strategies for International Markets* (Lexington, Mass.: D. C. Heath, 1980).

Disadvantages

On the other hand, exporting has a number of drawbacks. First, exporting from the firm's home base may not be appropriate if there are lower-cost locations for manufacturing the product abroad (i.e., if the firm can realize location economies by moving production elsewhere). Thus, particularly for firms pursuing global or transnational strategies, it may be preferable to manufacture in a location where the mix of factor conditions is most favorable from a value creation perspective and to export to the rest of the world from that location. This, of course, is not so much an argument against exporting as an argument against exporting from the firm's home country. Many U.S. electronics firms have moved some of their manufacturing to the Far East due to the availability of low-cost, highly skilled labor there. They then export from that location to the rest of the world, including the United States.

A second drawback to exporting is that high transport costs can make exporting uneconomical, particularly for bulk products. One way of getting around this is to manufacture bulk products regionally. This strategy enables the firm to realize some economies from large-scale production and at the same time to limit its transport costs. For example, many multinational chemical firms manufacture their products regionally, serving several countries from one facility.

Another drawback to exporting is that tariff barriers can make it uneconomical. Similarly, the threat of tariff barriers by the host-country government can make it very risky. Indeed, it was an implicit threat of the U.S. Congress to impose tariffs on imported Japanese autos that led to many Japanese auto firms' decisions to set up manufacturing plants in the United States. As a consequence, by 1990 almost 50 percent of all Japanese cars sold in the United States were manufactured locally—up from 0 percent in 1985.

A fourth drawback to exporting arises when a firm delegates its marketing in each country where it does business to a local agent. (This is common for firms that are just beginning to export.) Foreign agents often carry the products of competing firms and, as a result, have divided loyalties. In such cases, the foreign agent may not do as good a job as the firm would if it managed its marketing itself. There are ways around this problem, however. One way is to set up a wholly owned subsidiary in the country to handle local marketing. By doing this, the firm can exercise tight control over marketing in the country while reaping the cost advantages of manufacturing the product in a single location.

Turnkey Projects

Firms that specialize in the design, construction, and start-up of **turnkey plants** are common in some industries. In such a transaction, the contractor agrees to handle every detail of the project for a foreign client, including the training of operating personnel. At completion of the contract, the foreign client is handed the "key" to a plant that is ready for full operation—hence the term *turnkey*. This is actually a means of exporting process technology to other countries. Indeed, in a sense it is just a very specialized kind of exporting. Turnkey projects are most common in the chemical, pharmaceutical, petroleum refining, and metal refining industries, all of which use complex, expensive production-process technologies.

Advantages

The know-how required to assemble and run a technologically complex process, such as refining petroleum or steel, is a valuable asset. The main advantage of turnkey projects is that they are a way of earning great economic returns from that asset. The strategy is particularly useful in cases where FDI is limited by host-government regulations. For example, the governments of many oil-rich countries have set out to build their own petroleum refining industries and, as a step toward that goal, have placed severe restrictions on FDI in their oil and refining sectors. Since many of these countries lacked petroleum refining technology, however, they had to gain it by entering into turnkey projects with foreign firms that had the technology. Such deals are often attractive to the selling firm, since without them, they would probably have no way to earn a return on their valuable know-how in that country.

A second advantage of pursuing a turnkey strategy, as opposed to a more conventional type of FDI, is that it may make a good deal of sense in a country where the political and economic environment is such that a longer-term investment might expose the firm to unacceptable political and/or economic risks (e.g., the risk of nationalization or of economic collapse).

Disadvantages

Three main drawbacks are associated with a turnkey strategy. First, by definition, the firm that enters into a turnkey deal will have no long-term interest in the foreign country. This can be a disadvantage if that country subsequently proves to be a major market for the output of the process that has been exported. One way around this is to take a minority equity interest in the operation set up by the turnkey project.

Second, the firm that enters into a turnkey project with a foreign enterprise may inadvertently create a competitor. For example, many of the Western firms that sold oil refining technology to firms in Saudi Arabia, Kuwait, and other "Gulf" states now find themselves competing head to head with these firms in the world oil market. Third, and related to the second point, if the firm's process technology is a source of competitive advantage, then selling this technology through a turnkey project is also selling competitive advantage to potential and/or actual competitors.

Licensing

International licensing is an arrangement whereby a foreign licensee buys the rights to manufacture a firm's product in their country for a negotiated fee—normally, royalty payments on the number of units sold. The licensee then puts up most of the capital necessary to get the overseas operation going.[2]

Advantages

The advantage of licensing is that the firm does not have to bear the development costs and risks associated with opening up a foreign market. Licensing is a very attractive option for firms lacking the capital to develop operations overseas. In addition, licensing can be attractive when a firm is unwilling to commit substantial financial resources to an unfamiliar or politically volatile foreign market.

Disadvantages

On the other hand, licensing has three serious drawbacks. First, it does not give a firm the tight control over manufacturing, marketing, and strategy that is required for

---

[2] For a general discussion of licensing, see F. J. Contractor, "The Role of Licensing in International Strategy," *Columbia Journal of World Business*, Winter 1982, pp. 73–83.

realizing experience curve and location economies (as global and transnational firms must do; see Chapter 12). Licensing typically involves each licensee setting up its own manufacturing operations. This severely limits the firm's ability to realize experience curve and location economies by manufacturing its product in a centralized location. Thus, when these economies are important, licensing may not be the best way to expand overseas.

Second, competing in a global market may require a firm to coordinate strategic moves across countries by using profits earned in one country to support competitive attacks in another (again, see Chapter 12). By its very nature, licensing severely limits a firm's ability to do this. A licensee is unlikely to allow a multinational firm to use its profits (beyond those due in the form of royalty payments) to support a different licensee operating in another country.

A third problem with licensing is one that we first encountered in Chapter 6 when we reviewed the economic theory of FDI. This is the risk associated with licensing technological know-how to foreign companies. Technological know-how constitutes the basis of many multinational firms' competitive advantage. Most firms wish to maintain control over how their know-how is used, and a firm can quickly lose control over its technology by licensing it. Many firms have made the mistake of thinking they could maintain control over their know-how within the framework of a licensing agreement. RCA Corporation, for example, once licensed its color TV technology to a number of Japanese firms. The Japanese firms quickly assimilated the technology and used it to enter the U.S. market. Now the Japanese have a bigger share of the U.S. market than the RCA brand does. Similar concerns are now surfacing over the 1989 decision by Congress to allow Japanese firms to produce the advanced FSX fighter plane under license from McDonnell Douglas. Critics of the decision fear the Japanese will use the FSX technology to support the development of a commercial airline industry that will compete with Boeing and McDonnell Douglas in the global marketplace.

Franchising

In many respects, franchising is similar to licensing, although franchising tends to involve much longer-term commitments than licensing does. Also, whereas licensing is pursued primarily by manufacturing firms, franchising is employed primarily by service firms (e.g., McDonald's and Hilton International have both expanded internationally by franchising).[3] By a franchising agreement, a franchisor sells limited rights to the use of its brand name to a franchisee in return for a lump sum payment and a share of the franchisee's profits. In contrast to most licensing agreements, the franchisee agrees to abide by strict rules as to how it does business. Thus when McDonald's enters into a franchising agreement with a foreign firm, it expects that firm to run its restaurants in an identical manner to those run under the McDonald's name elsewhere in the world.

Advantages

The advantages of franchising as an entry mode are very similar to those of licensing. Specifically, the firm is relieved of the costs and risks of opening up a foreign market on its own. Instead, the franchisee typically assumes those costs and risks. Thus, using a franchising strategy, a service firm can build up a global presence quickly and at a low cost.

---

[3] J. H. Dunning and M. McQueen, "The Eclectic Theory of International Production: A Case Study of the International Hotel Industry," *Managerial and Decision Economics* 2 (1981), pp. 197–210.

Disadvantages

The disadvantages, though present, are less pronounced than in the case of licensing. Since franchising is used by service companies, there is no reason to consider the need for coordination of manufacturing to achieve experience curve and location economies. On the other hand, franchising may inhibit the firm's ability to take profits out of one country to support competitive attacks in another.

A more significant disadvantage of franchising is quality control. The foundation of franchising arrangements is that the firm's brand name conveys a message to consumers about the quality of the firm's product. Thus, a business traveler checking in at a Hilton International hotel in Hong Kong can reasonably expect the same quality of room, food, and service that she would receive in New York. The Hilton name is supposed to guarantee consistent product quality. This presents a problem in that foreign franchisees may not be as concerned about quality as they are supposed to be, and the result of poor quality can extend beyond lost sales in a particular foreign market to a decline in the firm's worldwide reputation. For example, if the business traveler has a bad experience at the Hilton in Hong Kong, she may never go to another Hilton hotel and may urge her colleagues to do likewise. The geographical distance of the firm from its foreign franchisees, however, can make poor quality difficult for the franchisor to detect. In addition, the sheer number of franchisees—in the case of McDonald's, tens of thousands—can make quality control difficult. Due to these factors, quality problems may persist.

One way around this disadvantage is to set up a subsidiary in each country or region in which the firm expands. The subsidiary might be wholly owned by the company or a joint venture with a foreign company. In either case, the subsidiary assumes the rights and obligations to establish franchises throughout the particular country or region. The combination of close proximity and the smaller number of franchises to oversee reduces the quality control challenge. In addition, because the subsidiary is at least partly owned by the firm, the firm can place its own managers in the subsidiary to help ensure that it is doing a good job of monitoring the franchises in that country or region. This organizational arrangement has proven very satisfactory in practice and is being used by McDonald's, Kentucky Fried Chicken, Hilton International, and others to expand their international operations.

Joint Ventures

Establishing a joint venture with a foreign firm has long been a popular mode for entering a new market. The most typical joint venture is a 50/50 venture, in which each party holds 50 percent ownership and contributes a team of managers to share operating control. Some firms, however, have sought joint ventures in which they have a majority share and thus tighter control.[4] For a description of how one company, the bicycle manufacturer Schwinn, used a joint venture to enter a foreign market, see Box 14.1.

Advantages

Joint ventures have a number of advantages. First, a firm is able to benefit from a local partner's knowledge of the host country's competitive conditions, culture, language, political systems, and business systems. Thus, for many U.S. firms, joint ventures have involved the U.S. company providing technological know-how and products, and the local partner providing the marketing expertise and the local knowledge necessary for

[4] For a review of the literature of joint ventures, see B. Kogut, "Joint Ventures: Theoretical and Empirical Perspectives," *Strategic Management Journal* 9 (1988), pp. 319–32.

BOX 14.1

Schwinn Enters the Hungarian Market

Joint ventures with host-country firms have many features that make them an attractive means of entering a foreign market, but they also have pitfalls. Consider the case of Schwinn, the U.S. bicycle manufacturer, which set up a joint venture with the Csepel Bicycle Works of Hungary in 1989 to manufacture bicycles for sale in Eastern Europe. Schwinn chose to work with Csepel because the Hungarian enterprise had a good reputation and access to relatively inexpensive, skilled labor.

The joint venture, Schwinn-Csepel, was capitalized at $2.1 million, Schwinn putting in 51 percent and Csepel 49 percent. Negotiations over the structure of the venture proved to be time consuming and tedious—they took well over a year—because there were no uniform procedures for setting up joint ventures in Hungary. Joint venture laws changed several times during the negotiations, and they have changed several times since. Nobody—lawyers, government officials, company officials—could keep track of precisely what had to be done to conform with Hungary's confused and rapidly changing joint venture laws.

Since the venture was formally incorporated in June 1989, further regulatory changes have played havoc with its plans. The joint venture agreement called for Schwinn to import component parts from the United States, assemble bicycles in Hungary, and then sell them throughout Eastern Europe. However, just as Schwinn-Csepel was starting production, the budget-conscious Hungarian government changed import taxes. Import taxes on component parts were levied that included a 15 percent import duty, a 25 percent value added tax (VAT), and a 2 percent handling charge. With nearly 300 different component parts coming in each day and no computers in the customs office, Schwinn-Csepel had to establish a five-person department to calculate import taxes. Moreover, although the VAT on re-exported bikes is refunded, six months may pass before this occurs. In effect, Schwinn-Csepel is making an interest-free loan to the Hungarian government that amounts to millions of dollars.

The venture has also been plagued by unanticipated productivity problems. Productivity is significantly lower than at Schwinn's North American plants; the percentage of defects is higher; and workers are apathetic. Worse still, the venture inherited a management problem. Many of the managers of the former Csepel Bicycle Works, although not all ex-communists, are products of the old communist system. Traditions of secrecy and favoritism and a lack of attention to productivity and profitability have persisted.

Despite these problems, the venture is beginning to make inroads. The venture sold about 250,000 bicycles in 1991, half of those in Hungary. The company has built up a dealer network of 55 shops, whose owners guarantee servicing and spare parts—unheard of in the old days of communist rule. There is no other Western competition, and competing bicycles built by other Eastern European firms are poorly built and relatively expensive. Consequently, Schwinn-Csepel's U.S. managers still believe their venture will succeed, but they warn other firms contemplating similar moves into the Eastern European market that they should expect the unexpected.

Source: "A Bicycle Made by Two," The Economist, *June 8, 1991, p. 73.*

competing in that country. Second, when the development costs and/or risks of opening a foreign market are high, a firm might gain by sharing these costs and/or risks with a local partner. Third, in many countries, political considerations make joint ventures the only feasible entry mode. For example, historically, many U.S. companies have found it was much easier to get permission to set up operations in Japan if they had a Japanese partner than if they tried to enter on their own. (Texas Instruments and IBM are notable exceptions.) Furthermore, research suggests that joint ventures with local partners face a low risk of nationalization.[5] This appears to be because local equity partners, who may have some influence on host-government policy, have a vested interest in speaking out against nationalization.

Disadvantages

Despite these advantages, there are two major disadvantages with joint ventures. First, just as with licensing, a firm that enters into a joint venture risks giving control of its technology to its partner. The joint venture between Boeing and a consortium of Japanese firms to build the 767 airliner raised fears that Boeing was unwittingly giving away its commercial airline technology to the Japanese. However, joint venture agreements can be constructed to minimize this risk. One option is to hold majority ownership in the venture. This allows the dominant partner to exercise greater control over its technology. The drawback with this is that it can be difficult to find a foreign partner who is willing to settle for minority ownership.

A second disadvantage is that a joint venture does not give a firm the tight control over subsidiaries that it might need to realize experience curve or location economies. Nor does it give a firm the tight control over a foreign subsidiary that it might need for engaging in coordinated global attacks against its rivals. For illustration, consider the entry of Texas Instruments (TI) into the Japanese semiconductor market. When TI established semiconductor facilities in Japan, it did so for the dual purpose of checking Japanese manufacturers' market share and limiting their cash available for invading TI's global market. In other words, TI was engaging in global strategic coordination. To implement this strategy, TI's subsidiary in Japan had to be prepared to take instructions from corporate headquarters regarding competitive strategy. The strategy also required the Japanese subsidiary to run at a loss if necessary. Few if any potential joint venture partners would have been willing to accept such conditions, since it would have necessitated a willingness to accept a negative return on their investment. Thus, to implement this strategy, TI set up a wholly owned subsidiary in Japan.

Wholly Owned Subsidiaries

In a wholly owned subsidiary, the firm owns 100 percent of the stock. Establishing a wholly owned subsidiary in a foreign market can be done two ways. The firm can either set up a completely new operation in that country or it can acquire an established firm and use that firm to promote its products in the country's market.

Advantages

There are three clear advantages of wholly owned subsidiaries. First, when a firm's competitive advantage is based on technological competence, a wholly owned subsidiary will normally be the preferred entry mode, since it reduces the risk of losing control over that competence. (See Chapter 6 for more details.) For this reason, many high-tech firms prefer this entry mode for overseas expansion (e.g., firms in the semiconductor, electronics, and pharmaceutical industries).

Second, a wholly owned subsidiary gives a firm the kind of tight control over operations in different countries that is necessary for engaging in global strategic coor-

[5] D. G. Bradley, "Managing Against Expropriation," *Harvard Business Review*, July–August 1977, pp. 78–90.

dination (i.e., using profits from one country to support competitive attacks in another). Third, a wholly owned subsidiary may be required if a firm is trying to realize location and experience curve economies (as firms pursuing global and transnational strategies try to do). As we saw in Chapter 12, when cost pressures are intense, it may pay a firm to configure its value chain in such a way that the value added at each stage is maximized. Thus, a national subsidiary may specialize in manufacturing only part of the product line or certain components of the end product, exchanging parts and products with other subsidiaries in the firm's global system. Establishing such a global production system requires a high degree of control over the operations of each affiliate. The various operations must be prepared to accept centrally determined decisions as to how they will produce, how much they will produce, and how their output will be priced for transfer to the next operation. Since licensees or joint venture partners are unlikely to accept such a subservient role, establishment of wholly owned subsidiaries may be necessary.

Disadvantages

On the other hand, establishing a wholly owned subsidiary is generally the most costly method of serving a foreign market. Firms doing this must bear the full costs and risks of setting up overseas operations. The risks associated with learning to do business in a new culture are less if the firm acquires an established host-country enterprise. However, acquisitions raise a whole set of additional problems, including those associated with trying to marry divergent corporate cultures. These problems may more than offset any benefits derived by acquiring an established operation.[6]

SELECTING AN ENTRY MODE

As the preceding discussion demonstrated, there are advantages and disadvantages associated with all of the entry modes; they are summarized in Table 14.1. Due to these advantages and disadvantages, trade-offs are inevitable when selecting an entry mode. For example, when considering entry into an unfamiliar country with a track record for nationalizing foreign-owned enterprises, a firm might favor a joint venture with a local enterprise. Its rationale might be that the local partner will help it establish operations in an unfamiliar environment and will speak out against nationalization should the possibility arise. However, if the firm's core competence is based on proprietary technology, entering a joint venture might risk losing control of that technology to the joint venture partner—in which case the strategy may seem very unattractive. Despite the existence of such trade-offs, it is possible to make some generalizations about the optimal choice of entry mode. That is what we do in this section.

Core Competencies and Entry Mode

We saw in Chapter 12 that firms often expand internationally to earn greater returns from their core competencies—transferring the skills and products derived from their core competencies to foreign markets where indigenous competitors lack those skills. We say that such firms are pursuing an international strategy. The optimal entry mode for these firms depends to some degree on the nature of their core competencies. In

[6] For a review of the kinds of problems encountered when making acquisitions, see Chapter 9 in C. W. L. Hill and G. R. Jones, *Strategic Management Theory* (Boston: Houghton-Mifflin, 1992).

Table 14.1
Advantages and Disadvantages of Entry Modes

Entry Mode	Advantage	Disadvantage
Exporting	Ability to realize location and experience curve economies	High transport costs Trade barriers Problems with local marketing agents
Turnkey contracts	Ability to earn returns from process technology skills in countries where FDI is restricted	Creating efficient competitors Lack of long-term market presence
Licensing	Low development costs and risks	Lack of control over technology Inability to realize location and experience curve economies Inability to engage in global strategic coordination
Franchising	Low development costs and risks	Lack of control over quality Inability to engage in global strategic coordination
Joint ventures	Access to local partner's knowledge Sharing development costs and risks Politically acceptable	Lack of control over technology Inability to engage in global strategic coordination Inability to realize location and experience economies
Wholly owned subsidiaries	Protection of technology Ability to engage in global strategic coordination Ability to realize location and experience economies	High costs and risks

particular, a distinction can be drawn between firms whose core competency is in technological know-how and those whose core competency is in management know-how.

Technological Know-How

As was initially observed in Chapter 6, if a firm's competitive advantage (its core competence) is based on control over proprietary technological know-how, licensing and joint venture arrangements should be avoided if possible so that the risk of losing control over that technology is minimized. Thus, if a high-tech firm sets up operations in a foreign country to profit from a core competency in technological know-how, it will probably do so through a wholly owned subsidiary.

This rule should not be viewed as hard and fast, however. One exception is when a licensing or joint venture arrangement can be structured so as to reduce the risks of a firm's technological know-how being expropriated by licensees or joint venture partners. We will see how this might be achieved later in the chapter when we examine the structuring of strategic alliances. Another exception exists when a firm perceives its technological advantage to be only transitory—when it expects rapid imitation of its core technology by competitors. In such case, the firm might want to license its technology as rapidly as possible to foreign firms to gain global acceptance for its technology before the imitation occurs. Such a strategy has some advantages. By licensing its technology to competitors, the firm may deter them from developing their own, possibly superior, technology. Further, by licensing its technology, the firm may be able to establish its technology as the dominant design in the industry (as Matsushita did with its VHS format for VCRs). In turn, this may ensure a steady stream of royalty payments. Such situations apart, however, the attractions of licensing are probably outweighed by the risks of losing control over technology, and thus licensing should be avoided.

Management Know-How

The competitive advantage of many service firms is based on management know-how (e.g., McDonald's, Hilton International). For such firms, the risk of losing control over their management skills to franchisees or joint venture partners is not that great. The reason is that these firms' valuable asset is their brand name, and brand names are generally well protected by international laws pertaining to trademarks. Given this, many of the issues arising in the case of technological know-how are of no concern here. As a result, many service firms favor a combination of franchising and subsidiaries to control the franchises within particular countries or regions. The subsidiaries may be wholly owned or joint ventures, but most service firms have found that joint ventures with local partners work best for the controlling subsidiaries. This is because a joint venture is often politically more acceptable and brings a degree of local knowledge to the subsidiary.

Pressures for Cost Reductions and Entry Mode

The greater the pressures for cost reductions are, the more likely a firm will want to pursue some combination of exporting and wholly owned subsidiaries. By manufacturing in those locations where factor conditions are optimal and then exporting to the rest of the world, a firm may be able to realize substantial location and experience curve economies. The firm might then want to export the finished product to marketing subsidiaries based in various countries. These subsidiaries will typically be wholly owned and have the responsibility for overseeing distribution in their particular countries. Setting up wholly owned marketing subsidiaries is preferable to joint venture arrangements and to using foreign marketing agents, because it gives the firm the tight control over marketing that might be required for coordinating a globally dispersed value chain. It also gives the firm the ability to use the profits generated in one market to improve its competitive position in another market. In other words, firms pursuing global or transnational strategies tend to prefer establishing wholly owned subsidiaries.

STRATEGIC ALLIANCES

The term *strategic alliances* refers to cooperative agreements between potential or actual competitors. In this section we are concerned specifically with strategic alliances between firms from different countries. Strategic alliances run the range from formal joint ventures, in which two or more firms have equity stakes, to short-term contractual agreements in which two companies agree to cooperate on a particular task (such as developing a new product). Without a doubt, collaboration between competitors is fashionable; the 1980s saw a virtual explosion in the number of strategic alliances. Examples include:

- A cooperative arrangement between Boeing and a consortium of Japanese companies to produce the 767 wide-bodied commercial jet.
- An alliance between General Electric and Snecma of France to build a family of low-thrust commercial aircraft engines.
- An agreement between Siemens and Philips to develop new semiconductor technology.
- An agreement between ICL, the British computer company, and Fujitsu of Japan to develop a new generation of mainframe computers capable of competing with IBM's products.

- An alliance between Eastman Kodak and Canon of Japan under which Canon manufactures a line of medium-volume copiers for sale under Kodak's name.
- An agreement between Texas Instruments and Kobe Steel, Inc., of Japan to make logic semiconductors in Japan.
- An agreement between Motorola and Toshiba to pool their technological know-how in the manufacture of microprocessors.

The Advantages of Strategic Alliances

Firms ally themselves with actual or potential competitors for various strategic purposes.[7] First, as noted earlier in the chapter, strategic alliances may facilitate entry into a foreign market. For example, Motorola initially found it very difficult to gain access to the Japanese cellular telephone market. In the mid-1980s the firm complained loudly about formal and informal Japanese trade barriers. The turning point for Motorola came in 1987 when it allied itself with Toshiba to build microprocessors. As part of the deal, Toshiba provided Motorola with marketing help—including some of its best managers. This helped Motorola in the political game of securing government approval to enter the Japanese market and getting radio frequencies assigned for its mobile communications systems. Motorola no longer complains about Japan's trade barriers. Although privately the company admits they still exist, with Toshiba's help Motorola has become skilled at getting around them.[8]

Another reason firms make strategic alliances is that it allows them to share the fixed costs (and associated risks) of developing new products or processes. This was a factor in the formation of the Ford–Mazda alliance (see the opening case). Motorola's alliance with Toshiba also was partly motivated by a desire to share the high fixed costs of setting up an operation to manufacture microprocessors. The microprocessor business is so capital intensive—Motorola and Toshiba each contributed close to $1 billion to set up their facility—that few firms can afford the costs and risks by themselves. Similarly, the alliance between Boeing and a number of Japanese companies to build the 767 was motivated by Boeing's desire to share the estimated $8 billion investment required to develop the aircraft. (For another example of such an alliance, see the discussion of the IBM, Toshiba, and Siemens alliance in Box 14.2.)

Third, an alliance is a way to bring together complementary skills and assets that neither company could easily develop on its own. This was a factor in the Ford–Mazda alliance, to which Ford contributed its marketing and design know-how and Mazda its engineering and manufacturing know-how. Another example is the alliance between France's Thompson and Japan's JVC to manufacture videocassette recorders. JVC and Thompson are trading core competencies; Thompson needs product technology and manufacturing skills, while JVC needs to learn how to succeed in the fragmented European market. Both sides believe there is an equitable chance for gain. Similarly, in 1990 AT&T struck a deal with NEC Corporation of Japan to trade technological skills. AT&T will give NEC some of its computer-aided design technology and NEC will give AT&T access to the technology underlying its advanced logic computer chips. Such trading of core competencies seems to underlie many of the most successful strategic alliances.

---

[7] See K. Ohmae, "The Global Logic of Strategic Alliances," *Harvard Business Review*, March–April 1989, pp. 143–54; G. Hamel, Y. L. Doz, and C. K. Prahalad, "Collaborate with Your Competitors and Win!" *Harvard Business Review*, January–February 1989, pp. 133–39; and W. Burgers, C. W. L. Hill, and W. C. Kim, "Alliances in the Global Auto Industry," *Strategic Management Journal*, in press, 1993.

[8] "Asia Beckons," *The Economist*, May 30, 1992, pp. 63–64.

The IBM, Toshiba, and Siemens Alliance

BOX 14.2

On July 18, 1992, three of the world's largest high-tech companies, IBM, Toshiba, and Siemens, announced a strategic alliance to build a new generation of semiconductor chips. These three companies are, respectively, the world's largest computer company and chipmaker, Japan's second-largest chipmaker, and Europe's third-largest semiconductor producer. The goal of the alliance is to develop a semiconductor chip onto whose tiny silicon surface will be etched what amounts to a street map of the entire world. Those electronic streets will link some 600 transistors. Targeted to be introduced in 1998, each chip will store 256 million bits of data which corresponds to about two copies of the complete works of Shakespeare. This technology will have the capability to create microprocessors with the power of today's supercomputers.

The main reason for the alliance is clear: to share the enormous costs and risks involved in the venture. The cost of developing the chip is estimated at about $1 billion. Factories to produce the chip in economical volumes will cost another $1 billion each. In addition to sharing these costs, the companies also hope that jointly developing the chip will improve its chances of becoming an accepted standard in an industry where being the standard is *everything.*

Sources: "Chip Diplomacy," The Economist, *July 18, 1992, p. 65; and O. Port, "Talk about Your Dream Team,"* Business Week, *July 27, 1992, pp. 59–60.*

Fourth, it can make sense to form an alliance that will help the firm establish technological standards for the industry that will benefit the firm. For example, in 1992 Philips NV allied with its global competitor, Matsushita, to manufacture and market the digital compact cassette (DCC) system Philips had developed. Philips' motive was that this linking with Matsushita would help it establish the DCC system as a new technological standard in the recording and consumer electronics industries. The issue is important, because Sony has developed a competing "mini compact disc" technology that it hopes to establish as the new technical standard. Since the two technologies do very similar things, there is probably room for only one new standard. The technology that becomes the new standard will be the one that succeeds. The loser will probably have to write off investments in the billions of dollars. Philips sees its alliance with Matsushita as a tactic for winning the race.

The Disadvantages of Strategic Alliances

The advantages we have discussed can be very significant. Despite this, some commentators have criticized strategic alliances on the grounds that they give competitors a low-cost route to new technology and markets. For example, Robert Reich and Eric Mankin have argued that strategic alliances between U.S. and Japanese firms are part of an implicit Japanese strategy to keep higher-paying, higher value added jobs in Japan while gaining the project engineering and production process skills that underlie the competitive success of many U.S. companies.[9] They argue that Japanese successes in the machine tool and semiconductor industries were largely built on U.S. technology acquired through various strategic alliances. And they argue that, increasingly, U.S. managers are aiding the Japanese in achieving their goals by entering alliances that channel new inventions to Japan and provide a U.S. sales and distribution network for the resulting

[9] R. B. Reich and E. D. Mankin, "Joint Ventures with Japan Give Away Our Future," *Harvard Business Review,* March–April 1986, pp. 78–90.

products. Although such deals may generate short-term profits, Reich and Mankin argue, in the long run the result is to "hollow out" U.S. firms, leaving them with no competitive advantage in the global marketplace.

Reich and Mankin have a point. Alliances do have risks. Unless a firm is careful, it can give away more than it receives. On the other hand, there are so many examples of apparently successful alliances between firms—including alliances between U.S. and Japanese firms—that their position seems more than a little extreme. It is difficult to see how the Motorola–Toshiba alliance, the Ford–Mazda alliance, and the 25-year-old Fuji–Xerox alliance to build and market photocopiers in Asia fit Reich and Mankin's thesis. In all of these cases, both partners seem to have gained from the alliance. Since Reich and Mankin undoubtedly do have a point, the question becomes, Why do some alliances benefit both firms while others benefit one firm and hurt the other? The next section provides an answer to this question.

MAKING ALLIANCES WORK

The benefits a firm receives from a strategic alliance seems to be a function of three factors: partner selection, alliance structure, and the manner in which the alliance is managed. We will look at each of these issues in turn.

Partner Selection

One of the keys to making a strategic alliance work is to select the right kind of ally. A good ally, or partner, has three principal characteristics. First, a good partner helps the firm achieve its strategic goals—whether they be market access, sharing the costs and risks of new product development, or gaining access to critical core competencies. In other words, the partner must have capabilities that the firm lacks and that it values. Second, a good partner shares the firm's vision for the purpose of the alliance. If two firms approach an alliance with radically different agendas, the chances are great that the relationship will not be harmonious, will not flourish, and will end in divorce.

Third, a good partner is unlikely to try to opportunistically exploit the alliance for its own ends; that is, to expropriate the firm's technological know-how while giving away little in return. In this respect, firms with reputations for "fair play" to maintain probably make the best allies. For example, IBM is involved in so many strategic alliances that it would not pay the company to trample roughshod over individual alliance partners. Such action would tarnish IBM's hard-won reputation of being a good ally and would make it more difficult for IBM to attract alliance partners in the future. Since IBM attaches great importance to its alliances, it is unlikely to engage in the kind of opportunistic behavior that Reich and Mankin highlight. Similarly, their reputations make it less likely (but by no means impossible) that such Japanese firms as Sony, Toshiba, and Fuji, which have histories of alliances with non-Japanese firms, would opportunistically exploit an alliance partner.

To select a partner with these three characteristics, a firm needs to conduct some comprehensive research on potential alliance candidates. To increase the probability of selecting a good partner, the firm should:

1. Collect as much pertinent, publicly available information on potential allies as possible.
2. Collect data from informed third parties. These include firms that have had alliances with the potential partners, investment bankers who have had dealings with them, and some of their former employees.

Figure 14.1
Structuring Alliances to Reduce Opportunism

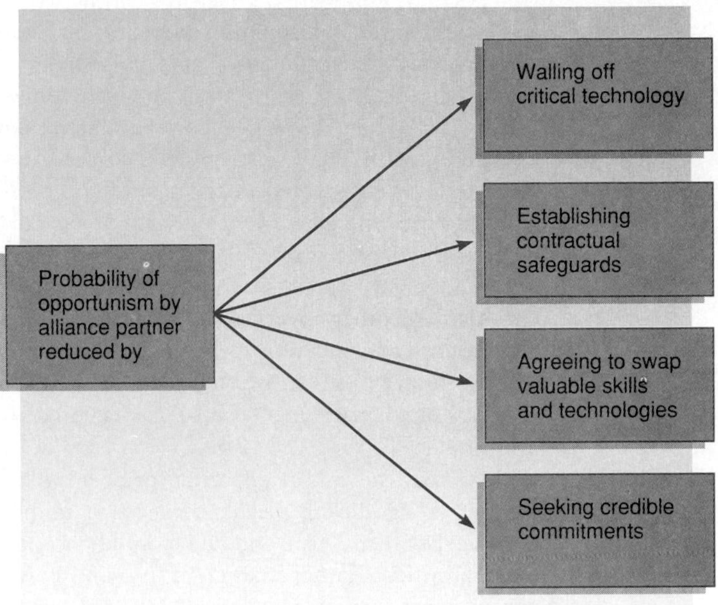

3. Get to know the potential partner as well as possible before committing to an alliance. This should include face-to-face meetings between senior managers (and perhaps middle-level managers) to ensure that the "chemistry" is right.

Alliance Structure

Having selected a partner, the alliance should be structured so that the firm's risks of giving too much away to the partner are reduced to an acceptable level. Figure 14.1 depicts the four safeguards against opportunism by alliance partners that we discuss here. (Opportunism includes the "theft" of technology and/or markets that Reich and Mankin describe.) First, alliances can be designed to make it difficult (if not impossible) to transfer technology not meant to be transferred. Specifically, the design, development, manufacture, and service of a product manufactured by an alliance can be structured so as to "wall off" sensitive technologies to prevent their leakage to the other participant. In the alliance between General Electric and Snecma to build commercial aircraft engines, for example, GE reduced the risk of "excess transfer" by walling off certain sections of the production process. The modularization effectively cut off the transfer of what GE regarded as key competitive technology, while permitting Snecma access to final assembly. Similarly, in the alliance between Boeing and the Japanese to build the 767, Boeing walled off research, design, and marketing functions considered central to its competitive position, while allowing the Japanese to share in production technology. Boeing also walled off new technologies not required for 767 production.[10]

[10] T. W. Roehl and J. F. Truitt, "Stormy Open Marriages Are Better," *Columbia Journal of World Business,* Summer 1987, pp. 87–95.

Second, contractual safeguards can be written into an alliance agreement to guard against the risk of opportunism by a partner. For example, TRW, Inc., has three strategic alliances with large Japanese auto component suppliers to produce seat belts, engine valves, and steering gears for sale to Japanese-owned auto assembly plants in the United States. TRW has clauses in each of its alliance contracts that bar the Japanese firms from competing with TRW to supply U.S.-owned auto companies with component parts. By doing this, TRW protects itself against the possibility that the Japanese companies are entering into the alliances merely as a means of gaining access to the North American market to compete with TRW in its home market.

Third, both parties to an alliance can agree in advance to swap skills and technologies that the other covets, thereby ensuring a chance for equitable gain. Cross-licensing agreements are one way to achieve this goal. For example, in the alliance between Motorola and Toshiba, Motorola has licensed some of its microprocessor technology to Toshiba, and in return Toshiba has licensed some of its memory chip technology to Motorola.

Fourth, the risk of opportunism by an alliance partner can be reduced if the firm extracts a significant *credible commitment* from its partner in advance. The long-term alliance between Xerox and Fuji to build photocopiers for the Asian market perhaps best illustrates this. Rather than enter into an informal agreement or some kind of licensing arrangement (which Fuji initially wanted), Xerox insisted that Fuji invest in a 50/50 joint venture to serve Japan and East Asia. This venture constituted such a significant investment in people, equipment, and facilities that Fuji was committed from the outset to making the alliance work in order to earn a return on its investment. By agreeing to the joint venture, Fuji essentially made a credible commitment to the alliance. Given this, Xerox felt secure in transferring its photocopier technology to Fuji.

Managing the Alliance

Once a partner has been selected and an appropriate alliance structure has been agreed on, the task facing the firm is to maximize its benefits from the alliance. As in all international business deals, an important factor is sensitivity to cultural differences (see Chapter 3). Many differences in management style are attributable to cultural differences, and managers need to make allowances for these in dealing with their partner. Beyond this, maximizing the benefits from an alliance seems to involve building trust between partners and learning from partners.

Building Trust

Part of the "trick" of managing an alliance successfully seems to be to build interpersonal relationships between the firms' managers. This is one lesson that can be drawn from the strategic alliance between Ford and Mazda. Ford and Mazda have set up a framework of meetings within which their managers not only discuss matters pertaining to the alliance, but which also provide sufficient "nonwork" time to allow the managers to get to know each other better. The belief is that the resulting friendships help build trust and facilitate harmonious relations between the two firms. Moreover, personal relationships foster an informal management network between the two firms. (Chapter 13 discusses informal management networks.) This network can then be used to help solve problems arising in more formal contexts (such as in joint committee meetings between personnel from the two firms).

Learning from Partners

After a five-year study of 15 strategic alliances between major multinationals, Gary Hamel, Yves Doz, and C. K. Prahalad concluded that a major determinant of how much a company gains from an alliance is its ability to learn from its alliance partner.[11] They focused on a number of alliances between Japanese companies and Western (European or American) partners. In every case in which a Japanese company emerged from an alliance stronger than its Western partner, the Japanese company had made a greater effort to *learn*. Indeed, few Western companies studied seemed to *want* to learn from their Japanese partners. They tended to regard the alliance purely as a cost-sharing or risk-sharing device, rather than as an opportunity to learn how a potential competitor does business.

For example, consider the alliance between General Motors and Toyota to build the Chevrolet Nova constituted in 1985 and still operating today. This alliance is structured as a formal joint venture, called *New United Motor Manufacturing, Inc.*, and each party has a 50 percent equity stake. The venture owns an auto plant in Fremont, California. According to one of the Japanese managers, Toyota quickly achieved most of its objectives from the alliance: "We learned about U.S. supply and transportation. And we got the confidence to manage U.S. workers."[12] All that knowledge was then quickly transferred to Georgetown, Kentucky, where Toyota opened a plant of its own in 1988. On the other hand, it may be that all GM got was a new product, the Chevrolet Nova. Some GM managers complained that the knowledge they gained through the alliance with Toyota has never been put to good use inside GM. They believe they should have been kept together as a team to educate GM's engineers and workers about the Japanese system. Instead, they have been dispersed to various GM subsidiaries.[13]

To maximize the learning benefits of an alliance, a firm must *try* to learn from its partner and then apply the knowledge within its own organization. It has been suggested that all operating employees should be well briefed on the partner's strengths and weaknesses and should understand how acquiring particular skills will bolster their firm's competitive position. Hamel, Doz, and Prahalad note that this is already standard practice among Japanese companies. For example, they made this observation:

> We accompanied a Japanese development engineer on a tour through a partner's factory. This engineer dutifully took notes on plant layout, the number of production stages, the rate at which the line was running, and the number of employees. He recorded all this despite the fact that he had no manufacturing responsibility in his own company, and that the alliance did not encompass joint manufacturing. Such dedication greatly enhances learning.[14]

For such learning to be of value, it must be diffused throughout the organization (as was seemingly not the case at GM following the GM–Toyota joint venture). To achieve this, the managers involved in the alliance should be explicitly used to educate their colleagues in the firm about the skills of the alliance partner.

---

[11] Hamel, Doz, and Prahalad, "Collaborate with Competitors."

[12] B. Wysocki, "Cross-Border Alliances Become Favorite Way to Crack New Markets," *The Wall Street Journal*, March 4, 1990, p. A1.

[13] Ibid.

[14] Hamel, Doz, and Prahalad, "Collaborate with Competitors."

SUMMARY OF CHAPTER

This chapter has been concerned with two related topics: the optimal choice of entry mode to serve a foreign market and the issue of strategic alliances. The two topics are related in that several entry modes (e.g., licensing and joint ventures) are strategic alliances. Most strategic alliances, however, involve more than just issues of market access. More specifically, the following points have been made in this chapter:

1. There are six ways of entering a foreign market: exporting, turnkey projects, licensing, franchising, joint venturing, and setting up a wholly owned subsidiary.
2. Exporting has the advantages of facilitating the realization of experience curve economies and of avoiding the costs of setting up manufacturing operations in another country. Disadvantages include high transport costs and trade barriers and problems with local marketing agents. The latter can be overcome if the firm sets up a wholly owned marketing subsidiary in the host country.
3. Turnkey projects allow firms to export their process know-how to countries where FDI might be prohibited, thereby enabling the firm to earn a greater return from this asset. The disadvantage is that the firm may inadvertently create efficient global competitors in the process.
4. The main advantage of licensing is that the licensee bears the costs and risks of opening up a foreign market. Disadvantages include the risk of losing technological know-how to the licensee and a lack of tight control over licensees (which may be required for realizing location and experience curve economies).
5. The main advantage of franchising is that the franchisee bears the costs and risks of opening up a foreign market. Disadvantages center on problems of quality control of distant franchisees.
6. Joint ventures have the advantages of sharing the costs and risks of opening up a foreign market and of gaining local knowledge and political influence. Disadvantages include the risk of losing control over technology and a lack of tight control (which may be required for realizing location and experience curve economies).
7. The advantages of wholly owned subsidiaries include tight control over operations (which is consistent with realizing location and experience curve economies) and tight control over technological know-how. The main disadvantage is that the firm must bear all of the costs and risks of opening up a foreign market.
8. The optimal choice of entry mode depends on the strategy of the firm.
9. When technological know-how constitutes a firm's core competence, wholly owned subsidiaries are preferred, since they best control technology.
10. When management know-how constitutes a firm's core competence, foreign franchises controlled by joint ventures seem to be optimal. This gives the firm the cost and risk benefits associated with franchising, while enabling it to monitor and control franchisee quality effectively.
11. When the firm is pursuing a global or transnational strategy, the need for tight control over operations in order to realize location and experience curve economies suggests wholly owned subsidiaries as the best entry mode.
12. Strategic alliances are cooperative agreements between actual or potential competitors.
13. The advantage of alliances are that they facilitate entry into foreign markets, enable partners to share the fixed costs and risks associated with new products and processes, facilitate the transfer of complementary skills between companies, and can help firms establish technical standards.
14. The disadvantage of a strategic alliance is that the firm risks giving away technological know-how and market access to its alliance partner in return for very little.
15. The disadvantages associated with alliances can be reduced if the firm selects partners carefully, paying close attention to the issue of reputation.
16. The disadvantages associated with alliances can also be reduced if the firm structures the alliance so as to avoid unintended transfers of know-how. This can be done by walling off sensitive technologies, by writing safeguards into the alliance agreements, by agreeing in advance to engage in reciprocal swaps of technological know-how, and by seeking credible commitments from alliance partners.
17. Two of the keys to making alliances work seem to be (*i*) building trust and informal communications networks between partners and (*ii*) taking proactive steps to learn from alliance partners.

DISCUSSION QUESTIONS

1. Licensing proprietary technology to foreign competitors is the best way to give up a firm's competitive advantage. Discuss.
2. What kind of companies stand to gain the most from entering into strategic alliances with potential competitors? Why?
3. Discuss how the need for control over foreign operations varies with firms' strategies and core competencies. What are the implications for the choice of entry mode?
4. A small Canadian firm that has developed some valuable new medical products using its unique biotechnology know-how is trying to decide how best to serve the European Community market. Its choices are

   a. Manufacture the product at home and let foreign sales agents handle marketing.

   b. Manufacture the products at home and set up a wholly owned subsidiary in Europe to handle marketing.

   c. Enter into a strategic alliance with a large European pharmaceutical firm. The product would be manufactured in Europe by the 50/50 joint venture and marketed by the European firm.

   The cost of investment in manufacturing facilities will be a major one for the Canadian firm, but it is not outside its reach. If these are the firm's only options, which one would you advise it to choose? Why?

Philips NV

Established in 1891, the Dutch company Philips NV is one of the world's largest electronics enterprises. Its businesses are grouped into four main divisions: lighting, consumer electronics, professional products (computers, telecommunications, and medical equipment), and components (including chips). In each of these areas it ranks alongside the likes of Matsushita, General Electric, Sony, and Siemens as a global competitor. By the late 1980s the company had several hundred subsidiaries in 60 countries, operated manufacturing plants in more than 40 countries, employed approximately 300,000 people, and manufactured thousands of products. Despite this global reach, however, Philips was a company in deep trouble by 1990. After a decade of deteriorating performance, Philips lost $2.2 billion on revenues of $28 billion that year. A major reason for this seems to have been Philips' inability to adapt to the changing competitive conditions in the global electronics industry during the 1970s and 80s.

TRADITIONAL ORGANIZATION

To trace the roots of Philips' current troubles, we must go back to World War II. Until World War II the foreign activities of Philips had been managed from its head office in Eindhoven, the Netherlands. However, the Netherlands were occupied by Germany during the war, and cut off from their home base, Philips' various national organizations began to operate independently. In essence, each major national organization developed into a self-contained company with its own manufacturing, marketing, and R&D functions.

Following the war, top management believed the company could be most successfully rebuilt through its national organizations. There were several reasons for this. First, high trade barriers made it logical that self-contained national organizations should be established in each major national market. Second, it was felt that strong national organizations allowed Philips to be responsive to local demands in each country in which it competed. And third, given the substantial autonomy that the various national organizations had gained during the war, top management felt that reestablishing centralized control might prove difficult and yield few benefits.

At the same time, top management felt the need for some centralized control over product policy and R&D to achieve some coordination among the national organizations. Its response was to create a number of worldwide product divisions (of which there were 14 by the mid-1980s). In theory, basic R&D and product development policy were the responsibility of the product divisions, whereas the national organizations were responsible for day-to-day operations in their particular countries. Product strategy in a given country was meant to be determined jointly by consultation between the responsible national organization and the product divisions. The national organizations implemented strategy.

Another feature of Philips' organization was duumvirate leadership. In most national organizations, top-management responsibilities and authority were shared by two managers—one responsible for "commercial affairs" and the other for "technical activities."

Source: Charles W. L. Hill.

This form of management had its origins with the company's founders, Anton and Gerard Philips. Anton was a salesman, and Gerard an engineer. Throughout the company there seemed to be vigorous informal competition between technical managers and sales managers, each attempting to outperform the other. As Anton once noted,

> the technical management and the sales management competed to outperform each other. Production tried to produce so much that sales would not be able to get rid of it; sales tried to sell so much that the factory would not be able to keep up.[1]

The top decision-making and policy-making body in the company was a 10-person board of management. Although the board members shared general management responsibility, they typically maintained a special interest in one of the functional areas of the company (e.g., R&D, manufacturing, marketing). Traditionally, most of the members of this board were Dutchmen who had come up through the Eindhoven bureaucracy, although most had extensive foreign postings, typically as a top manager of one of the company's national organizations.

ENVIRONMENTAL CHANGE

From the 1960s onward a number of significant changes occurred in Philips' competitive environment that would profoundly affect the company. First, due to the efforts of the General Agreement on Tariffs and Trade (GATT), trade barriers fell worldwide. In addition, in Philips' home base, Europe, the emergence of the European Economic Community, of which the Netherlands was an early member, led to a further reduction in trade barriers between the countries of Western Europe.

Second, during the 1960s and 70s a number of new competitors emerged in Japan. Taking advantage of GATT's success in lowering trade barriers, the Japanese companies produced most of their output at home and exported it to the rest of the world. The resulting economies of scale allowed them to reduce unit costs to below those achieved by Western competitors (such as Philips) that manufactured in multiple locations. This significantly increased competitive pressures in most of the business areas in which Philips competed.

Third, due to technological changes, the costs of R&D and manufacturing increased rapidly. The introduction of transistors and then integrated circuits called for significant capital expenditures in production facilities—many of them running into hundreds of millions of dollars. To realize scale economies, substantial levels of output had to be achieved. Moreover, the pace of technological change was declining, and product life cycles were shortening. This gave companies in the electronics industry less time to recoup their capital investments before the next generation of products came along.

Finally, as the world moved from a series of fragmented national markets toward a single global market, uniform global standards for electronic equipment began to emerge. This showed itself most clearly in the videocassette recorder business, where three standards initially battled for dominance: the Betamax standard produced by Sony, the VHS standard produced by Matsushita, and Philips's V2000 standard. Ultimately, the VHS standard was most widely accepted by consumers, and the others were abandoned.

---

[1] *The Philips Group: 1987,* Harvard Business School case 388-050.

For Philips and Sony, both of which had invested substantially in their own standard, this was a significant defeat. Philips' attempt to establish its V2000 format as an industry standard was effectively killed off by the decision of its own North American national organization, over Eindhoven's objections, to manufacture according to the VHS standard.

ORGANIZATIONAL AND STRATEGIC RESPONSES

By the early 1980s Philips realized that if it was to survive, it was going to have to radically restructure its business. Its high cost structure was due to the amount of duplication across national organizations, particularly in the area of manufacturing. Moreover, as the V2000 incident demonstrated, the company's attempts to compete effectively were being hindered by the strength and autonomy of its national organizations.

The first attempt at change came in 1982, when Wisse Dekker was appointed CEO. Dekker quickly pushed for manufacturing rationalization, creating international production centers that served a number of national organizations, and closing many small, inefficient plants. He also pushed Philips to enter into more collaborative alliances with other electronics firms to share the costs and risks of developing new products. In addition, Dekker accelerated the movement away from dual leadership in national organizations (commercial and technical), replacing it with a single general managership. Furthermore, Dekker tried to "tilt" Philips' matrix away from national organizations by creating a corporate council where the heads of product divisions would join the heads of the national organizations to discuss issues of importance to both. At the same time, he gave the product divisions more responsibility to determine companywide research and manufacturing activities.

In 1986 Dekker was succeeded by Cor van de Klugt. One of van de Klugt's first actions was to specify that profitability would be the central criteria for evaluating performance in the firm. The product divisions were given primary responsibility for achieving profits. This was followed in late 1986 by his termination of the American Trust, the "subcorporation" that had been given control of North American operations during World War II and still held it as of 1986. By terminating the trust, van de Klugt in theory reestablished Eindhoven's control over its North American subsidiaries. Then, in May 1987, van de Klugt announced a major restructuring. He designated four production divisions—lighting, consumer electronics, components, and telecommunications and data systems—as "core divisions," the implication being that other activities would be sold off. At the same time he reduced the size of the management board. Its policy-making responsibility was devolved to a new group management committee comprising the remaining board members plus the heads of the core product divisions. No heads of national organizations were appointed to this body, thereby further tilting power away from the national organizations and toward the product divisions.

Despite these changes, Philips' competitive position continued to deteriorate. Many outside observers attributed this to the huge head office bureaucracy at Eindhoven (comprising more than 3,000 employees in 1989). They argued that although van de Klugt had changed the organizational chart, much of the change was superficial. Real power, they argued, still lay with the Eindhoven bureaucracy and their allies in the national organizations. In support, they pointed out that Philips' work force had declined by less than 10 percent since 1986, far from the 30 percent reduction many analysts were calling for.

Alarmed by a 1989 loss of $1.06 billion, the board forced van de Klugt to resign in May 1990. He was replaced by Jan Timmer. Timmer quickly announced that he would cut Philips' worldwide work force by 10,000 to 283,000 and launch a $1.4 billion restructuring. Investors were unimpressed—many of them thinking the company should cut four or five times as many jobs—and reacted by knocking down the share price by 7 percent. Since then, however, Timmer has made some progress. In mid-1991 he sold off Philips' minicomputer division—which at the time was losing $1 million per day—to Digital Equipment. He also announced plans to reduce costs by $1.2 billion by cutting the work force by 55,000. In addition, he entered into a strategic alliance with Matsushita, the Japanese electronic giant, to manufacture and market the digital compact cassette (DCC). Developed by Philips and scheduled for introduction in late 1992, the DCC reproduces the sound of a compact disc on a tape. The DCC's great selling point is that users will be able to play their old analog tape cassettes on the new system. The DCC's chief rival is Sony's portable compact disc system, the "mini-disc." Many observers expect a replay of the classic battle between the VHS and Betamax videorecorder standards in the coming battle between the DCC and the mini-disc. If the DCC wins, it could be the remaking of Philips.

DISCUSSION QUESTIONS

1. What were the drawbacks of Philips' post-World War II organization?
2. What international strategy was Philips pursuing in the 1960s? What strategy *should* it have been pursuing?
3. Why did Dekker and van de Klugt try to tilt Philips' matrix away from the national organizations and toward the product divisions?
4. Identify the forces opposed to change at Philips.
5. Was it a good move for Philips to ally itself with Matsushita to manufacture and market the DCC? Wouldn't it have been better to go it alone?

SOURCES

Aguilar, F. J., and M. Y. Yoshino. *The Philips Group: 1987.* Harvard Business School case 388-050.

Bartlett, C. A., and S. Ghoshal. *Managing across Borders: The Transnational Solution* (Boston, Mass.: Harvard Business School Press, 1989).

Kapstein, J. and J. Levine, "A Would-Be World Beater Takes a Beating." *Business Week,* July 16, 1990, pp. 41–42.

Levine, J. "Philips' Big Gamble." *Business Week,* August 5, 1991, pp. 34–36.

"Philips Fights the Flab." *The Economist.* April 7, 1992, pp. 73–24.

Honda Motor Company

Established in 1948 to manufacture motorcycles, Honda Motor Company has grown into a corporation with $25 billion annual sales worldwide. It is now the 10th-largest automobile company in the world. In 1990 Honda held a 4 percent share of the global market for automobiles. Despite its success, Honda has always been viewed as something of a newcomer in Japan; unlike the other major Japanese automobile companies, it was

---

Source: Charles W. L. Hill and Maria Gonzalez.

not established until after World War II. Hence, it lacked the extensive contacts with other companies that Nissan and Toyota, who were associated with Japan's prewar *zibatsu* (business groups), enjoyed. Honda did not enter the automobile business itself until the 1960s, and then it was over the objections of Japan's powerful Ministry of Trade and Industry (MITI). MITI did not want to see another competitor in what it perceived to be an already very competitive domestic automobile market. Consequently, MITI tried hard to dissuade Honda from entering the business but to no avail. However, MITI's resistance meant that among other things, Honda had little official support for setting up an export network.

Another problem confronting Honda was the strong competition it faced at home. Marketing muscle and control over distribution systems are very important in Japan. As an upstart outsider, Honda found it difficult to break into the well-established distribution system. Most auto dealers in Japan have an exclusive arrangement with a single automobile company. Few dealers were willing to carry Honda cars lest they bring down the wrath of their existing supplier—Toyota, Nissan, or one of the other established automobile companies. Thus, the only way for Honda to build a distribution network in Japan was to buy land and build new outlets, which proved costly, particularly in urban Japan where land is very expensive. Consequently, Honda realized that its growth potential in Japan was limited, and so it turned its attention overseas. So successful was this strategy that by 1990 more than 60 percent of its total sales were made outside Japan. In addition to its Japanese facilities, Honda had 77 manufacturing plants in 40 countries outside of Japan by that time.

HONDA'S INTERNATIONAL EXPANSION

Honda's initial expansion overseas was in motorcycle sales, not automobiles. Honda first expanded into nearby Asian markets and then in the 1960s into the United States and Europe. In 1962 Honda established a facility to manufacture mopeds in Belgium for sale in the European market. This was the first major direct investment by a Japanese company in manufacturing facilities in an advanced industrialized nation. The Belgian experience was to provide many valuable lessons for Honda.

A number of factors underlay Honda's decision to manufacture mopeds in Belgium: the European market was very large (accounting for 85 percent of the world's non-Japanese motorcycle ownership in 1960); Honda was confident that it could manage European employees; and Honda believed it had a good product that would sell well in Europe. Actually, it took more than a decade for the Belgian venture to show a profit. Among the many problems Honda encountered were these:

- Its mopeds did not match the needs of Europeans, so demand was low.
- It had put too much distinctive design and technology into the moped, and thus local manufacturers were unable to supply parts of the right specifications.
- A series of misunderstandings between management and labor led to a rash of industrial disputes.

After this experience, Honda concluded that if it was going to establish manufacturing facilities overseas, it needed to localize the product so it was consistent with local demand and supply conditions, and it needed to develop a much better understanding of the local management practices and social conditions.

In the mid-1970s Honda began to think seriously about further major investments in industrialized countries. By this time, the company had made significant inroads into the U.S. automobile and motorcycle markets by exporting from Japan, so the United States

Honda's North American Automobile Plants, 1991

Location	Opened	Annual Capacity
Marysville, Ohio	1982	360,000
Alliston, Ontario	1987	80,000
East Liberty, Ohio	1989	150,000

seemed the natural choice. In addition, Honda saw the establishment of U.S. manufacturing facilities as a hedge against a rise in the value of the yen and any future trade disputes between Japan and the United States. (As it turned out, in the early 1980s the Japanese automobile companies agreed to abide to voluntary restraints on imports into the United States.)

Honda's first major U.S. investment was a motorcycle plant in Ohio, where production began in 1979. Over the next decade this was followed by the establishment of two automobile plants and an engine plant, all in Ohio. During this period Honda also established an automobile plant in Ontario, Canada, and by 1991, Honda had the capacity to produce close to 600,000 cars a year in North America. In total, by 1992 Honda had invested more than $3 billion in U.S. manufacturing facilities and had created more than 11,000 jobs in the Ohio region and 3,000 elsewhere in the United States. Of the 659,659 cars that Honda sold in the United States in 1991, 401,195 were built in North America. In 1990 its North American-manufactured cars helped Honda overtake Chrysler and become the number-three passenger car company in the United States with a market share 9.22 percent. In 1991 the Honda Accord, which is manufactured in Ohio, was the best-selling passenger car model in North America. Honda claims its American-built cars have a domestic content of 75 percent; that is, three quarters of the sticker price goes for U.S. labor, components, and other costs. In 1987 Honda began exporting Accords and Acuras from Ohio to Japan, and by 1991, 14,500 U.S.-built Hondas were sent to Japan. (GM exported 5,600 autos to Japan that year, and Ford only 1,100 autos.) Overall, in 1991 Honda of America exported 27,000 vehicles to 10 countries, including Japan, Israel, and 6 European nations. Honda's plans call for the company to export 40,000 cars per year from the United States by the end of 1992. In addition to car exports, Honda's Marysville plant exported 24 percent of the 55,000 motorcycles it produced in 1991.

Aside from its North American operations, Honda has made substantial investments in Europe in recent years—most notably in Great Britain, where it is building a facility with the capacity to produce 100,000 autos per year. This is scheduled to open in 1994. Like Toyota and Nissan, which are also building facilities there, Honda views Great Britain as a convenient site from which to serve the European Community market.

HONDA'S STRATEGY

Localization

Honda claims its strategy for operating overseas consists of four target concepts: localization of products, profit, production, and management.

Localization of products means developing, manufacturing, and marketing products best suited to the demands of local consumers. Honda sees subtle but important differences between countries in the way a product is used and what consumers expect of it. To localize products so they appeal to local consumers' tastes and preferences, Honda has invested in R&D centers in North America, Europe, and Southeast Asia. These centers do not just customize products designed in Japan; they take the lead in designing products for their local market. For example, the Acura was designed in the United States for sale in the U.S. market. Similarly, the new Honda Accord Wagon was designed, developed, and engineered in California and Ohio and is being built exclusively in the United States.

Localization of profits means reinvesting profits earned in a country *in* that country. This is clearly seen in the case of Honda's North American operations, with profits being used to finance the expansion of North American-based production capacity. It is not clear, however, if the company has pursued this practice elsewhere.

Localization of production means establishing significant production centers in each major market (country or region) where Honda does businesses. Honda stresses that when it talks about local production, it does not mean "screwdriver plants" that simply assemble parts manufactured in another country. Rather, Honda claims, it strives to increase the ratio of local content in its locally manufactured cars over time. In part, the rationale for localizing production is to provide some protection against currency fluctuations and trade barriers.

Localization of management means a number of things. First, it means local people should play a major role in the management of foreign subsidiaries. In the United States, for example, Honda's operations are headed by an American. Second, it means local managers and employees should have a good understanding of Honda's corporate philosophy. And third, it means managers dispatched from Honda's head office (in Japan) should become part of the local community by understanding local culture and ways of thinking.

Policies for Manufacturing outside of Japan

When establishing manufacturing facilities outside of Japan, Honda attaches particular importance to three policies. The first policy is to establish good human relations between the management and the work force. Management encourages employees to communicate problems directly to them. The management staff wear the same white work clothing and eat in the same cafeteria as other employees do. The second policy is to maintain and promote harmony with the local community by getting involved in local activities and helping to build the local community infrastructure. The third policy is to give top priority to maintaining high product quality. This calls for designing products that are easy to assemble, transferring the best production equipment and quality-control practices from its Japanese plants to its foreign operations, and building a strong commitment to quality control among all employees. To achieve the last goal Honda engages in substantial on-the-job training in production techniques, product design, quality control, and the like.

EMERGING TRADE TENSIONS

Despite its substantial investments in Ohio, Honda has recently run headlong into a potentially serious dispute with the U.S. Customs Service. In 1992 Customs researchers argued that Honda was overstating the local content of the cars it built in Ohio. At the heart of the dispute lies the claim that Honda cars are mostly a collection of Japanese parts handled by Americans but designed, engineered, and fabricated in Japan. Take Honda's Civic as an example. Honda claims that its Civics, built in Ohio, have 75 percent U.S. content. However, a study by the University of Michigan concluded that only 16 percent of the 1989 Civic parts were made by U.S.-owned suppliers based in the United States. Adding 20 percent to this figure for local labor costs, depreciation, and

What Went into a 1989 Honda Civic?

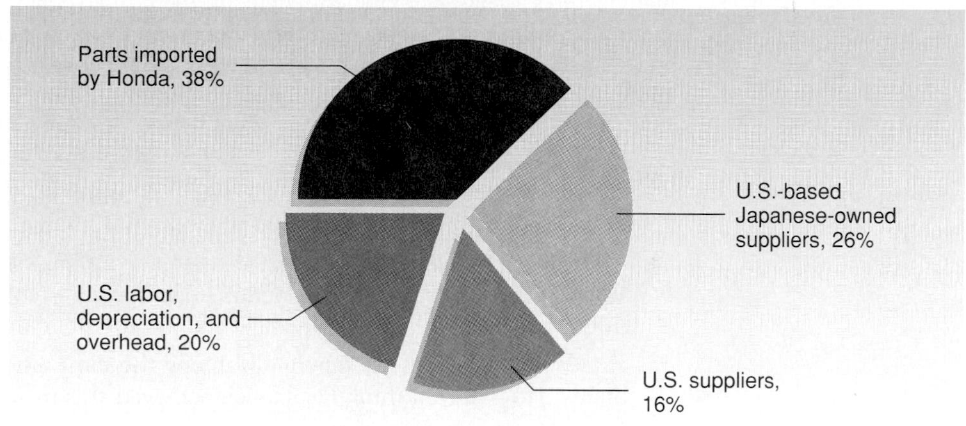

overhead suggests that, in total, only 36 percent of the content of the Civics is "local content." However, the University of Michigan does not regard parts produced in the United States by Japanese-owned suppliers as local content. If these are added to the calculation of local content, then the Civic might be argued to have 62 percent U.S. content—considerably more than the 36 percent claimed by the University of Michigan study, but still less than the 75 percent claimed by Honda.

The U.S. Customs Service has also criticized Honda for overstating the U.S. content of the engines produced at its Anna, Ohio, plant. According to Customs, 58 percent of the parts that go into these engines are imported by Honda (primarily from Japan), 37 percent are produced by Japanese-owned U.S.-based suppliers, and 5 percent are produced by U.S.-owned U.S.-based suppliers. On this basis, according to Customs, at most only 42 percent of the Anna engines can be considered U.S. content, and 5 percent would be a better figure. Yet when Honda ships engines to its assembly plant in Alliston, Ontario, the company claims that the U.S. content of the engines is more than 50 percent. According to the North American Free Trade Agreement, parts with more than 50 percent local content are reclassified as 100 percent North American when they cross the border. The engines are then placed into cars assembled in Ontario, which are then shipped back into the United States for resale. On the basis of the classification of the engine as 100 percent North American, Honda claims that the cars shipped from Canada are 75 percent North American. As such, they escape the imposition of import duties. It is this 75 percent figure, established on the basis of misleading statements about the U.S. content of Anna engines, that the Customs Service is challenging. According to Customs, Honda owes $20 million in import duties on cars shipped from Ontario to the United States since 1986.

Honda's response is to point out that the U.S. Customs Service is ignoring the input of local labor, depreciation, and overhead in the Anna engines. When this is added in, the total figure for U.S. content is over 50 percent. Honda also points out that U.S. Customs has not yet adopted rules for calculating local origin—a point the Customs Service acknowledges. Thus, according to Honda, there is nothing to say that they can't count labor inputs and parts supplied by U.S.-based Japanese suppliers as being of U.S. origin. Moreover, Honda notes it is ironic that the Customs Service has chosen to focus on an engine it is producing in Ohio at a time when Chrysler, GM, and Ford are all importing small engines for their cars. Honda is, in fact, the only auto maker that manufactures a small fuel-efficient engine in the United States. Honda also argues that it spent $2.9 billion purchasing parts from more than 240 American parts suppliers in 1992, and that its plans are to purchase $5 billion of parts per year from American suppliers by 1995.

DISCUSSION QUESTIONS

1. In terms of the strategies discussed in Chapter 12, what kind of strategy is Honda pursuing? What are the benefits of its strategy? What are the costs?
2. What is the reasoning behind Honda's decision to establish production facilities in the United States?
3. Honda's Ohio plants are reportedly among the most efficient in the United States. How do you think has Honda achieved this in such a short time?
4. Is the Honda Civic an American car? Is it more or less "American" than the Pontiac Le Mans, which, although designed in the United States, is built by Dawoo Motors of Korea, largely of parts manufactured in Southeast Asia?
5. Should parts produced in the United States by Japanese-owned suppliers be counted as "U.S. content"?
6. Does Honda's presence in Ohio benefit the U.S. economy?
7. Do you think the Customs Service was correct to focus attention on Honda?

REFERENCES

Honda in America. Company publication, Honda of America, Ohio. 1992.

Ingrassia, P., and C. Chandler. "Japan's Car Makers Now See Advantages in Restraining Growth." *The Wall Street Journal,* January 7, 1992, pp. 1, 6.

Magnusson, P.; J. B. Treece; and W. C. Symonds. "Honda: Is It an American Car?" *Business Week,* November 18, 1991, pp. 105–12.

Mair, A.; R. Florida; and M. Kenney. "The New Geography of Automobile Production: Japanese Transplants in North America." *Economic Geography* 64, pp. 352–73.

Patterson, G. A. "Domestic? Car Firms Play Games with the Categories." *The Wall Street Journal,* November 11, 1991, p. A1.

Reich, R. "The Myth of Made in the USA." *The Wall Street Journal,* July 5, 1991, p. A6.

Sugiura, H. "How Honda Localizes Its Global Strategy." *Sloan Management Review,* Fall 1990, pp. 77–82.

"Taking Root and Blooming." *The Economist,* April 15, 1992, p. 79.

Toy, S.; N. Gross; and J. B. Treece. "The Americanization of Honda." *Business Week,* April 25, 1992, pp. 90–96.

Whitlock, S. N. "Of Honda and the Japanese Presence in America." *Business Week,* December 16, 1991, p. 7.

PART SIX

Business Operations

Exporting, Importing, and Countertrade

CHAPTER 15

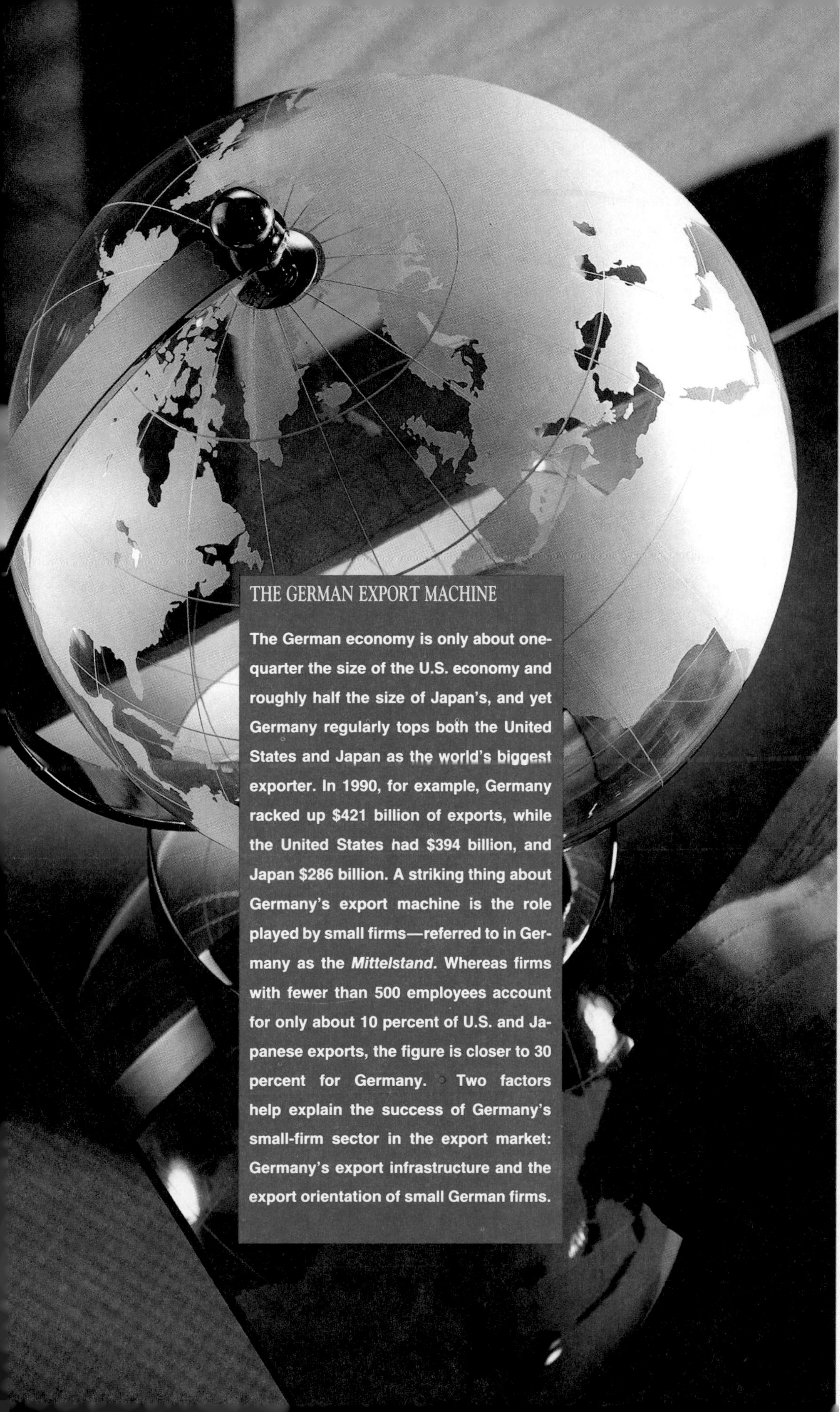

THE GERMAN EXPORT MACHINE

The German economy is only about one-quarter the size of the U.S. economy and roughly half the size of Japan's, and yet Germany regularly tops both the United States and Japan as the world's biggest exporter. In 1990, for example, Germany racked up $421 billion of exports, while the United States had $394 billion, and Japan $286 billion. A striking thing about Germany's export machine is the role played by small firms—referred to in Germany as the *Mittelstand.* Whereas firms with fewer than 500 employees account for only about 10 percent of U.S. and Japanese exports, the figure is closer to 30 percent for Germany. Two factors help explain the success of Germany's small-firm sector in the export market: Germany's export infrastructure and the export orientation of small German firms.

With regard to infrastructure, Germany's export network is perhaps second to none. German embassies, banks, trade associations, and chambers of commerce in dozens of countries serve as foreign eyes and ears for small businesses. They systematically funnel details of export opportunities to small German firms via newsletters, databases, and trade associations. Once an opportunity has been identified, trade associations, export trading companies, and banks all offer small firms extensive assistance with translation services and the documentation required to export. For example, industry associations provide standard contracts in many languages and translation and legal assistance with foreign contracts at no charge to members. They also allow German firms to use their foreign offices and secretarial services free of charge when negotiating deals. For financing export deals, German firms can turn to a banking system that is well attuned to their needs. Specialized banks and Mittelstand departments of large banks provide export financing and arrange for credit and political-risk insurance. • This is in stark contrast to the U.S. export infrastructure; it is characterized by a lack of coordination among dozens of competing and often poorly staffed federal, state, and local agencies. Consider Benton Corporation, a Pittsburgh manufacturer of navigational testing devices with revenues of about $4 million per year. Ron Ekas, Benton's international marketing manager, sought information as to how to export the firm's products and was given a list of potential distributors by the Pittsburgh office of the U.S. Department of Commerce. His subsequent quest for working capital to finance an export deal took him from Duquesne University to the Small Business Administration, from the Pennsylvania Commerce Department to the Export–Import Bank, and back again. Ekas says he "got right in the middle of a big loop. Everyone sent me to other places to look for help." • The U.S. infrastructure has suffered from poor funding. The state of Illinois, which once boasted one of the country's most successful export agencies, cut funding for its export agencies by 22 percent in 1992 because of state budget problems. Similarly, government funding of the 18 federal agencies that help promote U.S. exports has not kept pace with inflation in recent years. • Perhaps more important than infrastructure in explaining Germany's success, however, is the export orientation of German firms. Unlike the United States, with its largely self-contained, continental economy, Germany sits at the center of the patchwork of countries that make up Europe. Proximity to these foreign markets fosters an awareness of export opportunities. This orientation is further strengthened by the movement of the European Community toward closer economic integration. At the same time, small German firms have become adept at global niche marketing, at customizing their products to the needs of foreign customers, and at staying on the cutting edge of technology. • For example, consider Wilhelm Zuleeg, a German textile firm with annual revenues of $18 million. This firm competes profitably in an industry dominated by low-cost Asian imports and managed to increase its exports from 0 percent to 25 percent of revenues in three years. The explanation for this success can be seen in Zuleeg's technological prowess; its state-of-the-art computer-controlled factory churns out textile products with a minimum of labor input. The largely automated factory has only 85 employees—compared to several hundred in a more traditionally run enterprise. An example of global niche marketing is provided by the Munich firm Panther, which makes computer-controlled camera operator's chairs for use in the film industry. These chairs give photographers the ability to program the chair's movement. Started in 1987, the firm had 50 percent of the European market and 10 percent of the U.S. market by 1991. As a final example, consider G. W. Barth, a Ludwigsburg-based manufacturer of cocoa bean roasting machinery that employs just 65 people. During the 1980s Barth invested $1.8 million on complex new technology designed to boost the yields and fine-tune the temperature controls of its machinery. This small company had captured 70 percent of the global market for such machines by 1991, up from 25 percent in 1981. *Sources: W. J. Holstein and K. Kelly, "Little Companies, Big Exports,"* Business Week, *April 13, 1992, pp. 70–72; W. J. Holstein, "Why Johann Can Export, but Johnny Can't,"* Business Week, *November 4, 1991, pp. 64–65; G. E. Schares et al., "Think Small,"* Business Week, *November 4, 1991, pp. 58–65; and R. A. Mosbacher, "Opening Export Doors for Smaller Firms,"* Seattle Times, *July 24, 1991, p. A7.*

INTRODUCTION

In the previous chapter we reviewed exporting from a strategic perspective. We considered exporting as just one of a range of strategic options for profiting from international expansion. In this chapter we are more concerned with the "nuts and bolts" of exporting (and importing). We take the choice of strategy as a given and look instead at "how to export."

As seen in the opening case, one problem smaller U.S. firms face when considering exporting is that the United States does not have an export network comparable to that of Germany, where smaller firms play such a large role in the export market. German firms wishing to export are guided through the process by government agencies, banks, and trade associations, all of whom work together to coordinate their efforts. In the United States, while a number of government agencies do offer assistance to would-be exporters, a lack of coordination between the agencies complicates the process. Although both state and federal governments are trying to rectify this problem, a solution is not yet at hand.[1] As a result, it can be difficult for small U.S. firms to find their way through the maze of problems that confront any first-time exporter. Whereas large multinational enterprises have long been conversant with the steps that must be taken to export successfully, smaller enterprises can find the process quite intimidating.

Among other things, the firm wishing to export must identify foreign market opportunities, familiarize itself with the mechanics of export and import financing, learn where it can get financing and export credit insurance, and learn how it should deal with foreign exchange risk. The whole process is made all the more problematic by the fact that many countries' currencies are not freely convertible. As a result, there is the problem of arranging payment for exports to countries with weak currencies. This brings us to the complex topic of **countertrade,** by which payment for exports is received in goods and services rather than money. In this chapter we will discuss all of these issues with the exception of foreign exchange risk, which was covered in Chapter 9.

Despite the difficulties facing first-time exporters, all of the evidence suggests that smaller U.S. firms have increased their export orientation aggressively in recent years. One reason for this is that exporting has become easier over the years. The gradual decline in trade barriers under the umbrella of GATT, along with regional economic agreements such as the European Community and the North American Free Trade Association, have increased export opportunities. At the same time, the advent of

[1] C. W. Thurston, "U.S. Agency Set to Unveil Plan for Unified Export Strategy," *Journal of Commerce,* November 30, 1991, pp. 1A, 3A.

BOX 15.1

Examples of Small and Medium-Sized U.S. Exporters

Firm	Products	Sales ($ millions)	Exports as Percent of Sales
Molex	Electrical connectors	292	63%
Royal Appliance	Dirt Devil mini vacuum cleaner	273	4
Loctite Corporation	Super Glue	267	47
Invacare	Wheelchairs, home medical equipment	263	10
United Air Specialists	Air cleaners	30	40
Lubricating Systems	Lubricating fluids	6.5	20
Joseph Industries	Lift-truck transmissions	6	10
Midwest Tropical	Aquariums	5.5	25
Life Corporation	Emergency oxygen kits	5	50
Treatment Products	Auto wax	5	25
Sharper Finish	Laundry/ironing equipment	3	60

Note: Sales figures are for last available year, which is 1990 or 1991 in most cases.

Sources: W. J. Holstein, and K. Kelly, "Little Companies, Big Exports," Business Week, *April 13, 1992, pp. 70–72; R. A. Mosbacher, "Opening Export Doors for Smaller Firms,"* Seattle Times, *July 24, 1991, p. 7A; and R. A. King, "You Don't Have to Be a Giant to Score Big Overseas,"* Business Week, *April 13, 1987, pp. 62–63.*

modern communications and transportation technologies have alleviated the logistical problems associated with exporting. Small manufacturers are increasingly using fax machines, international 800 numbers, and international air express services to reduce the costs of exporting. As a consequence, it is no longer unusual to find small U.S. businesses that are thriving as exporters. Some examples are given in Box 15.1.

In the remainder of this chapter we will trace the steps that firms such as those identified in Box 15.1 have taken in establishing themselves as players in export markets. We begin by looking at the problem of identifying export opportunities. Then we switch our attention to the mechanics of export and import financing. This is followed by a review of assistance programs that can help firms finance their export program and insure against the risks associated with exporting. The chapter closes with an examination of countertrade.

IDENTIFYING EXPORT OPPORTUNITIES

One of the biggest impediments to exporting is the simple lack of knowledge of the opportunities available. Oftentimes there are many markets for a firm's product, but because they are in countries separated from the firm's home base by culture, language, distance, and time, the firm does not know of them. The problem of identifying export opportunities is made all the more complex by the fact that 180 countries with widely differing cultures compose the world of potential opportunities. Faced with such complexity and diversity, it is perhaps not surprising that firms sometimes hesitate to proactively seek out export opportunities.

An International Comparison

The way to overcome ignorance is to collect information. In the opening case we saw that German trade associations, government agencies, and commercial banks perform information-gathering functions, helping small firms identify export opportunities. A similar function is provided by the Japanese Ministry of International Trade and Industry (MITI), which is always on the lookout for export opportunities. In addition, many Japanese firms are affiliated in some way with the *sogo shosha,* Japan's great trading houses. The sogo shosha have offices all over the world, and they proactively, continuously seek out export opportunities for their affiliated companies large and small.[2] The great advantage of German and Japanese firms is that they can draw on the large reservoirs of experience, skills, information, and other resources of their respective export-oriented institutions.

Unlike their German and Japanese competitors, many U.S. firms are relatively blind when they seek export opportunities; they are information disadvantaged. In part, this difference reflects historical differences. Both Germany and Japan have long made their living as trading nations, whereas until recently the United States has been a relatively self-contained continental economy in which international trade played a minor role. This is changing; both imports and exports now play a much greater role in the U.S. economy than they did 20 years ago. As yet, however, the United States has not evolved an institutional structure for promoting exports similar to that of either Germany or Japan.

Some Information Sources

Despite this disadvantage, U.S. firms can increase their awareness of export opportunities. The most comprehensive source of information is probably the U.S. Department of Commerce and its district offices all over the country. Within that department are two organizations dedicated to providing businesses with intelligence and assistance for attacking foreign markets: the International Trade Administration and its "sister," the United States and Foreign Commercial Service Agency.

Among other things, these agencies provide the potential exporter with a "Best Prospects" list, which lists the names and addresses of potential distributors in foreign markets along with businesses they are in, the products they handle, and their contact person. In addition, the Department of Commerce has assembled a "Comparison Shopping Service" for 14 countries that are major markets for U.S. exports. (Figure 15.1 shows the eight largest and the eight fastest-growing markets for U.S. exports.) For a small fee, a firm can receive a customized market research survey on a product of its choice. This survey provides information on marketability, the competition, comparative prices, distribution channels, and names of potential sales representatives. Each study is conducted on-site by an officer of the U.S. Department of Commerce.

The Department of Commerce also organizes trade events that help potential exporters make foreign contacts and explore export opportunities. The department organizes exhibitions at international trade fairs, which are held regularly in major cities worldwide. The department also has a "matchmaker' program, in which department representatives accompany groups of U.S. businesspeople abroad to meet with qualified agents, distributors, and customers.

In addition to the Department of Commerce, nearly every state and many large cities maintain active trade commissions whose purpose is to promote exports. Most of these provide business counseling services, information-gathering service, technical assistance, and financing service. Unfortunately, many have fallen victim to budget cuts or to turf battles for political and financial support with other export agencies.

[2] M. Y. Yoshino and T. B. Lifson, *The Invisible Link* (Cambridge, Mass.: MIT Press, 1986).

Figure 15.1a
The Eight Largest Markets for U.S. Exports, 1991 ($ billions)

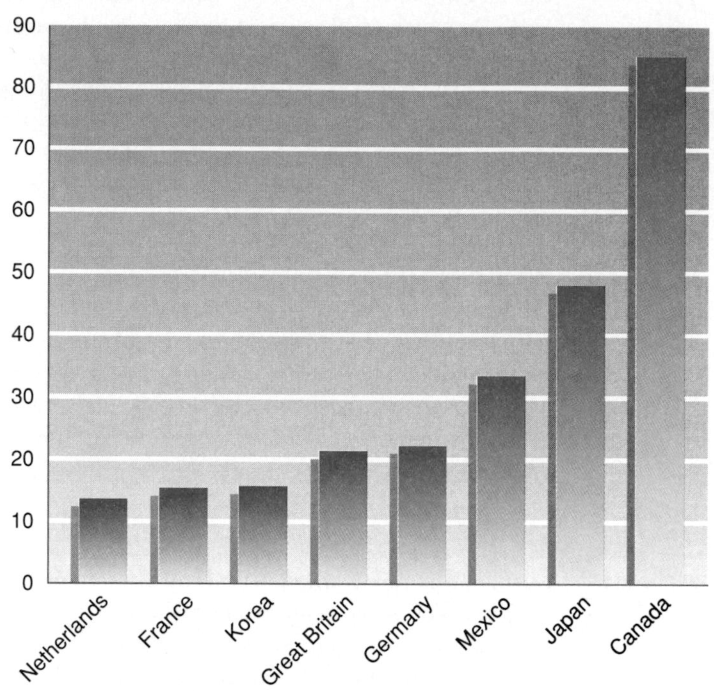

Source: Department of Commerce.

Figure 15.1b
The Eight Fastest-Growing Markets for U.S. Exports, 1986 to 1991

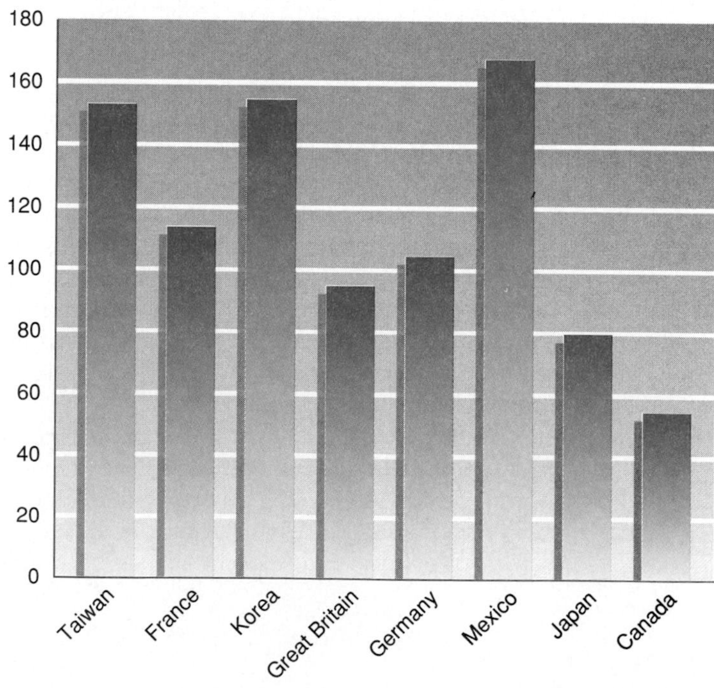

Source: W. J. Holstein and K. Kelly, "Little Companies, Big Exports," Business Week, *April 13, 1992, p. 70.*

A number of private organizations are also beginning to gear up to provide more assistance to would-be exporters. Most significant, commercial banks and major accounting firms are more willing to assist small firms in starting export operations than they were a decade ago. In addition, large multinationals that have been successful in the global arena are typically more than willing to discuss opportunities overseas with the owners or managers of small firms.[3]

EXPORT AND IMPORT FINANCING

Mechanisms for financing exports and imports have evolved over the centuries in response to a problem that can be particularly acute in international trade: the lack of trust that exists when one must put faith in a stranger. In this section we examine the financial devices that have evolved to cope with this problem in the context of international trade: the letter of credit, the draft (or bill of exchange), and the bill of lading. Then we will trace the 14 steps of a typical export-import transaction.

Lack of Trust

Firms engaged in international trade face the problem of having to trust someone they may have never seen, who lives in a different country, who speaks a different language, who abides by (or does not abide by) a different legal system, and who could be very difficult to track down if he or she defaults on an obligation. Consider, for example, a U.S. firm exporting to a distributor in France. The U.S. businessman might be concerned that if he ships the products to France before he receives payment for them from the French businesswoman, she might take delivery of the products and not pay him for them at all. Conversely, the French importer might worry that if she pays for the products before they are shipped, the U.S. firm might keep the money and never ship the products—or might ship defective products. In short, neither party to the exchange completely trusts the other. This lack of trust is exacerbated by the distance between the two parties—in space, language, and culture—and by the problems of using an underdeveloped international legal system to enforce contractual obligations.

Due to the (quite reasonable) lack of trust between the two parties, each has their own preferences as to how they would like the transaction to be configured. To make sure he is paid, the manager of the U.S. firm would prefer the French distributor to pay for the products before he ships them (see figure 15.2). Alternatively, to ensure she receives the products, the French distributor would prefer not to pay for them until they arrive (see Figure 15.3). Thus, each party has an entirely different set of preferences. Unless there is some way of establishing trust between the parties, the transaction might never take place.

The problem is solved by using a third party trusted by both—normally a reputable bank—to act as an intermediary. What happens can be summarized as follows (see Figure 15.4). First, the French importer obtains the bank's promise to pay on her behalf, knowing the U.S. exporter will trust the bank. This promise is known as a **letter of credit.** Having seen the letter of credit, the U.S. exporter now ships the products to France. Title to the products is given, in due course, to the bank in the form of a document called a **bill of lading.** In return, the U.S. exporter tells the bank to pay for the products, which the bank does. The document for requesting this payment is referred to as a **draft.** The bank, having paid for the products, now passes the title on to the French importer, whom the bank trusts. At that time or later, depending on their agreement, the

[3] L. W. Tuller, *Going Global* (Homewood, Ill.: Business One Irwin, 1991).

Figure 15.2
Preference of the U.S. Exporter

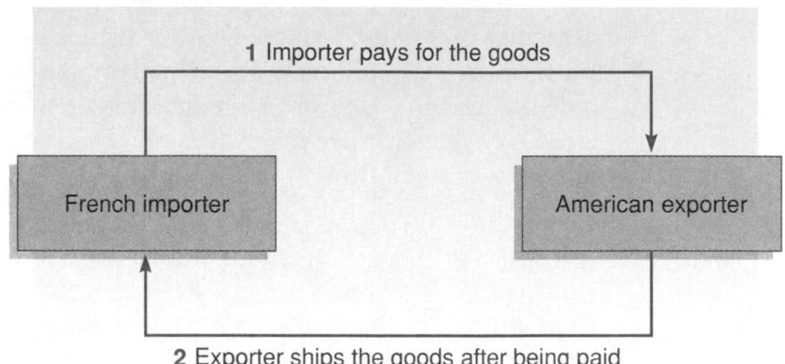

Figure 15.3
Preference of the French Importer

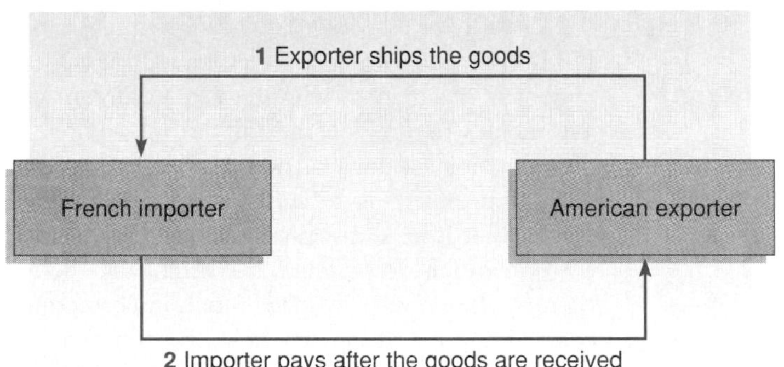

Figure 15.4
The Use of a Third Party

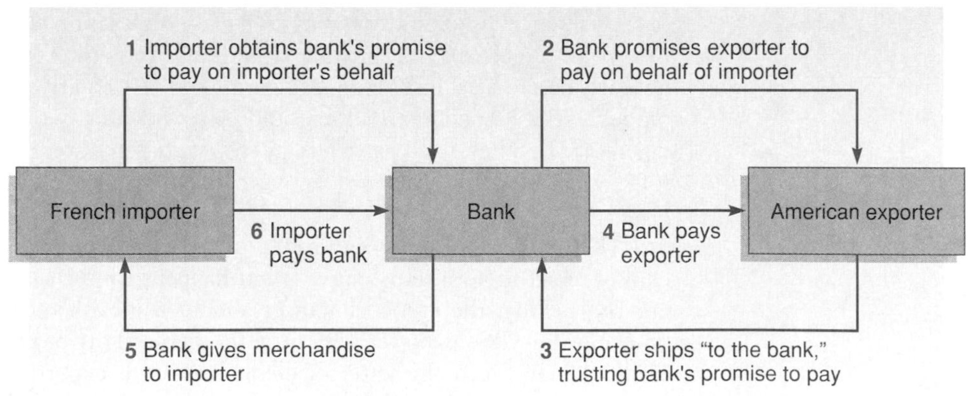

Source: Adapted from Eitman, Stonehill, and Moffett, Multinational Business Finance *(Reading, Mass.: Addison-Wesley, 1991), p. 520.*

importer reimburses the bank. In the remainder of this section, we will examine how this system works in more detail.

Letter of Credit

A letter of credit, abbreviated as *L/C,* stands at the center of international commercial transactions. Issued by a bank at the request of an importer, the letter of credit states that the bank will pay a specified sum of money to a beneficiary, normally the exporter, on presentation of particular, specified documents.

For illustration, consider once again the example of the U.S. exporter and the French importer. The French importer applies to her local bank, let's say the Bank of Paris, for the issuance of a letter of credit. The Bank of Paris then undertakes a credit check of the importer. If the Bank of Paris is satisfied with her creditworthiness, it will issue a letter of credit. However, the Bank of Paris might require a cash deposit or some other form of collateral from her first. In addition, the Bank of Paris will charge the importer a fee for this service. Typically this amounts to between 0.5 percent and 2 percent of the value of the letter of credit, depending on the importer's creditworthiness and the size of the transaction. (As a rule, the larger the transaction, the lower the percentage.)

Let us assume the Bank of Paris is satisfied with the French importer's creditworthiness and agrees to issue a letter of credit. The letter states that the Bank of Paris will pay the U.S. exporter for the merchandise so long as it is shipped in accordance with certain, specified instructions and conditions. At this point the letter of credit becomes a financial contract between the Bank of Paris and the U.S. exporter. The Bank of Paris then sends the letter of credit to the U.S. exporter's bank, let's say the Bank of New York. The Bank of New York tells the exporter that it has received a letter of credit and that he can go ahead and ship the merchandise. After the exporter has shipped the merchandise, he draws a draft against the Bank of Paris in accordance with the terms of the letter of credit, attaches the required documents, and presents the draft to his own bank, the Bank of New York, for payment. The Bank of New York then forwards the letter of credit and associated documents to the Bank of Paris. If all of the terms and conditions contained in the letter of credit have been complied with, the Bank of Paris will honor the draft and will send payment to the Bank of New York. When the Bank of New York receives the funds, it will pay the U.S. exporter.

As for the Bank of Paris, once it has transferred the funds to the Bank of New York, it will collect payment from the French importer. Alternatively, the Bank of Paris may allow the importer some time to resell the merchandise before requiring payment. This is not an unusual practice, particularly when the importer is a distributor and not the final consumer of the merchandise, since it helps the importer's cash flow position. Of course, the Bank of Paris will treat such an extension of the payment period as a loan to the importer and will charge an appropriate rate of interest.

The great advantage of this system is that both the French importer and the U.S. exporter are likely to trust reputable banks, even if they do not trust each other. Once the U.S. exporter has seen a letter of credit, he knows that he is guaranteed payment and will ship the merchandise. Moreover, an exporter may find that having a letter of credit will facilitate obtaining pre-export financing. For example, having seen the letter of credit, the Bank of New York might be willing to lend the exporter funds to process and prepare the merchandise for shipping to France. This loan may not have to be repaid until the exporter has received his payment for the merchandise. As for the French importer, the great advantage of the letter of credit arrangement is that she does not have to pay out funds for the merchandise until the documents have arrived and unless all conditions stated in the letter of credit have been satisfied. The drawback for the importer is the fee she must pay the Bank of Paris for the letter of credit. In addition, since the letter of credit is a financial liability against her, it may reduce her ability to borrow funds for other purposes.

Draft

A draft, sometimes referred to as a **bill of exchange,** is the instrument normally used in international commerce to effect payment. A draft is simply an order written by an exporter instructing an importer, or an importer's agent, to pay a specified amount of money at a specified time. In the example of the U.S. exporter and the French importer, the exporter writes a draft that instructs the Bank of Paris, the French importer's agent, to pay for the merchandise shipped to France. The person or business initiating the draft is known as the **maker** (in this case, the U.S. exporter). The party to whom the draft is presented is known as the **drawee** (in this case, the Bank of Paris).

International practice is to use drafts to settle trade transactions. This differs from domestic practice in which a seller usually ships merchandise on an open account, followed by a commercial *invoice* that specifies the amount due and the terms of payment. In domestic transactions the buyer can often obtain possession of the merchandise without signing a formal document acknowledging his or her obligation to pay. In contrast, due to the lack of trust in international transactions, payment or a formal promise to pay is required before the buyer can obtain the merchandise.

Drafts fall into two categories, sight drafts and time drafts. A **sight draft** is payable on presentation to the drawee. A **time draft** allows for a delay in payment—normally 30, 60, 90, or 120 days. It is presented to the drawee, who signifies acceptance of it by writing or stamping a notice of acceptance on its face. Once accepted, the time draft becomes a promise to pay by the accepting party. When a time draft is drawn on and accepted by a bank, it is called a **banker's acceptance.** When it is drawn on and accepted by a business firm, it is called a **trade acceptance.**

Time drafts are *negotiable* instruments; that is, once the draft is stamped with an acceptance, the maker can sell the draft to an investor at a discount from its face value. Going back to our example, imagine the agreement between the U.S. exporter and the French importer calls for the exporter to present the Bank of Paris (through the Bank of New York) with a time draft requiring payment 120 days after presentation. The Bank of Paris stamps the time draft with an acceptance. Imagine further that the draft is for $100,000.

The exporter can either hold onto the accepted time draft and receive $100,000 in 120 days or he can sell it to an investor, let's say the Bank of New York, for a discount from the face value. If the prevailing discount rate is 7 percent, the exporter could receive $96,500 by selling it immediately (7 percent per annum discount rate for 120 days for $100,000 equals $3,500, and $100,000 − $3,500 = $96,500). The Bank of New York would then collect the full $100,000 from the Bank of Paris in 120 days. The exporter might choose to sell the accepted time draft immediately if he needed the funds to finance merchandise in transit and/or to cover cash flow shortfalls.

Bill of Lading

The third key document for financing international trade is the bill of lading. The **bill of lading** is issued to the exporter by the common carrier transporting the merchandise. It serves three purposes: it is a receipt, a contract, and a document of title. As a *receipt,* the bill of lading indicates that the carrier has received the merchandise described on the face of the document. As a *contract,* it specifies that the carrier is obligated to provide a transportation service in return for a certain charge. As a *document of title,* it can be used to obtain payment or a written promise of payment before the merchandise is released to

Figure 15.5 *A Typical International Trade Transaction*

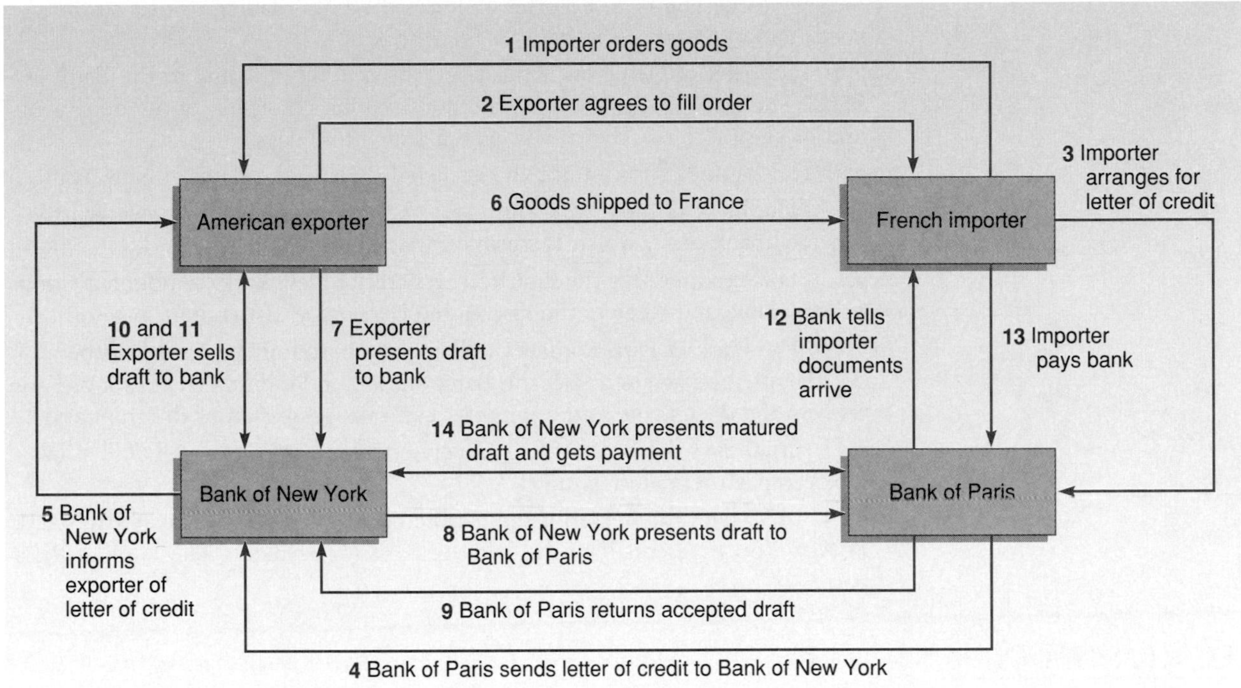

the importer. The bill of lading can also function as collateral against which funds may be advanced to the exporter by its local bank prior to or during shipment and before final payment by the importer.

A Typical International Trade Transaction

Now that we have received all of the elements of an international trade transaction, let us see how the whole process works in a typical case, sticking with the example of the U.S. exporter and the French importer. The typical transaction involves 14 distinct steps; see Figure 15.5. The steps are enumerated here.

Step 1: The French importer places an order with the U.S. exporter, and asks the American if he would be willing to ship under a letter of credit.

Step 2: The U.S. exporter agrees to ship under a letter of credit, and specifies relevant information such as prices and delivery terms.

Step 3: The French importer applies to the Bank of Paris for a letter of credit to be issued in favor of the U.S. exporter for the merchandise the importer wishes to buy.

Step 4: The Bank of Paris issues a letter of credit in the French importer's favor and sends it to the U.S. exporter's bank, the Bank of New York.

Step 5: The Bank of New York advises the U.S. exporter of the opening of a letter of credit in his favor.

Step 6: The U.S. exporter ships the goods to the French importer on a common carrier. An official of the carrier gives the exporter a bill of lading.

Step 7: The U.S. exporter presents a 90-day time draft drawn on the Bank of Paris in accordance with its letter of credit and the bill of lading to the Bank of New York. The U.S. exporter endorses the bill of lading so title to the goods is transferred to the Bank of New York.

Step 8: The Bank of New York sends the draft and bill of lading to the Bank of Paris. The Bank of Paris accepts the draft, taking possession of the documents and promising to pay the now-accepted draft in 90 days.

Step 9: The Bank of Paris returns the accepted draft to the Bank of New York.

Step 10: The Bank of New York tells the U.S. exporter that it has received the accepted bank draft, which is payable in 90 days.

Step 11: The exporter sells the draft to the Bank of New York at a discount from its face value and receives the discounted cash value of the draft in return.

Step 12: The Bank of Paris notifies the French importer of the arrival of the documents. She agrees to pay the Bank of Paris in 90 days. The Bank of Paris releases the documents so the importer can take possession of the shipment.

Step 13: In 90 days the Bank of Paris receives the importer's payment, so it has funds to pay the maturing draft.

Step 14: In 90 days the holder of the matured acceptance (in this case, the Bank of New York) presents it to the Bank of Paris for payment. The Bank of Paris pays.

EXPORT ASSISTANCE

Prospective U.S. exporters can draw on two forms of government-backed assistance to help finance their export programs. They can get financing aid from the Export–Import Bank and export credit insurance from the Foreign Credit Insurance Association.

Export–Import Bank

The Export–Import Bank, often referred to as *Eximbank,* is an independent agency of the U.S. government. Its mission is to provide financing aid that will facilitate exports, imports, and the exchange of commodities between the United States and other countries. Eximbank pursues this mission with various loan and loan-guarantee programs.

Eximbank guarantees repayment of medium- and long-term loans U.S. commercial banks make to foreign borrowers for purchasing U.S. exports. The Eximbank guarantee makes the commercial banks more willing to lend cash to foreign enterprises.

Eximbank also has a direct lending operation under which it lends dollars to foreign borrowers for use in purchasing U.S. exports. In some cases it grants loans that commercial banks would not if it sees a potential benefit to the United States in doing so. The foreign borrowers use the loans to pay U.S. suppliers and repay the loan to Eximbank with interest.

Export Credit Insurance

For reasons outlined earlier, exporters clearly prefer to get letters of credit from importers. However, at times an exporter who insists on a letter of credit is likely to lose an order to one who does not require a letter of credit. Thus, particularly when the importer is in a strong bargaining position and able to play competing suppliers off against each other, an exporter may have to forgo a letter of credit.[4] Obviously the lack of a letter of credit

---

[4] For a review of the conditions under which a buyer has power over a supplier, see M. E. Porter, *Competitive Strategy* (New York: Free Press, 1980).

Countertrade Examples

BOX 15.2

Saudi Arabia agreed to buy 10 747 jets from Boeing with payment in crude oil, discounted at 10 percent below posted world oil prices.

General Electric won a contract for a $150 million electric generator project in Romania by agreeing to market $150 million of Romanian products in markets to which Romania did not have access.

The Venezuelan government negotiated a contract with Caterpillar Tractor under which Venezuela would trade 350,000 tons of iron ore for Caterpillar earth-moving equipment.

Albania offered such items as spring water, tomato juice, and chrome ore in exchange for $60 million fertilizer and methanol complex.

Philip Morris ships cigarettes to the Russian Republic, for which it receives chemicals that can be used to make fertilizer. Philip Morris ships the chemicals to China, and in return, China ships glassware to North America for retail sale by Philip Morris.

Source: J. R. Carter and J. Gagne, "The Do's and Don'ts of International Countertrade," Sloan Management Review, *Spring 1988, pp. 31–37.*

exposes the exporter to the risk that the foreign importer will default on payment. The exporter can insure against this possibility by buying export credit insurance. If the customer defaults, the insurance firm will cover a major portion of the loss.

In the United States, export credit insurance is provided by the Foreign Credit Insurance Association (FCIA), an association of private commercial institutions operating under the guidance of the Export–Import Bank. The FCIA provides coverage against commercial risks and political risks. Losses due to commercial risk result from the buyer's insolvency or payment default. Political losses arise from actions of governments that are beyond the control of either buyer or seller.

COUNTERTRADE

We first encountered the topic of countertrade in Chapter 9 in our discussion of currency convertibility. There we noted that many currencies are not freely convertible into other currencies, primarily due to government restrictions. The main reason that a government restricts the convertibility of its currency is to preserve its foreign exchange reserves so they can service international debt commitments and purchase crucial imports. In the early 1990s more than 80 countries had major restrictions on the ability of residents and nonresidents to convert domestic currency into foreign currency, while another 30-plus countries had limited convertibility restrictions.[5]

This is obviously problematic for exporters. Nonconvertibility implies that the exporter may not be able to be paid in his or her home currency—and few exporters would desire payment in a currency that is not convertible. Countertrade is increasingly the solution of choice for problems posed by nonconvertibility. *Countertrade* denotes a whole range of barterlike agreements; its principle is to trade goods and services for other goods and services when they cannot be traded for money. Some specific examples of countertrade are given in Box 15.2.

[5] *Exchange Agreements and Exchange Restrictions* (Washington, D.C.: International Monetary Fund, 1989).

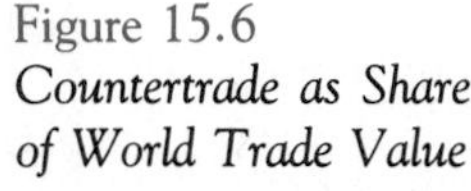

Figure 15.6
Countertrade as Share of World Trade Value

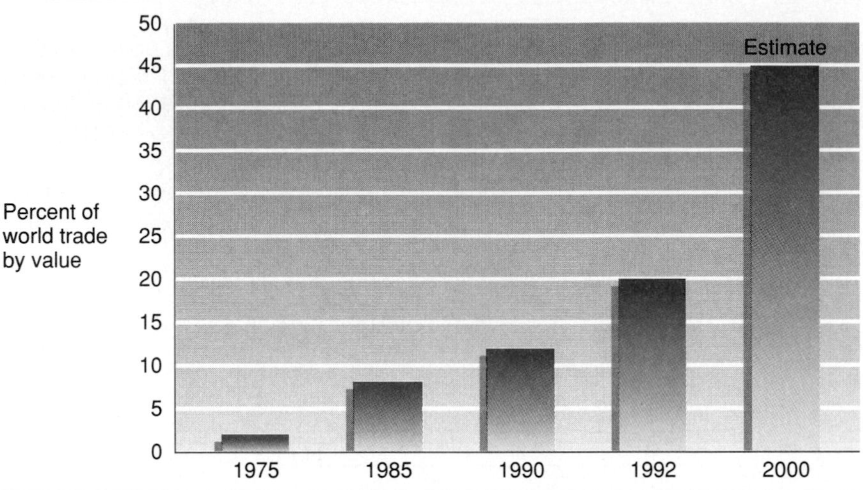

Source: G. Platt, "Worldwide Cash, Credit Crunch Lifts Countertrade," Journal of Commerce, *April 21, 1992, pp. 1A, 2A.*

The Growth of Countertrade

In the modern era, countertrade arose in the 1960s as a way for the U.S.S.R. and the communist states of Eastern Europe, whose currencies were generally nonconvertible, to purchase imports. During the 1980s the technique grew in popularity among many developing nations who lacked the foreign exchange reserves required to purchase necessary imports. Today, reflecting their own shortages of foreign exchange reserves, many of the successor states to the U.S.S.R.'s and the Eastern European communist nations are engaging in countertrade to purchase their imports. As a result, according to some estimates, more than 20 percent of world trade by value in 1992 was in the form of countertrade, up from only 2 percent in 1975 (see Figure 15.6). Moreover, because of a lack of hard currency and foreign exchange reserves in many developing nations, some commentators predict that by the year 2000, countertrade's share of world trade could rise to as much as 40 to 50 percent—although many others argue that this figure is an exaggeration. In any event, current estimates by the American Countertrade Association suggest that countertrade accounts for 20 percent of all U.S. export deals by value.[6]

Given the importance of countertrade as a means of financing world trade, it is apparent that prospective exporters will have to engage in this technique from time to time to gain access to international markets. Many developing and Third World nations may have no other way of doing business.[7]

Types of Countertrade

With its roots in the simple trading of goods and services for other goods and services, countertrade has evolved into a diverse set of activities that can be categorized as five distinct types of trading arrangements: barter, counterpurchase, offset, switch trading, and compensation or buyback.[8] The popularity of each of these arrangements, as

[6] G. Platt, "Worldwide Cash, Credit Crunch Lifts Countertrade," *Journal of Commerce,* April 21, 1992, pp. 1A, 2A; and S. Neumeier, "Why Countertrade Is Getting Hotter," *Fortune,* June 29, 1992, p. 25.

[7] J. R. Carter and J. Gagne, "The Do's and Dont's of International Countertrade," *Sloan Management Review,* Spring 1988, pp. 31–37.

[8] For details, see Carter and Gagne, "Do's and Dont's"; and J. F. Hennart, "Some Empirical Dimensions of Countertrade," *Journal of International Business Studies,* 1990, pp. 240–60.

Figure 15.7
Countertrade Practice, 1986

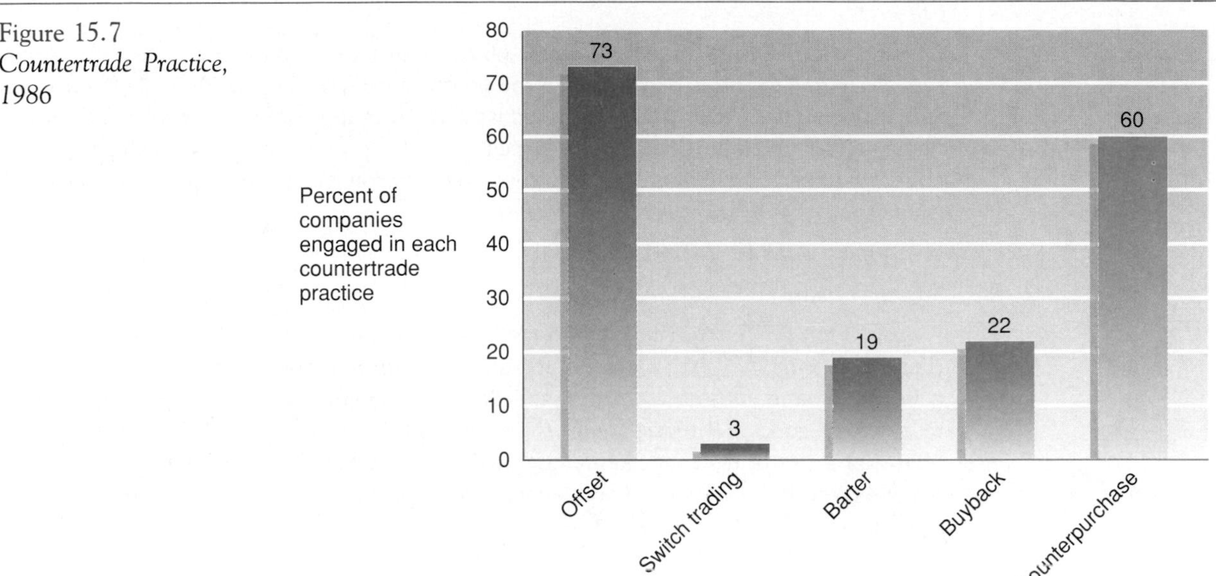

Source: J. R. Carter and J. Gagne, "The Do's and Don'ts of International Countertrade," Sloan Management Review, *Spring 1988, pp. 31–37, Table 2.*

indicated in a 1986 survey of multinational corporations, is summarized in Figure 15.7. Many countertrade deals involve not just one arrangement, but elements of two or more. We will consider each arrangement in turn.

Barter

Barter is the direct exchange of goods and/or services between two parties without a cash transaction. Although barter is the simplest arrangement, in practice it is not common. Its problems are twofold. First, if goods are not exchange simultaneously, one party ends up financing the other for a period of time. Second, firms engaged in barter run the risk of having to accept goods they do not want, cannot use, or have difficulty reselling at a reasonable price. For these reasons, barter is viewed as the most restrictive countertrade arrangement. It is primarily used for one-time-only deals in transactions with trading partners who are not creditworthy or trustworthy.

Counterpurchase

Counterpurchase is a reciprocal buying agreement. It occurs when a firm agrees to purchase a certain amount of materials back from a country to which a sale is made. For illustration, suppose that a U.S. firm sells some products to China. China pays the U.S. firm in dollars, but in exchange, the U.S. firm agrees to spend some of its proceeds from the sale on textiles produced by China. Thus, although China must draw on its foreign exchange reserves to pay the U.S. firm, it knows it will receive some of those dollars back from the U.S. firm due to the counterpurchase agreement. In a recent counterpurchase agreement, Rolls-Royce sold jet parts to Finland. As part of the deal, Rolls-Royce agreed to use some of the proceeds from the sale to purchase Finnish-manufactured TV sets that it would then sell in Great Britain.

Offset

Offset is similar to counterpurchase insofar as one party agrees to purchase goods and services with a specified percentage of the proceeds from the original sale. The difference is that this party can fulfill the obligation with any firm in the country to which the sale is being made. From an exporter's perspective this is more attractive than a straight counterpurchase agreement, since it gives the exporter greater flexibility to choose the goods that it wishes to purchase.

Switch Trading

Switch trading refers to the use of a specialized third-party trading house in a countertrade arrangement. When a firm enters into a counterpurchase or offset agreement with a country, it often ends up with what are called *counterpurchase credits,* which can be used to purchase goods from that country. Switch trading occurs when a third-party trading house buys the firm's counterpurchase credits and sells them to another firm that can make better use of them. For example, a U.S. firm concludes a counterpurchase agreement with Poland for which it receives some number of counterpurchase credits for purchasing Polish goods. The U.S. firm cannot use and does not want any Polish goods, however, so it sells the credits to a third-party trading house at a discount. The trading house finds a firm that can use the credits and sells them at a profit.

In one example of switch trading, Poland and Greece had a counterpurchase agreement that called for Poland to buy the same U.S.-dollar value of goods from Greece that it sold to Greece. However, Poland could not find enough Greek goods that it required, so it ended up with a dollar-dedominated counterpurchase balance in Greece that it was unwilling to use. A switch trader bought the right to 250,000 counterpurchase dollars from Poland for $225,000 and sold them to a European sultana (grape) merchant for $235,000, who used them to purchase sultanas from Greece.

Compensation or Buybacks

A **buyback** occurs when a firm builds a plant in a country—or supplies technology, equipment, training, or other services to the country—and agrees to take a certain percentage of the plant's output as partial payment for the contract. For example, Occidental Petroleum negotiated a deal with the U.S.S.R. under which Occidental would build several ammonia plants in the U.S.S.R. and as partial payment receive ammonia over a 20-year period. (This was before the breakup of the U.S.S.R.)

The Pros and Cons of Countertrade

The main attraction of countertrade is that it can give a firm a way to finance an export deal when other means are not available. Given the problems that many developing and Third World nations have in raising the foreign exchange necessary to pay for imports, countertrade may be the only option available when doing business in these countries. Moreover, even when countertrade is not the only option for structuring an export transaction, it must be borne in mind that many countries prefer countertrade to cash deals. Thus if a firm is unwilling to enter into a countertrade agreement, it may lose an export opportunity to a competitor that is willing to make a countertrade agreement. Put another way, countertrade allows U.S. firms to remain competitive with large Japanese and European trading companies, who for historical reasons are the masters of countertrade.

On the other hand, the drawbacks of countertrade agreements are fairly substantial. Other things being equal, all firms would prefer to be paid in hard currency. Countertrade contracts may involve the exchange of unusable or poor-quality goods that the firm cannot dispose of profitably. For example, a few years ago one U.S. firm got burnt when 50 percent of the television sets it received in a countertrade agreement with Hungary were defective and could not be sold. In addition, even if the goods it receives are of high quality, the firm still needs to dispose of them profitably. To do this, countertrade requires the firm to invest in an in-house trading department dedicated to arranging and managing countertrade deals. This in itself can be expensive and time consuming.

Given these drawbacks, the option of countertrade is most attractive to large, diverse, multinational enterprises that can use their worldwide network of contacts to dispose of goods acquired in countertrading. In point of fact, the masters of countertrade are Japan's giant trading firms, the sogo shosha, who use their vast networks of affiliated companies to profitably dispose of goods acquired through countertrade agreements. The trading firm of Mitsui & Company, for example, has about 120 affiliated companies in almost every sector of the manufacturing and service industries. As a result, if one of Mitsui's affiliates receives goods in a countertrade agreement that it cannot itself consume, Mitsui & Company will normally be able to find another affiliate that can profitably use them. The opportunity available to firms affiliated with trading houses such as Mitsui to access a network of similarly affiliated companies greatly increases their ability to enter into countertrade agreements. As a result, firms affiliated with one of Japan's sogo shosha often have a competitive advantage in countries where countertrade agreements are preferred. In addition, Western firms that are large, diverse, and have a global reach (e.g., General Electric and Philip Morris) have a similar profit advantage from countertrade agreements. On the other hand, unless there is no alternative, small and medium-sized exporters should probably try to avoid countertrade deals if possible, since they lack the worldwide network of operations that may be required to profitably utilize or dispose of goods acquired through them.[9]

SUMMARY OF CHAPTER

In this chapter we have examined the steps that firms must take to establish themselves as exporters. The specific points we have made include the following:

1. One of the biggest impediments to exporting is ignorance of foreign market opportunities.
2. The way to overcome ignorance is to gather information. In the United States a number of institutions, most important of which is the U.S. Department of Commerce, can help firms gather information and in the matchmaking process.
3. Firms engaged in international trade must do business with people they cannot trust, people who may be very difficult to track down if they default on an obligation.
4. Due to the lack of trust, each party to an international transaction has a different set of preferences regarding the configuration of the transaction.
5. The problems arising from lack of trust between exporters and importers can be solved by using a third party that is trusted by both—normally a reputable bank.
6. A letter of credit is issued by a bank at the request of an importer. It states that the bank promises to pay a beneficiary, normally the exporter, on presentation of documents specified in the letter.
7. A draft is the instrument normally used in international commerce to effect payment. It is an order written by an exporter instructing an importer, or an importer's

[9] D. J. Lecraw, "The Management of Countertrade: Factors Influencing Success," *Journal of International Business Studies*, Spring 1989, pp. 41–59.

agent, to pay a specified amount of money at a specified time.

8. Drafts are either sight drafts or time drafts. Time drafts are negotiable instruments.
9. A bill of lading is issued to the exporter by the common carrier transporting the merchandise. It serves as a receipt, a contract, and a document of title.
10. U.S. exporters can draw on two types of government-backed assistance to help finance their exports: loans from the Export-Import bank and export credit insurance from the FCIA.
11. Countertrade includes a whole range of barterlike agreements. It is primarily used when a firm exports to a country whose currency is not freely convertible and who may lack the foreign exchange reserves required to purchase the imports.
12. By some estimates, countertrade accounted for 20 percent of world trade by value in 1990.
13. There are five types of countertrade: barter, counterpurchase, offset, switch trading, and buyback.
14. The main attraction of countertrade is that it gives a firm a way to finance an export deal when other means are not available. A firm that insists on being paid in hard currency may be at a competitive disadvantage vis-à-vis one that is willing to engage in countertrade.
15. The main disadvantage of countertrade is that the firm may receive unusable or poor-quality goods that cannot be disposed of profitably.
16. As an option, countertrade is most attractive to large diverse, multinational enterprises that can use their worldwide network of contacts to profitably dispose of goods acquired in a countertrade agreement. It is less attractive to small and medium-sized exporters that lack access to such networks.

DISCUSSION QUESTIONS

1. A firm based in Washington State wants to export a shipload of finished lumber to the Philippines. The would-be importer cannot get sufficient credit from domestic sources to pay for the shipment but insists that the finished lumber can quickly be resold in the Philippines for a profit. Outline the steps the exporter should take to effect this export to the Philippines.

2. An alternative to using a letter of credit is export credit insurance. What are the advantages and disadvantages of using export credit insurance rather than a letter of credit for exporting
   a. A luxury yacht from California to Canada?
   b. Machine tools from New York to the Ukrainian Republic?
3. How do you explain the growing popularity of countertrade? Under what scenarios might its popularity increase still further by the year 2000? Under what scenarios might its popularity decline by the year 2000?

Global Manufacturing and Materials Management

CHAPTER 16

BOSE CORPORATION

Bose Corporation manufactures some of the world's best high-fidelity speakers. The Massachusetts corporation annually generates about $300 million in revenues. Its worldwide esteem is evidenced by the fact that Bose speakers are best-sellers in Japan, the world leader in consumer electronics. Bose's core competence is its electronic engineering skills, but the company attributes much of its business success to tightly coordinated materials management. • Bose purchases most of its electronic and nonelectronic components from independent suppliers scattered around North America, the Far East, and Europe. Roughly 50 percent of its purchases are from foreign suppliers, the majority of them in the Far East. Bose attempts to coordinate this globally dispersed supply chain so that

material holding and transportation costs are minimized. In general, this requires component parts to arrive at Bose's Massachusetts assembly plant *just in time* to enter the production process. All the same, Bose must remain responsive to customer demands, which requires the company to respond quickly to increase in customer demand for certain speakers. If it does not, it can lose a big order to competitors. Since Bose does not want to hold extensive inventories at its Massachusetts plant, this need for responsiveness requires Bose's globally dispersed supply chain to respond rapidly to increased demand for component parts. • Responsibility for coordinating the supply chain to meet both objectives—minimizing transportation and inventory holding costs and yet responding quickly to customer demands—falls on Bose's materials management function. This function achieves coordination by means of a sophisticated logistics operation. Most of Bose's imports from the Far East come via ships to the West Coast and then across North America to its Massachusetts plant via train. Most of the company's exports also move by ocean freight, but Bose does not hesitate to use air freight when goods are needed in a hurry. • To control this supply chain, Bose has a long-standing relationship with W. N. Procter, a Boston-based freight forwarder and customs broker. Procter handles customs clearance and shipping from suppliers to Bose. Procter provides Bose up-to-the-minute electronic data interchange (EDI) capabilities, which gives it the ability to track parts as they move through its global supply chain. Whenever a shipment leaves a supplier, it is entered in this "ProcterLink" system. Bose is then able to fine-tune its production scheduling so supplies enter the production process just in time. ProcterLink is more than a simple tracking system, however. The EDI system also allows Bose to run simulations that allow its logistics managers to examine a variety of factors, such as the effect of duties on the cost of goods sold. • Procter provides several other services to Bose, such as selecting overseas agents who can help move goods out of the Far East. Procter's well-established network of overseas contacts is especially useful when shipments must be expedited through foreign customs. Moreover, Procter is electronically linked into the U.S. customs system, which allows it to clear freight electronically as much as five days before a ship arrives at a U.S. port, or hours before an international air freight shipment arrives. This can get goods to Bose's manufacturing plant several days sooner. • Just how well this system can work was demonstrated recently when a Japanese customer doubled its order for Bose speakers. Bose needed to gear up its manufacturing immediately, but many of the essential components were far from Massachusetts. Using ProcterLink, Bose located the needed parts in its supply chain, pulled them out of the normal delivery chain, and airfreighted them to the manufacturing line to satisfy the accelerated schedule. As a result, Bose was able to fill the doubled order for its Japanese customer. *P. Bradley, "Global Sourcing Takes Split-Second Timing,"* Purchasing, *July 20, 1989, pp. 52–58.*

INTRODUCTION

In Chapter 12 we introduced the concept of the value chain and discussed a number of value creation activities—including production, marketing, materials management, R&D, human resources, and information systems. In this chapter we will be examining two of these activities, production and materials management, attempting to clarify how they might be performed internationally to (1) lower the costs of value creation and (2) add value by better serving customer needs. We will discuss the contributions of

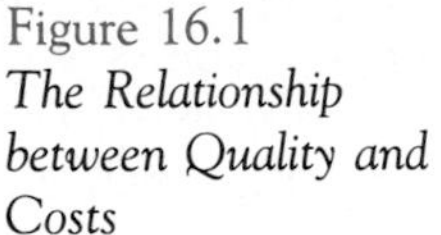

Figure 16.1
The Relationship between Quality and Costs

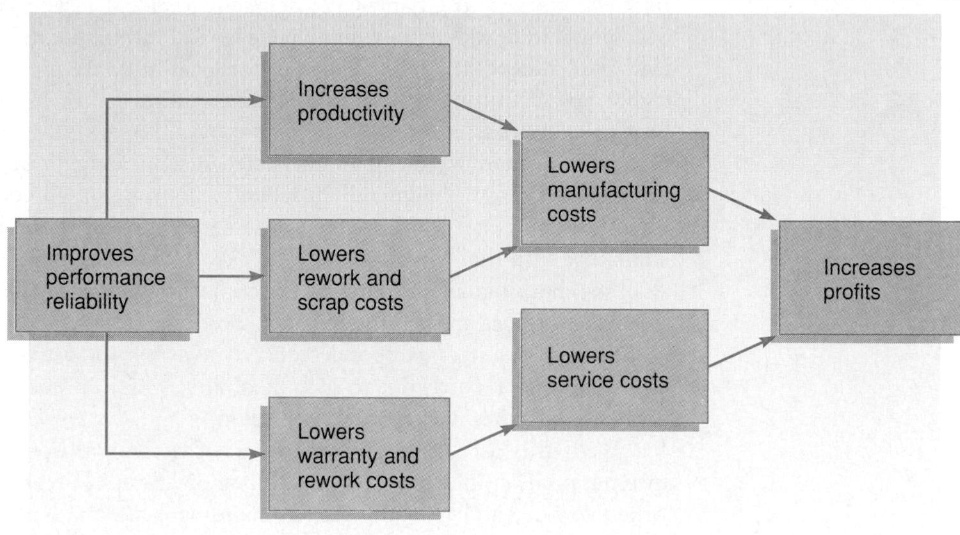

Source: Adapted from David A. Garvin, "What Does Product Quality Really Mean?" Sloan Management Review *26 (Fall 1984), Figure 1, p. 37.*

information technology to these activities. In the two chapters that follow we will look at other value creation activities in this international context (marketing, R&D, and human resource management).

In Chapter 12 we defined production as "the activities involved in creating a product." We used the term *production* to denote both service and manufacturing activities, since one can produce a service or produce a physical product. In this chapter we focus more on manufacturing than on service activities, so we will use the term *manufacturing* rather than *production.* As for materials management, recall that we defined it as "the activity that controls the transmission of physical materials through the value chain, from procurement through production and into distribution." Manufacturing and materials management are closely linked, since a firm's ability to perform its manufacturing function efficiently depends on a continuous supply of high-quality material inputs, for which materials management is responsible.

More specifically, the objectives of both manufacturing and materials management are to lower costs *and* to increase product quality by eliminating defective products from both the supply chain and the manufacturing process. Moreover, it should be noted that these objectives are not independent of each other. As illustrated in Figure 16.1, the firm that improves its quality control will also reduce its costs of value creation. Improved quality control reduces costs in three ways:

1. Productivity increases, because time is not wasted manufacturing poor-quality products that cannot be sold. This saving leads to a direct reduction in unit costs.
2. Increased product quality means lower rework and scrap costs.
3. Greater product quality means lower warranty and rework costs.

The net effect is to lower the costs of value creation by reducing both manufacturing and service costs.

In addition to the objectives of lowering costs and improving quality, two other objectives have particular importance in international businesses. First, manufacturing and materials management must be able to accommodate demands for local responsiveness. As we saw in Chapter 12, demands for local responsiveness arise from national differences in consumer tastes and preferences, infrastructure, distribution channels, and host-government demands. Demands for local responsiveness create pressures to decentralize manufacturing activities to the major national or regional markets in which the firm does business.

Second, manufacturing and materials management must be able to respond quickly to shifts in customer demand. In recent years **time-based competition** has grown more important. In other words, when consumer demand is prone to large and unpredictable shifts, the firm that can adapt most quickly to these shifts will gain an advantage. As we shall see, both manufacturing and materials management play critical roles here. Indeed, this issue surfaced in the opening case. Bose's materials management function, by its use of information systems, responded quickly to a shift in customer demand. Bose's competitive advantage is partly due to such flexibility, which in turn is in no small part due to its well-run materials management operation.

With this as background, in this chapter we will look at three key issues facing international businesses: (1) where to manufacture, (2) which components to make and which to buy, and (3) how best to coordinate a globally dispersed manufacturing and supply system.

WHERE TO MANUFACTURE

A key decision facing an international firm is where to locate its manufacturing activities to achieve the twin goals of minimizing costs and improving product quality. For the firm that considers international production to be a feasible option, a number of factors must be considered. These factors can be grouped under three broad headings: country factors, technological factors, and product factors.

Country Factors

We reviewed country-specific factors in some detail earlier in the book and we will not dwell on them here. Suffice it to say that political economy, culture, and relative factor costs differ from country to country. In Chapter 4, for example, we saw that due to differences in factor costs, certain countries have a comparative advantage for producing certain products. In Chapters 2 and 3 we saw how differences in political economy and national culture influence the benefits, costs, and risks of doing business in a country. It follows that, *other things being equal,* a firm should locate its various manufacturing activities in those locations where the economic, political, and cultural conditions, including relative factor costs, are more conducive to the performance of those activities. In Chapter 12 we referred to the benefits derived from such a strategy as *location economies.* We argued that one result of the strategy is the creation of a global web of value creation activities.

Of course, other things are not equal. Other country factors that impinge on location decisions include formal and informal trade barriers (see Chapter 6) and rules and regulations regarding foreign direct investment (see Chapter 7). Thus, for example, although relative factor costs may make a country look attractive as a location for performing a manufacturing activity, regulations prohibiting foreign direct investment may eliminate this option. Similarly, a consideration of factor costs might suggest that a firm should source production of a certain component part from a particular country, but trade barriers could make this uneconomical.

Another country factor that must be borne in mind is expected future movements in its currency's exchange rate (see Chapters 9 and 10). Adverse changes in exchange rates can quickly alter a country's attractiveness as a manufacturing base. In particular, currency appreciation can transform a low-cost location into a high-cost location. Many Japanese corporations have grappled with this problem in recent years. The relatively low value of the yen on foreign exchange markets between 1950 and 1980 helped strengthen Japan's position as a low-cost location for manufacturing. Since the early 1980s, however, the yen's appreciation against the dollar has increased the dollar cost of products exported from Japan, making Japan less attractive as a manufacturing location. In response, many Japanese firms have been moving their manufacturing offshore to lower-cost locations in East Asia.

Technological Factors

The technology we are concerned with in this subsection is **manufacturing technology**—the technology that performs specific manufacturing activities. The type of technology a firm uses in its manufacturing can be pivotal in location decisions. For example, due to technological constraints, in some cases it is feasible only to perform certain manufacturing activities in one location and serve the world market from there. In other cases, the technology may make it feasible to perform an activity in multiple locations. Three characteristics of a manufacturing technology are of interest here: the level of its fixed costs, its minimum efficient scale, and its flexibility.

Fixed Costs

As we noted in Chapter 12, in some cases the fixed costs of setting up a manufacturing plant are so high that a firm must serve the world market from a single location, or from a very few locations. For example, it can cost as much as $1 billion to set up a plant to manufacture semiconductor chips. Given this, serving the world market from a single plant sited at a single (optimal) location makes sense.

On the other hand, a relatively low level of fixed costs can make it economical to perform a particular activity in several locations at once. One advantage of this is that the firm can better accommodate demands for local responsiveness. Manufacturing in multiple locations may also help the firm avoid the risks of becoming too dependent on any one location. Being too dependent on one location is particularly risky in a world of floating exchange rates.

Minimum Efficient Scale

The concept of economies of scale tell us that as plant output expands, unit costs decrease. The reasons for this relationship include the greater utilization of capital equipment and the productivity gains that come with greater specialization of employees within the plant.[1] In general, however, it is well known that beyond a certain level of output, few additional scale economies are available.[2] Thus, the "unit cost curve" declines with output until a certain output level is reached, at which point further increases in output realize little reduction in unit costs. The level of output at which most plant-level scale economies are exhausted is referred to as the **minimum efficient scale** of output. This is the scale of output a plant must operate at to realize all major plant-level scale economies. (See Figure 16.2)

---

[1] For a review of the technical arguments, see D. A. Hay and D. J. Morris, *Industrial Economics: Theory and Evidence* (Oxford: Oxford University Press, 1979).

[2] Ibid.

Figure 16.2
A Typical Unit-Cost Curve

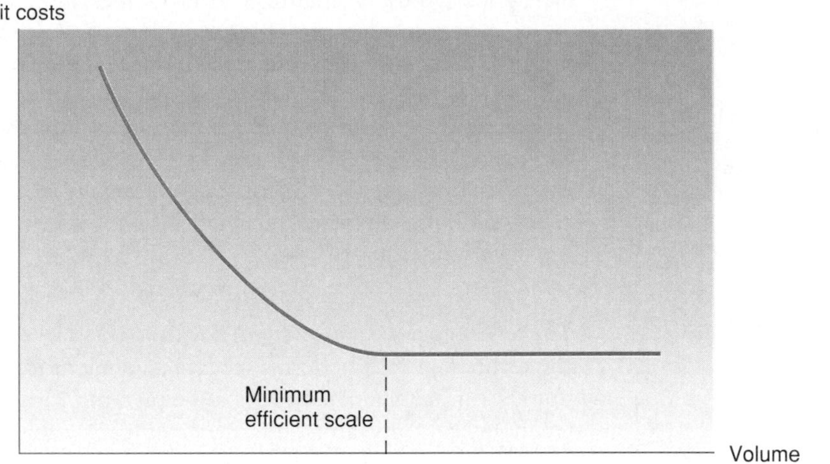

In the present context the implications of this concept are as follows: the larger the minimum efficient scale of a plant is, the greater is the argument for centralizing production in a single location or a limited number of locations. Alternatively, when the minimum efficient scale of production is relatively low, it may be economical to manufacture a product at several locations. As in the case of low fixed costs, the advantages are allowing the firm to better accommodate demands for local responsiveness or to hedge against currency risk by manufacturing the same product in several locations.

Flexible Manufacturing Technologies

The term *flexible manufacturing technology* refers to a range of computer-based technologies designed to (1) increase the utilization of individual machines through better scheduling, (2) reduce setup times for complex equipment, and (3) improve quality control at all stages of the manufacturing process.[3] Flexible manufacturing technologies allow the firm to produce a wider variety of end products at a cost that at one time could only be achieved through the mass production of a standardized output. Moreover, firms using flexible technologies frequently produce fewer defective products than firms using mass production technology.

Flexible manufacturing technologies vary in sophistication and complexity. We will look at the two most common technologies, flexible machine cells and flexible manufacturing systems. A third type, lean production, is profiled in Box 16.1.

A **flexible machine cell** is a grouping of various types of machinery, a common materials handler, and a centralized cell controller (computer). Each cell normally contains four to six machines, each capable of performing several operations. A typical cell is dedicated to producing a family of parts or products. Since the settings on machines are computer controlled, each cell is able to switch quickly from producing one part or product to another.

Improved capacity utilization and reductions in work-in-progress and waste are major benefits of flexible machine cells. Improved capacity utilization is due to reduced setup times and to the computer-controlled coordination of production flow between machines

---

[3] See P. Nemetz and L. Fry, "Flexible Manufacturing Organizations: Implications for Strategy Formulation," *Academy of Management Review* 13, (1988), pp. 627–38, N. Greenwood, *Implementing Flexible Manufacturing Systems* (New York: Halstead Press, 1986); and J. P. Womack, D. T. Jones, and D. Roos, *The Machine that Changed the World* (New York: Rawson Associates, 1990).

(which eliminates bottlenecks). The tight coordination between machines also reduces work-in-progress (e.g., stockpiles of partly finished products). Reductions in waste arise from the ability of computer-controlled machinery to identify how best to transform inputs into outputs while producing a minimum of unusable waste material. As a consequence of all these factors, whereas a free-standing machine might be used 50 percent of the time, the same machine placed in a cell can be used more than 80 percent of the time and produce the same end product with half the waste. This increases productivity and decreases production costs.

Flexible manufacturing systems are more complex than cells. A flexible manufacturing system achieves centralized coordination of a number of independent cells by utilizing a sophisticated, centralized computer—that is, a computer responsible for coordinating the activities of all the cells in a workplace. Flexible manufacturing systems are designed for the efficient production of small batches of products or parts. The enhanced coordination of production flow from cell to cell allows for improved logistics in materials handling over what can be achieved by each cell individually. In addition, when several cells operate in parallel to perform the same function, the production process will not come to a halt if a single cell breaks down. The results include further reductions in work-in-progress and increases in capacity utilization and productivity. The net effect is reduced costs. At the same time, the centrally controlled materials handling system allows the introduction of superior statistical quality control procedures.

The benefits of flexible manufacturing technology can be dramatic. Here are some examples:[4]

- Allen Bradley can manufacture more than 750 variations of its industrial controls in a single factory.
- Panasonic Bicycle Company of Japan is able to produce more than 11,000 bicycle design variations to suit each customer's body height, size, and color preference with no factory downtime.
- Following the introduction of a flexible manufacturing system, General Electric's locomotive operations reduced the time needed to produce a locomotive motor frame from 16 days to 16 hours.
- Ingersoll Milling Machine Company can produce 25,000 part designs, mostly in lots of one, and many one-of-a-kind designs to support its world dominance in the specialized production machinery market.
- IBM's flexible manufacturing plant in Austin, Texas, can turn out a laptop computer in less than six minutes, with 75 percent greater efficiency than a conventional plant.
- Caterpillar Tractor cut its unit costs by 22 percent between 1982 and 1986 following the introduction of cell-based flexible manufacturing technologies.
- After introducing a flexible manufacturing system, Fireplace Manufacturers, Inc., one of the country's largest fireplace businesses, reduced scrap by 60 percent, increased inventory turnover threefold, and increased labor productivity by more than 30 percent.

It is clear from these examples that adopting flexible manufacturing technologies can help improve a firm's competitive position. Most important for an international business, flexible manufacturing technologies can help the firm customize products for different

[4] Sources: J. D. Goldhar and D. Lei, "The Shape of 21st Century Global Manufacturing," *Journal of Business Strategy,* March/April 1991, pp. 37–41; "Factories that Turn Nuts into Bolts," *U.S. News and World Report,* July 14, 1986, pp. 44–45; and J. Kotkin, "The Great American Revival," *Inc.,* February 1988, pp. 52–63.

Lean Production in the Automobile Industry

To get a feeling for the power of flexible manufacturing technologies, consider the experience of the automobile industry. Historically, this industry has used mass production techniques to produce component parts and assemble cars. One reason for this was that anywhere from several hours to several days was needed to set up production equipment. Given this, the cost economies of long production runs were considerable. For example, because it took a full day to set up stamping machinery, Ford would stamp 50,000 right-door panels in a single production run and then store the parts in a warehouse until they were needed.

The impetus for changing this system came from a Japanese mechanical engineer, Ohno Taiichi, who was a major influence at Toyota from the 1950s to the 1980s. After visiting Ford's U.S. plants, Ohno was convinced that the basic mass production philosophy was flawed. He saw five problems with it:

1. Long production runs create massive inventories that must be stored in large warehouses. This is expensive because of the cost of warehousing and because inventories tie up capital in unproductive uses.
2. If initial machine settings are wrong, long production runs result in the production of a large number of defects.
3. The monotony of assembly-line tasks generates defects, since workers become lax about quality control. In addition, since assembly-line workers are not responsible for quality control, they have little incentive to minimize defects.
4. The extreme division of labor results in the employment of specialists such as foremen, quality inspectors, and tooling specialists, whose jobs could logically be performed by assembly-line workers.
5. The mass production system is unable to accommodate consumer preferences for product diversity.

The production system that Ohno developed at Toyota to deal with these flaws has since been dubbed *lean production.* It has four main characteristics: short setup times, organization of the work force, the *kanban* system, and assembly-line quality control.

Short Setup Times

Ohno developed a number of techniques to reduce setup times for production equipment. Using a system of levers and pulleys, he reduced the time required to change dies on stamping equipment from a full day in 1950 to three minutes by 1971! This made small production runs economical, which in turn allowed Toyota to better respond to consumer demands for product diversity. Small production runs also eliminate the need to hold large inventories, thereby reducing warehousing

national markets. The importance of this advantage cannot be overstated. When flexible manufacturing technologies are available, a firm can manufacture products customized to various national markets at a single factory sited at the optimal location. Moreover, it can do this without absorbing a significant cost penalty. Thus, the idea that manufacturing facilities must be established in each major national market in which the firm does

BOX 16.1

costs. Furthermore, small product runs and the lack of inventory mean that defective parts are produced in small numbers and enter the assembly process immediately. This allows defects to be traced back to their source and the problem to be corrected right away.

Organization of the Work Force

Ohno grouped the work force into teams. Each team was given a set of assembly tasks to perform, and team members were trained to perform all tasks for which the team was responsible. The teams were also given responsibility for house cleaning, minor tool repair, and quality inspection. The performance of teams was assessed on the basis of their ability to achieve output *and* quality goals. The introduction of teams reduced the need for specialists, boosted productivity, improved quality control at all stages in the manufacturing process, and had a beneficial impact on employee motivation and moral.

The *Kanban* System

Under the *kanban* system, parts are delivered to the assembly line in containers. As each container is emptied, it is sent back to the previous step in the manufacturing process, where it becomes the signal to make more parts. This "just-in-time" system minimizes work-in-progress and increases inventory turnover. The elimination of buffer inventories means defective components show up immediately, at the next stage of the production process. The visibility of defects speeds up the process of tracing defects back to their source and correcting quality problems.

Assembly-Line Quality Control

Rather than detecting and dealing with product defects at the end of the assembly line—the traditional practice in mass production plants—product defects are corrected on the assembly line by assembly line workers. The workers have the authority to stop the line to fix a defect, which tends to give them an incentive to be concerned about quality control.

These process innovations have resulted in higher levels of productivity and product quality than are attainable with mass production. This is illustrated in the table, which compares General Motors's Framingham plant, a traditional mass production plant, with Toyota's lean-production plant at Takaoka.

	General Motors	Toyota
Assembly hours per car	31	16
Assembly defects per 100 cars	135	45
Inventories of parts (average)	2 weeks	2 hours

Sources: M. A. Cusumano, The Japanese Automobile Industry *(Cambridge, Mass.: Harvard University Press, 1989); Ohno Taiichi,* Toyota Production System *(Cambridge, Mass.: Productivity Press, 1990); and J. P. Womack, D. T. Jones, and D. Roos,* The Machine that Changed the World *(New York: Rawson Associates, 1990).*

business to provide products that satisfy the specific consumer tastes and preferences (part of the rationale for a multidomestic strategy) is becoming outdated (see Chapter 12).

Summary

Pulling all of this material together, we see that a number of technological factors support the economic arguments for concentrating manufacturing facilities in a few choice locations, or even in a single location. Most important, other things being equal, when

Fixed costs are substantial,

The minimum efficient scale of production is high, and/or

Flexible manufacturing technologies are available,

the arguments for concentrating production at a few choice locations are strong. This is true even when substantial differences in consumer tastes and preferences exist between national markets, since flexible manufacturing technologies allow the firm to customize products to national differences at a single facility.

Alternatively, when

Fixed costs are low,

The minimum efficient scale of production is low, and

Flexible manufacturing technologies are not available,

the arguments for concentrating production at one or a few locations are not as compelling. In such cases, it may make more sense to manufacture in each major market in which the firm is active if this helps the firm better respond to local demands. However, this holds only if the increased local responsiveness more than offsets the cost disadvantages of not concentrating manufacturing. With the advent of flexible manufacturing technologies, such a strategy is becoming less and less attractive. In sum, technological factors are making it feasible, and indeed necessary, for firms to concentrate their manufacturing facilities at optimal locations. Trade barriers and transportation costs are probably the major brakes on this trend.

Product Factors

Two product features impact location decisions. The first is the product's **value-to-weight ratio** because of its influence on transportation costs. Many electronic components have high value-to-weight ratios; they are expensive and they do not weigh very much. Thus, even if they are shipped halfway around the world, their transportation costs account for a very small percentage of total costs. Given this, other things being equal, there is great pressure to manufacture these products in the optimal location and to serve the world market from there. The opposite holds for products with low value-to-weight ratios. Refined sugar, certain bulk chemicals, paints, and petroleum products all have low value-to-weight ratios; they are relatively inexpensive products that weigh a lot. Accordingly, when they are shipped long distances, transportation costs account for a large percentage of total costs. Thus, other things being equal, there is great pressure to manufacture these products in multiple locations close to major markets to reduce transportation costs.

The other product feature that can influence location decisions is whether the product serves **universal needs,** needs that are the same all over the world. Examples include many industrial products (e.g., industrial electronics, steel, bulk chemicals) and modern consumer products (e.g., handheld calculators and personal computers). Since there are few national differences in consumer taste and preference for such products, the need for local responsiveness is reduced. This increases the attractiveness of concentrating manufacturing at an optimal location.

Locating Manufacturing Facilities

In sum, there are two basic strategies for locating manufacturing facilities: concentrating them in the optimal location and serving the world market from there, and decentralizing them in various regional or national locations that are close to major markets. The appropriate strategic choice is determined by the various country, technological, and product factors we have discussed in this section. They are summarized in Table 16.1. As can be seen, **concentration of manufacturing** makes most sense when:

Table 16.1
Location Strategy and Manufacturing

	Favored Manufacturing Strategy	
	Concentrated	**Decentralized**
Country factors		
Differences in political economy	Substantial	Few
Differences in culture	Substantial	Few
Differences in factor costs	Substantial	Few
Trade barriers	Few	Many
Technological factors		
Fixed costs	High	Low
Minimum efficient scale	High	Low
Flexible manufacturing technology	Available	Not available
Product factors		
Value-to-weight ratio	High	Low
Serves universal needs	Yes	No

1. Differences between countries in factor costs, political economy, and culture have a substantial impact on the costs of manufacturing in various countries.
2. Trade barriers are low.
3. Important exchange rates are expected to remain relatively stable.
4. The production technology has high fixed costs, a high minimum efficient scale, or a flexible manufacturing technology exits.
5. The product's value-to-weight ratio is high.
6. The product serves universal needs.

Alternatively, **decentralization of manufacturing** is appropriate when:

1. Differences between countries in factor costs, political economy, and culture do not have a substantial impact on the costs of manufacturing in various countries.
2. Trade barriers are high.
3. Volatility in important exchange rates is expected.
4. The production technology has low fixed costs, low minimum efficient scale, and flexible manufacturing technology is not available.
5. The product's value-to-weight ratio is low.
6. The product does not serve universal needs (that is, significant differences in consumer tastes and preferences exist between nations).

In practice, location decisions are seldom clear cut. For example, it is not unusual for differences in factor costs, technological factors, and product factors to point toward concentrated manufacturing while at the same time a combination of trade barriers and volatile exchange rates points toward decentralized manufacturing. Indeed, this is probably the case in the world automobile industry. Although the availability of flexible manufacturing technologies (see Box 16.1) and cars' relatively high value-to-weight ratios suggest concentrated manufacturing, the combination of formal and informal trade barriers and the uncertainties of the world's current floating exchange rate regime (see Chapter 10) have inhibited firms' ability to pursue this strategy.

For these reasons, Honda is establishing "top-to-bottom" manufacturing operations in its three major markets: Japan, North America, and Western Europe. Honda is able to treat Western Europe as a single market because of the European Community's success in removing trade barriers and stabilizing exchange rates in the member-countries.

Figure 16.3
The Ford Fiesta Production Network in Europe

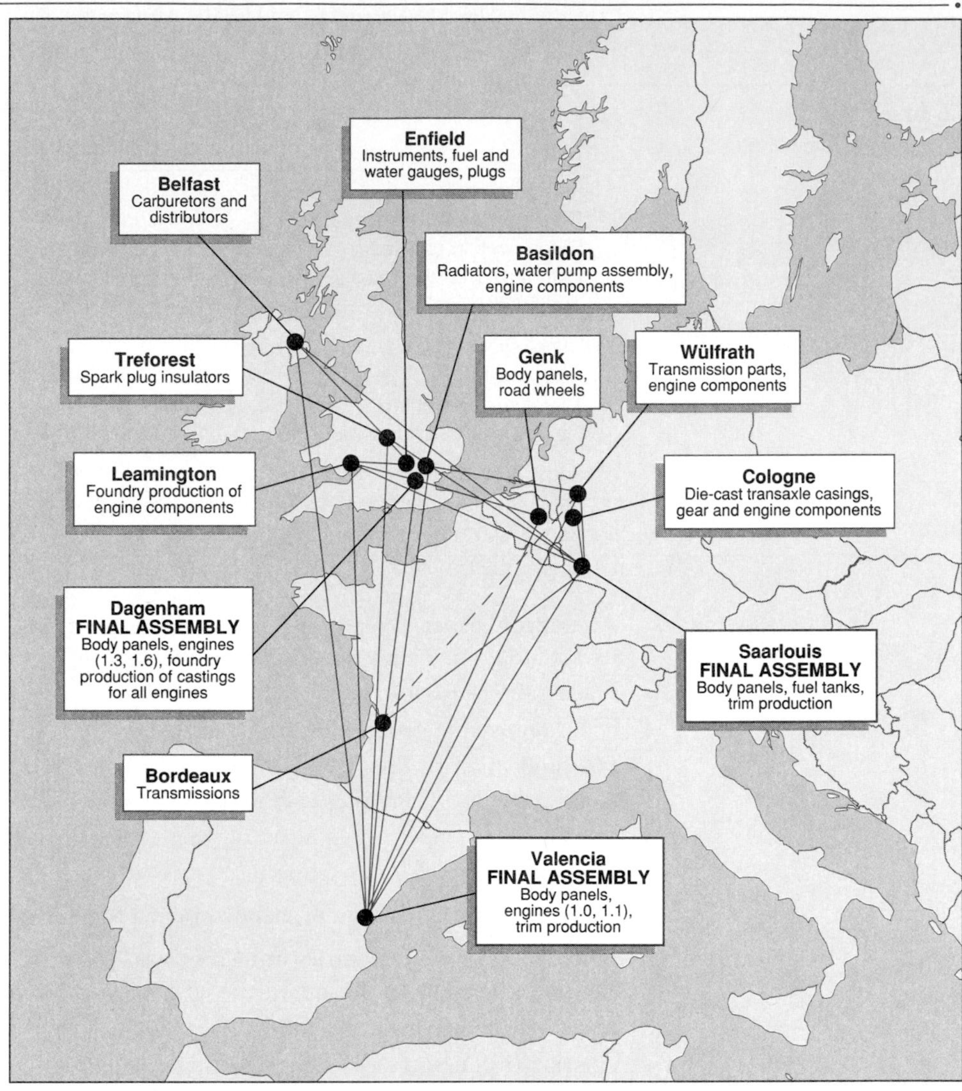

Source: Peter Dicken, Global Shift *(New York: The Guilford Press, 1992), p. 300.*

Another auto firm that treats Western Europe as a single market is Ford. Figure 16.3 shows how Ford of Europe dispersed the various manufacturing activities for its Fiesta to different locations in Western Europe. (This figure shows only the geographical pattern of the network within Ford itself; independent component suppliers are not shown.) Note that some components are single sourced to take advantage of economies of scale. For example, all carburetors are supplied by the Belfast plant; all transmissions are built at Bordeaux; Basildon supplies radiator assemblies; Treforest makes spark plugs. At the same time, final assembly operations are performed at three locations: Dagenham in Great Britain, Saarlouis in Germany, and Valencia in Spain. Ford reasons that it can better customize the product to local needs by doing this. Also, it can make up for shortfalls of production at one location by shipping cars from one of the other locations. In any event, the result is a complex network of cross-border flows of finished vehicles and components. Presumably, Ford locates the various activities in particular locations because it believes these are the most favorable locations for performing those activities.

MAKE-OR-BUY DECISIONS

International businesses also face *sourcing* decisions, decisions about whether they should make or buy the component parts that go into their final product. That is, should the firm **vertically integrate** backward and manufacture its own component parts, or should it **outsource** them—buy them from independent suppliers? Make-or-buy decisions are important factors of many firms' manufacturing strategies. In the automobile industry, for example, the typical car contains more than 10,000 components, so automobile firms constantly face make-or-buy decisions. Ford of Europe, for example, produces only about 45 percent of the value of the Fiesta in its own plants. The remaining 55 percent, mainly accounted for by component parts, comes from independent suppliers.

Make-or-buy decisions pose plenty of problems for purely domestic businesses but even more problems for international businesses. These decisions in the international arena are complicated by the volatility of countries' political economies, exchange rate movements, changes in relative factor costs, and the like. In this section we examine the arguments for making components and for buying them, and we consider the trade-offs involved in these decisions. Then we discuss strategic alliances as an alternative to manufacturing component parts within the company.

The Advantages of Make

The arguments that support making component parts in-house—vertical integration—are threefold. Specifically, vertical integration may facilitate investments in highly specialized assets, protect proprietary product technology, and facilitate the scheduling of adjacent processes.

Facilitating Specialized Investments

We first encountered the concept of specialized assets in Chapter 6 when we looked at the economic theory of vertical foreign direct investment. A variation of that concept explains why firms might want to make their own components rather than buy them.[5] The argument is that when one firm must invest in specialized assets to supply another, mutual dependency is created. In such circumstances, each party fears the other will abuse the relationship by seeking more favorable terms.

As an illustration, imagine Ford of Europe has developed a new, high-performance, high-quality, and uniquely designed carburetor. The carburetor's increased fuel efficiency will help sell Ford cars. Ford must decide whether to make the carburetor in-house or to contract out the manufacturing to an independent supplier. Manufacturing these uniquely designed carburetors requires investments in equipment that can be used only for this purpose; it cannot be used to make carburetors for any other auto firm. Thus, investment in this equipment constitutes an investment in specialized assets.

Let us first examine this situation from the perspective of an independent supplier who has been asked by Ford to make this investment. The supplier might reason that once it has made the investment it will become dependent on Ford for business—since Ford is the only possible customer for the output of this equipment. The supplier perceives this as putting *Ford* in a strong bargaining position and worries that once the specialized investment has been made, Ford might use this fact to squeeze down prices for

[5] The material in this section is based primarily on the transaction cost literature of vertical integration; for example, O. E. Williamson, *The Economic Institutions of Capitalism* (New York: The Free Press, 1985).

the carburetors. Given this risk, the supplier declines to make the investment in specialized equipment.

Now take the position of Ford. Ford might reason that if it contracts out production of these carburetors to an independent supplier, it might become too dependent on that supplier for a vital input. Since specialized equipment is required to produce the carburetors, Ford cannot easily switch its orders to other suppliers who lack that equipment. (It would face high switching costs.) Ford perceives this as increasing the bargaining power of the *supplier* and worries that the supplier might use its bargaining strength to demand higher prices.

Thus, the mutual dependency that out-sourcing would create in this case makes Ford nervous, and it serves to scare away potential suppliers. The problem here is lack of trust, of course. Neither party completely trusts the other to play fair. As a result, Ford might reason that the only safe way to get the new carburetors is to manufacture them itself. Indeed, it may be unable to persuade *any* independent supplier to manufacture them. Thus, Ford decides to make rather than buy.

In general, we can predict that when substantial investments in specialized assets are required to manufacture a component, the firm will prefer to make the component internally rather than contract it out to a supplier. A growing amount of empirical evidence supports this prediction.[6]

Proprietary Product Technology Protection

Proprietary product technology is technology unique to a firm. If it enables the firm to produce a product containing superior features, proprietary technology can give the firm competitive advantage. Obviously the firm would not want this technology to fall into the hands of competitors. If the firm contracts out the manufacture of components containing proprietary technology, it runs the risk that those suppliers will expropriate the technology for their own use or that they will sell it to the firm's competitors. Thus, to maintain control over its technology, the firm might prefer to make such component parts in-house.

For example, IBM integrated backward into the manufacture of microcircuits to protect the innovations incorporated in its PS/2 personal computer system. The information pathways and graphics of the PS/2 machines are created by proprietary chips, manufactured by IBM itself, that will be difficult for competitors to decipher. By taking this step, IBM hoped to avoid the widespread copying of its machines that occurred with its original PC system.

Improved Scheduling

The weakest argument for vertical integration is that production cost savings result from it because it makes planning, coordination, and scheduling of adjacent processes easier.[7] This is particularly important in firms with just-in-time inventory systems (which we discuss later in the chapter). In the 1920s, for example, Ford profited from tight coordination and scheduling made possible by backward vertical integration into steel foundries, iron ore shipping, and mining. Deliveries at Ford's foundries on the Great Lakes were coordinated so well that ore was turned into engine blocks within 24 hours.

---

[6] For a review of the evidence to the mid-1980s, see Williamson, *Economic Institutions*.

[7] A. D. Chandler, *The Visible Hand* (Cambridge, Mass.: Harvard University Press, 1977).

This substantially reduced Ford's production costs by eliminating the need to hold excessive ore inventories.

For international businesses that source worldwide, scheduling problems can be exacerbated by the time and distance between the firm and its suppliers. This is true whether the firms use their own subunits as suppliers or independent suppliers. *Ownership* is not the issue here. As we saw in the opening case, Bose has achieved tight scheduling with its globally dispersed parts suppliers without going to all the trouble of vertical integration. Thus, although this argument for vertical integration is often made, it is not compelling.

The Advantages of Buy

The advantages of buying component parts from independent suppliers are that it gives the firm greater flexibility and that it benefits the organization in several ways.

Strategic Flexibility

The great advantage of buying component parts from independent suppliers is that the firm can maintain its flexibility, switching orders between suppliers as circumstances dictate. This is particularly important in the international context, where changes in exchange rates and trade barriers can alter the attractiveness of supply sources over time. One year Hong Kong might be the lowest-cost source for a particular component, and the next year, Mexico may be.

Sourcing component parts from independent suppliers can also be advantageous when the optimal location for manufacturing a product is beset by political risks. Under such circumstances, foreign direct investment to establish a component manufacturing operation in that country would expose the firm to all kinds of political risks. The firm can avoid many of these risks by buying from an independent supplier in that country, thereby maintaining the flexibility to switch sourcing to another country in the event that a war, revolution, or other political change alters that country's attractiveness as a supply source.

It should be noted, however, that maintaining strategic flexibility has its downside. Specifically, if a supplier perceives the firm will change suppliers in response to changes in exchange rates, trade barriers, or general political circumstances, that supplier might not be willing to make specialized investments in plant and equipment that would ultimately benefit the firm.

Organizational Benefits

Vertical integration into the manufacture of component parts increases an organization's scope, and the resulting increase in organizational complexity can be costly. There are three reasons for this. First, the greater the number of subunits in an organization, the greater are the problems of coordinating and controlling those units. Coordinating and controlling subunits requires top management to effectively process large amounts of information about subunit activities. The greater the number of subunits, the more information top management must process and the harder it is for them to do this well. Theoretically, when the firm becomes involved in too many activities, headquarters management will be unable to effectively control all of them, and the resulting inefficiencies will more than offset any advantages derived from vertical integration.[8] This problem

[8] For a review of these arguments, see C. W. L. Hill and R. E. Hoskisson, "Strategy and Structure in the Multiproduct Firm," *Academy of Management Review* 12 (1987), pp. 331–41.

can be particularly serious in an international business, where the problem of controlling subunits is exacerbated by distance and differences in time, language, and culture.

Second, the firm that vertically integrates into component part manufacture may find that because its internal suppliers have a captive customer in the firm, they will lack an incentive to reduce costs. The fact that they do not have to compete for orders with other suppliers may result in *high* operating costs. Indeed, the managers of the supply operation may be tempted to pass on any cost increases to other parts of the firm in the form of higher transfer prices, rather than looking for ways to reduce those costs.

Third, leading on from the previous point, vertically integrated firms have to determine appropriate prices for goods transferred to subunits within the firm. This is a challenge in any firm, but it is even more complex in international businesses. Different tax regimes, exchange rate movements, and headquarters ignorance about local conditions all increase the complexity of transfer pricing decisions in the international business. This complexity enhances internal suppliers' ability to manipulate transfer prices to their advantage, passing cost increases downstream rather than looking for ways to reduce costs.

The firm that buys its components from independent suppliers can avoid all of these problems. The firm that sources from independent suppliers has fewer subunits to control. The incentive problems that occur with internal suppliers do not arise when independent suppliers are used. Independent suppliers know they must continue to be efficient if they are to win business from the firm. Moreover, since independent suppliers' prices are set by market forces, the transfer pricing problem does not exist. In sum, the bureaucratic inefficiencies that can arise when firms vertically integrate backward and manufacture their own components are avoided by buying component parts from independent suppliers.

Trade-offs

It is clear that trade-offs are involved in make-or-buy decisions. The benefits of manufacturing components in-house seem to be greatest when highly specialized assets are involved or when vertical integration is necessary for protecting proprietary technology. In any other circumstances, the potentials for strategic inflexibility and organizational problems suggest that it may be better to contract out component part manufacturing to independent suppliers. Since issues of strategic flexibility and organizational control loom even larger for international businesses than purely domestic ones, it follows that an international business should be particularly wary of vertical integration into component part manufacture.

Strategic Alliances with Suppliers

Several international businesses have tried to reap some of the benefits of vertical integration without the associated organizational problems by entering into strategic alliances with key suppliers. For example, in recent years we have seen an alliance between Kodak and Canon, under which Canon builds photocopiers for sale by Kodak; an alliance between Apple and Sony, under which Sony builds laptop computers for Apple; and an alliance between IBM and Epson, under which Epson provides key component parts for IBM's PROPRINTER. By these alliances, Kodak, Apple, and IBM have committed themselves to long-term relationships with these suppliers, which have, no doubt, encouraged the suppliers to undertake specialized investments. Recall from our earlier discussion that a lack of trust inhibits suppliers from making specialized investments to supply a firm with inputs. Strategic alliances are a way to build trust between the firm and its suppliers. Trust is built when a firm makes a credible commitment to continue purchasing from a supplier on reasonable terms. For example, the firm may invest money in a supplier—perhaps by taking a minority shareholding—to signal its intention to build a productive, mutually beneficial long-term relationship.

This kind of arrangement between the firm and its parts suppliers was pioneered in Japan by large auto companies such as Toyota. Many of the Japanese automakers have cooperative relationships with their suppliers that go back for decades. In these relationships the auto companies and their suppliers collaborate on ways to increase value-added by, for example, implementing just-in-time inventory systems or cooperating in the design of component parts to improve quality and reduce assembly costs. These relationships have been formalized when the auto firms acquired minority shareholdings in many of their key suppliers to symbolize their desire for long-term cooperative relationships with them. At the same time, the relationship between the firm and each key supplier remains market mediated and terminable if the supplier fails to perform up to standard. By pursuing such a strategy, the Japanese automakers have been able to capture many of the benefits of vertical integration—particularly those arising from investments in specialized assets—without suffering the organizational problems that come with formal vertical integration. The parts suppliers also benefit from these relationships, since they grow with the firm they supply and they share in its success. As a result of these strategies, Toyota manufactures only 27 percent of its component parts in-house, compared to 50 percent at Ford and 70 percent at GM. Of these three firms, Toyota appears to spend the least on component parts—suggesting it has captured many of the benefits that induced Ford and GM to vertically integrate while avoiding organizational inefficiencies. For example, in 1985 U.S. manufacturers spent an average of $3,350 on parts, materials, and services for small cars, whereas the average Japanese company spent $2,750—a cost saving of $600 that was achieved mainly through more efficient vendor relations.[9]

In general, the trends toward just-in-time systems (JIT), computer-aided design (CAD), and computer-aided manufacturing (CAM) seem to have increased pressures for firms to establish long-term relationships with their suppliers. JIT, CAD, and CAM systems all rely on close links between firms and their suppliers supported by substantial specialized investment in equipment and information systems hardware. To get a supplier to agree to adopt such systems, a firm must make some kind of credible commitment to an enduring relationship with the supplier. In other words, it must build trust with the supplier. It can do this within the framework of a strategic alliance.

One final word. Alliances are not all good. Like formal vertical integration, a firm that enters into long-term alliances may limit its strategic flexibility by the commitments it makes to its alliance partners. Moreover, as we saw in Chapter 14 when we considered alliances between competitors, a firm that allies itself with another firm risks giving away key technological know-how to a potential competitor.

COORDINATING A GLOBAL MANUFACTURING SYSTEM

Until this point in the chapter we have been discussing aspects of manufacturing strategy. Now it is time to turn our attention to the topic of materials management. **Materials management** encompasses the activities necessary to get materials to a manufacturing facility, through the manufacturing process, and out through a distribution system to the

[9] C. W. L. Hill, "Cooperation, Opportunism, and the Invisible Hand," *Academy of Management Review* 15 (1990), pp. 500–13.

Figure 16.4
Material Costs as a Percentage of Turnover in Eight Industries

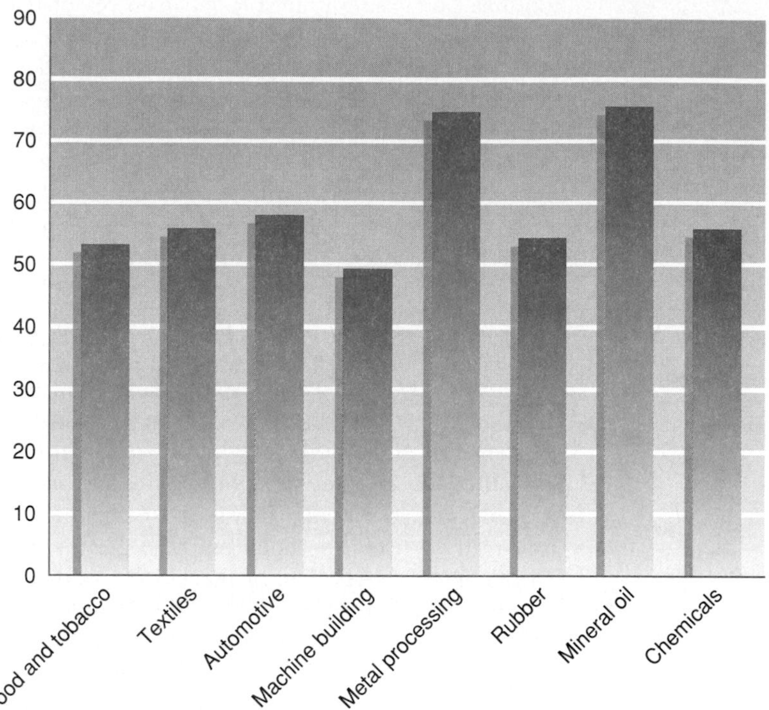

end user.[10] The objective of materials management is to achieve this at the lowest possible cost, thereby lowering the costs of value creation and helping the firms establish a competitive advantage.

The potential for reducing costs through more efficient materials management are enormous. For the typical manufacturing enterprise, material costs account for between 50 and 70 percent of revenues (see Figure 16.4 for a breakdown by industry). Even a small reduction in these costs can have a substantial impact on firm profitability. According to one estimate, for a firm with revenues of $1 million, a return on investment rate of 5 percent, and materials costs that are 50 percent of sales revenues, a $15,000 increase in total profits could be achieved either by increasing sales revenues 30 percent *or* by reducing materials costs by 3 percent.[11] In a saturated market it would be much easier to reduce materials costs by 3 percent than to increase sales revenues by 30 percent.

The materials management task is a major undertaking in a firm with a globally dispersed manufacturing system and global markets. Consider the example of Bose Corporation presented in the opening case. Bose purchases component parts from suppliers scattered over North American, Europe, and the Far East. It assembles its high-fidelity speakers in Massachusetts and ships them to customers the world over. Bose's materials management function must coordinate the flow of component parts so they arrive at the assembly plant just in time to enter the production system. Then they must oversee the timely distribution of finished speakers to customers around the globe. These

[10] R. Narasimhan and J. R. Carter, "Organization, Communication and Coordination of International Sourcing," *International Marketing Review* 7 (1990), pp. 6–20.

[11] H. F. Busch, "Integrated Materials Management," *IJPD & MM 18 (1990), pp. 28–39.*

BOX 16.2

BMW's Parts Distribution Network

An important component of consumer satisfaction is speed of service, and this is especially so in the U.S. automobile industry. Americans have become so dependent on their cars that they demand very quick service when their cars need repairs. To satisfy these demands, BMW has applied materials management techniques to its parts distribution network. BMW's aim is to get spare parts to a dealer within 24 hours so a customer's car can be fixed.

BMW serves its 420 automobile dealers and 290 motorcycle dealers in North America from parts distribution centers (PDCs) located in New Jersey, Texas, and California. Each dealer can access its regional PDC via a computer link. If the regional PDC does not have the needed part, the computer inventory system automatically checks availability in the next-closest PDC. The first PDC to have the part will ship it to the dealer via overnight air express.

If the search for a spare part is unsuccessful in the United States, the request is automatically transferred to BMW's world parts depot in Germany. This is not uncommon. BMW's parts list contains close to 100,000 items, and it would be very costly for the U.S. PDCs to maintain full inventories. BMW needs a system that can quickly fill requests for slow-moving parts while freeing the U.S. PDCs to concentrate on the more active half of the stock list. Accordingly, when parts that are not available in the United States are needed, BMW arranges for air express shipments via Federal Express from Germany to the U.S. dealer. Parts are normally delivered in 24 to 36 hours by this system. Federal Express moves 60-plus BMW parts each night from Germany directly to U.S. dealers.

Source: J. Barks, "Savvy Strategies for International Logistics: BMW," Distribution, *January 1992, pp. 46–47.*

tasks are complicated by the vast distances involved and by the fact that component parts and finished products are shipped across national borders, where they must pass Customs. Moreover, as shown in the opening case, from time to time Bose must be able to interrupt the normal supply chain to accelerate the delivery of key components to respond to sudden upsurges in demand for Bose's products. Another example of how efficient materials management can help a firm achieve competitive advantage, BMW, is given in Box 16.2.

In the remainder of this section we will see how firms such as Bose can manage materials efficiently. First, we will look at the just-in-time inventory system's role in influencing the performance of the materials management function. Then we will discuss the role of organization and information technology in facilitating an efficient materials management function.

The Power of Just-in-Time

Pioneered by Japanese firms during the 1950s and 60s, just-in-time inventory systems now play a major role in most manufacturing firms. The basic philosophy behind **just-in-time (JIT)** systems is to economize on inventory holding costs by having materials arrive at a manufacturing plant just in time to enter the production process, and not before. The major cost saving comes from speeding up inventory turnover; this reduces inventory holding costs, such as warehousing and storage costs. For example, Ford's switch to JIT systems in the early 1980s reportedly brought the firm a huge one-time savings of $3 billion. Minimal inventory now turns over nine times a year at Ford instead of the former six, which reduced carrying costs by a third almost immediately.

In addition to the cost benefits, JIT systems can also help firms improve product quality. Under a JIT system, parts enter the manufacturing process immediately; they are

Figure 16.5
Potential Materials Management Linkages

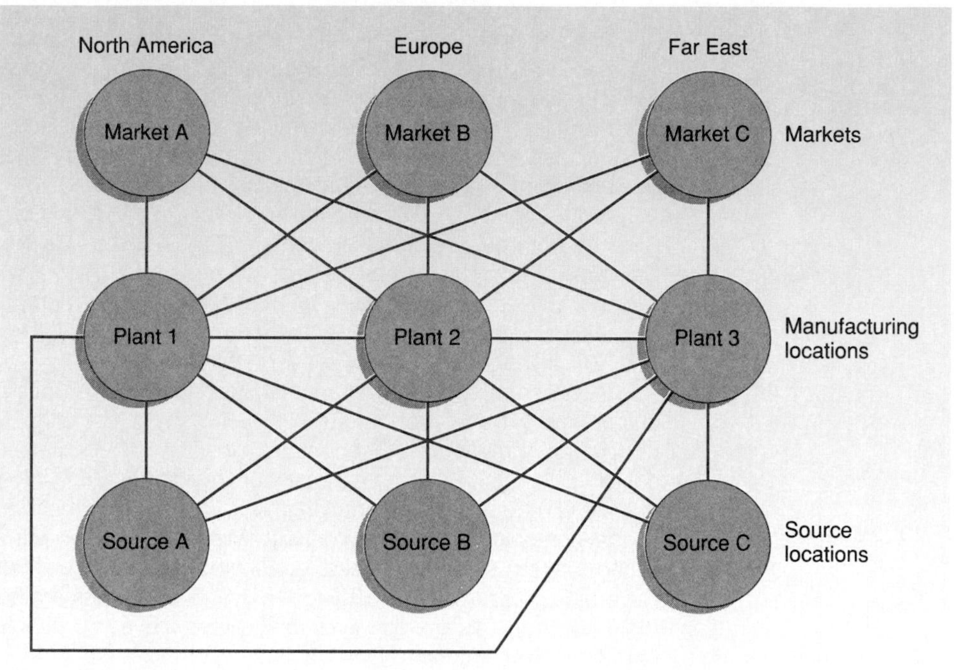

not warehoused. This allows defective inputs to be spotted right away. The problem can then be traced to the supply source and fixed before more defective parts are produced. Under a more traditional system, the practice of warehousing parts for months before they are used allows a large number of defective parts to be produced by a supplier before a problem is recognized.

The drawback of a JIT system is that it leaves a firm without a buffer stock of inventory. Although buffer stocks are expensive to store, they can help tide a firm over shortages bought about by disruption among suppliers (such as a labor dispute in a key supplier). Buffer stocks can also help a firm respond quickly to increases in demand. However, there are ways around these limitations. To reduce the risks associated with depending on one supplier for an important input, some firms source these inputs from several suppliers. As for responding quickly to increases in consumer demand, the experience of Bose Corporation shows that it is possible to do this while maintaining a JIT system—even if it involves shipping component parts by air express rather than overland or by ship.

The Role of Organization

As the number and dispersion of domestic and foreign markets and sources grow, the number and complexity of organizational linkages increase correspondingly. In a fully fledged multinational enterprise, the challenge of managing the costs associated with purchases, currency exchange, inbound and outbound transportation, production, inventory, communication, expediting, tariffs and duties, and overall administration is indeed massive. This is due to the number and complexity of organizational linkages that need to be managed. Figure 16.5 shows the linkages that might exist for a firm that sources, manufactures, and sells internationally. Each linkage represents a flow of materials, capital, information, decisions, and people. Given the complexity, the question is, How best can the firm be organized to achieve tight coordination of the various stages of the value creation process?

A major requirement seems to be to legitimize materials management by separating it out as a *function* and giving it equal weight, in organizational terms, with other, "more traditional" functions such as manufacturing, marketing, and R&D. According to materials management specialists, the idea behind establishing a separate materials management function is that purchasing, production, and distribution are not separate activities but three aspects of one basic task: controlling the flow of materials and products *from* sources of supply *through* manufacturing and distribution *into* the hands of customers.

Despite the apparent cost and quality control advantages of having a separate materials management function, by no means do all U.S. firms actually operate with such a function.[12] Those that do not include many firms in which purchasing costs, inventories, and customer service levels are important, interdependent aspects of establishing competitive advantage. Such firms typically operate with a traditional organizational structure similar to the one in Figure 16.6a. In such an organization, purchasing, production planning and control, and distribution are not integrated. Indeed, planning and control are part of the manufacturing function, whereas distribution is part of the marketing function. Such companies will be unable to establish materials management as a major strength and consequently may face higher costs. Figure 16.6b shows the structure of a typical organization in which materials management is a separate function. Note that purchasing, planning and control, and distribution are integrated within the materials management function. Such an arrangement allows the firm to transform materials management into an important strength.

Having established the legitimacy of materials management, the next question is, How best can its influence be structured in a multinational enterprise? In practice, authority is either centralized or decentralized.[13] Under a centralized solution, most materials management decisions are made at the corporate level, which can ensure efficiency and adherence to overall corporate objectives. This is the case at Bose Corporation, for example. In large, complex organizations with many manufacturing plants, however, a centralized materials management function may soon become overloaded and unable to perform its task effectively. In such cases, a decentralized solution is needed.

A decentralized solution delegates most materials management decisions to the level of individual manufacturing plants within the firm, although corporate headquarters retains responsibility for overseeing the function. The great advantage of decentralizing is that it allows plant-level materials management groups to develop the knowledge and skills needed for interacting with foreign suppliers that are important to their particular plant. This can lead to better decision making. The disadvantage is that a lack of coordination between plants can result in less than optimal global sourcing. It can also lead to duplication of materials management efforts across plants. These disadvantages can be attenuated, however, if the firm has information systems that enable headquarters to facilitate coordination of the various plant-level materials management groups.

The Role of Information Technology

As we saw in the opening case on Bose Corporation, information systems play a crucial role in modern materials management. By tracking component parts as they make their

---

[12] J. G. Miller and P. Gilmour, "Materials Managers: Who Needs Them?" *Harvard Business Review*, July–August 1979, pp. 57–67.

[13] Narasimhan and Carter, "International Sourcing."

Figure 16.6a
Traditional Organizational Structure

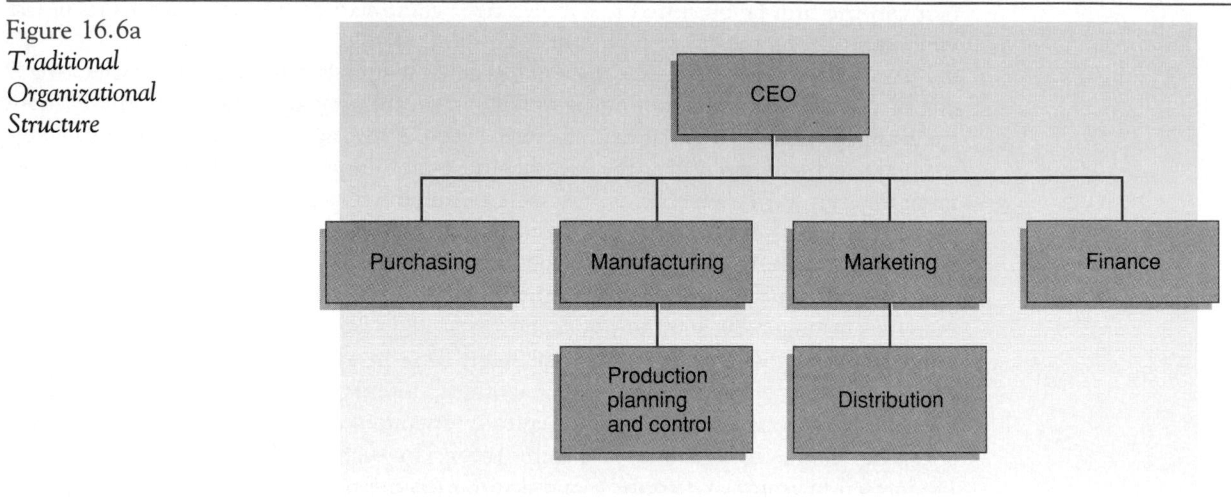

Figure 16.6b *Organizational Structure with Materials Management as a Separate Function*

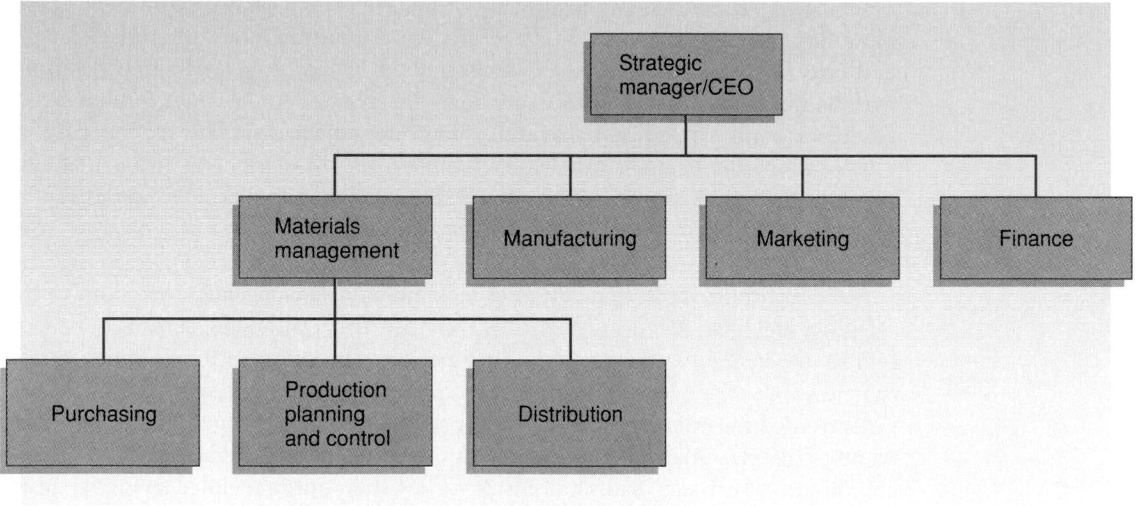

way across the globe toward an assembly plant, information systems enable a firm to optimize its production scheduling according to when components are expected to arrive. By locating component parts in the supply chain precisely, good information systems allow the firm to accelerate production when needed by pulling key components out of the regular supply chain and having them air expressed to the manufacturing plant.

Firms are increasingly using electronic data interchange (EDI) to help coordinate the flow of materials into manufacturing, through manufacturing, and out to customers. At a minimum, EDI systems require computer linkages between a firm, its suppliers, and its shippers. Sometimes customers also are integrated into the system. These electronic linkages are then used to place orders with suppliers, to register parts leaving a supplier, to track them as they travel toward a manufacturing plant, and to register their arrival. Suppliers typically use an EDI link to send invoices to the purchasing firm. One consequence of an EDI system is that suppliers, shippers, and the purchasing firm are able to communicate with each other in "real time" (with no time delay), which vastly increases the flexibility and responsiveness of the whole supply system. The second consequence is that much of the paperwork between suppliers, shippers, and the purchasing firm is eliminated. Furthermore, good EDI systems can help a firm decentralize materials management decisions to the plant level. It does this by giving corporate-level managers the information they need for coordinating and controlling decentralized materials management groups.

SUMMARY OF CHAPTER

This chapter has explained how efficient manufacturing and materials management functions can help improve an international business's competitive position by lowering the costs of value creation and by performing value creation activities in such ways that value-added is maximized. We looked closely at three issues central to international manufacturing and materials management: where to manufacture, what to make and what to buy, and how to coordinate a globally dispersed manufacturing and supply system. The following points were made in the chapter:

1. The choice of an optimal manufacturing location must consider country factors, technological factors, and product factors.
2. Country factors include the influence of factor costs, political economy, and national culture on manufacturing costs.
3. Technological factors include the fixed costs of setting up manufacturing facilities, the minimum efficient scale of production, and the availability of flexible manufacturing technologies.
4. Product factors include the value-to-weight ratio of the product and whether the product serves universal needs.
5. Location strategies either concentrate or decentralize manufacturing. The choice should be made in light of country, technological, and product factors. All location decisions involve trade-offs.
6. A key issue in many international businesses is determining which component parts should be manufactured in-house and which should be out-sourced to independent suppliers.
7. The advantages of making components in-house are that it facilitates investments in specialized assets and helps the firm protect its proprietary technology. It may improve scheduling between adjacent stages in the value chain, also.
8. The advantages of buying components from independent suppliers are that it facilitates strategic flexibility and helps the firm avoid the organizational problems associated with extensive vertical integration.
9. Several firms have tried to attain the benefits of vertical integration and avoid its associated organizational problems by entering into long-term strategic alliances with key suppliers.
10. Although alliances with suppliers can give a firm the benefits of vertical integration without dispensing entirely with the benefits of a market relationship, alliances have drawbacks. The firm that enters into a strategic alliance may find its strategic flexibility limited by commitments to alliance partners.
11. Materials management encompasses all the activities that move materials to a manufacturing facility, through the manufacturing process, and out through a distribution system to the end user. The materials management function is complicated in an international business by distance, time, exchange rates, custom barriers, and other things.
12. Efficient materials management can have a major impact on a firm's bottom line.
13. Just-in-time systems generate major cost savings from reduced warehousing and inventory holding costs. In addition, JIT systems help the firm spot defective parts and remove them from the manufacturing process, thereby improving product quality.
14. For a firm to establish a good materials management function, it needs to legitimize materials management within the organization. It can do this by giving materials management equal footing with other functions in the firm.
15. Information technology, particularly electronic data interchange, plays a major role in materials management. EDI facilitates the tracking of inputs, allows the firm to optimize its production schedule, allows the firm and its suppliers to communicate in real time, and eliminate the flow of paperwork between a firm and its suppliers.

DISCUSSION QUESTIONS

1. An electronics firm is considering how best to supply the world market for microprocessors used in consumer and industrial electronic products. A manufacturing plant costs approximately $500 million to construct and requires a highly skilled work force. The total value of the world market for this product over the next 10 years is estimated to be in the range of $10 to $15 billion. The tariffs prevailing in this industry are currently low. What kind of manufacturing strategy do you think the firm should adopt—concentrated or decentralized? What kind of location(s) should the firm favor for its plant(s)?
2. A chemical firm is considering how best to supply the world market for sulfuric acid. A manufacturing plant costs approximately $20 million to construct and requires a moderately skilled work force. The total value of the world market for this product over the next 10 years is estimated to be in the range of $20 to $30 billion dollars. The tariffs prevailing in this industry are moderate. Should the firm favor concentrated manufacturing or decentralized manufacturing? What kind of location(s) should the firm seek for its plant(s)?
3. A firm must decide whether to make a component part in-house or to contract it out to an independent supplier. Manufacturing the part requires a nonrecoverable investment in specialized assets. The most efficient suppliers are located in countries with currencies that many foreign exchange analysts expect to appreciate substantially over the next decade. What are the pros and cons of (*a*) manufacturing the component in-house and (*b*) out-sourcing manufacture to an independent supplier? Which option would you recommend? Why?
4. Explain how an efficient materials management function can help an international business compete more effectively in the global marketplace.

Global Marketing and R&D

CHAPTER 17

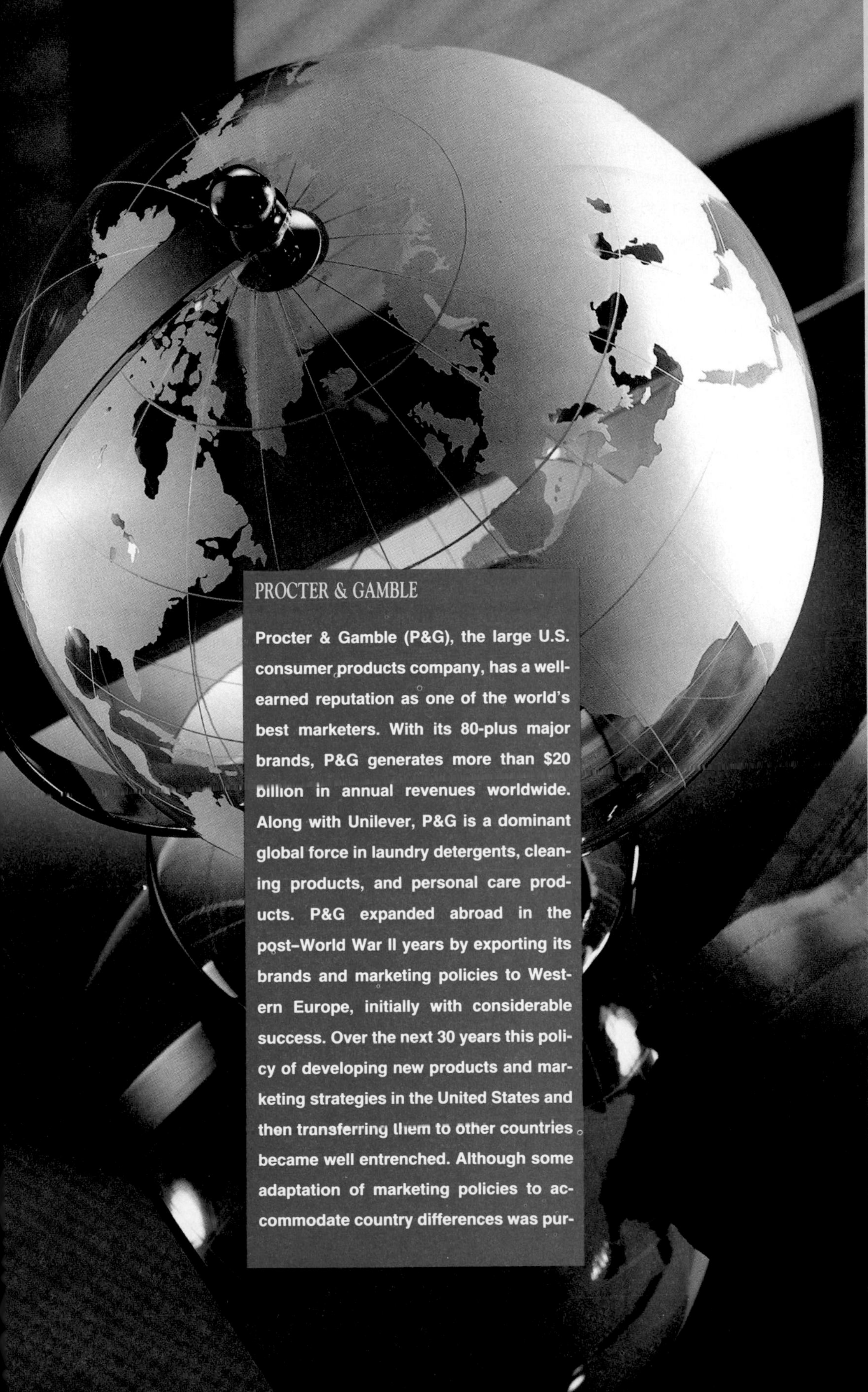

PROCTER & GAMBLE

Procter & Gamble (P&G), the large U.S. consumer products company, has a well-earned reputation as one of the world's best marketers. With its 80-plus major brands, P&G generates more than $20 billion in annual revenues worldwide. Along with Unilever, P&G is a dominant global force in laundry detergents, cleaning products, and personal care products. P&G expanded abroad in the post–World War II years by exporting its brands and marketing policies to Western Europe, initially with considerable success. Over the next 30 years this policy of developing new products and marketing strategies in the United States and then transferring them to other countries became well entrenched. Although some adaptation of marketing policies to accommodate country differences was pursued, by and large this adaptation was fairly minimal. • The first signs that this policy was no longer effective emerged in the 1970s, when P&G suffered a number of major setbacks in Japan. By 1985, after 13 years in Japan, P&G was still losing $40 million a year there. It had introduced disposable diapers in Japan and at one time had commanded an 80 percent share of the market, but yet by the early 1980s it held a miserable 8 percent. Three large Japanese consumer-products companies were dominating the market. P&G's problem was that its diapers, developed in the United States, were too bulky for the tastes of Japanese consumers. With this in mind, Kao, a Japanese company, had developed a line of trim-fit diapers that appealed more to Japanese tastes. Kao introduced its product with a marketing blitz and was quickly rewarded with a 30 percent share of the market. As for P&G, it realized that it would have to modify its diapers if it were to compete in Japan. So it did, and the company now has a 30 percent share of the Japanese market. Moreover, ironically, P&G's trim-fit diapers have become a best-seller in the United States. • P&G had a similar experience in marketing education in the Japanese laundry detergent market. In the early 1980s P&G introduced its Cheer laundry detergent in Japan. Developed in the United States, Cheer was promoted in Japan with the U.S. marketing message—that Cheer works in all temperatures and produces lots of rich suds. The problem was that many Japanese consumers wash their clothes in cold tap water, which made the claim of working in all temperatures irrelevant. Moreover, many Japanese add fabric softeners to their water, which reduces detergents' sudsing action—so Cheer did not suds up as advertised. After a disastrous launch, P&G knew it had to adapt its marketing message. Cheer is now promoted as a product that works effectively in cold water with fabric softeners added, and it is one of P&G's best-selling products in Japan. • P&G's experience with disposable diapers and laundry detergents in Japan forced the company to rethink its product development and marketing philosophy. The company now admits that its U.S.-centered way of doing business no longer works. Since the late 1980s P&G has been delegating more responsibility for new product development and marketing to its major subsidiaries in Japan and Europe. The company is more responsive to local differences in consumer tastes and preferences and more willing to admit that good new products can be developed outside the United States. • Despite the apparent changes at P&G, it is still not clear that P&G has achieved the revolution in thinking required to alter its long-standing practices. Its recent venture into the Polish shampoo market seems to illustrate that the company still has a way to go. In summer 1991 P&G entered the Polish market with its Vidal Sasson Wash & Go, an "all-in-one" shampoo and conditioner that is a best-seller in the United States and Europe. The product launch was supported by a U.S.-style marketing blitz on a scale never before seen in Poland. At first the campaign seemed to be effective as P&G captured more than 30 percent of the shampoo market, but early in 1992 sales suddenly plummeted. Then came the rumors—Wash & Go causes dandruff and hair loss—allegations P&G has strenuously denied. Next came the jokes. One doing the rounds in Poland is "I washed my car with Wash & Go, and the tires went bald." And when President Lech Walesa proposed about that time that he also be named prime minister, critics derided the idea as a "two-in-one solution, just like Wash & Go." • Where did P&G go wrong? The most common theory is that it promoted Wash & Go too hard in a country that has little enthusiasm for brash U.S.-style advertising. A poll by Pentor, a private market research company in Warsaw, found that almost three times more Poles disliked P&G's commercials than liked them. Pentor also argues that the high-profile marketing campaign backfired because years of Communist party propaganda have led Polish consumers to suspect that advertising is simply a way to move goods nobody wants. Some also believe Wash & Go, which was developed for U.S. consumers who shampoo daily, was far too sophisticated for Polish consumers who are less obsessed with personal hygiene. Underlying all of these criticisms is the idea that P&G once again stumbled because it transferred a product and marketing strategy wholesale from the United States to another country without modifying it to the tastes and preferences of local consumers. 🌐 *Sources: Guy de Jonquieres and C. Bobinski, "Wash and Get into a Lather in Poland,"* Financial Times, *May 28, 1992, p. 2; "Perestroika in Soapland,"* The Economist, *June 10, 1989, pp. 69–71; "After Early Stumbles P&G Is Making Inroads Overseas,"* The Wall Street Journal, *February 6, 1989, p. B1; and C. A. Bartlett and S. Ghoshal,* Managing across Borders: The Transnational Solution *(Boston, Mass.: Harvard Business School Press, 1989).*

INTRODUCTION

In the last chapter we looked at the roles of global manufacturing and materials management in an international business. In this chapter we continue our focus on specific business functions by examining the roles of marketing and research and development (R&D) in an international business. Specifically, our focus is on how marketing and R&D can be performed so they will reduce the costs of value creation and add value by better serving customer needs.

In Chapter 12 we spoke of the tension existing in most international businesses between the needs to reduce costs and at the same time to respond to local conditions, which tends to raise costs. This tension has been a persistent theme in most chapters since then, and it continues to be in this chapter. Most important, a global marketing strategy, which views the world's consumers as similar in their tastes and preferences, is consistent with the mass production of a standardized output. By mass producing a standardized output, the firm can realize substantial unit cost reductions from experience curve and other scale economies. On the other hand, ignoring country differences in consumer tastes and preferences can lead to failure. As we saw in the opening case, Procter & Gamble found this out more than once. Thus, an international business's marketing function needs to determine when product standardization is appropriate and when it is not. Similarly, the firm's R&D function needs to be able to develop globally standardized products when appropriate as well as products customized to local requirements when they are needed.

We are considering marketing and R&D within the same chapter because of their close relationship. A critical aspect of the marketing function is identifying gaps in the market so that new products can be developed to fill those gaps. Developing new products requires R&D; thus the linkage between marketing and R&D. Specifically, new products should be developed with market needs in mind, and only marketing can define those needs for R&D personnel. Moreover, only marketing can tell R&D whether to produce globally standardized or locally customized products. Consistent with this, academic research has long maintained that a major factor of success for new product introductions is the closeness of the relationship between marketing and R&D. The closer the linkage, the greater the success rate.[1]

[1] For example, see R. W. Ruekert and O. C. Walker, "Interactions between Marketing and R&D Departments in Implementing Different Business-Level Strategies," *Strategic Management Journal* 8(1987), pp. 233–248.

The opening case illustrates this principle quite well. Procter & Gamble's R&D function has traditionally been centralized in the United States, and most of its new products have been developed there. The linkages between R&D and foreign marketing operations have been weak; new products have been developed for the U.S. market and then "thrown over the wall" to foreign markets. The result: many of P&G's products have not been sufficiently customized to the tastes and preferences of consumers in other nations, and they have failed to gain market share. P&G erred in assuming consumers in the rest of the world are like Americans. A good marketing function can point this out to the R&D function, which, in response, can customize products to local conditions.

With all of this as background, in this chapter we examine the roles of marketing and R&D in international businesses. We begin by reviewing the debate on the globalization of markets. Then we discuss the four elements that constitute a firm's marketing mix: product attributes, distribution strategy, communication strategy, and pricing strategy. The marketing mix is the set of choices the firm offers to its targeted market(s). Many firms vary their marketing mix from country to country depending on differences in national culture, economic development, product standards, distribution channels, and so on. The chapter closes with a look at new product development in an international business and at the implications of this for the organization of the firm's R&D function.

THE GLOBALIZATION OF MARKETS?

In a now-famous *Harvard Business Review* article, Theodore Levitt waxed lyrically about the globalization of world markets.[2] Levitt's arguments are worth quoting at some length, since they have become something of a lightning rod for the debate about the extent of globalization. According to Levitt:

> A powerful force drives the world toward a converging commonalty, and that force is technology. It has proletarianized communication, transport, and travel. The result is a new commercial reality—the emergence of global markets for standardized consumer products on a previously unimagined scale of magnitude.
>
> Gone are accustomed differences in national or regional preferences. . . . The globalization of markets is at hand. With that, the multinational commercial world nears its end, and so does the multinational corporation. The multinational corporation operates in a number of countries and adjusts its products and practices to each—at high relative costs. The global corporation operates with resolute consistency—at low relative cost—as if the entire world were a single entity; it sells the same thing in the same way everywhere.
>
> Commercially, nothing confirms this as much as the success of McDonald's from the Champs Elysees to the Ginza, of Coca-Cola in Bahrain and Pepsi-Cola in Moscow, and of rock music, Greek salad, Hollywood movies, Revlon cosmetics, Sony television, and Levi's jeans everywhere.
>
> Ancient differences in national tastes or modes of doing business disappear. The commonalty of preference leads inescapably to the standardization of products, manufacturing, and the institutions of trade and commerce.

Is Levitt correct? If he is, this clearly has major implications for the marketing strategies pursued by international business. The consensus among academics seems to be that Levitt overstates his case.[3] Although Levitt may have a point when it comes to many

---

[2] T. Levitt, "The Globalization of Markets," *Harvard Business Review*, May–June 1983, pp. 92–102.

[3] For example, see S. P. Douglas and Y. Wind, "The Myth of Globalization," *Columbia Journal of World Business*, Winter 1987, pp. 19–29; and C. A. Bartlett and S. Ghoshal, *Managing across Borders: The Transnational Solution* (Boston, Mass.: Harvard Business School Press, 1989).

basic industrial products—such as steel, bulk chemicals, and semi-conductor chips—at present globalization seems to be the exception rather than the rule in most consumer goods markets and many industrial markets. Even a firm such as McDonald's, which Levitt holds up as the archetypal example of a consumer products firm that sells a standardized product worldwide, in fact modifies its menu from country to country in light of local consumer preferences.[4]

On the other hand, Levitt is probably correct to assert that modern transportation and communications technologies are serving to converge the tastes and preferences of consumers in the more advanced countries of the world. The popularity of sushi in Los Angeles and hamburgers in Tokyo certainly support this. In the very long run, such technological forces may lead to the evolution of a global culture. At present, however, the continuing persistence of cultural and economic differences between nations acts as a major brake on any trend toward global consumer tastes and preferences. In addition, trade barriers and differences in product and technical standards also constrain a firm's ability to sell a standardized product to a global market. We discuss the sources of these differences in the next section when we look at how products must be altered from country to country. For now, note that these differences are so substantial that Levitt's globally standardized markets seem a long way off in many industries.

PRODUCT ATTRIBUTES

A product can be viewed as a bundle of attributes.[5] For example, the attributes that make up a car include power, design, quality, performance, fuel consumption, and comfort; the attributes of a hamburger include taste, texture, and size; a hotel's attributes include atmosphere, quality, comfort, and service. Products sell well when their attributes match consumer needs (and when their prices are appropriate). BMW cars sell well to people who have high needs for luxury, quality, and performance, precisely because BMW builds those attributes into its cars. If consumer needs were the same the world over, a firm could simply sell the same product worldwide. Actually, however, consumer needs vary from country to country depending on culture and the level of economic development. In addition, a firm's ability to sell the same product worldwide is further constrained by countries' differing product standards. In this section we review each of these issues and discuss how they influence product attributes.

Cultural Differences

We discussed the topic of countries' cultural differences in Chapter 3. There we pointed out that countries differ along a whole range of dimensions, including social structure, language, religion, and education. And as alluded to in Chapter 2, these differences have important implications for marketing strategy. For example, "*ham*burgers" do not sell well in Islamic countries, where the consumption of ham is forbidden by Islamic law. More generally, with regard to country differences in consumer tastes and preferences, the most important aspect of countries' cultural differences is probably the impact of *tradition*. Tradition is particularly important in foodstuffs and beverages. For example, reflecting differences in traditional eating habits, the Findus frozen food division of Nestle, the Swiss food giant, markets fish cakes and fish fingers in Great Britain, but *beef bourguignon* and *coq au vin* in France and *vitèllo con funghi* and *braviola* in Italy. Similarly, in addition

[4] "Slow Food," *The Economist*, February 3, 1990, p. 64.

[5] This approach was originally developed in K. Lancaster, "A New Approach to Demand Theory," *Journal of Political Economy* 74 (1965), pp. 132–57.

to its normal range of products, Coca-Cola in Japan markets "Georgia," a cold coffee in a can, an "Aquarius," a tonic drink, products that appeal to traditional Japanese tastes.

For historical and idiosyncratic reasons, a whole range of other cultural differences exist between countries. For example, scent preferences differ from one country to another. S. C. Johnson & Son, a manufacturer of waxes and polishes, encountered resistances to its lemon-scented Pledge furniture polish among older consumers in Japan. Careful market research revealed that the polish smelled similar to latrine disinfectant used widely in Japan in the 1940s. Sales rose sharply after the scent was adjusted.[6]

At the same time, there is some evidence of the trends Levitt talked about. Tastes and preferences are becoming more cosmopolitan. Coffee is gaining ground against tea in Japan and Great Britain, while American-style frozen dinners have become popular in Europe (with some fine-tuning to local tastes). Taking advantage of these trends, Nestle has found that it can market its instant coffee, spaghetti bolognese, and Lean Cuisine frozen dinners in essentially the same manner in both North America and Western Europe. However, there is no market for Lean Cuisine dinners in most of the rest of the world, and there may never be. The diet-conscious Asian is difficult to find. Although some cultural convergence has occurred, particularly among the advanced industrial nations of North America and Western Europe, Levitt's global culture is still a long way off.

Economic Differences

Just as important as differences in culture are differences in the level of economic development. We discussed the extent of country differences in economic development in Chapter 2. Consumer behavior is influenced by the level of economic development of a country. Firms based in highly developed countries such as the United States tend to build a lot of extra performance attributes into their products. These extra attributes are not usually demanded by consumers in less-developed nations, where the preference is for more basic products. Thus cars sold in less-developed nations typically lack many of the features found in the West—such as air-conditioning, power steering, power windows, radios, and cassette players. At the same time, for most consumer durables, product reliability may be a more important attribute in less-developed nations, where such a purchase may account for a major proportion of a consumer's income, than it is in advanced nations.

The other side of the coin is that, contrary to Levitt's suggestions, consumers in the most developed countries are often not willing to sacrifice their preferred attributes for lower prices. Consumers in the most advanced countries often shun globally standardized products that have been developed with the lowest common denominator in mind. They are willing to pay more for products that have additional features and attributes customized to their tastes and preferences. For example, demand for top-of-the-line four-wheel-drive sports utility vehicles—such as Chrysler's Jeep, Ford's Explorer, and Toyota's Land Cruiser—is almost totally restricted to the United States. This is due to a combination of factors, including the high income level of U.S. consumers, the country's vast distances, the relatively low cost of gasoline, and the culturally grounded "outdoor" theme of American life.

Product and Technical Standards

Notwithstanding the forces that are creating some convergence of consumer tastes and preferences (at least among advanced, industrialized nations), Levitt's vision of global

[6] V. R. Alden, "Who Says You Can't Crack Japanese Markets?" *Harvard Business Review*, January–February 1987, pp. 52–56.

markets may still be a long way off due to national differences in product and technological standards.

Differing product standards mandated by governments can rule out mass production and marketing of a standardized product. For example, Caterpillar, the U.S. construction equipment firm, manufactures backhoe-loaders for all of Europe in Great Britain. These tractor-type machines have a bucket in front and a digger at the back. Several special parts must be built into backhoe-loaders that will be sold in Germany: a separate brake attached to the rear axle, a special locking mechanism on the backhoe operating valve, specially positioned valves in the steering system, and a lock on the bucket for traveling. These extras account for 5 percent of the total cost of the product in Germany.[7] Interestingly enough, the European Community (EC) is currently trying to harmonize such divergent product standards among its member-nations. If the EC is successful, the need to customize products will be reduced, at least within the boundaries of the EC.

Differences in technical standards also constrain the globalization of markets. Some of these differences result from idiosyncratic decisions made at particular points in history, rather than government actions. Their long-term effects are nonetheless profound. For example, video equipment manufactured for sale in the United States will not play videotapes recorded on equipment manufactured for sale in Great Britain, Germany, and France (and visa versa). The reason: different technical standards for frequency of television signals emerged in the 1950s that require television and video equipment to be customized to countries' prevailing standards. RCA stumbled in the 1970s when it failed to account for this in its marketing of TVs in Asia. Although several Asian countries had adopted the U.S. standard, Singapore, Hong Kong, and Malaysia had adopted the British standard. The result: people who bought RCA TVs in those countries could receive a picture but no sound![8]

DISTRIBUTION STRATEGY

A critical element of a firm's marketing mix is its distribution strategy, the means it chooses for delivering the product to the consumer. The way the product is delivered is determined by the firm's entry strategy, which we discussed in Chapter 14. In this section we examine a typical distribution system, discuss how its structure varies between countries, and look at how appropriate distribution strategies vary from country to country.

A Typical Distribution System

Figure 17.1 illustrates a typical distribution system consisting of a channel that includes a wholesale distributor and a retailer. If the firm manufactures its product in the particular country, it can sell directly to the consumer, to the retailer, or to the wholesaler. The same options are available to a firm that manufactures outside the country. Alternatively, this firm may decide to sell to an import agent, who then deals with the wholesale distributor, the retailer, or the consumer. The factors that determine the firm's choice of channel are considered later in this section.

Differences between Countries

The main differences between countries' distribution systems are threefold: retail concentration, channel length, and channel exclusivity.

---

7 A Bumpy Ride over Europe's Traditions," *Financial Times*, October 31, 1988, p. 5.

8 "RCA's New Vista: The Bottom Line," *Business Week*, July 4, 1977, p. 44.

Figure 17.1
A Typical Distribution System

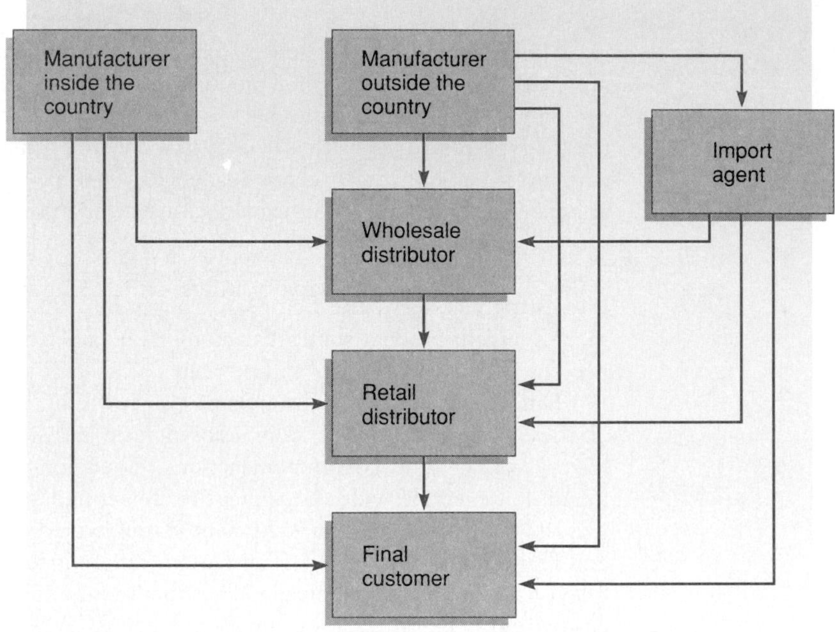

Retail Concentration

In some countries the retail system is very concentrated, whereas in other countries it is fragmented. In a concentrated system, a few retailers supply most of the market. A fragmented system is one in which there are many retailers, no one of which has a major share of the market. In Germany, for example, four retail chains control 65 percent of the market for food products. In neighboring Italy, retail distribution is very fragmented, with no chain controlling more than 2 percent of the market.

Many of the differences in concentration are rooted in history and tradition. In the United States, for example, the importance of the automobile and the relative youth of many urban settlements has resulted in a retail system centered around large stores or shopping malls to which people can drive. This has facilitated the concentration of the system. Japan's much greater population density, together with the large number of urban centers that grew up before the advent of the automobile, has resulted in a more fragmented retail system of many small stores that serve local neighborhoods and to which people frequently walk. In addition, the Japanese legal system protects small retailers. By law, small retailers can effectively block the establishment of a large retail outlet by petitioning their local government.

It should be recognized that there is a tendency for greater retail concentration in developed countries. Three factors that contribute to this are the increases in car ownership, number of households with refrigerators and freezers, and number of two-income households that accompany development. All of these factors have changed shopping habits and facilitated the growth of large retail establishments sited away from traditional shopping areas. Due to such trends, between 1980 and 84 supermarket chains increased their share of the total food market from 75 to 81 percent in Great Britain, from 58 to 67 percent in West Germany, and from 44 to 60 percent in the Netherlands.[9]

[9] "Retailing: Grocer Power," *The Economist,* January 10, 1987, p. 56.

Channel Length

Channel length refers to the number of intermediaries between the producer (or manufacturer) and the consumer. If the producer sells directly to the consumer, the channel is very short. If the producer sells through an import agent, a wholesaler, and a retailer, a long channel exists. The choice of a short or long channel is primarily a strategic decision for the producing firm. However, putting this aside for the moment (we well return to this subject later), it should be noted that some countries have longer distribution channels than others. The most important determinant of channel length is the degree to which the retail system is fragmented. Fragmented retail systems tend to promote the growth of wholesalers to serve retailers, which lengthens channels.

The reason for this is "simple economics." Basically, the more fragmented the retail system, the more expensive it is for a firm to make contact with each individual retailer. Imagine, for example, a firm that sells toothpaste in a country where there are 50,000 small retailers. To sell directly to the retailers, the firm would have to build a huge sales force. This would be very expensive, particularly since each sales call would yield a very small order. Imagine, however, that there are 50 wholesalers in the country who supply retailers not only with toothpaste but with all other personal care and household products. Since these wholesalers carry a wide range of products, they get bigger orders with each sales call. Thus, it becomes worthwhile for them to deal directly with the retailers. Accordingly, it makes economic sense for the firm to sell to the wholesalers and the wholesalers to deal with the retailers.

As a result of such factors, countries with fragmented retail systems also tend to have long channels of distribution. The classic example is Japan, where there are often two or three layers of wholesalers between the firm and retail outlets. In contrast, in countries like Great Britain, Germany, and the United States where the retail system is far more concentrated, channels are much shorter. Indeed, when the retail sector is very concentrated it makes sense for the firm to deal directly with retailers, cutting out wholesalers altogether. This is because a relatively small sales force is required to deal with a concentrated retail sector, and the orders generated from each sales call can be large. Such circumstances tend to prevail in the United States, where large food companies sell directly to supermarkets rather than going through wholesale distributors.

Channel Exclusivity

An exclusive distribution channel is one that is difficult for outsiders to access. For example, it is often difficult for a new firm to get access to shelf space in U.S. supermarkets. This occurs because retailers tend to prefer to carry the products of long-established manufacturers of foodstuffs with national reputations, rather than gamble on the products of unknown firms. How exclusive a distribution system is varies between countries. Japan's system is often held up as an example of a very exclusive system. In Japan, relationships between manufacturers, wholesalers, and retailers often go back decades. Many of these relationships are based on the understanding that distributors will not carry the products of competing firms. In return, the distributors are guaranteed an attractive markup by the manufacturer. As many U.S. and European manufacturers have learned, the close ties that result from this arrangement can make access to the Japanese market very difficult.

Choosing a Distribution Strategy

A choice of distribution strategy determines which channel the firm will use to reach potential consumers. Should the firm try to sell directly to the consumer or should it go through retailers; should it go through a wholesaler; should it use an import agent? The optimal strategy is determined by the relative costs and benefits of each alternative. In turn, the relative costs and benefits of each alternative vary from country to country depending on the three factors we have just discussed: retail concentration, channel length, and channel exclusivity.

The first point to note is that—since each intermediary in a channel adds its own markup to the products—there is generally a critical linkage between channel length, the final selling price, and the firm's profit margin. The longer a channel, the greater is the aggregate markup, and the higher the price that consumers are charged for the final product. To ensure that prices do not get too high due to markups by multiple intermediaries, a firm might be forced to operate with lower profit margins. Thus, if price is an important competitive weapon, and if the firm does not want to see its profit margins squeezed, other things being equal, the firm would prefer to use a shorter channel.

However, the benefits of using a longer channel often outweigh these drawbacks. As we have seen, one benefit of using a longer channel is that it economizes on selling costs when the retail sector is very fragmented. Thus, it makes sense for an international business to use longer channels in countries where the retail sector is fragmented and shorter channels in countries where the retail sector is concentrated.

Another benefit of using a longer channel is market access—the ability to enter an exclusive channel. Import agents may have long-term relationships with wholesalers, retailers, and/or important consumers and thus be better able to win orders and get access to a distribution system than the firm on its own. Similarly, wholesalers may have long-standing relationships with retailers and, therefore, be better able to persuade them to carry the firm's product than the firm itself would.

It should be noted that import agents are not limited to independent trading houses; any firm with a strong local reputation could serve just as well. For example, to break down channel exclusivity and gain greater access to the Japanese market, in 1991 and 92 Apple Computer signed distribution agreements with five large Japanese firms including business equipment giant Brother Industries, stationery leader Kokuyo, Mitsubishi, Sharp, and Minolta. These firms are using their own long-established distribution relationships with consumers, retailers, and wholesalers to push Apple Macintosh computers through the Japanese distribution system. As a result, Apple's share of the Japanese market increased from less than 1 percent in 1988 to 6 percent in 1991, and it is projected to reach 13 percent by 1994.[10]

If such an arrangement is not possible, the firm might want to consider other, less traditional alternatives to gaining market access. Frustrated by channel exclusivity in Japan, some foreign manufacturers of consumer goods have attempted to sell directly to Japanese consumers using direct mail and catalogs. REI, a Northwest retailer of outdoor clothing and equipment, had trouble persuading Japanese wholesalers and retailers to carry its products. So instead it began a direct-mail campaign in Japan that is proving very successful.

COMMUNICATION STRATEGY

Another critical element in the marketing mix is communicating the attributes of the product to prospective customers. A number of communications channels are available to a firm; they include direct selling, sales promotion, direct marketing, and advertising. A

[10] N. Gross and K. Rebello, "Apple? Japan Can't Say No," *Business Week*, June 29, 1992, pp. 32–33.

firm's communications strategy is partly defined by its choice of channel. Some firms rely primarily on direct selling, others on point-of-sale promotions or direct marketing, others on mass advertising; still others use several channels simultaneously to communicate their message to prospective customers. In this section we will look first at the barriers to international communication. Then we will survey the various factors that determine which communications strategy is most appropriate in a particular country. After that we discuss the topic of global advertising.

Barriers to International Communications

International communication occurs whenever a firm uses a marketing message to sell its products in another country. The opening case reports some of Procter & Gamble's expensive lessons in international communication. The effectiveness of a firm's international communication can be jeopardized by three potentially critical variables: cultural barriers, source effects, and noise levels.

Cultural Barriers

Cultural barriers can make it difficult to communicate messages across cultures. We have discussed some sources and consequences of cultural differences between nations, in Chapter 3 and in the previous section of this chapter. Due to cultural differences, a message that means one thing in one country may mean something quite different in another. For example, when Procter & Gamble promoted its Camay soap in Japan in 1983 it ran into unexpected trouble. In a TV commercial, a Japanese man walked into the bathroom while his wife was bathing. The woman began telling her husband all about her new beauty soap, but the husband, stroking her shoulder, hinted that suds were not on his mind. This ad had been very popular in Europe, but it flopped in Japan because it is considered very bad manners there for a man to intrude on his wife.[11] Benetton, the Italian clothing manufacturer and retailer, is another firm that has run into cultural problems with its advertising. The company launched a worldwide advertising campaign in 1989 with the theme "United Colors of Benetton" that had won awards in France. One of its ads featured a black woman breast-feeding a white baby, and another one showed a black man and a white man handcuffed together. Benetton was surprised when the ads were attacked by U.S. civil rights groups for promoting white racial domination. Benetton had to withdraw its ads and it fired its advertising agency, Eldorado of France.

The best way for a firm to overcome cultural barriers is to develop cross-cultural literacy (see Chapter 3). In addition, it should employ some local input in developing its marketing message; for example, it could use a local advertising agency. Alternatively, if the firm uses direct selling rather than advertising to communicate its message, it would be well advised to develop a local sales force whenever possible. Indeed, cultural differences limit a firm's ability to use the same marketing message the world over. What works well in one country may be offensive in another.

Source Effects

Source effects occur when the receiver of the message (the potential consumer in this case) evaluates the message based on the status or image of the sender. Source effects can be damaging for an international business when potential consumers in a target country

---

[11] "After Early Stumbles P&G Is Making Inroads Overseas," *The Wall Street Journal,* February 6, 1989, p. B1.

have a bias against "foreign firms." For example, a wave of "Japan bashing" swept the United States in 1992. Worried that U.S. consumers might view their advertisements negatively, Honda responded by creating advertisements that emphasized the U.S.-content of its cars to show how "American" the company had become. In fact, many international businesses try to counter negative source effects by deemphasizing their foreign origins. When British Petroleum acquired Mobil Oil's extensive network of U.S. gas stations, it changed its name to *BP*, thereby diverting attention away from the fact that one of the biggest operators of gas stations in the United States is a British firm.

Source effects are by no means always negative; they can be positive. French wine, Italian clothes, and German luxury cars benefit from nearly universal positive source effects. Far from downplaying their national origins, in such cases it may pay a firm to emphasize its foreign origins. In Japan, for example, there is currently a boom in demand for high-quality foreign goods, particularly those from Europe. It has become an index of chic to carry a Gucci handbag, sport a Rolex watch, drink expensive French wine, and drive a BMW.

Noise Levels

Noise tends to reduce the probability of effective communication. In this context, *noise* refers to the amount of other messages competing for a potential consumer's attention, and this too varies across countries. In highly developed countries such as the United States, noise from firms competing for the attention of target consumers is extremely high. In contrast, fewer firms vie for the attention of prospective customers in developing countries, and the noise level is lower.

Push versus Pull Strategies

The main decision with regard to communications strategy is the choice between a push strategy and a pull strategy. A **push strategy** emphasizes personal selling rather than mass media advertising in the promotional mix. Although very effective as a promotional tool, personal selling requires intensive use of a sales force and is thus relatively costly. A **pull strategy** depends more on mass media advertising to communicate the marketing message to potential consumers.

Although some firms employ only a pull strategy and others only a push strategy, still other firms combine direct selling with mass advertising to maximize communication effectiveness. Factors that determine the relative attractiveness of push and pull strategies include product type relative to consumer sophistication, channel length, and media availability.

Product Type and Consumer Sophistication

A pull strategy is generally favored by firms in consumer goods industries that are trying to sell to a large segment of the market. For such firms, mass communication has cost advantages, and direct selling is rarely used. In contrast, a push strategy is favored by firms that sell industrial products or other complex products. One of the great strengths of direct selling is that it allows the firm to educate potential consumers about the features of the product. This may not be necessary in advanced nations where a complex product has been in use for some time, where the product's attributes are well understood, and where consumers are sophisticated. However, customer education may be very important when consumers have less sophistication toward the product, which can be the case in developing nations, or in more advanced nations when a complex product is being introduced.

Channel Length

The longer the distribution channel, the more intermediaries there are that must be persuaded to carry the product for it to reach the consumer. This can lead to inertia in the channel, which can make entry very difficult. Moreover, using direct selling to push a product through many layers of a distribution channel can be very expensive. In such circumstances, a firm may try to pull its product through the channels by using mass advertising to create consumer demand—the theory being that once demand is created, intermediaries will feel obliged to carry the product.

Whereas U.S. distribution channels are relatively short, in other countries they can be quite long. As discussed earlier, in Japan products often pass through two, three, or even four wholesalers before they reach the final retail outlet. This can make it difficult for foreign firms to break into the Japanese market. Not only must the foreigner persuade a Japanese retailer to carry her product, she may also have to persuade every intermediary in the chain to carry the product. Mass advertising may be one way to break down channel resistance in such circumstances.

Media Availability

A pull strategy relies on access to advertising media. In the United States, a large number of media are available, including print media (newspapers and magazines) and electronic media (television and radio). Moreover, the rise of cable television in the United States has facilitated extremely focused advertising targeted at particular segments of the market (e.g., MTV for teens and young adults, Lifetime for women, ESPN for sports enthusiasts). With a few exceptions such as Canada and Japan, this level of media sophistication is not found outside the United States. Even many advanced nations have far fewer electronic media available for advertising. In Scandinavia, for example, no commercial television or radio stations existed in 1987; all electronic media were state owned and carried no commercials. Similarly, in Great Britain BBC television and radio services are state owned and carry no commercials. In many developing nations the situation is even more restrictive, since mass media of all types are typically more limited. Obviously, a firm's ability to use a pull strategy is limited in some countries by media availability. In such circumstances, a push strategy is more attractive.

Media availability is limited by law in some cases. Few countries allow advertisements for tobacco and alcohol products on television and radio, though they are usually permitted in print media. When the leading Japanese whiskey distiller, Suntory, entered the U.S. market, it had to do so without television, its preferred medium. The firm spends about $50 million annually on television advertising in Japan.

The Push-Pull Mix

In sum, the optimal mix between push and pull strategies depends on product type and consumer sophistication, channel length, and media sophistication. Push strategies tend to be emphasized:

- For industrial products and/or complex new products.
- When distribution channels are short.
- When few print or electronic media are available.

Pull strategies tend to be emphasized:

- For consumer goods.

- When distribution channels are long.
- When sufficient print and electronic media are available to carry the marketing message.

Global Advertising

In recent years, largely inspired by the work of visionaries such as Theodore Levitt, there has been a great deal of discussion about the pros and cons of standardizing advertising worldwide. One of the most successful standardized campaigns has been Philip Morris's promotion of Marlboro cigarettes. The campaign was instituted in the 1950s, when the brand was repositioned, to assure smokers that the flavor would be unchanged by the addition of a filter. The campaign theme of "Come to where the flavor is. Come to Marlboro country." was a worldwide success. Marlboro built on this when it introduced "the Marlboro man," a rugged cowboy smoking his Marlboro while riding his horse through the great outdoors. This ad proved successful in just about every major market around the world, and it helped propel Marlboro to the top of the world market share table.

For Standardized Advertising

The support for global advertising is threefold. First, it has significant economic advantages. Standardized advertising lowers the costs of value creation by spreading the fixed costs of developing the advertisements over a large number of countries. For example, in the early 1980s Levi Strauss paid an advertising agency $550,000 to produce a series of TV commercials. By reusing this series in many countries, rather than developing a series for each country, the company enjoyed significant cost savings. Similarly, over a 20-year period Coca-Cola's advertising agency, McCann-Erickson, claims to have saved Coca-Cola $90 million in costs by using certain elements of its campaign globally.

Second, there is the concern that creative talent is scarce and hence that one large effort to develop a campaign will produce better results than 40 or 50 smaller efforts.

A third justification for a standardized approach is that many brand names are global. With the substantial amount of international travel today and the considerable overlap in media across national borders, many international firms want to project a single image to avoid confusion caused by local campaigns that conflict with each other. This is particularly important in regions such as Western Europe, where travel across borders is as common as travel across state lines in the United States.

Against Standardized Advertising

There are two main arguments against globally standardized advertising. First, as we have seen repeatedly in this chapter and in Chapter 3, cultural differences between nations are such that a message that works in one nation can fail miserably in another. Due to cultural diversity, it is extremely difficult to develop a single advertising theme that is effective worldwide. Messages directed at the culture of a given country may be more effective than global messages.

Second, country differences in advertising regulations may effectively block the implementation of standardized advertising. For example, Kellogg could not use a television commercial it produced in Great Britain to promote its cornflakes in many other European countries. A reference to the iron and vitamin content of its cornflakes was not permissible in the Netherlands, where claims relating to health and medical benefits are outlawed. A child wearing a Kellogg T-shirt had to be edited out of the commercial before it could be used in France, since French laws forbid the use of children

BOX 17.1

Pitfalls in Global Marketing: Polaroid's Experience

Polaroid introduced its SX-70 instant camera in Europe in the mid-1970s with the same marketing strategy, TV commercials, and print ads it had used in North America. Polaroid's headquarters believed the camera served a universal need—the pleasure of instant photography—and that the communication strategy should thus be the same the world over. The television commercials featured testimonials of personalities well-known in the United States. Few of these personalities were known in Europe, however, and managers of Polaroid's European operations pointed this out to headquarters. Unperturbed by these concerns, headquarters management set strict guidelines to discourage deviation from the global plan. Nonetheless, the European personnel were proved correct. The testimonials by "unknown" personalities left consumers cold. The commercials never achieved much impact in raising awareness of Polaroid's instant camera. Even though the camera later became successful in Europe, local management believes the misguided introductory campaign in no way helped its performance.

The lesson was remembered a decade later when Polaroid's European management launched a pan-European program to reposition Polaroid's instant photography from the "party camera" platform to a serious, "utilitarian" platform. This time headquarters did not assume *it* had the answers. Instead, it looked for inspiration in the various advertising practices of its European subsidiaries, and it found it in the strategy of one of its smallest subsidiaries in Switzerland. With considerable success, the Swiss subsidiary had promoted the functional uses of instant photography as a means of communicating with family and friends. A task force was set up to test this concept in other markets. The tests showed that the Swiss strategy was indeed transferable and that it produced the desired impact. Thus was born Europe's "Learn to Speak Polaroid" campaign, one of the firm's most successful advertising efforts. Ultimately, non-European subsidiaries, including those in Japan and Australia, liked the strategy so much that they adopted it.

What made this campaign different than the SX-70 campaign a decade earlier was the decentralized decision making. Instead of headquarters imposing upon Europe an advertising campaign developed in the United States, the European subsidiaries were able to develop their own campaign. Equally important, even after the pan-European program was adapted, European managers had the freedom to adapt the campaign to local tastes and needs. For example, where tests showed that the "Learn to Speak Polaroid" tag did not convey the intended meaning in the local language, the subsidiary was free to change it.

Source: Kamran Kashani, "Beware the Pitfalls of Global Marketing," Harvard Business Review, *September-October 1989, pp. 91–98.*

in product endorsements. Furthermore, the key line, "Kellogg's makes their cornflakes the best they have ever been," was disallowed in Germany because of a prohibition against competitive claims.[12]

Dealing with Country Differences

Given the arguments for and against the feasibility of globally standardized advertising, the question arises as to whether it might be possible to capture some of the benefits of global standardization while recognizing differences in countries' cultural and legal environments. As it turns out, some firms have been experimenting with this. A firm

12 "Advertising in a Single Market," *The Economist,* March 24, 1990, p. 64.

may select some features for all of its advertising campaigns and localize other features. By doing so, it may be able to save on some costs and build international brand recognition and yet customize its advertisements to different cultures.

For example, Pepsi-Cola used this approach in its 1986 advertising campaign. The company wanted to use modern music to connect its products with local markets. Pepsi hired popular U.S. singer Tina Turner and rock stars from six countries to team up in singing and performing the Pepsi-Cola theme song in a big rock concert. In the commercials the local rock stars appear with Tina Turner. Except for the footage of the local stars, all the commercials are identical. For other countries, local rock stars are spliced into the footage so they appear to be on the stage with Tina Turner. By shooting the commercials all at once, Pepsi saved on production costs. The campaign was extended to 30 countries, which relieved the local subsidiaries or bottlers of having to develop their own campaigns.[13]

PRICING STRATEGY

International pricing strategy is an important component of the overall international marketing mix. In this section we look at three aspects of international pricing strategy. First, we examine the case for pursuing price discrimination, charging different prices for the same product in different countries. Second, we look at what might be called *strategic pricing.* Third, we briefly review some of the regulatory factors—such as government-mandated price controls and antidumping regulations—that limit a firm's ability to charge the prices it would prefer in a country.

Price Discrimination

In an international context, price discrimination exists whenever consumers in different countries are charged different prices for the same product. In essence, price discrimination involves charging whatever the market will bear; in a competitive market, prices may have to be lower than in a market where the firm has a monopoly. As a practice, price discrimination can help a company maximize its profits. It makes economic sense to charge different prices in different countries.

Two conditions are necessary for profitable price discrimination. First, the firm must be able to keep its national markets separate. If it cannot do this, individuals or businesses may undercut its attempt at price discrimination by engaging in arbitrage. Arbitrage occurs when an individual or business capitalizes on a price differential for a firm's product between two countries by purchasing the product in the country where prices are lower and reselling it in the country where prices are higher. For example, many automobile firms have long practiced price discrimination in Europe. At one point a Ford Escort cost $2,000 more in Germany than it did in Belgium. This policy broke down when car dealers bought Escorts in Belgium and drove them to Germany, where they sold them at a profit for slightly less than Ford was selling Escorts in Germany. To protect the market share of its German auto dealers, Ford had to bring its German prices into line with those being charged in Belgium. In other words, Ford could not keep these markets separate.

Interestingly enough, however, Ford still practices price discrimination between Great Britain and Belgium. A Ford car can cost up to $3,000 more in Great Britain than in Belgium. In this case, arbitrage has not been able to equalize the price, because right-

[13] "Advertising: Tina Turner Helps Pepsi's Global Effort," *The New York Times,* March 10, 1986, p. D13.

Figure 17.2
Elastic and Inelastic Demand Curves

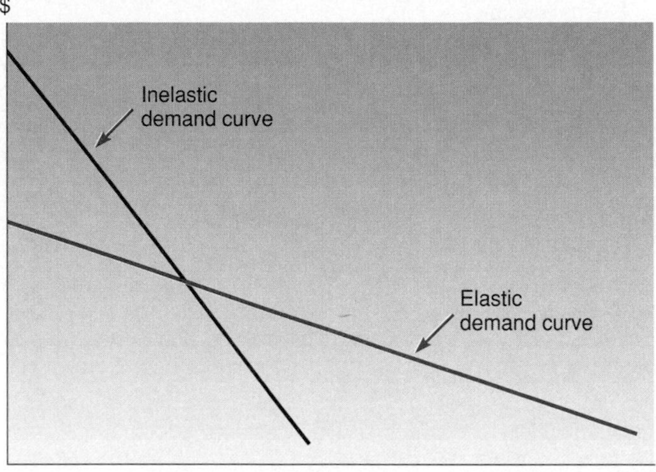

hand-drive cars are sold in Great Britain and left-hand-drive cars in the rest of Europe. Because there is no market for left-hand-drive cars in Great Britain, Ford has been able to keep the markets separate.

The second necessary condition for profitable price discrimination is different price elasticities of demand in different countries. The **price elasticity of demand** is a measure of the responsiveness of demand for a product to changes in price. Demand is said to be *elastic* when a small change in price produces a large change in demand; it is said to be *inelastic* when a large change in price produces only a small change in demand. Elastic and inelastic demand curves are illustrated in Figure 17.2. As a general rule, for reasons that will be explained shortly, a firm can charge a higher price in a country where demand is inelastic.

The Determinants of Demand Elasticity

The elasticity of demand for a product in a given country is determined by a number of factors, of which income level and competitive conditions are perhaps the two most important. With regard to income levels, price elasticity tends to be greater (more elastic) in countries with low income levels. The reason for this is that consumers with limited incomes tend to be very price conscious; they have less to spend, so they look much more closely at price. Thus, price elasticities for products such as television sets are greater in countries such as India, where a television set is still a luxury item, than in the United States, where it is considered a necessity.

With regard to competitive conditions, in general, the more competitors there are, the greater consumers' bargaining power will be and the more likely consumers will be to buy from the firm that charges the lowest price. Thus a large number of competitors causes high elasticity of demand. In such circumstances, if a firm raises its prices above those of its competitors, consumers will switch to the competitors' products. The opposite is true when a firm faces few competitors. When competitors are limited, consumers' bargaining power is weaker and price is less important as a competitive weapon. Thus a firm may charge a higher price for its product in a country where competition is limited than in a country where competition is intense.

Figure 17.3 *Price Discrimination*

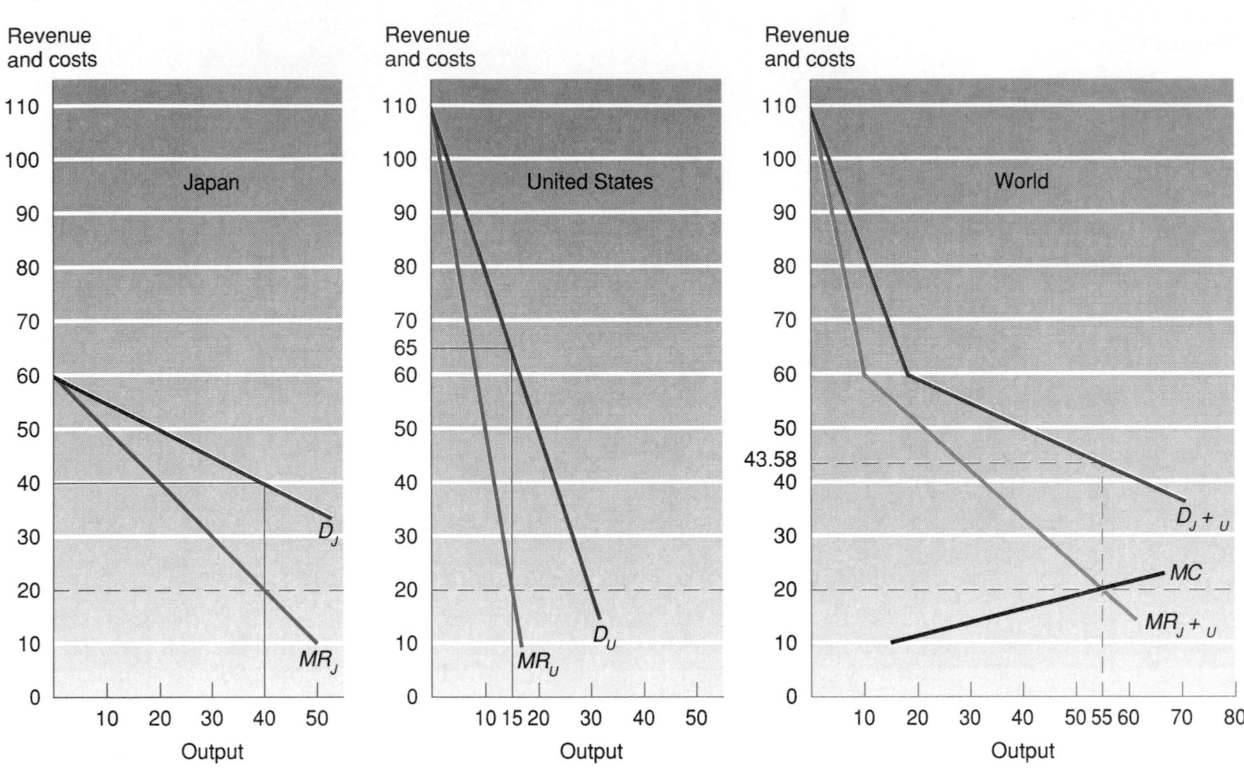

Profit Maximizing under Price Discrimination

For those readers with some grasp of economic logic, we can offer a more formal presentation of the above argument. (Readers unfamiliar with basic economic terminology may want to skip this subsection.) Figure 17.3 shows the situation facing a firm that sells the same product in only two countries, Japan and the United States. The Japanese market is very competitive, so the firm faces an elastic demand curve (D_J) and marginal revenue curve (MR_J). The U.S. market is not competitive, so there the firm faces an inelastic demand curve (D_U) and marginal revenue curve (MR_U). Also shown in the figure are the firm's total demand curve (D_{J+U}), total marginal revenue curve (MR_{J+U}), and marginal cost curve (MC). The total demand curve is simply the summation of the demand facing the firm in Japan and the United States, as is the total marginal revenue curve.

To maximize profits, the firm must produce at the output where $MR = MC$. In Figure 17.3 this implies an output of 55 units. If the firm does not practice price discrimination, it will charge a price of \$43.58 to sell an output of 55 units. Thus, without price discrimination the firm's total revenues are

$$\$43.58 \times 55 = \$2,392.50.$$

Now look what happens when the firm decides to engage in price discrimination. It will still produce 55 units, since that is where $MR = MC$. However, the firm must now allocate this output between the two countries to take advantage of the difference in demand elasticity. Proper allocation of output between Japan and the United States can be determined graphically by drawing a line through their respective graphs at $20 to indicate that $20 is the marginal cost in each country (see Figure 17.3). To maximize profits in each country, prices are now set *in each country* at that level where the marginal revenue *for that country* equals marginal costs. In Japan this is a price of $40, and the firm sells 40 units. In the United States the optimal price is $65, and it sells 15 units. Thus, reflecting the different competitive conditions, the price charged in the United States is over 50 percent more than the price charged in Japan. More important, look at what happens to total revenues. With price discrimination, the firm earns revenues of

$$\$40 \times 40 \text{ units} = \$1{,}600$$

in Japan and

$$\$65 \times 15 \text{ units} = \$975$$

in the United States. By engaging in price discrimination, the firm can thus earn total revenues of

$$\$1{,}600 + \$975 = \$2{,}575,$$

which is $182.50 more than the $2,392.50 it earned before. Price discrimination pays!

Strategic Pricing

The concept of strategic pricing has two aspects, which we will refer to as *predatory pricing* and *experience curve pricing.* Both predatory pricing and experience curve pricing can result in problems with antidumping regulations. Accordingly, once we have reviewed predatory and experience curve pricing, we will take a look at antidumping rules and other regulatory policies.

Predatory Pricing

Predatory pricing is the use of price as a competitive weapon for the purpose of driving weaker competitors out of a national market. Once the competitors have left the market, the firm can raise prices and enjoy high profits. For such a pricing strategy to work, the firm must normally have a profitable position in another national market, which it can use to subsidize aggressive pricing in the market it is trying to monopolize. Many Japanese firms have been accused of pursuing this strategy. The argument runs similarly to this: because the Japanese market is protected from foreign competition by high informal trade barriers, Japanese firms can charge high prices and earn high profits at home. They then use these profits to subsidize aggressive pricing overseas, the aim of which is to drive competitors out of those markets. Once this has occurred, so it is claimed, the Japanese firms then raise prices. For example, Matsushita has been accused of using this strategy to enter the U.S. TV market. As one of the major TV producers in Japan, Matsushita was able to earn high profits at home. It then used these profits to subsidize the losses it made in the United States during its early years there, when it priced low to increase its market penetration. Ultimately, Matsushita became the world's largest manufacturer of TVs.[14]

Experience Curve Pricing

We first encountered the experience curve in Chapter 12. There we saw that as a firm builds up its accumulated production volume over time, so unit costs fall due to

[14] These allegations were made on a PBS "Frontline" documentary telecast in the United States in May 1992.

"experience effects." Further, you will recall that learning effects and economies of scale underlie the experience curve. Price comes into the picture, since aggressive pricing (along with aggressive promotion and advertising) is a way to build up accumulated sales volume rapidly and thus move down the experience curve. In turn, firms further down the experience curve have a cost advantage vis-à-vis firms further up the curve.

Many firms pursuing an experience curve pricing strategy on an international scale price low worldwide in attempting to build global sales volume as rapidly as possible, even if this means taking large losses initially. Such a firm believes that several years in the future, when it has moved down the experience curve, it will be making substantial profits and, moreover, have a cost advantage over its less-aggressive competitors.

Regulatory Influences on Prices

Firms' abilities to engage in either price discrimination or strategic pricing may be limited by national or international regulations. Most important, a firm's freedom to set its own prices is constrained by antidumping regulations and competition policy.

Antidumping Regulations

Both predatory pricing and experience curve pricing can run afoul of antidumping regulations. Technically speaking, **dumping** occurs whenever a firm sells a product for a price that is less than the cost of producing it. Most regulations, however, define *dumping* more vaguely. For example, a country is allowed to bring antidumping actions against an importer under Article 6 of GATT so long as two criteria are met: sales at "less than fair value" and "material injury to a domestic industry." The problem with this terminology is that it does not indicate what is a fair value. The ambiguity has led some to argue that selling abroad at prices below those in the country of origin, as opposed to below cost, is dumping.

It was such logic that led the Bush administration to place a 25 percent duty on imports of Japanese light trucks in 1988. The Japanese manufacturers protested that they were not selling below cost. Admitting that their prices were lower in the United States than in Japan, they argued that this simply reflected the intensely competitive nature of the U.S. market (i.e., different price elasticities). In a similar example, the European Commission found Japanese exporters of dot matrix printers to be in violation of dumping regulations. To correct what they saw as dumping, the EC placed a 47 percent import duty on imports of dot matrix printers from Japan. According to EC rules, this import duty must be passed on to European consumers as a price increase.[15]

From the perspective of an international business, the important point is that antidumping rules set a floor under export prices and limit firms' ability to pursue strategic pricing. Indeed, the rather vague terminology used in most antidumping actions suggests that a firm's ability to engage in price discrimination also may be challenged under antidumping legislation.

Competition Policy

Most industrialized nations have regulations designed to promote competition and to restrict monopoly practices. These regulations can be used to limit the prices that a firm can charge in a given country. For example, during the 1960s and 70s the Swiss pharmaceutical manufacturer Hoffmann-LaRoche had a monopoly on the supply of

---

15 "Printers Reflect Pattern of Trade Rows," *Financial Times,* December 20, 1988, p. 3.

Valium and Librium tranquilizers. In 1973 the company was investigated by the British Monopolies and Mergers Commission, which is responsible for promoting fair competition in Great Britain. The commission found that Hoffmann-LaRoche was overcharging for its tranquilizers and ordered the company to reduce its prices 35 to 40 percent. Hoffmann-LaRoche maintained unsuccessfully that it was merely engaging in price discrimination. Similar actions were later brought against Hoffmann-LaRoche by the German cartel office and by the Dutch and Danish governments.[16]

NEW PRODUCT DEVELOPMENT

Firms that successfully develop and market new products can earn enormous returns. Some examples are

- Xerox's 25-year domination of the photocopier market.
- Du Pont's steady stream of inventions such as cellophane, nylon, Freon (used in all air-conditioners), and Teflon.
- Sony's development of the Walkman and compact disc.
- Bausch & Lomb's development of contact lenses.
- Matsushita's development of the videocassette recorder.

In the late 20th century, competition is as much about technological innovation as anything else. The pace of technological change has accelerated since the industrial revolution in the 18th century, and it continues to do so today. The result has been a dramatic shortening of product life cycles. Technological innovation is both creative and destructive.[17] An innovation can make established products obsolete overnight. At the same time, an innovation can make a host of new products possible. Witness recent changes in the electronics industry. For 40 years before the early 1950s, vacuum valves were a major component in radios and then in record players and early computers. The advent of transistors destroyed the market for vacuum valves, but at the same time it created new opportunities connected with transistors. Transistors took up far less space than vacuum valves, creating a trend toward miniaturization that continues today. The transistor held its position as the major component in the electronics industry for just a decade. In the 1970s microprocessors were developed, and the market for transistors declined rapidly. At the same time, however, the microprocessor created yet another set of new product opportunities—handheld calculators (which destroyed the market for slide rules), compact disc players, and personal computers, to name a few.

This process of "creative destruction" unleashed by technological change makes it absolutely critical that the firm stay on the leading edge of technology, lest it lose out to a competitor's innovations. As we explain in the next subsection, this not only creates a need for the firm to invest in R&D, it also requires the firm to establish R&D activities at those locations around the globe where expertise is concentrated. Moreover, as we shall see, leading-edge technology on its own is not enough to guarantee a firm's survival. The firm must also apply that technology in developing products that satisfy consumer needs. To do that, the firm needs to build close links between marketing and R&D. This is difficult enough for the domestic firm, but it is even more problematic for the interna-

[16] J. F. Pickering, *Industrial Structure and Market Conduct* (London: Martin Robertson, 1974).

[17] The phrase was first used by economist Joseph Schumpeter in *Capitalism, Socialism, and Democracy* (New York: Harper Brothers, 1942).

tional business competing in an industry where consumer tastes and preferences differ from country to country. With all of this in mind, we now move on to examine the issues of locating R&D activities and building links between R&D and marketing.

The Location of R&D

By and large, ideas for new products are stimulated by the interactions of scientific research, demand conditions, and competitive conditions. Other things being equal, the rate of new product development seems to be greater in countries where:

- More money is spent on basic and applied research and development.
- Demand is strong.
- Consumers are affluent.
- Competition is intense.[18]

Basic and applied Research & Development discovers new technologies and then commercializes them. Strong demand and affluent consumers create a potential market for new products. Intense competition between firms stimulates innovation as the firms try to beat out their competitors and reap potentially enormous first-mover advantages that result from successful innovation.

For most of the post–World War II period, the country that ranked highest on these criteria was the United States. The United States devoted a greater proportion of its gross domestic product (GDP) to R&D than any other country did. Its scientific establishment was the largest and most active in the world. U.S. consumers were the most affluent in the world, the market was large, and competition among U.S. firms was brisk. Due to these factors, the United States was the **lead market**—the market where most new products were developed and introduced. Accordingly, it was the best location for R&D activities; it was where the action was.

Since the late 1970s things have been changing fast. The U.S. monopoly on new product development has disappeared. Although U.S. firms are still at the leading edge of many new technologies, Japanese and European firms are catching up. When the Japanese government's Economic Planning Agency surveyed 110 critical leading-edge technologies in 1991, it concluded that U.S. firms dominated 43 of them; Japanese firms, 33; and European firms, the remaining 34.[19] Both Japan and Germany are now devoting a greater proportion of their GDP to nondefense R&D than is the United States. In 1990 Japan spent 3 percent of its GDP on nondefense R&D ; Germany, 2.7 percent; and the United States, 1.8 percent.[20] In addition, both Japan and the European Community are large, affluent markets, and the wealth gap between them and the United States is closing.

In sum, it is no longer appropriate to consider the United States the lead market. Indeed, it is questionable if any country is. To succeed today, it is often necessary to simultaneously introduce new products in all major industrialized markets. Moreover, since leading-edge research is now carried out in many locations around the world, the argument for centralizing R&D activity in the United States is now much weaker than it was two decades ago. (It used to be argued that centralized R&D eliminated duplication.) Much leading-edge research is now occurring in Japan and Europe, and it makes sense for many firms to disperse their R&D activities to those locations. Such dispersion allows a

---

[18] See D. C. Mowery and N. Rosenberg, *Technology and the Pursuit of Economic Growth* (Cambridge, U.K.: Cambridge University Press, 1989); and M. E. Porter, *The Competitive Advantage of Nations* (New York: The Free Press, 1990).

[19] Can America Compete?" *The Economist*, January 18, 1992, pp. 65–66.

[20] C. Farrell, "Industrial Policy," *Business Week*, April 6, 1992, pp. 70–75.

firm to stay close to the center of leading-edge activity to gather scientific and competitive information and to draw on local scientific resources. This may result in some duplication of R&D activities, but the cost disadvantages of duplication are outweighed by the advantages of dispersion.

For example, to expose themselves to the research and new product development work now being done in Japan, many U.S. firms have recently set up satellite R&D centers in Japan. Kodak's $65 million R&D center in Japan employs approximately 200 people. The company hired about 100 professional Japanese researchers and directed the lab to concentrate on electronic imaging technology. A few of the U.S. firms that have established R&D facilities in Japan are Corning, Texas Instruments, IBM, Digital Equipment, Procter & Gamble, Upjohn, Pfizer, Du Pont, and Monsanto.[21] At the same time, to internationalize their own research and gain access to U.S. research talent, Japanese firms have begun to make heavy investments in U.S.-based research facilities.

Linking R&D and Marketing

It has been estimated that 80 to 88 percent of all new products fail to earn an economic return.[22] Thus, although a firm that is successful at developing new products may earn enormous returns, new product development is a very risky business with a high failure rate. Despite this, some firms seem consistently better than others at successfully introducing new products. Firms such as 3M, Sony, and Matsushita have well-earned reputations for successful innovation. One reason for these firms' success seems to be that they build close links between their R&D activities and their marketing function to ensure new products are tailored to consumer needs. Many new products fail because they are not adequately commercialized. For example, many of the early personal computers failed to sell because the user needed to be a computer programmer to be able to use them; their technology had not been commercialized. Steve Jobs of Apple Computer realized that if the technology could be made "user friendly," the market for it would be enormous.

The need to adequately commercialize new technologies poses special problems in the international business, since commercialization may require different versions of a new product to be produced for different countries. To do this, the firm must build close links between its R&D centers and its various country operations. This may require R&D centers in North America, Asia, and Europe that are closely linked by formal and informal integrating mechanisms with marketing operations in each country in their regions. (Chapter 13 discusses formal and informal integrating mechanisms.) As we saw in the opening case, Procter & Gamble stumbled when it introduced new products in Japan and Poland, because there was little linkage between its overseas marketing operations and its domestic R&D and marketing functions. In addition, the various R&D centers also need to be linked by formal and informal integrating mechanisms so that advances achieved at one center can be quickly diffused throughout the firm.

SUMMARY OF CHAPTER

This chapter has discussed the marketing and R&D functions in international business. A persistent theme of the chapter is the tension that exists between the need to reduce costs and the need to be responsive to local conditions, which raises costs. Specifically, the following points have been made.

1. Theodore Levitt has argued that, due to the advent of modern communications and transport technologies, consumer tastes and preferences are becoming global, which is creating global markets for standardized consumer products.

---

[21] "When the Corporate Lab Goes to Japan," *The New York Times*, April 28, 1991, sec. 3, p. 1.

[22] E. Mansfield, "How Economists See R&D," *Harvard Business Review*, November-December 1981, pp. 98-106.

2. Levitt's position is regarded as extreme by many commentators, who argue that substantial differences still exist between countries.
3. A product can be viewed as a bundle of attributes. Product attributes need to be varied from country to country to satisfy different consumer tastes and preferences.
4. Country differences in consumer tastes and preferences are due to differences in culture and economic development. In addition, differences in product and technical standards may require the firm to customize product attributes from country to country.
5. A distribution strategy decision is an attempt to define the optimal channel for delivering a product to the consumer.
6. Significant country differences exist in distribution systems. In some countries the retail system is concentrated; in others it is fragmented. In some countries channel length is short; in others it is long. Access to some countries' distribution channels is difficult to achieve.
7. The longer the channel, the greater the aggregate markup and the higher the price consumers must pay for the product. Despite this, the benefits of using a longer channel may outweigh the drawbacks.
8. The benefits of using a longer channel are that longer channels may economize on selling costs and assist the firm to gain market access.
9. A critical element in the marketing mix is communication strategy, which defines the process the firm will use in communicating the attributes of its product to prospective customers.
10. Barriers to international communication include cultural differences, source effects, and noise levels.
11. A communication strategy is either a push strategy or a pull strategy. A push strategy emphasizes personal selling, whereas a pull strategy emphasizes mass media advertising.
12. Whether a push strategy or a pull strategy is optimal depends on the type of product, consumer sophistication, channel length, and media availability.
13. A globally standardized advertising campaign, which uses the same marketing message all over the world, has economic advantages, but it fails to account for differences in culture and the various governments' advertising regulations.
14. Price discrimination exists when consumers in different countries are charged different prices for the same product. Price discrimination can help a firm maximize its profits.
15. For price discrimination to be effective, the national markets must be separate and their price elasticities of demand must differ.
16. Predatory pricing is the use of profit gained in one market to support aggressive pricing in another market for the purpose of driving competitors out of that market.
17. Experience curve pricing is the use of aggressive pricing for the purpose of building accumulated volume as rapidly as possible to move the firm down the experience curve rapidly.
18. The ability of a firm to engage in price discrimination or strategic pricing is limited by governments' antidumping regulations and competition policies.
19. New product development is a high-risk, potentially high-return activity. To build up a competency in new product development, an international business must do two things: *(i)* disperse R&D activities to those countries where new products are being pioneered and *(ii)* integrate R&D with marketing.

DISCUSSION QUESTIONS

1. Imagine you are the marketing manager for a U.S. manufacturer of disposable diapers. Your firm is considering entering the European market, concentrating on the major EC countries. Your CEO believes the advertising message that has been effective in the United States will suffice in Europe. Outline your objections to this.
2. By the end of this century we will have seen the emergence of enormous global markets for standardized consumer products. Do you agree with this statement? Justify your answer.
3. You are the marketing manager of a food products company that is considering entering the South Korean market. The retail system in South Korea tends to be very fragmented. Moreover, retailers and wholesalers tend to have long-term ties with South Korean food companies, which makes access to distribution channels difficult. What distribution strategy would you advise the company to pursue? Why?
4. Price discrimination is indistinguishable from dumping. Discuss the accuracy of this statement.

Global Human Resource Management

CHAPTER 18

COLGATE-PALMOLIVE, INC.

Colgate–Palmolive, the $6-billion-a-year personal products giant, earns nearly two thirds of its revenues outside the United States. For years Colgate succeeded, as many U.S. multinationals have, by developing products at home and then "throwing them over the wall" to foreign subsidiaries. Each major foreign subsidiary was responsible for local manufacturing and marketing. Senior management positions in these subsidiaries were typically held by Americans, and practically all of the company's U.S.-based managers were U.S. citizens. • In the early 1980s Colgate realized that if it was going to succeed in the rapidly changing international business environment, it would have to develop more of a transnational orientation. Its competitors, such as Procter & Gamble, Unilever, and Kao, were themselves trying to become transnational companies, and Colgate needed to follow suit. One of the most important aspects of becoming a transnational is developing an international cadre of executive managers who are as at home working in one culture as in another and who have the ability to rise above their ethnocentric perspectives. • As a first step toward building such a cadre, Colgate began recruiting college graduates in 1987 and putting them through an intensive international training program. The typical recruit holds an M.B.A. from a U.S. university, speaks at least one foreign language, has lived outside the United States, and has strong computer skills and business experience. Over one quarter of the participants are foreign nationals. • The trainees spend 24 months in a U.S. program. During three-month stints, they learn global business development secrets of, for example, Colgate toothpaste, compiling a guide for introducing a new product or revamping an existing one in various national markets. Participants also receive additional language instruction and take international business trips. When they have completed the program, the participants become associate product managers in the United States or abroad. Unlike most U.S. companies, Colgate does not send foreign-born trainees to their native countries for their initial jobs. Instead, it is more likely that a French national will remain in the United States, a U.S. national will be sent to Germany, and a British national will go to Spain. The foreigners receive the same generous expatriate compensation packages the Americans do, even if they are assigned to their home country. One problem that has emerged is that this extra pay can create resentment among locally hired managers of foreign subsidiaries. Colgate is trying to resolve this problem by urging its foreign subsidiaries to send their brightest young managers to the training program. • In addition to the management training program, Colgate has taken a number of other steps to develop its international cadre of managers. In Europe, for example, the company is trying to develop "Euromanagers," managers who have experience working in several European countries. This is a departure from the established practice of having managers spend most (if not all) of their working careers in their home country. Also, Colgate now makes efforts to ensure that project teams contain managers from several different countries. ⊕ *Sources: J. S. Lublin, "Managing Globally: Younger Managers Learn Global Skills,"* The Wall Street Journal, *March 31, 1992, p. B1; and B. Hagerty, "Companies in Europe Seeking Executives Who Can Cross Borders in a Single Bound,"* The Wall Street Journal, *January 25, 1991, p. B1.*

INTRODUCTION

Continuing our survey of specific functions within an international business, this chapter examines international human resource management (HRM). HRM refers to the activities an organization carries out to utilize its human resource effectively.[1] These activities include determining the firm's human resource strategy, staffing, performance evaluation, management development, compensation, and labor relations. None of these activities are performed in a vacuum; all are related to the strategy of the firm, for, as we will see, HRM has an important strategic component. Through its influence on the character, development, quality, and productivity of the firm's human resources, the

[1] P. J. Dowling and R. S. Schuler, *International Dimensions of Human Resource Management* (Boston, Mass.: PSW-Kent, 1990).

HRM function can help the firm achieve its primary strategic goals of reducing the costs of value creation and adding value by better serving customer needs.

The strategic role of HRM is complex enough in a purely domestic firm, but it is more complex in an international business, where staffing, management development, performance evaluation, and compensation activities are complicated by profound differences between countries in labor markets, culture, legal systems, economic systems, and the like (see Chapters 2 and 3). For example,

- Compensation practices may have to vary from country to country depending on prevailing management customs.
- Labor laws may prohibit union organization in one country and mandate it in another.
- Equal employment legislation may be strongly pursued in one country and not in another.

Moreover, if it is to build a cadre of international managers, the HRM function must deal with a host of issues related to expatriate managers. (An *expatriate* manager is a citizen of one country who is working abroad in one of the firm's subsidiaries.)

With all this as background, in this chapter we will look closely at the role of HRM in an international business. We begin by briefly discussing the strategic role of HRM. Then we turn our attention to four major tasks of the HRM function—staffing policy, management training and development, performance appraisal, and compensation policy. Throughout these sections we will point out the strategic implications of each of these tasks. The chapter closes with a look at international labor relations and the relationship between the firm's management of labor relations and its overall strategy.

THE STRATEGIC ROLE OF INTERNATIONAL HRM

In Chapter 12 we examined four strategies pursued by international businesses—the multidomestic, the international, the global, and the transnational. Recall that multidomestic firms try to create value by emphasizing local responsiveness; international firms, by transferring core competencies overseas; global firms, by realizing experience curve and location economies; and transnational firms, by doing all of these things simultaneously. In Chapter 13 we discussed the organizational requirements for implementing each of these strategies. Table 18.1, identical to Table 13.2, summarizes the relationships between international strategies, structures, and controls.

We now must admit that none of the structures or controls summarized in Table 18.1 mean very much if the human resources that support them are not appropriate. Without the right kind of people in place, organizational structure is just a hollow shell. In Chapter 13 we explained that formal and informal structure and controls must be congruent with a firm's strategy for the firm to succeed. Now we will show that success also requires HRM policies to be congruent with the firm's strategy and with its formal and informal structure and controls. For example, a transnational strategy imposes very different requirements for staffing, management development, and compensation practices than a multidomestic strategy does.

The opening case alluded to the relationship between strategy, structure, and HRM. Like many other consumer products firms, Colgate-Palmolive is trying to become a transnational organization. As indicated in Table 18.1, firms pursuing a transnational strategy need, among other things, to build a strong corporate culture and an informal management network for transmitting information within the organization. Through its employee selection, management development, performance appraisal, and compensation

Table 18.1
Strategy, Structure, and Control Systems

Structure and Controls	International Strategy			
	Multidomestic	International	Global	Transnational
Centralization of operating decisions	Decentralized	Core competency centralized. Rest decentralized	Some centralized	Mixed centralized and decentralized
Horizontal differentiation	Worldwide area structure	Worldwide product division	Worldwide product division	Informal matrix
Need for coordination	Low	Moderate	High	Very high
Integrating mechanisms	None	Few	Many	Very many
Performance ambiguity	Low	Moderate	High	Very high
Need for cultural controls	Low	Moderate	High	Very high

policies, the HRM function can help develop these things. For example, Colgate's management development program, by creating a cadre of international managers with experience in various nations, should help to establish an informal management network. In addition, management development programs can serve to build a corporate culture that supports strategic goals. In short, HRM has a critical role to play in implementing strategy. In each section that follows we will review the strategic role of HRM in some detail.

STAFFING POLICY

Staffing policy is concerned with the selection of employees for particular jobs. At one level this involves selecting individuals who have the skills required to do particular jobs. At another level, staffing policy can be a tool for developing and promoting corporate culture.[2] By *corporate culture* we mean the organization's norms and value systems. We first encountered the concept in Chapter 13 when we discussed the use of "cultural controls" in businesses, noting that strong cultural controls help the firm pursue its strategy. In particular, we noted that firms pursuing transnational and global strategies have high needs for a strong unifying culture, whereas the need is somewhat lower for firms pursuing an international strategy and lowest of all for firms pursuing a multidomestic strategy (see Table 18.1).

Thus, in firms pursuing transnational and global strategies, we might expect the HRM function to pay significant attention to selecting individuals who not only have the skills required to perform particular jobs but who also "fit" the prevailing culture of the firm. IBM, for example, which is positioned toward the transnational end of the strategic spectrum, is not just concerned with hiring people who have the skills required for performing particular jobs; it wants to hire individuals whose behavioral styles, beliefs, and value systems are consistent with those of IBM. This is true whether an American is being hired, an Italian, a German, or an Australian and whether the hiring is for a U.S. operation or a foreign operation. The belief is that if employees are predisposed toward

[2] E. H. Schein, *Organizational Culture and Leadership* (San Francisco: Jossey-Bass, 1985).

the organization's norms and value systems by their personality type, the firm—which has a significant need for integration—will experience fewer problems with performance ambiguity.

By the same token, the need for integration is substantially lower in a multidomestic firm. As a result, there is less performance ambiguity there and, therefore, not the same need for cultural controls. In theory, this means the HRM function can pay less attention to building a unified corporate culture. In multidomestic firms, the culture can be allowed to vary from national operation to national operation. (Although it should be pointed out that given the questionable viability of a multidomestic strategy in today's world, this might not be the best policy to pursue. Chapter 12 discusses the viability of this strategy.)

Types of Staffing Policy

Research has identified three types of staffing policies in international businesses: the ethnocentric approach, the polycentric approach, and the geocentric approach.[3] We will review each policy and link it to the strategy pursued by the firm. As we will see, the most attractive staffing policy is probably the geocentric approach, although there are several impediments to adopting it.

The Ethnocentric Approach

An ethnocentric staffing policy is one in which all key management positions are filled by parent-country nationals. This practice was very widespread at one time. Firms such as Procter & Gamble, Philips NV, and Matsushita originally followed it. In the Dutch firm Philips, for example, all important positions in most foreign subsidiaries were at one time held by Dutch nationals who were referred to by their non-Dutch colleagues as the *Dutch mafia.* In many Japanese firms today, key positions in international operations are still held by Japanese nationals.

Firms pursue an ethnocentric staffing policy for three reasons. First, the firm may believe there is a lack of qualified individuals in the host country to fill senior management positions. This argument is heard most often when the firm has operations in less developed countries. Second, the firm may see an ethnocentric staffing policy as the best way to maintain a unified corporate culture. Many Japanese firms, for example, prefer their foreign operations to be headed by expatriate Japanese managers because these managers will have been socialized into the firm's culture while employed in Japan. Similarly, until recently Procter & Gamble preferred to staff important management positions in its foreign subsidiaries with U.S. nationals who had been socialized into P&G's corporate culture by years of employment in its U.S. operations. Such reasoning tends to predominate when a firm places a high value on its corporate culture.

Third, if the firm is trying to create value by transferring core competencies to a foreign operation, as firms pursuing an international strategy are, it may feel that the best way to do this is to transfer parent-country nationals who have knowledge of that competency to the foreign operation. For illustration, imagine what might occur if a firm tried to transfer a core competency in marketing to a foreign subsidiary without supporting the transfer with a corresponding transfer of home-country marketing management personnel. The transfer would probably fail to produce the anticipated benefits, because the knowledge underlying a core competency cannot easily be articulated and written

[3] D. A. Heenan and H. V. Perlmutter, *Multinational Organizational Development* (Reading, Mass.: Addison-Wesley, 1979); and D. A. Ondrack, "International Human Resources Management in European and North American Firms," *International Studies of Management and Organization* 15(1985), pp. 6–32.

down. Such knowledge often has a significant *tacit dimension*; it is acquired through experience over time. Just like the great tennis player who cannot instruct others how to become great tennis players simply by writing a handbook, the firm that has a core competency in marketing—or anything else—cannot just write a handbook that tells a foreign subsidiary how to build the firm's core competency anew in a foreign setting. It must also transfer management personnel to the foreign operation so they can *show* foreign managers how to become good marketers, for example. In large part, the need to transfer managers overseas arises because the knowledge that underlies the firm's core competency resides in the heads of its domestic managers. In turn, they have acquired this knowledge through years of experience, not by reading a handbook. Thus, if a firm is to transfer a core competency to a foreign subsidiary, it must also transfer the appropriate managers.

Despite this rationale for pursuing an ethnocentric staffing policy, the policy is now on the wane in most international businesses. There are two reasons for this. First, an ethnocentric staffing policy limits advancement opportunities for host-country nationals. In turn, this can lead to resentment, lower productivity, and increased turnover among that group. Resentment can be greater still if, as often occurs, expatriate managers are paid significantly more than home-country nationals.

Second, an ethnocentric policy can lead to "cultural myopia," the firm's failure to understand host-country cultural differences that require different approaches to marketing and management. The adaptation of expatriate managers can take a long time, during which they may make major mistakes. For example, expatriate managers may fail to appreciate how product attributes, distribution strategy, communications strategy, and pricing strategy should be adapted to host-country conditions. The result may be some costly blunders. The opening case to Chapter 17 described how this occurred at Procter & Gamble on a number of occasions. In response, P&G is now hiring more host-country nationals to senior management positions in its foreign operations.

The Polycentric Approach

A polycentric staffing policy requires host-country nationals to be recruited to manage subsidiaries, while parent-country nationals occupy key positions at corporate headquarters. In many respects a polycentric approach is a response to the shortcomings of an ethnocentric approach. One advantage of adopting a polycentric approach is that the firm is less likely to suffer from cultural myopia. Host-country managers are unlikely to make the mistakes arising from cultural misunderstandings that expatriate managers are vulnerable to. A second advantage is that a polycentric approach may be less expensive to implement. Expatriate managers can be very expensive to maintain (see Box 18.1). Insofar as host-country nationals do not require the same level of expenditures, using them can reduce the costs of value creation.

However, a polycentric approach also has its drawbacks. Host-country nationals have limited opportunities to gain experience outside their own country and thus cannot progress beyond senior positions in their own subsidiary. As in the case of an ethnocentric policy, this may cause resentment. Perhaps the major drawback with a polycentric approach, however, is the gap that can form between host-country managers and parent-country managers. Language barriers, national loyalties, and a range of cultural differences may isolate the corporate headquarters staff from the various foreign subsidiaries. The lack of management transfers from home to host countries, and vice versa, can exacerbate this isolation and lead to a lack of integration between corporate headquarters and foreign subsidiaries. The result can be a "federation" of largely independent national

BOX 18.1

The Price of an Expatriate

An expatriate executive can cost a firm up to three times as much as a domestic executive. For example, consider an employer's typical first-year expenses for transferring a U.S. executive to Japan. Assume the U.S. executive has an annual salary of $100,000 and a family of four.

Expense	Amount
Direct Compensation	
Base salary	$100,000
Foreign service premium	15,000
Goods and services differential	30,000
Housing costs in Tokyo	40,000
Transfer Expenses	
Relocation allowance	$ 10,000
Airfare to Tokyo	5,000
Moving household goods	30,000
Other	
Company car	$ 20,000
Schooling (two children)	20,000
Annual home leave	5,000
Japanese personal income tax	45,000
TOTAL	$320,000

Yes, the first year's cost to the firm would be $320,000. Thereafter, the annual cost of keeping the expatriate in Japan would be about $275,000. Thus, it is small wonder that many firms are trying to reduce their use of expatriates. At the same time, however, the need to build an international cadre of executives requires increased use of expatriates.

units with only nominal links to the corporate headquarters. Within such a federation, the coordination required to transfer core competencies or to pursue experience curve and location economies may be difficult to achieve. Thus, although a polycentric approach may be effective for firms pursuing a multidomestic strategy, it is inappropriate for other strategies.

Moreover, the federation that may result from a polycentric approach can be a force for inertia within the firm. For example, after decades of pursing a polycentric staffing policy, food and detergents giant Unilever found that shifting from a multidomestic strategic posture to a transnational posture was very difficult. The reason: Unilever's foreign subsidiaries had evolved into quasi-autonomous operations, each with its own strong national identity. These "little kingdoms" objected strenuously to corporate headquarters' attempts to limit their autonomy and to rationalize global manufacturing.[4]

The Geocentric Approach

A geocentric staffing policy seeks the best people for key jobs throughout the organization, regardless of nationality. As we saw in the opening case, Colgate-Palmolive is now pursuing a geocentric staffing policy. There are a number of advantages to this policy. First, it enables the firm to make the best use of its human resources. Second, and perhaps more important, a geocentric policy enables the firm to build a cadre of international executives who feel at home working in a number of different cultures. In turn, the creation of such a cadre may be a critical first step toward building a strong unifying corporate culture and an informal management network, both of which are required for global and transnational strategies (see Table 18.1). Put another way, firms pursuing a geocentric staffing policy may be better able to create value from the pursuit of experience curve and location economies and from the multidirectional transfer of core competencies than firms pursuing other staffing policies. In addition, the multinational composition of the management team that results from geocentric staffing tends to reduce cultural myopia and to enhance local responsiveness. Thus, other things being equal, a geocentric staffing policy seems the most attractive.

However, despite this, a number of problems limit the firm's ability to pursue a geocentric policy. One problem is that many countries want foreign subsidiaries to employ their citizens. To achieve this goal, they use immigration laws to require the employment of host-country nationals if they are available in adequate numbers and have the necessary skills. Most countries (including the United States) require firms to provide extensive documentation if they wish to hire a foreign national instead of a local national. This documentation can be time consuming, expensive, and at times futile. A further problem is that a geocentric staffing policy can be very expensive to implement. There are increased training costs, relocation costs involved in transferring managers from country to country, and the need for a compensation structure with a standardized international base pay level that may be higher than national levels in many countries. (If you haven't yet read Box 18.1, you might want to do so now.) In addition, the higher pay enjoyed by managers placed on an international "fast track" may be a source of resentment within a firm.

Summary

The advantages and disadvantages of the three approaches to staffing policy are summarized in Table 18.2. Note that an ethnocentric approach is compatible with an international strategy, a polycentric approach is compatible with a multidomestic strategy, and a geocentric approach is compatible with both global and transnational strategies. (See Chapter 12 for details of the strategies.)

The Expatriate Problem

Two of the three staffing policies we have discussed—the ethnocentric and the geocentric—rely on extensive use of expatriate managers. With an ethnocentric policy, the expatriates are all home-country nationals who are transferred abroad. With a geocentric approach, the expatriates need not be home-country nationals; the firm does not base transfer decisions on nationality. A prominent issue in the international staffing literature is *expatriate failure*—the premature return of an expatriate manager to his or her home country. Here we briefly review the evidence on expatriate failure before discussing a number of ways in which the expatriate failure rate can be minimized.

Expatriate Failure Rates

Expatriate failure represents a failure of the firm's selection policies to identify individuals who will not thrive abroad. The costs of expatriate failure are high. One estimate is that

---

[4] C. A. Bartlett, and S. Ghoshal, *Managing across Borders: The Transnational Solution,* (Boston, Mass.: Harvard Business School Press, 1989).

Table 18.2
Comparison of Staffing Approaches

Staffing Approach	Strategic Appropriateness	Advantages	Disadvantages
Ethnocentric	International	Overcomes lack of qualified managers in host nation Unified culture Helps transfer core competencies	Produces resentment in host country Can lead to cultural myopia
Polycentric	Multidomestic	Alleviates cultural myopia Inexpensive to implement	Limits career mobility Isolates headquarters from foreign subsidiaries
Geocentric	Global and Transnational	Uses human resources efficiently Helps build strong culture and informal management network	National immigration policies may limit implementation Expensive

the average cost per failure to the parent firms can be as high as three times the expatriate's annual domestic salary *plus* the cost of relocation (which is affected by currency exchange rates and location of assignment).[5] Research also suggests that expatriate failure is a persistent and recurring problem in international businesses. In one study, R. L. Tung surveyed a number of U.S., European, and Japanese multinationals.[6] Her results, summarized in Table 18.3., suggest that 76 percent of U.S. multinationals experience expatriate failure rates of 10 percent or more, with 7 percent of U.S. multinationals experiencing a failure rate of more than 20 percent. Tung's work also suggests that U.S.-based multinationals experience a much higher expatriate failure rate than either European or Japanese multinationals.
multinationals experiencing a failure rate of more than 20 percent. Tung's work also suggests that U.S.-based multinationals experience a much higher expatriate failure rate than either European or Japanese multinationals.

Tung asked her sample of multinational managers to indicate reasons for expatriate failure. For U.S. multinationals, the reasons, in descending order of importance, were

1. Inability of spouse to adjust.
2. Manager's inability to adjust.
3. Other family problems.
4. Manager's personal or emotional maturity.
5. Inability to cope with larger overseas responsibility.

Managers of European firms gave only one reason consistently to explain expatriate failure: the inability of the manager's spouse to adjust to a new environment. For the Japanese firms, the reasons for failure, in descending order of importance, were

1. Inability to cope with larger overseas responsibility.
2. Difficulties with new environment.

---

[5] M. G. Harvey, "The Multinational Corporation's Expatriate Problem: An Application of Murphy's Law," *Business Horizons* 26(1983), pp. 71–78.

[6] R. L. Tung, "Selection and Training Procedures of U.S., European, and Japanese Multinationals," *California Management Review* 25(1982), pp. 57–71.

Table 18.3
Expatriate Failure Rates

Recall Rate Percent	Percent of Companies
U.S. multinationals	
20–40%	7%
10–20	69
<10	24
European multinationals	
11–15%	3%
6–10	38
<5	59
Japanese multinationals	
11–19%	14%
6–10	10
<5	76

Source: Data from R. L. Tung, "Selection and Training Procedures of U.S., European, and Japanese Multinationals," California Management Review *25 (1982), pp. 57–71.*

3. Personal or emotional problems.
4. Lack of technical competence.
5. Inability of spouse to adjust.

Perhaps the most striking difference between these lists is that "inability of spouse to adjust" was the number-one reason for expatriate failure among U.S. and European multinationals but only the number-five reason among Japanese multinationals. Tung comments that this difference is not surprising, given the role and status to which Japanese society traditionally relegates the wife and the fact that most of the Japanese expatriate managers in the study were men.

The inability of expatriate managers' spouses to adjust to a foreign posting seems to be related to a number of factors. Often spouses find themselves in a foreign country without the familiar network of family and friends. Language differences make it difficult for them to make new friends. While this may not be too great a problem for the manager, who can make friends at work, it can be difficult for the spouse who might feel trapped at home. The problem is often exacerbated by immigration regulations prohibiting the spouse from taking employment.

Expatriate Selection

One way of reducing expatriate failure rates is through improved selection procedures for screening out inappropriate candidates in advance. In a review of the research on this issue, Mendenhall and Oddou state that a major problem in many firms is that HRM managers tend to fall into the trap of equating domestic performance with overseas performance potential, selecting candidates for foreign postings accordingly.[7] Domestic performance and overseas performance potential are not the same thing, of course. An executive who performs well in a domestic setting may not be able to adapt to managing in a different cultural setting. From their review of the research, Mendenhall and Oddou identified four dimensions that seem to predict success in a foreign posting: self-orientation, others-orientation, perceptual ability, and cultural toughness.

[7] M. Mendenhall and G. Oddou, "The Dimensions of Expatriate Acculturation: A Review," *Academy of Management Review* 10(1985), pp. 39–47.

1. *Self-orientation.* The attributes of this dimension strengthen the expatriate's self-esteem, self-confidence, and mental well-being. Expatriates with high self-esteem, self-confidence, and mental well-being were more likely to succeed in foreign postings. Mendenhall and Oddou concluded that such individuals were able to adapt their interests in food, sport, and music; had interests outside of work that could be pursued (e.g., hobbies); and were technically competent.
2. *Others-orientation.* The attributes of this dimension enhance the expatriate's ability to interact effectively with host-country nationals. The more effectively the expatriate interacts with host-country nationals, the more likely he or she is to succeed. Two factors seem to be particularly important here: *relationship development* and *willingness to communicate.* Relationship development refers to the ability to develop long-lasting friendships with host-country nationals. Willingness to communicate refers to the expatriate's willingness to use the host-country language. Although language fluency helps here, an expatriate need not be fluent to show willingness to communicate. Making the effort to use the language is what is important. Such gestures tend to be rewarded with greater cooperation by host-country nationals.
3. *Perceptual ability.* This is the ability to understand why people of other countries behave in the way they do; that is, the ability to empathize with them. This dimension seems critical for managing host-country nationals. Expatriate managers who lack this ability tend to treat foreign nationals as if they were home-country nationals. As a result, they may experience significant management problems and considerable frustration. As one expatriate executive from Hewlett-Packard observed, "It took me six months to accept the fact that my staff meetings would start 30 minutes late, and that it would bother no one but me." According to Mendenhall and Oddou, well-adjusted expatriates tend to be nonjudgmental and nonevaluative in interpreting the behavior of host-country nationals and willing to be flexible in their management style, adjusting it as cultural conditions warrant.
4. *Cultural toughness.* This dimension refers to the fact that how well an expatriate adjusts to a particular posting tends to be related to the country of assignment. Some countries are much "tougher" postings than others because their cultures are more unfamiliar and uncomfortable. For example, many Americans regard Great Britain as a relatively easy foreign posting, and for good reason—U.S. and British cultures have much in common. On the other hand, many Americans find postings in non-Western cultures—such as India, Southeast Asia, and the Middle East—to be much tougher.[8] The reasons are many, including poor health care and housing standards, inhospitable climate, a lack of Western entertainment, and language difficulties. It is also important to stress that many cultures are extremely male dominated and thus may be particularly difficult postings for female Western managers.

Mendenhall and Oddou point out that standard psychological tests can be used to assess the first three of these dimensions, whereas a comparison of cultures can give managers a feeling for the fourth dimension. Their basic point is that in addition to domestic performance, these four dimensions should be given weight when selecting a manager for foreign posting. There is evidence, however, that current practice does not conform to Mendenhall and Oddou's recommendations. Tung's research, for example, showed that only 5 percent of the firms in her sample used formal procedures and

[8] I. Torbiorin, *Living Abroad: Personal Adjustment and Personnel Policy in the Overseas Setting* (New York: John Wiley, 1982).

psychological tests to assess the personality traits and relational abilities of potential expatriates.[9]

One factor that Mendenhall and Oddou do not address is the problem of expatriate failure due to a spouse's inability to adjust. According to a number of other researchers, a review of the family situation should be a part of the expatriate selection process.[10] Tung found that at the time of her study, 52 percent of the firms in the sample were interviewing both the candidate and his or her spouse when evaluating a candidate's suitability for an overseas posting. Although this percentage may seem high, remember that "inability of spouse to adjust" was the number-one reason given for expatriate failure. Given this, it is surprising that the figure was not higher.

TRAINING AND MANAGEMENT DEVELOPMENT

Selection is just the first step in matching a manager with a job. The next step is training the manager to do the specific job. For example, an intensive training program might be used to give expatriate managers the skills required for success in a foreign posting. In contrast, management development is a much broader concept. It is intended to develop the manager's skills over his or her career with the firm. Thus, as part of a management development program, over a number of years a manager might be sent on several foreign postings to build up her cross-cultural sensitivity and experience. At the same time, along with a group of other managers in the firm, she might attend management education programs at regular intervals.

Historically, most international businesses have been more concerned with training than with management development. Moreover, they tended to focus their training efforts on preparing home-country nationals for foreign postings. Recently, however, the shift toward greater global competition and the rise of transnational firms have brought about changes in this. It is increasingly common for firms to provide general management development programs in addition to training for particular posts. In many international businesses, the explicit purpose of these management development programs is strategic. The belief is management development is a tool that can be used to help the firm achieve its strategic goals.

With this distinction between *training* and *management development* in mind, in this section we first examine the types of training managers receive for foreign postings. Then we discuss the connection between management development and strategy in the international business.

Training for Expatriate Managers

Earlier in the chapter we saw that the two most common reasons for expatriate failure were the inability of a manager's spouse to adjust to a foreign environment and the manager's own inability to adjust to a foreign environment. Training can help the manager and his or her spouse cope with both of these problems. *Cultural training, language training,* and *practical training* all seem to reduce expatriate failure. We discuss each of these kinds of training here.[11] First, however, we should note that despite the usefulness of these kinds of training, evidence suggests that many managers receive no

---

[9] R. L. Tung, "Selection and Training of Personnel for Overseas Assignments," *Columbia Journal of World Business* 16(1981), pp. 68–78.

[10] S. Ronen, "Training and International Assignee," in *Training and Career Development,* ed. I. Goldstein (San Francisco: Jossey-Bass); and R. L. Tung, "Selection and Training of Personnel for Overseas Assignments," *Columbia Journal of World Business* 16(1981), pp. 68–78.

[11] This section is based on Dowling and Schuler, *International Dimensions of Human Resource Management* (see footnote 1).

training at all before they are sent on foreign postings. One study found that only about 30 percent of managers sent on one- to five-year expatriate assignments received training before their departure.[12]

Cultural Training

Cultural training seeks to foster an appreciation for the host country's culture. The belief is that understanding a host country's culture will help the manager empathize with the culture, which will enhance her effectiveness in dealing with host-country nationals. It has been suggested that expatriates should receive training in the host country's culture, history, politics, economy, religion, and social and business practices.[13] If possible, it is also advisable to arrange for a familiarization trip to the host country before the formal transfer, since this seems to ease culture shock. Given the problems related to spouse adaptation, it is important that the spouse, and perhaps the whole family, be included in cultural training programs. (For an example of cultural training at a large U.S. multinational, Honeywell, see Box 18.2.)

Language Training

English is the language of world business; it is quite possible to conduct business all over the world using only English. For example, in ABB, a Swiss electrical equipment giant, the company's top 13 managers hold frequent meetings in different countries. Since they share no common first language, they speak only English, a foreign tongue to all but one.[14] Despite the prevalence of English, however, an exclusive reliance on English diminishes an expatriate manager's ability to interact with host-country nationals. As noted earlier in the chapter, a willingness to communicate in the language of the host country, even if the expatriate is far from fluent in the language, can help build rapport with local employees and improve the manager's effectiveness. Despite this, J. C. Baker's study of 74 executives of U.S. multinationals found that only 23 believed knowledge of foreign languages was necessary for conducting business abroad.[15] Those firms that did offer foreign language training for expatriates believed it improved their employees' effectiveness and enabled them to relate more easily to a foreign culture, which in turn fostered a better image of the firm in the host country.

Practical Training

Practical training is aimed at helping the expatriate manager and her family ease themselves into day-to-day life in the host country. The sooner a day-to-day routine is established, the better are the prospects that the expatriate and her family will adapt successfully. One of the most critical needs is for a support network of friends for the expatriate. Where an expatriate community exists, firms often devote considerable effort to ensuring the new expatriate family is quickly integrated into that group. The expatriate community can be a useful source of support and information and can be invaluable in helping the family adapt to a foreign culture.

---

[12] Ibid.

[13] G. Baliga and J. C. Baker, "Multinational Corporate Policies for Expatriate Managers: Selection, Training, and Evaluation," *Advanced Management Journal*, Autumn 1985, pp. 31–38.

[14] C. Rapoport, "A Tough Swede Invades the U.S.," *Fortune*, June 20, 1992, pp. 67–70.

[15] J. C. Baker, "Foreign Language and Departure Training in U.S. Multinational Firms," *Personnel Administrator*, July 1984, pp. 68–70.

BOX 18.2

Honeywell's Intercultural Training Program

Honeywell, the large Minnesota-based high-technology firm, receives more than one third of its $5 billion sales revenue from foreign operations. As a result, the firm needed to develop intercultural training for managers who live and travel abroad. The president of Honeywell Control Systems, Jim Renier, working with the corporate human resource development staff, initiated a program in 1981 to advance both international managerial skills and intercultural awareness.

Analysis

A need analysis was developed that surveyed most of the employees who traveled extensively, lived abroad, or interacted regularly with those from abroad. This survey was designed to determine cultural barriers as well as strengths and weaknesses of management practices in worldwide operations, in order to design an effective program that could assist employees in preparing to live abroad and to reenter the home country when their assignments were completed. The results of the survey were analyzed by using standard statistical procedures and by collecting anecdotal data that respondents provided. Evidently, the top executives needed to be kept informed of the changing economic and market conditions, exchange rates, and ethical practices in the countries in which Honeywell operates.

Seminar

A seminar was developed for top executives and management to discuss issues such as matrix management, international marketing, foreign currency and risk management, and cultural values. The survey also indicated the need to address cross-cultural problems that Honeywell American employees experienced overseas. To raise cross-cultural awareness, a training program was designed to focus on three specific areas.

1. *Culture-specific information*—data covering other countries and particularly the country one would be entering.
2. *Cultural general information*—values, practices, and assumptions of countries other than the United States.
3. *Self-specific information*—identifying one's own cultural paradigm including values, assumptions, and perceptions about others.

In addition to seminars and training programs, videopacks on "how to enter another culture" and "cultural grams" about specific countries and cultures are provided to those going overseas for self-study. This cross-cultural program has lessened the cultural gap between expatriate and native personnel and increased the employees' efficiency and productivity on a worldwide basis.

Source: W. C. Kim and R. A. Mauborgne, "Cross-Cultural Strategies," Journal of Business Strategy, *1988, page 33.*

Management Development and Strategy

Management development programs are designed to increase the overall skill levels of managers through a mix of ongoing management education and rotations of managers through a number of jobs within the firm to give them varied experiences. Put another way, management development programs are attempts to improve the overall productivity and quality of the firm's management resources.

Increasingly, international businesses are using management development as a strategic tool. This is particularly true in firms pursuing a transnational strategy—as increasing numbers are. As we have seen, in such firms there are needs for a strong unifying corporate culture and for informal management networks to assist in coordination and control (see Table 18.2). In addition, transnational firm managers need to be able to detect pressures for local responsiveness, and that requires them to understand the culture of a host country.

In the first instance, management development programs help build a unifying corporate culture by socializing new managers into the norms and value systems of the firm. Colgate's 24-month international management training program is an example of this (see the opening case). In-house company training programs and intense interaction during off-site training can foster esprit de corps—shared experiences, informal networks, perhaps a company language or jargon—as well as develop technical competencies. These training events often include songs, picnics, and sporting events that promote feelings of togetherness. These rites of integration may include "initiation rites" wherein personal culture is stripped, company uniforms are donned (e.g., T-shirts bearing the company logo), and humiliation is inflicted (e.g., a pie in the face). The aim of all these activities is to strengthen a manager's identification with the company.[16]

Bringing managers together in one location for extended periods of time and rotating them through different jobs in several countries helps the firm build an informal management network. (Chapter 13 explained the importance of such networks in transnational firms.) As an example, consider the Swedish telecommunications company L. M. Ericsson. Interunit cooperation is extremely important in Ericsson, particularly for transferring know-how and core competencies from the parent to foreign subsidiaries, from foreign subsidiaries to the parent, and between foreign subsidiaries. To facilitate cooperation, Ericsson has a long-standing policy of transferring large numbers of people back and forth between headquarters and subsidiaries. Ericsson sends a team of 50 to 100 engineers and managers from one unit to another for a year or two. This process establishes a network of interpersonal contacts. This policy is effective for both solidifying a common culture in the company and coordinating the company's globally dispersed operations.[17]

PERFORMANCE APPRAISAL

A particularly thorny issue in many international businesses is of how best to evaluate its expatriate managers' performance.[18] In this section we look at this issue and consider some guidelines for appraising expatriate performance.

Performance Appraisal Problems

The intrusion of unintentional bias makes it difficult to evaluate the performance of expatriate managers objectively. In most cases, two groups evaluate the performance of expatriate managers, host-nation managers and home-office managers, and both are subject to bias. The host-nation managers may be biased by their own cultural frame of reference and set of expectations. For example, Oddou and Mendenhall report the case of a U.S. manager who introduced participative decision making while working in an Indian subsidiary.[19] The manager subsequently received a negative evaluation from host-

[16] S. C. Schneider, "National v. Corporate Culture: Implications for Human Resource Management," *Human Resource Management* 27 (Summer 1988), pp. 231–46.

[17] Bartlett and Ghoshal, *Managing across Borders*.

[18] The main sources for this section are: G. Oddou and M. Mendenhall, "Expatriate Performance Appraisal: Problems and Solutions," in *International Human Resource Management*, ed. Mendenhall and Oddou (Boston: PWS-Kent, 1991); and Dowling and Schuler, *International Dimensions*.

[19] Oddou and Mendenhall, "Expatriate Performance."

country managers. The reason: Due to the strong social stratification that exists in India, managers are seen as experts who should not have to ask subordinates for details. The local employees apparently viewed the U.S. manager's attempt at participatory management as an indication that he was incompetent and did not know his job. This negatively affected his host-country manager's evaluation of his performance.

Home-country managers' appraisals may be biased by distance and, in some cases, by their own lack of experience working abroad. Due to distance, home-office management is often not aware of what is going on in a foreign operation. Accordingly, they tend to rely on "hard" data in evaluating an expatriate's performance—data such as the subunit's productivity, profitability, or market share. The problem with using such criteria is that they may reflect factors outside the expatriate manager's control (e.g., adverse changes in exchange rates, economic downturns). Moreover, hard data do not take into account many less-visible "soft" variables that are also important, such as an expatriate's ability to develop cross-cultural awareness and to work productively with local managers.

Due to such biases, many expatriate managers appear to feel that headquarters management evaluates them unfairly and does not fully appreciate the value of their skills and experience. This could be one reason many expatriates believe a foreign posting does not benefit their careers. In one study of personnel managers in U.S. multinationals, 56 percent of the managers surveyed stated that a foreign assignment is either detrimental or immaterial to one's career.[20]

Guidelines for Performance Appraisal

According to Oddou and Mendenhall, several things can reduce bias in the performance appraisal process.[21] First, most expatriates appear to believe more weight should be given to an on-site manager's appraisal than to an off-site manager's appraisal. Due to proximity, an on-site manager is more likely to be able to evaluate the soft variables that are important aspects of an expatriate's performance. The evaluation may be especially valid when the on-site manager is of the same nationality as the expatriate, since cultural bias should be alleviated.

In practice, however, home-office managers often write performance evaluations after receiving input from on-site managers. When this is the case, Oddou and Mendenhall recommend that a former expatriate who served in the same location should be involved in the appraisal process to help reduce bias. Finally, Oddou and Mendenhall argue that when the policy is for foreign on-site managers to write performance evaluations, home-office managers should be consulted before an on-site manager completes a formal termination evaluation. This makes sense, because it gives the home-office manager the opportunity to balance what could be a very hostile evaluation based on a cultural misunderstanding.

COMPENSATION

Two issues are raised in every discussion of compensation practices in an international business. One is how compensation should be adjusted to reflect national differences in economic circumstances and compensation practices. The other issue is how expatriate managers should be paid. In this section we consider each issue in turn.

---

20 "Expatriates Often See Little Benefit to Careers in Foreign Stints, Indifference at Home," *Wall Street Journal*, December 11, 1989, p. B1

21 Oddou and Mendenhall, "Expatriate Performance."

National Differences in Compensation

Substantial differences exist in the compensation of executives at the same level in various countries. Figure 18.1 compares the gross pay of general managers of $30 million companies in the United States and nine European countries. As can be seen, U.S. executives are paid significantly more than executives in most other countries except for Switzerland. Indeed, the average U.S. executive is paid twice as much as his or her British counterpart. Figure 18.2 compares the average 1991 remuneration for CEOs of firms with sales in excess of $250 million in 11 countries. Again the United States is at the top of the list. The average U.S. CEO received more than $750,000 in total compensation, compared with about $400,000 for the average Japanese CEO and under $300,000 for the average Australian CEO. Notice, however, that much of the difference between U.S. CEOs and the other CEOs is that the U.S. CEOs receive a substantial proportion of their pay in the form of long-term incentives such as stock options. This reflects the belief—which has gained wider currency in the United States than elsewhere—that performance-related bonuses motivate managers to do a better job.

These differences in compensation practices raise a perplexing question for an international business: should the firm pay executives in different countries according to the prevailing standards in each country, or should it equalize pay on a global basis? The problem does not really arise in firms pursuing ethnocentric or polycentric staffing policies. In ethnocentric firms the issue can be reduced to that of how much home-country expatriates should be paid (which we will consider later). As for polycentric firms, the lack of managers' mobility among national operations implies that pay can and should be kept country-specific. There would seem to be no point in paying executives in Great Britain the same as U.S. executives if they never work side by side.

However, this problem is very real in firms with geocentric staffing policies. Recall that a geocentric staffing policy is consistent with a transnational strategy. One aspect of this policy, from the HRM perspective, is the need for a cadre of international managers. By definition, this cadre may comprise managers of many different nationalities. Should all members of such a cadre be paid the same salary and the same incentive pay? For a U.S.-based firm this would mean raising the compensation of foreign nationals to U.S. levels, which, given the high pay rates prevailing in the United States, could be very expensive. On the other hand, if the firm does not equalize pay, it could cause considerable resentment among foreign nationals who are members of the international cadre and work side by side with U.S. nationals. You might recall that this issue arose in the opening case on Colgate-Palmolive, and Colgate decided to pay all members of its international cadre the same rate. However, this has caused resentment among foreign executives who see some of their compatriots receiving much higher pay. Notwithstanding such complications, in general, if the firm is serious about building an international cadre, it may have to pay its international executives the same basic salary irrespective of their country of origin or assignment.

Expatriate Pay

The most common approach to expatriate pay is the **balance sheet approach.** This approach equalizes purchasing power across countries so employees can enjoy the same living standard in their foreign posting that they enjoyed at home. In addition, the approach provides financial incentives to offset qualitative differences between assignment locations.[22] Figure 18.3 shows a typical balance sheet. Note that home-country outlays for the employee are designated as income taxes, housing expenses, expenditures for goods and services (food, clothing, entertainment, etc.), and reserves (savings,

---

[22] C. Reynolds, "Compensation of Overseas Personnel," in *Handbook of Human Resource Administration*, ed. J. J. Famularo (New York: McGraw-Hill, 1986).

Figure 18.1
Compensation of General Managers of $30 Million Firms in Selected Countries (in $000)

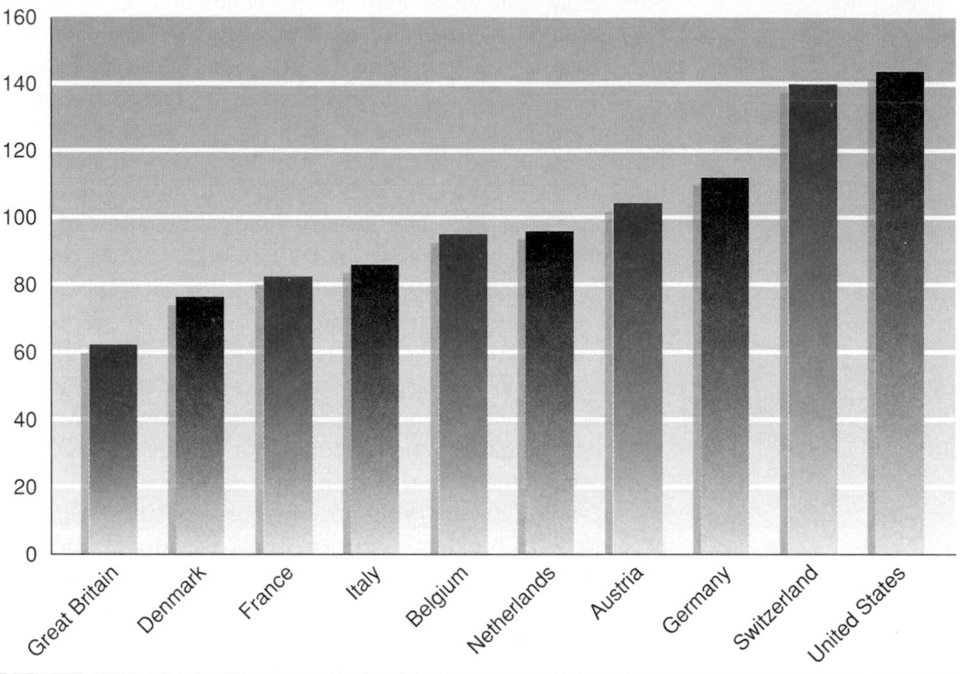

Source: Data from G. Oddou and M. Mendenhall, "Expatriate Performance Appraisal: Problems and Solutions," International Human Resource Management, *ed. M. Mendenhall and G. Oddou (Boston: PSW-Kent, 1991).*

Figure 18.2
Average Remuneration of CEOs of Firms with More than $250 Million is Sales, 1991 (in $000)

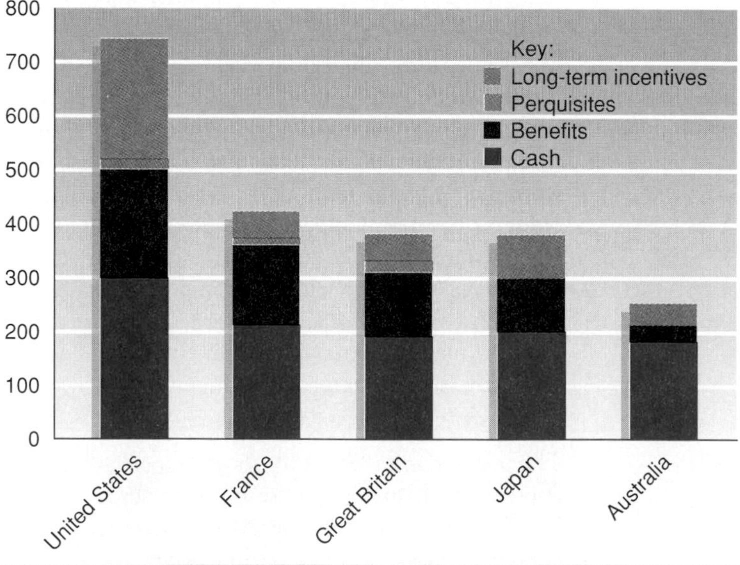

Source: Data estimates from Towers Perrin.

pension contributions, etc.) The balance sheet approach attempts to provide expatriates with the same standard of living in their host countries as they enjoy at home *plus* a financial inducement (i.e., premium, incentive) for accepting an overseas assignment.

The components of the typical expatriate compensation package are a base salary, a foreign service premium, allowances of various types, tax differentials, and benefits. We

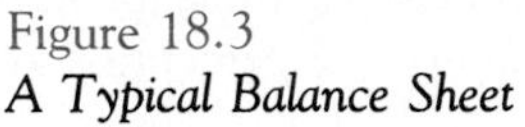
Figure 18.3
A Typical Balance Sheet

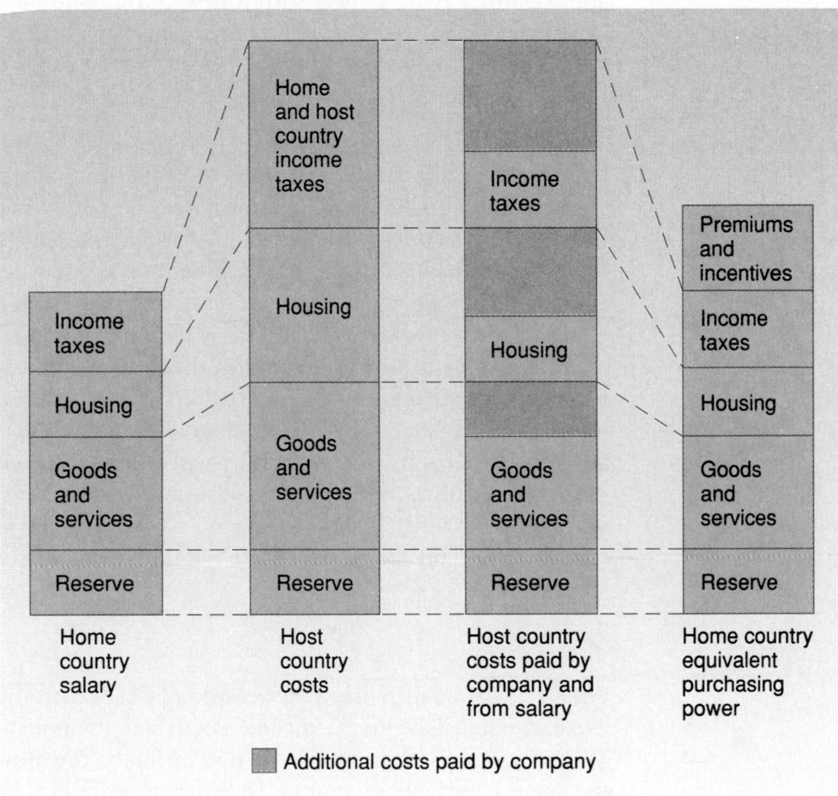

Source: C. Reynolds, "Compensation of Overseas Personnel," in Handbook of Human Resource Administration, 2nd ed, ed. J. J. Famularo (New York: McGraw-Hill, 1986), p. 51.

shall briefly review each of these components.[23] For now note that an expatriate's total compensation package may amount to three times what he or she would cost the firm in a home-country posting. (Box 18.1 provides some figures on this.) Because of the high cost of expatriates, many firms have reduced their use of them in recent years. However, their ability to do so is often limited by their desire to build a cadre of international managers. Thus, a firm's ability to reduce its use of expatriates may be limited, particularly if it is pursuing an ethnocentric or geocentric staffing policy.

Base Salary

An expatriate's base salary is normally in the same range as the base salary for a similar position in the home country. The base salary is normally paid in either the home-country currency or in the local currency.

Foreign Service Premium

A foreign service premium is extra pay the expatriate receives for working outside his or her country of origin. It is offered as an inducement to accept foreign postings. It compensates the expatriate for having to live in an unfamiliar country isolated from family

[23] M. Helms, "International Executive Compensation Practices," in *International Human Resource Management*, ed. M. Mendenhall and G. Oddou (Boston: PWS-Kent, 1991).

and friends, having to deal with a new culture and language, and having to adapt new work habits and practices. Many firms pay foreign service premiums as a percentage of base salary ranging from 10 to 30 percent after tax.

Allowances

Four types of allowances are often included in an expatriate's compensation package: hardship allowances, housing allowances, cost-of-living allowances, and education allowances. A *hardship allowance* is paid when the expatriate is being sent to a difficult location. A *difficult* location is usually defined as one where such basic amenities as health care, schools, and retail stores are grossly deficient by the standards of the expatriate's home country. A *housing allowance* is normally given to ensure that the expatriate can afford the same quality of housing in the foreign country as at home. In locations where housing is very expensive (e.g., London, Tokyo), this allowance can be substantial—as much as 10 to 30 percent of the expatriate's total compensation package. A *cost-of-living allowance* ensures that the expatriate will enjoy the same standard of living in the foreign posting as at home. An *education allowance* ensures that an expatriate's children receive adequate schooling (by home-country standards). Host-country public schools are sometimes not suitable for an expatriate's children, in which case they must attend a private school.

Taxation

Unless a host country has a reciprocal tax treaty with the expatriate's home country, the expatriate may have to pay income tax to *both* the home- and host-country governments. When a reciprocal tax treaty is not in force, the firm typically pays the expatriate's income tax in the host country. In addition, firms normally make up the difference when a higher income tax rate in a host country reduces an expatriate's take-home pay.

Benefits

Many firms also ensure that their expatriates receive the same level of medical and pension benefits abroad that they received at home. This can be very costly for the firm, since many benefits that are tax deductible for the firm in the home country (e.g., medical and pension benefits) may not be deductible out of the country.

INTERNATIONAL LABOR RELATIONS

The HRM function of an international business is typically responsible for international labor relations. From a strategic perspective, the key issue in international labor relations is the degree to which organized labor is able to limit the choices of an international business. Most significant, a firm's ability to integrate and consolidate its global operations to realize experience curve and location economies can be limited by organized labor. Put another way, a firm's ability to pursue a transnational or global strategy can be significantly constrained by the actions of labor unions. Prahalad and Doz give the example of General Motors, which bought peace with labor unions by agreeing not to integrate and consolidate their operations in the most efficient manner.[24] In the early 1980s General Motors made substantial investments in Germany—matching its new investments in Austria and Spain—at the demand of the German metal workers' unions.

---

[24] C. K. Prahalad and Y. L. Doz, *The Multinational Mission* (New York: The Free Press, 1987).

One task of the HRM function is to foster harmony and minimize conflict between the firm and organized labor. With this in mind, this section is divided into three parts. First, we review the concerns of organized labor about multinational enterprises. Second, we look at how organized labor has tried to deal with these concerns. And third, we look at how international businesses manage their labor relations to minimize labor disputes.

The Concerns of Organized Labor

Labor in general is typically most concerned about pay, job security, and working conditions, and labor unions try to get better pay, greater job security, and better working conditions for their members through collective bargaining with management. The unions' bargaining power is derived largely from their ability to threaten to disrupt production, either by a strike or some other form of work protest (e.g., refusing to work overtime). This threat is credible, however, only insofar as management has no alternative but to employ union labor.

A principal concern of domestic unions about multinational firms is that the multinational can counter their bargaining power with the power to move production to another country. Ford, for example, very clearly threatened British unions with a plan to move manufacturing to Continental Europe unless British workers abandoned work rules that limited productivity, showed restraint in negotiating for wage increases, and curtailed strikes and other work disruptions.[25]

Another concern of organized labor is that an international business will keep highly skilled tasks in its home country and farm out only low-skilled tasks to foreign plants. Unions feel that if their members perform only low-skilled tasks, those tasks could just as well be performed by workers in yet another country. Indeed, such a practice makes it relatively easy for an international business to switch production from one location to another as economic conditions warrant. Consequently, the bargaining power of organized labor is once more reduced.

A final union concern arises when an international business attempts to import employment practices and contractual agreements from its home country. When these practices are alien to those traditional in the host country, organized labor fears the change will reduce its influence and power. This concern has surfaced in response to Japanese multinationals that have been trying to export their style of labor relations to other countries. For example, much to the annoyance of the United Auto Workers (UAW), most Japanese auto plants in the United States are not unionized. As a result, union influence in the auto industry is on the decline.

The Strategy of Organized Labor

Organized labor has responded to the increased bargaining power of multinational corporations by taking three actions: (1) trying to establish international labor organizations, (2) lobbying for national legislation to restrict multinationals, and (3) trying to achieve international regulations on multinationals through such organizations as the United Nations. None of these efforts have been very successful.

In the 1960s organized labor began to establish a number of International Trade Secretariats (ITSs) to provide worldwide links for national unions in particular industries. Their long-term goal was to be able to bargain transnationally with multinational firms. Organized labor believed that by coordinating union action across countries through an ITS, it could effectively counter the power of a multinational corporation by threatening to disrupt production on an international scale. For example, Ford's threat to move production from Great Britain to other European locations would not have been credible if the unions in various European countries had united to oppose it.

---

[25] Ibid.

In practice, however, the ITSs have had virtually no real success. The reason is that although national unions may want to cooperate, they also compete with each other to attract investment from international businesses, and hence jobs for their members. For example, in attempting to gain new jobs for their members, national unions in the auto industry often court auto firms that are seeking locations for new plants. One reason Nissan chose to build its European production facilities in Great Britain rather than Spain was that the British unions agreed to greater concessions than the Spanish unions did. As a result of such competition between national unions, cooperation is difficult to establish.

A further impediment to cooperation has been the wide variation in union structure across countries. Trade unions developed independently in each country. As a result, the structure and ideology of unions tends to vary significantly from country to country, as does the nature of collective bargaining. For example, in Great Britain, France, and Italy many unions are controlled by left-wing socialists, who view collective bargaining through the lens of "class conflict." In contrast, most union leaders in Germany, the Netherlands, Scandinavia, and Switzerland are far more moderate politically. The ideological gap between union leaders in different countries has made cooperation difficult, since divergent ideologies are reflected in radically different views about the role of a union in society and the stance unions should take toward multinationals.

Organized labor has also met with only limited success in its efforts to get national and international bodies to regulate multinationals. Such international organizations as the International Labor Organization (ILO) and the Organization for Economic Cooperation and Development (OECD) have adopted codes of conduct for multinational firms to follow in labor relations. However, these guidelines are not as far-reaching as many unions would like; moreover, they do not provide any enforcement mechanisms. Not surprisingly, many researchers report that such guidelines are of only limited effectiveness.[26]

Approaches to Labor Relations

International businesses differ markedly in their approaches to international labor relations. Perhaps the main difference is the degree to which labor relations activities are centralized or decentralized in the firms. Historically, most international businesses have decentralized international labor relations activities to their foreign subsidiaries, since labor laws, union power, and the nature of collective bargaining varied so much from country to country. It made sense to decentralize the labor relations function to local managers. The belief was that there was no way central management could effectively handle the complexity of simultaneously managing labor relations in a number of different environments.

Although this logic still holds, there is now a trend toward greater centralized control over international labor relations in international businesses. In part, this trend reflects international firms' attempts to rationalize their global operations. The general rise in competitive pressure in industry after industry has made it more important for firms to control their costs. Since labor costs account for such a large percentage of total costs, many firms are now using the threat to move production to another country in their negotiations with unions to change work rules and limit wage increases (as Ford did in Europe). Because such a move would involve major new investments and plant closures, this bargaining tactic requires the input of headquarters management. Thus, the level of centralized input into labor relations is increasing.

---

[26] For a review see Dowling and Schuler, *International Dimensions*; and Prahalad and Doz, *Multinational Mission*.

In addition, there is growing realization that the way work is organized within a plant can be a major source of competitive advantage. Much of the competitive advantage of Japanese automakers, for example, has been attributed to the use of self-managing teams, job rotation, cross-training, and the like in their Japanese plants.[27] To replicate their domestic performance in foreign plants, the Japanese firms have tried to replicate their work practices there. This often brings them into direct conflict with traditional work practices in those countries, as sanctioned by the local labor unions, so the Japanese firms have often made their foreign investments contingent on the local union accepting a radical change in work practices. To achieve this, the headquarters of many Japanese firms bargains directly with local unions to get union agreement to changes in work rules before committing to an investment. For example, before Nissan decided to invest in northern England, it got a commitment from British unions to agree to a change in traditional work practices. By its very nature, pursuing such a strategy requires centralized control over the labor relations function.

SUMMARY OF CHAPTER

This chapter has focused on human resource management in international businesses. HRM activities include human resource strategy, staffing, performance evaluation, management development, compensation, and labor relations. None of these activities are performed in a vacuum; all must be appropriate to the firm's's strategy. The following points were made in the chapter:

1. Firm success requires HRM policies to be congruent with the firm's strategy and with its formal and informal structure and controls.
2. Staffing policy is concerned with selecting employees who have the skills required to perform particular jobs. Staffing policy can be a tool for developing and promoting a corporate culture.
3. An ethnocentric approach to staffing policy fills all key management positions in an international business with parent-country nationals. The policy is congruent with an international strategy. A drawback is that ethnocentric staffing can result in cultural myopia.
4. A polycentric staffing policy uses host-country nationals to manage foreign subsidiaries and parent-country nationals for the key positions at corporate headquarters. This approach can minimize the dangers of cultural myopia, but it can create a gap between home- and host-country operations. The policy is best suited to a multidomestic strategy.
5. A geocentric staffing policy seeks the best people for key jobs throughout the organization, regardless of their nationality. This approach is consistent with building a strong unifying culture and informal management network and is thus well suited to both global and transnational strategies. Immigration policies of national governments may limit a firm's ability to pursue this policy.
6. A prominent issue in the international staffing literature is expatriate failure, defined as the premature return of an expatriate manager to his or her home country.
7. The costs of expatriate failure can be substantial. The main reason for expatriate failure among Western firms seems to be the expatriate's spouse's inability to adapt to a foreign culture.
8. Expatriate failure can be reduced by selection procedures that screen out inappropriate candidates. The most successful expatriates seem to be those who have high self-esteem and self-confidence, get along well with others, are willing to attempt to communicate in a foreign language, and can empathize with people of other cultures.
9. Training can lower the probability of expatriate failure. It should include cultural training, language training, and practical training, and it should be provided to both the expatriate manager and the spouse.
10. Management development programs attempt to increase the overall skill levels of managers through a mix of ongoing management education and rotation of managers through different jobs within the firm to give them varied experiences.
11. Management development is often used as a strategic tool to build a strong unifying culture and informal management network, both of which support transnational and global strategies.

[27] See J. P. Womack, D. T. Jones, and D. Roos, *The Machine that Changed the World* (New York: Rawson Associates, 1990).

12. It can be difficult to evaluate the performance of expatriate managers objectively due to the intrusion of unintentional bias. A number of steps can be taken to reduce this bias.
13. Substantial country differences exist in the average pay for executives at the same level. U.S. executives generally receive substantially greater compensation than executives of similar rank in other countries.
14. Country differences in compensation practices raise a difficult question for an international business: Should the firm pay executives in different countries according to the standards in each country or equalize pay on a global basis? This dilemma does not arise in firms pursuing ethnocentric or polycentric staffing policies, but it can be serious in firms with geocentric staffing policies.
15. The most common approach to expatriate pay is the balance sheet approach. This approach aims to equalize purchasing power so employees can enjoy the same living standard in their foreign posting that they had at home.
16. Another component of the balance sheet approach is financial incentives and allowances that offset qualitative differences between assignment locations.
17. A key issue in international labor relations is the degree to which organized labor is able to limit the choices available to an international business. A firm's ability to pursue a transnational or global strategy can be significantly constrained by the actions of labor unions.
18. A principal concern of organized labor is that the multinational can counter union bargaining power with threats to move production to another country.
19. Organized labor has tried to counter the bargaining power of multinationals by forming international labor organizations. In general, these efforts have not borne fruit.
20. Traditionally labor relations have been decentralized to individual foreign subsidiaries of multinationals. Now there is a trend toward greater centralization, which enhances the bargaining power of the multinational vis-à-vis organized labor.

DISCUSSION QUESTIONS

1. What are the main advantages and disadvantages of the ethnocentric, polycentric, and geocentric approaches to staffing policy? When is each approach appropriate?
2. Identify the key aspects of a successful expatriate training and development program.
3. What is the link between an international business's strategy and its compensation practices?
4. In what ways can organized labor constrain the strategic choices of an international business? How can an international business limit these constraints?

Accounting in the International Business

CHAPTER 19

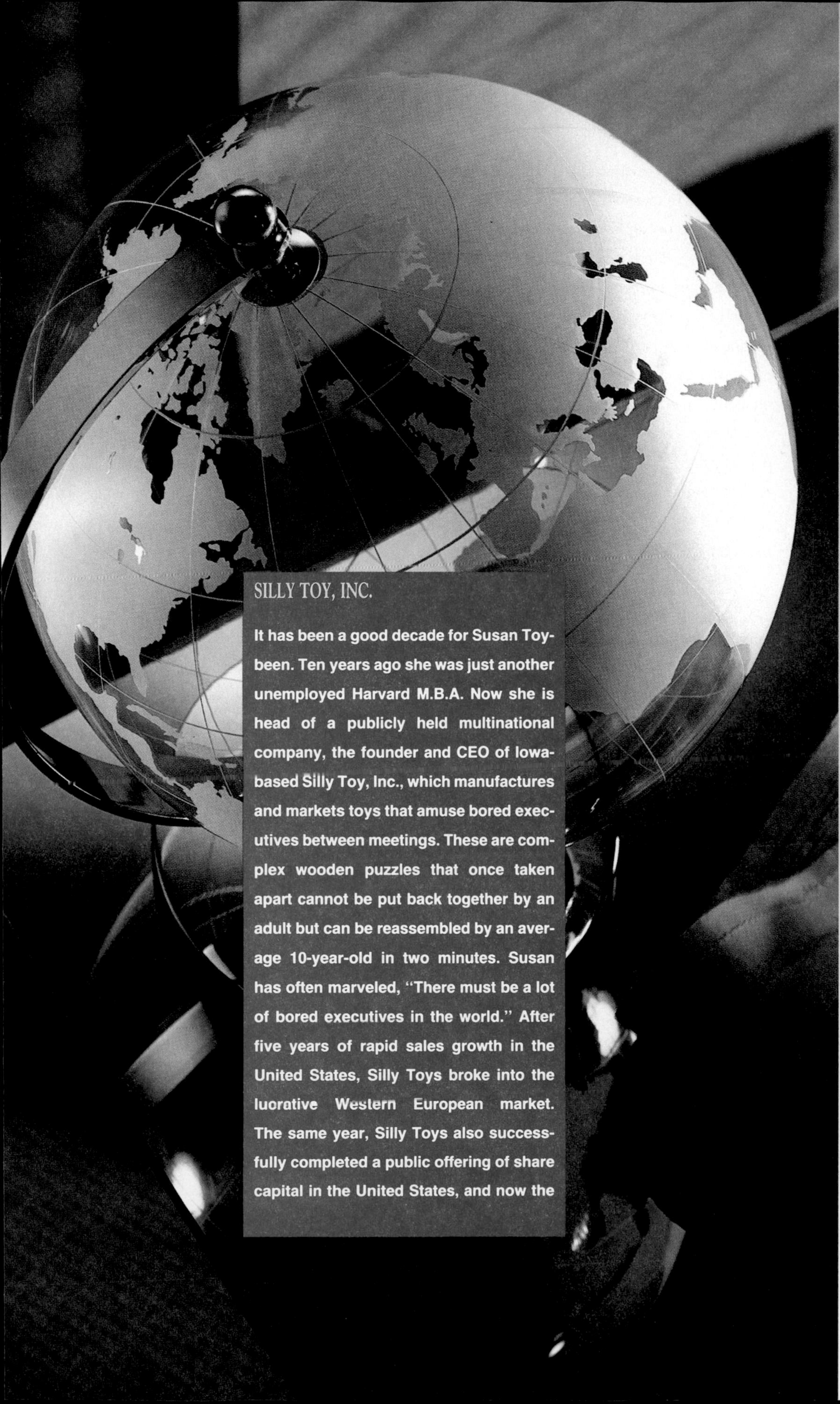

SILLY TOY, INC.

It has been a good decade for Susan Toybeen. Ten years ago she was just another unemployed Harvard M.B.A. Now she is head of a publicly held multinational company, the founder and CEO of Iowa-based Silly Toy, Inc., which manufactures and markets toys that amuse bored executives between meetings. These are complex wooden puzzles that once taken apart cannot be put back together by an adult but can be reassembled by an average 10-year-old in two minutes. Susan has often marveled, "There must be a lot of bored executives in the world." After five years of rapid sales growth in the United States, Silly Toys broke into the lucrative Western European market. The same year, Silly Toys also successfully completed a public offering of share capital in the United States, and now the company is listed on the over-the-counter (OTC) exchange. • The European business grew so rapidly that last year Susan set up a subsidiary, Silly Toys Europe (STE), in Toddington, Great Britain, to manufacture toys for sale in Europe. STE is 50 percent owned by Silly Toys, Inc., and 50 percent owned by European investors who can trade STE shares through the London Stock Exchange. • Unfortunately, Susan's day was just now ruined by her corporate controller, Manfred Frankenfurter. Manfred, once an unemployed Harvard M.B.A. himself, told Susan that Silly Toys, Inc., must prepare a second set of financial statements for last year that conform to the Fourth and Seventh Directives of the European Community (EC), at an additional cost of $50,000.

"Why can't we just use our U.S. reports?" Susan asked. "After all, Manfred, if they're good enough for the SEC they ought to be good enough for the EC."

"Unfortunately, they're not," replied Manfred. "The EC Directives require not only a different way of presenting our financial statements but also some extra disclosures that we don't have to put in our reports here."

"Like what?" barked Susan, trying, without success, to put together a puzzle that she herself designed.

"Well, for one thing, they want a value added statement," replied Manfred.

"A what!" exclaimed an annoyed Susan.

"A *value added statement,*" said Manfred. "We have to show the value we add to the materials and services that we purchased, and then we have to show how we disposed of the value that we added."

"How we disposed of the value added?" Susan was really lost now. "I don't remember learning this stuff at Harvard."

"That's right," replied Manfred, who was wondering how his boss could be so dense, "how we disposed of value added. The Europeans want to know how much of our value added went to employees as salaries, pensions, and the like; how much to government as taxes; how much went to providers of capital as interest to creditors and as dividends to shareholders; and how much we reinvested in the business."

Susan looked confused.

"Look," said Manfred, "I've brought you the value added statement for ICI to show you the kind of thing we have to do." Manfred slid ICI's value added statement over to Susan. "See," he said, "they show their value added, and they show how they disposed of it."

Susan glanced at the document. "Okay," she said, changing tack, "what if we just follow the International Accounting Standards Committee *Standards* when we prepare our year-end statements? Will that keep us from having to do two sets of report?"

"I'm afraid not," said Manfred. "Neither the SEC nor the EC accept the IASC *Standards* in place of its own. The SEC won't accept the EC *Standards,* and the EC doesn't accept the SEC *Standards.*"

"Good grief, how stupid!" responded Susan. "Well, the EC can just shove it. I don't see any benefit in preparing two sets of financial statements just because the stupid EC can't agree with the stupid SEC on a stupid format. It'd cost us too much money. Our U.S. reports will do the job quite adequately. And damn this stupid puzzle!" Susan flung it at the wall.

Table 19.A
Value Added Statement of Imperial Chemical Industries (ICI)

Sources and Disposal of Value Added

	Notes	1988 £m	1987 £m	Percentage change
SOURCES OF INCOME				
Sales turnover		11,699	11,123	+5%
Royalties and other trading income		154	144	+7%
Less: materials and services used		(7,591)	(7,338)	+3%
VALUE ADDED BY MANUFACTURING AND TRADING ACTIVITIES		4,262	3,929	+8%
Share of profits less losses of related companies		162	157	+3%
TOTAL VALUE ADDED		4,424	4,086	+8%
DISPOSAL OF TOTAL VALUE ADDED				
EMPLOYEES	1			
Pay, plus pensiion and national insurance contributions, and severance costs		2,274	2,145	
Profit-sharing bonus	2	63	54	
		2,337	2,199	+6%
GOVERNMENTS	3			
Corporate taxes		540	504	
Less: grants		(29)	(31)	
		511	473	+8%
PROVIDERS OF CAPITAL				
Interest cost of net borrowings		162	142	
Dividends to shareholders		341	277	
Minority shareholders in subsidiaries		49	48	
		552	467	+18%
RE-INVESTMENTS IN THE BUSINESS				
Depreciation and provision in respect of extraordinary item		528	464	
Profit retained		496	483	
		1024	947	+8%
TOTAL DISPOSAL		4,424	4,086	

NOTES

1 The average number of employees in the Group worldwide increased by 2 percent. The number employed in the UK decreased by 2 percent.

2 The 1988 UK bonus rate was 9.2p per £1 of renumeration (1987, 8.6p).

3 Does not include tax deducted from the pay of employees. Income tax deducted from the pay of UK employees under PAYE amounted to £152m in 1988 (1987, £158m).

This table, which is used for calculating the bonus under the Employees' Profit-Sharing Scheme, is based on the audited accounts. It shows the total value added to the cost of materials and services purchased from outside the Group and indicates how this increase in value has been disposed of.

"Here we go again," thought Manfred. "Susan, you're missing the point. Half the STE stock is held by Europeans. They expect to see this information, and we want to keep *them* happy. More to the point, remember that STE has a quote on the London Exchange; we *have* to produce a report that conforms to the EC format to meet *their* regulations."

Susan's shoulders slumped, defeated. "Okay, Manfred," she said. "Go ahead and do it—and, will you hand me that puzzle before you leave?"

Figure 19.1
Accounting Information and Capital Flows

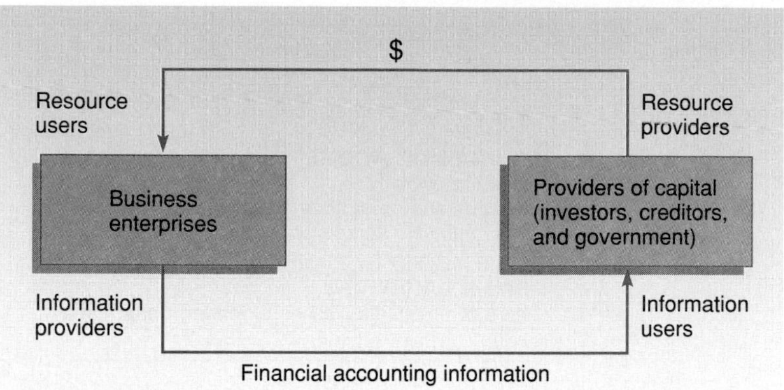

INTRODUCTION

Accounting has often been referred to as "the language of business."[1] This language finds expression in profit and loss statements, balance sheets, budgets, investment analysis, and tax analysis. Accounting information is the means by which firms communicate their financial position to the providers of capital—investors, creditors, and government. It enables the providers of capital to assess the value of their investments, or the security of their loans, and to make decisions about future resource allocations (see Figure 19.1). Accounting information is also the means by which firms report their income to the government, so the government can assess how much tax the firm owes. Furthermore, it is the means by which the firm can evaluate its performance, control its internal expenditures, and plan for future expenditures and income. Thus, it is no exaggeration to say that a good accounting function is critical to the smooth running of the firm.

International businesses are confronted with a number of accounting problems that do not confront purely domestic businesses. In the Silly Toys opening case, Susan Toybeen has just faced one of these problems, the lack of consistency in the accounting standards of different countries. We begin this chapter by looking at the source of these country differences. Then we shift our attention to the attempts currently under way to establish international accounting and auditing standards—the International Accounting Standards Committee *Standards* referred to in the case.

Having done this, we will examine the problems arising when an international business with operations in more than one country must produce consolidated financial statements. As we will see, these firms face special problems because, for example, the accounts for their operations in France will be in francs, in Italy they will be in lira, and in Japan they will be in yen. If the firm is based in the United States, it will have to decide what basis to use for translating all of these accounts into U.S. dollars.

The last issue we discuss in the chapter is that of control in an international business. We touched on the issue of control in Chapter 13 in rather abstract terms. Here we look at control from an accounting perspective.

---

[1] G. G. Mueller, H. Gernon, and G. Meek, *Accounting: An International Perspective* (Homewood, Ill.: Richard D. Irwin, 1991).

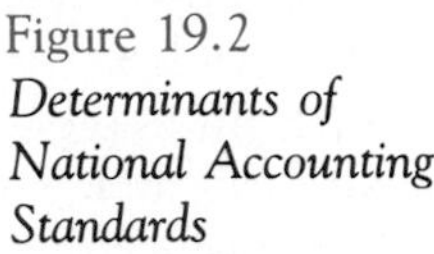

Figure 19.2
Determinants of National Accounting Standards

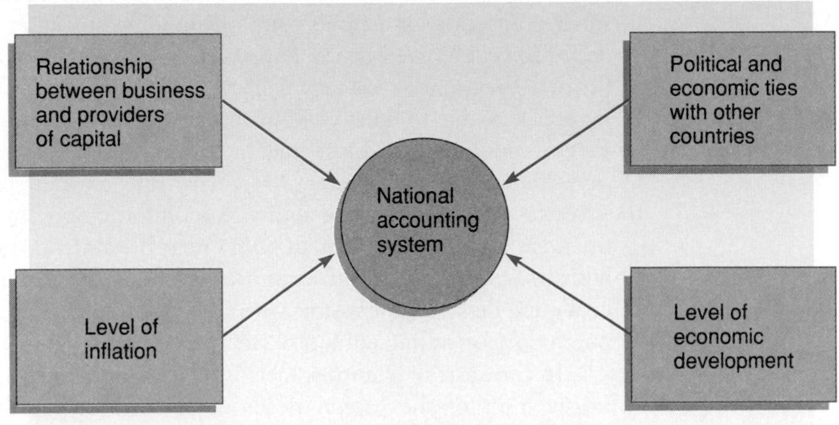

COUNTRY DIFFERENCES IN ACCOUNTING STANDARDS

Accounting is shaped by the environment in which it operates. Just as different countries have different political systems, economic systems, and cultures, so they also have different accounting systems. In each country, the accounting system has evolved in response to the demands for accounting information in that country. An example of these differences underlies the opening case. Another example of differences in accounting conventions concerns employee disclosures. In many European countries, government regulations require firms to publish detailed information about their training and employment policies, whereas there is no such requirement in the United States.

Although many factors can influence the development of a country's accounting system, there appear to be four main variables:

1. The relationship between business and the providers of capital.
2. Political and economic ties with other countries.
3. The level of inflation.
4. The level of a country's economic development.

See Figure 19.2. We will review each of these variables in turn.

Relationship between Business and Providers of Capital

As we have said, there are three main external sources of capital for business enterprises —individual investors, banks, and government. In most advanced countries all three sources are of some importance. In the United States, for example, business firms can raise capital by selling shares and bonds to individual investors through the stock market and the bond market. They can also borrow capital from banks and, in rather limited cases (particularly to support investments in defense-related R&D), from the government. The importance of each source of capital varies from country to country. In some countries, such as the United States, individual investors are the major source of capital; in others, banks play a greater role; in still others, the government is the major provider of capital. A country's accounting system tends to reflect the relative importance of these three constituencies as providers of capital.

Consider the case of the United States and Great Britain. Both of these countries have well-developed stock and bond markets in which firms can raise capital by selling stocks and bonds to individual investors. Most individual investors purchase only a very small proportion of a firm's total outstanding stocks or bonds. As such, they have no desire to be involved in the day-to-day management of the firms in which they invest. Rather, they leave that task to professional managers. The problem with this arrangement is that due to their lack of contact with the management of the firms in which they invest, individual investors may lack the information required to assess how well their investments are performing. Moreover, due to their small stake in firms, individual investors generally lack the ability to get information on demand from management. The financial accounting system in both Great Britain and the United States evolved to cope with this problem. In both countries the financial accounting system is oriented toward providing individual investors with the information they need for making decisions about purchasing or selling corporate stocks and bonds.

In contrast, in countries such as Switzerland, Germany, and Japan, a few large banks satisfy most of the capital needs of business enterprises. Individual investors play a relatively minor role. In these countries the role of the banks is so important that a bank's officers often have seats on the boards of firms to which it lends capital. In such circumstances, the information needs of the capital providers are satisfied in a relatively straightforward way—through personal contacts, direct visits, and information provided at board meetings. Consequently, although government regulations in these countries mandate some public disclosure of a firm's financial position, and so firms still prepare financial reports, the reports tend to contain less information than those of British or U.S. firms. Moreover, since banks are the major providers of capital, financial accounting practices are oriented toward protecting a bank's investment. Thus, assets are valued conservatively and liabilities are overvalued (in contrast to U.S. practice) to provide a cushion for the bank in the event of default.

In still other countries, the national government has historically been an important provider of capital, and this has influenced accounting practices. This is the case in France and Sweden, where the national government has often stepped in to loan or invest in firms whose activities are deemed in the "national interest." In these countries, financial accounting practices tend to be oriented toward the needs of government planners.

Political and Economic Ties with Other Countries

Similarities in the accounting systems of countries are sometimes due to the countries' close political and/or economic ties. For example, the U.S. system has influenced accounting practices in Canada and Mexico. U.S.-style accounting systems are also used in the Philippines, which was once a U.S. protectorate. Another significant force in accounting worldwide has been the British system. The vast majority of former colonies of the British empire have accounting practices modeled on Great Britain's. Similarly, the European Community has been attempting to harmonize accounting practices in its member-countries. At present the accounting systems of EC members such as Great Britain, Germany, and France are quite different, but due to the EC's attempts to achieve harmonization, they may all converge on some norm eventually.

Inflation Accounting

In many countries, including Germany, Japan, and the United States, accounting is based on the **historic cost principle.** This principle assumes the currency unit used to report financial results is not losing its value due to inflation. Firms record sales, purchases, and the like at the original transaction price and make no adjustments in the amounts later. The historic cost principle affects accounting most significantly in the area of asset valuation. If inflation is high, the historic cost principle yields an underestimate of a firm's assets. One result of this is that depreciation charges based on these underestimates can be inadequate for replacing assets when they wear out or become obsolete.

The appropriateness of this principle varies inversely with the level of inflation in a country. The high level of price inflation in many industrialized countries during the 1970s created a need for accounting methods that adjust for the effects of inflation. A number of industrialized countries adopted new practices. One of the most far-reaching approaches was adopted in Great Britain in 1980. Called *current cost accounting*, it adjusts all items in a financial statement—assets, liabilities, costs, and revenues—to factor out the effects of inflation. The method uses a general price index to convert historic figures into current values. The standard was not made compulsory, however, and once Great Britain's inflation rate fell in the 1980s, most firms stopped providing the data.

Level of Development

Developed nations tend to have sophisticated business systems comprising large, complex organizations, whose accounting problems are far more difficult than those of small organizations. Developed nations also tend to have sophisticated capital markets in which business organizations raise funds from investors and banks. These providers of capital require—indeed, *demand*—that the organizations they invest in and lend to provide comprehensive reports of their financial activities. The work forces of developed nations tend to be highly educated and skilled, and they can thus be trained to perform complex accounting functions. For all of these reasons, accounting in developed countries tends to be far more sophisticated than it is in less developed countries, where the accounting standards may be fairly primitive.

Accounting Clusters

Due to the combined impact of the variables we have discussed, very few countries have identical accounting systems. Notable similarities between nations do exist, however, and three groups of countries with similar standards can be identified (see Figure 19.3).[2] One group might be called the *British-American-Dutch group*. Great Britain, the United States, and the Netherlands are the trendsetters in this group. All of these countries have large, well-developed stock and bond markets where firms raise capital from investors. Thus, these countries' accounting systems are tailored to providing information to individual investors. A second group might be called the *Europe-Japan group*. Firms in these countries have very close ties to banks, which supply a large proportion of their capital needs. Therefore, their accounting practices are geared to the needs of banks. A third group might be the *South American group*. The countries in this group have all experienced persistent and rapid inflation. Consequently, they have adopted inflation accounting principles.

NATIONAL AND INTERNATIONAL STANDARDS

The diverse accounting practices discussed in the previous section have been enshrined in national accounting and auditing standards. **Accounting standards** are rules for preparing financial statements; they define what is useful accounting information. **Auditing standards** specify the rules for performing an **audit**—the technical process by which an independent person (the *auditor*) gathers evidence for determining if a set of financial accounts conforms to required accounting standards and if it is also reliable.

[2] Mueller, Gernon, and Meek, *Accounting*.

Figure 19.3 *Accounting Clusters*

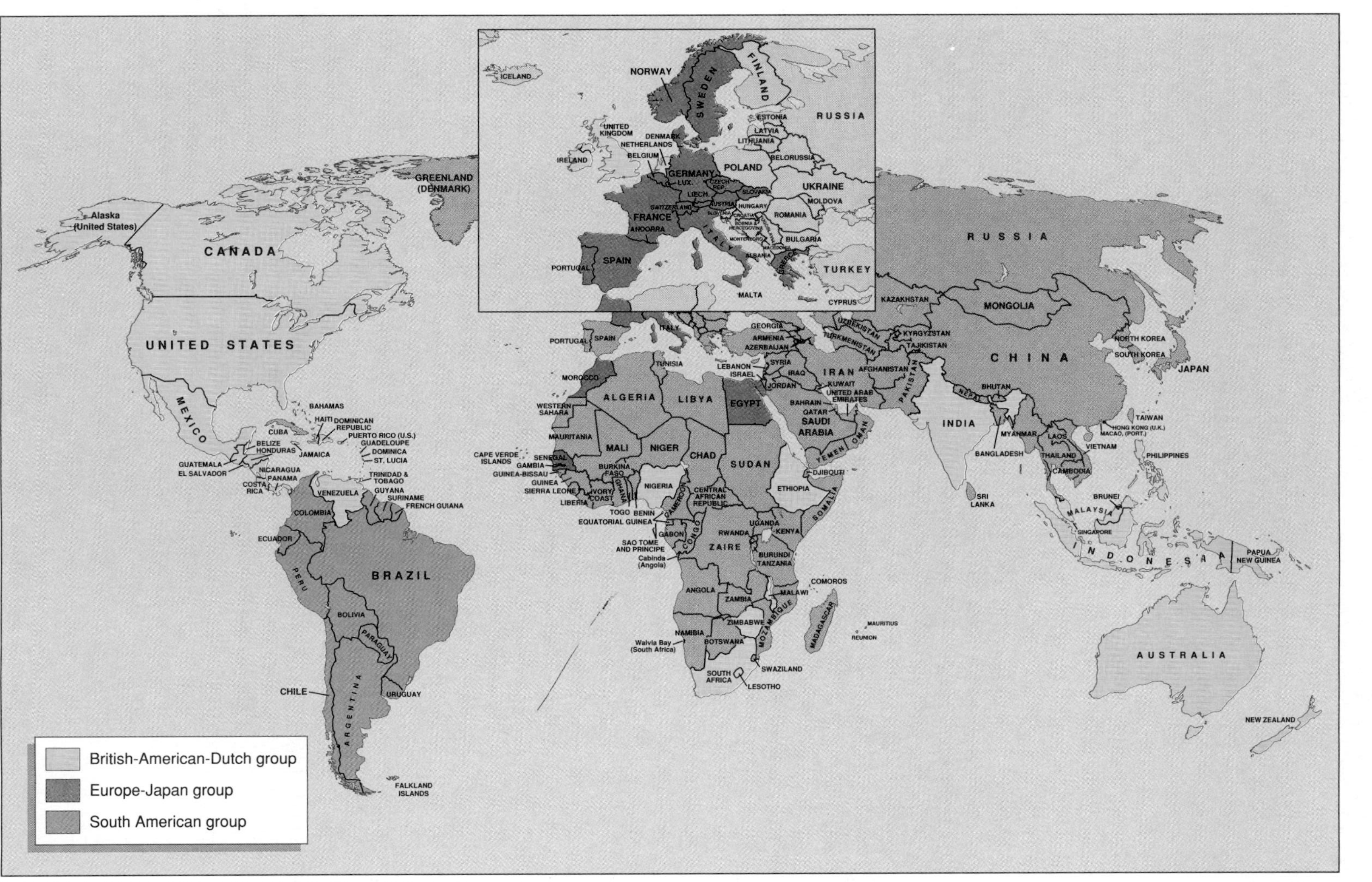

Consequences of the Lack of Comparability

An unfortunate result of national differences in accounting and auditing standards is the general lack of comparability of financial reports from one country to another. For example, consider the following:

- Dutch standards favor the use of current values for replacement assets; Japanese law generally prohibits revaluation and prescribes historic cost.
- Capitalization of financial leases is required practice in Great Britain, but it is not practiced in France.
- Whereas research and development costs must be written off in the year they are incurred in the United States, in Spain they may be deferred as an asset and need not be amortized as long as benefits that will cover them are expected to arise in the future.
- German accountants treat depreciation as a liability, whereas British companies deduct it from assets.

Such differences would not matter very much if **transnational financial reporting** was limited; that is, if there was little need for a firm headquartered in one country to report its financial results to citizens of another country. However, as you might recall from Chapter 11, one of the striking developments of the last two decades has been the development of global capital markets. As a result of this, we have seen the growth of both transnational financing and transnational investment.

Transnational financing occurs when a firm based in one country enters another country's capital market to *raise capital* from the sale of stocks or bonds. A Danish firm raising capital by selling stock through the London Stock Exchange is an example of transnational financing. **Transnational investment** occurs when an investor based in one country enters the capital market of another nation to *invest* in the stocks or bonds of a firm based in that country. An investor based in Great Britain buying General Motors stock through the New York Stock Exchange would be an example of transnational investment.

The rapid expansion of transnational financing and investment in recent years has been accompanied by a corresponding growth in transnational financial reporting. For example, in addition to its Danish financial reports, the Danish firm raising capital in London must issue financial reports that serve the needs of its British investors. Similarly, the U.S. firm with a large number of British investors might wish to issue reports that serve the needs of those investors. However, the lack of comparability between accounting standards in different nations can lead to a lot of confusion. For example, the Danish firm that issues two sets of financial reports, one set prepared under Danish standards and the other under British standards, may find that its financial position looks significantly different in the two reports, and its investors may have difficulty identifying the firm's true worth. Two examples of the confusion that can arise from this lack of comparability appear in Box 19.1.

In addition to the problems this lack of comparability gives investors, it can give the firm some major headaches. For one thing, the firm may have to explain to its investors why its financial position looks so different in the two accountings. Beyond this, an international business may find it extremely difficult to assess the financial positions of important foreign customers, suppliers, and competitors due to the lack of comparability in their financial statements.

International Standards

In light of the problems we have been discussing, substantial efforts have been made in recent years to harmonize accounting standards across countries. Perhaps the most

Two Examples of Confusion Arising from Different Accounting Standards

BOX 19.1

U.S.-based SmithKline Beckman (SKB) merged with the British company Beecham in 1989. After the merger SKB had quotations on both the London and New York Stock Exchanges, so it had to prepare financial reports in accordance with both U.S. and British standards. SKB's postmerger earnings, properly prepared in accordance with British accounting standards, were 130 million pounds sterling—quite a bit more than the 87 million pounds sterling reported in SKB's statement prepared in accordance with U.S. accounting standards. The difference resulted primarily from the income statement effects of different asset bases arising from treating the merger as a *pooling* of assets for British purposes and as a *purchase* of assets for U.S. purposes. Even more confusing, the differences resulted in a shareholders' equity of 3.5 billion sterling in the United States, but a negative 300 million sterling in Great Britain! Not surprisingly, after these figures were released, SKB's stock was trading 17 percent lower on the London Stock Exchange than on the New York Stock Exchange!

Another example is that of Telefonica, Spain's largest industrial company. In the mid-1980s Telefonica was the first company in the world to float a multicountry stock offering simultaneously. In 1990 it reported net income under U.S. accounting standards of 176 billion pesetas, more than twice the 76 billion pesetas it reported under Spanish accounting standards. The difference was mainly due to an "add-back" of the incremental depreciation on assets carried at historic cost in the United States but reflecting more recent market value in the Spanish report. The effect of this difference on shareholders' equity was in the opposite direction; the equity reported in the U.S. accounts was 15 percent less than the equity reported in the Spanish accounts.

Source: S. F. O'Malley, "Accounting across Borders," Financial Executive, *March/April 1992, pp. 28–31.*

significant body that is pushing for this is the **International Accounting Standards Committee (IASC).** The IASC is composed of representatives of 106 professional accounting groups in 79 countries. Governed by a 14-member board of representatives from 13 countries plus a representative from the International Federation of Financial Analysts, the IASC is responsible for formulating international accounting *Standards.* Other areas of interest to the accounting profession worldwide—including auditing, ethical, educational and public sector standards—are handled by the **International Federation of Accountants (IFAC),** which has the same membership.

The IASC was begun in 1973 as an outgrowth of an effort by Canada, the United States, and Great Britain to develop international accounting standards. The IFAC was established in 1977, when it was determined that the IASC did not have the expertise to deal with broader professional issues. The two organizations work closely, but they are operated and funded separately.

As of mid-1992, the IASC had issued 31 international accounting *Standards.*[3] To issue a new *Standard,* 75 percent of the 14 members of the board must agree. It can be difficult to get three-quarters agreement, particularly since members come from different cultures and legal systems. To get around this problem, most IASC statements provide two acceptable alternatives. Arthur Wyatt, chairman of the IASC, says, "It's not much

[3] See P. D. Fleming, "The Growing Importance of International Accounting Standards," *Journal of Accountancy,* September 1991, pp. 100–106.

of a standard if you have two alternatives, but it's better than having six. If you can get agreement on two alternatives, you can capture the 11 required votes and eliminate some of the less used practices."[4]

Another hindrance to the development of international accounting standards is that compliance with the IASC *Standards* is voluntary; the IASC has no power to enforce its *Standards*. Despite this, support for the IASC and recognition of its *Standards* is growing around the world. Increasingly, the IASC is regarded as an effective voice for defining acceptable worldwide accounting principles. Japan, for example, began requiring financial statements to be prepared on a consolidated basis after the IASC issued its initial *Standards* on the topic.

Among all countries, the impact of the IASC *Standards* has probably been least noticeable in the United States. This is because most of the 31 *Standards* issued by the IASC have been consistent with *Opinions* already articulated by the U.S. **Financial Accounting Standards Board (FASB).** The FASB is the principal body that writes the generally accepted accounting principles by which the financial statements of U.S. firms must be prepared. In sharp contrast, some of the IASC *Standards* have had a significant impact on practices in many other countries, because they eliminated a commonly used alternative.

Another body that promises to have substantial influence on the harmonization of accounting standards, at least within Europe, is the European Community (EC). In accordance with its plans for closer economic and political union, the EC is attempting to harmonize the accounting principles of its 12 member-countries. The EC does this by issuing **Directives,** EC laws that the member-states are obligated to incorporate into their own national laws. Since EC Directives have the power of law, we might assume the EC has a better chance of achieving harmonization than the IASC does. In practice, however, the EC is experiencing some implementation difficulties. These difficulties arise from the wide variation in accounting practices among EC member-countries. Accounting practices in Great Britain, for example, are closer to those of the United States than to those of France or Germany. Despite these difficulties, developments in the EC should be watched closely, since if the EC is successful in achieving harmonization (in all probability, it eventually will be), the accounting principles adopted in the EC could be a major influence on future IASC pronouncements.

MULTINATIONAL CONSOLIDATION AND CURRENCY TRANSLATION

A consolidated financial statement combines the separate financial statements of two or more companies to yield a single set of financial statements as if the individual companies were really one. Most multinational firms are composed of a parent company and a number of subsidiary companies located in various other countries. Typically, such firms issue consolidated financial statements, which merge the accounts of all the companies, rather than issuing individual financial statements for the parent company and each subsidiary. In this section we examine the consolidated financial statements and then move on to look at the related issue of foreign currency translation.

Consolidated Financial Statements

Many firms find it advantageous to organize themselves as a set of separate legal entities (companies). For example, a firm may separately incorporate the various components of its business in order to limit its total legal liability or to take advantage of corporate tax

[4] Ibid., p. 101.

regulations. Multinationals are often required by the countries in which they do business to set up a separate company in each country. Thus the typical multinational comprises a parent company and a number of subsidiary companies located in different countries, most of which are wholly owned by the parent. The point, however, is that although the subsidiaries may be separate *legal* entities, they are not separate *economic* entities. Economically, all of the companies in a corporate group are interdependent. For example, if the French subsidiary of a U.S. parent company experiences substantial financial losses that suck up corporate funds, the cash available for investment in that subsidiary, the U.S. parent company, and other subsidiary companies will obviously be limited. Thus, the purpose of consolidated financial statements is to provide accounting information about a group of companies that recognizes their economic interdependence.

Transactions among the members of a corporate family are not included in consolidated financial statements; only assets, liabilities, revenues, and expenses with external third parties are shown. By law, however, separate legal entities are required to keep their own accounting records and to prepare their own financial statements. Thus transactions with other members of a corporate group must be identified in the separate statements so they can be excluded when the consolidated statements are prepared. The process involves adding up the individual assets, liabilities, revenues, and expenses reported on the separate financial statements and then eliminating the intragroup ones. For example, consider these items selected from the individual financial statements of a parent company and one of its foreign subsidiaries:

	Parent	Foreign Subsidiary
Cash	$1,000	$ 250
Receivables	3,000*	900
Payables	300	500*
Revenues	7,000†	5,000
Expenses	2,000	3,000†

Notes: * *Subsidiary owes parent $300.*
† *Subsidiary pays parent $1,000 in royalties for products licensed from parent.*

The $300 receivable that the parent includes on its financial statements and the $300 payable that the subsidiary includes on its statements represent an intragroup item. These items cancel each other out and thus are not included in consolidated financial statements. Similarly, the $1,000 the subsidiary owes the parent in royalty payments is an intragroup item that will not appear in the consolidated accounts. The adjustments are as follows:

			Eliminations		
	Parent	Subsidiary	Debit	Credit	Consolidated
Cash	$1,000	$ 250			$ 1,250
Receivables	3,000*	900		$ 300	3,600
Payables	300	500*	$ 300		500
Revenues	7,000†	5,000		1,000	11,000
Expenses	2,000	3,000†	1,000		4,000

Notes: * *Subsidiary owes parent $300.*
† *Subsidiary pays parent $1,000 in royalties for products licensed from parent.*

Thus, for example, while simply adding the two sets of accounts would suggest that the group of companies has revenues of $12,000 and receivables of $3,900, once intragroup transactions are removed from the picture, these figures drop to $11,000 and $3,600, respectively.

Preparing consolidated financial statements is becoming the norm for multinational firms. Investors realize that without consolidated financial statements, a multinational firm could conceal losses in an unconsolidated subsidiary, thereby hiding the economic status of the entire group. For example, the parent company in our illustration could increase its profit merely by charging the subsidiary company higher royalty fees. Since this has no affect on the group's overall profits, such a practice amounts to little more than window dressing—it may make the parent company look good. If the parent does not issue a consolidated financial statement, however, the true economic status of the group is obscured by such a practice. With this in mind, the IASC has issued two *Standards* requiring firms to prepare consolidated financial statements, and in most industrialized countries this is now required.

Currency Translation

Foreign subsidiaries of multinational firms normally keep their accounting records and prepare their financial statements in the currency of the country in which they are located. Thus the Japanese subsidiary of a U.S. firm will prepare its accounts in yen, a French subsidiary in francs, an Italian subsidiary in lira, and so on. Consequently, when a multinational prepares consolidated accounts, it must convert all of these financial statements into the currency of its home country. As we saw in Chapter 9, however, the problem is that exchange rates vary, often on a day-to-day basis, in response to changes in economic circumstances. This raises the difficult question of what exchange rate should be used when translating financial statement currencies. There are two main methods used to do this, the current rate method and the temporal method.

The Current Rate Method

Under the **current rate method**, the exchange rate *at the balance sheet date* is used to translate the financial statements of a foreign subsidiary into the home currency of the multinational firm. Although this may seem a logical choice, it is incompatible with the historic cost principle, which, as we saw earlier in the chapter, is a generally accepted accounting principle in many countries, including the United States. For an example of why this is so, consider the case of a U.S. firm that invests $100,000 in a French subsidiary. Assume the exchange rate at the time is $1 = FFr 5. The subsidiary converts the $100,000 into francs, which gives it FFr 500,000. It then goes out and purchases some land with this money. Subsequently, the dollar depreciates against the franc, so that by year-end, $1 = FFr 4. If this exchange rate is used to convert the value of the land back into U.S. dollars for the purpose of preparing consolidated accounts, the land will be valued at $125,000. The piece of land would appear to have increased in value by $25,000, although in reality the increase would be simply a function of an exchange rate change. Thus the consolidated accounts would present a somewhat misleading picture.

The Temporal Method

One way to avoid this problem is to use the temporal method to translate the accounts of a foreign subsidiary. The **temporal method** translates assets valued in a foreign currency into the home-country currency using the exchange rate that exists *when the assets are purchased.* Referring to our example, the exchange rate of $1 = FFr 5, the rate on the day the French subsidiary purchased the land, would be used to convert the value of the land back into U.S. dollars at year-end. However, although the temporal method will ensure the dollar value of the land does not fluctuate due to exchange rate changes, it brings with it a serious problem of its own. Since the various assets of a foreign subsidiary will in all probability be acquired at different times, and since exchange rates seldom remain stable for long, different exchange rates will probably have to be used to translate those foreign assets into the multinational's home currency. Consequently, the multinational's balance sheet may not balance!

To understand this, consider the case of a U.S. firm that on January 1, 1994, invests \$100,000 in a new Japanese subsidiary. The exchange rate at that time is \$1 = ¥100. The initial investment is therefore ¥10 million, and the Japanese subsidiary's balance sheet looks like this on January 1, 1994:

	Yen	Exchange Rate	U.S. Dollars
Cash	10,000,000	(\$1 = ¥100)	100,000
Owners' equity	10,000,000	(\$1 = ¥100)	100,000

Assume that on January 31, when the exchange rate is \$1 = ¥95, the Japanese subsidiary invests ¥5 million in a factory (i.e., fixed assets). Then on February 15, when the exchange rate in \$1 = ¥90, the subsidiary purchases ¥5 million of inventory. The balance sheet of the subsidiary will look like this on March 1, 1994:

	Yen	Exchange Rate	U.S. Dollars
Fixed assets	5,000,000	(\$1 = ¥95)	52,632
Inventory	5,000,000	(\$1 = ¥90)	55,556
Total	10,000,000		108,187
Owners' equity	10,000,000	(\$1 = ¥100)	100,000

As can be seen, although the balance sheet balances in yen, it does not balance when the temporal method is used to translate the yen-denominated balance sheet figures back into dollars. In translation, the balance sheet debits exceed the credits by \$8,187. How to cope with the gap between debits and credits is an issue of some debate within the accounting profession. It is probably safe to say that no satisfactory solution has yet been adopted. The practice currently used in the United States is explained next.

Current U.S. Practice

U.S.-based multinational firms must follow the requirements of *Statement 52,* "Foreign Currency Translation," issued by the U.S. Financial Accounting Standards Board (FASB) in 1981. Under *Statement 52,* a foreign subsidiary is classified either as a *self-sustaining,* autonomous subsidiary or as *integral* to the activities of the parent company. (A link can be made here with the material on strategy discussed in Chapter 12. Firms pursuing multidomestic and international strategies are most likely to have self-sustaining subsidiaries, whereas firms pursuing global and transnational strategies, by the very nature of those strategies, are most likely to have integral subsidiaries.) According to *Statement 52,* the local currency of a self-sustaining foreign subsidiary is to be its functional currency. The balance sheet for such subsidiaries is translated into the home currency using the exchange rate in effect at the *end* of the firm's financial year, whereas the income statement is translated using the *average* exchange rate for the firm's financial year. On the other hand, the functional currency of an integral subsidiary is to be U.S. dollars. The financial statements of such subsidiaries are translated at various historic rates using the temporal method (as we did in the example), and the dangling debit or credit increases or decreases consolidated earnings for the period.

ACCOUNTING ASPECTS OF CONTROL SYSTEMS

One of the principal roles of any corporate headquarters is to control subunits within the organization to ensure they achieve the best possible performance. In the typical firm, the control process is annual and involves three main steps:

1. Head office and subunit management jointly determine subunit goals for the coming year.

Table 19.1
*Importance of Financial Criteria Used to Evaluate Performance of Foreign Subsidiaries and Their Managers**

Item	Subsidiary	Manager
Return on investment (ROI)	1.9	2.2
Return on equity (ROE)	3.0	3.0
Return on assets (ROA)	2.3	2.3
Return on sales (ROS)	2.1	2.1
Residual income	3.4	3.3
Budget compared to actual sales	1.9	1.7
Budget compared to actual profit	1.5	1.3
Budget compared to actual ROI	2.3	2.4
Budget compared to actual ROA	2.7	2.5
Budget compared to actual ROE	3.1	3.0

* Importance of criteria ranked on a scale from: 1 = very important to 5 = unimportant
Source: F. Choi, and I. Czechowicz, "Assessing Foreign Subsidiary Performance: A Multinational Comparison," Management International Review *4 (1983), p. 16.*

2. Throughout the year the head office monitors subunit performance against the agreed goals.
3. If a subunit fails to achieve its goals, the head office intervenes in the subunit to learn why the shortfall occurred, taking corrective action when appropriate.

The accounting function plays a critical role in this process. Most of the goals for subunits are expressed in financial terms and are embodied in the subunit's budget for the coming year. The budget is thus the main instrument of financial control. The budget is typically prepared by the subunit, but it must be approved by headquarters management. During the approval process, headquarters and subunit managements debate the goals that should be incorporated in the budget. One of the functions of headquarters management is to ensure a subunit's budget contains challenging but realistic performance goals. Once a budget is agreed to, accounting information systems are then used to collect data throughout the year so a subunit's performance can be evaluated against the goals contained in its budget.

In most international businesses, many of the firm's subunits are foreign subsidiaries. The performance goals for the coming year are thus set by negotiation between corporate management and the managers of foreign subsidiaries. According to one survey of control practices within multinational enterprises, the most important criterion for evaluating the performance of a foreign subsidiary is the subsidiary's actual profits compared to budgeted profits (see Table 19.1).[5] This is closely followed by a subsidiary's actual sales compared to budgeted sales and its return on investment. Interestingly enough, the same criteria were also found useful in evaluating the performance of the subsidiary managers (see Table 19.1). This is a point that we will return to and discuss later in this section. First of all, however, we will examine two factors that can seriously complicate the control process in an international business: exchange rate changes and transfer pricing practices.

Exchange Rate Changes and Control Systems

Most international businesses require all budgets and performance data within the firm to be expressed in the "corporate currency," which is normally the home currency. Thus the French subsidiary of a U.S. multinational would probably submit for approval a budget prepared in U.S. dollars, rather than French francs, and performance data throughout the year would be reported to headquarters in U.S. dollars. One can see why this practice

[5] F. Choi and I. Czechowicz, "Assessing Foreign Subsidiary Performance: A Multinational Comparison," *Management International Review* 4 (1983), pp. 14–25.

is pursued; it facilitates comparisons between subsidiaries in different countries, and it makes things easier for headquarters management. However, it also allows exchange rate changes during the year to introduce substantial distortions into the control process. For example, the French subsidiary may fail to achieve the profit goals contained in its budget not because of any inherent performance problems, but merely because of a decline in the value of the franc against the dollar. The opposite can occur, also, and a foreign subsidiary will look better than it actually is.

The Lessard-Lorange Model

According to research by Donald Lessard and Peter Lorange, a number of methods are available to international businesses for dealing with this problem.[6] Lessard and Lorange point out three exchange rates that can be used in the budget-setting process and in the subsequent tracking of performance to translate foreign currencies into the corporate currency:

The **initial rate,** the spot exchange rate when the budget is adopted.

The **projected rate,** the spot exchange rate forecasted for the end of the budget period (i.e., the forward rate).

The **ending rate,** the spot exchange rate when the budget and performance are being compared.

These three exchange rates imply nine possible combinations (see Figure 19.4). Lessard and Lorange ruled out four of the nine combinations as illogical and unreasonable; they are shaded in Figure 19.4. For example, it would make no sense to use the ending rate to translate the budget and the initial rate to translate actual performance data. Any of the remaining five combinations might be used for the budget-setting and performance evaluation process.

With three of these five combinations—II, PP, and EE—the same exchange rate is used for translating both budget figures and performance figures into the corporate currency. All three combinations have the advantage that a change in the exchange rate during the year does not distort the control process. This is not true for the other two combinations, IE and PE. In those cases, exchange rate changes can introduce distortions. The potential for distortion is greater with IE; the ending spot exchange rate used to evaluate performance against the budget may be quite different from the initial spot exchange rate used to translate the budget. The distortion is less serious in the case of PE, since the projected exchange rate takes into account future exchange rate movements.

Of the five combinations, Lessard and Lorange recommend that firms use the projected spot exchange rate to translate both the budget and performance figures into the corporate currency, combination PP. The projected rate in such cases will typically be the forward exchange rate as determined by the foreign exchange market (see Chapter 9 for the definition of *forward rate*) or some company-generated forecast of future spot rates—which Lessard and Lorange refer to as the **internal forward rate.** The internal forward rate may differ from the forward rate quoted by the foreign exchange market if the firm wishes to bias its business in favor of, or against, the particular foreign currency.

Transfer Pricing and Control Systems

In Chapter 12 we reviewed the various strategies that international businesses pursue. We saw that two of these strategies, the global strategy and the transnational strategy, give rise to a globally dispersed web of productive activities. Firms pursuing these strategies

[6] D. Lessard, and P. Lorange. "Currency Changes and Management Control: Resolving the Centralization/Decentralization Dilemma," *Accounting Review,* July 1977, pp. 628–37.

Figure 19.4
Possible Combinations of Exchanges Rates in the Control Process

Rate used for translating budget	Rate used to translate actual performance for comparison with budget →	Initial (I)	Projected (P)	Ending (E)
	Initial (I)	(II) Budget at initial Actual at initial	Budget at intial Actual at projected	(IE) Budget at initial Actual at ending
	Projected (P)	Budget at projected Actual at initial	(PP) Budget at projected Actual at projected	(PE) Budget at projected Actual at ending
	Ending (E)	Budget at ending Actual at initial	Budget at ending Actual at projected	(EE) Budget at ending Actual at ending

disperse each value creation activity to its optimal location in the world. Thus a product might be designed in one country, some of its components manufactured in a second country, other components manufactured in a third country, all assembled in a fourth country, and then sold worldwide.

Obviously, the volume of intrafirm transactions in such firms is very high. Such firms are continually shipping component parts and finished goods between subsidiaries in different countries. This poses a very important question: How should goods and services transferred between subsidiary companies in a multinational firm be priced? The price at which such goods and services are transferred is referred to as the **transfer price.**

The choice of transfer price can critically affect the performance of two subsidiaries that exchange goods or services. For illustration, consider this example: A French manufacturing subsidiary of a U.S. multinational imports a major component from Brazil. It incorporates this part into a product that it sells in France for the equivalent of $230 per unit. The product costs $200 to manufacture, of which $100 goes to the Brazilian subsidiary to pay for the component part. The remaining $100 are costs incurred in France. Thus the French subsidiary earns $30 profit per unit.

	Before Change in Transfer Price	**After 20 percent Increase in Transfer Price**
Revenues per unit	$230	$230
Cost of component per unit	100	120
Other costs per unit	100	100
Profit per unit	$ 30	$ 10

Now look at what happens if corporate headquarters decides to increase transfer prices by 20 percent ($20 per unit). The French subsidiary's profits will fall by two thirds from $30 per unit to $10 per unit. Thus, the performance of the French subsidiary is wholly dependent on the transfer price for the component part imported from Brazil, and the transfer price is controlled by corporate headquarters. Clearly then, when setting budgets and reviewing a subsidiary's performance, corporate headquarters must keep in mind the distorting effect of transfer prices.

How should transfer prices be determined? We discuss this issue in detail in the next chapter. We will see there that international businesses often manipulate transfer prices to minimize their worldwide tax liability, minimize import duties, and avoid government restrictions on capital flows. For now, however, it is enough to note that the transfer price must be taken into account when setting budgets and evaluating a subsidiary's performance.

Separation of Subsidiary and Manager Performance

Table 19.1 suggests that in many international businesses, the same quantitative criteria are used to assess the performance of both a foreign subsidiary and its managers. Many accountants, however, argue that although it is perfectly legitimate to compare subsidiaries against each other on the basis of return on investment (ROI) or other indicators of profitability, it may not be appropriate to use these for comparing and evaluating the managers of different subsidiaries. Foreign subsidiaries do not operate in uniform environments; their environments have widely different economic, political, and social conditions, all of which influence the costs of doing business in a country and hence the subsidiaries' profitability. Thus the manager of a subsidiary in an adverse environment that has an ROI of 5 percent may actually be doing a better job than the manager of a subsidiary in a benign environment that has an ROI of 20 percent. Although the firm might want to pull out of a country where its ROI is only 5 percent, it may also want to recognize the manager's achievement of any profits at all in such an adverse environment.

Accordingly, it has been suggested that the evaluation of a subsidiary should be kept separate from the evaluation of its manager.[7] The manager's evaluation should involve a degree of subjectivity that considers how hostile or benign the country's environment is for that business. Further, managers should be evaluated in local currency terms after making allowances for those items over which they have no control (e.g., interest rates, tax rates, inflation rates, transfer prices, exchange rates).

SUMMARY OF CHAPTER

The central focus of this chapter has been on financial accounting within the multinational firm. We have explained why accounting practices and standards differ from country to country and have surveyed the efforts now under way to harmonize countries' accounting practices. We have discussed the rationale behind consolidated accounts and have looked at the problem of currency translation. We have reviewed several issues related to the use of accounting-based control systems within international businesses. More specifically, the following points have been made:

1. Accounting is the language of business: the means by which firms communicate their financial position to the providers of capital and to governments (for tax purposes). It is also the means by which firms evaluate their own performance, control their expenditures, and plan for the future.
2. Accounting is shaped by the environment in which it operates. Each country's accounting system has evolved in response to the local demands for accounting information.
3. Four main factors seem to influence the type of accounting system a country has: (*i*) the relationship between business and the providers of capital, (*ii*) political and economic ties with other countries, (*iii*) the level of inflation, and (*iv*) the level of a country's development.
4. National differences in accounting and auditing standards have resulted in a general lack of comparability in countries' financial reports.
5. This lack of comparability has become a problem as transnational financing and transnational investment have grown rapidly in recent decades (a consequence of the globalization of capital markets). Due to the lack of comparability, a firm may have to explain to investors why its financial position looks very different on financial reports that are based on different accounting practices.
6. The most significant push for harmonization of accounting standards across countries has come from the International Accounting Standards Committee

[7] Mueller et al., *Accounting*.

(IASC). So far, the IASC's success, while noteworthy, has been limited.

7. Consolidated financial statements provide financial accounting information about a group of companies that recognizes the companies' economic interdependence.
8. Transactions among the members of a corporate family are not included on consolidated financial statements; only assets, liabilities, revenues, and expenses generated with external third parties are shown.
9. Foreign subsidiaries of a multinational firm normally keep their accounting records and prepare their financial statements in the currency of the country in which they are located. When the multinational prepares its consolidated accounts, these financial statements must be translated into the currency of its home country.
10. Under the current rate translation method, the exchange rate at the balance sheet date is used to translate the financial statements of a foreign subsidiary into the home currency. This has the drawback of being incompatible with the historic cost principle.
11. Under the temporal method, assets valued in a foreign currency are translated into the home currency using the exchange rate that existed when the assets were purchased. A problem with this approach is that the multinational's balance sheet may not balance.
12. In most international businesses, the annual budget is the main instrument by which headquarters controls foreign subsidiaries. Throughout the year headquarters compares a subsidiary's performance against the financial goals incorporated in its budget, intervening selectively in its operations when shortfalls occur.
13. Most international businesses require all budgets and performance data within the firm to be expressed in the corporate currency. This enhances comparability, but it leads to distortions in the control process if the relevant exchange rates change between the time a foreign subsidiary's budget is set and the time its performance is evaluated.
14. According to the Lessard–Lorange model, the best way to deal with this problem is to use a projected spot exchange rate to translate both budget figures and performance figures into the corporate currency.
15. Transfer prices also can introduce significant distortions into the control process and thus must be taken into account when setting budgets and evaluating a subsidiary's performance.
16. Foreign subsidiaries do not operate in uniform environments, and some environments are much tougher than others. Accordingly, it has been suggested that the evaluation of a subsidiary should be kept separate from the evaluation of the subsidiary manager.

DISCUSSION QUESTIONS

1. Why do the accounting systems of different countries differ? Why do these differences matter?
2. Why are transactions among members of a corporate family not included in consolidated financial statements?
3. The following are selected amounts from the separate financial statements of a parent company (unconsolidated) and one of its subsidiaries

	Parent	**Subsidiary**
Cash	$ 180	$ 80
Receivables	380	200
Accounts payable	245	110
Retained earnings	790	680
Revenues	4,980	3,520
Rent income	0	200
Dividend income	250	0
Expenses	4,160	2,960

Notes: 1. Parent owes subsidiary $70.
2. Parent owns 100% of subsidiary. During the year subsidiary paid parent a dividend of $250.
3. Subsidiary owns the building that parent rents for $200.
4. During the year parent sold some inventory to subsidiary for $2,200. It had cost parent $1,500. Subsidiary, in turn, sold the inventory to an unrelated party for $3,200.

Given this,

a. What is the parent's (unconsolidated) net income?
b. What is the subsidiary's net income?
c. What is the consolidated profit on the inventory that the parent originally sold to the subsidiary?
d. What are the amounts of consolidated cash and receivables?

4. Why might an accounting-based control system provide headquarters management with biased information about the performance of a foreign subsidiary? How can these biases best be corrected?

Financial Management in the International Business

CHAPTER 20

FINANCIAL MANAGEMENT AND COMPETITIVE ADVANTAGE

The connection between a firm's finance function and competitive advantage is often poorly understood. As the following examples show, however, there is often a close, fundamental relationship between an international business's financial management and its competitive advantage in the global marketplace.

EXAMPLE 1
FOREIGN EXCHANGE TRADING

FMC Corporation, a Chicago-based producer of chemicals and farm equipment, counts on overseas business for 40 percent of its sales. FMC attributes some of its success overseas to aggressive trading in the forward foreign exchange market. By trading in currency futures, FMC can provide overseas customers with stable long-term prices for three years or more, regardless of what happens to ex-

change rates in the intervening period. Ralph DelZenero, FMC's foreign exchange specialist, says, "Some of our competitors change their prices on a relatively short-term basis depending on what is happening with their own exchange rate. . . . We want to provide longer-term pricing as a customer service—they can plan their budgets knowing what the numbers will be—and we can hopefully maintain and build our customer base." • FMC also offers its customers the option of paying in any of several currencies as a convenience to them and as an attempt to retain customers. If customers could pay only in dollars, they might give their business to a competitor that offered pricing in a variety of currencies. By adopting this policy, FMC's customers "don't have to deal with the hassle of foreign exchange movements," says Mr. DelZenero. "FMC does that for them." • By offering customers multicurrency pricing alternatives, FMC implicitly accepts the responsibility of managing foreign exchange risk for its business units that sell overseas. To do this, it has set up what amounts to an in-house bank to manage the operation, monitoring currency rates daily and managing its risks on a portfolio basis. This bank handles more than $1 billion in currency transactions annually, which means the company can often beat the currency prices quoted by commercial banks. *Lawrence Quinn, "Currency Futures Trading Helps Firms Sharpen Competitive Edge,"* Crain's Chicago Business, *March 2, 1992, p. 20.*

EXAMPLE 2
GLOBAL CASH MANAGEMENT

A French manufacturer that imported raw materials and sold the finished products throughout Europe undertook a study to find ways to conserve cash. The company's management found it was able to free the French franc equivalent of $3.5 million in funds and to reduce interest and bank charges by $500,000 by improving its global cash management procedures. • The manufacturer's target bank balance, which had been $1 million, is now zero. The remainder of the $3.5 million savings has resulted from speeding up the movement of money from customers and delaying the time it takes to debit its accounts to reflect payment to suppliers. Neither the company's customers nor its suppliers are affected by these changes in timing, which simply move cash through the international banking system more rapidly. *J. J. Dyment, "International Cash Management,"* Harvard Business Review, *May–June 1978, p. 143.*

EXAMPLE 3
CASH MANAGEMENT

Monsanto, a U.S.-based chemical manufacturer with annual sales of $8.7 billion, has a very big presence in Europe. In 1989 its Europe–Africa division boasted an annual turnover of $1.8 billion, which accounted for 21 percent of worldwide sales. In the mid-1980s Monsanto centralized its European cash management system in Brussels. By centralizing cash management, rather than having each European subsidiary manage its own cash reserves, Monsanto was able to reduce its average precautionary cash balance in Europe from $30 million per month to $8 million per month. The company is now seeking ways to speed the movement of that $8 million through the region, which should further reduce its working capital needs. *J. Geanuracus, "Monsanto: An Advanced Cash Management System for a Unified Europe,"* Business International Money Report, *April 9, 1990, 140; and J. Geanuracus, "Monsanto: Cash Management Reduces Working Capital, Cuts Down Banking Needs,"* Business International Money Report, *May 7, 1990, pp. 170, 172.*

INTRODUCTION

The focus of this chapter is on financial management in the international business. Included within the scope of financial management are three sets of related decisions:

Investment decisions, decisions about what activities to finance.

Financing decisions, decisions about how to finance those activities.

Money management decisions, decisions about how to manage the firm's financial resources most efficiently.

In an international business all of these decisions are complicated by the fact that countries have different currencies, different tax regimes, different regulations concerning the flow of capital across their borders, different norms regarding the financing of business activities, different levels of economic and political risk, and so on. Financial managers in the international business must consider all of these factors when deciding which activities to finance, how best to finance those activities, how best to manage the firm's financial resources, and how best to protect the firm from political and economic risks (including foreign exchange risk).

Good financial management can be an important source of competitive advantage as the examples in the opening case show. This is certainly true in a purely domestic business, but due to the added complexity of competing in multiple markets, it is even more true in an international business. In Chapter 12 we talked about the value chain and pointed out that creating a competitive advantage requires a firm to reduce its costs of value creation and/or add value by improving its customer service. What must now be explicitly recognized is that good financial management can help the firm both to reduce the costs of creating value and to add value by improving customer service. By reducing the firm's cost of capital, eliminating foreign exchange losses, minimizing the firm's tax burden, minimizing the firm's exposure to unnecessarily risky activities, and managing the firm's cash flows and reserves in the most efficient manner, the finance function can reduce the costs of creating value. Moreover, as the example of FMC in the opening case illustrates, good financial management can also enhance customer service and thereby add value.

With all of this in mind, we begin this chapter by looking at investment decisions in an international business. We will be most concerned here with the issue of capital budgeting, but not with a highly technical exposition of it. Rather, our objective is to identify the range of factors that can complicate capital budgeting decisions in an international business, as opposed to a purely domestic business. Most important, we will discuss how such factors as political and economic risk complicate capital budgeting decisions.

Then we turn our attention to financing decisions in an international business, focusing on the financial structure of foreign affiliates—the mix of equity and debt financing. We will see that financial structure norms for firms vary widely from country to country. We will discuss the advantages and disadvantages of localizing the financial structure of a foreign affiliate to make it consistent with the norms of the country in which it is based.

Next we examine money management decisions in an international business. We will look at the objectives of global money management, the various ways businesses can move money across borders, and some techniques for managing the firm's financial resources efficiently.

The chapter closes with a section on managing foreign exchange risk. Of course, foreign exchange risk was discussed in Chapter 9, but there our focus was on how the foreign exchange market works and the forces that determine exchange rate movements.

In this chapter we focus on the various tactics and strategies international businesses use to manage their foreign exchange risk.

INVESTMENT DECISIONS

A decision to invest in activities in a given country must consider a large number of economic, political, cultural, and strategic variables. We have been discussing this issue throughout much of this book. We first touched on this issue in Chapters 2 and 3 when we discussed how the political, economic, legal, and cultural environment of a country can influence the benefits, costs, and risks of doing business there and thus its attractiveness as an investment site. We returned to the issue in Chapter 6 with a discussion of the economic theory of foreign direct investment. We identified a number of factors that determine the economic attractiveness of a foreign investment opportunity. Building on this, in Chapter 7 we looked at the political economy of foreign direct investment and we considered the role that government intervention can play in foreign investment. In Chapter 12 we pulled much of this material together when we considered how a firm can reduce its costs of value creation and/or increase its value added by investing in productive activities in other countries. And finally, we returned to the issue again in Chapter 14 when we considered the various modes for entering foreign markets. Against this background, one role of the financial manager in an international business is to try to quantify the various benefits, costs, and risks that are likely to flow from an investment in a given location. This is done by using capital budgeting techniques.

Capital Budgeting

The purpose of capital budgeting is to quantify the benefits, costs, and risks of an investment. This enables top managers to compare, in a reasonably objective fashion, different investment alternatives within and across countries so they can make informed choices about where in the world the firm should invest its scarce financial resources. Capital budgeting for a foreign project uses the same theoretical framework that domestic capital budgeting uses; that is, the firm must first estimate the cash flows associated with the project over time. In most cases the cash flows will at first be negative, since the firm will be investing heavily in production facilities. After some initial period, however, the cash flows will become positive as investment costs decline and revenues grow. Once the cash flows have been estimated, they must be discounted to determine their net present value using an appropriate discount rate. The most commonly used discount rate is either the firm's cost of capital or some other required rate of return. So long as the net present value of the discounted cash flows is greater than zero, the firm should go ahead with the project.[1]

Although this might sound quite straightforward, in practice capital budgeting is a very complex and imperfect process. Among the factors complicating the process for an international business are these:

1. A distinction must be made between cash flows to the project and cash flows to the parent company.
2. Political and economic risks, including foreign exchange risk, can significantly change the value of a foreign investment.
3. There is a connection between cash flows to the parent and the source of financing that must be recognized.

---

[1] For details of capital budgeting techniques see R. A. Brealy and S. C. Myers, *Principles of Corporate Finance* (New York: McGraw-Hill, 1988).

We look at the first two of these issues in this section. Discussion of the connection between cash flows and the source of financing is postponed until the next section, where we discuss the source of financing.

Project and Parent Cash Flows

A theoretical argument exists for analyzing any foreign project from the perspective of the parent company, since cash flows to the project are not necessarily the same thing as cash flows to the parent company. The project may not be able to remit all of its cash flows to the parent for a number of reasons. For example, cash flows may be blocked from repatriation by the host-country government, they may be taxed at an unfavorable rate, or the host government may require a certain percentage of the cash flows generated from the project to be reinvested within the host nation. While none of these restrictions affect the net present value of the project itself, they do affect the net present value of the project to the *parent company*, since they limit the cash flows that can be remitted to it from the project.

When evaluating a foreign investment opportunity, the parent should be interested in the cash flows it will *receive*—as opposed to those the project generates—because the cash flows it receives are ultimately the basis for dividends to stockholders, investments elsewhere in the world, repayment of worldwide corporate debt, and so on. The parent needs to keep in mind that its stockholders will not perceive blocked earnings as contributing to the value of the firm, and creditors will not count them when calculating the parent's ability to service its debt.

Having said all this, it must be recognized that the problem of blocked earnings is not as serious as it once was. The worldwide move toward greater acceptance of free market economics (first discussed in Chapter 2) has reduced the number of countries in which governments are likely to prohibit the affiliates of foreign multinationals from remitting cash flows to their parent companies. In addition, as we will see later in the chapter, firms have a number of options for circumventing host-government attempts to block the free flow of funds from an affiliate.

Adjusting for Political and Economic Risk

When analyzing a foreign investment opportunity, the company must consider the risks that stem from its foreign location. These risks include, most importantly, political risk and economic risk. We will discuss these before looking at how capital budgeting methods can be adjusted to take risks into account.

Political Risk

We initially encountered the concept of **political risk** in Chapter 2. There we defined it as the likelihood that political forces will cause drastic changes in a country's business environment that adversely affect the profit and other goals of a business enterprise. So defined, political risk tends to be greater in countries experiencing social unrest or disorder and countries where the underlying nature of the society makes the likelihood of social unrest high. When political risk is high, there is a high probability that a change will occur in the country's political environment that will endanger foreign firms there.

In extreme cases, political change may result in the expropriation of the assets of foreign firms. This occurred to U.S. firms in the aftermath of the Iranian revolution of 1979. Social unrest may also result in economic collapse, which can effectively render worthless a firm's assets. This has occurred to many foreign companies' assets as a result of the bloody war following the breakup of Yugoslavia. In less extreme cases, political changes may result in increased tax rates, the imposition of exchange controls that limit or block a subsidiary's ability to remit earnings to its parent company, the imposition of price controls, and government interference in existing contracts. The likelihood of any of these events impairs the attractiveness of a foreign investment opportunity.

Many firms devote considerable attention to political risk analysis and to quantifying political risk. For example, Union Carbide, the U.S. multinational chemical giant, has an elaborate procedure for incorporating political risk into its strategic planning and capital budgeting process.[2] Similarly, *Euromoney* magazine publishes an annual "Country Risk Rating," which incorporates assessments of political and other risks (see Table 20.1 and Box 20.1). The problem with all attempts to forecast political risk, however, is that they try to predict a future that by its nature can only be guessed at—and in many cases, the guesses are wrong. For example, few people foresaw the 1979 Iranian revolution, the collapse of communism in Eastern Europe, or the dramatic breakup of the Soviet Union, yet all of these events have had a profound impact on the business environments of the countries involved. This is not to say that political risk assessment is without value; merely to point out that it is more art than science.

Economic Risk

Like political risk, we first encountered the concept of **economic risk** in Chapter 2. There we defined it as the likelihood that economic mismanagement will cause drastic changes in a country's business environment that adversely affect the profit and other goals of a particular business enterprise. In practice, the biggest problem arising from economic mismanagement seems to be inflation. Historically many governments have fallen into the trap of expanding their domestic money supply in misguided attempts to stimulate economic activity. The result has all too often been too much money chasing too few goods, and then price inflation. In turn, as we saw in Chapter 9, sooner or later price inflation is reflected in a drop in the value of a country's currency on the foreign exchange market. This can be a serious problem for a foreign firm with assets in that country, since the value of the cash flows it receives from those assets will fall as the country's currency depreciates on the foreign exchange market. The likelihood of this occurring decreases the attractiveness of foreign investment in that country.

There have been many attempts to quantify countries' economic risk and long-term movements in their exchange rates. *Euromoney*'s annual Country Risk Rating (Table 20.1) incorporates an assessment of economic risk in its calculation of each country's overall level of risk. As we saw in Chapter 9, there have in fact been extensive empirical studies of the relationship between countries' inflation rates and their currencies' exchange rates. These studies show that in the long run there is a relationship between a country's relative inflation rates and changes in its currency's exchange rates. However, the relationship is not as close as theory would predict, it is not reliable in the short-run and is not totally reliable in the long run. So, as with political risk, any attempts to quantify economic risk must be tempered with some healthy skepticism.

---

[2] For details see E. G. Roberts, "Country Risk Assessment: The Union Carbide Experience," in *Global Risk Assessment*, Book 3, ed. J. Rogers (Riverside, Calif.: Global Risk Assessments, 1988).

Risk and Capital Budgeting

In analyzing a foreign investment opportunity, the additional risk that stems from its location can be handled in at least two ways. The first method is to treat all risk as a single problem by increasing the discount rate applicable to foreign projects in countries where political and economic risks are perceived as high. Thus, for example, a firm might apply a 6 percent discount rate to potential investments in Great Britain, the United States, and Germany, reflecting those countries' economic and political stability, and it might use a 10 percent discount rate for potential investments in Russia, reflecting the political and economic turmoil in that country. In effect, the higher the discount rate, the higher the projected net cash flows must be for an investment to have a positive net present value.

Adjusting discount rates to reflect a location's riskiness seems to be fairly widely practiced. For example, a study of large U.S. multinationals found that 49 percent of them routinely added a premium percentage for risk to the discount rate they used in evaluating potential foreign investment projects.[3] However, critics of this method argue that it penalizes early cash flows too heavily and does not penalize distant cash flows enough.[4] They point out that if political or economic collapse were expected in the near future, the investment would not take place anyway. (This is borne out today in the case of Russia; Western companies are not investing there because they perceive imminent danger of political and economic collapse.) So for any investment being considered seriously, the political and economic risk being assessed is not of the immediate-possibility type but, rather, risk that is some distance in the future. Accordingly, it can be argued that rather than using a higher discount rate to evaluate such risky projects—which penalizes early cash flows too heavily—it is better to revise future cash flows from the project downward to reflect the possibility of adverse political or economic changes sometime in the future. Put another way, rather than revising the discount rate upward to reflect higher risk, advocates of this approach argue that future cash flows several years out should be revised downward to reflect higher risk. Surveys of actual practice within multinationals suggest that the practice of revising future cash flows downward is just about as popular as that of revising the discount rate upward.[5]

FINANCING DECISIONS

When considering its options for financing a foreign investment, an international business must consider two factors. The first is how the foreign investment will be financed. Most important, if external financing is required, the firm must decide whether

---

[3] J. C. Backer and L. J. Beardsley, "Multinational Companies' Use of Risk Evaluation and Profit Measurement for Capital Budgeting Decisions," *Journal of Business Finance,* Spring 1973, pp. 34–43.

[4] For example, see D. K. Eiteman, A. I. Stonehill, and M. H. Moffett, *Multinational Business Finance* (Reading, Mass.: Addison-Wesley, 1922).

[5] M. Stanley and S. Block, "An Empirical Study of Management and Financial Variables Influencing Capital Budgeting Decisions for Multinational Corporations in the 1980s," *Management International Review* 23(1983), pp. 61–71.

The *Euromoney* Country Risk Method

BOX 20.1

Euromoney's assessment of country risk makes use of three categories. These are analytical indicators 40 percent, credit indicators 20 percent, and market indicators 40 percent. These offer a broad but sensitive evaluation of the relative risks faced by exposure in these countries.

Analytical Indicators

This is made up of political risk 20 percent, economic risk 10 percent, and economic indicators 10 percent. Political risk is a measure of stability and the potential fall out from any instability. The economic indicators consist of three key ratios: the debt-service-to-export ratio as a measure of liquidity, and balance-of-payments-to-GNP and external-debt-to-GNP as measures of solvency. As these are historical, the prospective view of economic performance to 1993 is used to gauge economic risk.

Credit Indicators

This is made up of payment record 15 percent and ease of rescheduling 5 percent. Ease of rescheduling indicates a country's general creditworthiness in the face of temporary liquidity problems.

Market Indicators

These consist of access to bond markets (FRN, straight, and Yankee) 15 percent, availability of short-term finance 10 percent, and access to and discount available on forfeiting 15 percent. Bond market access is fine-tuned by considering access to syndicated loans, credit ratings, and secondary market spreads. The attitudes of the market to countries will incorporate analytical and credit indicators—but its favor can be crucial to sustaining a country's economy as well as maintaining liquidity for its sovereign debt in the secondary markets.

Special thanks to all those who supplied data to produce the ranking. Those not wishing to remain anonymous are: Country Risk Analysis, ASLK-CGER Bank; Nicolas Clavel, Citicorp Investment Bank; Kit Brownlees, Investment Insurance International; Kansallis-Osake-Pankki, Lehman Brothers International; Midland Bank Aval; Paul Forrest, Mitsubishi Bank; David Kern, Chief Economist and Head of Market Intelligence, National Westminster Bank; Salomon Brothers Bond Market Research; and Union Bank of Switzerland. Ranking compiled by Laura Irvine.

Source: Euromoney, *September 1991.*

Table 20.1 *Euromoney Magazine's Country Risk Ratings, 1991*

Rank 1991	Rank 1990	Country	Rating 1991	Rating 1990
1	1	Japan	95.7	91.9
2	6	Switzerland	94.7	87.6
3	3	Netherlands	94.6	89.9
4	18	Germany	93.9	82.7
5	3	France	93.8	89.9
6	3	Austria	93.7	89.9
7	10	USA	93.4	85.7
8	2	Luxembourg	93.1	91.1
9	10	Denmark	92.6	85.7
10	9	Canada	92.3	85.8
11	14	Norway	92.3	84.9
12	7	Sweden	92.0	87.4
13	13	Belgium	91.9	85.4
14	17	United Kingdom	91.8	83.5
15	8	Finland	91.8	86.2
16	16	Italy	89.5	83.6
17	20	Spain	89.1	81.9
18	10	Ireland	88.0	85.7
19	15	Singapore	86.2	84.8
20	24	Australia	85.3	74.4
21	21	Taiwan	83.8	79.2
22	31	Iceland	82.6	69.0
23	26	New Zealand	82.6	73.5
24	21	Portugal	77.6	79.2
25	19	Korea, South	76.7	82.0
26	23	Malaysia	76.0	75.8

Rank 1991	Rank 1990	Country	Rating 1991	Rating 1990
27	27	Thailand	73.3	72.2
28	29	Hong Kong	72.3	71.2
29	25	Malta	72.2	73.9
30	37	Greece	65.2	64.7
31	35	Bermuda	60.1	65.2
32	34	Indonesia	57.3	65.7
33	28	Brunei	56.5	72.1
34	47	Mexico	55.8	58.6
35	39	Czechoslovakia	54.1	61.7
36	51	South Africa	54.0	55.0
37	43	Saudi Arabia	53.9	60.0
38	60	Israel	53.8	49.9
39	30	Cyprus	53.6	70.0
40	53	Turkey	53.1	54.0
41	43	Bahrain	52.9	60.0
42	49	UAE	52.7	56.0
43	36	China	52.5	65.1
44	40	Hungary	52.0	60.8
45	64	Venezuela	51.8	46.1
46	41	Botswana	50.8	60.3
47	52	Chile	50.3	54.4
48	45	Oman	49.8	59.0
49	50	Barbados	49.4	55.3
50	70	Qatar	47.5	44.8
51	46	India	45.9	58.7
52	65	Zimbabwe	44.0	46.0
53	57	Salomon Islands	43.3	52.4
54	62	Trinidad and Tobago	42.8	47.6
55	38	Nauru	41.8	63.1
56	56	Pakistan	41.3	52.7
57	73	Poland	40.5	43.0
58	92	Iran	40.5	33.8
59	32	Mauritius	40.2	66.5
60	74	Morocco	40.0	42.5
61	66	Colombia	40.0	45.0
62	42	Uruguay	39.8	60.1
63	48	Fiji	39.6	57.0
64	59	Tunisia	39.1	50.0
65	66	Brazil	38.2	45.0
66	66	Swaziland	38.2	45.0
67	61	Papua New Guinea	37.8	48.5
68	75	Sri Lanka	37.6	42.4
69	72	Kenya	37.5	43.2
70	127	Namibia	37.4	18.9
71	55	Paraguay	37.0	53.0
72	105	Kuwait	36.9	27.9
73	88	Gabon	36.9	35.8
74	91	Ghana	36.7	33.9
75	82	Belize	35.9	38.0
76	81	Jamaica	35.3	39.0
77	89	Costa Rica	35.1	35.0
78	94	Argentina	34.9	33.3
79	109	Guatemala	34.6	26.0
80	79	Egypt	34.5	39.6
81	77	Philippines	33.9	41.4
82	83	Senegal	33.1	37.8
83	63	Algeria	31.9	47.0
84	78	Malawi	31.7	40.0
85	97	Ecuador	31.6	30.0
86	84	Cameroon	31.6	37.0
87	93	Tanzania	31.4	33.7
88	95	Nigeria	31.0	33.0
89	71	Romania	30.7	43.3
90	109	Honduras	30.2	26.0
91	58	Panama	30.2	50.8
92	98	Gambia	29.5	28.9
93	87	Lesotho	29.0	36.0
94	86	Mali	29.0	36.8
95	102	Niger	28.7	28.6
96	80	Bangladesh	28.7	39.3
97	104	Dominican Republic	28.6	28.0
98	115	Djibouti	28.6	25.2
99	103	Bolivia	27.7	28.3
100	98	Sierra Leone	27.2	28.9
101	98	Peru	27.0	28.9
102	96	Jordan	25.7	31.0
103	121	Syria	25.2	22.3
104	106	Congo	24.5	27.4
105	120	Mauritania	24.4	22.8
106	115	Ivory Coast	24.2	25.2
107	112	Angola	24.0	25.0
108	119	Zambia	23.8	23.0
109	113	Madagascar	23.6	25.4
110	124	Uganda	23.1	19.4
111	54	USSR	22.9	53.4
112	101	Libya	22.8	28.7
113	107	Chad	22.7	27.2
114	90	Bulgaria	22.6	34.7
115	111	El Salvador	22.2	25.7
116	130	Nicaragua	22.2	14.5
117	117	Myanmar (Burma)	21.2	25.0
118	113	Cuba	20.7	25.4
119	132	Mozambique	20.3	13.6
120	85	Rwanda	18.6	36.9
121	76	Yugoslavia	18.2	42.2
122	118	Haiti	17.4	23.2
123	124	Guyana	16.9	19.4
124	130	Sudan	16.8	14.5
125	108	Albania	16.7	27.0
126	123	Lebanon	15.4	19.6
127	122	Zaire	15.2	21.5
128	126	Ethopia	13.9	19.3
129	129	Liberia	8.5	17.3
130	128	Iraq	1.9	18.4

Source: Euromoney, *September 1991.*

to borrow from sources in the host country or from sources elsewhere. The second factor that must be considered is how the financial structure of the foreign affiliate should be configured.

Source of Financing

If the firm is going to seek external financing for a project, it will want to borrow funds from the lowest-cost source of capital available. As we saw in Chapter 11, increasingly, firms are turning to the global capital market to finance their investments. By virtue of its size and liquidity, the cost of capital is typically lower in the global capital market than in many domestic capital markets—particularly those that are small and relatively illiquid. Thus, for example, a U.S. firm making an investment in Denmark may finance the investment by borrowing through the London-based Eurobond market rather than the Danish capital market.

In practice, however, host-country government restrictions may rule out this option. The governments of many countries require, or at least prefer, foreign multinationals to finance projects in their country by local debt financing or local sales of equity. In countries where liquidity is limited, this effectively raises the cost of capital used to finance a project. Thus, with regard to capital budgeting decisions, the discount rate must be adjusted upward to reflect this. However, this is not the only possibility. In Chapter 8 we saw that some governments court foreign investment by offering foreign firms low-interest loans. Obviously this lowers the cost of capital. Accordingly, with regard to capital budgeting decisions, the discount rate should be revised downward in such cases.

In addition to the impact of host-government policies on the cost of capital and financing decisions, the firm may wish to consider local debt financing for investments in countries where the local currency is expected to depreciate on the foreign exchange market. The amount of local currency required to meet interest payments and retire principle on local debt obligations is not affected when a country's currency depreciates. However, if foreign debt obligations must be served, the amount of local currency required to do this will increase as the currency depreciates, and this effectively raises the cost of capital. (*Note:* We looked at this issue first in Chapter 11 when we considered foreign exchange risk and the cost of capital.) Thus, although the initial cost of capital may be greater with local borrowing, it may be better to borrow locally if the local currency is expected to depreciate on the foreign exchange market.

Financial Structure

There is a quite striking difference in the financial structures of firms based in different countries. By **financial structure** we mean the mix of debt and equity used to finance a business. It is well known, for example, that Japanese firms rely far more on debt financing than do most U.S. firms. Table 20.2 reproduces the results of a study comparing debt ratios for 677 firms in nine industries in 23 countries.[6] As can be seen, there is wide variation in the average debt ratios of firms based in different countries. The average debt ratio of firms based in Italy, for example, is more than double that of firms based in Singapore.

It is not altogether clear why the financial structure of firms should vary so much across countries. One possible explanation is that different tax regimes determine the relative attractiveness of debt and equity in a country. For example, if dividends are taxed

[6] W. S. Sekely and J. M. Collins, "Cultural Influences on International Capital Structure," *Journal of International Business Studies,* Spring, pp. 87–100.

Table 20.2 *Debt Ratios for Selected Industries and Countries (in order of increasing debt)*

	Alcoholic Beverages	Auto-mobiles	Chemicals	Electrical	Foods	Iron & Steel	Nonferrous Metals	Paper	Textiles	Country Mean
Singapore		.22		.57	.28	.28	.38			.34
Malaysia	.20	.60	.41		.30	.38	.30	.77	.69	.37
Argentina		.42		.44	.35	.32				.38
Australia	.29	.50	.52	.51	.45	.53	.34	.48	.54	.46
Chile			.33	.28	.70	.48	.50	.47		.46
Mexico	.18		.47	.57	.59	.53	.47	.47		.47
South Africa	.59	.50	.51		.46	.53	.32	.42	.69	.50
Brazil		.66	.48	.53	.57	.61		.37		.54
United Kingdom	.45	.73	.50	.60	.55	.51	.57	.56	.52	.55
United States	.51	.58	.55	.54	.56	.54	.58	.58	.50	.55
Benelux	.41	.62	.60	.51	.64	.61	.49	.65	.54	.56
Canada	.55		.45	.52		.69	.61	.68		.58
India	.08	.75	.55			.49	.69	.74	.48	.60
Switzerland				.63	.54	.64				.60
West Germany		.57	.56	.66	.49	.60	.70	.70	.65	.62
Denmark	.66		.47	.74	.69	.52	.61	.74		.63
Spain		.59	.64	.45	.66	.82	.70	.85	.43	.64
Sweden	.79	.75	.67	.67	.63	.67	.64	.61	.60	.68
France	.56	.67	.72	.72	.78	.73	.67	.74	.74	.71
Finland	.40	.82	.71	.73	.77	.73	.72	.76	.82	.72
Pakistan		.87	.87				.71	.66	.70	.72
Norway			.76	.67	.79	.62		.82	.75	.74
Italy		.49	.65	.79	.85	.87	.86	.77	.83	.76
Industry mean	.49	.58	.56	.59	.62	.61	.58	.63	.70	

Note: Debt ratio *is defined as total debt divided by total assets at book value.*

Source: W. S. Sekely, and J. M. Collins, "Cultural Influences on International Capital Structure," Journal of International Business Studies *19 (1988), p. 91.*

highly, a preference for debt financing over equity financing would be expected. However, according to recent empirical research, country differences in financial structure do not seem related in any systematic way to country differences in tax structure.[7] Another possibility is that these country differences may reflect deep-seated cultural norms.[8] This explanation may be valid, although the mechanism by which culture influences capital structure has not yet been explained.

In any event, the interesting question for the international business is whether it should conform to local capital structure norms. For example, should a U.S. firm investing in Italy adopt the higher debt ratio typical of Italian firms for its Italian subsidiary, or should it stick with its more conservative practice? In truth, there are few good arguments for conforming to local norms. One advantage claimed for conforming to host-country debt norms is that management can more easily evaluate its return on equity relative to local competitors in the same industry. However, this seems a rather weak rationale for what is an important decision. Another point often made is that conforming

[7] J. Collins and W. S. Sekely, "The Relationship of Headquarters, Country, and Industry Classification to Financial Structure," *Financial Structure,* Autumn 1983, pp. 45–51; and J. Rutterford, "An International Perspective on the Capital Structure Puzzle," *Midland Corporate Finance Journal,* Fall 1985, p. 72.

[8] Sekely and Collins, "Cultural Influences."

to higher host-country debt norms can improve the image of foreign affiliates that have been operating with too little debt and thus appear insensitive to local monetary policy. Just how important this point is, however, has not been established. In general, then, the best recommendation is that an international business should adopt a financial structure for each foreign affiliate that minimizes its cost of capital, irrespective of whether that structure is consistent with local practice.

THE OBJECTIVES OF GLOBAL MONEY MANAGEMENT

Money management decisions attempt to manage the firm's global cash resources—its working capital—most efficiently. In this section we take a brief look at the two objectives of global money management—the efficiency objective and the tax objective. Then in the next section we will see how an international business can transfer liquid funds around the world. After that we will turn our attention to two techniques of global money management—centralized depositories and multilateral netting.

The Efficiency Objective

A principal objective of global money management is to utilize the firm's global cash resources as efficiently as possible. Essentially this involves minimizing cash balances and reducing transaction costs.

Minimizing Cash Balances

For any given period a firm must hold certain cash balances. This is necessary for serving any accounts and notes payable during that period and as a contingency against unexpected demands on cash. Of course, the firm does not sit on its cash reserves. It typically invests them in money market accounts so it can earn interest on them. However, it must be able to withdraw its money from those accounts freely. Such accounts typically offer a relatively low rate of interest. In contrast, the firm could earn a higher rate of interest if it could invest its cash resources in longer-term financial instruments (e.g., six-month certificates of deposit). The problem with longer-term instruments, however, is that the firm cannot withdraw its money before the instruments mature without suffering a financial penalty.

Thus, the firm faces a dilemma. If it invests its cash balances in money market accounts (or the equivalent), it will have unlimited liquidity but earn a relatively low rate of interest. If it invests its cash in longer-term financial instruments (certificates of deposit, bonds, etc.), it will earn a higher rate of interest, but liquidity will be limited. Obviously, in an ideal world the firm would have minimal liquid cash balances. We will see later in the chapter that by centrally managing its total global cash reserves through a centralized depository (as opposed to letting each affiliate manage its own cash reserves), an international business can in effect reduce the amount of funds it must hold in liquid accounts and thereby increase its rate of return on its cash reserves.

Reducing Transaction Costs

Transaction costs are the cost of exchange. Every time a firm changes cash from one currency into another currency it must bear a transaction cost—the commission fee it pays to foreign exchange dealers for performing the transaction. Most banks also charge a **transfer fee** for moving cash from one location to another; this is another transaction cost. Since many international businesses have subsidiaries in different countries around

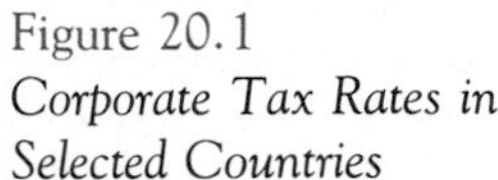

Figure 20.1
Corporate Tax Rates in Selected Countries

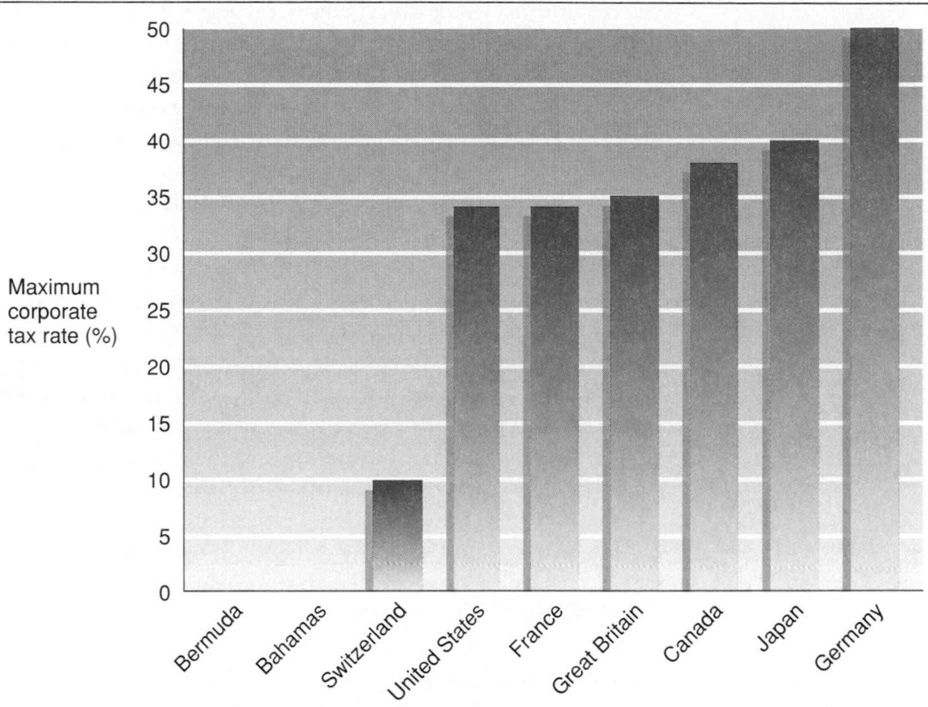

Source: Corporate Taxes: A Worldwide Summary, 1991, *Price Waterhouse, 1285 Avenue of the Americas, New York.*

the globe that are continually trading with each other, the commission and transfer fees arising from intrafirm transactions can be quite substantial. As we will see later in the chapter, a technique called *multilateral netting* can be used to reduce the number of transactions between the firm's subsidiaries, thereby reducing the total transactions costs arising from foreign exchange dealings and transfer fees.

The Tax Objective

Different countries have different tax regimes. To illustrate this, Figure 20.1 shows the maximum tax rate on corporate income in selected countries. As can be seen, the tax rate varies from a high of 50 percent in Germany to a low of 0 percent in the Bahamas and Bermuda (the Bahamas and Bermuda are tax havens). The picture is actually much more complex than the one presented in Figure 20.1. For example, in Germany and Japan the tax rate is lower on income distributed to stockholders as dividends (36 and 35 percent, respectively), whereas in France the tax on profits distributed to stockholders is higher (42 percent).

Many nations follow the worldwide principle that they have the right to tax income earned outside of their boundaries by entities based in their country. Thus, for example, the U.S. government can tax the earnings of the German subsidiary of an enterprise incorporated in the United States. The worldwide principle results in double taxation when the income of a foreign subsidiary is taxed both by the host-country government and by the parent company's home government. However, double taxation is to some extent mitigated by tax credits, tax treaties, and the deferral principle.

A **tax credit** allows an entity to reduce the taxes paid to the home government by the amount of taxes paid to the foreign government. A **tax treaty** between two countries is an agreement specifying what items of income will be taxed by the authorities of the country where the income is earned. For example, a tax treaty between the United States and Germany may specify that a U.S. firm need not pay tax in Germany on any earnings from its German subsidiary that are remitted to the United States in the form of dividends. A **deferral principle** specifies that parent companies are not taxed on foreign source income until they actually receive a dividend.

For the international business with activities in a large number of different countries, the various tax regimes and the myriad of tax treaties existing between countries have important implications for how the firm should structure its internal payments system among the foreign subsidiaries and the parent company. As we will see in the next section, the firm can use such devices as *transfer prices* and *fronting loans* to minimize its global tax liability. In addition, the *form in which income is remitted* from a foreign subsidiary to the parent company (e.g., royalty payments versus dividend payments) can be structured to minimize the firm's global tax liability.

Some firms use **tax havens** such as the Bahamas and Bermuda to minimize their tax liability. A tax haven is a country with an exceptionally low, or even no, income tax and thus can be used by international businesses to avoid or defer income taxes. They do this by establishing a 100 percent-owned, nonoperating subsidiary in the tax haven. In turn, the tax haven subsidiary will own the common stock of the operating foreign subsidiaries. This allows all transfers of funds from foreign operating subsidiaries to the parent company to be funneled through the tax haven subsidiary. By this means, the tax levied on foreign source income by a firm's home government, which might normally be paid when a dividend is declared by a foreign subsidiary, can be deferred under the deferral principle until the tax haven subsidiary pays the dividend to the parent. In theory, this dividend payment can be postponed indefinitely if foreign operations continue to grow and require new internal financing from the tax haven affiliate. For U.S-based enterprises, however, U.S. regulations tax U.S. shareholders on the overseas income of the firm *when it is earned,* regardless of when the parent company in the United States receives it. This regulation effectively eliminates U.S.-based firms' ability to use tax haven subsidiaries to avoid tax liabilities in the manner just described.

MOVING MONEY ACROSS BORDERS

Pursuing the joint objectives of utilizing the firm's cash resources most efficiently and minimizing the firm's global tax liability requires the firm to be able to transfer funds from one location to another around the globe. International businesses use a number of techniques to transfer liquid funds across borders. These include dividend remittances, royalty payments and fees, transfer prices, and fronting loans. Some firms rely on more than one of these techniques to transfer funds across borders—a practice known as **unbundling.** By using a mix of techniques to transfer liquid funds from a foreign subsidiary to the parent company, unbundling allows an international business to recover funds from its foreign subsidiaries without piquing host-country sensitivities with large "dividend drains."

Before we consider the various means for moving liquid funds from location to location, we must point out that a firm's ability to select a particular policy is severely limited when a foreign subsidiary is part-owned either by a local joint venture partner or by local stockholders. In either case, serving the legitimate demands of the local co-owners of a foreign subsidiary may limit the firm's ability to impose the kind of dividend policy, royalty payment schedule, or transfer pricing policy that would be optimal for the parent company.

Dividend Remittances

Payment of dividends is probably the most common method by which firms transfer funds from foreign subsidiaries to the parent company. Typically the dividend policy varies with each subsidiary depending on such factors as tax regulations, foreign exchange risk, the age of the subsidiary, and the extent of local equity participation. For example, the higher the rate of tax levied on dividends by the host-country government, the less attractive this option becomes relative to other options for transferring liquid funds. With regard to foreign exchange risk, firms sometimes require foreign subsidiaries based in "high-risk" countries to speed up the transfer of funds to the parent through accelerated dividend payments. This is basically a way of moving corporate funds out of a country whose currency is expected to depreciate significantly. The age of a foreign subsidiary influences dividend policy in that older subsidiaries tend to remit a higher proportion of their earnings in dividends to the parent, presumably because a subsidiary has fewer capital investment needs as it matures. Local equity participation is a factor because local co-owners' demands for dividends must be recognized.

Royalty Payments and Fees

Royalties represent the remuneration paid to the owners of technology, patents, or trade names for the use of that technology or the right to manufacture and/or sell products under those patents or trade names. It is quite common for a parent company to charge its foreign subsidiaries royalties for the technology, patents, or trade names it has transferred to them. Royalties may be levied as a fixed monetary amount per unit of the product the subsidiary sells or as a percentage of a subsidiary's gross revenues.

A **fee** is compensation for professional services or expertise supplied to a foreign subsidiary by the parent company or another subsidiary. Fees are sometimes differentiated into "management fees" for general expertise and advice and "technical assistance fees" for guidance in technical matters. Fees are usually levied as fixed charges for the particular services provided.

Royalties and fees have certain tax advantages over dividends, particularly when the corporate tax rate is higher in the host country than in the parent's home country. Royalties and fees are often tax deductible locally (because they are viewed as an expense), so arranging for payment in royalties and fees will reduce the foreign subsidiary's tax liability. In contrast, if the foreign subsidiary compensates the parent company by dividend payments, local income taxes must be paid before the dividend distribution, and withholding taxes must be paid on the dividend itself. Although the parent can often take a tax credit for the local withholding and income taxes it has paid, part of the benefit can be lost if the subsidiary's combined tax rate is higher than the parent's.

Transfer Prices

In any international business there are normally a large number of transfers of goods and services between the parent company and foreign subsidiaries and between foreign subsidiaries. This is particularly likely in firms pursuing global and transnational strategies, since these firms are likely to have dispersed their value creation activities to various "optimal" locations around the globe (see Chapter 12). As noted in Chapter 19, the price at which goods and services are transferred between entities within the firm is referred to as the **transfer price.**

Transfer prices can be used to position funds within an international business. For example, funds can be *moved out* of a particular country by setting high transfer prices for goods and services supplied to a subsidiary in that country, and by setting low transfer prices for the goods and services sourced from that subsidiary. Conversely, funds can be *positioned in* a country by the opposite policy: setting low transfer prices for goods and services supplied to a subsidiary in that country, and setting high transfer prices for the goods and services sourced from that subsidiary. This movement of funds can be between the firm's different subsidiaries or between the parent company and a subsidiary.

Benefits of Manipulating Transfer Prices

At least four gains can be derived by manipulating transfer prices.

1. The firm can reduce its tax liabilities by using transfer prices to shift earnings from a high-tax country to a low-tax one.
2. The firm can use transfer prices to move funds out of a country where a significant currency devaluation is expected, thereby reducing its exposure to foreign exchange risk.
3. The firm can use transfer prices to move funds from a subsidiary to the parent company (or a tax haven) when financial transfers in the form of dividends are restricted or blocked by host-country government policies.
4. The firm can use transfer prices to reduce the import duties it must pay when an *ad valorem* tariff is in force—a tariff assessed as a percentage of value. In this case, low transfer prices on goods or services being imported into the country are required. Since this lowers the value of the good or services, it lowers the tariff.

Problems with Transfer Pricing

It must also be recognized that significant problems are associated with pursuing a transfer pricing policy. For one thing, few governments are favorably disposed to it. When transfer prices are used to reduce a firm's tax liabilities or import duties, most governments feel they are being cheated of their legitimate income. Similarly, when transfer prices are manipulated to circumvent government restrictions on capital flows (e.g., dividend remittances), governments perceive this as breaking the spirit—if not the letter—of the law. Accordingly, a number of governments have passed fairly restrictive legislation that seriously limits international businesses' ability to manipulate transfer prices in the manner just described. The United States, for example, has strict regulations governing transfer pricing practices. According to Section 482 of the Internal Revenue Code, the Internal Revenue Service (IRS) can reallocate gross income, deductions, credits, or allowances between related corporations to prevent tax evasion or to reflect more clearly a proper allocation of income. Under the IRS guidelines and subsequent judicial interpretation, the burden of proof is on the taxpayer to show that the IRS has been arbitrary or unreasonable in reallocating income. The correct transfer price, according to the IRS guidelines, is an **arms-length price**—the price that would prevail between unrelated firms transacting in a market setting. Clearly, such a strict interpretation of what is a correct transfer price theoretically limits a firm's ability to manipulate transfer prices to achieve the benefits we have discussed. In reality, however, there is a feeling that transfer pricing is still widely practiced; Box 20.2 provides an example.

A further problem associated with transfer pricing is related to management incentives and performance evaluation. In brief, the practice is inconsistent with a policy of treating each subsidiary in the firm as a profit center. When transfer prices are manipulated by the firm and, as a result, deviate significantly from the arm's length price, the performance of each subsidiary may depend as much on transfer prices as it does on other pertinent factors—such as management effort. Thus a subsidiary told to charge a high transfer price for a good supplied to another subsidiary will appear to be doing better than it actually is, while the subsidiary purchasing the good will appear to be doing worse.

BOX 20.2

Washington Accuses Foreign Multinationals of Transfer Pricing Violations

According to testimony given at hearings held by the House Ways and Means Oversight subcommittee in July 1990, foreign-based multinationals, through elaborate transfer pricing schemes, underpaid the U.S. government by as much as $35 billion during the 1980s. Japanese companies were cited as the principal offenders, followed by German, Canadian, and British companies. Toyota, Toshiba, Sony, Mitsubishi, Fuji Bank, and Siemens were among the foreign multinationals cited for abusing the U.S. tax code. Yamaha, the Japanese motorcycle manufacturer, for example, paid just $123 in U.S. taxes one year, and the IRS claimed that it should have paid more than $27 million!

Some of the schemes foreign-based multinationals are using to pay little or no taxes include charging U.S. subsidiaries for inflated or nonexisting freight, insurance, interest, and other expenses. In one example, a Japanese multinational was accused of double-billing its U.S. subsidiary for insurance on motorcycle inventory. In another case, U.S. officials testified that a foreign automaker charged its U.S. subsidiary $15 interest per vehicle even though interest payments were not required under the distribution agreement.

In response, foreign multinationals argue that they have done nothing wrong. Certainly, it will take years of litigation to determine whether the United States has a case. But one thing is clear: multinationals' use of transfer pricing policies has come under increasing scrutiny in the United States and elsewhere. As foreign multinationals face closer scrutiny in the United States, so other countries seem likely to scrutinize U.S. multinationals more closely in response. Numerous officials testified at the hearings that Congress should be aware that U.S. companies routinely engage in similar transfer pricing schemes in other countries. According to Lawrence Gibbs, a former IRS commissioner and international tax lawyer, the countries in which U.S. multinationals do the most business—Canada, Japan, Germany, and Great Britain—all have higher corporate tax rates than the United States, and that gives U.S. multinationals a lot of incentive to use transfer prices improperly. Echoing the theme, a Treasury Department official noted that many of the measures proposed to limit transfer pricing abuses by foreign multinationals in the United States open the door to retaliation against U.S. multinationals.

Source: E. Neumann, "Washington Escalates the Transfer Pricing War," Business International Money Report, *July 23, 1990, p. 277–79.*

Unless this is explicitly recognized when performance is being evaluated, serious distortions in management incentive systems can occur. In this case, for example, managers in the selling subsidiary may be able to use high transfer prices to mask inefficiencies, whereas managers in the purchasing subsidiary may become disheartened by the effect of high transfer prices on their subsidiary's profitability.

Despite these problems, research suggests that many international businesses do not use arm's length pricing but instead use some cost-based system for pricing transfers among their subunits (typically cost plus some standard markup). A survey of 164 U.S. multinational firms found that 35 percent of the firms used market-based prices, 15 percent used negotiated prices, and 65 percent used a cost-based pricing method. (The figures add up to more than 100% because some companies use more than one method.)[9]

[9] M. F. Al-Eryani, P. Alam, and S. Akhter, "Transfer Pricing Determinants of U.S. Multinationals," *Journal of International Business Studies*, 1990, pp. 409–25.

This is significant, since only market and negotiated prices could reasonably be interpreted as arm's length prices. This does not imply the remaining 65 percent of firms manipulate transfer prices. Nevertheless, the opportunity for price manipulation is much greater with cost-based transfer pricing methods.

Finally, an important ethical dimension to the transfer pricing debate must be noted. Although a firm may be *able* to manipulate transfer prices to avoid tax liabilities or circumvent government restrictions on capital flows across borders, this does not mean the firm *should* do so. Since the practice often violates at least the spirit, if not the letter, of the law in many countries, the ethics of engaging in transfer pricing are often dubious at best.

Fronting Loans

A **fronting loan** is a loan between a parent and its subsidiary channeled through a financial intermediary, usually a large international bank. In a *direct* intrafirm loan, the parent company loans cash directly to the foreign subsidiary, and the subsidiary repays it at a later date. By contrast, in a fronting loan the parent company deposits funds in an international bank, and the bank then lends the same amount to the foreign subsidiary. Thus a U.S. firm might deposit $100,000 in a London bank. The London bank might then loan that $100,000 to a subsidiary of the firm in India. From the bank's point of view the loan is risk free, since it has 100 percent collateral in the form of the parent's deposit. In effect, the bank "fronts" for the parent—hence the name. The bank makes a profit by paying the parent company a slightly lower interest rate on its deposit than it charges the foreign subsidiary on the borrowed funds.

Firms use fronting loans for two reasons. First, fronting loans can circumvent host-country government restrictions on the remittance of funds from a foreign subsidiary to the parent company. Whereas a host government may restrict a foreign subsidiary from repaying a loan to its parent in order (for example) to preserve the country's foreign exchange reserves, it is less likely to restrict a foreign subsidiary's ability to repay a loan to a large international bank. To stop payment to an international bank would hurt the country's credit image, whereas halting payment to the parent company would probably have a minimal impact in its image. Consequently, international businesses sometimes use fronting loans when they want to lend funds to a subsidiary based in a country with a fairly high probability of political turmoil that might lead to restrictions on capital flows (i.e., where the level of political risk is high).

The second reason for using a fronting loan is that it can provide tax advantages. Consider an example. A tax haven (Bermuda) subsidiary that is 100 percent owned by the parent company deposits $1 million in a London-based international bank at 8 percent interest. The bank in turn lends the $1 million to a foreign operating subsidiary at 9 percent interest. The country where the foreign operating subsidiary is based taxes corporate income at 50 percent (see Figure 20.2).

Under this arrangement, interest payments net of income tax will be as follows:

1. The foreign operating subsidiary pays $90,000 interest to the London bank. Deducting these interest payments from its taxable income results in a net after-tax cost of $45,000 to the foreign operating subsidiary.
2. The London bank receives the $90,000. It retains $10,000 of this for its services and pays $80,000 interest on the deposit to the Bermuda subsidiary.
3. The Bermuda subsidiary thus receives $80,000 interest on its deposit, tax free.

The net result is that $80,000 in cash has been moved from the foreign operating subsidiary to the tax haven subsidiary. Because the foreign operating subsidiary's after tax-

Figure 20.2
An Example of the Tax Aspects of a Fronting Loan

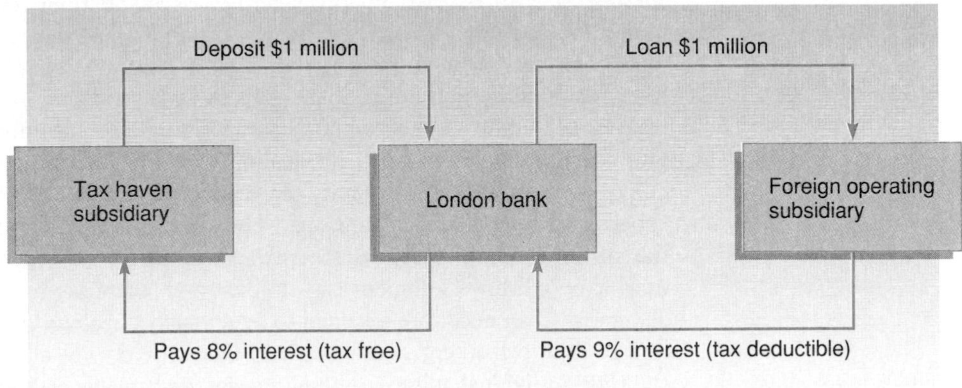

cost of borrowing is only $45,000, the parent company has been able to move an additional $35,000 out of the country by using this arrangement. If the tax haven subsidiary had made a direct loan to the foreign operating subsidiary, the host government may well have disallowed the interest charge as a tax-deductible expense by ruling that it was in reality a dividend to the parent disguised as an interest payment.

TECHNIQUES FOR GLOBAL MONEY MANAGEMENT

We have now discussed the objectives of global money management and the various methods international businesses use to move money across borders. Building on this material, we now look at two money management techniques firms use in attempting to manage their global cash resources in the most efficient manner: centralized depositories and multilateral netting.

Centralized Depositories

Every business needs to hold some cash balances for servicing accounts that might be paid and for insuring against unanticipated negative variation from its projected cash flows. The critical issue for an international business is whether each of its foreign subsidiaries should hold its own cash balances or whether cash balances should be held at some centralized depository. In general, firms prefer to hold cash balances at a centralized depository for three reasons.

First, by pooling cash reserves centrally the firm is able to deposit larger amounts. Recall that cash balances are typically deposited in liquid accounts, such as overnight money market accounts. Since interest rates on such deposits normally increase with the size of the deposit, by pooling cash centrally the firm should be able to earn a higher interest rate than it would if each subsidiary managed its own cash balances.

Second, if the centralized depository is located in a major financial center (e.g., London, New York, or Tokyo), it should have access to information about good short-term investment opportunities that the typical foreign subsidiary would lack. Moreover, the financial experts at a centralized depository should be able to develop investment skills and know-how that managers in the typical foreign subsidiary would lack. Thus, the firm should be able to make better investment decisions if it pools its cash reserves at a centralized depository.

Third, by pooling its cash reserves, the firm is able to reduce the total size of the cash pool it must hold in highly liquid accounts, which enables the firm to invest a larger amount of cash reserves in longer-term, less liquid financial instruments that earn a higher interest rate. To understand why, consider an example. (Although this explanation seems technical, it requires only a basic grasp of statistics.) A U.S. firm has three foreign subsidiaries—one in Spain, one in Italy, and one in Germany. Each subsidiary maintains a cash balance that includes an amount for dealing with its day-to-day needs plus a precautionary amount for dealing with unanticipated cash demands. The firm's policy is that the total required cash balance is equal to *three standard deviations* of the expected day-to-day-needs amount. The three-standard-deviation requirement reflects the firm's estimate that, in practice, there is a 99.87 percent probability that the subsidiary will have sufficient cash to deal with both day-to-day and unanticipated cash demands. Cash needs are assumed to be *normally distributed* in each country and *independent* of each other (e.g., cash needs in Germany do not affect cash needs in Italy).

The individual subsidiaries' day-to-day cash needs and the precautionary cash balances they should hold are as follows (in millions of dollars):

	Day-to-Day Cash Need (*A*)	**One Standard Deviation (*B*)**	**Required Cash Balance [*A* + (3 × *B*)]**
Spain	$10	$1	$13
Italy	6	2	12
Germany	12	3	21
Total	$28	$6	$46

Thus the Spanish subsidiary estimates that it must hold $10 million to serve its day-to-day needs. The standard deviation of this is $1 million, so it is to hold an additional $3 million as a precautionary amount. This gives a total required cash balance of $13 million. The total of the required cash balances for all three subsidiaries is $46 million.

Now consider what might occur if the firm decided to maintain all three cash balances at a centralized depository in London. Since *variances* are *additive* when probability distributions are independent of each other, the standard deviation of the combined precautionary account would be

$$\begin{aligned}\text{Standard deviation of combined precautionary account} &= \sqrt{1{,}000{,}000^2 + 2{,}000{,}000^2 + 3{,}000{,}000^2} \\ &= \sqrt{14{,}000{,}000} \\ &= \$3{,}741{,}657\end{aligned}$$

Therefore, if the firm used a centralized depository, it would need to hold $28 million for day-to-day needs plus (3 × $3,741,657) as a precautionary amount, or a total cash balance of $39,224,972. In other words, the firm's total required cash balance would be reduced from $46 million to $39,224,972, a saving of $6,775,028. This is cash that could be invested in less liquid, higher-interest accounts or in tangible assets. The saving arises simply due to the statistical effects of summing the three independent, normal probability distributions. A real-world illustration of this is the example of Monsanto that we discussed in the opening case. There we saw that by adopting a centralized depository to manage its European cash reserves, Monsanto reduced its required precautionary balance from $30 million per month to $8 million per month.

It must be remembered, however, that a firm's ability to establish a centralized depository that can serve short-term cash needs might be limited by government-imposed restrictions on capital flows across borders (e.g., controls put in place to protect a country's foreign exchange reserves). Moreover, the transaction costs of moving money into and out of different currencies can limit the advantages of such a system. Despite this,

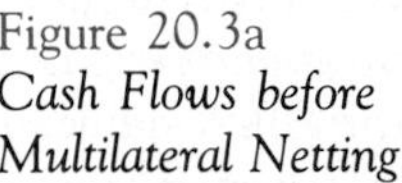

Figure 20.3a
Cash Flows before Multilateral Netting

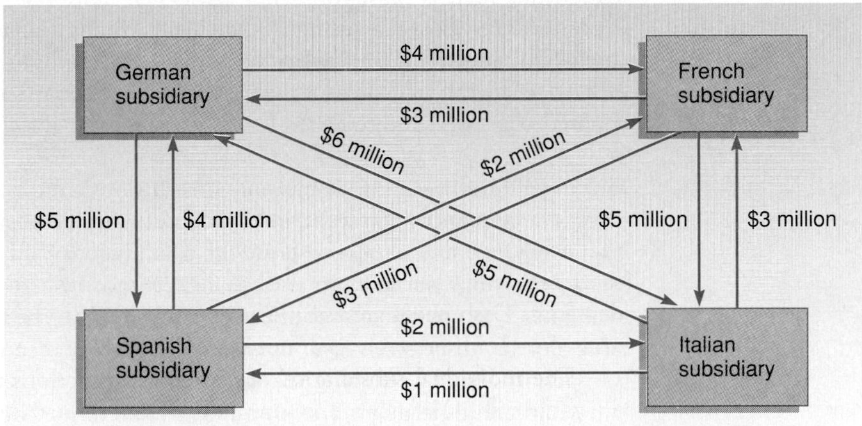

Figure 20.3b *Calculation of Net Receipts (all amounts in millions)*

Receiving Subsidiary	Paying Subsidiary: Germany	France	Spain	Italy	Total Receipts	Net Receipts* (payments)
Germany	—	$ 3	$4	$5	$12	($3)
France	$ 4	—	2	3	9	(2)
Spain	5	3	—	1	9	1
Italy	6	5	2	—	13	4
Total payments	$15	$11	$8	$9		

Net receipts = total payments − total receipts.

Figure 20.3c
Cash Flows after Multilateral Netting

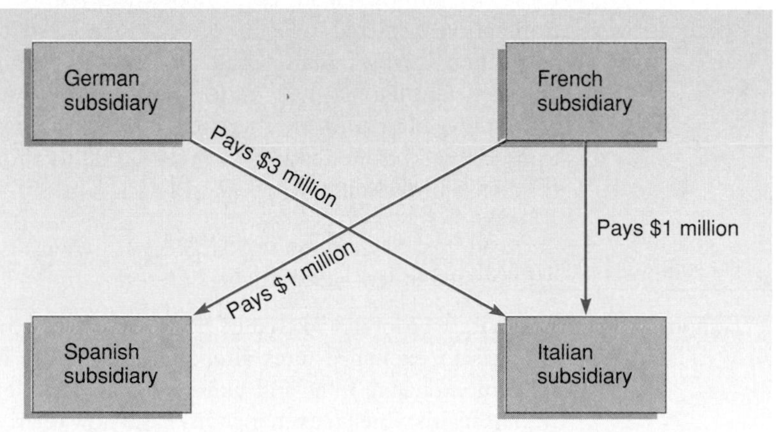

many firms hold at least their subsidiaries' precautionary cash reserves at a centralized depository, having each subsidiary hold its own day-to-day-needs cash balance in many cases. Furthermore, the globalization of the world capital market and the general removal of barriers to the free flow of cash across borders (particularly among advanced industrialized countries) are two trends likely to increase the use of centralized depositories.

Multilateral Netting

Multilateral netting allows a multinational firm to reduce the transaction costs that arise when a large number of transactions occur between its subsidiaries in the normal course of business. These transaction costs are the commissions paid to foreign exchange dealers for foreign exchange transactions and the fees charged by banks for transferring cash between locations. The volume of such transactions is likely to be particularly high in a firm that has a globally dispersed web of interdependent value creation activities. Netting reduces transaction costs by reducing the number of transactions that occur.

Multilateral netting is an extension of bilateral netting. Under **bilateral netting,** if a French subsidiary owes a Mexican subsidiary $6 million and the Mexican subsidiary simultaneously owes the French subsidiary $4 million, a bilateral settlement will be made with a single payment of $2 million from the French subsidiary to the Mexican subsidiary, the remaining debt being cancelled out.

Under **multilateral netting,** this simple concept is extended to the transactions between multiple subsidiaries within an international business. Consider, for example, a firm that wants to establish multilateral netting among four European subsidiaries based in Germany, France, Spain, and Italy. These subsidiaries all trade with each other, so at the end of each month a large volume of cash transactions must be settled. Figure 20.3a shows how the payment schedule might look at the end of a given month. Figure 20.3b is a payment matrix that summarizes the obligations among the subsidiaries. Note that a total of $43 million needs to flow among the subsidiaries. If the transaction costs (foreign exchange commissions plus transfer fees) amount to 1 percent of the total funds to be transferred, this will cost the parent firm $430,000. However, this amount can be significantly reduced by multilateral netting. Using the payment matrix (Figure 20.3b), the firm can determine the payments that need to be made among its subsidiaries to settle these obligations. Figure 20.3c shows the results. By multilateral netting, the myriad transactions depicted in Figure 20.3a is reduced to just three; the German subsidiary pays $3 million to the Italian subsidiary, and the French subsidiary pays $1 million to the Spanish subsidiary and $1 million to the Italian subsidiary. The total funds that flow among the subsidiaries are therefore reduced from $43 million to just $5 million, and the transaction costs are reduced from $430,000 to $50,000, a saving of $380,000 achieved through multilateral netting.

MANAGING FOREIGN EXCHANGE RISK

The nature of foreign exchange risk was discussed in Chapter 9. There we described how changes in exchange rates alter the profitability of trade and investment deals, how forward exchange rates and currency swaps enable firms to insure themselves to some degree against foreign exchange risk, and how relative inflation rates determine exchange rate movements. It is now time to revisit this topic. This time, however, our perspective is different. In this section we focus on the various strategies international businesses use to *manage* their foreign exchange risk. Buying forward, the strategy most discussed in Chapter 9, is just one of these. We will examine the types of foreign exchange exposure, the tactics and strategies firms adopt in attempting to minimize their exposure to foreign exchange risk, and things firms can do to develop policies for managing foreign exchange risk.

Types of Foreign Exchange Exposure

When we speak of **foreign exchange exposure,** we are referring to the risk that future changes in a country's exchange rate will adversely affect the firm. As we saw in Chapter 9, changes in foreign exchange values often affect the profitability of international trade and investment deals. Foreign exchange exposure is normally broken down into three categories: transaction exposure, translation exposure, and economic exposure. Each of those is explained here.

Transaction Exposure

Transaction exposure is typically defined as the extent to which the income from individual transactions is affected by fluctuations in foreign exchange values. Such exposure includes obligations for the purchase or sale of goods and services at previously agreed prices and the borrowing or lending of funds in foreign currencies. Consider this example of transaction exposure: A U.S. company has just contracted to import laptop computers from Japan. When the shipment arrives in 30 days, the company must pay the Japanese supplier ¥200,000 for each computer. The dollar/yen spot exchange rate today is $1 = ¥120. At this rate, each laptop computer would cost the importer $1,667 (i.e., 200,000/120 = 1,667). The importer knows it can sell each computer for $2,000 on the day they arrive, so as the exchange rate stands, the U.S. company looks set to make a gross profit of $333 on every computer it sells (2,000 − 1,667). If the dollar depreciates against the yen over the next 30 days, say to $1 = ¥95, the U.S. company will still have to pay the Japanese company ¥200,000 per computer, but in dollar terms that would be $2,105 per laptop computer—more than the computers could be sold for. A depreciation in the value of the dollar against the yen from $1 = ¥120 to $1 = ¥95 would transform this profitable transaction into an unprofitable one.

Translation Exposure

Translation exposure is the impact of currency exchange rate changes on the reported consolidated results and balance sheet of a company. This issue was discussed in some detail in Chapter 19 when we looked at currency translation practices. Translation exposure is basically concerned with the present measurement of past events. The resulting accounting gains or losses are said to be *unrealized*—they are "paper" gains and losses—but this is not to say they are unimportant. For example, consider a U.S. firm with a subsidiary in Mexico. If the value of the Mexican peso depreciates significantly against the dollar, as it did during the early 1980s, this can substantially reduce the dollar value of the Mexican subsidiary's equity. In turn, this would reduce the total dollar value of the firm's equity reported in its consolidated balance sheet. This would raise the apparent *leverage* of the firm (its debt ratio), which could increase the firm's cost of borrowing and restrict its access to the capital market. Thus, translation exposure can have a very negative impact on a firm.

Economic Exposure

Economic exposure is the extent to which a firm's future international business earning power is affected by changes in exchange rates. Economic exposure is concerned with the long-run effect of changes in exchange rates on future prices, sales, and costs. This is distinct from transaction exposure, which is concerned with the effect of changes in exchange rates on individual transactions—most of which are short-term affairs that will be executed within a few weeks or months. As an example of economic exposure, consider the effect of the wide swings in the value of the dollar on many U.S. firms' international competitiveness during the 1980s. The rapid rise in the value of the dollar on the foreign exchange market in the early 1980s adversely affected the price competitiveness of many U.S. producers in world markets. U.S. manufacturers that relied heavily on exports (such as Caterpillar Tractor) saw their export volume and world market share plunge. The reverse phenomenon has occurred since the mid-1980s, when the dollar has declined against most major currencies. The fall in the value of the dollar since 1985 has increased the price competitiveness of U.S. manufacturers in world markets and helped produce an export boom in the United States.

Tactics and Strategies for Reducing Foreign Exchange Risk

A number of strategies and tactics can help firms reduce their foreign exchange exposure. The *tactics,* which include the practice of buying forward and the use of leading and lagging, are best suited to alleviating transaction exposure and translation exposure. The *strategies,* which involve strategic decisions about the configuration of a firm's assets across countries, are best suited to reducing economic exposure.

Reducing Transaction and Translation Exposure

A number of tactics are available to firms for helping them minimize their transaction and translation exposure. These tactics primarily protect short-term cash flows from adverse changes in exchange rates. We discussed two of these tactics in Chapter 9, **buying forward** and using **currency swaps.** We will not discuss these two tactics here, except to note that they are important sources of insurance against the short-term effects of foreign exchange exposure. (For details, go back to Chapter 9.)

In addition to buying forward and using swaps, firms can adopt other tactics to minimize their foreign exchange exposure. One commonly used one is **leading and lagging** payables and receivables—that is, collecting and paying early or late depending on expected exchange rate movements. A **lead strategy** involves attempting to collect foreign currency receivables early when a foreign currency is expected to depreciate and paying foreign currency payables before they are due when a currency is expected to appreciate. A **lag strategy** involves delaying collection of foreign currency receivables if that currency is expected to appreciate and delaying payables if the currency is expected to depreciate. Put another way, leading and lagging involves accelerating payments from weak-currency to strong-currency countries, and delaying inflows from strong-currency to weak-currency countries.

Lead and lag strategies can be difficult to implement, however. For one thing, the firm must be in a position to exercise some control over payment terms if it is to use the tactic. Firms do not always have this kind of bargaining power, particularly when they are dealing with important customers who *are* in a position to dictate payment terms. Moreover, because lead and lag strategies can put pressure on a weak currency, many governments impose limits on leads and lags. For example, some countries set 180 days as a limit for receiving payments for exports or making payments for imports.

Several other tactics that can reduce transaction and translation exposure have already been discussed in this chapter. Specifically, we have explained that:

- Transfer prices can be manipulated to move funds out of a country whose currency is expected to depreciate.
- Local debt financing can provide a hedge against foreign exchange risk.
- It may make sense to accelerate dividend payments from subsidiaries based in countries with weak currencies.

- Capital budgeting techniques can be adjusted to deflect the negative impact of adverse exchange rate movements on the current net value of a foreign investment.

Reducing Economic Exposure

Reducing economic exposure requires strategic choices that go beyond the realm of financial management. The key to reducing economic exposure is to distribute the firm's productive assets to various locations around the globe so the firm's long-term financial well-being is not severely impacted by adverse changes in exchange rates. The post-1985 trend by Japanese automakers to establish productive capacity in North America and Western Europe can partly be seen as a strategy for reducing economic exposure (it is also a strategy for reducing trade tensions). Before 1985 most Japanese automobile companies concentrated their productive assets in Japan. However, the rise in the value of the yen on the foreign exchange market has transformed Japan from a low-cost to a high-cost manufacturing location over the last 10 years. In response, Japanese auto firms have moved many of their productive assets overseas in an attempt to ensure the prices of their cars will not be unduly impacted by further rises in the value of the yen. In general, then, reducing economic exposure necessitates that the firm ensure its assets are not too concentrated in countries where likely rises in currency values will lead to damaging increases in the foreign prices of the goods and services they produce. An example of how one company, Black & Decker, has pursued strategies for reducing its economic exposure is given in Box 20.3.

Developing Policies for Managing Foreign Exchange Exposure

The firm needs to develop a mechanism for ensuring it maintains an appropriate mix of tactics and strategies for minimizing its foreign exchange exposure. Although there is no universal agreement among firms as to the components of this mechanism, a number of common themes stand out.[10] First, central control of exposure is needed to protect resources efficiently and ensure that each subunit adopts the correct mix of tactics and strategies. Toward this end, many companies have set up in-house foreign exchange centers. Although such centers may not be able to execute all foreign exchange deals—particularly in large, complex multinationals where myriad transactions may be pursued simultaneously—they should at the very least set guidelines for the firm's subsidiaries to follow.

Second, there is a need to distinguish between, on one hand, transaction and translation exposure and, on the other, economic exposure. All too many companies seem to focus on reducing their transaction and translation exposure and to pay scant attention to economic exposure, which may have more profound long-term implications for the firm's well-being.[11] Firms need to develop strategies for dealing with economic exposure (see Box 20.3).

Third, the need to forecast future exchange rate movements cannot be overstated, though, as we saw in Chapter 9, this is a tricky business. No model comes close to perfectly predicting future movements in foreign exchange rates. The best that can be said is that in the short run, forward exchange rates provide reasonable predictions of exchange rate movements, whereas in the long run, fundamental economic factors—particularly relative inflation rates—should be watched, because they influence exchange rate movements. Some firms attempt to forecast exchange rate movements in-house; others rely on the attempts of outside forecasters. The most important thing to recognize however, is that all such forecasts are imperfect attempts to predict the future.

How Black & Decker Hedges against Economic Exposure

BOX 20.3

Black & Decker is one of the few multinationals known to actively manage its economic risk. The key to Black & Decker's strategy is flexible sourcing. In response to foreign exchange movements, Black & Decker is able to move production from one location to another to effect the most competitive pricing.

Black & Decker manufactures in more than a dozen locations around the world; these include major countries in Europe, Australia, Brazil, Mexico, and Japan. In total, more than 50 percent of the company's productive assets are based outside of North America. Although each of Black & Decker's factories focuses on one or two products to achieve economies of scale, there is considerable overlap. Moreover, on average, the company runs its factories at no more than 80 percent capacity. As a consequence, most of the company's factories have the capability to switch rapidly from producing one product to producing another or to add a product. This allows what is produced at a given factory to be changed over time in response to foreign exchange movements. For example, as the dollar depreciated during the latter half of the 1980s, the amount of imports into the United States from overseas subsidiaries was reduced, and the amount of exports from U.S. subsidiaries to other locations was increased.

According to the company, the ability to move production of a product in response to changes in foreign exchange movements is a source of competitive advantage. Black & Decker enjoys a much better long-term competitive position than one of its most significant competitors in the power tool business, Japan's Makita Electric Works, Ltd. This is because 90 percent of Makita's operations are located in Japan, and it exports heavily to the United States. Although Makita may benefit when the yen is depreciating, its margins are vulnerable during periods of yen strength. Black & Decker, in contrast, is not so vulnerable to appreciations in the value of the dollar.

Source: S. Arterian, "How Black & Decker Defines Exposure," Business International Money Report, *December 18, 1989, pp. 404, 405, 409.*

Fourth, firms need to establish good reporting systems so the central finance function (or in-house foreign exchange center) can monitor the firm's exposure positions on a regular basis. Such reporting systems should enable the firm to identify any exposed accounts, the exposed position by currency of each account, and the time periods covered.

Finally, on the basis of the information it receives from exchange rate forecasts and its own regular reporting systems, the firm should produce monthly foreign exchange exposure reports. These reports should identify how cash flows and balance sheet elements might be affected by forecasted changes in exchange rates. The reports can then be used by management as a basis for adopting tactics and strategies to hedge against undue foreign exchange risks.

---

[10] For details on how various firms manage their foreign exchange exposure, see the articles contained in the special foreign exchange issue of *Business International Money Report*, December 18, 1989, pp. 401–12.

[11] Ibid.

SUMMARY OF CHAPTER

This chapter has been concerned with financial management in the international business. We have discussed how investment decisions, financing decisions, and money management decisions are complicated by the fact that different countries have different currencies, different tax regimes, different levels of political and economic risk, and so on. Financial managers must account for all of these factors when deciding which activities to finance, how best to finance those activities, how best to manage the firm's financial resources, and how best to protect the firm from political and economic risks (including foreign exchange risk). More specifically, the following points have been made:

1. The process of using capital budgeting techniques to evaluate proposed foreign investments is complicated by several factors unique to an international business.
2. When using capital budgeting techniques to evaluate a potential foreign project, a distinction must be made between cash flows to the project and cash flows to the parent. The two will not be the same thing when a host-country government blocks the repatriation of cash flows from a foreign investment.
3. When using capital budgeting techniques to evaluate a potential foreign project, the firm needs to recognize the specific risks arising from its foreign location. These include political risks and economic risks (including foreign exchange risk).
4. Political and economic risks can be incorporated into the capital budgeting process either by using a higher discount rate to evaluate risky projects or by forecasting lower cash flows for such projects.
5. The cost of capital is typically lower in the global capital market than in domestic markets. Consequently, other things being equal, firms prefer to finance their investments by borrowing from the global capital market.
6. Borrowing from the global capital market may be restricted by host-government regulations or demands. In such cases, the discount rate used in capital budgeting must be revised upward to reflect this.
7. The firm may want to consider local debt financing for investments in countries where the local currency is expected to depreciate.
8. There are striking differences in the financial structures on firms based in different countries. This may be due to differences in tax regimes or in cultural practices. Despite the existence of such differences, the arguments for conforming to local debt norms are not strong.
9. The principal objectives of global money management are to utilize the firm's cash resources in the most efficient manner and to minimize the firm's global tax liabilities.
10. Firms use a number of techniques to transfer liquid funds across borders, including dividend remittances, royalty payments and fees, transfer prices, and fronting loans.
11. Dividend remittances are the most common method used for transferring funds across borders, but royalty payments and fees have certain tax advantages over dividend remittances.
12. There is evidence that the manipulation of transfer prices is frequently used by firms to move funds out of a country to minimize tax liabilities, hedge against foreign exchange risk, circumvent government restrictions on capital flows, and reduce tariff payments.
13. However, manipulating transfer prices in this manner runs counter to government regulations in many countries, it may distort incentive systems within the firm, and it has ethically dubious foundations.
14. Fronting loans involves channeling funds from a parent company to a foreign subsidiary through a third party, normally an international bank.
15. Fronting loans can circumvent host-government restrictions on the remittance of funds and provide certain tax advantages.
16. By holding cash at a centralized depository, the firm may be able to invest its cash reserves more efficiently. It can reduce the total size of the cash pool that it needs to hold in highly liquid accounts, thereby freeing cash for investment in higher-interest-bearing (less liquid) accounts or in tangible assets.
17. Multilateral netting reduces the transaction costs arising when a large number of transactions occur between a firm's subsidiaries in the normal course of business.
18. The three types of exposure to foreign exchange risk are transaction exposure, translation exposure, and economic exposure.
19. Tactics that insure against transaction and translation exposure include buying forward, using currency swaps, leading and lagging payables and receivables, manipulating transfer prices, using local debt financing, accelerating dividend payments, and adjusting capital budgeting to reflect foreign exchange exposure.
20. Reducing a firm's economic exposure requires strategic choices about how the firm's productive assets are distributed around the globe.
21. To manage foreign exchange exposure effectively, the firm must exercise centralized oversight over its foreign exchange hedging activities, recognize the difference

between transaction exposure and economic exposure, forecast future exchange rate movements, establish good reporting systems within the firm to monitor exposure positions, and produce regular foreign exchange exposure reports that can be used as a basis for action.

DISCUSSION QUESTIONS

1. How can the finance function of an international business improve the firm's competitive position in the global marketplace?
2. What actions can a firm take to minimize its global tax liability? On ethical grounds, can such actions be justified?
3. You are the CFO of a U.S. firm whose wholly owned subsidiary in Mexico manufactures component parts for your U.S. assembly operations. The subsidiary has been financed by bank borrowings in the United States. You have just been told by one of your analysts that the Mexican peso is expected to depreciate by 30 percent against the U.S. dollar on the foreign exchange markets over the next year. What actions, if any, should you take?
4. You are the CFO of a Canadian firm that is considering building a $10 million factory in Russia to produce milk. The investment is expected to produce net cash flows of $3 million each year for the next 10 years, after which the investment will have to close down due to technological obsolescence. Scrap values will be zero. The cost of capital will be 6 percent if financing is arranged through the Eurobond market. However, you have an option to finance the project by borrowing funds from a Russian bank at 12 percent.

   Analysts tell you that due to high inflation in Russia, the Russian ruble is expected to depreciate against the Canadian dollar. Moreover, analysts rate probability of violent revolution occurring in Russia within the next 10 years as high. How would you incorporate these factors into your evaluation of the investment opportunity? What would you recommend the firm do?

Cosa Bella, Inc.

It was early evening, June 1988, and Susan Maxwell, president of Cosa Bella, Inc. (CBI), was working late on a group of fanciful ceramic table accessories featuring handpainted fish and octopus designs. The Al Mare group of dinnerware and oversized platters had done well for CBI since its introduction last season, and Maxwell wanted to follow up quickly with a collection of serving bowls, candlesticks, and pitchers in related patterns. "What a long way we've come in five years," Maxwell thought, glancing at the display of Italian dinnerware that filled shelves lining one wall of her office. From the single dinnerware line, Campagna, discovered when she was on holiday in Italy with her mother and sister in May 1983, CBI had grown to be one of the largest importers and distributors of handcrafted Italian tableware and gifts in the United States. In 1988, CBI carried 22 lines from 20 manufacturers. Each special line, handcrafted by Italian artisans, reflected the sophisticated, tasteful image Maxwell felt was the key to her company's success.

Remembering that first trip to Italy, Maxwell smiled at how improbable the company's present success was. At 30, with a BA degree in education, an MS in recreational therapy, and five years' experience managing a small specialty retail shop in Charlottesville, Virginia, Maxwell had moved to New York to take interior design classes at the New York School of Interior Design. When her mother offered to take Susan and her sister Frances to Italy for three weeks, Susan jumped at the chance. As luck would have it, that holiday took Susan's career in a new direction.

The Maxwell women had been so taken with the colorful dinnerware used in the dining room of the tiny San Pietro Hotel that they hired a chauffeur and went in search of the factory where it was produced. The factory—Solimene—was located in San Felice Circeo, a small fishing village. There, with the assistance of their driver's rough translations, the Maxwells met Don Vincenza, patriarch of the family business. Solimene employed some 30 artisans to make the colorful ceramic articles the Maxwells had admired. The women spent two of their vacation days negotiating prices for container-loads of the dinnerware, still uncertain as to how they would sell it or, indeed, what was involved in importing goods from Italy to the United States. Filled with enthusiasm for their new project, however, the three forged ahead—and Cosa Bella (Italian for "thing of beauty") was founded.

In the course of their travels, the Maxwells met Fabio Puccinelli, a Florentine businessman with extensive import-export experience. Fabio would later become CBI's sole agent in Italy, acting as an invaluable link in coordinating the flow of merchandise from factories through the local freight carriers to customs officials. It was Fabio who first warned them, when they broached the idea of importing Solimene dinnerware to the United States, that although "Solimene makes extremely fine ceramics . . . they are

---

Source: This case was prepared by Sidney Taylor Smith under the direction of Professor Richard I. Levin, UNC Business School at Chapel Hill, as a basis for class discussion rather than to illustrate either effective or ineffective handling of an administrator situation. Names and company data have been disguised.

Table 1 *Quantity and C.I.F. Value of U.S. Imports of Tabletop Items*

	Quantity (000)		C.I.F. Value ($000)	
	1987	1986	1987	1986
Earthenware				
Coarse-grain and fine-grain, household ware	48,973	39,666	$344,868	$308,531
China				
Bone and nonbone tableware	20,958	20,493	$227,668	$234,058
Total earthenware and china	69,931	60,159	$572,536	$543,589

Source: U.S. Bureau of the Census, U.S. Imports for Consumption, *FT246, Annual 1986, 1987.*

notorious . . . indeed, they are the most difficult factory to work with in all of Italy." Undeterred by Fabio's warnings, the Maxwells returned to the States, determined to investigate the intricacies of customs brokers, freight forwarders, attorneys, bankers, and to learn something about the market for high-end specialty dinnerware.

BACKGROUND

In 1987 the United States imported $572.5 million worth of dinnerware and tabletop items, with the bulk of imports coming from suppliers in the Far East. The dinnerware/tabletop category has grown approximately 5 percent annually since 1980, with most growth attributable to increased prices due to the weakened buying power of the dollar. Imports represented 70 percent of the total U.S. dinnerware market in 1987, a 2.3 percent increase over 1986 levels. Table 1 shows quantity and C.I.F. value of imported dinnerware/tabletop items in 1986 and 1987.[1] Ceramic tableware from Italy represented about 3.5 percent of U.S. tableware imports in 1987.

Retail sales of tableware and table accessory products approaches $5.6 billion in 1987. The market for high-end tabletop items, giftware, and crystal was considered an important growth segment of this market by major retailers, who attributed its importance to the booming bridal market. Bloomingdale's alone generated $20 million in tabletop business in 1987 and credited its success in this category to a policy of selecting merchandise from suppliers with limited distribution, consistent delivery schedules, and extensive customer service.

Ceramics from European artisans are noted for their design quality, and Italian design is considered the best. Despite their high cost (as much as 20–25 percent more expensive than handcrafted ceramics from other Southern European countries), the U.S. market was receptive to high-quality Italian products. There are six importer/distributors of ceramic tableware in the United States, with three (including CBI) importing only Italian products. In addition to the handful of importer/distributors, most major department stores purchase directly from factories all over the world.

COSA BELLA

From the moment she signed the first contract with Solimene to produce the Campagna dinnerware line, Susan Maxwell was committed to keeping her new company bound to a

[1] C.I.F. values reflect the *cost* of goods plus *insurance* and *freight* to some U.S. port.

focused strategy. That strategy included an emphasis on handcrafted articles targeted to a sophisticated, upscale customer and dedication to customer service. Cosa Bella's first sale, in 1984, was to Neiman-Marcus. Better department stores with large tabletop and giftware departments (such as Neiman-Marcus, Gump, Bullock's, and Bloomingdale's) remained important accounts as CBI grew. Located in or close to major metropolitan areas, these retailers offered wide merchandise selections and such services as bridal registries. Most of these major retailers import some merchandise directly through their buying office in order to cut out the importer's costs, but CBI was successful in selling to these accounts on the basis of a distinctive product line and timely delivery of orders.

In order to ensure proper service to CBI accounts, Maxwell insisted that sales be handled internally rather than by independent giftware reps. CBI's three salespeople were responsible for developing accounts in three types of accounts: (1) specialty and gift stores, (2) department stores, and (3) catalog accounts. By 1988, specialty/gift shops accounted for 90 percent of sales, department stores accounted for 6 percent of CBI's sales, and catalog accounts represented 4 percent of sales. Sales to all three types of accounts were conducted out of permanent showrooms in Dallas, New York, Atlanta, and temporary booths at trade shows.

Maxwell carefully controlled the development of new product lines, making sure each addition to the CBI line was as special as the original Campagna line. To protect the uniqueness of the CBI product line, Maxwell negotiated verbal contracts with all suppliers to retain exclusive rights to all CBI patterns. In her five years of operation, Maxwell had added additional dinnerware lines, collections of terra-cotta cachepots and planters, heavy handblown crystal, and whimsical accessory lines. In 1988, CBI's 22 product lines reflected Maxwell's tireless search (three times a year) throughout Italy for the finest Italian crafts.

Maxwell had also carefully managed CBI's growth over the years. Conscious of her own limited experience in import-export and wholesale sales, Maxwell operated along conservative lines, relying on her policy of internally controlled sales to maintain CBI's reputation for customer service, and taking on very little debt to minimize CBI's financial risk. Maxwell credited much of CBI's success to her lean and loyal staff, which numbered 25 in 1988. Table 2 provides a list of key players on CBI's management team and a brief description of their responsibilities. Tables 3 and 4 show CBI's financial statements for 1984 through 1987.

SOLIMENE

Solimene had proved to be as difficult to work with as Fabio had predicted. Don Vincenza had passed much of the managerial responsibility for the factory to his 28-year-old son, who was blatantly unscrupulous in negotiating prices and in attempting to create a bidding war for Solimene's limited output. The Vincenzas raised their prices 10 percent each year. Shipments were erratic and often incomplete. Maxwell was troubled by the deterioration of her relationship with Solimene and was afraid that the Vincenzas were interested in replacing her business with sales to department stores (who could afford to pay more).

Maxwell tried many tactics to improve the service she receiv from Solimene, including paying for goods four months in advance of receipt. But she refused to negotiate any further with the Vincenzas once prices were agreed upon and orders booked, as that would place her in the difficult position of having to bid against retail buyers who might also be her customers. Furthermore, Maxwell was concerned by the prospect of shrinking gross margins on the Campagna product line. She felt that accepting the price increases would establish a dangerous precedent.

Table 2 *Cosa Bella Management Team*

Name	Title	Responsibilities
Susan Maxwell	President	General management, sales, product sourcing and design, supplier contract negotiations.
Penny Kearns	Financial controller	Responsible for preparation of financial statements, profitability analysis of product lines. Supervises letter of credit procedures. Responsible for Accounts Payable and Receivable.
Rick Kelly	Purchasing manager	Responsible for ordering merchandise, quality control, lead testing, and manufacturer relationships.
Robert Miles	Director of sales	Oversees sales and marketing. Sales responsibility for department stores.
Ellyn Brooks	Sales manager	Supervises all showrooms and showroom personnel. Sales responsibility for catalog accounts. Sales administration for trade shows and all CBI accounts.
Mark Hunter	Design coordinator	Showroom and office design. Trade show sales.
Frances Maxwell Robertson	Marketing/advertising director	Product brochure design. Art Director for all CBI advertising.
Lynn Kendrick	Office operations manager	Supervises office and warehouse employees. Order administration supervisor. Customer service coordinator.
Will Thompson	Warehouse manager	Supervises order filling and shipping process. Supervises quality control.

Table 3 *Cosa Bella, Inc., Income Statement ($000)*

	1984	1985	1986	1987
Sales	175.69	591.43	1265.56	2271.20
Cost of sales	35.51	205.03	530.68	924.36
Other cost of sales	6.36	29.96	96.54	198.89
Gross profit	133.82	356.44	638.35	1148.04
Operating expenses				
Office	14.34	21.69	33.70	52.64
Warehouse	11.53	60.75	108.87	210.19
Wages/employee benefits	53.48	120.97	265.23	456.43
Administration	12.80	54.38	74.14	81.24
Sales administration		18.12	31.41	41.96
Total operating expenses	92.15	275.91	513.35	842.45
Marketing and sales	15.72	71.21	104.09	261.64
Buying	13.97	21.91	26.19	46.33
Total expenses	121.84	369.03	643.63	1150.43
Other income	0.62	32.15	94.04	144.71
Net profit (loss) before tax	12.60	19.57	88.75	142.33

Table 4 *Cosa Bella, Inc., Balance Sheet*

Assets	**1984**	**1985**	**1986**	**1987**
Current assets				
Cash	8,052	17,287	65,483	149,694
Accounts receivable	19,335	106,707	212,037	286,099
Inventory	60,350	107,084	264,258	512,288
Prepaid expenses	0	1,786	3,033	4,453
Total current assets	87,737	232,864	544,811	952,534
Fixed assets				
Furniture and fixtures	1,710	11,262	15,017	16,804
Warehouse/office equipment	128	19,542	37,391	74,049
Automobile	6,222	24,886	45,772	45,772
Leasehold improvements	231	231	500	1,140
Less accum depreciation	−908	−12,991	−37,690	−45,833
Net book value	7,383	42,930	60,990	91,932
Other assets	63	63	11,946	9,885
Total assets	95,183	275,857	617,747	1,054,351
Liabilities and Stockholders' Equity				
Current liabilities				
Accounts payable	5,095	65,833	327,911	500,314
Taxes payable	1,951	24,337	38,345	14,337
Total current liabilities	7,046	90,170	366,256	514,651
Long-term debts				
Notes payable	81,000	141,664	162,777	378,155
Less current maturity	0	0	0	−58,500
Total long-term debt	81,000	141,664	162,777	319,655
Total liabilities	88,046	231,834	529,033	834,306
Stockholders' equity				
Capital stock	20,000	20,000	20,000	20,000
Undistributed tax income	−25,456	0	0	0
Retained earnings	0	4,451	4,450	68,715
Net profit or (loss)	12,593	19,572	64,264	131,330
Total stockholder's equity	7,137	44,023	88,714	220,045
Total liabilities and stockholders' equity	95,183	275,857	617,747	1,054,351

An additional concern was that the incidence of flawed merchandise from Solimene was steadily increasing. In 1988, nearly 15 percent of the goods received from Solimene were second-quality goods for which Maxwell paid full price. Solimene steadfastly refused to allow CBI's deductions for flawed merchandise, and Maxwell had not been successful in achieving a compromise on this issue.

DESUIR

In an effort to limit CBI's dependence on a single supplier, Maxwell developed relationships with many other factories in Italy, and found one factory—Desuir—that was managed by a young, enthusiastic, and accommodating couple. Desuir's annual output

Table 5
Cosa Bella, Inc., Representative FOB Prices, Solimene vs. Desuir

Style Number	Description	Solimene FOB Price	Desuir FOB Price	CBI Wholesale Price
1010	Mug	$ 2.60	$ 1.60	$ 6.50
1011	Pitcher	$ 8.40	$ 5.76	$22.00
1012	Casserole	$17.60	$11.12	$39.00

1. *Factory prices based on average 1987 exchange rate of 1250 lire = $1.00.*
2. *FOB—"free on board," meaning the buyer bears the cost of shipping from the FOB point specified by the seller to the receiving point of the buyer.*
3. *Landed cost per piece (including freight, duty, insurance, and agents' fees) averages 28% above FOB price on these articles.*

was expected to be just over $700,000 in value (factory cost) in 1988, of which CBI would buy about $250,000. Desuir's rapid growth was hampered by space limitations, but plans for expansion were being formulated. (In contrast, Solimene's annual production was valued at just over $400,000, and the Solimene facility was approximately 50 percent larger than Desuir's.) Maxwell planned to add a new line of dinnerware from Desuir, and expected to place orders for $750,000 from Desuir in 1989. She estimated that Desuir's total output would reach $1.3 million in value in 1989.

In early 1988, the owners of Desuir approached Maxwell about investing in Desuir so that they could more rapidly expand their production capacity. Maxwell understood that the Desuir management wanted confirmation of CBI's long-term commitment to their business relationship, and felt that such an investment would give CBI a measure of security as well, guaranteeing a steady supply of merchandise. No specific level of investment was discussed, and Maxwell was not certain how much CBI would have to invest to establish a strong position with Desuir. She estimated, however, that an investment of around $200,000 would cover the costs of Desuir's expansion and give CBI significant clout with Desuir.

Desuir had proved to be a reliable and efficient supplier of ceramic dinnerware and terra-cotta pots in the two years Maxwell had worked with them. Desuir's product quality was good and its shipment record was consistent. In an effort to ensure adequate inventories on key Campagna accessory pieces, Maxwell asked Desuir to copy the Campagna patterns (which Maxwell had developed at Solimene) on mugs, pitchers, casseroles, and serving pieces. While this had intensified the strained relations with Solimene, Maxwell felt that the ability to fill her customers' orders and the higher gross margins offered by Desuir made her actions justifiable. Table 5 reflects 1987 product costs from Solimene and Desuir for key accessory pieces. Table 6 indicates gross profit by pattern for representative product lines.

Despite Desuir's strengths, Maxwell had two reservations about making Desuir her primary supplier of ceramic dinnerware. The first had to do with her concern about incidences of lead contamination in Desuir ceramics.[2] FDA standards specified acceptable levels of extractable lead in ceramic ware used in the preparation, serving, or storage of food. "Action levels" (levels of lead contamination which required legal action and detainment of the entire shipment) varied according to category of ceramic ware. Table 7

[2] Potters have long used pulverized lead to enhance the sheen of ceramic articles. When these articles are not fired at high enough temperatures, the glazes can break down, exposing users of the article to potentially fatal lead poisoning. In 1971, the FDA established standards regarding acceptable levels of lead releases. Imported ceramics account for the majority of violations, often due to the use of traditional methods of formulating and firing glazes.

Table 6 *Cosa Bella, Inc., Schedule of Gross Profit by Pattern*

Product Line	Description	1984	1985	1986	1987
Campagna	Ceramic dinnerware and accessories				
Pattern #1		80.5%	74.6%	64.9%	67.4%
Pattern #2		79.7%	73.0%	66.7%	67.3%
Pattern #3		79.4%	75.3%	64.1%	67.6%
Pattern #4		79.5%	74.3%	66.8%	66.6%
Pattern #5		79.8%	76.1%	67.1%	66.2%
Pattern #6			73.1%	73.5%	67.9%
Insalata	Ceramic plates and serving pieces		53.3%	49.5%	46.5%
Ontano	Wooden accessories		54.0%	40.7%	46.7%
Puccinelli glass	Hand-blown stemware and accessories		49.1%	36.9%	45.9%
Buon Giorno	Ceramic dinnerware and accessories			72.0%	67.3%
De Simone	Decorative ceramic accessories			44.3%	50.8%
Fish	Whimsical fish platters			62.5%	65.8%
Veranda	Terracotta planters			62.5%	65.8%
Angeli	Planters				50.2%
Donatello	Handpressed bas reliefs				58.1%
Animale	Ceramic animal tureens				52.8%
Colore	Ceramic dinnerware and accessories				58.7%
Al Mare	Ceramic platters				67.3%

Note: 1987 margins on Campagna reflect weighted average of Solimene/Desuir FOB prices.

describes FDA standards for the flatware, small hollowware, and large hollowware categories.

CBI regularly tested shipments from all vendors at an independent lab in Richmond. CBI's tests had never found a contaminated piece in shipments sampled from Solimene. Unfortunately, in the past six months, one vividly colored platter made by Desuir had been tested by CBI's lab and identified as containing 7.1 parts per million of lead, slightly above legally accepted levels. Since only one piece out of the six tested was found to be contaminated, CBI management did not believe the problem was widespread. However, subsequent FDA tests of a shipment containing these pieces found that one out of three had excessive levels of extractable lead, indicating the problem was far more serious than CBI tests indicated. While Maxwell challenged the FDA test results, CBI promptly recalled the piece, which had been sold to accounts all over the United States.

Maxwell knew that certain glaze colors contained more lead than others, and thus postulated that the problem with Desuir could be the result of the requirements of certain brightly colored designs rather than simply bad firing by Desuir. Maxwell frequently reminded all of her suppliers of the stringent FDA requirements. Nevertheless, she was concerned that dependence on Desuir could prove risky if the FDA stepped up its inspections of imported ceramics. In 1987, the FDA prohibited importation of over 1,000 shipments of ceramic articles due to lead violations, a 20-fold increase since 1983.

Table 7
Food and Drug Administration Compliance Policy Guide No. 7117.87

Subject: Pottery (ceramics): imported and domestic—lead contamination

Background: Imported and domestic ceramic ware has been found to have significant quantities of extractable lead. The metal is extractable by acid foods and could cause chronic lead poisoning under continued food use.

Regulatory Action Guidance: The following represents the criteria for recommending legal action to the Division of Regulatory Guidance or for detaining imports.

The article 1. Is suitable to be used for liquid foods, and
2. Contains in 6 units examined a level of lead per ml of leaching solution exceeding the action level for the category specified.

Category	**Action Basis**	**Action Level Parts per Million**
Flatware	Average of 6 units	7.0
Small holloware	Any one of 6 units	5.0
Large holloware	Any one of 6 units	2.5

Note: The categories of ceramic articles, flatware, and holloware used in the preparation, serving, or storage of food are defined as follows:
Flatware: Ceramic articles which have an internal depth as measured from the lowest point to the horizontal plane passing through the upper rim, that does not exceed 25mm.
Holloware: Ceramic articles having an internal depth as measured from the lowest point to the horizontal plane passing through the upper rim, greater than 25mm.
Small holloware: A capacity less than 1.1 liter
Large holloware: A capacity of 1.1 liter or more

Maxwell's second concern was that if she decided to give up her relationship with Solimene in order to establish a stronger bond with Desuir, the Vincenzas would attempt to sell the Campagna patterns directly to major U.S. retailers. While Maxwell had a verbal understanding with the Vincenzas that the Campagna designs belonged exclusively to CBI, she was uncertain about which country's laws would protect her claim if the Vincenzas decided not to honor that agreement. On the other hand, Maxwell felt that given Solimene's erratic shipping record in 1987 and 1988, it was unlikely that the Vincenzas would suddenly flood the U.S. market if they lost or abandoned CBI's business. Maxwell did feel an emotional tie to the line around which CBI was founded. She was also keenly aware that demand for the Campagna line remained strong. Campagna remained CBI's number-one product line, representing 25 percent of sales in 1987 (see Table 8). Maxwell estimated that she could sell three to five times as much Campagna dinnerware if it were possible to get product.

Maxwell was confident that Desuir could produce dinnerware similar in quality to the Solimene product line. However, she was reluctant to risk losing her exclusive rights to the Campagna patterns. On the other hand, she was concerned by the prospect of passing on Solimene's steeply climbing prices to her customers and frustrated by Solimene's poor shipping record and high levels of flawed merchandise, all of which diminished her ability to serve her customers effectively. Maxwell felt that she must take some sort of action.

THE DECISION

In a May 30 meeting with CBI Controller Penny Kearns, Maxwell outlined three options (which she noted were not mutually exclusive) for dealing with the Solimene problem.

Her first option was to take no action per se, but to continue to search for ways to work with Solimene. Given the continuing popularity of the Campagna line, and the fact

Table 8
Cosa Bella, Inc., $ Sales of Campagna Line

	1984	1985	1986	1987
Pattern #1	$ 35,117	$ 66,606	$ 71,136	$ 72,319
Pattern #2	45,205	103,792	161,282	186,662
Pattern #3	36,035	57,436	78,813	106,081
Pattern #4	27,026	58,953	69,713	95,185
Pattern #5	32,300	56,320	63,601	85,392
Pattern #6		14,608	20,837	22,118
	$175,683	$357,715	$465,382	$567,757

that she had greatly minimized the company's dependence on a single supplier, this could be the safest course of action. While the relationship with Solimene appeared to be deteriorating, Maxwell knew that she was an important customer to Solimene, and they were not likely to drop her as a customer—at this point. Kearns also pointed out that the rustic Campagna look would not remain popular indefinitely, and when demand fell off, Solimene would undoubtedly be more accommodating.

Maxwell felt that her second option was to invest in Desuir. Italian policy toward foreign investment was quite liberal, as such investment was believed to contribute to economic growth, employment, and the level of technology. Maxwell felt that she could rely on her Italian agent to assist her in negotiating with the owners of Desuir. Maxwell's consultations with lawyers in the United States and Italy confirmed that Italian law "guarantees repatriation of foreign capital originally invested in new 'productive' enterprises in Italy and unlimited remittance of profits therefrom."[3] Furthermore, "Italy does not limit ownership in an Italian corporation or other business entity." Maxwell was excited by the idea of investment in Desuir, as she felt that being able to better control factory deliveries would strengthen CBI's customer service image. On the other hand, Kearns pointed out that CBI's growth would soon require moving to a larger warehouse/office. Kearns felt that building a larger, more modern warehouse would also improve CBI's service capabilities, and might prove to be a more secure investment. Maxwell felt that investment in Desuir was a strategic option that should be given careful thought. She knew that it might negatively impact her relations with other suppliers if they felt she was going to shift the bulk of her business to Desuir. It would almost certainly destroy her relationship with Solimene.

Maxwell's third option was to maintain the relationship with Solimene, but to investigate sourcing new lines from lower-cost producers in Spain and Portugal. The quality of ceramic imports from other countries had been improving, and Maxwell felt that she now had sufficient expertise in judging ceramics quality to select the best handcrafts available in those countries. Such a strategy could help improve CBI's gross margins, assuming she could sell the lower-cost Spanish and Portuguese articles for prices comparable to the Italian lines. Maxwell calculated that much of the initial advantage of purchasing lower-cost goods would be offset by increased travel and salary expenses. Sourcing goods from Spain/Portugal would require her to make two to three additional trips to Europe each year. Such a travel schedule would make it very difficult for her to maintain her central role in managing the home office, so Maxwell felt this plan would have to include hiring a dinner- and gift-ware merchandiser to help in sourcing, new design development, seeking local agents, and negotiating supplier contracts. Maxwell

[3] *Productive investments* are those defined as adding to Italy's stock of foreign capital.

estimated that an experienced merchandiser would require an annual salary in the neighborhood of $40,000.

Maxwell felt that there must be other options for either improving relations with Solimene or minimizing CBI's risk if she were forced to drop Solimene as a supplier. Yet nothing new had come out of her meetings with Kearns and other key advisers. With her meeting with the CBI board of directors less than a week away, Maxwell removed the stack of Al Mare platters from her desk and began to outline her proposal for dealing with the Solimene problem.

The Globalization of Xerox Corporation

In March 1960 Xerox Corporation shipped its first 914 series copiers, beginning one of the most successful new product introductions in history. Its photocopiers were protected from imitation by a wall of patents. Safe behind this wall, Xerox dominated the industry for the next 15 years. By the late 1970s Xerox was a multinational company with three main legs:

- The parent company, Xerox Corporation, designed and produced products in the United States for the North American market.
- Rank-Xerox, a 51 percent-owned Xerox company, developed and manufactured products for the European market.
- Fuji-Xerox, a 50/50 joint venture between Xerox and Fuji, developed and manufactured products for the Japanese and Asian market.

Each Xerox company controlled its own suppliers, manufacturing plants, and distribution channels. Each was, in effect, a self-contained entity.

By 1980, however, Xerox was facing problems. Its patents had expired, and many new competitors were entering its markets. Most significant, the Japanese companies Cannon and Ricoh had emerged as significant global competitors. Although Xerox still dominated the copier market, both Cannon and Ricoh were selling high-quality copiers at a price approximately equivalent to Xerox's cost for producing comparable products. Moreover, Xerox's market share had fallen by half, and its return on assets had slumped to 8 percent.

Xerox learned firsthand how far it had fallen behind when it began to produce and market a copier in the United States that had been designed by its Japanese affiliate, Fuji-Xerox. Xerox discovered that the reject rate for Fuji-Xerox parts was only a fraction of that for U.S.-produced parts. Visits to Fuji-Xerox revealed another important truth: quality in manufacturing does not increase real costs; it reduces costs by reducing defective products and service costs.

These developments forced Xerox to fundamentally rethink the way it did business. In 1982 Xerox launched the first of a series of initiatives that over the next decade were to transform its operations. As a consequence, Xerox became the first major U.S. company to win back market share from the Japanese. In 1989 it won the prestigious Malcolm Baldrige Award for quality, and by 1991 its return on assets had increased to 14 percent. The changes underlying this turnaround are detailed in the remainder of this case.

Source: Charles W. L. Hill.

MANAGING SUPPLY SOURCES

In 1981 Xerox had more than 5,000 individual suppliers worldwide. After reviewing Fuji-Xerox's management of suppliers, Xerox realized that if it consolidated its supply base, it could probably achieve three goals:

1. Simplifying the purchasing process would cut overhead in the purchasing area.
2. Having a single supplier produce a particular part for all of Xerox's worldwide operations would allow the supplier to achieve economies of scale in production. The resulting cost savings would be passed on to Xerox in the form of lower prices.
3. Cutting down the number of suppliers would make it easier for Xerox to work with its suppliers to improve the quality of component parts.

As a first step, in 1982 Xerox created multifunctional, multinational "commodity teams." These teams included buyers, engineers, cost experts, and quality control personnel from more than a dozen of its operating companies. Their first task was to reduce Xerox's supplier base from more than 5,000 to less than 500. The teams reduced it to 325 suppliers. In several cases the company decided to use a single supplier for a component. For example, the lamps for Xerox's copiers now come from a single supplier with plants in Asia, Europe, and the United States. Because the consolidation of suppliers simplified the purchasing process, overhead rates fell from 9 percent of total costs for materials in 1982 to about 3 percent by 1992.

Once the supplier base had been consolidated, Xerox launched a quality training effort with its suppliers. Xerox told them that its quality goal was to reduce the number of defective parts coming from them to below 1,000 defects per million. At the time, some suppliers' defect rates were as high as 25,000 per million parts. To implement this policy, Xerox took five steps:

1. Formally established a sole source policy whereby it would deal with only one supplier for a particular part around the world.
2. Entered into long-term (three to five years) contracts with its sole source suppliers, thus reinforcing the notion that it was in a supplier's best interest to work closely with Xerox.
3. Adopted a continuous supplier involvement program that involves suppliers in the design of new products.
4. Established multilevel communications with suppliers. In the past Xerox engineers were prohibited from talking to suppliers for fear they might discuss costs. Now engineers are required to talk with suppliers.
5. Minimized its use of competitive bidding. Xerox now establishes "target costs" for component parts based on its knowledge of what a part should cost to produce. The target cost is then the basis for negotiations with preferred suppliers. In the past, competitive bidding practices had tended to undermine efforts to work with selected suppliers on designs. A supplier that contributed to a design might be left out in the cold if a "garage shop down the street" submitted a slightly lower bid.

As a result of these steps, the company soon met its quality goal of 1,000 defects per million parts. Indeed, by 1992 its defect rate on parts from suppliers was below 300 per million. Moreover, overall material-related costs were down about 50 percent from the 1980 level—reflecting not only more-concentrated purchases, but also improved designs, new technology, and internal efficiencies, all of which were generated by working more closely with suppliers.

CHANGES WITHIN XEROX

At the same time Xerox was reorganizing its worldwide supplier relations, it was also reorganizing its operations. Borrowing heavily from Fuji-Xerox, the first step was to organize its plant workers into "Quality of Worklife" circles. After training the workers in interpersonal skills, group dynamics, and problem-solving techniques, the worklife circles were asked to evaluate situations ranging from working conditions to production problems, and to come up with recommendations for improvement.

Building on this, Xerox introduced its "Leadership Through Quality" program in 1983. The Quality of Worklife circles were merged into "Business Area Work Groups," with membership of these groups including both management and lower-level employees. The Business Area Work Groups were established throughout the hierarchy—from top management down to the factory floor—with each group's membership comprising adjacent levels in the hierarchy, and each group received training in quality improvement programs. Emphasis was on identifying quality shortfalls and the problems that caused them, determining the root causes of the problems, and then developing and implementing solutions for the problems. The training program began with the top-tier groups and then cascaded throughout the organization, gradually spreading worldwide to some 100,000 employees.

Also in 1983 Xerox adopted "Competitive Benchmarking," a process of measuring the company against the products, services, and practices of some of the most efficient global companies. For example, Xerox benchmarked L. L. Bean for distribution procedures, Deere and Company for central computer operations, Procter & Gamble for marketing, and Florida Power and Light for its quality improvement process. Approximately 240 functional areas are now benchmarked against comparable areas in other companies.

In 1985 and 1986 Xerox began to focus on its new product development process. One goal was to design products that are customized to local market conditions but also contain a large number of globally standardized parts. Another goal was to reduce the time needed to design new products and get them to the market. To achieve these goals, Xerox established multifunctional, multinational new product development teams. Each team was to manage the design, component sourcing, manufacturing, distribution, and after-sale customer service for its assigned new product on a worldwide basis. For example, one team designed a new product with a universal power supplier and multi-language displays to eliminate the cost of reengineering for new markets at a later date. In general, the use of design teams cut as much as a year from the overall product development cycle and saved millions of dollars.

One consequence of the new approach to product development was the 5100 copier, the first product jointly designed by Xerox and Fuji-Xerox for the world market and manufactured in U.S. plants. It was launched in Japan in November 1990 and in the United States the following February. The 5100's global design reportedly reduced the overall time-to-market and saved the company more than $10 million in development costs.

In 1988 Xerox created a multinational task force to review its progress toward global integration. This task force identified three levels of integration and used them as a basis for restructuring various operations at all facilities. All Xerox plants were required to:

1. Adopt global standards for basic processes that apply to all operations (e.g., use standard databases for materials management).
2. Maintain common business processes but, where necessary, tailor them to local needs (e.g., just-in-time programs).

3. Set site-specific processes for only those systems that must conform to local needs (e.g., government reporting requirements).

In 1989 Xerox calculated that it could eliminate $1 billion in inventory and $200 million in inventory-related costs by linking worldwide customer orders more closely with production. The company implemented a multinational program called "Central Logistics and Assets Management," the aim of which is to achieve tight integration between individual customer orders and plant production levels and thereby reduce the need for excessive inventory.

CONCLUSION

As a result of these steps, Xerox's competitive position improved markedly during the 1980s. Due to its improved quality, lower costs, and shorter product development time, Xerox was able to regain market share from its Japanese competitors and to boost its profits and revenues. Xerox's share of the U.S. copier market increased from a low of 10 percent in 1985 to 18 percent in 1991.

DISCUSSION QUESTIONS

1. What strategy was Xerox pursuing in 1979? In 1989?
2. From what source did Xerox receive guidance in transforming its organization in the 1980s? What does this reveal about the advantages of a multinational firm?
3. To what extent did taking a global, rather than local, perspective help Xerox improve its competitive position?
4. Evaluate the roles of global manufacturing, materials management, and R&D in Xerox's improved performance during the 1980s.

REFERENCES

Howard, R. "The CEO as Organizational Architect." *Harvard Business Review,* September–October 1992, pp. 106–23.

Kearns, D. "Leadership through Quality," *Academy of Management Executive* 4 (1990), no. 3, pp. 86–89.

McGrath, M. E., and R. W. Hoole, "Manufacturing's New Economies of Scale." *Harvard Business Review,* May–June 1992, pp. 94–102.

Rohan, T. "In Search of Speed." *Industry Week,* September 3, 1990, pp. 78–82.

Sheridan, J. "America's Best Plants." *Industry Week,* October 15, 1990, pp. 27–40.

———. "Suppliers: Partners in Prosperity," *Industry Week,* March 19, 1990, pp. 12–19.

Metalfabriken Brazil

For the first time in Brazil's history, direct foreign investment in the country turned negative in 1986 amid rumors of tighter rules on dividend remittances. There had seemed to be some light emerging in 1984 and 1985 as Brazil began to trade its way out of the

---

Source: This case was prepared by Professor Harold Crookell for illustrative classroom purposes.

Exhibit 1 *Brazil's Balance of Payments (in millions of U.S. dollars)*

	1973	1982	1984	1986
Balance of trade	182	800	13,100	8,400
Exports	6,198	20,200	27,000	22,400
Imports	−6,018	−19,400	−13,900	−14,000
(of which oil)	—	—	(6,900)	(3,000)
Other current items	−1,472	−17,100	−12,600	−12,400
Inflows	900	3,300	3,300	3,000
Outflows	−2,372	−20,400	−15,900	−15,400
(of which interest)	—	(12,600)	(10,200)	(9,100)
Current account balance	−1,290	−16,300	500	−4,000
Net capital movement	3,680	7,900	6,100	−1,000
Direct investment	820	2,500	1,100	−100
Long-term financing	4,760	12,500	13,600	12,500
Amortizations	−1,900	−7,000	−7,800	−13,200
Other	—	−100	−800	−200
Errors and omissions	−63	−400	400	200
Balance of payments	2,327	−8,800	7,000	−4,800
Reserves	6,389	3,900	11,500	5,800
External debt	12,218	80,000 E	92,400	101,000
Debt coefficient	1.0	3.8	3.0	4.25

Source: Economist *Intelligence Unit, Country Profile 1987–88 and quarterly report, January–March 1988.*

Exhibit 2 *Selected Economic Indicators of Brazil*

	1983	1984	1985	1986
GDP at market prices (billions of cruzado)	118	388	1,046	3,688
Real GDP growth (%)	−2.5	5.7	8.3	8.2
Consumer price inflation (%)	142	197	256	67
Exchange rate (average) (cruzado per U.S. dollar)	0.6	1.85	6.20	13.61
Exchange rate (average) (German marks per U.S. dollar)	2.55	2.85	2.94	2.17
Trade surplus with major trading partners in billions US$				
United States				2,670
Japan				630
United Kingdom				277
France				143
West Germany				−176

Source: Economist *Intelligence Unit, Country Profile 1987–88 and quarterly report, January–March 1988.*

massive foreign debt dilemma bequeathed to it by the preceding decade of high oil prices. In 1986, however, the gloom deepened as the country's trade surplus fell below its interest obligation, and external debt climbed over US$100 billion. As a consequence of outside pressure on Brazil to set its house in order, 1987 saw GDP growth slow substantially from the 8 percent level of the previous years, and inflation and devaluation began to accelerate yet again (see Exhibits 1 and 2 for details).

Exhibit 3 *Income Statements for Selected Years (in millions of cruzados and marks)*

	1984		1985		1986	
	0.65 Cruz	1.00 Marks	2.1 Cruz	1.00 Marks	6.3* Cruz	1.00 Marks
Sales	82.2	126.5	251.5	119.8	708.3	112.4
Cost of sales†	52.3	80.5	175.0	83.3	520.5	82.6
Gross profit	29.9	46.0	76.5	36.5	187.8	29.8
Selling and administrative	13.9	21.4	42.5	20.3	113.3	18.0
Profit before tax	16.0	24.6	34.0	16.2	74.5	11.8
Monetary correction on working capital‡	8.0	12.3	24.0	11.4	44.5	7.1
Income tax (30%)	2.4	3.7	3.0	1.4	9.0	1.4
Profit after tax	13.6	20.9	31.0	14.8	65.5	10.4
Dividends to Germany (before withholding tax)	6.4	9.8	15.5	7.4	32.5	5.2

* In the fall of 1987, the exchange rate was about 37.5 cruzados to 1 DM.

† Includes 25% foreign exchange tax, on imports of Cr 40 mln. in 1985 (partial year) and Cr 158 mln. in 1986.

‡ Part of the loss in value of working capital due to inflation is allowed as a tax deduction in Brazil.

Exhibit 4 *Balance Sheets for Selected Years (in millions of cruzados and marks)*

	1984		1985		1986	
	Cruz	Mark	Cruz	Mark	Cruz	Mark
Current assets						
Cash	3.1	4.8	12.5	5.9	28.8	4.6
Accounts receivable	12.1	18.7	39.5	18.8	125.5	19.9
Inventories	8.5	13.1	24.8	11.8	76.4	12.1
Current liabilities						
Short-term debt	(2.1)	(3.2)	(6.0)	(2.9)	(17.4)	2.8
Accounts payable	(6.5)	(10.0)	(20.0)	(9.5)	(57.5)	9.1
Net working capital	15.2	23.4	50.8	24.2	155.8	24.7
Fixed assets (net)	12.5	19.2	24.5	11.7	60.5	9.6
Long-term debt	(3.0)	(4.6)	(7.5)	(3.6)	(24.3)	(3.8)
Equity and retained earnings	24.7	38.0	67.8	32.3	192.0	30.5
Registered capital	40.0		156.0		275.0	

MFK IN BRAZIL

Simon Kirsch, who had served as general manager of MFK Brazil since its inception in 1975, felt that the deterioration in the country's economic condition warranted a review of the company's operating strategy. He was reluctant to consider any fundamental strategic change, because the company's Brazilian operations had been remarkably successful and profitable despite rapid domestic inflation. Recent years, however, had shown sales and profits declining in hard currency terms (see Exhibits 3 and 4). Success was achieved mainly by exploiting parent-company technology in Brazil and by exporting intermittently elsewhere in Latin America. In practice, MFK Brazil produced the parent company's line of specialized automatic lathes, importing key components and attachments from the parent company in Germany. The more advanced the model, the more dependent the Brazilian operation was on imported components. However, because of worsening foreign exchange problems in Brazil, the government in 1985 had imposed a 25 percent tax in cruzados on foreign exchange purchases to pay for imports. At the same time, export incentives were introduced that offset the foreign exchange tax. Any Brazilian firm that increased its exports over base year 1985 received a 25 percent rebate in cruzados of the value of the increase in its exports.

MFK PRODUCT LINE

MFK was a small, German-based producer of specialized automatic lathes with worldwide sales in 1986 of DM 870 million from four factories located in Germany, Switzerland, India, and Brazil. The company's success in world markets stemmed from its policy of in-house design and development of a unique and innovative product line. MFK lathes were basically cheaper than their competitors' and offered comparable performance although for a more limited range of common applications. Over the past decade the range of applications had been broadened gradually by the development of more sophisticated machines built on the same basic principle as the original MFK innovation and by the development of special attachments. The company had also developed a group of highly trained technical specialists both to maintain product standards in the factories and to help company sales reps sell the more complex machines to increasingly sophisticated industrial users.

When production began in Brazil in 1976, the factory was not much more than an assembly plant for the basic MFK lathe—the X20 model, capable of machining barstock between 15 and 25 mm in diameter. Components were imported from Germany. However, in order to qualify for government incentive grants at the time—a time when MFK Brazil was short of funds because of the unanticipated working capital demands of high inflation—Kirsch moved quickly to increase the level of local content in Brazilian-made X20s. He was able to move quickly because of the help he received from parent-company technical specialists. These specialists were always in short supply, but faced with the alternative of investing more capital in Brazil, the parent company agreed to extending specialist support, even though it meant a decline in component exports per unit sold. The hope from Germany's standpoint was that more X20s would be sold in Brazil than would otherwise be possible, and that the smaller volume of exports per unit sold would be offset by higher sales.

In 1978, MFK Brazil began assembly of the X50 lathe—for barstock between 40 and 60 mm—again largely on the basis of imported components and gradual "localization." In 1980, the parent company completed a major R&D project that resulted in a new, more advanced product line capable of closer tolerance work. The company decided to introduce the new line (AX20 and AX50) in addition to the existing line to see how different kinds of customers would react to the choice. Kirsch was not anxious to get into production of the new machines in Brazil at first, but demand for them—especially by foreign subsidiaries in Brazil—was stronger than expected. As a result, AX50s were imported in 1980 and AX20s the following year, and as sales grew, assembly and gradual "localization" of production began. By 1987, MFK Brazil was producing, with varying degrees of local content, the X20, X50, and AX20, and AX50 machines. Exhibit 5 shows the factory price and cost of each of these machines, together with the number sold and the level of import content. The sale of a machine usually involved selected attachments to increase its versatility, and the attachments were all imported from Germany because of their complexity.

Exhibit 5 *Price and Cost Data by Model*

	Factory Price* (Cr. 000s)		Factory Cost (Cr. 000s)		Number Sold		Imports as Percent of Factory Cost		Total Value† of Imports (Cr. 000s)	
	1984	1986	1984	1986	1984	1986	1984	1986	1984	1986
X20	29.0	205	21.3	149	690	790	14	11	2,057	12,948
X50	45.2	317	29.5	230	195	230	18	18	1,035	9,522
AX20	60.3	442	41.7	330	170	255	48	44	3,402	37,026
AX50	69.5	536	47.7	410	385	405	42	31	7,713	51,475
Total					1440	1680			14,207	110,971

* Price relates to the basic machine without attachments. Attachments constitute about 20 percent of total sales.

† These values represent imports of component parts only and include tariff and transportation costs paid in cruzados. All attachments were also imported.

MARKETING IN BRAZIL

Automatic lathes were not easy to sell. The sales force had to be trained not only to understand the technical capacity of the machines it sold, but more importantly, to recognize potential applications by studying a customer's production processes. The more sophisticated the machine, the wider its range of applications and hence the more skill required to sell it. Furthermore, the possible range of attachments in a sale added further to the machine's versatility. The MFK sales force was, therefore, supported (and trained) by a strong technical group in the factory, which in turn was supported and trained by parent-company technical specialists. The incentive to sell more sophisticated machines rather than to concentrate on simpler applications stemmed from the higher prices of the former and, hence, by application of the same commission rate, a higher net commission on each sale.

As a rule, the salesmen would identify the potential sale and bring the necessary information back to the technical group for quotation. The quoted price of course, depended on which attachments were added to the basic machine, which in turn depended on the tasks the machine had to perform.

Frequently, technical support staff would have to accompany salesmen to the customers' factories to determine more precisely what attachments were really needed. This was especially true with newer salesmen. All models of the basic machine were subject to Brazilian price controls, but the attachments were not. In general, the Price Review Board would allow price increases equivalent to documented cost increases, even if the cost increases were due largely to higher priced imports. The main problem with the system was that it consumed a lot of management time and involved a considerable time gap between cost increases and compensating price increases. As a result, there had been a gradual narrowing of profit margins on basic machines, which Kirsch had tried to offset by increasing the margins on attachments.

Customer financing was another major marketing problem in Brazil. The government-subsidized financing scheme, operating by FINAME, permitted credit-worthy customers to finance purchases of industrial equipment through the banking system at reduced interest rates. This was part of a Brazilian program to promote productivity and modernization. All MFK machines qualified under the scheme except the AX20, which failed because its import content was too high. Attachments sold with machines qualified as long as the machine qualified.

SALES FORCE

There were 24 field salesmen in the organization in 1987, four operating out of Rio and the rest out of Sao Paulo. Over 80 percent of the company's customers (and potential customers) were in the Sao Paulo region, where much of Brazil's industry had settled. Regions outside of Rio and Sao Paulo were serviced through independent Brazilian distributors. The distribution of Brazilian sales by region in 1986 was as follows:

Domestic Brazil Sales of MFK Lathes, 1986

Region	Number of Customers	Number of Machines Sold
Sao Paulo	1,490	1,135
Rio	164	170
Other	166	110
Total	1,820	1,415

In early 1987, Mr. Kirsch found it necessary to split Sao Paulo into five regions rather than three as had previously been the case and to increase the Sao Paulo sales force from 12 to 20. Two conditions prompted this move. First, the economic boom was slowing down due to inflationary problems brought on by the country's foreign exchange problems. And, second, the salesmen, because of the commission system, were earning salaries over 50 percent higher than the technical specialists who supported them. The new sales territories, of course, did not please the existing salesmen, but Kirsch wanted them to dig a little deeper for sales rather than skimming their territories, and he wanted them to invest more time with key customers and sell more attachments to them.

EXPORTING FROM BRAZIL

Kirsch was strongly committed to exporting from Brazil whenever market conditions in the rest of Latin America permitted it. He felt exports, especially of the X20, had made a major contribution to scale economies in the Brazilian factory, and export prices were not subject to Brazilian price controls. They were, however, subject to competitive pressure, particularly from an Argentine competitor who had virtually copied the X20 and X50 machines in the late 1970s. Over the years, an implicit understanding had evolved that he would not sell his version of the X20 in Brazil and MFK would not sell its X50 in Argentina. Shortly thereafter Kirsch began importing AX50s to reduce the Argentinian's share of the top end of the X50 market in Brazil. In third markets in Latin America the two firms competed actively. Data on MFK Brazil's exports appear in Exhibit 6.

One of the company's biggest export problems was the instability of Latin American markets. Despite efforts over many years, the area was still struggling to make free trade a reality. The major economies—Argentina, Brazil, and Mexico—all had major economic problems of their own, but were nevertheless still trying to reduce trade impediments within Latin America. Of the 11 nations that signed the 1980 Montevideo Treaty (ALADI), three (Bolivia, Ecuador, and Paraguay) were classified as least developed and were given special trade concessions. The other five intermediate economies belonged to Chile, Colombia, Peru, Uruguay, and Venezuela. MFK's parent company also exported to Latin America and had developed an informal understanding with Kirsch that the markets should go to whoever could supply them at the lower cost. For the most part, Germany had lower production costs than Brazil (see Exhibit 7) but faced approximately 25 percent higher tariffs to enter ALADI markets, and an even bigger differential in relation to Argentina. In 1986, Brazil and Argentina, concerned at the slow pace of multilateral negotiations, signed their own version of a freer trade agreement. As a result, Brazilian goods had an even greater advantage than German goods entering Argentina.

Exhibit 6 *Exports by Model and Country 1984 and 1986 (in millions of cruzados)*

	X20		**X50**		**AX20**		**AX50**		**Total**	
Argentina	1.3	14.4	—	1.0	1.0	6.0	1.2	5.5	3.5	26.9
Mexico	4.5	18.6	0.8	5.5	—	1.0	—	1.5	5.3	26.6
Chile	2.5	17.5	0.4	2.5	—	—	—	—	2.9	20.0
Colombia	1.0	9.5	0.3	—	—	—	—	—	1.3	9.5
Peru	—	6.5	—	1.0	—	—	—	—	—	7.5
Venezuela	1.2	10.0	1.0	5.0	—	—	—	—	2.2	15.0
Total	10.5	76.5	2.5	15.0	1.0	7.0	1.2	7.0	15.2	105.5

Exhibit 7
Prices and Costs in Germany by Model (in thousands of German Marks)

	Factory Prices		**Factory Cost**		**Number Produced**	
	1984	**1986**	**1984**	**1986**	**1984**	**1986**
X20	22.5	24.0	18.0	19.0	4,190	4,085
X50	33.5	35.0	25.7	27.0	3,275	2,915
AX20	44.0	46.5	33.0	35.0	3,850	3,615
AX50	54.0	57.0	40.0	42.5	3,595	3,420
Total					14,910	14,035

THE MANAGEMENT MEETING

Kirsch decided to call a meeting of his key executives in the fall of 1987 to discuss whether conditions in Brazil called for fundamental change in MFK's competitive strategy. Attending the meeting were José DaSilva and Philippe Garcia, in charge of marketing and finance, respectively, and Manfred Schmidt and Rolf Kruger, in charge of production and technical support.

Kirsch: So with inflation on the move again and Brazil's debt problems worsening by the week, I'm afraid we may be in for more import controls and perhaps some tightening of Brazil's dividend rules on foreign investment. How do those dividend rules work again, Philippe?

Garcia: You can pay foreign dividends up to 12 percent of registered capital at a 25 percent rate of withholding tax. Anything higher than 12 percent faces a higher rate of tax, up to 60 percent.

Kruger: How can you operate a business on a system like that? Inflation is going through the roof, and they allow you 12 percent on your original investment—then they take a quarter of it for tax. It's not worth the effort.

Garcia: Registered capital allows for inflation and reinvested profits. It's not that bad. And the 12 percent is after withholding tax. It's 16 percent gross.

Kruger: Well, why didn't we send a bigger dividend to Germany in 1986? It sounds like we could have.

Garcia: We probably could have, in retrospect, but we needed to keep more money on hand to meet the new foreign exchange tax, and the strength of the German mark has made the tax even higher.

Kruger: This country is just one stupid rule after another. People spend all their time chasing their shadows instead of getting on. . . .

Schmidt: Come on, Rolf. Don't get so worked up. Brazil didn't create high oil prices and high interest rates. If you ask me, this country is paying a hell of a price for other people's greed and mistakes.

Kruger: And its own!

Kirsch: What we have to decide is whether we can continue to do business on the strategy we have used so far. We import a lot more than we export and one of the rumors I've heard is that foreign-owned firms like us are going to have to earn their own foreign exchange needs.

DaSilva: The government's latest regulations are clearly intended to push foreign firms to import less and export more. Why don't we try to do that? Mount an export marketing effort throughout Latin America and speed up the local manufacture of imported components.

Kruger: That's it! Build a stronger business in Brazil at the expense of Germany. Great idea! And how do you propose to manage it?

DaSilva: Brazil's problems are serious. We have to do something to become more independent of imports. Manfred, couldn't the factory produce a lot of the components we now import? And why not launch an export drive?

Schmidt: We could do a little more in our own factory, but to make a real dent in imports will require some new equipment and training of our people.

Kruger: And who will have to do it? More technical specialists from Germany! And how long will that take? About 25 years, the speed people learn around here.

Schmidt: That's uncalled for, Rolf. We've got some first-class people on the shop floor. They could pick up the training fast enough.

Kruger: You've been in Brazil too long, Manfred. I think you've gone native. Look, I spent several weeks earlier this year visiting our agents in Argentina, Mexico, Chile, Peru, and Colombia. You know why our exports are not that great. They don't have the technical know-how to help their customers. I went personally to show customers what our machines can do and made all kinds of sales. Why do you think our exports are mainly X20's? Because they are the easiest to sell. It's simple, if we want to increase exports, we have to provide much stronger technical support in other Latin American countries. And where do you suppose the technical support is going to come from? And why do you suppose Germany has not already provided it to increase its own exports? Because there are better places to put it, that's why!

DaSilva: Another reason our X20 exports are stronger is our Argentinian competitor. He has done a good job of . . . .

Kruger: He's not worth powder to blow him to hell. Forget him. Let's stay with the real problem. We need three things: technicians, technicians, and technicians.

Kirsch: Look, José is right about one thing. Brazil is in foreign exchange trouble and we are part of the problem. What's more we have to increase our sales of attachments in Brazil because that's where the big profit is, and all the attachments are imported and require a lot of skill to sell. Maybe we just have to pick away at training as fast as we can. Reduce our imports and increase our exports gradually. We just have to get more technical support from Germany. But how can we convince them of that?

Garcia: I could prepare a very persuasive presentation on Brazil's economic problems and the risk they put us in.

Kruger: They'll cry all the way to the Bundesbank! Try money instead. Not cruzados. Real money.

Schmidt: Stuff it, Rolf!

Garcia: Actually there is a way we could get more foreign exchange to Germany.

Kirsch: You mean raise the dividend to the full 12 percent allowed.

Garcia: Yes, but more than that. The 12 percent allowance is based over a three year average, and dividends in 1985 and 1986 were below the limit. We could declare a dividend in 1987 high enough to bring the entire three years up to 12 percent net of withholding tax. Mind you, we may have to borrow to do it, and interest rates are going through the roof, but it could be done.

Kirsch: That's really useful, Philippe. Maybe we have something to bargain with if we present it right.

Kruger: But look at what you're doing. You are going to build a bigger, stronger Brazilian company with more assets and more profit just as the country is going to blow up. Everything will be trapped here. What good is that to the company?

Schmidt: Do you have a better idea?

Kruger: Ja wohl.

Schmidt: I don't think I want to hear it.

Kruger: Why not stop manufacturing everything in Brazil but the X20? Import the other models from Germany. Take our technical expertise out of the factory and put it to work marketing and exporting. Get Germany to let Brazil be a major global supplier of X20s. Exports go up, manufacturing costs come down, and the investment exposure in Brazil is reduced, too. Presto, the perfect solution!

Schmidt: I knew I didn't want to hear it. Do you realize, Rolf, that would destroy in one stroke five years of accumulated training and skill-building? Once you wipe out technical capability like that, it's lost forever.

DaSilva: The factory would become quite remote from the sales force. I can see it from Germany's point of view, but it is not good for Brazil.

Kirsch: I don't know whether that's the kind of business I'd enjoy presiding over, Rolf. But it's certainly an idea worth thinking about. In fact, it's been a very useful meeting, indeed. I just wish I knew what to do.

Glossary

A

absolute advantage A country has an absolute advantage in the production of a product when it is more efficient than any other country at producing it.

administrative trade policies Administrative policies, typically adopted by government bureaucracies, that can be used to restrict imports or boost exports.

ad valorem tariff A tariff levied as a proportion of the value of an imported good.

Andean Pact A 1969 agreement between Bolivia, Chile, Ecuador, Colombia, and Peru to establish a customs union.

antidumping regulations Regulations designed to restrict the sale of goods for less than their fair market price.

arbitrage The purchase of securities in one market for immediate resale in another to profit from a price discrepancy.

ASEAN (Association of South East Asian Nations) Formed in 1967, an attempt to establish a free trade area between Brunei, Indonesia, Malaysia, the Philippines, Singapore, and Thailand.

B

balance of payments accounts National accounts that track both payments to and receipts from foreigners.

barriers to entry Factors that make it difficult or costly for firms to enter an industry or market.

barter The direct exchange of goods or services between two parties without a cash transaction.

bill of exchange An order written by an exporter instructing an importer, or an importer's agent, to pay a specified amount of money at a specified time.

bill of lading (or draft) A document issued to an exporter by a common carrier transporting merchandise. It serves as a receipt, a contract, and a document of title.

Bretton Woods A 1944 conference in which representatives of 40 countries met to design a new international monetary system.

bureaucratic controls Achieving control through the establishment of a system of rules and procedures.

C

capital account In the balance of payments, records transactions involving the purchase or sale of assets.

CARICOM An association of English-speaking Caribbean states that are attempting to establish a customs union.

caste system A system of social stratification in which social position is determined by the family into which a person is born, and change in that position is usually not possible during an individual's lifetime.

centralized depository The practice of centralizing corporate cash balances in a single depository.

channel length The number of intermediaries that a product has to go through before it reaches the final consumer.

civil law system A system of law based on a very detailed set of written laws and codes.

class consciousness A tendency for individuals to perceive themselves in terms of their class background.

class system A system of social stratification in which social status is determined by the family into which a person is born and subsequent socioeconomic achievements. Mobility between classes is possible.

collectivism An emphasis on collective goals as opposed to individual goals.

COMECON Now-defunct economic association of Eastern European communist states headed by the former USSR.

command economy An economic system where the allocation of resources, including determination of what goods and services should be produced, and in what quantity, is planned by the government.

common law system A system of law based on tradition, precedent, and custom. When law courts interpret common law, they do so with regard to these characteristics.

common market A group of countries committed to (1) removing all barriers to the free flow of goods, services, and factors of production between each other and (2) the pursuit of a common external trade policy.

communist totalitarianism A version of collectivism advocating that socialism can only be achieved through a totalitarian dictatorship.

Communists Those who believe socialism can only be achieved through revolution and totalitarian dictatorship.

comparative advantage The theory that countries should specialize in the production of goods and services they can produce most efficiently. A country is said to have a comparative advantage in the production of such goods and services.

competition policy Regulations designed to promote competition and restrict monopoly practices.

controlling interest A firm has a controlling interest in another business entity when it owns more than 50 percent of that entity's voting stock.

core competence Firm skills that competitors cannot easily match or imitate.

counterpurchase A reciprocal buying agreement.

countertrade The trade of goods and services for other goods and services.

cross-cultural literacy Understanding how the culture of a country affects the way business is practiced.

cultural controls Achieving control by persuading subordinates to identify with the norms and value systems of the organization (self-control).

culture The complex whole that includes knowledge, belief, art, morals, law, custom, and other capabilities acquired by man as a member of society.

currency translation Converting the financial statements of foreign subsidiaries into the currency of the home country.

current account In the balance of payments, records transactions involving the export or import of goods and services.

current account deficit The current account of the balance of payments is in deficit when a country imports more goods and services than it exports.

current account surplus The current account of the balance of payments is in surplus when a country exports more goods and services than it imports.

current rate method Using the exchange rate at the balance sheet date to translate the financial statements of a foreign subsidiary into the home currency.

customs union A group of countries committed to (1) removing all barriers to the free flow of goods and services between each other and (2) the pursuit of a common external trade policy.

D

deferral principle Parent companies are not taxed on the income of a foreign subsidiary until they actually receive a dividend from that subsidiary.

diminishing returns Applied to international trade theory, the more of a good that a country produces, the greater the units of resources required to produce each additional item.

draft See bill of lading.

drawee The party to whom a bill of lading is presented.

E

economic risk The likelihood that events, including economic mismanagement, will cause drastic changes in a country's business environment that adversely affect the profit and other goals of a particular business enterprise.

economic union A group of countries committed to (1) removing all barriers to the free flow of goods, services, and factors of production between each other, (2) the adoption of a common currency, (3) the harmonization of tax rates, and (4) the pursuit of a common external trade policy.

economies of scale Cost advantages associated with large-scale production.

ecu A basket of EC currencies that serves as the unit of account for the EMS.

efficient market A market where prices reflect all available information.

ethnocentric staffing A staffing approach within the MNE in which all key management positions are filled by parent-country nationals.

Eurobonds A bond placed in countries other than the one in whose currency the bond is denominated.

Eurocurrency Any currency banked outside of its country of origin.

Eurodollar Dollar banked outside of the United States.

European Community (EC) An economic group of 12 European nations: Belgium, Great Britain, Denmark, France, Germany, Greece, the Netherlands, Ireland, Italy, Luxembourg, Portugal, and Spain. Established as a customs union, it is now moving toward economic union.

European Free Trade Association (EFTA) A free trade association including Finland, Austria, Norway, Sweden, Iceland, and Switzerland.

European Monetary System (EMS) EC system designed to create a zone of monetary stability in Europe, control inflation, and coordinate exchange rate policies of EC countries.

exchange rate The rate at which one currency is converted into another.

exchange rate mechanism (ERM) Mechanism for aligning the exchange rates of EC currencies against each other.

exclusive channels A distribution channel that outsiders find difficult to access.

expatriate manager A national of one country appointed to a management position in another country.

experience curve Systematic production cost reductions that occur over the life of a product.

experience curve pricing Aggressive pricing designed to increase volume and help the firm realize experience curve economies.

Export-Import Bank (Eximbank) Agency of the U.S. government whose mission is to provide aid in financing and facilitate exports and imports.

exporting Sale of products produced in one country to residents of another country.

externally convertible currency Nonresidents can convert their holdings of domestic currency into foreign currency, but the ability of residents to convert the currency is in some way limited.

F

factor endowments A country's endowment with resources such as land, labor, and capital.

factors of production Inputs into the productive process of a firm, including labor, management, land, capital, and technological know-how.

Financial Accounting Standards Board (FASB) The body that writes the generally accepted accounting principles by which the financial statements of U.S. firms must be prepared.

financial structure Mix of debt and equity used to finance a business.

Fisher effect Nominal interest rates (i) in each country equal the required real rate of interest (r) and the expected rate of inflation over the period of time for which the funds are to be lent (I). That is, $i = r + I$.

first-mover advantages Advantages accruing to the first to enter a market.

fixed exchange rates A system under which the exchange rate for converting one currency into another is fixed.

fixed-rate bond Offers a fixed set of cash payoffs each year until maturity, when the investor also receives the face value of the bond in cash.

flexible manufacturing technologies Manufacturing technologies designed to improve job scheduling, reduce setup time, and improve quality control.

floating exchange rates A system under which the exchange rate for converting one currency into another is continuously adjusted depending on the laws of supply and demand.

flow of foreign direct investment The amount of foreign direct investment undertaken over a given time period (normally one year).

folkways Routine conventions of everyday life.

foreign bonds Bonds sold outside the borrower's country and denominated in the currency of the country in which they are issued.

foreign direct investment (FDI) Direct investment in business operations in a foreign country.

foreign exchange market A market for converting the currency of one country into that of another country.

foreign exchange risk The risk that changes in exchange rates will adversely affect the profitability of a business deal.

foreign portfolio investment (FPI) Investment by individuals, firms, or public bodies (e.g., national and local governments) in foreign financial instruments (e.g., government bonds, foreign stocks).

forward exchange When two parties agree to exchange currency and execute a deal at some specific date in the future.

forward exchange rate The exchange rates governing forward exchange transactions.

free trade The absence of barriers to the free flow of goods and services between countries.

free trade area A group of countries committed to removing all barriers to the free flow of goods and services between each other, but pursuing independent external trade policies.

freely convertible currency A country's currency is freely convertible when the government of that country allows both residents and nonresidents to purchase unlimited amounts of foreign currency with the domestic currency.

fronting loans A loan between a parent company and a foreign subsidiary that is channeled through a financial intermediary.

G

gains from trade The economic gains to a country from engaging in international trade.

General Agreement on Tariffs and Trade (GATT) International treaty that committed signatories to lowering barriers to the free flow of goods across national borders.

geocentric staffing A staffing policy where the best people are sought for key jobs throughout an MNE, regardless of nationality.

global matrix structure Horizontal differentiation proceeds along two dimensions: product divisions and areas.

global strategy Strategy focusing on increasing profitability by reaping the cost reductions from experience curve and location economies.

globalization of markets Moving away from an economic system in which national markets are distinct entities, isolated by trade barriers and barriers of distance, time, and culture, and toward a system in which national markets are merging into one global market.

globalization of production Trend by individual firms to disperse parts of their productive processes to different locations around the globe to take advantage of differences in the cost and quality of factors of production.

gold par value The amount of currency needed to purchase one ounce of gold.

gross domestic product (GDP) The market value of a country's output attributable to factors of production located in the country's territory.

gross national product (GNP) The market value of all the final goods and services produced by a national economy.

H

Heckscher–Ohlin Theory Countries will export those goods that make intensive use of locally abundant factors of production and import goods that make intensive use of locally scarce factors of production.

historic cost principle Accounting principle founded on the assumption that the currency unit used to report financial results is not losing its value due to inflation.

home country The source country for foreign direct investment.

horizontal differentiation The division of the firm into subunits.

horizontal foreign direct investment Foreign direct investment in the same industry abroad as a firm operates in at home.

host country Recipient country of inward investment by a foreign firm.

human development index An attempt by the United Nations to assess the impact of a number of factors on the quality of human life in a country.

I

import quota A direct restriction on the quantity of a good that can be imported into a country.

individualism An emphasis on the importance of guaranteeing individual freedom and self-expression.

infant industry argument New industries in developing countries must be temporarily protected from international competition to help them reach a position where they can compete on world markets with the firms of developed nations.

integrating mechanisms Mechanisms for achieving coordination between subunits within an organization.

intellectual property Products of the mind, ideas (e.g., books, music, computer software, designs, technological know-how). Intellectual property can be protected by patents, copyright, and trademarks.

International Accounting Standards Committee (IASC) Organization of representatives of 106 professional accounting organizations from 79 countries that is attempting to harmonize accounting standards across countries.

international division Division responsible for a firm's international activities.

International Fisher Effect For any two countries, the spot exchange rate should change in an equal amount but in the opposite direction to the difference in nominal interest rates between countries.

International Monetary Fund (IMF) International institution set up to maintain order in the international monetary system.

international strategy Trying to create value by transferring core competencies to foreign markets where indigenous competitors lack those competencies.

J

joint venture A cooperative undertaking between two or more firms.

just-in-time (JIT) Logistics systems designed to deliver parts to a production process as they are needed, not before.

L

lag strategy Delaying the collection of foreign currency receivables if that currency is expected to appreciate, and delaying payables if that currency is expected to depreciate.

law of one price In competitive markets free of transportation costs and barriers to trade, identical products sold in different countries must sell for the same price when their price is expressed in terms of the same currency.

lead market Market where new products are first introduced.

lead strategy Collecting foreign currency receivables early when a foreign currency is expected to depreciate, and paying foreign currency payables before they are due when a currency is expected to appreciate.

lean production systems Flexible manufacturing technologies pioneered at Toyota and now used in much of the automobile industry.

learning effects Cost savings from learning by doing.

legal risk The likelihood that a trading partner will opportunistically break a contract or expropriate intellectual property rights.

Leontief Paradox The empirical finding that, in contrast to the predictions of the Heckscher-Ohlin theory, U.S. exports are less capital intensive than U.S. imports.

letter of credit Issued by a bank, indicating that the bank will make payments under specific circumstances.

licensing Occurs when a firm (the licensor) licenses the right to produce its product, use its production processes, or use its brand name or trademark to another firm (the licensee). In return for giving the licensee these rights the licensor collects a royalty fee on every unit the licensee sells.

local content requirement A requirement that some specific fraction of a good be produced domestically.

location economies Cost advantages from performing a value creation activity at the optimal location for that activity.

M

Maastricht Treaty Treaty agreed to in 1991, but not ratified by mid-1993, that committed the 12 member-states of the European Community to a closer economic and political union.

maker Person or business initiating a bill of lading (draft).

managed-float system An exchange rate system in which some currencies are allowed to float freely, but the majority are managed in some way by government intervention.

management networks A network of informal contacts between individual managers.

market economy The allocation of resources is determined by the invisible hand of the price system.

market imperfections Imperfections in the operation of the market mechanism.

market makers Financial service companies that connect investors and borrowers, either directly or indirectly.

market power Ability of a firm to exercise control over industry prices or output.

mercantilism An economic philosophy advocating that countries should simultaneously encourage exports and discourage imports.

MERCOSUR Pact between Argentina, Brazil, Paraguay, and Uruguay to establish a free trade area.

minimum efficient scale The level of output at which most plant-level scale economies are exhausted.

MITI Japan's Ministry of International Trade and Industry.

mixed economy Certain sectors of the economy are left to private ownership and free market mechanisms, while other sectors have significant government ownership and government planning.

mores Norms seen as central to a functioning of a society and to its social life.

multilateral netting A technique used to reduce the number of transactions between subsidiaries of the firm, thereby reducing the total transaction costs arising from foreign exchange dealings and transfer fees.

multinational enterprise (MNE) A firm that owns business operations in more than one country.

multidomestic strategy Emphasizing the need to be responsive to the unique conditions prevailing in different national markets.

N

new trade theory The observed pattern of trade in the world economy may be due in part to the ability of firms in a given market to capture first-mover advantages.

nonconvertible currency A currency is not convertible when both residents and nonresidents are prohibited from converting their holdings of that currency into another currency.

norms Social rules and guidelines that prescribe appropriate behavior in particular situations.

North American Free Trade Agreement (NAFTA) Proposed free trade area between Canada, Mexico, and the United States.

O

oligopoly An industry composed of a limited number of large firms.

output controls Achieving control by setting goals for subordinates, expressing these goals in terms of objective criteria, and then judging performance by a subordinate's ability to met these goals.

P

performance ambiguity Occurs when the causes of good or bad performance are not clearly identifiable.

personal controls Achieving control by personal contact with subordinates.

political economy The study of how political factors influence the functioning of an economic system.

political risk The likelihood that political forces will cause drastic changes in a country's business environment that adversely affect the profit and other goals of a particular business enterprise.

polycentric staffing A staffing policy in an MNE in which host-country nationals are recruited to manage subsidiaries in their own country, while parent-country nationals occupy key positions at corporate headquarters.

positive sum game A situation in which all countries can benefit, even if some benefit more than others.

predatory pricing Reducing prices below fair market value as a competitive weapon to drive weaker competitors out of the market ("fair" being cost plus some reasonable profit margin).

price discrimination The practice of charging different prices for the same product in different markets.

price elasticity of demand A measure of how responsive demand for a product is to changes in price.

product life-cycle theory The optimal location in the world to produce a product changes as the market for the product matures.

pull strategy A marketing strategy emphasizing mass media advertising as opposed to personal selling.

purchasing power parity (PPP) An adjustment in gross domestic product per capita to reflect differences in the cost of living.

push strategy A marketing strategy emphasizing personal selling rather than mass media advertising.

R

representative democracy A political system in which citizens periodically elect individuals to represent them in government.

right wing totalitarianism A political system in which political power is monopolized by a party, group, or individual that generally permits individual economic freedom but restricts individual political freedom, including free speech, often on the grounds that it would lead to a rise of communism.

S

sight draft A draft payable on presentation to the drawee.

Single European Act A 1987 act, adopted by members of the European Community, that committed member-countries to establishing an economic union.

Smoot-Hawley Tariff Enacted in 1930 by the U.S. Congress, this tariff erected a wall of barriers against imports into the United States.

Social Democrats Those committed to achieving socialism by democratic means.

social mobility The extent to which individuals can move out of the social strata into which they are born.

social structure The basic social organization of a society.

socialism A political philosophy advocating substantial public involvement, through government ownership, in the means of production and distribution.

sogo shosha Japanese trading companies; a key part of the *keiretsu*, the large Japanese industrial groups.

specialized asset An asset designed to perform a specific task, whose value is significantly reduced in its next-best use.

specific tariff Tariff levied as a fixed charge for each unit of a good imported.

spot exchange rate The exchange rate at which a foreign exchange dealer will convert one currency into another on that particular day.

stock of foreign direct investment The total accumulated value of foreign-owned assets at a given point in time.

strategic alliances Cooperative agreements between two or more firms.

strategic trade policy Government policy aimed at improving the competitive position of a domestic industry and/or domestic firm in the world market.

Structural Impediments Initiative A 1990 agreement between the United States and Japan aimed at trying to decrease nontariff barriers restricting imports into Japan.

subsidy Government financial assistance to a domestic producer.

swaps The simultaneous purchase and sale of a given amount of foreign exchange for two different value dates.

systematic risk Movements in a stock portfolio's value that are attributable to macroeconomic forces affecting all firms in an economy, rather than factors specific to an individual firm (unsystematic risk).

T

tax haven A country with exceptionally low, or even no, income taxes.

tax treaty An agreement specifying what items of income will be taxed by the authorities of the country where the income is earned.

temporal method Translating assets valued in a foreign currency into the home currency using the exchange rate that existed when the assets were originally purchased.

theocratic totalitarianism A political system in which political power is monopolized by a party, group, or individual that governs according to religious principles.

time-based competition Competing on the basis of speed in responding to customer demands and developing new products.

time draft A promise to pay by the accepting party at some future date.

trade creation Trade created due to regional economic integration; occurs when high-cost domestic producers are replaced by low-cost foreign producers in a free trade area.

trade deficit See current account deficit.

trade diversion Trade diverted due to regional economic integration; occurs when low-cost foreign suppliers outside a free trade area are replaced by higher-cost foreign suppliers in a free trade area.

trade surplus See current account surplus.

transaction costs The costs of exchange.

transaction exposure The extent to which income from individual transactions is affected by fluctuations in foreign exchange values.

transfer price The price at which goods and services are transferred between subsidiary companies of a corporation.

translation exposure The extent to which the reported consolidated results and balance sheets of a corporation are affected by fluctuations in foreign exchange values.

transnational corporation A firm that tries to simultaneously realize gains from experience curve economies, location economies, and global learning, while remaining locally responsive.

transnational financial reporting The need for a firm headquartered in one country to report its results to citizens of another country.

Treaty of Rome The 1957 treaty that established the European Community.

tribal totalitarianism A political system in which a party, group, or individual that represents the interests of a particular tribe (ethnic group) monopolizes political power.

turnkey project A project in which a firm agrees to set up an operating plant for a foreign client and hand over the "key" when the plant is fully operational.

U

unbundling Relying on more than one financial technique to transfer funds across borders.

V

value creation Performing activities that increase the value of goods or services to consumers.

values Abstract ideas about what a society believes to be good, right, and desirable.

vehicle currency A currency that plays a central role in the foreign exchange market (e.g., the U.S. dollar and Japanese yen).

vertical differentiation The centralization and decentralization of decision-making responsibilities.

vertical foreign direct investment Foreign direct investment in an industry abroad that provides inputs into a firm's domestic operations, or foreign direct investment into an industry abroad that sells the outputs of a firm's domestic operations.

vertical integration Extension of a firm's activities into adjacent stages of production (i.e., those providing the firm's inputs or those that purchase the firm's outputs).

voluntary export restraint (VER) A quota on trade imposed from the exporting country's side, instead of the importer's; usually imposed at the request of the importing country's government.

W

wholly owned subsidiary A subsidiary in which the firm owns 100 percent of the stock.

World Bank International institution set up to promote general economic development in the world's poorer nations.

worldwide area structure Organizational structure under which the world is divided into areas.

worldwide product division structure Organizational structure based on product divisions that have worldwide responsibility.

Z

zero sum game A situation in which an economic gain by one country results in an economic loss by another.

Index

L

M

Q

R

S

T

ICELAND
UNITED KINGDOM
IRELAND
GREENLAND (DENMARK)
Alaska (United States)
CANADA
SPAIN
PORTUGAL
UNITED STATES
PORTUGAL
SPAIN
MOROCCO
MEXICO
BAHAMAS
HAITI
DOMINICAN REPUBLIC
CUBA
PUERTO RICO (U.S.)
GUADELOUPE
DOMINICA
ST. LUCIA
BELIZE
HONDURAS
JAMAICA
GUATEMALA
EL SALVADOR
NICARAGUA
COSTA RICA
PANAMA
TRINIDAD & TOBAGO
VENEZUELA
GUYANA
SURINAME
FRENCH GUIANA
COLOMBIA
ECUADOR
PERU
BRAZIL
BOLIVIA
PARAGUAY
CHILE
ARGENTINA
URUGUAY
FALKLAND ISLANDS
WESTERN SAHARA
MAURITANIA
MALI
CAPE VERDE ISLANDS
SENEGAL
GAMBIA
GUINEA-BISSAU
GUINEA
SIERRA LEONE
LIBERIA
BURKINA FASO
IVORY COAST
GHANA
TOGO